TWO ACADEMIC LIVES

Alice Freeman Palmer Memorial in the Houghton Memorial Chapel at Wellesley College. After George Herbert Palmer died he, too, was cremated, his ashes were placed in the memorial, and his name and dates (1842–1933) were added to the base. (See also Note 5 on page 244)

TWO ACADEMIC LIVES

GEORGE HERBERT PALMER AND ALICE FREEMAN PALMER

A COMPILATION

ARTHUR J. LINENTHAL, M.D.

Privately Printed
Boston, Massachusetts
1995

This book is printed with Soy Ink on acid-free paper.

ISBN 0-9626606-1-2

Library of Congress Catalog Card Number: 94-96814

To Vi

and

Her Wellesley College Class of 1940

and

The Class of 1940 Scholarship Endowment Fund

"'Tis the good reader that makes the good book;
in every book he finds passages which seem confidences or asides
hidden from all else and unmistakably meant for his ear;
the profit of books is according to the sensibility of the reader;
the profoundest thought or passion sleeps as in a mine,
until it is discovered by an equal mind and heart."

Ralph Waldo Emerson
Success

Contents

Illustrations

Credits: Illustrations

frontispiece Album, private collection

1 Harvard University Archives, Portrait collection

2 A Service in Memory of Alice Freeman Palmer held by her Friends and Associates in Appleton Chapel Harvard University January Thirty-First MDCCCCIII, Boston, Houghton Mifflin and Co., 1903, facing page 32

3 Page from Chronicles

4 Page from Chronicles

5 Photograph from Chronicles

6 Page from Chronicles

7 Page from Chronicles

8 George Herbert Palmer, *Twenty-Five Portraits of Alice Freeman Palmer, 1855–1902, Cambridge, Riverside Press, 1904*

9 Page from Diary

10 Page from Diary

11 AJL Collection—in Special Collections at Wellesley College Library

12 Pomona College Archives

13 AJL Collection—in Special Collections at Wellesley College Library

14 Miss Margaret Lane, Boxford, Massachusetts

15 Harvard University Catalogue, 1900-01

Preface

About twenty-five years ago, I became an aficianado of George Herbert Palmer (1842–1933), professor of philosophy at Harvard University, and his wife, Alice Freeman Palmer (1855–1902), second president of Wellesley College. They were both widely influential in American academia. In addition to my own continuous association with Harvard for the sixty years since I matriculated as a college freshman in 1933, two other factors undoubtedly influenced my interest in the Palmers.

My father, Harvard College class of 1900 and Harvard Medical School class of 1904, studied philosophy with Professor Palmer and had a close personal relationship with him (see Note 1 on page 144).

Violet, my wife, a devoted, class of 1940 alumna of Wellesley College, shared my interest in the Palmers, encouraged my research, and made many important suggestions as she edited the manuscript. She and I are publishing this book, Wellesley College has accepted it with the copyright as a gift from us, and all receipts from the sale of the book will be added to the Class of 1940 Scholarship Endowment Fund.

In the late 1960s, during a summer vacation on Cape Cod, I happened to read my father's copy of *The Life of Alice Freeman Palmer*. Published in 1908, this is George Herbert Palmer's remarkable biography of his wife. In his introduction, Professor Palmer says that the book, "while ostensibly a biography, claims the many privileges of an autobiography." According to a contemporary reviewer, "we feel in reading Mrs. Palmer's life that it owes at every point an incalulable debt to Mr. Palmer's telling . . . We can recall no other husband who has paid such a tribute to his wife . . ." (*Harvard Graduates' Magazine,* 1907–

1908; 16 (June 1908): 654–656). A later reviewer writes: "Among shining tributes offered by husbands to wives, this book perhaps ranks second only to Shah Jehan's Taj Mahal" (A. D. Dickinson, *The Worlds's Best Books*, H. W. Wilson Co., 1953, page 265).

This reading triggered my great interest in the Palmers, and I began to collect books and articles by them and about them. As the demands of a busy professional life permitted, I also began, in a very preliminary fashion, to explore related archival material at Wellesley College and at Harvard University. In 1985 I retired from medicine in order to work, full-time, on another project which was completed in 1990 when my wife and I published *First A Dream: The History of Boston's Jewish Hospitals, 1895–1928*.

Then, finally, I was able to return to the Palmers, full-time, and to gather the material for this compilation.

In the preface to *Formative Types in English Poetry,* one of his numerous publications on poetry, Professor Palmer, then 76 years old, writes: "Perhaps a word of apology is needed here for venturing outside my province. My professional work has been in Philosophy. To the poets I have listened only as an amateur. Yet every one is wise, whatever his occupation, in cherishing some collateral interest which produces nothing for the market, is amenable to no social standard, and is valued simply for sweetening his own life. Such an unpaid invigorator has poetry been to me during a long life."

And so have the Palmers invigorated the life of this physician for these many years.

I am grateful for help from the staffs of numerous institutions and organizations: American Association of University Women; Amherst College; Appalachian Mountain Club; Beloit College, Colonel Robert H. Morse Library; Boston Public Library and the Kirstein Business Branch; Bowdoin College; Boxford Historic Document Center; Boxford Public Library; Bradford College; Bronx Community College; Brookline Historical Commission; Brookline Public Library; Broome County (New York) Historical Society; Brown University, John Hay Library; Bryn Mawr College, Mariam Coffin Canaday Library; Cambridge Historical Commission; Carleton College; Case Western Reserve University; Chautauqua Institution; Columbia University; Commission on Archives and History (Berkeley, California); Congregational Library (Boston); Dana Hall School; Dartmouth College; Elmira College, Gannett-Tripp Library; Fisk University; Forest Hills Cemetery (Boston); Grinnell College, Burling Library; Harvard University: Archives, Countway Library Archives, Department of Philosophy, Fogg Museum Archives, Fogg Museum Library, Gutman Library,

Houghton Library, Pusey Library, Widener Library, Woodberry Poet Room; Haverford College; Holyhood Cemetery Association (Boston); Houghton Mifflin Company; Knox College, Seymour Library; Little Compton (Rhode Island) Free Public Library; Massachusetts Medical Society; Museum of Fine Arts (Boston) Archives; Mount Holyoke College, Williston Memorial Library; New York State Library (Albany); New York University; Oberlin College; Old South Church (Boston); Parish of Christ Church (Andover, Massachusetts); Perkins School for the Blind; Pomona College; Pratt Institute; Princeton University, Seeley G. Mudd Manuscript Library; Radcliffe College, Arthur and Elizabeth Schlesinger Library; Reed College; St. Luke's Hospital (Saginaw, Michigan); Simmons College School of Social Work; Smith College; Swedenborgian Church: Headquarters, School of Religion Archives (Newton, Massachusetts); Union College, Schaffer Library; University of California, Berkeley, The Bancroft Library; University of Chicago, Joseph Regenstein Library; University of Iowa; University of Michigan, Michigan Historical Collections, Bentley Historical Library; University of Vermont; University of Washington Archives (Seattle); Vassar College; Wellesley College: Archives, Center for Research on Women, Margaret Clapp Library, Special Collections; Wheaton College; Windsor Central School District (New York); and Yale University.

I am also grateful to the following individuals for help in the research and in the preparation of the manuscript. At the Wellesley College Archives, Jean N. Berry and Wilma R. Slaight found answers to my innumerable questions and showed me additional material. Arnold P. Silverman and Theodore Berman, both dealers in used books, helped me assemble a large collection of related publications. The late G. William Patten crowned my collection with the gift of stenographer's transcripts of several lectures by Professor Palmer (see page 369). Gregory Barz, Minda Kutz, Aline A. Russotto, Joseph Webber, Michael Winship, and Richard J. Wolfe clarified confusing questions. Antiquarian book dealers at London's Bernard Quaritch, Ltd., were extremely helpful: throughout the years of this project, Richard A. Linenthal, our son, helped in so very many ways; Nicholas Poole-Wilson translated several book dedications from Latin or Greek; and Arthur Freeman and Theodore Hofmann gave me exciting material for my collection. Barbara L. Linenthal, our daughter, designed the dust jacket for the book.

The prints for the illustrations were prepared by the Photographic Services at Boston's Beth Israel Hospital and by O'Neill Photography in Natick, Massachusetts. The typography for this volume was done by Wellington Graphics in Westwood, Massachusetts, and the printing and binding by Thomson-Shore, Incorporated, in Dexter, Michigan.

Certain abbreviations appear in the compilation: **GHP** = George Herbert Palmer, **AFP** = Alice Freeman Palmer, *HGM* = *Harvard Graduates' Magazine,* ΦBK = Phi Beta Kappa. AJL Collection = the compiler's extensive collection of writings by and about the Palmers; this material is available for reference in Special Collections at the Wellesley College Margaret Clapp Library.

Chapters 1, 2, 3, 4, 5, and 10 contain previously unpublished writings by George Herbert Palmer and Alice Freeman Palmer. For permission to publish these writings, I am grateful to the institutions that have physical ownership of them: the Harvard University Archives, the Houghton Library at Harvard University, and the Wellesley College Archives. And I am grateful to Houghton Mifflin Company for permission to publish the letters in chapter 10 from Houghton Mifflin Company to George Herbert Palmer.

I am pleased to describe our gratifying contacts with members of the Freeman and Palmer families—a total of three grandnieces and one grandnephew—who own the copyrights to this unpublished material. Not only have they given written permissions to publish the writings, but they have expressed great interest in the compilation.

With the Freeman members, I have been in touch by telephone and correspondence. Elizabeth Novy Proulx, a grandniece of Alice Freeman Palmer, lives in Michigan. She has written that her sister, Barbara Novy Webster, also approves of the publication. From an entry in the Chronicles, Mrs. Proulx identified a ring that her mother had given her (see Note 4 on page 130). Recently, she sent me a copy of *The Saginaw Hall of Fame,* which lists Alice Freeman Palmer as one of the first five honorees, in 1964.

James Warren Freeman, a grandnephew, named after his great-grandfather, lives in New York State. He has written that his sister, Elizabeth Freeman Walter, also approves, and he has sent me information about the Freemans in Saginaw, Michigan, which is incorporated in Note 1 on page 53.

Violet and I have visited the two grandnieces of George Herbert Palmer, both alumnae of Wellesley College (see Biographical Summaries). Margaret Lane has lived for over fifty years in the Boxford house where the Palmers spent so much time, and we have seen her there several times. She was born after Mrs. Palmer died, but she shared with us her vivid memories of "Uncle George." She also talked about the house and the land, and we witnessed the bird activity around the house which the Palmers had enjoyed. In addition, she introduced us to the impressive Boxford Historic Document Center, with its Palmer-related material, which she was instrumental in founding.

Helen Palmer Avery, the other grandniece, was also born after Mrs. Palmer died; she, too, knew "Uncle George." She lives in Maryland and spends the summers in Wellfleet on Cape Cod. In June 1993, Violet and I had a wonderful visit there with her and her husband. Their summer home, where members of the Palmer family often visited, is the cottage which originally belonged to one of George Herbert Palmer's brothers, Julius A. Palmer, Jr. (see page 140). The Averys have modernized the secluded house which is located on high ground with a beautiful view of Gull Pond. Like the Boxford house, it contains numerous Palmer memorabilia.

These contacts have sharpened our impressions of George Herbert Palmer and Alice Freeman Palmer, and have added greatly to our enjoyment of this project.

Autobiographical Sketches

Introduction

Autobiographical Sketches

George Herbert Palmer (1842–1933) and Alice Freeman Palmer (1855-1902) each wrote an autobiographical sketch at the beginning of the diary for March 1900 (chapter 4). His sketch, covering eleven handwritten pages, appears in this compilation as chapter 1; hers, covering six pages, as chapter 2. This material was transcribed as exactly as possible. As in the Chronicles (chapters 3 and 5), punctuation varies and is often absent, abbrevations appear, and words may be shortened (e.g. Profssor).

In addition to these sketches and the diaries, entries in the Chronicles (chapters 3 and 5) are largely autobiographical, and much similar material is scattered throughout the compilation. In 1921, for example, in The Puritan Home, an article in the *Atlantic Monthly* (**GHP**-92), Professor Palmer describes his early family life; and in 1930, when he was eighty-eight years old, an autobiographical introduction to *Contemporary American Philosophy* (**GHP**-103), was also published as *The Autobiography of a Philosopher* (**GHP**-104). Some notes in the Chronicles include autobiographical excerpts from these and some of his other publications. The prefaces to Professor Palmer's books are often autobiographical, and his handwritten letters to Houghton Mifflin Company detail his relations with this publisher and his involvement in the publication process (chapter 10).

For Mrs. Palmer also, autobiographical material appears in Chronicle notes that include excerpts from certain of her publications. I have found one purely autobiographical piece by her, Why I Am An Optimist (**AFP**-15), and her poems in *A Marriage Cycle* are clearly autobiographical as her husband indicates in his preface (**AFP**-18).

George Herbert Palmer and Alice Freeman Palmer, prominent academic figures of the late nineteenth and early twentieth century, each had strong ties to both Wellesley College and Harvard University. When they were married, in 1887, Mrs. Palmer resigned from the presidency of Wellesley and lived in Cambridge for fifteen years. Here, she was an important figure on the Harvard scene. She found "life in the College Yard the most interesting thing in the world" (page 164), even as she became well known across the country and in Europe for her "special hobby," the education of girls (page 497). Mrs. Palmer died in 1902 at the age of forty-seven. Her husband, a renowned Harvard professor of philosophy, died thirty-one years later at the age of ninety-one. During those years he demonstrated an intense devotion to Wellesley; Katherine Lee Bates, professor of English at Wellesley, suggested that he made "continual restitution" to the college for having "won away her president" (page 250). After the terrible fire of 1914 destroyed College Hall, for example, Professor Palmer was chairman of a successful campaign for funds (**GHP**-77), and in 1924, as a memorial to his wife, he gave to the college the remarkable collection of first editions of English poetry that is in the Special Collections in Wellesley's Margaret Clapp Library (249n5).

Memorials to the Palmers abound. In Cambridge, for example, one can see the Dana-Palmer House near the Faculty Club; when this was their home, it was located across Quincy Street, on the site of the Lamont Library. In Emerson Hall, Winifred Rieber's large painting (86 inches wide, 78 inches high) of the Three Philosophers — Royce, James, and Palmer — hangs in lecture room 105, and Charles Hopkinson's portrait of Professor Palmer hangs in the Bechtel Room with those of other Harvard philosophers. Incidentally, Palmer Street, which runs from Church Street to Brattle Street, behind the main building of the Harvard Cooperative Society, was named, as early as 1854, after an unrelated, early nineteenth century Cambridge family.

Wellesley College has several such memorials. In the Margaret Clapp Library, Mrs. Rieber's paintings of the Palmers hang near each other in Special Collections, where there is also a replica of the bust of Alice Freeman Palmer that is in the Hall of Fame for Great Americans in New York City (286n1). A large portrait of Alice Freeman Palmer by Abbott Thayer is in the library's Reference Room with those of other Wellesley College presidents, and a dormitory, Freeman Hall, is named after her. The ashes of both Palmers are in the base of Daniel Chester

French's memorial to Alice Freeman Palmer in the Houghton Memorial Chapel (see frontispiece).

There are also memorials to Alice Freeman Palmer elsewhere: in Boxford, Massachusetts, the Alice Freeman Palmer House in which she and her husband spent so much time; at Bradford College, where she was an influential trustee, a copy of the Thayer portrait; in Windsor, New York, where she lived as a child and attended the Academy, the Alice Freeman Palmer Elementary School; for years, in Sedalia, North Carolina, a college preparatory school for black students, the Palmer Memorial Institute with an Alice Freeman Palmer building; in Saginaw, Michigan, inclusion in a 1989 publication, *The Saginaw Hall of Fame*; and at the University of Chicago, where she was Dean of Women, the Alice Freeman Palmer Chimes in the Mitchell Tower.

Chapter 1

Autobiographical Sketch

George Herbert Palmer

Life

I was born at 3 Crescent Place, Boston on March 19, 1842, the seventh of a family of five sons & four daughters of Julius Auboyneau Palmer & Lucy Manning Peabody. My father was a member of the firm of Palmer & Bachelders, dealers in jewelry & silver ware. My father was a poor boy from Rhode Island, who made a comfortable property. Unable himself to obtain the College Education he wished, he provided his children with every scholarly opportunity they desired.

I passed through the Mayhew Grammar School in Chardon St — a public School — & when 12 years old entered Phillips Academy at Andover, at that time under Dr Samuel Taylor. There I continued until 1856, when my eyes failed — the trouble being severe granulation of the lids. After a year spent with doctors at home, I was sent away for a voyage on a barque of 500 tons to Egypt & Sicily, eight months absence. My eyes being no better on my return, I went into business for a couple of years. A skilful doctor so much improved my sight that during the last two years I was able to do a little studying each day under a private tutor, H. G. Spa[u]lding, Harvard,1860 & I myself entered Harvard in September 1860. My natural affiliations were with Yale, where my Uncle Ray Palmer, & his son Charles Ray Palmer, had been valedictorians of their classes. At this time too Harvard was a Unitarian College, & I & my family were Orthodox Congregationalists. I have always been a member of Mt Vernon Church, Boston, at that time under the charge of Rev Edward N. Kirk.

During the early years of my college life I was obliged to use my eyes very carefully, & at no time throughout my course could I use them freely. Under the stupid required curriculum I maintained, however, a fair standing & also read pretty largely in English poetry — a subject which at that time was not taught in any college course. My tastes in Philosophy became pronounced in the Senior Year. My interest too in Latin & Greek as literature was so decided that I formed a partnership with a classmate & privately read largely in these languages. The class room technical drill was of little value for our purposes.

In college I was a member of "The Institute" "The Hasty Pudding" & "The Christian Brethren," this last subsequently changing its name to "the Christian Association." Of this society I was President during my Senior Year, & was at the same time the 'Leading Lady' in the many plays of the Hasty Pudding Society. We played in those days once a month at our rooms in the top of the North Entry of Stoughton Hall. But we gave no performances for the general public. Though I stood in the first half of my class my rank was never high, partly perhaps on account of my inability to use my eyes in the evening. I was of too low a grade to be elected to the ΦΒΚ & was elected as an Honorary Member after I became a professor.

From childhood I had always expected to lead a literary and learned life rather than one of trade, & I was uncertain whether to turn to teaching or the ministry. Being offered a place as submaster in the Salem High School on a salary of $900, I accepted it & taught there 1864–1865, greatly enjoying the work. In Sept 1865 I entered Andover Theological Seminary, desiring to prepare myself for the teaching of Philosophy but hoping to preach for a few years first. There were no graduate Schools in the country then nor opportunity for higher work in Philosophy. I formed a philosophical partnership with James H Lee & we devoted every morning to reading aloud together in Philosophy.

One of my sisters had married A. E. Bachelder, a business partner of my father. Her home in Brookline was largely my home during these years. There I often talked of my philosophic hopes. At the close of the winter of 1866 Mr Bachelder offered me $1000 to defray my expenses for a year at a German University. James Lee's father also gave him permission to go. We sailed in May 1866 & after a brief stay in England crossed to Holland, walked through Friesland & went up the Rhine to Stuttgardt where we had introductions to a German family. While living here we walked down to Tübingen one day & were so attracted by the beauty of the place that we abandoned our plan of settling at Halle & Berlin & entered the University of Tübingen.

Mr & Mrs Bachelder coming to Paris this summer, I joined them there & was taken sick with typhus fever which centered in the brain — where I had had serious trouble for several years. Indeed from childhood up I was of a very feeble constitution, with almost constant headaches. My life was now despaired of, but I was saved by the skilful & persistent care of Mme Hahnemann, the wife of the discoverer of Homoeopathy. But I went back to Tübingen much weakened & found the sanitary and food conditions there of the worst possible sort. As I was forbidden to do serious brain work, I began to amuse myself with reading Greek. I read the whole of Sophocles Aeschylus & Homer as well as large parts of Plato, & decided to make my thesis for the Doctorate on The Doctrine of Sin in Aeschylus. James Lee went home in the summer of 1867 & I was left alone. At this time there were not half a dozen English speaking students in the University. But I had become fascinated with it & was unwilling to go elsewhere. My father, seeing how badly I had been interrupted by illness, wished me to remain another year.

But I did not grow strong. And when in the winter of 1867–68 Mr Bachelder fell ill in Rome & I went down to see him, the Roman fever attacked me & left me a wreck. My hopes of study were over & I returned to America in April 1868. Gaining a trifle during the summer, I went back to Andover Seminary for a last year but broke down again with nervous prostration & withdrew in December with Mr & Mrs Bachelder to our country place at Boxford. I saw now that I could not take up the burdens of a parish; & when a tutorship in Greek was offered me by Pres. Eliot, I accepted it & began to work at Harvard in Sept. 1870, taking a room at 54 Thayer — a building opened that year.

June 15, 1871, I married Ellen Margaret Wellman, daughter of W'm A. Wellman of Brookline, to whom I had long been attached. I was receiving a salary of only $1000. I had no capital & she brought me none; but by private tutoring we managed to live & were never in debt. In Jan 1872 I was appointed curator of the Gray Engravings with a salary of $500.

In Oct. 1872 Professor Peterson, Asst. Prof. in Philosophy suddenly resigned. I offered to take his work & was appointed Instructor in Philosophy, having also charge of Forensics on a salary of $500. In 1873 I was appointed Asst. Prof. Philos. on a salary of $2000, besides the salaries for Forensics and Engravings. The first year of our married life my wife & I boarded on the corner of North Avenue & Holmes Place. In the autumn of 1872 we took the small house 3 Garden St. cor. Appian Way, where we lived throughout the remainder of her life. Receiving in 1872–73 $2000 for my services as tutor to the daughter of Nathan Matthews of Boston, we went abroad in the summer of 1873 & living at St Germain I perfected my French. In 1876 when the Gray Collection was moved to Boston I resigned the Curatorship, but my professors salary was raised in 1878 to $2500. I resigned the charge of Forensics in 1880.

My wife had always been delicate. Consumption was in her family. In the summer of 1877 at Boxford a hemorrhage occurred, followed by severe illness, & we were obliged to spend that winter in the South. She gained so much that in the Summer I went over to Glasgow to make the acquaintance of Professor Edward Caird whose philosophic writing had greatly attracted me. In the Autumn she sank again & died Feb. 10, 1879. Owing to the exceeding beauty of her character, mind, & person, the marriage had been an extremely intimate one. Through her prompting, I undertook the Greek Readings which finally resulted in my translation of the Odyssey. By her advice I gave up our house after her death & rebuilt the rooms 25, 26, & 27 Stoughton Hall & lived there until 1888.

In 1883 I was appointed Professor of Philosophy with a salary of $3000, which rose in 1886 to $3500, in 1888 to $4000, in 1892 to $4500, in 1897 to $5000. After the foundation of Radcliffe College $500 was paid me each year I gave a course there. A few hundred dollars a year came to me from my books, & still more — as years went on — from public lectures. From this last source I have received as much as $1500 in a single year. But I had only such capital as I could save from my salary until 1899, when Edwin H. Abbot gave me $11000 of rail road stock. I had been a second father to his son Philip Stanley, who was killed in climbing Mt Lefroy.

Dec, 23, 1887, I married Alice Elvira Freeman at the house of Governor Claflin in Boston. She was at that time President of Wellesley College, an office which she resigned for my sake, & came to live at 479 Broadway, cor. Prescott St., for the remainder of the College Year. That Summer we went abroad & remained fifteen months, keeping house in Paris Venice & Florence, but also visiting Greece Germany & England. On coming home we lived for the first year at 118 Brattle St, a half house which we hired; from 1890 to 1894 in the Deanery of the Episcopal Theological School; & after 1893 at 11 Quincy St., previously occupied by Prof A P Peabody D.D., a house which I very largely altered. In all these homes — & in that which continued through them all at Boxford — there was deep content, wide comradeship & ever vivid love, between my wise wife & myself. She had her own abounding life, & I had mine; & these we contributed to one another. The year 1895–96 we spent again abroad, & greatly enjoyed the 1500 miles we rode together on our bicycles.

In Dec. 1889, I was appointed Alford Professor of Philosophy, succeeding Profssor Bowen, who died the following January. On the foundation of the University of Chicago in 1892, Pres. Harper called me to its chair of Philosophy on a salary of $7000, offering to my wife also the Deanship of women at a salary of $5000. These offers we declined.

But the work of providing girls suitable opportunities of study at this University — the first where absolute equality was proposed — seemed to us both so important that she agreed to spend twelve weeks in several periods each year in Chicago, & in this way to become Dean at a salary of $3000. During these residences I was often able to be with her, & she continued this work for three years.

At its Centennial in 1887 Columbia University gave my wife the degree of L.H.D. — she had already received the degree of Ph.D. from Michigan University in 1882 — & Union College gave us both the degree of LL.D at its Centennial in 1895 — I having already received this degree from Michigan University in 1894. Western Reserve Univ. also conferred on me the degree of L.H.D in 1898.

In the spring of 1884 I published a translation of the first twelve books of the Odyssey, printing the Greek text on the opposite page — Houghton Mifflin & Co. In 1891 I brought out the whole of the Odyssey, through the same publishers, but I omitted the Greek text. A translation of the Antigone of Sophocles was also published by me through Houghton Mifflin & Co in 1899. I took an active part in the long discussion over the elective system at Harvard, printing three articles in defence of it in the Andover Review, & these in 1887 were gathered into a little volume entitled The New Education, Little Brown & Co. Boston. Two Commencement addresses of mine have also been published by T.Y. Crowell & Co, Boston — The Glory of the Imperfect & Self Cultivation in English. I have written articles from time to time for the Forum, the Atlantic Monthly & book notices for The Nation, & I now have in hand a critical edition of George Herbert & a volume on Ethics formed from the Noble Lectures, delivered this year. But I have made it my ambition to be a teacher rather than a writer, & I count it my most gratifying success to have deeply influenced many subsequently powerful lives.

My philosophic attitude is markedly idealistic. I have been much influenced by Caird, who has been a close friend & correspondent for 30 years; & by Hegel, whom I deeply honor & deeply dissent from; & by my remarkable staff of colleagues. When I began my teaching in Philosophy, Professor Bowen was the only other member of the Department. Now there are six full Professors, two Ass't Professors, five Instructors, & six Assistants. I am at present the Chairman.

[A section headed Boxford near the end of the diary—Chapter 4—fits here]

Since this is my last entry for the month, & I have often referred in these records to my house in the country, I had better write a little description of it. My mother was a Peabody. At Boxford, between 1640 & –50, Capt John Peabody — the first of that name in this country — settled on a farm which continued uninterruptedly in the Peabody name until it was inherited more than 200 years later by my mother. My grandfather Peabody owned it in my boyhood, he living with us in Boston in the winter, & we with him in the Summer. From my earliest childhood, therefore, Boxford was the name of the spot that was in my thought the most sacred, most free, most beautiful, & most happy. The little town is 28 miles from Boston on a branch of the Boston & Maine R.R. — a township 10 miles long by half a dozen wide, with two parishes, but containing in both only 700 people. It is largely covered with woods, has a sterile soil, in my part of the town few hills — its only beauty being its abundant water in ponds & brooks, & its splendid forests. Its little village, 3/4 of a mile from my house, has about a dozen houses, one store, one church, a public library of 2500 volumes, a town Hall, a parsonage, no doctor, no lawyer. Farming is the only occupation. There is no severe poverty, but no rich men. Nearly all the inhabitants have been here for many generations, & I have known most of them from boyhood.

My farm consists of something over 100 acres, half of it woodland — pine in front of the house along the brook, while behind the house is a good deal of oak, nut, & maple. The ancient house of my ancestors, built in 1660, was taken down by my father. The house my grandfather built is now occupied by my sister in summer. Next it is a farm house supposed to be over 200 years old & very quaint, which I own & occupy. I have made large changes in it to fit it to our convenience, especially adding a large piazza on the west side, overlooking the Run & the Park, on which I live all summer. I have fitted it up as a complete study. Next my house, still farther from my sister's, stands the farm house, half of it occupied by our farmer, who has been with us 43 years — his three children being born on the farm. His wife is Katy Bronte, a second cousin of Charlotte Bronte. The other half of the farm house (6 rooms) is now from time to time let in the summer. I occupied it for 21 years, during the life time of my first wife & for some years afterwards.

Here in Boxford we spend our Summers whenever we are in this country. Term Time is so busy with lectures and interruptions that during it I can do little serious study or writing. We generally arrive here about July 1, & then for three months I am free for private work. I take five or six hours a day in study, & take my exercise in gathering the morning vegetables, in running on my bicycle to the mail 3/4 of a mile away, in having a bath in the brook before supper, & especially in cutting paths in the woods. Each summer a new one is laid out or an old one renewed. I pay few visits within the town, seldom leave it, & make it my hermitage for study. Here I keep a library of a thousand volumes the year round. The house is in other respects completely furnished, much of the furniture of ancient patterns which have come down to me from my ancestors.

Again and again during the year we spend a few days here, though these seasons are less frequent than we could wish on account of the dangers of cold. We have no furnace. It would be difficult to keep one unrusted in a house so often closed. We depend almost entirely on our old fireplaces. But this year we spent Christmas week here. And here we came for a fortnight after our wedding, Dec. 23,1887. In the summer at my sister's large house, next door, there are usually my brother-in-law A. E. Bachelder & his wife, often my brother Rev. Frederic Palmer of Andover & his wife, & generally some young people.

Last summer I began work on a critical edition of George Herbert — for whom I was named by an uncle, a Professor in Amherst College, who was particularly fond of that old poet. His poems were given me when I was but a child, & without understanding them fully I then committed them largely to memory. My views of Herbert & his work through this long familiarity becoming somewhat different from those which are customary, I have wished to express them & to attempt to recast the study of Herbert. Finding the printed statements about Herbert's text untrustworthy, I have sent to England & had the Williams & the Bodleian Mss copied, & from Prof C. E. Norton have procured a copy of the first edition. With these I shall constitute my text & rearrange the order of the poems. The whole work, with the introductory essays & the notes, will occupy what leisure I can find for probably three summers.

So long a time will be required because most of next summer must be given to bringing out the Noble Lectures which I have just been giving at Cambridge. They have been delivered without notes, have been reported by a stenographer, & this report I shall then work over for publication. It will constitute a kind of first part of a discussion of the problems of Ethics which I dream of some day carrying on.

[He continues with 11 Quincy St.]

The Cambridge house in which we live perhaps deserves a few words. It stands on the West corner of Quincy St & Quincy Square & though the first house on that side is numbered 11 Quincy St. Who built it or precisely when, I do not know. I believe it came into the possession of Harvard College between 1830 & 1840, & was not then an old house. It was occupied by William Bond our first Professor of Astronomy, who set on its top a little observatory — still there — & who built on its South West corner a small house for transit circle observation. Here subsequently lived Professor Felton, Prof. F. D. Huntington, & after him for 33 years Prof. A. P. Peabody DD. Soon after his death his daughters built a house on Appleton St. & we moved into 11 Quincy St in Feb. 1893. I largely remodelled its interior, adding the transit house to my library, rebuilding entirely the dining room, upper entry, kitchen & pantries, & making some change in almost every room. Little had been previously done to the house for many years & it was greatly out of repair. The College undertook the expense of the exterior, I of the interior, but it was understood that all the four houses still remaining within the College grounds on Quincy St. may at any time be removed. The house on the North West corner of Quincy St. now occupied by Prof. Langdell is to go this year.

Chapter 2

Autobiographical Sketch

Alice Freeman Palmer

I, Alice Freeman Palmer, was born Feb. 21, 1855, and am therefore just over forty-five. My father was a country physician in the litte village of Windsor, in the Susquehanna valley of southern New York. There I prepared for college at the old Academy, and in 1872 entered the University of Michigan. A part of the Junior Year I taught in the High School of Ottawa, Illinois, but I returned to Ann Arbor and graduated with my class in 1876. I taught the following year in a Seminary in Geneva Lake, Wisconsin, then two years in the high school of Saginaw, Michigan, and then in 1879 became Professor of History in Wellesley College.

In 1881, on the death of the founder of the College in October, I was made Acting President, and in June 1882, President of the College. In 1887, Dec. 23, I left the College to marry Prof. George Herbert Palmer of Harvard. During these twelve years of married life we have been twice to Europe for a year's study and travel; the remaining years have been spent in Cambridge, my husband devoting himself to his students, in teaching and administrative duties during the academic year, and to study and writing during the summer. He cannot give time or strength to many social functions, or general engagements; we have not had children; I have therefore had time for educational work in which we are both interested:—

A. For more than ten years I have been one of the eight members of the State board of Education and am now on its special committees on Bridgewater, Fitchburg and Hyannis Normal Schools, and on granting State Scholarships. I am also called often to the legislative hearings on education and kindred subjects at the State House.

B. I have been, since my marriage, a trustee of Wellesley College; am one of the nine members on the Executive Board; one of the Committee on the Policy of the College, and am President of the Students Aid Society. Of course having been connected with the College twenty years, I must hold myself at its service in many indefinite ways.

C. President of the Woman's Education Association, Incorporated, of Boston and vicinity. For more than thirty years this company of women, now two hundred and fifty, has done many kinds of influential work especially for women's education. We hold six meetings in Boston, each year, sometimes more.

D. Have recently resigned as President of the Corporation of the International Institute for Girls in Spain, securing the Hon. S. B. Capen, Pres. of the American Board to take my place, as we are raising large sums of money. Am still a member of the Corporation, and Chairman of the Ways and Means Committee. But I am trying to do less work, on account of a serious accident, when a bicycler ran me down, striking my head, and producing hemorrhages [see page 139]. I have also

E. resigned from the presidency of the College Club of Boston, of four hundred members; from the chairmanship of many committees, and membership of several societies.

F. I am still, however, on the Standing Committee on Corporate Membership in the Collegiate Alumnae Association, on the Com. on Finance and Publication, and the Board of College Trustees, in the same body; Com. on Membership in Archaeological Association; the Treasurer of the Association to maintain an American Woman's Table at the Zoölogical Station in Naples; Vice-President of the Cantabrigia Club & the Round Table; on Committee on Membership of the Authors' Club of Boston; on the American Board of Commissioners for Foreign Missions, etc, etc, etc.

I try to limit my work to educational interests, and my writing and public speaking to those topics, or allied subjects. I have written four articles this year, and spoken very seldom in large meetings, but am now regaining my strength. It is our custom to receive constantly students, and college men and women at our table. I am always at home Tuesday afternoon and evening, and in addition I have this year given a reception to the Senior class of Radcliffe, inviting a hundred ladies of special distinction to meet them; have had twenty five ladies — "the Bee," to a supper; twenty ladies to a luncheon party; the Radcliffe Philosophical Club for an evening entertainment; and have given thus far since October five more formal dinners of ten each. But before the college year closes I must invite the College Club, the Round Table, The Authors' Club, my husband's classes in Harvard and

Radcliffe, and as many young people to dinner as we can take evenings for.

Perhaps this gives a fair idea of the way our days go, but in the summer at Boxford I have time for reading, writing, sewing and making jellies and preserves, — work of which I am very fond.

I dream of writing several books which I have much in my mind, but the demands are so pressing for daily help in the things which need doing in our confused city conditions now in this country that everything else waits. And unless I cut off these interests I must go back to lecturing again next year, as one seems to involve the other, and press constantly.

I have written the daily plain record of March which follows just as the hours have brought their various demands, but have not stopped to say how all days are good that are spent with my husband who illustrates perfectly his lectures on the nature of goodness, and is wiser than all his philosophy. Our interests are the same and we always share each other's work. — though he is essentially the scholar as I am not; but he has a rare gift of taking me into his many-sided life, and especially into his interests in other men — younger teachers and students to whom he is a father and friend. I cannot imagine a happier or more interesting life than we live, in the place of all in the world where we wish to be, doing the work that we wish to do. If any one who opens these bits of college life sixty years hence is busier, happier and fonder of Harvard's daily duties than we are, it will be because our dreams have come true, and the world has learned the art of living better than we know it now.

Chronicles and Diaries

Introduction

Chronicles and Diaries

Chronicles

The compiler transcribed this unpublished material (chapters 3 and 5) from a hardcover volume in the Wellesley College Archives. Its outside dimensions are $6x8^{3/4}x1^{1/8}$ inches, the binding is a medium brown cloth, and horizontal gold stamping on the spine reads "Journal." George Herbert Palmer's bookplate (see illustration on page 229) is on the inside of the front cover.

The pages, light brown and quite brittle, measure $5^{3/4}x8^{1/2}$ inches. Except for some blanks at the back of the volume, the pages all have handwritten entries by the Palmers. Photographs of four pages are included in chapter 3. Professor Palmer wrote with a pencil, Mrs. Palmer with a pen, and their writing is often difficult to decipher. Prospective entries began in September 1891, as Professor Palmer indicated on the opening page, and ended in 1929; earlier pages have a list of biographical dates and then retrospective entries starting in 1842, the year of George Herbert Palmer's birth.

The transcription reproduces the original as exactly as possible. Punctuation varies and is often absent, abbreviations are frequent, misspellings occur, words are occasionally shortened (e.g., fr for from, thru for through, c'd for could, th. for that), and a few entries are incomplete. A question mark may have two meanings: including parentheses, (?), as part of an entry or bracketed, [?], to indicate the transcriber's uncertainty about spelling.

The transcription is presented in two parts, chapters 3 and 5, so that the Diaries for March 1900, can appear in the proper chronologic sequence as chapter 4. Marginal initials, **GHP** or **AFP,** identify the writer of the entries that follow immediately. Brackets [ ] enclose references to publications, clarifications, and cross-references.

The picture of William Rainey Harper, first president of the University of Chicago, reproduced on page 94, is the only photograph in the original Chronicles.

Multiplication by a factor of about 15 will convert most of the dollar figures in the Chronicles to figures for the 1990s.

The superscript [Note] identifies an entry selected for annotation, and these **Notes** are presented immediately after the entries for a given year. A line down the left-hand margin of the notes distinguishes them from the entries. Throughout the compilation, the location of a note in the Chronicles is indicated by the page on which it begins, e.g., 87n2 identifies 1891, Note 2. An index to these notes starts on page 610.

Biographical Summaries of most of the personal names in the notes and elsewhere in the compilation start on page 569.

Diaries

The compiler transcribed, with some added paragraphing, the Autobiograpical Sketches (chapters 1 and 2) and Diaries (chapter 4) from unpublished material in the Harvard University Achives (HUA 900:13 "Chest of 1900").

George Herbert Palmer and Alice Freeman Palmer kept separate diaries for the month of March 1900; thirty carefully handwritten pages by him, fifty-seven by her (see illustrations on pages 191 and 175). The lined paper, $7^{3/4}$ x$10^{1/4}$ inches, was in perfect condition and both handwritings were much easier to read than in the Chronicles. For each day in March 1900, the diary entries are presented here in sequence, indicated by **GHP** or **AFP.** As in the Chronicles: punctuation varies and may be absent; abbreviations are frequent; and a question mark may have two meanings—including parentheses, (?), as part of the original text or bracketed, [?], to indicate the transcriber's uncertainty about spelling.

The Palmers often mention various "calls." These were personal visits that they received or made; a telephone was not installed in their home at 11 Quincy Street until January 14, 1905 (see entry on page 225).

The background of these diaries is described in a letter, dated February 22, 1900, that William C. Lane, librarian of Harvard College, sent to officers of the university:

> "At the last meeting of the University Council it was suggested that an attempt be made to bring together, *for the benefit of our successors at the close of the twentieth century* [compiler's italics], as complete a record as possible of the present daily life of the University . . .
>
> "Let each one during the month of March 1900, keep a careful journal of his daily doings, recording faithfully, and in as much detail as he can, all that goes on from day to day, including his college work, his professional interests, his family relations, his amusements, in fact all the elements of his life . . .
>
> "The journals when finished are to be brought to the College Library, placed flat in stout envelopes provided by the library, and sealed by the writers. They will be deposited in a zinc-lined chest (or chests), soldered up securely, locked by two different keys, and the keys placed, one in the keeping of the President, and the other in the hands of the Librarian.
>
> "The chest is to remain absolutely closed until the year 1925; and no general use of the records will be permitted earlier than 1960. Between 1925 and 1960, any individual record may be opened and used if the writer has died and his family or literary executors wish the material for biographical purposes. All other records shall remain intact and unopened until the year 1960" . . .

The letter continued with some details, such as, that "theme paper in common use in the College be employed or else paper of the same size," and that "contributions from other members of his family would serve to make the picture more complete." Mr. Lane was "aware that the carrying out of this plan asks much of a very busy company of men" He ended the letter: "Will you kindly inform me whether you will contribute to the success of this plan? Those whom I have consulted in advance have all promised to help."

Professor Palmer responded: "I like this scheme, burdensome as it certainly will be. And I do not see how it could be more wisely presented."

Chapter 3

The Chronicles

to March 1900, annotated

Chronicles
of Two Lives

George Herbert Palmer
(Left Page)
&
Alice Elvira Freeman
(Right Page)

Begun
Sept. 1891

GHP

Aug. 16, 1928, Delia Sharkey died at Boxford of cancer
Grandparents: Thomas Palmer b. 1773 d. June 17, 1857
Susanna Palmer b 1779 d. March 24, 1815
Jacob Peabody b 1778 d. Nov. 12, 1856
Julius Auboyneau Palmer b. June 14, 1803 d Feb. 14, 1872
Lucy Manning Peabody b Aug. 6, 1805 d Oct. 27, 1877
Anna M. Boland b. Oct. 17, 1917

Nov 12, 1827 Father and Mother married at Boxford
Nov 20, 1828 Harriet Amanda Palmer, Died Dec 7 1872
Feb 1 1831 Lucy Ann Palmer Died July 16, 1880
Dec. 21 1833 Jacob Peabody Palmer, Died Jan 15, 1901
Aug 20 1836 Julius Augustus Palmer. Died Sept17, 1837
July 28 1838 Julia Augusta Palmer. Died Jan 30 1881
March 1 1840 Julius Auboyneau Palmer. Died Jan 11, 1899
March 19 1842 George Herbert Palmer. Died May 7, 1933 [unidentified handwriting]
Feb 8 1845 Emily Jane Palmer. Died Feb. 17 1907
Aug. 6 1848 Frederic Palmer Died 1932

Dec 6, 1824 Augustus Edwin Bachelder, Died Sept. 22 1904
Aug 5 1848 Lily Wilkinson Bachelder. Died Dec 21, 1909
March 8, 1834 Mary Anne (Kimball) Palmer d. Jan 29 1882
Nov 28 1846 Mary (Towle) Palmer born
April 2, 1835 Ellen Margaret (Wellman) Palmer d. Feb 10, 1879
Feb 21, 1855 Alice Elvira (Freeman) Palmer d. Feb. 6, 1902
May 22 1877 Frederic Palmer marries Mary Towle
Oct 17, 1878 Eric Palmer born. Married June 19, 1907
Jan 6, 1877 Helen Wallace
Aug. 5, 1846 Lucy (Wilkinson) Bachelder. d. Dec. 21, 1909
July 20, 1869 Bertha Palmer m. May 12, 1902
July 2 1878 Lucy Sprague b. May 8 marries Wesley Clair Mitchell
Mar 6, 1915 Sprague Mitchell born
April 7, 1905 Margaret Lane
Feb. 22, 1907 Rosamond Lane
May 12 1908 Frederic Palmer 3d
Jan 22, 1910 Helen Wallace Palmer

AFP

Oct. 25, 1828 James Warren Freeman born

GHP
[adds] d. May 3, 1909
June 16, 1837 Elizabeth Josephine Higley Freeman born. d. Oct 18, 1910

Feb 21, 1855 Ellen Margaret Freeman Feb 10, 1879
Nov 22, 1856 (7) [unidentified handwriting]-Fred Warren Freeman-1942
Dec 11, 1858 — Ella Louise Freeman 1942 [unidentified handwriting]
Dec 28, 1860 — Roxie Estelle Freeman d. June 20, 1879
June 20 1879 — Charles Horace Talmage & Ella Louise Freeman married at Saginaw
Mar. 22, 1854 James Warren Freeman (d. May 3, 1909), Elizabeth Josephine Higley (d. 1910) married
Nathaniel Carter Towle, Dec. 1, 1805 - Apr 25 1898
Eunice Makepeace May 4, 1806 - Oct 19 1894
Barbara & Katherine French b Oct 2, 1882[Note 1]
Bertha Palmer marries W. C. Lane May 12, 1903
Eric Palmer " Helen Wallace June 19, 1907
Lewis K. Morse b. [1869]
Ednah Rich b. March 16, 1871

1836 Firm of Davis Palmer & Co formed
Sept 8, 1928 Rosamond Lane marries Milton Edward Lord in the Boxford church, the whole parish individually invited, Frederic Palmer Mr Bradford & ~~young~~ Mr. Worcester officiating. A large reception followed at the Lane's house.

Note

1. This list names only members of the Palmer and Freeman families and a few close friends. The names of these twins — Barbara French and Katherine French — do not appear again until the summer of 1901, when they were in Boxford with Augustus Bachelder, Lily Wilkinson Bachelder, and Mrs. Wilkinson. Thereafter, they are named frequently, the last time being in 1916.

Bachelder's first wife, Lucy Palmer Bachelder, died in 1880; she was George Herbert Palmer's sister. In 1887 Bachelder married Elizabeth (Lily) Wilkinson. Katherine Wilkinson, Elizabeth Wilkinson's sister, was already married to Peter French and their twin daughters — Barbara and Katherine — were born in 1882.

In the summer of 1897, the Chronicles show "Mrs. Wilkinson" (presumably Lily Wilkinson Bachelder's mother) and "2 little girls" in Boxford with Palmer's sister Emily. In 1894, the Bachelders moved from Boston to Andover. "Aug, Lily, Mrs Wilkinson & the two children" were at Emily's in Boxford during the summer in 1897, 1898, 1899, and 1900. In her application to Vassar College in 1901, Katherine French indicated that Augustus E. Bachelder was her guardian (although her father was still living), and that she lived in Andover with an aunt.

The "little girls" became "children," and when the "children" were eighteen years old, they finally became "Katherine" and "Barbara": Palmer's entries in 1901 and 1902 read: "In Boxford this summer were at Emily's Aug & Lily, Mrs. Wilkinson, Katherine & Barbara." Numerous subsequent entries refer to them by name.

1842

GHP

March 19 at 3 Crescent Place Boston. G.H.P. born**Note 1**

Note 1842

1. Throughout the Chronicles and in their Diaries (chapter 4), both George Herbert Palmer and Alice Freeman Palmer describe their close involvement in family matters.

When he was seventy-nine years old, Professor Palmer, who grew up with three brothers and four sisters, describes in his own childhood the background of a "tenacity of family affection": "In a family where there were few servants, each of us took part in household duties. There were rooms to be set in order, wood to be split, errands to be run. The older children must wait on the younger. In this way all were drawn together by common cares. Brothers and sisters became close friends. Affection was deep and openly expressed. With no fear of sentimentality, we kissed one another often, always on going to bed, on rising, and usually when leaving the house for even a few hours. We were generous with our small pocket-moneys, and wept when the ending vacation carried away to boarding-school a member of our group. The Puritan home cannot be rightly estimated without noting the tenacity of family affection, which its devout atmosphere directly contributed to induce" (**GHP**-92).

1845

GHP

Jan 12 Lydia Manning died — 2nd wife of grandfather. Mother of Uncle William She born Sept. 15, 1786

Lucy Manning — 1st wife my own grandmother died Oct 26, 1813, born Aug 21, 1780

Feb. 8 Emily J. Palmer born, 3 Crescent Place, Boston

Firm of Palmer & Bachelders formed [an accompanying envelope with a three cents postage stamp: addressed to Mr. George H. Palmer, 32 Brattle Hall, Theo Sem., Andover, Mass.,— Return to **Palmer Bachelders & Co.,** 162 Washington St., **Boston,** Mass., if not delivered within 10 days.]

1846

GHP

Nov 28 Mary Towle born

Firm of Palmer & Bachelders succeeds Davis Palmer & Co.

1848

GHP

Aug 6 Frederic Palmer born 3 Crescent Place, Boston

1852

GHP

Jule graduated at Mayhew School & entered Topsfield Academy

1853

GHP

Sept 1 Lucy married to Augustus E. Bachelder & went to live in Harrison Avenue

Apr. Jule entered Phillips Academy, Andover Lat Dept

1854

GHP

This summer I graduated at the Mayhew Grammer School Boston & entered Phillips Academy Andover[Note 1] boarding with Julius at Mrs. Willard's, 2nd house fr Old South Church. Here knew Henry Champion.

AFP

March 22, Father & Mother married at the old farm, Osborn Hollow, N.Y.

GHP

[adds] Both lived in Colesville, about 10 miles apart Became engaged on Dr. Freeman's 25th Birthday Osborn Hollow is now Sanitary Springs

Note 1854

1. Phillips Academy at Andover opened in 1778 to prepare boys for college, and the course of study was "constantly enlarged to keep

pace with the increased requirements of admission to college . . . The expenses of attendance at the school are much less than in the larger number of New England colleges, and no higher than in other academies of high standing. The annual tuition fees amount to sixty dollars for each student. The cost of board and room in private families seldom either exceeds eight dollars a week, or falls below six . . . For over a century Phillips Academy has sent more students to Harvard than any other Academy except Exeter. Under the present administration the instruction covers in every department more than the requirement for admission to Harvard . . . The students that have come to Harvard have been among the abler graduates of both institutions." The Andover Theological Seminary (see 32n1) "was organized in 1807 under the same board of trustees . . . [and] the buildings and grounds adjoin" (Charles F. Thwing, Phillips Academy at Andover, *Harvard Register*, 1881; 3 (No. 4, April): 205–209).

1855

GHP

May Jule left Latin for Eng Dept

Sept. Jule & I took lower back room - Lizzie Jenkins

Nov. Jule left Andover & entered Butler Keith & Hill I took room with Henry Champion

AFP

February 21. born at 10.30 P.M. on a farm in Colesville, Broome Co. N.Y.

GHP

[adds] named for her mother's mother (Elvira Frost) who was herself a teacher for 10 years

1856

GHP

Spring — Aug & Luc left Harrison Ave. Boston & took house in Harvard Avenue, Brookline

In June Champion going to Yale, I went to board with Rev John Taylor

In early spring Miss Amelia Buck [?Bush]

Oct. Jule entered Palmer & Bachelders

Nov. 12, 1856 — Jacob Peabody died. Born May 14, 1778

At the close of this year, or the beginning of the following I was obliged to leave Andover on account of failing eyes. I went back to Crescent Place & was put under charge of Dr. Williams. the occulist of Arlington St. The disease was granulation which had almost closed the lids & had begun to affect the ball. Dr. W. continually cauterized the formations — which were as large as peas — & five times cut them off. He then advised change of air — a voyage

AFP

Nov. 22. Fred Washington Freeman born, in Colesville, N.Y.

GHP

[corrects] Warren
~~Washington~~

1857

GHP

Summer Oak Wood on place sold for $5000.

June 17. Grandfather Thomas Palmer died at Little Compton [Rhode Island]

Nov 7 sailed with Julius in bark Wild Gazelle, 500 tons, Humphrey Master, for Alexandria Egypt, 42 days. Remained there six weeks, visiting Cairo, then to Messina, Sicily, where we laid 2 or 3 weeks & then in a voyage of 65 days reached home May 1

1858

GHP

My eyes being no better when I returned, after a summer at Boxford, I gave up hopes of education & entered house of Wellington Winter & Gross, wholesale dry goods, on Milk St, as boy to run errands & sweep store — $50 a year salary. Jule at same time entered Patterson Eager & Co. wholesale cloth merchants.

June 26 Sat. Narrowly escaped drowning in Coles Pond

AFP

Dec. 11. Ella Louise Freeman born

GHP

[adds] at Winsor — Windsor being 5 or 6 miles fr Colesville.

1859

GHP

Nov 17 Jacob & Annie married at Boxford at the Kimballs

May 23–27 3 Crescent Place sold. Jules — he going for the summer to Mahore [?] — & I took furnished room together at 1 Bulfinch St., The Albany, getting our meals at restaurants. This was my home from now on till I entered college, & Jule's till marriage.

Spring Aug & Luc moved to Linden Place Brookline.

This winter Aug and Luce spent at Mrs. Plimptons Tremont St. Boston & P. B. & Co. moved fr 91 Washington St to 162

My eyes improving under Dr. F. T. Talbot's care, I took a private tutor Henry G. Spaulding, valedictorian of the Harvard Class of 1860 &

by studying two hours a day & keeping out of doors the rest of the day — peddling small articles for P. B. & Co — I got into College with five conditions

Ellen Wellman engaged to David Wilder

1860

AFP

Dec. 28. Roxie Estelle Freeman born.

GHP

[adds] in Colesville

Sept. Entered Harvard College

Nov. 10 1860 Arthur Kimball Palmer born

1861

GHP

They were at this time living 3 miles fr Windsor at the Moore farm but moved into Winsor when Mr Freeman came from Albany

This year J. W. Freeman began to study medicine with the physician of the next town, & the next year entered Albany Medical Scool

1862

GHP

Summer. Old House torn down & barn built

Sept, Jule leaves Patterson Eager, goes into business in Alexandria, Va. In Nov. came home with fever Went back in Feb.

April — Ellen Wellman breaks engagement to David Wilder

1863

GHP

Oct. Jule finally returns fr Alexandria & goes into business with Tileston

Father builds barn at Boxford

Professor Oliver offers himself to Ellen Wellman

1864

AFP

May 3. Julius and Effie Wood married.

GHP

June. B. A. at Harvard[Note 1]

Sept. Became Submaster in Salem High School, with A. H. Davis as Master & Lois Wright Lady Principal. Had $1000 salary & boarded at Mrs. Doyle's, Summer st.

Dec. 15 James S. Kimball dies at Nashville. aged 21
27 December J. W. Freeman graduates from Albany Medical School and settles in Windsor

Note 1864

1. Twenty-six of the 99 graduates in 1864 were selected on the basis of grades during four years in college and during the senior year alone, to speak at "Performances for Commencement" on July 20, 1864. The Commencement parts were named according to the level of distinction achieved: the 2 graduates who ranked highest, each delivered an "oration"; the next 10, a "dissertation"; the next 5, a "disquisition"; and the last 9, an "essay."

George Herbert Palmer's grades in his senior year were much higher than those for his whole four years; 86 percent of the maximum compared to 74 percent. He presented an essay entitled "Utility as a Basis of Moral Science" (*HUArch*, HUC 6863.47, holograph, 8 pages):

"These two little words right and wrong are among the most familiar in every language. Yet since the earliest times philosophers have been enquiring about them, and are still far from agreed as to their meaning. The common people, relying on instinct, have felt the want of a precise definition but little in the common affairs of life. But if the separate commands of instinct or of conscience could be reduced to one general formula, this would plainly be of service in the minor acts of morality, and in correcting conscience when vitiated. It would also lay the foundation of a science of morals whose force might be understood as well as felt.

"I call your attention to one definition which, in its earliest form was proposed more than two thousand years ago by Epicurus, and which has since been further developed under the name of Utilitarianism, or the Greatest Happiness Principle. Though continually misrepresented and sneered at, it has ever grown in favor with the increase of knowledge and candor. Among others, Hume, Paley and Bentham supported it in past days, and in our time it has found an advocate in a philosopher of perhaps the widest influence of any now living, Mr. John Stuart Mill.

"The Utilitarian, then considers an act right or wrong in proportion as it is, in the long run, more or less expedient, or useful to mankind. If it be asked useful for what? we answer, in promoting the sum of human happiness. For a little reflection will show that in this word happiness is comprehended all that men prize, and that money is gained, and various pursuits engaged in, only as different means to the same great end. The popular expression, 'following a thing for its own sake,' only means, when analyzed, that the happiness in such cases is thought chiefly to attend the pursuit of the object, and not to lie so much in its attainment.

"There is a vulgar use of the word Utility, which has somewhat hindered its adoption as a standard of Morals, where the term is employed solely with reference to sordid ends, and immediate results . . . This narrow use of Utility, or expediency, is precisely the reverse of its philosophic sense, in which that alone is considered useful which enlarges the character and happiness of the individual and of the state.

"Great care must be taken, in applying this standard, to estimate the remote, and less evident, as well as the immediate results . . . A distinctive, and most honorable feature of the Utilitarian Morality is that it identifies the interests of society and of the individual. It is not a 'selfish system.' It calls upon every one to increase the sum of human happiness — his own included

"To such a reduction of Morals to Ultimate Expediency, the Christian may object that right acts should be performed as a service to God, and not merely with a view to our own happiness, or even to that of others. But Utilitarianism is only a means for applying the principles of revelation, and finding out what the Will of God is. It is not expected that the Greatest Happiness of all will be the governing motive for every act, but only its regulating test. So that Conscience, Utility, and God's Will may all work together harmoniously if we allow Conscience to prompt our acts, if we test them by Utility, and then perform them as consecrated services to our Heavenly Father."

1865

GHP

Father retires from Palmer Bachelders & Co

Jule leaves Tileston and forms partnership in cloth business with Eager Bartlett & Co.

Hedge in front of barn at Boxford set out

Professor Taft [?] offers himself to Ellen Wellman

Sept. Entered Andover Theol. Seminary[Note 1]

Sept 8 Franklin Sawyer Palmer born

AFP

Sept. Began school life in Windsor, going to the old Academy. Charles & Emma Eastman in charge. Ada Hotchkiss my teacher.[Note 2]

GHP

[adds] From her 5th year to this she went to district school on the Moor Farm

Notes 1865

1. "Ministers of colonial churches in America had been educated overseas or went to Harvard, Yale, and other colonial colleges. Late in the eighteenth century the time came when a distinctly theological school seemed preferable, and the Seminary was the answer to the need. Andover [opened in 1808] was the first such institution among the Congregationalists, the first in New England of any Christian denomination . . . It is impressive to call the roll of colleges that invited Andover men to be their presidents. In New England they include Bowdoin and Dartmouth, Middlebury and the University of Vermont; Amherst, Smith and Brown . . . In New York were Hamilton, Union, and Vassar. Five were in Ohio: Antioch, Marietta, Oberlin, Western Reserve, and Ohio Female College. Moving steadily westward one finds Andover alumni at Wabash, Indiana, Illinois and Knox in Illinois, Drury in Missouri, Washburn in Kansas, Colorado among the Rockies, and Pomona in California. In a more northerly latitude are

Adrian and Olivet in Michigan, Beloit in Wisconsin, Iowa College in Iowa, and Fargo in North Dakota. Howard University in Washington, D. C., Atlanta in Georgia, Rollins in Florida, Fisk in Tennessee, and state colleges in Alabama and Tennessee . . . the universities of Wisconsin and Kansas should be added. And overseas were Robert College in Constantinople and the Syrian Protestant College at Beirut.

"Among the personal names are some of the greatest presidents in the history of these institutions. It is enough to name Hyde of Bowdoin, Tucker of Dartmouth, Marsh of Vermont, Stearns and Harris of Amherst, Seelye of Amherst, and Wayland of Brown, men illustrious in the ecclesiastical as well as the educational history of New England." In 1908, the Andover Theological Seminary affiliated with the Harvard Divinity School and moved to Cambridge (Henry K. Rowe, *History of Andover Theological Seminary*, Newton, 1933, pages v, 137, 192, 195).

2. In December 1992, 137 years after Alice Freeman Palmer's birth in Colesville, 120 years after she graduated from the Windsor Academy, and 90 years after her death, she is still widely known and commemorated in Broome County, New York.

The *Echo* was started in 1884 by Windsor Academy alumni, with the motto, "Let the Past Ever Speak to the Present." This publication has long reported, often from newspaper sources, on Alice Freeman Palmer's activities: in 1887, about her marriage to George Herbert Palmer, called "A Wedding of Intellect"; in 1888, about a visit to New York City, where a newspaper reported that she "does not propose to drop educational work altogether"; in 1890, when she wrote to express her regrets that she could not attend an Academy reunion, and added: "It is hard to believe that the girls and boys of to-day are half as merry and eager a set as we were over our music lessons and our Latin verbs. If we should come back, they would look upon us as middle-aged people, and never dream that we are younger than they are, and twice as happy, too! One learns how to be happy when the thirties come. If not we are poor creatures"; again in 1890, with extracts from her Recognition Day address on "Education is Life," at Chautauqua (see **AFP**-3); in 1892, about her position as "Advisory Dean" at the new University of Chicago (see 98n5); in 1896, about her address at Knox College on "The Higher Education of Women" (see 110n2); in 1900, report of her address at a Windsor Academy reunion (see 154n5); and in 1904, an obituary which includes excerpts from the memorial service at Harvard in January 1903 (see **aboutAFPann**-5).

The Broome County Historical Society has other pertinent newspaper clippings: from the *Chicago Examiner*, June 9, 1908, about the Alice Freeman Chimes at the University of Chicago (see 238n2); from the *Saginaw Evening News*, early May 1909, about the death of her father, Dr. James Warren Freeman (see 53n1); and from the *Binghamton Press*, November 9, 1920, a long article entitled, "Colesville Native Accorded Niche in the Hall of Fame, name of Alice Freeman Palmer is added to American Immortals." This piece includes individual pictures of Mrs. Palmer, her father, and her mother (see 286n1).

In December 1924, seven months after a bust of Mrs. Palmer was unveiled in the Hall of Fame, the *Echo* issued a sixty-eight page Alice Freeman Palmer Memorial Edition — "To the memory of Alice Freeman Palmer Windsor Academy's most illustrious alumna is this, the twenty-first issue of 'The Echo' humbly dedicated." Features about Alice Freeman Palmer, several from **GHP**-57, include: a picture of the marble bust of her in the Hall of Fame; five pictures of her; from an August 1924, reunion of Windsor Academy and High School alumni, a description of a visit to her birthplace — "a pilgrimage which promises to become an annual hegira to the birthplace of Windsor Academy's most famous alumna"; recollections by several of her contemporaries [had she lived, Alice Freeman Palmer would have been sixty-nine years old at this time]; three poems about her; a sketch of her compiled from *The Life of Alice Freeman Palmer* (**GHP**-57); a statement that this biography of her "is a book which should be in the home of every alumnus and should be read by every person who prides himself with having resided in Windsor"; a plan for next year by the president of the alumni group to offer a copy of the biography as a prize for the best sketch of Mrs. Palmer by a pupil in Windsor High School's English class; and the formation of a memorial committee — "It is high time that this body of men and women, the alumni of the Windsor Academy and High School, began some real constructive measure to provide in Windsor a suitable memorial to Alice Freeman Palmer."

Much more recently, the 1983 summer issue of the Broome County Historical Society Newsletter featured a cover story about Alice Freeman Palmer, and included a picture of the Freeman Home — the Old Freeman Farmhouse — in Colesville.

And, finally, as recently as March 2, 1992, Windsor's Board of Education voted unanimously "that the elementary school located in Windsor be named the Alice Freeman Palmer Elementary School." Earlier, in 1931, the High School had been named in honor of Alice Freeman Palmer with a bronze plaque that reads:

To the memory of
Alice Freeman Palmer
Doctor of Philosophy, Laws, and Letters.
1855–1902
Alumna of Windsor Academy
President and Trustee of Wellesley College
Dean of Women Chicago University
Elected to the Hall of Fame
Erected by the Alumni
"Let the Past Ever Speak to the Present"

In 1992, with some rearrangements in the Windsor Central School District, one building now houses the Alice Freeman Palmer Elementary School, with the plaque, and the Windsor Central Middle School.

(Sources: Marjory B. Hinman, Librarian, Broome County Historial Society. Oliver N. Blaise, Jr., Superintendent of Schools, Windsor Central School District. Donald R. Davis, School District Clerk, Windsor Central School District. *Echo* and newspaper clippings as indicated above. Colored photograph of the plaque. Other material from the Broome County Historical Society is used elsewhere in this compilation and is identified as BCHSoc.)

1866

GHP

Summer Aug & Luc in Europe

May Jule dissolves partnership with Eager Bartlett & Co & June 15, 1866 sails for San Francisco

This winter 4 schools had a literary contest Each school writing articles & putting them in charge of a delegate to arrange & read at the public meeting. All the other schools chose mothers as delegates. Windsor chose her [Alice Freeman]. She carried off the prize by her arrangement, her own article & her effective reading.

1867

GHP

May. Sailed with James H. Lee for Germany, $1000 being given me by A. E. B. Father giving the rest. After 10 days in England & a walk thru Friesland we settled in Stuttgardt in family of Pastor Wagner for a month & then to Tübingen. In July went to Paris to meet Aug, Luc Hattie & Alice Moss. Fell sick there with typhus fever in the brain. Attended by Mme Hahnemann. Convalescing lived with Edw. Silsbee, frequently attending with him Paris Exposition of 1867. Fine art interest strong. Return to Tubingen in Oct. & relapse occurring went back to Silsbee in Paris for another two months, then to Tubingen once more. Too weak for hard study in Philos began to read Greek with Earp Herzog & German student & hoped finally to take Ph. D. on Doctrine of Sin in Aeschylus Trilogy

June 27. Robert Manning Palmer born

1868

GHP

This summer Lee went home & Aug & Luc came from America & after visiting me in Tubingen all 3 of us went to Dresden & Berlin, I returning to Tübingen at opening of Term. Pushing on work for degree

Rev. S. E. [?] Gammell settled at Boxford

1869

GHP

Feb 8 Aunt Lucy died

June 15 Hannah Lord died
Jan 10 She [Alice Freeman] joined Presbyterian church in Windsor where her father was an Elder

AFP

Engaged to T. D. Barclay, my teacher in the Windsor Academy — a graduate of Union & student at Princeton Seminary. The following year he went to Yale Theological Seminary

GHP

[adds] He taught at Windsor two years in all Barclay was a graduate of Monmouth College then had a year at Union & another year at Princeton
July 20 1869 Bertha Palmer [born]
June — I return fr. Germany ill. Summer at Boxford
Sept. Entered Andover Theol. Sem again in Senior Year. Fred entering Junior
Nov. Left Andover on account of illness, & joined Aug. & Luc at Boxford where we spent winter in fitting up old Briggs House [see 123n10], next father's, which Aug. had just bought from father
1928 — Fred took us all with Delia to Boxford on July 20 She died there Aug 16
This year or the next before leaving Windsor she [Alice Freeman] gave the church there a chandelier, going without a cloak & earning the money

1870

GHP

May Jule returns from voyaging & goes into business w. Father
Fall Aug. left Brookline House & bought 57 Chestnut St. Boston
Sept. Entered Harvard College as Tutor of Greek[Note 1, 2] Had room 54 Thayer Hall, then first occupied Salary $1000
Took this year 2 pupils fr whom obtained $1800

Notes 1870

1. In his autobiography (**GHP**-104, page 32–34), George Herbert Palmer describes the background of his first Harvard teaching appointment: "In May [1870] I sent out applications to several Western colleges for a place in Philosophy. None of them replied. One day I met Professor Kelsey, the temporary President of Michigan, Angell's predecessor . . . I asked if there were no opening in Philosophy at Michigan. He thought there might be, would look it up and write. While waiting for the letter, I asked Professor Gurney of Harvard if I might use his name as a reference. He readily gave it, but said he

thought I made a mistake in treating my subject as final and then looking for a college where it might be taught; better turn the matter round. Choose a first-class college and teach whatever they would accept . . . Daring advice! — which I resisted. But three days later, I received from President Eliot an appointment in Greek. I replied that I could not decide at once, but must await an expected letter from the West. 'And how long?' 'A fortnight. If nothing then comes, I shall be obliged to accept Harvard.' Nothing came. Twenty-five years later, President Angell showed me on the Faculty Record my appointment to an Assistant Professorship at Michigan and underneath it, in a different hand, 'Declined.' All were dead who knew the circumstances. The only explanation I can imagine is a letter lost in the mail . . . My entire career was thus changed by a single mishap. So interlocked are luck and purpose in the game of life."

2. Palmer writes: "When I told Professor Goodwin that an objection to my entering his department was that I knew no Greek and could not write a Greek sentence if my life depended on it, he was most kind, saying that teachers drilled in Greek grammar were common, but trained in Greek literature rare. One of these would not harm his department. It harmed me, though. Most of my time the first year had to be spent on moods and tenses. In an attempt to make my students perceive what these were for, I offered, as we finished a Book of the Odyssey, to translate the whole at a sitting for all who cared to come. A large number came. Copies of the text were provided and the closest possible rendering was used. Hence rose the voluntary Greek Readings, a plan soon adopted in other departments. In successive years I read the whole Odyssey through twice" (**GHP**-104, 34–35. **GHP**-7, facsimile letter).

1871

GHP

June15 — I married Ellen Margaret Wellman daughter of Wm A. & Susan Prescott Wellman, at the Swedenborgian Church, Brookline We took Aunt Lucy's house in Boxford for summer & in Sept went to board with Mrs Baker 1 Holmes Place Cambridge.[Note 1]

AFP

Feb. 16. Broke engagement with T. D. Barclay.

GHP

[adds] He wished to marry at once & she wanted to go through college first. He complained. He was for a long time a minister in Kent,

George Herbert Palmer, age 30 years, 1872.

Alice Elvira Freeman, age 17 years, 1872.

Conn He named his eldest girl for Alice. He married Miss White (?) — daughter of minister where he taught — about two years after the engagement was broken. It was broken with mutual consent.

Note 1871

1. At the time of their marriage, Ellen Margaret Wellman was 36 years old, George Herbert Palmer was 29. "She was deeply religious, a follower of Swedenborg and the mainstay of her litle church," (56n1) which was within walking distance of her home. Her father, William A. Wellman, was also an active member of the church. The Swedenborgian Church (also called The New Church), was at 58 Irving Street in Brookline, Massachusetts. A brick church with buttresses visible on the outside, it was built in 1860–1862, was sold in the 1950s, and now (1994), with additions, is The Latvian-Lutheran Church.

Emanuel Swedenborg (1688–1772), "natural scientist, neurophysiologist, and theologian, [was] better known for his writings in theosophy than in science." After his scientific work, "he gave himself to the contemplation of spiritual matters, especially to the work of making clear to mankind the true inner doctrines of the divine Word as he claimed they were revealed to him by direct insight into the spiritual world after 'heaven was opened' to him . . . And he was assured that to him alone had the true sense of the Scriptures been opened in this way . . . It was not Swedenborg's intention to establish a new sect" "The Swedenborgians, the religious sect based on the belief that Swedenborg had witnessed the last judgment, was founded after the death of their leader" (Emanuel Swedenborg, *Journal of the American Medical Association*, editorial, 1968; 206: 887–8. *The Columbia Encyclopedia*, New York, Columbia University Press, 3rd ed., 1963, page 2077).

1872

GHP

Jan Appointed Curator of Gray Coll. Engravings $500 salary
Samuel E. Herrick Pastor Mt Vernon Church 1872–1904

AFP

June. Father and I went to Ann Arbor for examinations & Commencement. Heavy conditions.[Note 1] Studied all summer with George Smith, who was preparing for Amherst.

September. Entered University of Michigan. Roomed alone in front parlor of little house opposite the Law School [50 State St.

(BCHSoc.)]. Angie Chapin [see 58n2] & Lucie Andrews roomed above, & Misses Belden & Mason in rear rooms.**Note** 2

Heavily conditioned in entrance Greek and made it up with Emma Hall, '74. In algebra, & studied with Mr. — '75. Other subjects made up by myself while carrying Freshman work.

December. Spent all vacation in Ann Arbor studying.

GHP

March 14 — Father died — Born June 14, 1803**Note** 3 — Father & mother had been boarding in Ashburton Place but went to 57 Chestnut St & died there

Sept. Hired house 3 Garden St & began housekeeping (cor. Appian Way)

This year took Miss Matthews, daughter of Nathan Matthews cor. Commonwealth Ave. & Arlington St Boston as private pupil — at $2000 a year**Note** 4 Resigned her at the close of year & henceforward took no private pupils

At beginning of this year (Sept) resigned Tutorship in Greek & became Instructor in Philos succeeding Ellis Peterson. Also instructed in Forensics. For latter $500; for former $1000 a year.**Note** 5

Dec. 7 Harriet Amanda Palmer died 57 Chestnut St. — Born Nov. 20, 1828

Sept Took house 3 Garden St Cambridge

" Fred graduates at Andover

Nov. 1st Boston Fire.**Note** 6 — P & B burned — Aug retired from firm Feb. 1, 1873 & P. & B. to store in Temple Place

Notes 1872

1. James B. Angell, who had been president of the university for only one year, interviewed Alice Freeman himself, and decided to admit her despite her inadequate preparation. In June 1871, at the beginning of his presidency, Angell had spoken "guardedly but optimistically of the experiment then less than six months in operation of the admission of women. Its development is being watched in the universities of the East, and when it proves successful a number of the schools of that section, and even some in Europe, may be expected again to follow the lead of Michigan" (Shirley W. Smith, *James Burrill Angell: An American Influence,* Ann Arbor, University of Michigan Press, 1954: 95).

2. Nineteen years later, in **AFP**-4, Alice Freeman Palmer writes about this co-educational college: "The girl who goes to the University of Michigan to-day, just as when I entered there in 1872, finds

her own boarding-place in one of the quiet homes of the pleasant little city whose interest centres in the 2,500 students scattered within its borders. She makes the business arrangements for her winter's fuel and its storage; she finds her washerwoman, or her laundry; she arranges her own hours of exercise, of study, and of sleep; she chooses her own society, clubs, and church. The advice she gets comes from another girl student of sophomoric dignity who chances to be in the same house, or possibly from a still more advanced young woman whom she met on the journey, or sat near in church on her first Sunday. Strong is the comradeship among these ambitious girls, who nurse one another in illness, admonish one another in health, and rival one another in study only less eagerly than they all rival the boys. In my time in college the little group of girls, suddenly introduced into the army of young men, felt that the fate of our sex hung upon proving that 'lady Greek' involved the accents, and that women's minds were particularly absorptive of the calculus and metaphysics. And still in those sections, where, with growing experience, the anxieties about co-education have been allayed, a healthy and hearty relationship and honest rivalry between young men and women exists. It is a stimulating atmosphere, and develops in good stock a strength and independent balance which tell in after life."

3. Almost fifty years after his father died, George Herbert Palmer wrote about him lovingly in the 1921 article, The Puritan Home (**GHP**-92):

"My father was a Boston merchant, who had come from the country and by diligence had climbed to a competence . . . To me the day [Sunday] was one of special happiness, because my father was then at home, and during almost every hour of the day was his children's companion. We gathered about him for cheerful talk after breakfast, and after the noon dinner he usually read to us from *The Pilgrim's Progress*, or some other benign and attractive book . . . Toward the end of the evening my father was apt to put his arm around one of the children and draw him [or her] into the library for a half-hour's private talk. Blessed and influential sessions these, serving the purpose of the Roman confessional! As frank as that and as peace-bringing, but freed from its formality, with no other authority recognized than a common allegiance to a Heavenly Father, the independence of us little ones guarded by the abounding wisdom, tenderness, trust, and even playfulness of our adored companion . . .

"To the family tie the Puritans gave great prominence. Marriage was a sacrament, and the family a divine institution, where each member was charged with the well-being of all. In my own family there was little authoritative restriction. With father and mother we children were on terms of tender and reverential intimacy. They joined us in our games, were sharers in our studies, friendships, and aspirations. To them we expressed freely our half-formed thoughts. If one of them took a journey, one of us was pretty sure to be a companion . . .

"My father was not a college graduate, eagerly as he had desired to be. He sent his brother [Ray, five years younger] to Yale and accepted a business life for himself. But he more than made up the regretted loss by diligent reading, and to all his children he gave the utmost education they would accept . . .

"The libraries of my father and grandfather were considerable, containing most of the important books in history, biography, divinity, and poetry. Physical science was then just starting. Of fiction there was little; until the beginning of the nineteenth century, novelists were few . . . From our family library none of the great English poets was absent. My grandfather loved Pope, my father Shakespeare and Byron, my mother Cowper. All three wrote respectable verse, as did several of the children. Most persons did. No one of us ever doubted that to be a poet or a composer of music was the highest attainment of human faculty, unless indeed that preeminence might be challenged by the minister, to whom these artistic seers were thought to be near of kin."

Julius A. Palmer, Sr. was born in Little Compton, Rhode Island. His parents, Thomas Palmer and Susanna Palmer Palmer, "distantly related to each other," were descendants of William Palmer, who landed from the ship "Fortune" at Plymouth, Massachusetts, in 1621. Julius went to Boston in 1819, and later became the senior member of the firm of Palmer, Batchelder & Company, jewellers. "He was an ardent temperance man and was several times selected as the temperance candidate for mayor of Boston. He was a representative to the Legislature from Boston in 1843 and in 1851 . . . Though living much of the time and doing business in Boston, [Palmer] was closely affiliated with [Boxford], where he held, occupied, and improved a valuable estate, and where he gave his encouragement to all good local undertakings. Retiring to Boxford on account of age and health, he was elected to the Senate from Essex County in 1869.

"Mr. Palmer was connected with many charitable, religious, and reformatory organizations, where he exercised marked influence on account of his intelligence and high personal character. He was an active member and deacon of the Mount Vernon Church, Boston" (Sidney Perley, *The History of Boxford, Essex County, Massachusetts, From the earliest settlement known to the present time,* Boxford, published by the author, 1880, Reprint edition, 1984, page 389 footnote).

In April 1872, one month after Julius A. Palmer died, the *Congregational Quarterly* published his scholarly, twenty-four page article on the history of the Hanover Church in Boston. He was one of the founders, in 1825, of this Orthodox Congregational Church at a time of increasing unitarianism (reprint in AJL Collection).

4. The $2000 — more than Palmer's $1500 academic salary for the year — made it possible for him and his wife to go abroad in the summer of 1873.

Nathan Matthews, born in 1815, a successful business man, "retired from commercial life to devote his whole attention to real estate development and operations . . . He was a main factor in the development of the Back Bay district of Boston, and from this and other successful operations he became . . . the largest individual taxpayer on real estate in the city" (G. R. Nutter, Nathan Matthews, *HGM,* 1927–28; 26 (March 1928): 382).

He gave Matthews Hall to Harvard. "The foundation was laid in the spring of 1870, and the building was opened to students at the beginning of the college year of 1872–73. Its cost was about $125,000, and the rent of the rooms is about one tenth of this amount. Among the conditions imposed by Mr. Matthews in making the gift was that one half of the net income should be devoted to scholarships. Fifteen scholarships, therefore, of the annual amount of three hundred dollars each, have been established, bearing the name of the donor. They are given to deserving scholars, those intending to enter the Episcopal ministry and sons of Episcopal ministers preferred" (Matthews Hall, *Harvard Register,* 1881; 3 (January to July): 288).

5. "When the establishment of a Graduate Department was first before the College Faculty, in 1872, there was much opposition. It was said that the University had insufficient funds to teach undergraduates properly, and that a graduate department would weaken the College. To which President Eliot replied, as Professor Palmer remembers, 'It will strengthen the College. As long as the main duty of the faculty is to teach boys, professors need never pursue their

subjects beyond a certain point. With graduate students to teach, they will regard their subjects as infinite, and will keep up that constant investigation which is necessary for the best teaching.'

"No prophecy of Eliot has been more amply fulfilled" (Charles H. Haskins, The Graduate School of Arts and Sciences, in Morison, *Development of Harvard University, 1869–1929*, page 461–2).

6. "The great Boston fire of November 6, 1872, started [on Wednesday] in a wooden elevator shaft and burned through Saturday night until Sunday noon, destroying sixty-five acres of buildings in the area bounded by the present Summer, Washington, Milk, and Broad streets. The fire engines were handicapped by lack of horses, due to an epidemic [of equine encephalitis] that incapacitated most of these animals. The gas was cut off, leaving the city in darkness, and buildings were blown up in an attempt to halt the flames, but still the fire raged. Thousands lost their property or their livelihood. Seven hundred and sixty-six buildings, of which sixty-seven were of brick or stone, were rapidly consumed. The demolished Fort Hill area formed an open space which acted as a stopgap in that section. The fire finally was halted near the old State House" (Marjorie Drake Ross, *The Book of Boston, The Victorian Period,* New York, Hastings House, 1964, page 86).

1873

AFP

January. Joined 1st Presbyterian church by letter from church in Windsor. Samuel W. Duffield. Pastor

GHP

This spring Fred Wellman married Sallie Pomeroy

Appointed Asst Prof Philosophy (till 1880)

In June Nell and I go abroad, rapidly through England & then settle at St. Germain in Laye at Pension Louis Quartorge for summer I had no French but by end of summer c'd read & understand anything without translating

Sept. Became Ass't Prof Philosophy $2000 salary

Oct. 22 Rev. Joshua Emery resigned at North Weymouth

1874

GHP

Aug and Luc buy cottage at Magnolia in Fall This summer they were in Europe, Nell & I in their Boxford house

This summer occurred fall from horse

We devoted summer to reading Elizabethan Drama
C. H. Moore & wife at Mill House
Oct 1874 Fred goes to Revere being settled there in March 1875

AFP

Nov. & Dec. Mr. Gleason, Mr. Hostetter, Mr. Cooper, Mr. Waldinger—
Many perplexities, all together deciding me to wish to leave college to teach the remainder of the year.

GHP

[adds] This year her father sold out at Windsor & moved to Otego

1875

AFP

January. — Left college & took Principalship of High School at Ottawa Illinois, Supt. of Schools Mr. Schriet. After getting settled, first informed my family. This was the year father's financial embarrassment began. Boarded at Mr. Toger's. Salary $700.

Went to Presbyterian Church. Taught all day, & all High School subjects except Chemistry & Greek which Mr. Schriet took. He was a hot-tempered German unable to control himself or the school. Took me to my church at a distance Sunday evenings, bringing me home. This I allowed not knowing how to avoid it, until he embarrassed me by falling in love.

June. Left Ottawa to return to Ann Arbor for 75's commencement. Went home for the summer vacation to Otego. Had lost all Junior examinations & the last half year's work. Tried to study but father and Stella were sick.

GHP

[adds] in September she returned to College.
April 26 1st Greek reading fr. the Odyssey [see 37n2]
This spring Hollis Hall burned. We took in to house Jayne & Finck who were burned out & contributed $200 to fund for rebuilding
This 1st summer of Aug and Luc at Magnolia
Boxford piazza built
Sept Give room to G. E. Woodberry - $1^1/_2$ years[Note 1]

Note 1875

1. Charles F. Thwing comments (**aboutGHPann**-6, page 446): "There is one element in Palmer less frequently found in the teachers of American colleges than in the dons of Oxford and Cambridge. It is the element of picking out undergraduate friends, joining one's self to them, and them to one's self, unto the common benefit and hap-

piness . . . This student association, entered into in undergraduate days, was continued, in the case of Palmer, into the graduate years."

Thwing (page 447) quotes a letter that Palmer (then 83 years old) wrote in 1925 on the occasion of George Edward Woodberry's 70th birthday: "Just fifty years ago in one of my classes I noticed a young fellow of exceptional promise. As I had in my house at 3 Garden Street more rooms than I needed, I offered one to him and he became a member of my household. Mrs. Palmer [Ellen Wellman Palmer] as well as I became warmly attached to him. His literary interests were then forming and he was reaching out toward that perfection of style in prose and verse which has ever since distinguished him. Often we three read together the masterpieces of English poetry, and in the discussions which followed he took an active part." Thwing adds: "Such intimacies of friendship, begun in undergraduate years and enriched in all the following times, represent the best in method and means and result of all education and other relationships."

Woodberry "believed that many students who faced literature as a chore of the curriculum would find an enduring delight in poetry if it were made available to them as a recreation for their leisure and pleasure outside their regular study." In his memory, the Woodberry Poetry Room was opened in Widener Library in 1931 and was moved to Lamont Library in 1949 (J. Broberg, The Poetry Room at Harvard University, *Recorded Sound*, No. 27, July, 1967).

1876

AFP

January. Took mid-year examinations in Senior Studies — Political Economy & International Law,— Dr. Angell; Constitutional History, England & U. S. —Prof. Adams; Masterpieces of English Literature,— Prof. Moses Coit Tyler; Philosophy, Dr. Cocker; Italian, Prof. Morris; English Themes,— Prof. Tyler; Greek Tragedys, Prof. D'Ooge. Teachers' Seminaries in Latin & Greek. 20 hours weekly, examinations & with extras.

In February made up Plato, Quintilian, Physics, English Themes &c of Junior year's work — lost by going to teach.

March. Commencement speakers anounced. Ten — 8 men & two women — Annie Ekin and I.

At the Law Commencement graduated Arthur Woodcock, Mr. McDivitt, Will Coman, Clark Gleason, Frank Hostetter, Mr. Allison.

At Medical Commence. Misses Baker, Ballintine, Conklin, Hall & Mosher, all dear friends.

Farewell supper in the rooms of Kate & Will Coman, [see 58n2]

April Studied on Junior work all the recess. Chose subject of Com. oration — "The relation of Science & Poetry."**Note 1**

May Promised to teach with Will Warner in his mother's Seminary for Young Ladies in Geneva Lake, Wisconsin. Another classmate, Albert Pearson was to teach the Music. We were to take our sisters, Ella & Eva whose board & tuition were to count for 300 of the 800 salary.

GHP

June Resigned Curatorship of Gray Collection, it going to Boston

This spring E. H. Abbot goes to Milwaukee after failure

This summer we studied Boxford trees & mushrooms

June Frank [Francis Lewis] Wellman graduated & T. C. Williams.

AFP

June Graduated Univ. of Mich. A. B.

after taking examinations on 18 hrs. weekly Junior & 20 weekly Senior studies.

To the hard work of the year was added great anxiety for father's money matters, constantly growing worse, & his health and Stella's. Perplexities about some classmates were very heavy, especially Melvin Cooper — entering Auburn Theological Seminary & Charles Woodridge — the Medical School. The latter, whom I clearly disliked, had offered himself at regular intervals since the spring of '73, & in '76 had appealed to Dr. Angell, Dr. Cocker & others for influence in his behalf, thus making me miserably shy of them.

July Went home to Otego for the last time to spend a summer. Prepared Ella & myself for the year in Wisconsin.

Sept. Started early & we spent a fortnight in Philadelphia as guests of the Marstons. Mr. M was Commissioner for Wis. Charles Talmage escorted us, & there we met at the Marstons, a dozen Ann Arbor friends, chiefly of '75 & '76.

Sept. Went to Geneva Lake, Wisconsin with Ella.

GHP

[adds] Charlie & Ella were already engaged.

Nov. Gave room to S. Shepherd — Woodberry leaving. [see 46n1]

This year, Dr. Everett going abroad, I gave a course in the Divinity School in his place, going over Kant's Critique of Pure Reason.

Note 1876

1. Even many years later, James B. Angell, President of the University of Michigan, remembered: "She spoke on 'The Conflict Between Science and Poetry.' [S]he attempted to set forth the contrast between the intellectual methods of the scientific investigator on the

one hand and those of the creative poet on the other, and to show that the imagination which so richly served the poet might well be of service to the scientist in constructing theories to guide him in his quest after truth . . . [S]he was very timid and anxious about delivering her speech to the audience of three thousand . . . But she had hardly uttered two sentences when it was clear to me that she had the whole audience hanging upon her lips, as in her later years she always held her audiences spellbound to the very last syllable that she uttered" (**aboutAFPann**-5, pages 36–37).

1877

AFP

June-Sept. Spent in Ann Arbor with Sam and Lucy Andrews. keeping house. I studying for M. A. Degree. Ella went to Otego for summer.

Did not return for examinations the following year on account of Stella's illness. Never took the degree.

Was offered instructorship in Math. in Wellesley wh I declined. [see 61n1]

Sept. Went to E. Saginaw High School as preceptress with J. C. Jones as Supt. of Schools, C. T. Beatty as Principal & Annie Clark as assistant. Salary $700.[Note 1, 2]

Father made assignment, giving up everything.

Oct. Got Ella position in Hoyt Grammer School at $500. & sent for her. We boarded at Mrs. B. Thompson's.

GHP

May 22. Frederic Palmer and Mary Towle married in Brookline, Irving St.

Oct 24, 1877 Mother, Lucy Manning Peabody died Born Aug 6, 1805 — She died at 57 Chestnut St

Sept 8 Nell had hemorrhage at Boxford & I brought her to Cambridge where she was sick until I took her to south.[Note 3]

AFP

Dec. Rented house on Jefferson St. for Father & Mother. Sent for whole family.

Notes 1877

1. "East Saginaw, Michigan, [Saturday] September 8th. 1877 —
My dear Cousin Staub: —

Will you excuse a very hurried letter this afternoon, or wait until I have some time? I think I will decide for you, and send it now, as you are not near enough to judge how long it may be before I have even a few minutes again. You must know that I am settled down school-teaching again. Can you picture me as Preceptress of a High

School of one hundred and forty, and going in and out of these busy streets: E. Saginaw has 20,000 inhabitants, and just across the river, though no one could tell where one ends and the other begins, is Saginaw City with 11,000 more.

"I have a very pleasant boarding place in the home of the Mayor of the city and I think I shall enjoy my work when I become accustomed to it. It is so different from my experience in boarding school last year. In some ways it is much harder work also. I have charge of a room all day and have night classes, principally composed of Juniors and Seniors. I wish you could see my flowers. I have had several little bouquets brought me during the first week of school, but yesterday I was completely overwhelmed when a member of the school board came up the stairs where I was standing, and gave me a monstrous bouquet — in size, I mean, the flowers and their arrangement were entirely exquisite. It fills my room with the fragrance of heliotrope, day lilies and tube roses.

"You can see how good the people are to their teachers here— and that they will be inclined to be charitable. But I think I have said enough about myself, except that I am delighted with the prospect of your coming east next winter. It was very good in you to answer my letter so soon, and I was really glad to hear from you. I shall not forgive you if you come home again without coming to see me. You can take East Saginaw into your route between Chicago and Detroit very easily, and I shall be very glad to see you, and recall 'the days of our childhood' before you 'bundled on the shoulder straps and sword,' as the Jubilee singers have it, and I grasp the [?], and become accustomed to being called 'an old maid.' Ah ! [?], 'the days of our youth are the days of our glory,' so improve there, my brave cousin.

"I do not wonder that you are getting tired of such campaigns as you described in your letter. I so hope you will have no more like it, and will take care of yourself. I imagine that the climate is not very good, especially for one who has not strong lungs. I am in the most malarious part of Mich. and am told that I will surely have the ague, but I am inclined to be as obstinate as possible on that point. And I certainly think the west better for people with consumptive tendencies. Father intends to go to Iowa to live this fall, if possible; if not, next spring. Yet I can hardly bear to think of not having my <u>home</u> among the old hills in New York. It has been so long since I have been in Windsor I know very little about it, and I think that I should dread to go back there now, and see all the changes. "Married or dead" is the story of our old classmates. I have heard nothing directly from your people in a long time. Is Miss Sage still at home? And Mollie must be a young lady, now, almost old enough to marry.

"I have just seen 'Othello' very finely acted, Lawrence Barrett acting Iago. But I despise the character so thoroughly that no amount of genius can make me enjoy it really. We have many nice concerts, lectures, etc here, but I haven't time to indulge, except occasionally.

I send a picture, Staub.— the best one I have, but it isn't very clear. If you want to know how I look, I think you will have to come and see for yourself. I do not know that I have changed much, however. I do not curl my hair now, and so I suppose I look older than when you saw me last, as indeed I ought to — I haven't seen Louise in a long time. She is looking for a school again and talks of going back to Cortland if she does not succeed in finding one. I hear from home often. Ella and her Charlie are having a delightful time, I suppose. It makes me almost homesick to think of myself so long and far away from them all.

Thank you for your kind wishes, Staub. If 'the road winds uphill all the way' and is so long — the end comes to every journey, and 'after the battle — rest.' And, too, work is good for strong hands and young hearts — and I am content.

"I do hope you will write soon again. About what time do you expect to have leave of absence? You must tell me just when you are coming before hand so that I can get my work out of the way and have a chance to see you. But I shall hear from you more than once, ?letters before then — Yours sincerely — Alice E. F-." (from a copy of the original letter in the Old Ouaquaga Historical Society, Harpursville, New York. BCHSoc).

2. James B. Angell, president of the University of Michigan reminisces: "It so happened that I had occasion, I think in the year 1879, to visit the high school in East Saginaw, of which [Alice Freeman] was then principal. I attended a class in English Literature which she was teaching. The class was largely composed of boys of from fifteen to eighteen years of age, in whom one would perhaps hardly expect much enthusiasm for the great masters of English Literature. But it was soon apparent that she had those boys, as she always had her classes, completely under her control and largely filled with her own enthusiasm. They showed that at their homes they had been carefully and lovingly reading some of the great masterpieces, and were ready to discuss them with intelligence and zest. I have never witnessed finer work of the kind with a class of that sort.

"When I returned home, I wrote to Mr. Durant that he *must*

appoint the woman whose remarkable work I had been witnessing, that he could not afford to let her slip out of his hand. Whether my letter led to his decision to call her to Wellesley, I do not know. But he did call her and she went. The rest is matter of history" (**about AFPann**-5, pages 39–40).

3. Ellen Margaret Wellman and Alice Elvira Freeman each suffered from tuberculosis of the lungs before her marriage to George Herbert Palmer.

Ellen became his first wife in June 1871, when she was thirty-six years old. She probably contacted the infection when she nursed her brother who died from "quick consumption" in 1866. The final stage of her progressive illness from tuberculosis was marked by a hemorrhage from the lungs in September 1877, and she died in February 1879, at the age of forty-three.

Alice became Professor Palmer's second wife in December 1887, when she was almost thirty-three. On her mother's side there was "a tendency to consumption," and she wrote that "[o]ne of Papa's lungs has failed." Professor Palmer wrote that "her lungs were her weak part, and that from the time she went to college she had a constant cough. She took cold easily." Her youngest sister, Stella, became ill with progressive pulmonary tuberculosis in 1875, was often nursed by Alice, and died from the disease in June 1879, at the age of eighteen. In February 1880, eight months after Stella died, Alice had a hemorrhage from the lungs and the doctors thought that she, too, had tuberculosis. Unlike Ellen, Ellen's brother, and Alice's sister, however, although Alice had a chronic cough, her disease was not progressive. Her death — in December 1902, at the age of forty-seven — almost twenty-three years after the hemorrhage, was caused by an unrelated condition (Entries in the Chronicles; **GHP**-57, pages 20, 55, 79–81, 84, 329; 56n1; 217n3).

1878

GHP

Feb. 8 take Nell to Nassau St. Augustine Jacksonville Aiken Richmond Return May 12 Her father dies that day.

Our servant Sarah, who had been with us all our married life leaves us & returns to Ireland

AFP

Jan. 1. Father, Mother, Fred & Stella arrived with some household goods early in the morning & came to Mrs. Thompson's. Spent the vacation getting settled, in Jef. St.

Fred soon found work in a store, & Father began practice.**Note 1** Mother took some teachers to board.

June. Offered position at Wellesley in Math. Salary in Saginaw raised to $800. Mr. Beatty

GHP

June Fred leaves Revere & Congregationalism

Oct goes to Emmanuel Ch Boston as Assistant

May 31-July 11 in Glasgow for work with Edw. Caird whose book on Kant I had read in the winter & whose acquaintance I now made.**Note 2** Six weeks absent fr Nell

Aug 24 Received Dr. Knight's report th. no hope for Nell.

July 2 Lucy Sprague born

AFP

Ella & Charles Horace Talmage married at sunset in Jefferson St. house East Saginaw. Went on Great Lakes for wedding journey.

Sept. Moved to new house on Webster St. near the Thompsons

GHP

[adds] mayor where Alice and Ella formerly boarded.

AFP

Had some teachers boarding with us.

GHP

Oct 17 Eric Palmer born in Brookline

Aug. sells Chestnut St. house & spent winter 86 Charles St

Sept. Reappointed Asst Prof Philos on salary $2500

Throughout this autumn Nell dying & I watching with her We keep Boxford horse & buggy for daily rides

Oct. Augusta & Lucy enter Bost. Univ Med. School

AFP

Dec. 1878 Again invited to Wellesley for Greek. Declined. [see61n1]

Notes 1878

1. The late 1870s were eventful years for Alice Elvira Freeman, her parents, and her three siblings. Her mother was eighteen years old when Alice, the oldest of the four children, was born. 1877: Alice became preceptress at the East Saginaw High School in Michigan; her father declared bankruptcy; she rented a house for her family in Saginaw. 1878: her parents, her brother, Fred, and her sister, Roxie Estelle or "Stella," moved to Saginaw; her sister, Ella Louise, married Charles Talmage. 1879: Stella died; Alice went to Wellesley College as professor of history.

Starting in 1878, Alice's parents, Dr. James Warren Freeman (age 50) and Elizabeth Higley Freeman (age 41), and brother Fred (age 22) developed strong, permanent roots in Saginaw. Dr. Freeman practiced as a family physician for about thirty years, until shortly before his death in 1909. The funeral ceremonies, held in the Presbyterian Church, of which Dr. Freeman had been "a member for 31 years and an elder for 30 years . . . were peculiarly fitting [his] life and career . . . There was a large congregation assembled, and splendid tributes were paid . . . by the pastor of the church and by his son-in-law, Dr. Palmer, the attendance and the unusually numerous floral tributes also assisting in voicing the sense of the community in the loss sustained by the removal of this notable man" (clipping from *Saginaw Evening News*, BCHS).

In 1882 Fred completed the study of medicine at the University of Michigan and began to practice with his father in Saginaw. When he died in 1942, Dr. Fred Warren Freeman was acclaimed as "Beloved family physician, counselor and friend of hundreds of Saginawians for more than half a century of practice."

Alice's mother, Elizabeth Higley Freeman, also made an important contribution to the health of the community, as she became the moving spirit in establishing "A Working Woman's Home and Hospital" in Saginaw. As the wife and mother of two family physicians, she became aware of the need for such an institution; there was no hospital in the Saginaw Valley for women and children. "Young girls from the country are coming to the city in search of employment. To such the temptations of a city are peculiarly dangerous. With little or no money, unless employment presents itself at once, the advantages of a place where they can find a home and help cannot be overestimated . . . No occupation ensures permanent employment. Girls are liable at any time to discharge from one cause or another. Nor is there security against illness, which may assail at any time. The fear of such liabilities to women who are self-dependent is terrible . . . "

Other women for whom "the hospital would prove a blessing" were also identified: "The wife of the poor mechanic who cannot afford the services of a nurse at a time when, of all others, [that is, for childbirth] the best of care is needed, can, in such an institution, find, for a moderate sum, skilled care and nourishing food. Hundreds of women, wives of woodsmen, are left alone at times to meet the trials and perils of maternity, dependent on chance or a neighbor's kindness."

"Mrs. Dr. Freeman" was president of the Working Woman's Home and Hospital Association, which raised the funds to start the institution in 1888. Two years later, she was also chairman of the Association's building committee which planned and solicited funds for a new building to expand the service. *The Saginaw Evening News*, on October 9, 1890, described a well-attended public reception on the formal opening of the New Home and Hospital for Working Women, and added that "it is evident that the noble work which has been done by Mrs. J. W. Freeman and her charitable lady friends is appreciated as it should be."

At the very time when Mrs. Freeman was receiving this accolade, her daughter, Alice, having left Saginaw eleven years before, had already been president of Wellesley College, had married George Herbert Palmer, and had recently accepted leadership positions with a number of women's organizations.

Sometime between 1920 and 1935 the Woman's Home and Hospital Association became St. Luke's Hospital Association of Saginaw, and later St. Luke's Healthcare Association. Now, in 1993, St. Luke's is a 262-bed general hospital (medicine, surgery, and obstetrics), accreditated by the Joint Commission on Accreditation of Healthcare Organizations and a member of the American Hospital Association.

(For information in this note I am grateful to James Warren Freeman of Fairport, New York and Ms. Carol Moulton, Executive Secretary, St. Luke's Hospital in Saginaw, Michigan.)

2. This was "the first of six summers [only two other visits, in 1879 and 1880, are entered in the Chronicles] . . . [that Palmer] spent with this stimulating friend . . . What I sought him for chiefly was his Hegelianism . . . Our procedure was always the same. We took a furnished house and had the owner cook for us, often in the English Lake Country, sometimes in the Highlands . . . After a simple breakfast we worked in our respective rooms at our respective studies till luncheon time . . . [Then] we must walk for three hours . . . It always rained. I have gone six weeks without seeing the sun. These walks were our seasons of earnest discussion [Caird] was prodigiously learned. He loved the English poets too, but more still Dante and Goethe. In religion a Presbyterian, in politics an extreme liberal, [he was] a propagandist for woman's education and suffrage" (**GHP**-104, pages 67–69).

1879

GHP

Feb. 10 Nell died & was buried in Garden St graveyard**Note** [1] Benj. Worcester reading service

Feb 24 Louis Dyer came & took meals with me till I abandoned the house

AFP

May. R. B. McKnight

GHP

May 18 1879 Arthur Kimball Palmer died [18 years old]

June join Cairds at Dingwall, Scotland

April. Left Garden St & took rooms 25 & 27 Stoughton Hall Having meals served in room by Reid, my man.

June. Fred leaves Emmanuel Ch. & in Oct goes to Lonsdale [Rhode Island]

Aug & Luc went this spring for last visit to Europe — 1 year

AFP

June 20. Roxie Estelle Freeman died. 2.30 a.m.

July. Went to Wellesley College as Professor of History. Sarah Eastman my assistant. Roomed with Angie Chapin, instructor in Greek.[Note 2]

This my first coming east of New York.

Notes 1879

1. In his autobiography (**GHP**-104, page 36–40), George Herbert Palmer writes of "an influence which was the chief formative agency of the first half of my life . . . For ten years I followed Ellen Margaret Wellman, of Brookline. She lived but a few doors from my sister [Lucy] and was an intimate in my sister's household. No doubt I am prejudiced, but I believe every one living in Brookline at that time ackowledged her as preëminent in fascination and accomplishments. A little creature, weighing less than a hundred pounds, all grace, vivacity, and charm, abounding in health and spirits, totally unacquainted with fear either of man or nature, all she said or did was unique, though never queer.

"Those were the days when girls did not go to college or take part in public affairs. But the education the best of them gave themselves induced a refinement all their own. Miss Wellman was exquisite in all things, as a musician, actress, dancer, talker. She had read widely and with discerning taste. French was nearly as familiar to her as English. With all her brilliancy, too, and perpetual humor, she was deeply religious, a follower of Swedenborg and the mainstay of her little church. Several years older than I, she allowed me during my Harvard and Andover days all the friendship I could ask until a catastrophe occurred, parting us for a time, but ultimately uniting.

"A favorite brother of hers [Henry C. Wellman] was in the class below me at Harvard . He looked forward to a scholarly life, but was struck down the year after graduation with quick consumption. He was bitterly rebellious. With her usual unselfish ardor she abandoned all other interests to identify herself with him. She must be his only nurse. She did not leave his room by day and slept on the floor beside him at night. When he died [in 1866] he was at peace with himself and God. Up to that time she had never known a day's illness; from that time she knew no day of health, and she never regretted the sacrifice.

"The following year she spent in the Azores with little improvement in health but great enjoyment. Her ability to enjoy, no weakness could check. I was abroad all this time. We exchanged a few letters, only a few. But when I came home, broken, too, the love of years could no longer be hidden. It had ripened in us both. Through much opposition from both families on grounds of age, religion, and health, we came to our joyful wedding on June 1, 1871.

"The specifically intellectual profits of an ideally happy marriage cannot be summarized. They are too subtle and permeating. But I will venture to name a few of the more conspicuous. Inclusive of all else was the whole-hearted companionship which gave a deeper significance to all I did. She taught me to talk; for we talked all day, seldom of trivialities or gossip, but of things worth talking about. Able to go about but little, she entered the more completely into my work. The publication of my Odyssey was due to her urging, and to her it is dedicated. Innumerable students were drawn by her to our home, and her swift sympathies contributed something to the modern friendly Harvard spirit. Then, too, I felt it an enlargement that the sources from which we instinctively drew our spiritual sustenance were so different. She read her Swedenborg every day and in the early years hoped to see me a convert. But at the last I think she liked me better as I was.

"I should add also that the knowledge that we could be together only a short time sanctified those precious years and deepened their influence. For two years after her hemorrhage came, she could only speak in whispers. But this in no wise checked her gaiety or charm. We talked of her approaching death as freely as of any other incident. She advised me, after it should occur, to take rooms in the College buildings, herself selected the rooms, and planned how our furniture should be disposed. On February 10, 1879, she died. For eight and a half year's thereafter . . . I lived among my boys in Stoughton Hall."

Palmer's entry for September 1, 1899: "I had Ellens body removed from the tomb in the Old Cambridge Burying Ground where it had lain for twenty years to her family lot in Forest Hills — fulfilling my promise to her."

2. In October 1899, at the inauguration of Wellesley's President Caroline Hazard, James B. Angell, president of the University of MIchigan, was one of the speakers: "[T]he relations between the University of Michigan and Wellesley College have been remarkably close. When President Durant began his great work here, the number of college-trained women in the country was small. He encountered some difficulty for a time in finding suitable women for his Faculty. As early as 1874 he began to make inquiries of me concerning the few women who were graduating from the University of Michigan. I think the first one he received on my recommendation was Mary Sheldon, widely known before her death [in 1898] as Mary Sheldon Barnes, the author of school histories prepared on an original plan. He was so pleased with her that he invited several others. Finally he wrote me that he would take any one I should be willing to recommend. This was welcome news to me. It will perhaps interest you to know that under this general commission I warmly recommended to him one of our graduates, whom I found teaching English in a Michigan High School with such marked success as to fill me with admiration. She is known to you — and to whom is she not known? — as Alice Freeman Palmer [who was present on the occasion]. Professor Chapin, Professor Coman, Associate Professor Chandler, Associate Professor Case, and others who are not now with you, have worthily represented us on your Faculty" (*A Record of the Exercises Attending the Inauguration of Caroline Hazard, Litt. D., as President of Wellesley College III October MDCCCXCIX*, Cambridge, Riverside Press, 1899, page 20–21. See also Mary B. Jenkins, Wellesley class of 1903, Michigan Women at Wellesley, *Wellesley Alumnae Magazine*, vol. 10, No. 2, December 1925, 57–59).

For the six graduates from the University of Michigan whom Angell names, the following table shows the year of graduation, the starting year at Wellesley, the initial subject taught, the field in which professorship was reached, and the year that emeritus status began:

Mary S. Case	1884	1884	Latin	History of Philosophy	1924
Eva Chandler	1878	1879	Math	Mathematics	1920
Angie C. Chapin	1875	1879	Greek	Greek	1919
Katharine Coman	1880	1880	Rhetoric	Political & Social Sci	1913
Alice E. Freeman	1876	1879	History	History, Political Sci	
Mary D. Sheldon	1874	1876	English Literature, professor, 1876–1877; History, professor, 1877–1879		

1880

GHP

Feb. Corporation granted me 26 Stoughton Hall which I rebuilt as a dining room

Bought Mrs. Bacon's house in village & gave it to Boxford as public library[Note 1]

AFP

February. Had hemorrhage in upper lobe of right lung. Sick in hospital & consulted Dr. H. I. Bowditch. He said I would not live six months & advanced So. France. I went to the old farm & Aunt Sarah [in Colesville, New York] & spent March there, consulting Dr. Willard Parker in New York. He told me I could live if I had enough character & pluck to do it.

Returned to college first week in April after Easter Recess & carried my full work. 15 lectures in History (including the entire college) daily Bible class, morning domestic work & class advisor for 80.

GHP

July 16 Lucy Ann (Palmer) Bachelder died Born Feb1 1831 They returning fr years absence in Europe

Mr Gammell resigned at Boxford & ws succeeded by Mr Alcott.

This summer Aug. let his Boxford house to Irving Winslow & the following year sold it to him.

June-Sept I in Borrowdale England wth Cairds.

Oct Fred leaves Lonsdale & in Dec. settled at Jenkintown [Pennsylvania]

Sept. Resigned work in Forensics

Called to Mills Professorship of Philosophy at University of California, $4500, Declined[Note 2]

Notes 1880

1. In 1873, the Boxford Public Library was established in a rented room, by people who contributed books and money. "In 1880 a small wooden cottage was purchased and fitted up for the use of the library. The entire expense was $360, and the amount was secured by subscription, Prof. George H. Palmer of Harvard College, a summer resident of the town, being the leading donor . . . Professor Palmer gave a collection of about 100 volumes as a memorial of his wife, Ellen Margaret Palmer; and among the other leading donors have been Miss Augusta Palmer [Julia Augusta Palmer] . . . and Mrs. A. E. Bachelder [Lucy Palmer Bachelder]" (C.D. Tillinghast, The Free Public Libraries of Massachusetts, 1891, in Massachusetts Board of Education, *Fifty-Fourth Annual Report*, 1889–1900, Janu-

ary, 1891, page 31. Tillinghast was assistant secretary of the board; Alice Freeman Palmer is listed as one of the eight members).

Professor Palmer describes the library in 1900 (**GHP**-39): "It cannot then be said that the natural conditions of Boxford are exceptionally favorable. It is an average country town. But let us see what man has done here to make life worth living during the last ten years . . . A little before the beginning of this period a public library has been started, and the people — always great readers of books and magazines — have been spending $100 a year on novels, histories, biographies and general literature. Our collection now numbers 2,200 volumes, with no rubbish and few books not in frequent use. Different ladies give their services as librarians, and so stop all cost of care and circulation."

In the 1980s a large addition to the original building created a beautiful, modern library. The historical collection includes many books by members of the Palmer family. George Herbert Palmer has given some volumes from his library as well as copies of a number of his own publications. Copies of *Self-Cultivation in English* (**GHP**-34) and *The Glory of the Imperfect* (**GHP**-19) each have the same large bookplate:

Boxford Public Library

In Memory of
Ellen Margaret Palmer
This Book
Is given to the Town she loved
by her Husband

2. From 1880 (age 38) to 1892 (age 50), Palmer's entries indicate that he declined six offers of academic positions: 1883, Phillips Academy Exeter, Principalship; 1883, Smith College, Professorship of Philosophy; 1884, Johns Hopkins University, Professorship; 1888, Kansas State University, Chancellorship; 1892, University of California, President; and 1892, University of Chicago, Head Professor of Ethics.

1881

GHP

Jan 30 Julia Augusta Palmer died at 86 Charles St

A. V. G. Allen took house in Boxford.

AFP

Oct. Mr. Durant died.

Nov. 15. was appointed Vice & Acting President for the year and Miss Howard was given a leave of absence.**Note** 1

Note 1881

1. Regarding Miss Howard's presidency since 1875: "No one could have had a more difficult time than our first president, that stately lady of the old school, brought up under the seminary standards of the Mid-Victorians, dominated on the one hand by the masterful personality of the founder [Henry Durant] and beset on the other by the hundreds of students, already clamoring, even as now [1924], for freedom of self-expression" (**aboutAFPann**-20).

1882

GHP

Jan 29 Mary Anne (Kimball) Palmer died

Rev. Joshua Emery died at Kansas City, Apr. 24. born Aug. 5, 1807

Augustus buys house 105 Mt Vernon St Boston

Rev Samuel Herrick comes to Mt. Vernon Church

AFP

June. Elected President of Wellesley College.**Note** 1

" Michigan University gave me Ph. D. Father & Fred present.**Note** 2

GHP

This summer — Fred in Europe, Mary & Eric with me at Boxford — I built kitchen & two chambers on my house

The Ballous in the old house

Notes 1882

1. Alice Freeman Palmer's official relations with Wellesley College: summer 1877, declined instructorship in mathematics; June 1878, declined position in mathematics; December 1878, declined position in Greek; July 1879, accepted professorship in history, 1879–1883; professor of political science, 1883–1886; November 1881, appointed acting president; June 1882, elected president; December 1887, resigned when she married Professor Palmer; president, Student Aid Society (1898); trustee, 1884–1902; member, executive committee, 1889–1902.

2. A resolution in the minutes of the Board of Regents of the University of Michigan: "Resolved, that the honorary degree of Doctor of Philosophy be and the same is hereby conferred upon Alice Elvira Freeman, A. B., a graduate of this University, late professor of History in, and now president of, Wellesley College, Mass."

1883

GHP

Took my sabbatical year of vacation from Harvard**Note 1** & went to work on my Odyssey. During the summer at Boxford with Fred & Mary & made this my home through the year, letting my Stoughton rooms to Adams Claflin. Spent much time fitting up the old Boxford house which I bought this autumn.

Sept. Appointed Professor of Philosophy $3000 Salary was raised in 1886 to $3500; in 1888 to $4000 in 1892 to 4500 — in 1897 to 5000 — in 1905 to 5500

All Professors appointed at this time received lower salary because of poverty of College**Note 2**

In May of this year the Principalship of Phillips Academy Exeter was offered me at a salary of $3500 & house, I to have no formal teaching unless I wished and in early September a Professorship of Philosophy at Smith College on $2500 salary. [see 60n2]

Dec. Mr. Kendall came to Boxford as minister.

Notes 1883

1. Harvard was the first university to establish the Sabbatical Year, in 1878. "Each seventh year . . . a professor may take to himself on half pay. He need not teach or study, he may travel or remain at home, he may even decline the proffered vacation and go on with customary work and salary; but the opportunity is given to freshen and enrich himself, and by doing so to enrich his subsequent teaching."

In December 1887, when Professor Palmer married Alice E. Freeman, "her obvious need after so many years of labor was entire rest and change of scene." Although Palmer had had a sabbatical only five years before [in 1883], the university authorities, "perceiving Mrs. Palmer's needs offered [him] another prematurely." They were away from June 1888 to September 1889, and again in 1895 to 1896. Their next sabbatical started in September 1902; Mrs. Palmer died in Paris on December 6th of that year (**GHP**-104, page 72. **GHP**-57, page 191–192. 217n3).

2. Ten years later, in 1893, Harvard's "poverty" continued: "the joint account of the University, College, and Library was overdrawn by about $25,000, owing to new instructors, some advances in salaries, remodeling of buildings, and last, but by no means least, the World's Fair exhibit [see 87n3]. As most of the College officers have modest salaries, and are always forced to live simply and count coppers

carefully, it is depressing to begin a year under the necessity of economizing rigidly for the University as well as for self. Since no reductions can be made in salaries, either in number or amount, economy in College outlays means a little less relief for the older professors from blue-book reading, theme-sorting and similar harassing chores which lessen their effectiveness as teachers and investigators. To the younger men retrenchment means added work and perhaps less pay than they had hoped to receive. To the administrative officers it means less clerical assistance, longer hours, and more exacting work. To needy students it means less College aid from monitorships, and fewer temporary jobs in the Office and laboratories."

Early in 1894, "the College was surprised by the announcement that the Corporation, from motives of economy due to a deficit of nearly $25,000 last year, had requested the resignations of the following gentlemen: [two professors and four instructors were named]. The resignations will take effect at the end of the present academic year . . . From this action on the part of the Corporation it is inferred that henceforth the tenure of office of professors is not a life tenure, as has hitherto been generally assumed" (*HGM*, 1893–94; 2 (December 1893): 230–231; (March 1894): 443–444).

One hundred years later, in the 1990s, Harvard University faces daunting financial problems "confronting virtually all higher-education institutions, such as mounting costs for salaries, financial aid, and scientific equipment; limits on how much tuition and fees can rise; and a national recession that hampers fundraising." As only one example, from the area of student financial aid: "Although the Harvard-Radcliffe Financial Aid Office was already prepared to offer more than $28 million in grant aid last year, by mid-year it had to scramble to come up with an additional $1.5 million of Harvard-Radcliffe funds to meet an unexpected demand for grant assistance . . . a fight is being waged on many fronts to protect vital programs from the debilitating effects of budget cuts" (President Rudenstine discusses academic planning and priority setting. Pressures on financial aid. *Harvard Gazette*, December 13, 1991, pages 1, 7, 11).

1884

GHP

Visited Fred & Jenkintown for some weeks this winter & also Theodore Williams who was living with Mrs. Scudder & Miss Dalton in New York

In spring my Odyssey published [**GHP**-1]

In August I go with Edwin & Philip Abbot to England for six weeks

AFP

June. My class at W. C. graduated; Edith Tufts President**Note** 1

GHP

Dr. Freeman tells me that he went with Alice in order to prevent Gleason & Hostetter from following her

AFP

July 12.-to Sept 1. Spent in England Scotland & Wales with Electa Dye. Father went with us by City of Rome as far as Keswick & then returned by the same steamer. We were at Castlerigg Cottage; there met the "Country Parsons" from Oxford & Cambridge. Went through the Lakes, on to Scotland, and returned by Durham & York to London for International Conference on Education to which I had been appointed delegate from American Colleges by U. S. Com. of Ed. at Washington. Earl Ray presided. I was called on to speak three times.**Note** 2 James Russel Lowell asked to make me a discusser which I declined.

Met Mrs. Henry Sidgwick & Miss Helen Gladstone, & accepted invitation to spend a week at Newnham College with them & Miss Clough. Mr. Hammond, Fellow & lecturers at Trinity gave me a lunch in his rooms. Met Archen [?] Hinde. They took me through the libraries & private gardens. Miss Clough took me rowing on the Cam.**Note** 3

Electa & I walked in Shakespeare Country, a few days in Wales & sailed by City of Rome, reaching N. Y. Sept 1.

GHP

Dec. 17 Party at Prof Horsfords. Alice & I meet

This year Pres Gilman authorized Stanley Hall to ask if I would allow my name to be presented to the Trustees of Johns Hopkins University for a Professorship, I declined, tho' assured I should be elected. [see 60n2]

Christmas of this year to June 6 acquaintance with Mary Whitall Smith

Notes 1884

1. The class of 1884 elected Wellesley's president, Alice Freeman, an honorary member. In 1903, Edith S. Tufts, the president of the class, writes: "To the members of the class of '84, the death of Alice Freeman Palmer brings a sense of personal loss. We owe to her, as our honorary member, much that was best, much that we value most in our college course" (**aboutAFPann**-6). Years later, in 1924, Edith Tufts adds: " I ought to remember just how we of '84 asked her to be our honorary member, but it has slipped my mind whether we sent an embassy or a letter, and I forget, too, how she accepted.

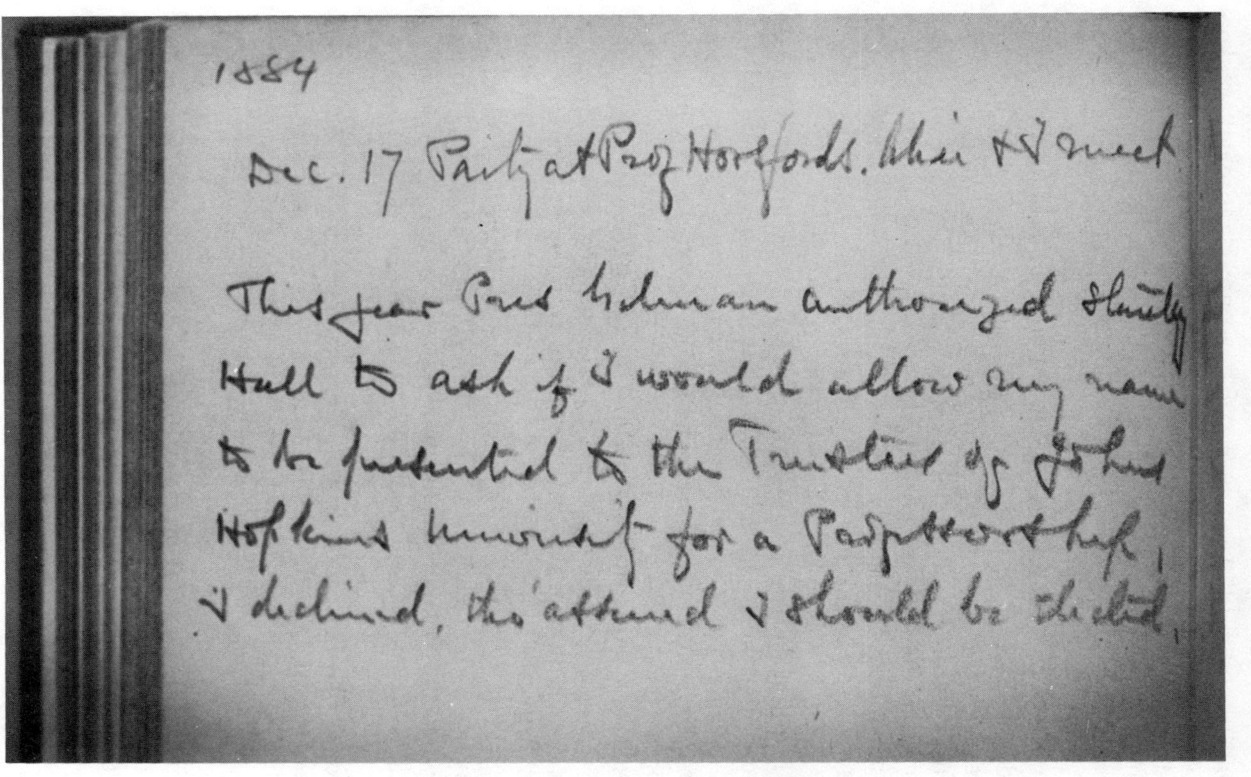

1884

Dec. 17 Party at Prof. Horsford's. Whist & I went.

This year Pres. Gilman authorized Stanley Hall to ask if I would allow my name to be presented to the Trustees of Johns Hopkins University for a Professorship. I declined, tho' assured I should be elected.

George Herbert Palmer's entries, 1884. (actual size)

But no '84 can forget the pride we had in her acceptance, nor the delightful fellowship we enjoyed with our president in college days and afterwards" (**aboutAFPann**-20).

Subsequent entries show that Eben N. Horsford was an honorary member of the class of 1886, and both George Herbert Palmer and Lyman Abbott, of the class of 1888. (See **aboutAFPann**-19)

2. On August 8, Henry Sidgwick, English philosopher, "went to London to listen to International Educationists in Conference . . . Room crowded The internal conversation was hardly a debate . . . the nations are at such different stages in the development of the question of female education. Two Frenchmen disputed whether woman was to be specially trained for her function as 'mère.' The lowest point was reached by a German who praised the institution in Dresden (?) where they are taught to wash babies.

"The best speech was by Miss Freeman, Principal of Wellesley College. I gathered from her that the practical question in the United States is not whether women are to have a University education, but whether they are to have it in mixed classes with men. It appears that, speaking broadly, the Western States have gone for mixed education — the University of Michigan (*e.g.*) is open to both sexes equally — while the more dignified universities in the Eastern States are still resisting the invasion of women, and separate colleges for them, like Wellesley, are flourishing. Miss Freeman holds that the two systems should go on side by side being adapted respectively to different kinds of women. Parents should choose." (Arthur Sidgwick and Eleanor M. Sidgwick, *Henry Sidgwick: A Memoir*, London, Macmillan and Co., 1906, page 384). (See also **AFP**-4)

3. Anne Jemima Clough was the first principal (in 1871) of a house for women students, later Newnham College, at Cambridge University in England. "In 1870 members of Cambridge University had prepared a scheme of lectures [for women] . . . and as these lectures drew to Cambridge women from a distance, a house was provided, under the charge of women, for their accommodation. As the undertaking grew, the Association for Promoting the Higher Education of Women in Cambridge was formed to take charge of it, Newnham Hall was opened, and . . . [soon] took permanent form as Newnham College. In this college in 1879, 82 women were receiving instruction, largely in the lectures of the University and its colleges. [In 1889 and 1890, Ellen Fitz Pendleton studied at Newnham College. She became President of Wellesley College in 1911 (Florence Con-

verse, *The Story of Wellesley,* Boston, Little Brown & Co., 1915: 114).] It was about 1878 or 1879 that the movement took its start in Oxford, and two halls, Lady Margaret Hall and Somerville Hall, were opened for women, and opportunities of instruction by University men were given, more or less informally and privately" (Joseph B. Warner, Radcliffe College, *HGM*, 1893–94; 2 (March 1894): 332).

1885

GHP

June go to California to conduct Harv. Examinations[Note 1] — Stop in Jenkintown, Denver, Manitou, Salt Lake City, Lake Tahoe, San Francisco, YoSemite Valley (a fortnight with Prof Stringham), Portland, Yellowstone Park, Milwaukee (with Edwin Abbot), & home Aug. 5

Spent rest of summer at Magnolia where Fred & Mary had Augustus cottage. I writing my first article on Education [**GHP**-10]

AFP

April, Moved to my new rooms in Norumbega — fitted up by the class of 1886 (Prof. Horsford.) [see **aboutAFPann**-1]

GHP

Sept. Salary raised to $3500

Nov. Article on The New Education pub. in Andover Rev. Novemb [**GHP**-10]

Note 1885

1. "The June examinations for admission to Harvard College, the Lawrence Scientific School, the Law School, and the Medical School [were] held simultaneously in Cambridge, Exeter, N. H., New York, N. Y., Philadelphia, Penn., Cinncinati, Ohio, Chicago, Ill., and San Francisco, Cal., on the Thursday, Friday, and Saturday following the last Wednesday in June." A representative from Cambridge was present to be in charge of the examinations and to answer any general questions about the University. "A fee of five dollars [was] to be paid in advance by every candidate . . . examined for admission to Harvard College at any place other than Cambridge."

In 1881, the prescribed, written examination for admission to Harvard College consisted of one hour for each of the following topics: on Thursday, Caesar and Virgil, Latin at sight and Composition, Translation of Xenophon at sight or Goodwin's Reader (pp. I-III) and Iliad I., II., and Sentences to be translated into Greek; on Friday, Algebra, Arithmetic, English, Ancient History and Geography, and Plane Geometry; on Saturday, French or German, and Physics (*Harvard Register*, 1881; 3 (January to July): 108–109. *HGM*, 1896–1897; 5 (September 1896): 75–76).

1886

GHP

May 10 Vote of Corporation that morning Prayers be made voluntary
March, visit Wellesley for 1st time, with Gilman, talk with Alice
May 28 Prof Horsfords Library Day at Wellesley
June 25 Alice comes to Class Day
July 16–20 Alice visits Boxford for 1st time with Mrs. Claflin
July 29 with her in the Wellesley Woods

AFP

28 June, Library Day in honor of Prof. Horsford.
Prof. Horsford's class graduated. [see 64n1]

GHP

Dec. 1st article on Limitations of the Elective System pub. in Andover Rev [**GHP**-11]

1887

GHP

Jan. 2nd article Limitations of Elect Syst And Rev. [**GHP**-12][Note 1]

This spring my Educational articles published in volume by Little Brown & Co Boston [**GHP**-13]

AFP

Columbia gives me L. H. D. at its Centennial Celebration [Note 2]

GHP[Note 3]

Sept 28 Augustus & Lilly married at Poughkeepsie

Dec 23 [Friday] Married to Alice E. Freeman at Gov. Wm Claflins 63 Mt Vernon St Boston at 11.30 A.M. by Revs S. W. Herrick, Frederic Palmer, & C. H. Talmage. Reception & wedding breakfast 12–2 Took 4.45 train for Boxford where spent 10 days in my rooms, Katie cooking for us. Took furnished house in Cambridge 479 Broadway, cor. Prescott St until June, $1000 a year

Edwin Abbot gave wedding present of $500 & Prof Horsford sent us on wedding day $5000 for European journey & portrait of Alice for Wellesley

Dec. 23 Married at Gov. Claflins Mt Vernon St., Boston, by Frederic Palmer, Charles Talmage & S. E. Herrick

Notes 1887

1. Miss Freeman and Professor Palmer first met on December 17, 1884, and two years later it was clear that they would be married. On January 25, 1887, George Herbert Palmer wrote to his close friend, William C. Lane:

Dear Will:

I want you and your mother to know that sometime — when, I do not know myself — I am going to marry Alice Freeman of Wellesley. We have been friends for a long time, drawn together first by our common work, then, as aims and tastes were felt to be in harmony, finding our intimacy deepen, until we have finally crossed the shadowy line which separates friends from lovers. When you spoke to me so kindly last winter, I could not honestly admit that I was engaged, nor on reflection did I think I ought to deny it. I was puzzled to describe my status. Those who understand what true marriage means do not know much about engagements.

We thought we ought not to let our wishes appear until the Wellesley Trustees were consulted. This could not properly be done till the college closed. So we have put ourselves on the hard fare of seeing one another but rarely, and & have not told our most intimate friends what we were thinking about. I have tried, however, by mentioning Miss Freeman's name from time to time to let you see that she was more & more my very dear friend & that I like everybody admired her exceptional powers and character. You have understood me, I am sure, & will recognize this seemingly sudden step as an equable growth & no abandonment of anything once held dear. Whether I can make it for Miss Freeman the enlargement of life it is for me, the years must show.

Will you still keep the matter entirely private — you & your mother — for a few weeks more?

Faithfully yours,
G. H. Palmer

Cambridge
Jan 25, 1887

The Freeman-Palmer correspondence from January until June, when they announced their engagement, shows how difficult the period was for both of them (**GHP**-109. **AFP**-20). On February 21, however, Miss Freeman's thirty-second birthday, Professor gave her an engagement ring which she proceeded to wear (**GHP**-57, page 170), and he also used that date for the preface of *The New Education*, his volume of educational essays (**GHP**-13) which was published in the spring.

(I am grateful to Miss Margaret Lane for permission to present this transcript of the letter from her great-uncle, George Herbert Palmer, to her father, William C. Lane.)

2. No citation is available from Columbia University.

In January when Miss Freeman first heard from Columbia about the award, Professor Palmer wrote to her: "how pleased I am with the proposed degree from Columbia. Such a thing is altogether unique. I know of no other case where an honorary degree has been given by a great eastern college to a woman" (**GHP**-109, page 103).

From The Centennial of Columbia College, editorial in *Boston Medical and Surgical Journal*, 1887; 116 (April 14): 364: "This week Columbia College is celebrating, with appropriate ceremonies, the one hundredth anniversary of its revival after the Revolution. In 1787 it was reorganized by an act of the State Legislature which confirmed the royal charter granted in 1754 for the establishment of a college in New York and also changed the name of the institution from King's College to Columbia College"

3. Vida Dutton Scudder describes how George Herbert Palmer introduced her to her academic career at Wellesley College: "My mother was the close friend of his sister Emily, and we were spending the summer in one of his old houses in Boxford. Those sweet houses! The New England quiet surrounding them, the meadows, the brook and the pine-woods, the syringa by the door! . . . How well I recall the peaceful evenings, when Professor Palmer, in one of the most beautiful voices ever granted a man, read aloud to us, now Shakespeare's sonnets (I knew most of them by heart; my college roommate [Smith College, class of 1884] and I used to recite them together while we made our beds), now a passage from his growing translation of the Odyssey. His celestial simplicity took an interest in everyone; he extended friendliness to me. I owe him much. Chief among those debts I reckon one remark, which cleared some prickly brambles from my relations with my fellows. 'I am defeated,' said that very wise gentleman, whose culture was as sensitive and wide as any I have ever met; 'I am defeated and know it, if I meet any human being from whom I find myself unable to learn anything.' Simply and humbly he said it; and the listening girl, still fastidious despite her growing desire to draw near to the dispossessed, was a bit awestruck. I wonder yet whether the sentiment be not a trifle exaggerated; but he meant it, and it betrayed the secret of that extraordinary sympathetic insight which distinguished him from his perhaps more famous colleagues in one of the most distinguished groups Harvard has known.

"Perhaps such insight guided his suggestion to my mother that I apply for a position to teach English literature at Wellesley College.

He was engaged, so he confided to her — but I think the knowledge was common property — to the most wonderful woman in the world: Miss Alice Freeman, President of the College. She would be marrying him presently; but the privilege of working under her might still be known for a short time. Should he send Vida with an introduction to this marvelous person?

"I was a very frightened young woman; but I saw Miss Freeman, and she was gracious to me . . . So in the autumn of 1887 I became a Wellesley instructor; engaged to teach a course in the modern English poets—'modern' in those days meant the Romantic Revival and the Victorian Age—at the munificent salary of five hundred dollars a year. That seemed to me a great deal of money; I was scared, amused, and a little ashamed, when told that I was to earn it" (Vida Dutton Scudder, *On Journey*, New York, E. P. Dutton & Co., 1937: 94–96).

1888

GHP

Wedding receptions 2 Wednesdays in Jan, 2 in Feb

Pres. Eliot gave us a Faculty Lunch at his house day after our first at home

April 7 Fred takes parish at Andover[Note 1]

June 1888-Sept1889 Sabbatical Year

This year was offered the Chancellorship of Kansas State University. Declined [see 60n2]

AFP

George's class at Wellesley graduated Lyman Abbott other honorary member, Christable Lee — President (Safford.) [see 64n1]

GHP

Sept. Salary raised to $4000

Note 1888

1. Innumerable entries throughout the Chronicles document the close relationship of George Herbert Palmer and Alice Freeman Palmer with "Fred" and his immediate family. Frederic Palmer, the youngest of the Palmer siblings, was six years younger than his brother, George. Fred and Mary were married in 1877 and first met Alice Freeman in September 1886, at Wellesley College when Professor Palmer was courting her. She reported, "How much I like them both! What very good friends we could be!," and George responded that they "were much drawn to you" (**GHP**-109, pages 45, 55). In December 1887, Reverend Palmer was one of the three

clergymen who married Alice Elvira Freeman and George Herbert Palmer.

For sixteen years after he graduated from Andover Theological Seminary in 1872, Reverend Frederic Palmer had a succession of placements: in Revere, Massachusetts; then, leaving Congregationalism, in Boston's Emmanuel Church (Episcopal); in Lonsdale, Rhode Island; in Jenkintown, Pennsylvania; and, finally, in 1888, as Rector of Christ Church (Episcopal) in the town of Andover, Massachusetts.

The Parish of Christ Church in Andover was established in 1835. Its first church, a wooden structure, was destroyed by fire in February 1886, but the rectory was saved. The present structure, at 25 Central Street, consecrated in January, 1887, was designed and constructed by Henry Walker Hartwell and William Cummings Richardson, "well-known Boston architects." "It is of the Byzantine Romanesque style of architecture built of reddish granite from Braggville with trimming of Kibbe stone from Longmeadow." The entire cost was $42,000. Under the National Historic Preservation Act of 1966, the church was designated a National Register Church in 1982 (*The Parish of Christ Church, Andover, Massachusetts, 1835–1987,* compiled by the Christ Church Historical Commission, booklet, 34 pages).

For twenty-five years, from 1888 to 1913, Frederic Palmer was Rector of the Andover church. In 1904, he described the community, with a population of about seven thousand as "unique, in that it combines the activity of a manufacturing village wth the intellectual atmosphere of a college town . . . [with] Phillips Academy, with some four hundred boys preparing for college; Abbot Academy, with about one hundred girls; and the Andover Theological Seminary, fitting students for the Congregational ministry." Many business men commuted daily from Andover to Boston, twenty miles away (*Parish of Christ Church,* page 20). In his diary for Friday, March 23, 1900, Professor Palmer writes: "I rise early & catch the train leaving Boston at 7:30 & breakfast with my brother, Fred, in Andover. He has been sick with a cold this week. Reaching Cambridge again at 11.30" (page 188).

During these years, the Rectory in Andover, only seven miles from the Palmer houses in Boxford and easily reached from Cambridge by train, was a site of frequent activities by the large Palmer family. Chronicle entries indicate, for example, that seventeen family members celebrated Christmas there in 1894, and that there were Christmas celebrations at the Rectory in 1896, 1898, 1899,

1900, and 1905. Professor Palmer lived there for more than a month after his wife died in 1902, and sister Emily died there in 1907.

During his years in Andover, Frederic Palmer published *The Winning of Immortality* (1910) and, with his wife, *Poems* (1912); both were dedicated to George Herbert Palmer (**dedctdGHPann**-3 and 4).

In 1913, soon after his twenty-fifth anniversary at Christ Church, Frederic Palmer resigned from the parish, to become editor of the *Harvard Theological Review.* He and his wife moved to Cambridge and lived at 11 Quincy Street with Professor Palmer, who retired from the Harvard faculty in June 1913.

In the graveyard next to Christ Church in Andover, tombstones mark the graves of Frederic Palmer, Mary Towle Palmer, Frederic Palmer, Jr., and Helen Wallace Palmer.

1889

GHP

Sept. Agnes Lockhart came to us as second girl

Sept 15 Took lease for one year of 118 Brattle St fr. Miss Susan Wyman, furnished, $1000 a year

Dec. Appointed Alford Professor [of Natural Religion, Moral Philosophy, and Civil Polity][Note 1] succeedg Bowen who died the following Jan.

AFP

Special occupations Sept. to June

Wellesley trustee & Exec. Committee

State Board of Education, First meeting October[Note 2]

President of Collegiate Alumnae Assoc. [Association of Collegiate Alumnae, = A. C. A.][Note 3]

President of Woman's Home Missionary Assoc.

Drawing room talks. nine - entire charge of presiding at meetings

Lenten Talks at St. James' Cambridge, four

Addresses at Cambridge churches.

GHP

Speeches in 1889–90

Oct. 7 Christian Association
" 21 Harvard Philosophical Club
Nov. 8 Andover Club Dinner
" 16 Wellesley Lecture on Homer
Dec. 19 Round Table - on Arnold
Jan. 20 Mr. Brimmers on Delphi
Jan. 29 Miss Phillips' on Libraries

Jan. 30 Andover Theol Sem Prayer for Colleges
" 31 Fall River Harvard Club
Feb. 12 State House on Libraries
" 15 Chicago Harvard Club
Mar 10 Bost Univ. Theol School on Tact
" 27 Sanders Theatre Introducing Rev. W. R. Salter
Apr 21 Cambridge Club Dinner Boston on the Annex[Note 4]
" 26 School Masters Club Boston on Literature
" 30 Harv. Conference - on Neces. Elements of t. Religious Life
May Rev. C. H. Talmage's Church meeting Address.

Notes 1889

1. George Herbert Palmer's official relations with Harvard University: A.B., A.M., 1864; ΦΒΚ (honorary); Doctor of Laws (honorary), 1906; tutor, Greek, 1870–1872; instructor, philosophy, 1872–1873; curator, Gray Collection of Engravings, 1872–1876; assistant professor, philosophy, 1873–1883; professor, philosophy, 1883–1889; Alford Professor of Natural Religion, Moral Philosophy, and Civil Polity, 1889–1913 [This professorship was first awarded in 1817. Palmer, the fifth appointee, was succeeded in 1914 by Josiah Royce]; overseer, 1913–1919.

2. "She was appointed [to the Massachusetts State Board of Education] by Governor Ames and held the position during the remaining thirteen years of her life . . . [and] became the senior member of the Board Indirectly through the reports which the Board makes to the Legislature and through its recommendations, the whole of the education of the State is affected . . . Mrs. Palmer's special gift of seizing a situation and understanding a personality was of greatest value in the sort of work which this Board does. Her reports at the Board meetings and her addresses at the teachers' institutes which were held under its auspices make one of her very important contributions to the cause of education . . . She was assiduous at meetings and made long journeys to make speeches in behalf of some measure in towns where she felt it necessary for the enlightenment and direction of public opinion.

"Her colleagues on the Board have commemorated her in a minute which reads, in part:

Her first concern was for the children of the state, that they should have the best facilities for the acquisition of knowledge in the training of their intellectual powers and the development of their characters; her next was for the teachers, especially for those in the humbler places; that everything should be done to make their calling comfortable and dignified. She was courageous before committees of the legislature in advocating the measures deemed wise by the Board and in seeking to avoid the evils of mischievous legislation."

"One of her colleagues has said, 'She was the most persuasive debator I ever knew.'" (Caroline Hazard, *From College Gates*, Boston, Houghton Mifflin Co., 1925: 218–221).

3. The original objective of the Association of Collegiate Alumnae—"the first association of college and university trained women in the world"— as stated in its constitution in 1882, was "to unite alumnae of different institutions for practical educational work." The early accomplishments were significant, as shown by "six policies which have been carried on for half a century: first, that of conducting research by means of committees; second, that of forming new committees for the study of new problems; third, that of admitting properly qualified institutions to membership; fourth, that of welcoming branches of the Association formed in various parts of the country; fifth, that of asking distinguished people to present the results of their study before the branches of the parent organization; and sixth, that of encouraging through study groups (for such some of the committees proved to be) investigation which should be concerned with an aspect of education whether elementary, advanced, rural or industrial."

The first preliminary meeting to discuss such an association was held in Boston, Massachusetts, on November 28, 1881. Seventeen women represented eight institutions: Boston University, Cornell University, Oberlin College, Smith College, University of Michigan, University of Wisconsin, Vassar College, and Wellesley College. Miss Marion Talbot, representing Boston University, was secretary of the meeting. Miss Alice E. Freeman represented the University of Michigan; only thirteen days before the meeting, she had been appointed acting president of Wellesley College. The group accepted a motion by Miss Freeman "that a meeting be called for the purpose of organizing an association of women college graduates, with headquarters in Boston." On January 14, 1882, sixty-five alumnae of the eight institutions, who lived in New England or New York, attended a meeting in Boston, adopted a constitution for the association, and elected officers. Miss Talbot was elected secretary and held this position until 1892. Miss Freeman, who was elected one of the five directors, held other subsequent positions (she became Alice Freeman Palmer in December 1887): president, 1885–1887 and 1889–1890; chairmanship or membership on several committees (see 79n2); and general secretary (that is, executive officer), 1901–1902.

The Association of Collegiate Alumnae was incorporated in Massachusetts as a charitable organization in 1899 and merged with the Southern Association of College Women in 1921 to become the American Association of University Women (Marion Talbot and Lois Kimball Mathews Rosenberry, *The History of the American Association of University Women*, Boston, Houghton Mifflin Co., 1931, pages 9–12, 14, 28, 31, 425).

Marion Talbot presents this tribute to Alice Freeman Palmer: "The record of her work in the Association brings into strong relief a trait which marks her as one of the great of her time. She was preëminently a seer. To persons, her gift was to reveal undreamed-of resources; to every organization which felt her power and influence, she disclosed visions of work to be done and good to be wrought. Nor had these visions anything quixotic about them. Her gracious manner and instant charm were balanced by a judgment which was sound and convincing. Great was her service, greater her inspiration" (Talbot, Alice Freeman Palmer as member of the Association of Collegiate Alumnae, in **about AFPann**-4, page 12).

4. In this first systematic listing of his various speeches, Professor Palmer mentions the Annex where he had been teaching since 1879. He was one of many Harvard faculty members who had agreed "to repeat for women one of more of their college courses." In 1882, this informal arrangement had been incorporated as "The Society for the Collegiate Instruction of Women . . . to promote the education of women, with the assistance of the instructors of Harvard University . . . The name 'Harvard Annex' had been early attached to the enterprise, no one knows by whom, and against this popular knickname the long, formal title of the corporation could make no headway" (Dorothy Elia Howells, *A Century to Celebrate: Radcliffe College, 1879–1979*, Cambridge, Radcliffe College, 1978: 42. Warner, Radcliffe College, *HGM*, 1893–94; 2 (March 1894): 329–345).

Alice Freeman Palmer also taught at the Annex (her first related entry is in October 1891) and she describes it in 1891 (**AFP**-4), as "a recent and interesting experiment in the education of girls, whose future is yet difficult to predict. Only a few cases [of this type of college] exist, and as the Harvard Annex is the most conspicuous, by reason of its dozen years of age and nearly 200 students, I shall describe it as the typical example. In the Harvard Annex, groups of young women undertake courses of study in classes whose instruction is furnished entirely by members of the Harvard faculty. No college officer is obliged to give this instruction, and the Annex staff of teachers is, therefore, liable to considerable variation from year to year. Though the usual four classes appear in its curriculum, the large majority of its students devote themselves to special subjects. A wealthy girl turns from fashionable society to pursue a single course in history or economics; a hard-worked teacher draws inspiration during a few afternoons each week from a famous Greek or Latin professor; a woman who has been long familiar with French literature explores with a learned specialist some single period in the history of the language. Because the opportunities for advanced and detached study are so tempting, many ladies living in the neighborhood of the Annex enter one or more of its courses. There are consequently among its students women much older than the average of those who attend the colleges . . .

"It is impossible to estimate either favorably or adversely the permanent worth of an undertaking still in its infancy. Manifestly, the opportunities for the very highest training are here superb if they happen to exist at all. In this however, is the incalculable feature of the system. The Annex lives by favor, not by right, and it is impossible to predict what the extent of favor may at any time be . . . The fact that favor rules, and not rights, peculiarly hampers scientific and laboratory courses, and for its literary work obliges the Annex largely to depend on its own library. Yet when all these weaknesses are confessed—and by none are they confessed more frankly than by the wise and devoted managers of the Annex themselves—it should be said that hitherto they have not practically hindered the formation of a spirit of scholarship, eager, free and sane to an extraordinary degree. The Annex girl succeeds in remaining a private and unobserved gentlewoman, while still, in certain directions, pushing her studies to an advanced point seldom reached elsewhere."

1890

AFP

Special duties

This year (academic) was

Trustee of Wellesley & Executive Committee

State Board of Education, Com. on Bridgewater
Pres. of Woman's Home Missionary Association
Pres. " Woman's Educational Assoc. Elected January 1891.**Note** 1
Chairman of Com. on Fellowships,**Note** 2 & member of Com on Admission to A.C.A.**Note** 3
Drawing room talks. 4 by Mrs. Whitman, Mrs. E. S. P. Ward & Miss Annette Rogers & myself.
Sitting to Miss Whitney for bust. finished June, 1891.
George & I raised money $1350.00 for founding Domestic Science Dept. at Wellesley.**Note** 4

GHP

Fred, Mary & Eric spend summer abroad in Switzerland & Venice
Prof & Mrs. W. G. Hale had the old house
Sept. 1 Took Dean Gray's house, 3 Mason St. unfurnished at $1200 rent & spent last of the summer in furnishing it
Gave rooms in it through the year to Wm Lee, son of J. H. Lee, & to Jo Wellmans son Hiller. They left in October of following year
This was my last summer in the farm house where I had lived 20 years.
My complete Odyssey published [**GHP**-2]

AFP

May. Went west to speak at Indianapolis & elsewhere for money -
First Time I took money for speaking was this spring when I first spoke on Greece - & to Dana Hall, $15.
June. Made Commencement address at Wellesley - $50.
October. Made Commemoration address at Woman's College in Baltimore, $100
August. Recognition address at Chautauqua N. Y. - $75. [**AFP**-3]**Note** 5
Temperance rally in Cambridge at Union Hall.
May Wrote article for Christian Union, - $15. [**AFP**-2]
255.00 [by **GHP**]
Sept. 1. Miss Shafer broke down with bronchitis & did not return to Wellesley until June 1891. Miss Lord, at her request, acted as President.

GHP

Aug. 1 Alice & I at Fryeburg Me for a speech apiece at Chautauqua Afterwards went to Fabyans, slept on Mt Washington, the next night with Ella & Charley Talmage at Marlboro N. H.

Notes 1890

1. The Woman's Education Association was organized in 1872 and incorporated in Massachusetts in 1877. "Organized for promotion of better education of women. Stimulates interest by regular meet-

ings. Undertakes new educational enterprises, which if proved useful, are put on an independent basis, or continued. Gives one fellowship for study in Europe or this country. Sends travelling libraries and collections of photographs throughout the state. Also prepares semi-annual lists of new books suitable for small libraries. Has one school visitor. Aids in developing helpful connections between the school and outside institutions, such as the Public Library and the Museum of Fine Arts" (*A Directory of the Charitable and Beneficent Organizations of Boston*, 6th edition, Boston, Old Corner Book Store, 1914, page 327).

2. In the 1880s the A.C.A. (Association of Collegiate Alumnae) investigated "the subject of the graduate study for women in spite of the view frequently held that women were not mentally equal even to college work . . . very few graduate courses of any kind were open to women, and no positions on college faculties outside of women's colleges could be obtained by them. It was a distinctly masculine procession that was advancing into the field for research and scholarship."

In 1890, with 1,275 members, alumnae of fifteen institutions, the A.C.A. began a European fellowship program "with the effort to secure the opportunity of foreign study for American university women when foreign study was the gate to expanding knowledge." Alice Freeman Palmer was chairman of the Committee on Fellowships for many years, and under her leadership "the policy became firmly established — that aid to graduate study was a chief concern of the A.C.A., and that it could be counted on for aid to any organization which wished to further such a program." Marion Talbot writes: "The work which most claimed [Mrs. Palmer's] interest was that of securing fellowships for women . . . with ardor tempered by discrimination, she labored to open to women new approaches to advanced scholarship. Her successor as Chairman of the Fellowship Committee says, 'During all the years of work, in the midst of discouragement and trials, she was fertile in resource, quick to respond, most helpful with suggestions; while in the arousing of public interest and in the securing of funds, she rendered valuable aid.'" In her diary entries for March 18, 19, 24, 27, and 29, 1900 [chapter 4], Mrs. Palmer describes such fellowship-related activities.

In the late 1890s A.C.A. joined twelve other colleges and universities to form the Naples Table Association for Promoting Laboratory Reseach by Women. The purpose of this association was to support a Woman's Table at the Zoölogical Station in Naples, Italy.

"This station, founded in 1892 by Dr. Anton Dohrn for the collection of biological material and for the study of all forms of salt-water plant and animal life, had developed into an international institution for scientific research." As Mrs Palmer indicates in her diary entry for March 26, 1900, she was treasurer of this Table Association (Marion Talbot, *More Than Lore, Reminiscences of Marion Talbot, Chicago, University of Chicago Press, 1936: 127–128. Ruth W. Tryon, Investment in Creative Scholarship: A History of the Fellowship Program of the American Association of University Women, 1890–1956,* Washington, D. C., American Association of University Women, 1957, pages x, 184. Talbot and Rosenberry, *History,* page 148. Alice Upton Pearmain, The Zoological Station at Naples: A Table and a Research Prize of One Thousand Dollars for Women, *The Association of Collegiate Alumnae Magazine,* Series III, No. 14, February 1907, 1–13).

3. In 1897, with Mrs. Palmer as chairman, the A.C.A.'s Committee on Corporate Membership "admitted Radcliffe College, the University of Chicago, the University of Minnesota, and Leland Stanford, Jr., University." At the same time the committee stated some principles regarding such admissions: "First: An institution is invited to join the Association for the educational strength it can bring. The policy of admitting weak institutions on the ground that they are growing rapidly and that admission to our membership would hasten that growth has not been borne out by results in the past. Second: An institution is invited to join the Association for the benefit of educational standards *in the whole country and not for local influence.* The power of our Association lies in the help it may give toward lifting up and unifying standards of education in the country at large and not in aiding this branch and that institution at the sacrifice of such standards" (Talbot and Rosenberry, *History,* pages 71–72).

In her diary for March 29 and 30, 1900, Mrs. Palmer describes activities concerned with such admissions.

4. The Palmers' interest in Domestic Science reflected the influence of an intensive research program carried out by the Sanitary Science Club of the Association of Collegiate Alumnae, organized in November 1883, "for the study of home sanitation." The Club's report, edited by Ellen H. Richards and Marion Talbot, and published in 1887, introduced the "hygiene of the home [as] a subject of growing importance and interest. As one of the problems of social and eco-

nomic science it is beginning to receive the attention it may rightly claim. The women of our country should not only follow the discussions which are carried on by sanitary congresses, boards of health, and other authorities, but, by combining theory with practice, as few others can, aid in solving the great questions which seriously affect the interests of the home and the family . . . The day is past [the report concludes] when sickness was held to be a direct interference of Providence, as retributive punishment. Pestilence, fevers, and weakness are, indeed, penalties for sin, but it is for the sin of ignorance. In this age of scientific enlightenment and invention and wide-spread information, ignorance of the primary conditions of health and vigor is unpardonable. A knowledge of sanitary principles should be regarded as an essential part of every woman's education, and obedience to sanitary laws should be ranked, as it was in the Mosaic Code, as a religious duty."

In 1888, Miss Talbot received the S. B. degree from the Massachusetts Institute of Technology, and in a lecture series to students at Lasell Seminary in 1889, she "*called their attention to a new theory of disease which has recently been suggested and which was called the 'germ theory.' [She] told the students that it had not been generally accepted, but it would be worthwhile for them to note whether it made any progress.*" [compiler's italics]

In 1890, through the initiative of Mrs. Palmer, Marion Talbot was "appointed instructor in domestic science at Wellesley College and for two years gave to the Seniors a three-hour course" which included lectures by Miss Talbot and by visiting experts. "The topics studied have been the situation and surroundings of the house, methods of ventilation and heating, principles and practice of drainage and plumbing, house furnishing, the chemistry of cleaning, food principles, methods of preserving foods, the scientific principles involved in the preparation of foods, methods of detecting food adulterations, household art, clothing, and domestic service."

Miss Talbot resigned in July 1892, to go to Chicago with Mrs. Palmer (see 98n5). The course at Wellesley was not continued because "women able to conduct courses in Domestic Science [were] so few that the vacancy caused by this resignation could not be filled." Later, from 1900 to 1915, Olive Davis was appointed lecturer on Domestic Science.

Early in 1905, the president of the University of Missouri described his attempts to fill a faculty position "with a good title and a good salary to teach home economics. [He goes on] I found Miss Talbot in this subject, but she was wedded to the University of

Chicago. There was Mrs. Ellen Richards, but she could not have been detached from the Massachusetts Institute of Technology. One or two other illustrious women I found, but they were beyond my reach. The number of them was not great. Among women obtainable, I found a woeful dearth of those that represented such scholarly attainments as we demanded for other things."

(Ellen H. Richards and Marion Talbot, eds., *Home Sanitation, a Manual for Housekeepers* by the Sanitary Science Club of the Association of Collegiate Alumnae, Boston, Ticknor and Co., 1887, pages 3, 7, 73. Talbot, *More Than Lore,* Chicago, University of Chicago Press, 1936: 145–146. Wellesley College President's Reports: 1891, pages 10–11; 1892, pages 13–14; 1893, page 6. R. H. Jesse, The Position of Household Economics in the Academic Curriculum, *The Association of Collegiate Alumnae Magazine,* 1905; 10 (January): 24–29.)

5. Chautauqua, on the west shore of Chautauqua Lake in western New York, was established in 1874 as a summer training place for Sunday School teachers of the main Protestant denominations. Soon, it expanded into a summer center of popular education, music, and recreation. Since 1878, the Chautauqua Literary and Scientific Circle (CLSC) provided, year-round, "a way for out-of-school people to approximate the reading of college graduates." Recognition Day was "a sort of graduation day for CLSC members who in that year had completed four years of planned reading and coordinated studies." Similar Chautauquas developed in many parts of the United States (Rebecca Richmond, *Chautauqua : An American Place,* New York, Duell, Sloan & Pearce, 1943. Information and quotations from the Chautauqua Institution).

In presenting his Doubts about University Extension, in 1892 (**GHP-**22), Professor Palmer praised the "fundamental consequence" of Chautauqua, even though it was not able to provide the same education as a college: "Its work, indeed, has had a different aim; and, amusing as that work often appears, it ought to be understood and acknowledged as of fundmental consequence in our hastily settled and heterogeneous land. Chautauqua sends its little books and papers into stagnant homes from Maine to California, and gives the silent occupants something to think about. Conversation springs up; and with it fresh interests, fresh hopes. A new tie is formed between young and old, as together they pursue the same studies, and in the same graduating class walk through the Golden Gate.

"Any man who loves knowledge and his native land must be glad at heart when he visits a summer assembly of Chautauqua: there listens to the Orator's Recognition Address; attends the swiftly successive Round Tables upon Milton, Temperance, Geology, the American Constitution, the Relations of Science and Religion, and the Doctrine of Rent; perhaps assists at the Cooking School, the Prayer Meeting, the Concert, and the Gymnastic Drill; or wanders under the trees among the piazzaed cottages, and sees the Hall of Philosophy and the wooden Doric Temple shining on their little eminences; and, best of all, perceives in what throngs have gathered here the butcher, the baker, and the candlestick-maker, — a throng themselves, their wives and daughters a throng — all heated in body, but none the less aglow for learning and a good time.

"The comic aspect of this mixture of science, fresh air, flirtation, Greek reminiscence, and devoutness are patent enough; but the way in which the multitude is being won to discard distrust of knowledge, and to think of it rather as the desirable goal for all, is not so generally remarked by scholarly observers. Yet this is the mighty fact. The actual product in education may not be large; enthusiasm and the memory may be more stimulated than the rational intelligence. But minds are set in motion; an intellectual world, beyond the domestic and personal, begins to appear; studious thought forms its fit friendship with piety, gladness, and the sense of a common humanity; a groundwork of civilization is prepared.

"To find a popular movement so composite and aspiring, we must go back to the mediæval Crusades or the Greek Mysteries. In these alone do we observe anything so ideal, so bizarre, so expressive of the combined intellectual and religious hopes of a people. In many Chautauqua homes pathetic sacrifices will be made in the next generation to send the boys and girls to a real college."

1891

GHP

Left farm house after 21 years occupancy

Built piazza & repaired old house & adopt'd it as own, my former rooms being fitted up by Em & occupied this summer by Fred & Mary

Read Greek this summer: Plato - Apology Crito, Phaedo, Meno & the Republic; Aristotle the whole Nicom. Ethics & Epictetus Eucheindion

In early July two addresses before Summer School of Theology in Cambridge on Parables $10.00

August 4 speeches at Fryeburg Me on Geo. Herbert, Homer, Reasons for going to College, and the work of Chautauqua $50.00

Article published in Christian Union Ownership of Books (written in Spring Recess) $25.00 [**GHP**-17]

Wrote also brief article for Congregationalist on Manliness of Boyhood $25.00 [**GHP**-21] & began Univ. Extension

June Atlantic contained my article Reminiscences of Prof Sophocles for which rec'd $75.00. [**GHP**-16] Subscription raised money at once for portrait.

June - Gave Comencement addresses at Wells College (Aurora, N. Y.) & at Western Reserve Univ. Cleveland, O. on The Glory of the Imperfect $75 each. Cleveland reported & printed through D. C. Heath & Co. Boston [**GHP**-18]

AFP

From May to Sept. George & I earned by writing & speaking $915.00. of this $765 was clear profit.

In August wrote article for Sept. Forum. [**AFP**-4]

Aug. 8. Spent Sunday with Miss Whiting, Shelburne N. H. - Monday rode through the Glen. Tuesday & Wednesday spoke four times (& George four) at Fryeburg, Chautauqua for $50.00 each

Aug. 20. Recognition Address at Epping, N. H. $20

915.00 [entered by **GHP**]

GHP

Also June. Commencement Address at Worcester Academy on the Manliness of Boyhood $25.00

This year left Administrative Board of College & became Chairman of Committee on Entertainments Seminary on Greek Ethics not taken.

This year I had 1st third (Logic) of Phil. 1 ending Dec. 10. After which had only 3 hours a week. Constructive Ethics Single pupils in Ethical Research 3 hours on Ethics in Annex & on Wed evenings went over with 11 Episc. Div. students the week's work in Ethics. This I give them.

Boxford Town Hall opened this summer[Note 1]

This year Bertha Palmer lived with us & attended Annex, we receiving $75 & whatever furniture Jacob had previously lent us[Note 2]

AFP

Speeches

Sept. 3. Bridgewater Normal School. Presided.
" 17. Boxford Greece

Oct. 10. Haverhill. Greece. $25.00
" 19. Cambridge. North Ave. Ch. "Missions."

Oct 20. Cambridge. Annex First address of yr.
Emmanuel Society
" 22. A. C. A. Boston "Fellowships."
" 23. " " " " Reports.
" 28. Missionary Assoc. Boston, Ann meeting
" 30. Teachers' Assoc. Tremont Temple. 10
Nov. 9. Andover. "Ideals in Education." 25.
" 11. Newark. "Ethics of Missions." 20
" 12. Garden City - Greece. 30.
" 13. Norwalk - Girls' Education. 15.
" 14. Providence. Outlook in Schools. 10.

100

" " Tremont Temple. W. C. T. U. [Woman's Christian Temperance Union]
" 18. Cambridge. Dedication of School.
" " Boston. Boot & Shoe Club.
" 22. Cambridge. Y. W. C. A. Religious Life.
" 28. Boston. Influence of Teachers' Manners.
" 30. Cambridge. Temperance Rally.

Dec. 17. N. E. A. Boston. College Education
" 18. Portland Womans' Club. Greece. 31.00
" 19. Skowhegan. Womans' Clubs. Italy (Housekeeping) 29.00
" 21. Bath. (Greece.) 26.50

310.00 [entered by **GHP**]

GHP

Speeches & Articles 1891–2

Pamphlet - The Glory of the Imperfect. D. C. Heath & Co [**GHP**-18]
Barnes' Rural Poems - Christian Union, Dec. 26, 1891 $25.00 [**GHP**-20]
Doubts about University Extension, Atlantic Monthly March $55.00 [**GHP**-22]
The Manliness of Boyhood, Congregationalist, Feb. 18 $25.00 [**GHP**-21]
Public Support of College Vices (McClure) 25.00 [**GHP**-23]
Review of Jowett's Plato in N. Y. Nation July 7 [**GHP**-25] for both
" " Burnet's Early Greek Phil. " " Aug 11 [**GHP**-27] 7[?]
Philosophy in the Colleges - New York Independent Aug 4 15 [**GHP**-26]
Oct Melrose W. C. T. U. Glory of Imperfect $15.00
Oct 22, 1891 Before Y. M. C. A. "Holy Heedlessness"
Oct 19, " " Unitarian Ministers Union "The Value of Sects"
Dec. 26, Preached at Brunswick Me. On "Patience"

Jan. 9, Sat. Morning Club Boston On "Criticism"
Feb. 3, Williston Seminary The Manliness of Boyhood $10.00
Feb 4, Westfield Normal School Self Training in t Use of English $10.00
Feb 23, Prospect Union Wordsworth
Feb. 18 ~~In the Congregationalist Manliness of Boyhood $25.00~~
Feb. 25, Annex English Club On Criticism
March 25, Montclair N. J. New Education $50.00
April 21, Round Table, Private Rights to a Public Press
May 23. Sen. Philos. Club Wordsworth
June 1. Mt. Vernon Church Semicentenial. The Puritan Home
June 15. Elmira College Commencement Cultivation of Tact [**GHP**-24] $75.00
June 28. Class Supper
July 19-Aug 2 West Chop Normal Institute $200.00 (14 lectures)
Sept 11 Preached in Boxford pulpit on Church Going

507.00

AFP

Speeches continued

Dec. 28.	Bangor.	"Life among College Girls."	25.00
" 29.	"	Housekeeping in Italy.	10.00
" 29.	Augusta.	Life among College Girls.	30.50
" 30.	Belfast.	" " " "	25.00
			176.50

Oct. Nov. Dec. earnings by speaking. $301.50

During this winter I devoted large amounts of time to the Women's Education Com. which had six public meetings & six Ex. Com. meetings, at wh. I presided, beside planning the $500.00 Fellowship which was raised.

I also had many meetings as Educational Com. to the World's Fair consulting College Presidents, Public School men, etc.[Note 3]

Wellesley & State Board of Education gave me much anxiety, and I consulted much in their interests, raising $2000. for Wellesley (1500 for gymnasium & 500 for Miss Talbot's work [see 80n4]) With all this I spoke very little in public & wrote nothing except enormous correspondence.

Notes 1891

1. Professor Palmer describes the Town Hall in 1900 (**GHP**-39): "About ten years ago $3,000 were spent on the building of a Town Hall, plain but exactly fitted to our needs. Here we have had num-

berless lectures, concerts, lantern shows, dramatic entertainments — the best of them devised and carried out by our vivacious young people. The green in front of the Town Hall has proved a good place to gather the entire population for Fourth of July fireworks, which are paid for by general subscription; and this year the hall itself took us all in afterward for music and ice-cream."

2. Bertha Palmer, Professor Palmer's niece, graduated from Wellesley College in 1891. Following her year at the Annex she received an M. A. degree in English and Ethics from Wellesley in 1893. Her thesis topic was The Nature of Creative Criticism Ethically Considered (Wellesley College Archives). Her poem, entitled Friendship, is included in Cordelia C. Nevers, *Wellesley Lyrics*, published by Cordelia C. Nevers, 1896: 125, and another poem by her (as Bertha Palmer Lane), entitled Age, appears in Martha Hale Shackford, *Wellesley Verse, 1875–1925*, New York, Oxford University Press, 1925: 56.

3. For six months in 1893, from May 1st to October 30th, a lake shore area (Jackson Park) on Chicago's south side was the site of the World's Columbian Exposition to celebrate the 400th anniversary of the discovery of America. "[T]he area of the Exposition was 633 acres . . . far and away the largest up to that time. Added to the dozen or so major buildings and their dependencies, and to the 19 foreign-government and 38 state-government buildings, the service structures and individual exhibitors' pavilions . . . brought the total of separate buildings to about 200. It was estimated that to see everything in the fair once quickly, a visitor would need about three weeks and would have to walk over 150 miles" (*The Chicago World's Fair of 1893: A Photograph Record*, with text by Stanley Appelbaum, New York, Dover Publications, 1980: 5).

In July 1891, the governor of Massachusetts appointed Alice Freeman Palmer, another woman, and three men, as a Board of Managers "for the purpose of exhibiting the arts, industries, institutions, resources, products and general development of the Commonwealth . . . at the Exposition." The planning process began at once, and by the spring of 1893, the State had appropriated a total of $175,000 for this major undertaking. Some of the State's exhibits were displayed in a specially-constructed Massachusetts State Building, while many exhibits were placed elsewhere in the Exposition.

Mrs. Palmer's main responsibility was for "an exhibit which should worthily represent the educational features of the State" In

July 1892, during the planning period, she also accepted an appointment as the first Dean of Women, part-time, at the University of Chicago which was just opening (see 98n5). During her frequent visits to Chicago in 1892 and 1893, she served both the University and the Exposition; the Exposition grounds were within walking distance of the University campus.

The Massachusetts Educational exhibit, located in the Department of Liberal Arts, presented extensive material about public schools, normal schools, and the Board of Education. In the same department were exhibits of universities, colleges and technical schools of the State. The four women's colleges were represented: the Harvard Annex, Mount Holyoke, Smith, and Wellesley. "Wellesley sent the largest [of these four exhibits] and one of the most attractive. She was also the only one of the smaller colleges to furnish an attendant . . . The graduates of Wellesley manifested the greatest enthusiasm in behalf of their *alma mater*. Weekly receptions were held at the exhibit, under the auspices of the Chicago Alumnae Association, being always attended by large numbers of former students." And the college received an award "for excellence of equipment and of work of undergraduates and graduates."

The extensive Harvard University exhibit occupied 4,500 square feet of floor space and was designed to command "the attention of the student in search of training, the teacher in search of methods, and the expert in search of accurate knowledge of experiments tried and results achieved."

In summary from the Board of Managers: "Its members cannot refrain from saying that there was perhaps no State exhibit in the department of education which was more highly commended and called forth more praise than did that of Massachusetts. The medals and awards made by the Bureau having the supervision of such matters testify to the good opinion in which Massachusetts and her works are held in the minds of the committee which passed upon the exhibit of the Commonwealth" (Massachusetts Board of World Fair Managers, *Report*, Boston, Wright & Potter Printing Co., State Printers, 1894. Wellesley College, President's Report, 1894, page 12. Edward Cummings, The Harvard Exhibit at the World's Fair, *HGM*, 1893–94; 2 (September 1893): 50–63. **AFP**-6).

From an article about this fair a century later, in 1993: "No world's fair before or since has captured the national imagination as completely. Not even the Centennnial fair of 1876 or the New York World's Fair of 1939 so shaped the way the nation saw itself and the world. The Exposition was one of the epochal events of its time. It is hard for us today to grasp the impact a simple world's fair could have on the nation — an impact combining the appeal of a moon launch and the Bicentennial celebration. In its half-year of existence, it drew 27 million visitors — a number approaching half the American population" (Phil Patton, 'Sell the cookstove if necessary, but come to the Fair,' *Smithsonian*, 1993; 24 (No. 3, June): 38–50).

1892

GHP

Jan. 1 J. H. Lee takes house on Hilliard St.

Jan. 20 Uncle Charles H Peabody died at New Bedford (82)

Jan 26 Agnes Herrick engaged to J. B. Fletcher

Feb 29, Pres. Eliot sends for me & says he has been asked to name a President for the University of California & to offer suggestions for making this office a powerful & secure one. He asked if he may name me. I declined. [see 60n2]

March 12 — Pres. Harper visits us & urges us to accept positions in the Univ. of Chicago, I to be Head Professor of Ethics with a salary of $7000, teaching graduates 6–8 hours a week; Alice to be Dean of the Womens Dept & Professor of History with a salary of not less than $3000 & probably $5000.**Note 1**

April 6–12 Spring Recess. Alice & I visit Chicago A. afterwards going to Saginaw for a visit & then lecturing through the West until May.

May 5. Alice returned & that evening we telegraphed Harper that we declined & May 7 printed letter in Crimson.**Note 2** [see 95n2]

July-Sept Fred in Farm House, preaching in Andover Mrs. Wilkinson & 2 little girls with Emily, sometimes Brother.

AFP

Addresses & articles etc.

January 12. Quill Club. N. Y.	Education.	20.00
" 15. Brooklyn Heights Seminary	"	25.00

Friday

Feb 19. Mrs. Underhill's, Lowell, $25.00

" 22. U. of Mich. dinner speech.

March 2. Quincy. on foundation of Woodward School

" 9. Hearing in State House on World's Fair appropriation.

Apr 3. Mr. Beach's Church. Lenten service for girls.

" 5. Lowell, "Opportunities for Women" $25.00

" 15. Teachers of East Saginaw.

" 17. Congregational Church, Saginaw.

" 23. Madison. Phases of College Life. $25.00

Apr 24. " Congregational Ch.
" 26. Northfield. Journeys in Greece.**Note 3** 25.00
" 27. Minneapolis. Education High School,
University 25.00
" 29. Duluth. " 25.00
" 30. St. Paul. " 25.00
May 2. Chicago. " 25.00
" 3. Ann Arbor. U. of M. Girls
" 4. Buffalo. St. Margaret's 25.00
For expenses 50.00

320.00
176.00
310.00

806.00 [entered by **GHP**]

Was sick three weeks in March and in the week from Apr. 6 May 5

West Chop. July 19. Aug. 2. Martha's Vineyard - $400 & expenses. with a three roomed cottage

GHP

Aug. 20 Bought Bicycle & learned to ride

August E. L. Bradford settles in Boxford. Marries in September

We did not come to Boxford until July 3 & accordingly Alice had only 2 months here A good deal of time was devoted to the study of birds, she observing 80 species. We also began to look up trees.

This summer Rob't Herrick spent in Europe broken in health,**Note 4** Edw. Abbot & Philip there too

Fred Mary Alice & I read aloud every evening Grant's Memoirs. Privately we also read Sherman's Memoirs & Dodges Birds Eye View of Civil War

I read much in Ethics — Alexander, Dewey, Muirhead, Gilman, Hyde, Sidgwicks Hist of Ethics, Much of Hegel's Phenomenologie & the first vol. entire of Thenings Zweck im Recht

Our joint income this year about $6000

AFP

May 13. Exeter. Domestic Economy. $25.00
" 19. Boston University. "Western Education"
" 25. Mothers' Club " "
" 27. Dorchester. Life among College Girls.

June 6. Cleveland. Education & Home. $50.
" 7. Shelbyville. " " 120.

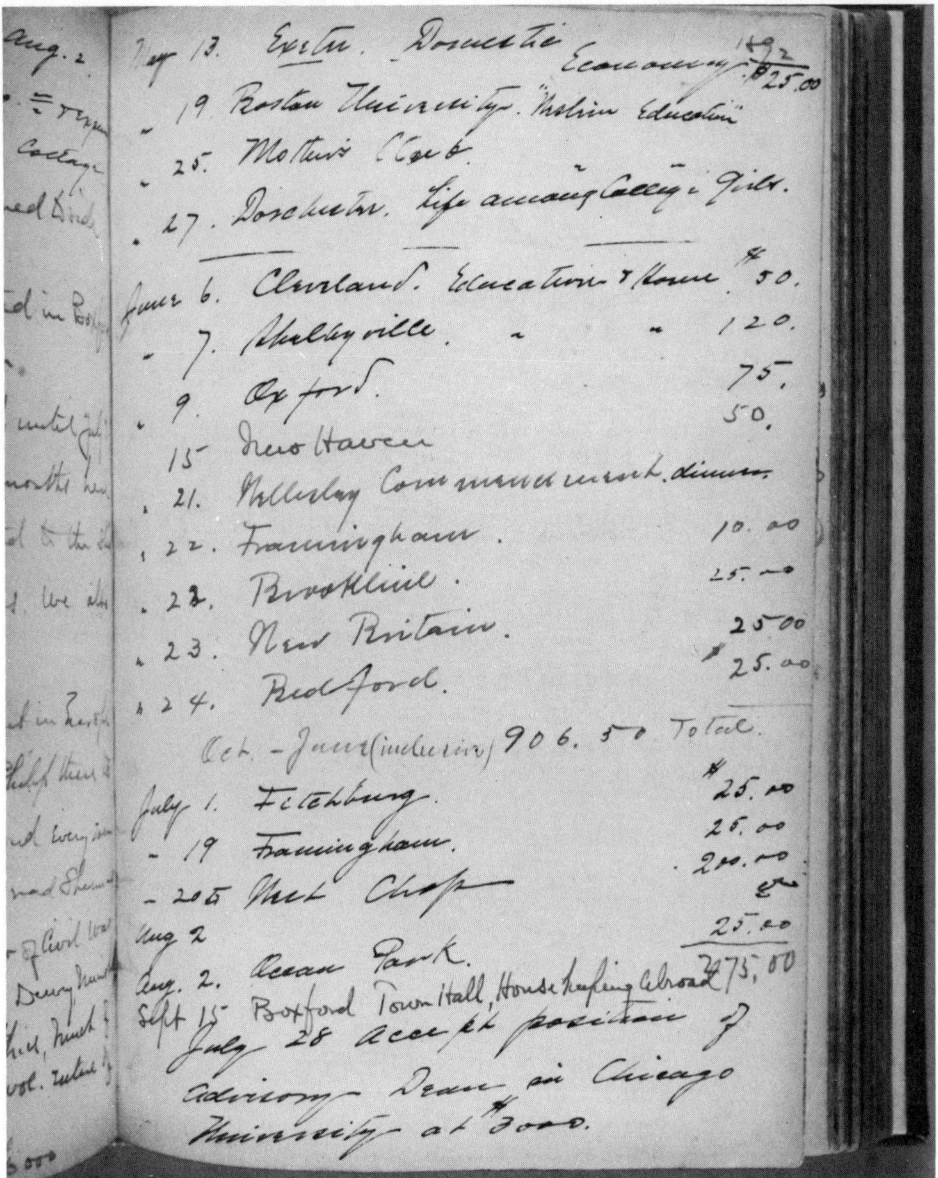

Alice Freeman Palmer's entries, 1892. Professor Palmer wrote the year, 1892, in the upper right-hand corner; the entry for Sept 15; and the total, 275.00, for the four, lower right-hand figures. (reduced size)

June 9. Oxford. 75.
" 15. New Haven 50.
" 21. Wellesley Commencement. dinner.
" 22. Framingham 10.00
" 22. Brookline. 25.00
" 23. New Britain. 25.00
" 24. Bedford. $25.00
Oct.-June (inclusive) 906.50 Total
July 1. Fitchburg. $25.00
" 19. Framingham. 25.00
" 20 to Aug 2 West Chop [on Martha's Vineyard] 200.00
Aug. 2. Ocean Park. 25.00

275.00

GHP

[adds] Sept 15 Boxford Town Hall, Housekeeping Abroad

AFP

July 28 Accepted position of Advisory Dean in Chicago University at $3000.[Note 5]

GHP

Sept. Bertha enters the Brearly School J. H. Croswell Master, as Instructor in English
Mt Vernon Church moves to Back Bay
Dec. 1 Salary raised to $4500 Course in Annex $400
March 9 Aunt Margaret dies
Sept. 19 Alice leaves Boxford for Chicago[Note 6]
Oct 18 Returns
Dec 30-Jan 2 Alice in Chicago
1893 Jan 1, 1893 Prof E. N. Horsford dies
" Jan 21-Feb 21 A. in Chicago, Saginaw & Ann Arbor I absent fr. Cambridge Jan 21-Feb. 7
" April 12–30 Alice in Chicago
" May 10 Effie Wood Palmer dies [see 142n5]

Speeches & Articles 1892–3

Review of Hyde's Ethics Christian Union Oct. 22 12.00 [**GHP**-28]
Forum. Jan. Can Moral conduct be taught in Schools 100.00 [**GHP**-29]
Harvard Christian Association Address of Welcome Oct. 4
Oct. 10 Providence Congreg. Club "The Old Liberalism & the New" 40.00
" 14 N. E. Assoc. of Colleges & Preparatory Schools on Ethical training in School & College

Oct. 25 Emmanuel Society, Harvard Annex, Ethical Training
Nov. 11 Round Table, Boston " " 10.00
" 25 Mass. Teachers Assoc. Springfield " "
" 25 J. MacDuffe's School " Odyssey Bk VI[Note 7]
" 21 Brooklyn Institute "Nature & Aim of Philosophy" 40.00
Dec. 15 Womans Educ. Soc. 117 Marlborough St Boston Ethical Training
" 26 Self Cultivation in English Bangor Lecture Course 36.00
Jan. 4. [1893] Mother's Club of Cambridge Ethical Training
" 7. Wheaton Fem Sem at Norton Cultivation in English 25.00
" 12 Worcester Academy. Homer 25.00
" 14 Vassar Students Aid Society Homer
" 19 Homer reading at Miss Markhams School[Note 7]
" 23-Feb. 5 In Chicago 6 speeches, 5 Readings
Feb 26 Brookline Fortnightly Club - Criticism
Mar. 6 Harv. Religious Union — Jones Very
" 12 Rev D. N. Breachs [?] Church Evening - Patience
" 17 Harv. Grad Club — Criticism
" 24 Phillips Academy Andover — Harvard University
Apr 25 Miss Emerson's School18 Newbury St Boston English[Note 7] 25.00
May 31 Annex Grad Club on Graduate Study 25.00

412.00
Oct. 16 Western Reserve Univ. 50.00
Dec 12 Newark N. J. 50.00
Feb. West End Womans Club Chicago 50.00
March 25 Sat. Morning Club Boston
Dec. Emmanuel Club Annex
May Lawrence 17.00
June 2 Miss Norths School Brooklyn 50.00
" 14 Hardy School Duluth 100.00
317.00

Notes 1892

1. William Rainey Harper was the first president of the University of Chicago, which opened on October 1, 1892. In recruiting the faculty, he "sought big men, men already distinguished and recognized as exceptionally able . . . He wanted the very best and ablest, the most distinguished scholars and teachers he could find. The more eminent they were the more he wanted them . . . He seemed incapable of taking No! for an answer . . . He was also a born diplomat and would continue a negotation long after a less purposeful man would have abandoned it, and would, oftener than not, con-

Pres. Harper

tinue it to a successful conclusion He had a very wide acquaintance among college and university professors . . . [and] he scoured the academic world for great scholars who would dare exchange comfortable and safe positions for the hazards and excitements of a new undertaking." He obtained a wide knowledge of many people, including the Palmers, when he was principal of Chautauqua's College of Liberal Arts from 1886 to 1892 (Thomas Wakefield Goodspeed, *A History of the University of Chicago, Founded by John D. Rockfeller: The First Quarter Century*, Chicago, University of Chicago Press, 1916: 200–203. Talbot, *More Than Lore*, page 2. See 82n5).

Harper's offers to the Palmers, which would have doubled their annual joint income, from $6,000 to $12,000, exemplified a problem in Cambridge, as new universities, such as Stanford and the University of Chicago, offered much higher salaries to attract Harvard men. While the Palmers hesitated, "much was said of the immediate need of making Harvard salaries more nearly what they ought to be, but when they refused the offers, there seemed to be a disposition to underrate their sacrifices, while striving to prove that, after all, meagre salaries in Cambridge are more attractive than good pay in other centres of culture" (*HGM*, 1892–1893; 1 (October 1892): 43–65, 110).

Chicago's original faculty did include Frank Bigelow Tarbell who went directly from Harvard, as well as William Gardner Hale and James Laurence Laughlin, both of whom had gone to Cornell after teaching at Harvard. The recruitment of the two men from Cornell was greatly facilitated when Harper convinced Chicago's trustees to raise the salary of a Head Professor from $6,000 to $7,000 (Goodspeed, *Chicago*, pages 206–207).

President Harper studied and reported on "The Pay of American College Professors" (*Forum*, 1893; 16 (September): 96–109). He concluded "that the professor in the American college does not to-day receive justice at the hands of those whom he serves, and for whose benefit he devotes his life. When there are considered (1) the grave responsibilities which rest upon him, (2) the numerous demands, of every kind, made of him, it is evident that he deserves, at the lowest, an increase of about fifty per cent in his pay, over the present rates. The average should be not $1,400, but $2,000. The 'most highly paid' professor should receive, not $4,000, but $7,000, while those who today get $1,800 and $2,000 should receive $2,500 and $3,000."

2. On the front page of the *Harvard Crimson* , Saturday, May 7, 1892, under the heading, Professor Palmer will Remain at Harvard:

"*To the Editors of the Crimson:*

"Gentlemen: Can you allow me a little space in your paper to announce to my Harvard friends that last night I declined the professorship recently offered to me at Chicago.

"It is a superb university which is rapidly rising there. Its millionaire founder, sagacious and self-effacing; its young, resourceful, and winning President; its capable Trustees, who, though two-thirds of them are drawn from a single sect [Baptist], serve under a constitution which provides that 'no particular religious profession shall ever be held as a requisite for election to any professorship'; its enthusiastic city, already contributing nearly half of its great endowment; its distinguished Faculty, selected from all parts of this and other lands; its commanding position in the middle region of the country, where it stands as a new Harvard, Yale, or Johns Hopkins, attending to that expensive highest instruction which the smaller colleges cannot of themselves supply; all these things must lead a lover of learning to welcome the new foundation as a splendid addition to the educational resources of the country, and may well make any man eager to serve upon its staff.

"But long service in a single place begets duties to that place, duties strong if undefinable. And without disparaging other colleges, a Harvard man may fairly feel that there is something in his own university which renders it incomparable, potent over the future, compulsive of loyalty and of love.

Very truly yours,
G. H. Palmer"

3. Before this speech at Carleton College in Northfield, Minnesota, Chronicle entries show that Mrs. Palmer had given several talks about Greece: in the spring of 1890 — the first time she was paid for speaking — and four times in 1891.

The background of these talks was a visit to Greece, probably during the Palmers' sabbatical from June 1888 to September 1889. Professor Palmer describes the visit: "One spring we spent in Greece, going to Ithaca, to Delphi, and Olympia. Greek had early been a favorite of Mrs. Palmer's, and she came to the enjoyment of that unique sculpture and architecture not unprepared. It is impossible to knock the beauty out of a piece of marble which a Greek hand has touched. While a fragment remains, the master is there. She at least found no difficulty in overlooking absent heads and legs, and easily turned her mind to the loveliness that is left. Greek gravestones she learned to know in Athens for the first time, and she was deeply moved by their method of proclaiming no grief but resting in some remembered scene from the life of him who had gone. She gathered all procurable photographs of them, as of the splendid tombs of Italy, and placed them together in a book which she called her Graveyard. Yet she enjoyed Greece not merely because the Greeks had enjoyed it, but for the same reasons as they. Its colored soils, the noble outlines of its heights, its atmosphere, its ever present sea, its olive trees, intoxicated her and kept her from regretting its generally absent verdure. She interested herself too in its present conditions and people. Dr. Schliemann was hospitable.

The accomplished sister of Prime Minister Tricoupis became her friend" (**GHP**-57, page 200–201).

In 1873 Heinrich Schliemann, a German archaeologist, had discovered about 1200 gold artifacts, which he thought belonged to King Priam, who ruled Troy around 1200 B.C. and are described in Homer's *Iliad.* The collection was seized from a Berlin museum by Soviet troops at the end of World War II. Not until August 1993, did the Russian Minister of Culture reveal that the treasures had been in a secret Russian vault (Celestine Bohlen, *Display of Troy's Riches to Take Time, New York Times*, August 28, 1993, page 9).

From *The Carletonia* (1892; 12 (No, 3, May 13): 9–10): "A distinguished luminary appeared upon the intellectual horizon of Carleton College, Tuesday, April 26 [1892], in the person of Mrs. Alice Freeman Palmer, president of Wellesley College until 1887. Under the auspices of the Associated Collegiate Alumnae, she was billed to lecture that evening, her subject being, 'A Journey Through Greece.' Mrs. Palmer reached Northfield in time to attend the annual dinner . . . to the Senior class, and her presence added much to that ever-enjoyable occasion

"Mrs. Palmer's lecture in the evening, although heralded with enthusiasm, and looked forward to with pleasure, exceeded the anticipations of all. Her subject was one of interest to all, and especially to classical students and lovers of the Greek masterpieces, whose minds the very names of Athens and Olympus, Parnassus and Pieria, throng with images of the heroes and heroines of the old Hellenic myths.

"Mrs. Palmer's manner as a lecturer is most charming, being easy, graceful, and conversational; she is vivid in description, and most happy in her choice of themes, not dealing with dry statistics, but representing the Greece of today in its life, manners, and appearance, with so much artistic vividness and perspicacity, as almost to transport her listeners into that classic fairy-land."

4. This is the first of Professor Palmer's numerous entries about Robert Herrick and his family during the next twenty-two years. Herrick graduated from Harvard College in 1890, taught English at the Massachusetts Institute of Technology until 1903, and then joined the faculty of the new University of Chicago as professor of English and rhetoric. In 1894 he married Harriet Emery, who was George Herbert Palmer's cousin (their mothers were sisters - Lucy

Peabody Palmer and Harriet Peabody Emery). They named their first child, Alice Palmer Herrick; their second child, Harriet, died at an early age. The Herricks visited New England and had a house in Boxford. The last entry notes that Robert and Harriet Herrick separated in 1914.

"Coming to Chicago . . . at the urging of William Rainey Harper, Herrick anticipated an exciting intellectual environment, but his experience proved to be bitter-sweet. Personal and family problems, combined with a dislike for the Midwest and the city of Chicago, produced almost immediate dissatisfaction and periodic despair.

"While Herrick often chafed under his teaching obligations, he benefited from the University's intellectual ferment and the unusual freedom from teaching responsibilities that Harper had provided him. During his tenure at Chicago, Herrick produced thirteen novels [Palmer notes that he read the Man Who Wins and Gospel of Freedom], spending lengthy periods of time in Europe and in the East while he wrote" (Frank Yoder, *The University of Chicago Faculty: A Centennial View*, Chicago, The University of Chicago Library, 1991, pages 26–27, including a picture of Robert Herrick).

5. Harper's "difficulties in the way of securing Alice Freeman Palmer were well-nigh insuperable. But because she was brilliant and famous and certain to win the admiration and affection of the entire University he wanted her, and in the face of all discouragement secured her." The arrangements specified that "Mrs. Palmer will reside at the University, in all, twelve weeks during the year; she will, however, while absent, retain an active share in the administration." Harper accepted Mrs. Palmer's suggestion that Miss Marion Talbot come to Chicago as her assistant and to be the dean of women while she [Mrs. Palmer] was absent. Marion Talbot was also appointed assistant professor of sanitary science. "The duties of the office included supervision of the housing and food of the woman students, their conduct, and the choice of their studies. [Mrs. Palmer's] belief in coeducation made this position especially attractive to her" (Goodspeed, *Chicago*, page 203. Talbot, *More Than Lore*, pages 4, 157, 158).

6. Mrs. Palmer, Miss Marion Talbot, and Professor William Gardner Hale traveled to Chicago together, and Miss Talbot writes that "quite a crowd of friends assembled at the station in Boston to see us off on September 19, 1892 . . . We carried our friends' good wishes for us in our undertaking, even though some of them quietly

intimated that the pioneer conditions of life and education in the Middle West, for such they were supposed to be at that time, — out there on the edge of the prairie, as it seemed to the dwellers on Beacon Hill — would not hold us long from the well-tried and highly approved mores of the Athens of America. But we were confident and light hearted. Even Mr. Hale's remark as we sped through the Berkshire forests, 'Goodbye, Trees,' failed to give us concern. When we reached Hyde Park station the following afternoon, we were met by J. Laurence Laughlin, our old friend and associate. He waved a magazine in the air as he approached us on the platform, and said, 'We have a real University; here is the student paper!' Ten days before the University opened!" (Talbot, *More Than Lore,* pages 6–7).

7. In the Chronicles both Professor and Mrs. Palmer identify the many different settings in which they gave addresses. These three schools, for example, prepared girls for admission to college. Mr. and Mrs. John McDuffe's Magnolia Terrace School for Girls, in Springfield, Massachusetts was "recommended for college preparation by presidents and secretaries of Radcliffe, Smith, and Wellesley," and Miss Frances V. Emerson's School provided "College Preparatory, Regular and Advanced Courses" (Advertisements in *HGM*, 2: 1893–1894).

1893

GHP

Speeches & articles continued

June 1 Miss Tichnor's Soc. for Home Studies Congrat. to Teachers
" 2 Riverview Acad on Harv. Univ. 50.00
" 15 West End Institute New Haven, English 50.00
" 23 Bangor High School, Going to College 50.00
July 24–31 Chautauqua N. Y. Pleasure 6+4 [**GHP**-30] 200.00
Aug 6 Boxford Pulpit, Holy Heedlessness
" 23 Peabody Reunion in Pine Grove - Heredity

350.00

This vacation I read:-
Minto's Logic
Davidson's Aristotle (as Educator)
Guyan Morals sans Sanction
" Morale Anglaise
Stimthal's Ethick
Pater's Plato & Platonism
James' Psychology 2 vols

Howell's Quality of Mercy
Fuller's Pratt Portraits
Perley's History of Boxford
Stephen's Liberty Equality & Fraternity
Kirkups History of Socialism
Taussigs Silver Situation in the U. S.
Mackenzies Manual of Ethics
Janet's Theory of Morals

June 1–22 Alice in Chicago & I with her from June 1 to 15
July 1 We go to West Chop [on Martha's Vineyard] for a fortnight at $500 & expenses; but so few persons appear that we persuade the management to give up the School paying us $250
July 24–31 We spend at Chautauqua N. Y. Alice speaking 6 times; I, 10 $400.00 We paying all expenses - about 100.00
Course in Radcliffe $500[Note 1]
Our joint income this year $9300.00
Fred Mary & Eric spent most of August in the Farm House
Aug. 23 Peabody Reunion

Books Read Term Time 1893–4

G. Smith's United States
Quincy's Hist Harvard College 2 vols
A. Sidgwick's Process of Argument
Wendell's Life of Cotton Mather
Jebb's Growth & Influence of Classic Greek Poetry
Lang's Homer & the Epic
Crawfords Cigarette Makers Romance
Lowells Letters 2 vols
Earle's Fashions & Customs of Old New England
The Heavenly Twins by Sarah Grand
Mrs. Wards Marcella 2 vols
A Superfluous Woman by Sarah Grand
Ships that pass in the Night - Miss Harvaden
Kidd's Evolutionary Socialism
Wylies Evolution of English Criticism
Meredith's Richard Feverel

Sept 13-Oct 19, Alice & I leave Boxford for Chicago, I return Sept 23 Alice Oct. 19
Dec 30-Jan 21 [1894] Alice in Chicago
Mar. 27-Apr. 27 " " "

Addresses 1893–4

Harv. Xn Association Parl. of Religion Oct. 26
Nov. 22 Prospect Union — Study of Poetry
Jan 31. Wheaton Seminary Criticism[Note 2] 25.00
March 11 Wellesley — Shaksperes Sonnets, Barnes G. Herbert
Apr. 19 Harv. Religious Union — G. Herbert
" 24 Annex Emmanuel Society — Shaksperes Sonnets
March 30 & 31 Reading fr Odyssey at Annex Play[Note 3]
" 18 Trinity Chapel Atlanta University
June 15. Courtland School Bridgport, English 35.00
" 28 Michigan University — English 55.00
" " Commencement Dinner
July 1 Convocation Dinner Chicago

115.00

Dec 1893 Article for Johnsons Cyclopedia on Harv Univ. - copy of book given me [**GHP**-31]

Addresses & Articles

Emmanuel Society - Annex - Oct.
Dec. 9 School Masters Club, Women teachers in Grammar Schools
March 18 Trinity Chapel Atlanta University

Notes 1893

1. This is the first reference to Radcliffe. It was becoming clear that the [Annex — see 76n4] was no longer an experiment. "President Eliot [of Harvard] in a speech to the Women's Education Association in November 1892, said that a sum no less than $250,000 would be necessary in order to consider making the Annex a part of Harvard. Thereupon the Women's Education Association, under the presidency of Alice Freeman Palmer [elected in January 1891] . . . announced that it was prepared to help the Annex raise that amount. The fund drive was well under way when, in 1893, Harvard entered into negotiations with the Annex for the establishment of an independent college for women" (Howells, *A Century to Celebrate*, page 13).

"On December 6, 1893, the Board of Overseers of Harvard College, by a unanimous vote, gave its consent to an arrangement to be made between the University and the Society for the Collegiate Instruction of Women . . . What should be the nature of the connection between the two bodies was the next question and the chief one . . . It was not easy to express or define this arrangement by a comprehensive phrase. It finally took the shape of a visitatorial power, to be assumed by the University over the new college. This power is, of course, but vaguely described in the word visitatorial, but it is nevertheless, in fact, most substantial, and with the understanding which has been established by fifteen years of experience, it is effectual and insures a close union in essential matters. In this view the vagueness of the term is, and was meant to be, favorable to the growth of whatever further connection may hereafter be developed."

The name Radcliffe College, "though not connected with anything in the history of the enterprise, was suggested, in the absence of any name obviously appropriate, by its association with an incident in the early history of Harvard College." In 1643, the wife of the Lord Mayor of London, Lady Moulson, whose maiden name was Anne Radcliffe, gave Harvard £100 for a scholarship. This gift, "probably the first ever made to Harvard College by a woman, established its first scholarship, and being made, as it was, in England, to aid the infant college in the distant New World, it was a conspicuous evidence of interest in learning. This incident, although its connection with the present college for women is certainly of the slightest, has supplied an acceptable name, and enough of pleasant association to justify it" (Joseph B. Warner, Radcliffe College, *HGM*, 1893–94; 2 (March 1894): 329–345).

Three hundred and fifty years later, this gift, "one of Harvard's first endowment funds . . . is currently valued at $48,000 and still provides scholarships to Harvard undergraduates" (Q & A on the Endowment, *Harvard Gazette*, February 14, 1992, page 7).

2. His entries show that Professor Palmer gave numerous lectures at Wheaton, and that he also spoke about "Criticism" elsewhere. In his *Autobiography* (**GHP**-104, page 125–126), he writes: "Criticism became my sacred word . . . Its simplest definition is the sense of inadequacy. Slightly modified as the Glory of the Imperfect, it appeared as the title of one of my earliest papers [**GHP**-18]. Combined with appreciation of beauty — beauty in poetry, pictures, architecture, or landscape — it becomes a mighty engine, successively revealing what is adequate or harmonious and teasing us to bring this perfection to birth. It has been my guiding principle in many fields. I have altered successfully five houses. I never planned one from the ground up. I need something to begin with and improve. This ethical sense of a better in alliance with its twin sister, the aesthetic, trains practical judgment and makes one a generally useful person, resorted to by many for advice. Such advisory work has brought me much happiness and has enabled me to find situations for a large

number of teachers. My recommendations are accepted because they are not generalities, but indicate just the work of which a candidate is capable."

The following text is from a handwritten summary of his lecture at Wheaton: "Each literary epoch has had its characteristic form of expression. There has been a time of poetry, a time of romances, and a time when one who wished to give his opinions on some subject, issued a pamphlet. General thought now expresses itself through critical articles and novels, and professional critics are especially numerous.

"In business life, it is sometimes said that a retail merchant is unnecessary, that he creates nothing, but merely turns goods over from the producer to the consumer, who could more economically make the transaction without him. On the contrary, the middleman helps the producer by finding out the taste of his customers, and saves the time of the consumer, both by bringing things where he can conveniently get them and by making it his duty to know about the products which he sells. 'The critic is the middleman in fine art, his office is interpretation, he must have both knowledge and sympathy, and his work is a positive, not a negative one.'

"Probably for the reason that it is always easier to tell what is lacking than to discern the different elements of what is present, a critic is often thought to be a fault-finder, one who looks for the flaws, and tells us the good qualities which a certain book or picture does not contain. This person is not without his use; but the really fine critic is not destructive, he is constructive, his trained intellect can point out to us special merits, and his approbation is a stamp of value.

"Criticism may be divided into several branches, but while one critic deals chiefly with one kind, and another with another, the broadest unites them all. Professional criticism is the expression of emotions aroused by its object; it is good only in so far as it is unprejudiced and sincere, and valuable in proportion to the brightness and sensibility of the critic. Historical criticism studies the author and ascertains the circumstances under which his work was done; it is eminently a scholarly kind, but, like the criticism of expression, uses no criterion and holds up no standard. The remaining kinds, on the contrary, all involve some form of comparison; the Traditional compares a man's work with that of his predecessors, brings experience to bear upon the present, and asks if all is in harmony with established ideas; the Artistic compares with nature, demands a true relationship between all the parts, and asks whether the best means has been taken to convey the thought intended; while the Moral inquires if the purpose were a high one and justified the labor spent, and compares the artist's accomplishment with his ideal.

"The deepest criticism is the bringing of an author to the standard of his own laws, and is applicable to life, and as advantageous to character, as it is to works of art" (Seminary notes, *The Rushlight*, Winter term, 1894).

3. Public entertainment by the Radcliffe Glee Club, a presentation entitled "Pictures from Homer": "Students in Grecian costumes recited dramatically the Greek Verses, Professor Palmer read, between the scenes, selections from his translation of the Odyssey" (*HGM*, 1893–94; 2 (June 1894): 555). A 4x4 inch picture, probably from this performance, entitled "Earliest Greek play, about 1893," shows six young women in Grecian costumes (Howells, A Century to Celebrate, page 72).

1894

GHP

Jan 5-Feb 21 workmen altering 11 Quincy St Dr Peabody's old house which we took at $750 rent & spent $2600.00 on repairing it.[Note 1] Having nearly 5 years more lease of 3 Mason St. we agreed to give it up to Dean Hodges, the Trustees paying us $1000 for the repairs we had made upon it.

In middle of June Robt Herrick married Harriet Emery

June 28 I deliver Commencement Oration at Michigan University, which confers on me degree of L. L. D.[Note 2] Alice obliged to remain in Cambridge on account of sickness

July 7 We move to Boxford, where Mrs. Lane & Will occupy the farm house.

Aug 9–11 At Plymouth together — School of Ethics

Sept 15–17 Leominster with Talmages

This summer Augustus sells his house in Boston & hires home in Andover

Closed Hotel Placidia & drove Mr Kimball out of Boxford for liquor selling

Jan. 20 [1894] — Helen A. Shafer, Pres. Wellesley, dies

Feb 21, 1894 I give Alice the bronze Relief of myself executed by Anne Whitney I paying $350.00 for it.[Note 3]

Summer Speeches & Reading

July 29 Sermon in Boxford - Work
Aug. 5 " " " Fear of God
" 26 " " " Drinking of his Cup
Aug. 10 Address. at Plymouth School of Ethics The School as an Ethical Instrument

Books Read

Bradley's Appearance & Reality
Hutchinson's Hist. of Massachusetts 2 vols
Fiske's Beginnings of New England
" American Revolution 2 vols
Farina Faute di Picche (Italian)
Jane Barlow's Irish Idylls
Three Episodes in New Eng. History C. F. Adams 2 vols
Fiske's Critical Period in Amer. Hist
J. Seth's Study of Ethical Principles
Banath's Physical Ethics
Ritchie's Principles of State Interference
Fiske's History of the United States
Tarde Les Lois de l Invitation

Books Read by me Term 1894–5

Ladds Primer of Psychology
Trilby of Du Maurier
Parkmans Frontenac
Phelps Romantic Movement
Fuller's Cliff Dwellers
Paulsens German Universities
Huxleys Ethics & Evolution
Maeterlincks Plays
The Bard of the Dimbovitza
Deweys Study of Ethics
Hydes Social Theology
Tylers Shakesperes Sonnets
Balfours Foundations of Belief
Watsons Comte Mill & Spencer
Nordaus Dégénérescence
An Experiment in Altruism

Speeches & Articles 1894–95

Oct. 4 Welcome to Xn Assocation
" 11 Andover Club
Nov 12 Phil Conference — Positions f. teaching Philos.

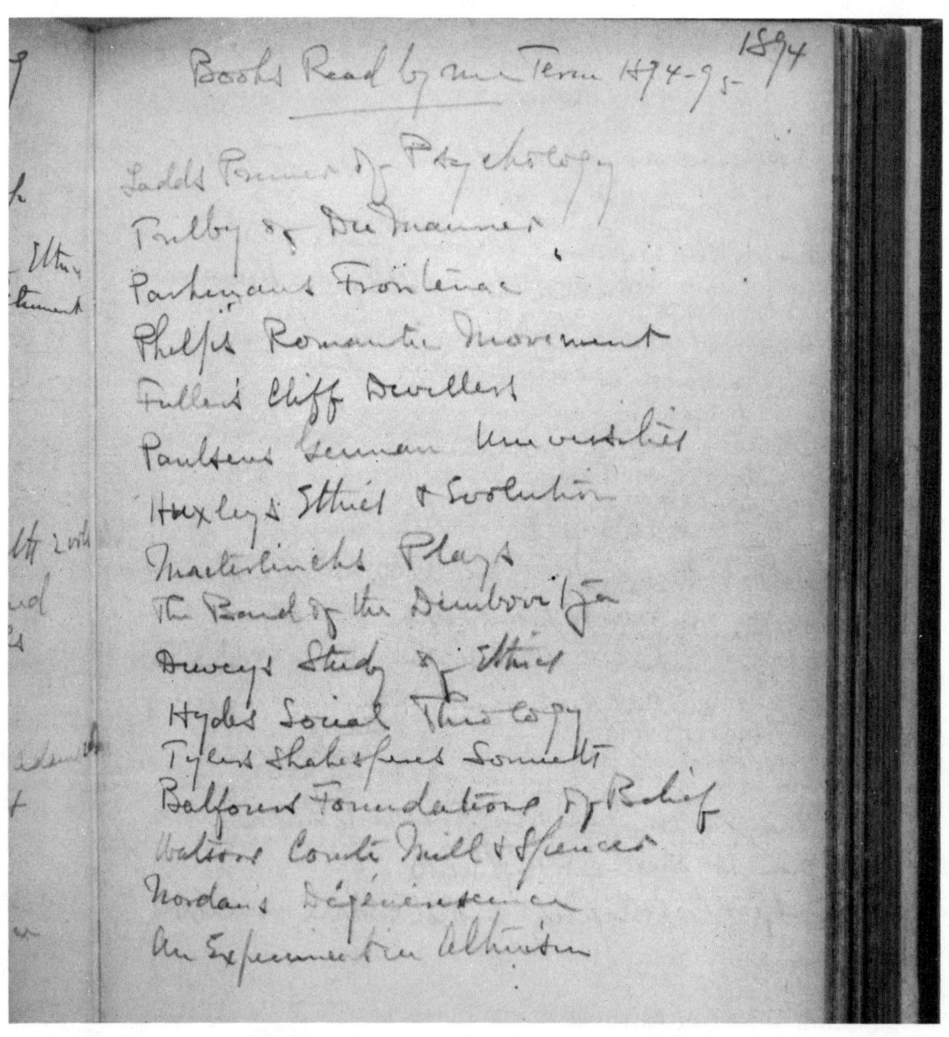

Books Read by me Term 1894-95 1894

Ladd's Primer of Psychology
Trilby of Du Maurier
Parkman's Frontenac
Phelps's Romantic Movement
Fuller's Cliff Dwellers
Paulsen's German Universities
Huxley's Ethics & Evolution
Maeterlinck's Plays
The Bard of the Dimbovitza
Dewey's Study of Ethics
Hyde's Social Theology
Tyler's Shakespeare Sonnets
Balfour's Foundations of Belief
Watson's Comte Mill & Spencer
Nordau's Dégénérescence
An Experiment in Altruism

George Herbert Palmer's entries, 1894–95. (reduced size)

Nov. 23 Signet Graduate Club — Colleges at Harvard
Dec. 15 Graduate Club " " "
Jan 9 [1895] Prospect Union The Odyssey
Jan 24 Michigan University " "
Jan 31 Univ Chicago Graduates Prayer for Colleges
Feb 1 Chicago Quadrangle Club Odyssey Bk VI
" 6 Kelley Hall The Odyssey Bk XIX
" 7 Cleveland O. Self Cultivation in English $100.00
" 8 Buffalo 20th Cent. Club Ethics of Happiness $100.00
" " Chicago 20th Cent Club Sonnets of Shakspeare $100.00
Mar. 2 New York Rev P. Grants Descriptive Sciences & Ethics $300.00
" 9 " " " " " Law & " &
" 16 " " " " " Aesthetics & " expen-
" 23 " " " " " Religion & " ses
May 29 Mrs. Hayes School Boston Cultivation in English 25.00
June. 18 Saginaw High School " " " 50.00
July 11 & 12 Cottage City [now Oak Bluffs, Martha's Vineyard]
English & Ethical Training in Schools 50.00
725.00

Sept. 21 We leave Boxford for Cambridge Find Prof Laughlin & Agatha there The latter spends year with us & goes to Miss Ingalls School.
Sept 27 Alice goes to Chicago
Oct 30 Reaching home
Dec 31-Feb 20 [1895] Alice in Chicago
Jan 22-Feb. 13 Agatha & I Chicago at Laughlins
Dec 6 All family dined with Augustus on his 70th birthday at his new house in Andover
Christmas Mary & Fred entertained 17 of us
Dec. Alice sends formal resignation of her Deanship of Chicago

Notes 1894

1. The house, built in 1823 on a knoll on the west side of Quincy Street, was occupied for about ten years by the Dana family [Richard Henry Dana], was sold to Harvard College in 1835, was the home of a succession of Harvard professors, and served for a time as the College observatory. A report in 1911, stated that "Professor Palmer-has improved the house considerably. He has put in modern appliances has changed the position of the room, used in observatory times for the transit circle, so that it now joins the main house at

right angles . . . uses this room for his library . . . and [the house] has now the qualities of a very comfortable dwelling, rather than the scientific aspect of an observatory."

After living in the house for almost forty years, George Herbert Palmer died there in 1933, and it became known as the Dana-Palmer House. In 1946, when plans were made to build the Lamont Library on the site, "outcry against destruction of the Dana-Palmer House was loud and immediate; students, alumni, and Cambridge residents joined in denouncing the demolition of one of the last remaining wooden structures in the Yard" James B. Conant, in *My Several Lives, Memoirs of a Social Inventor*, New York, Harper & Row, 1970: 406, describes this "storm in an academic coffeepot," and adds that Mr. Lamont gave "an additional $75,000 to move the house across the street; this was done in June, 1947." (The Dwelling-Houses in the College Yard, *Harvard Alumni Bulletin*, 1911–1912; 14 (No. 3, October 18, 1911): 36–40. Jean R. Stern, A Brief History of the Dana-Palmer House, typescript, 4 pages, March, 1946).

Thomas W. Lamont, class of 1892 in Harvard College, who provided these funds, writes about his college years: "Then there were three courses in philosophy, that department at Harvard being far outstanding among all the universities of the country. Philosophy seemed rather out of my line, for I was given to action rather than to meditation and speculation. It was the men — all three of them falling in my classification of giants — rather than the subjects that attracted me — George Herbert Palmer, Josiah Royce, and William James. (George Santayana was just beginning as an instructor). Professor Palmer taught us ethics in a most alluring manner. I had already known him through his perfectly corking metrical translation of Homer's *Odyssey* " (Thomas W. Lamont, *My Boyhood in a Parsonage,* New York, Harper & Bros., 1946: 181–182).

As a Christmas gift in 1894, the Palmers' friend, William DeWitt Hyde, president of Bowdoin College, sent "a copy of a picture of Christ sitting by the shore in conversation with a fisherman." Professor Palmer acknowledged the gift: "It is very beautiful and to me entirely new. Who is the painter? . . . It hangs in my Library, with St. George and Dr. Peabody and Caird and Erasmus and Hegel, with Ellen too and Alice, each telling their own special way of winning the world to righteousness" (Charles T. Burnett, *Hyde of Bowdoin,* Boston, Houghton Mifflin Co., 1931: 273–274). A photograph of the library at 11 Quincy Street shows a number of pictures hanging on one wall (**GHP**-57).

2. A citation for his honorary degree is not available from the archives at the University of Michigan. His commencement address was on Self-Cultivation in English (**GHP**-34).

3. The Wellesley College Archives has a 24 x18$^{1/2}$ inch plaster, left profile bust relief of George Herbert Palmer. On May 31, 1894, Palmer wrote to Miss Whitney: "Here is the check. You wrote that the price was $350, yet I have suspicions that by some covert generosity you are preventing my playing the part I had so much in mind of a thorough going customer. At any rate I know our gains are not level with this little outgo. In no other way would the sum have purchased so long a pleasure. Alice will enjoy the likeness, & I the fine art, as long as our eyes can see. And always we shall be the happier for having you a member of our household" (Wellesley College Archives, 3P Anne Whitney Papers).

1895

GHP

In June ends my 25th year of continuous service at Harvard, the College having paid me $75,500

June 19 Dr. Fred Freeman at Saginaw marries Alice Wiggins, I officiating [The Palmers' diaries —chapter 4 — for March 7 and 10, 1900, note a visit in Cambridge from Alice Wiggins' father, who was "engaged in great lumber operations" in Nova Scotia.]

June 27. Union College celebrates its Centennial Harvard sends me as delegate. Alice goes to Chicago & Saginaw taking Agatha Laughlin home, I follow a week later to Saginaw, then to Chicago to wedding of Prof Laughlin & Mary Cramer then we both spend 4 days at Schenectady & receive each an LL. D Prof Hale receiving one also[Note 1]

This summer Fred & Mary in farm house Hurd of England preaching for him in Aug. We visit Arthur Marsh in early July, leave Boxford Aug. 7 & sail Steamer Maasdam Netherlands Line for Bologne Aug [incomplete entry]

Wellesley Commencement Mrs J. J. Irving accepts Presidency of Wellesley

Our property now is $8000 saved & RR stock nominally $10000 given me by E. H. Abbot

See 1898–99

Alices Lectures

Knox College Feb. 15 Note 2		
Jackson " 18	25.00	
Buffalo " 19	25.00	
Brunswick Mar 23		
Manchester N. H. Apr 10	25.00	[figure by **AFP**]
Hartford " 11–13	60.00	" " "
Fitchburg " 26	25.00	" " "
Summersworth May 1	25.00	" " "
AFP		
Lewiston May 2	25.00	
North Abington	25.00	
GHP		
Chicago Miss Brooks School June	50.00	
July 11 & 12 Cottage City	50.00	
	360.00	

Notes 1895

1. Union College does not have citations for the honorary degrees. In a description of the Centennial dinner, *The Schenectady Daily Union* has this paragraph: "The next speaker was Prof. George Herbert Palmer, of Harvard, and as he rose from his chair the students present gave the Harvard yell. Prof. Palmer said his was a most agreeable duty and he tendered to 'Old Union' Harvard's heartiest congratulations on the grounds of kinship and honor. For kinship because both institutions believed in freedom of religion, a most sound principle. On the grounds of honor because he believed the success of any college was the success of all colleges. The speaker then said 'I feel personally under deep obligation to Union. A long while ago a Union man who was in charge of a school believed he had one pupil—a woman, who deserved a higher education [see **AFP**'s entry, page 36]. He used his influence and gained her parents' consent to send her to Michigan university. She finally became the president of Wellesley and my wife. I always have known that in Union there is strength, now I am persuaded of it.' "

2. On Friday, February 15, 1895, Knox College in Galesburg, Illinois, 185 miles southwest of Chicago, celebrated the fifty-ninth anniversary of its founding in 1837. Mrs. Palmer came from Chicago where she was on a visit as the University's Dean of Women. Late in the afternoon she attended a reception in honor of her and other guests, and in the evening she delivered an address on "The Higher Educa-

tion of Women." The Presbyterian church was filled when President Finley introduced Alice Freeman Palmer.

The weekly college newspaper summarized her presentation: "The Advancement of women is progressing with surprising rapidity, and noticeably so along educational lines. Because of her advance in other respects, women must be better educated also, to keep pace with it. There is a great demand for knowledge. Women have great use for better education. The speaker emphasized the importance of having the best educated teachers for the youth of the land. Over ninety per cent of these teachers are women.

"Mrs. Palmer spoke in high terms of the college and the anniversary. After the lecture, many remained to greet the speaker in the parlors. [Lucius Brown reported: "It was a pleasure for me to meet Mrs. Palmer for the first time and our relations to old Windsor Academy made us friends immediately." (BCHSoc.)] She goes abroad with her husband soon for pleasure and study. Mr. Palmer is at the head of the Philosophical department at Harvard and in accordance with the custom there of allowing one year in seven for rest and study, he will take the coming year for travel abroad with his estimable wife" (*The Knox Student*, February 6, 13, 20, 1895. Program of exercises for Founders' Day 1837–1895).

1895–96

GHP

See volume on Absence in Europe**Note 1** [I have not found this volume]

<u>Deaths during our absence</u>

Mrs Claflin June 1896 [see **aboutAFPann**-4 for a "message" that Mrs. Palmer delivered at a memorial service for her close friend, Mrs. Claflin].

Philip S. Abbot Aug. 3 1896**Note 2**

Aunt Hattie Sept 1896

Notes 1895–96

1. From Vienna, on June 3, 1896, Alice Freeman Palmer wrote a long letter to James B. Angell, who was being honored on his twenty-fifth anniversary as president of the University of Michigan:

"Austria and Ann Arbor are not very far apart after all! And now that June has come how often I wish that we could change the one for the other! For this is the month when you celebrate twenty-five years at the dear old place; and all the world will come to tell you how good it has been, and how thankful and glad we are. My husband and I want to join the great company and swell the chorus, and it is bitterly hard to miss it all. And it is my twentieth anniversary too! I suppose my class will all be there, counting their gray heads, and wondering why '76 has grown so old, and you so young! That is certainly the most curious phenomenon of my time and has caused me much speculation.

"When a man comes to his silver wedding day I suppose his wife feels at liberty to tell him just how good she thinks he is! Why may not your friends venture now to say out boldly how much they love you, and how grateful they are for you, and what you have done and been, all the while they have been keeping silence?

"To me you have always been the ideal College President! As an undergraduate I watched you from the immeasurable distance and felt the power that made for righteousness and peace, and unconsciously trusted that all the place was good and safe to be in because you stood there at the head of it! And since, as a woman I came a little closer to College Presidents, and had occasion to study a great many of them and their work, I have better understood how rare and how fine is the combination of qualities and of forces which you have brought to my University.

"To my mind, the quality of your character and influence explains the unquestionable fact that the University of Michigan has accomplished more than any other place on either side of the Atlantic, for the wisest solution of the many problems of the education of girls and women.

"The indirect influences going out from Ann Arbor have been more subtly good and far-reaching than any man can calculate; and chiefly because, while all the time the doctors have been discussing our bodies, and the clergymen have been warning us about our souls, and many men have been brutal, and many more sentimental, and all of us women ignorant of best ways, and groping in the dark,—all of this important, struggling quarter of a century there has stood quietly in his place at the head of the University of Michigan a *man, who has been so much a gentleman, that all men about him have been more just and courteous; and all women more hopeful and dutiful and large minded!*

"There the air has been clearer, and life has been simpler, and work more strenuous, because of our President's intellectual honesty and hospitality, and his uncommon common sense. Why should not we women, and every child or scholar we have, rise up and bless our good Angell,—our Mr. Great Heart?

"It is more and more amazing to me that you could have done so much at Ann Arbor in so many widely different directions, especially on the sadly deficient resources you have had to work with all these years. In all these years not a single educational reform has escaped your influence; you have found time and means for bettering every scholar in Michigan, from the kindergarten into his professional life,—and so of helping on the reign of right reason everywhere; whether in California or Massachusetts, which are rivals in indebtedness to you,—not to mention China indeed! [In 1880–1881, Angell was Envoy Extraordinary and Minister Plenipotentiary of the United States at Peking] How many secrets you keep hidden down somewhere in your fountain of perpetual youth! Some time you must tell us about it,—but not yet; for there is *Arbitration* to be brought about, and English and Americans to be taught how to be brothers—and your Committee has work to do! And are we too selfish to ask for twenty-five years more? You have been so generous already, be generous still! Let us find you at the heart of things for many a year to come. Let other feet run the errands, and other hands write the letters—don't answer this!—but please sit in the beautiful new library, or on the wide piazza under the trees, and write the wise books so long growing in your brain;—and, not the least, the story of these twenty-five years for the thousands who, like me, owe everything to *your* University of Michigan.

"We had your good letter wth the greatest pleasure, as probably my husband has said. His congratulations and good wishes and love go to you with mine, and he wishes that he might sit down with your other sons-in-law and drink to your health on your anniversary day" (Shirley W. Smith, *James Burrill Angell*: *An American Influence,* Ann Arbor, University of Michigan Press, 1954, pages 151, 245–247.).

2. Philip Stanley Abbot, son of Edwin Hale Abbot and a member of the Appalachian Mountain Club, died from a fall while climbing Mount Lefroy in the Canadian Rockies; he was one month short of his twenty-ninth birthday.

Charles E. Fay, one of three men who were climbing with him, describes Abbot's enthusiasm on a visit to the "Canadian Alps" in 1895, and the circumstances of his death:

"Knowing the best of Switzerland by an intimate experience possessing thus the truest criterions of comparison and kept by his native clear-sightedness and strong common-sense from unsober overestimates of what presently filled his eye . . . [he] rejoiced as at a new and priceless discovery in the realization that within four days of the Atlantic seaboard there lies another and a virgin Switzerland."

In 1894, another member of the Club, climbing on Mount Lefroy, had reached a gorge, — "a true pass, —one of the highest and grandest of the Continental Divide" — had named it "Death-Trap Col" [renamed "Abbot Pass" after the tragedy], and had decided that ascent to the peak from that side of the gorge was impracticable. "This seeming prohibition was to Abbot an alluring invitation. The game of ascending Mt. Lefroy by any other way than this was not worth the candle to him, at least not until this way should have been shown to be beyond our powers by an actual test."

"All scepticism and reluctance succumbed to [Abbot's] enthusiasm and witty logic . . . [and] after a long debating of the pros and cons [the group decided] to attack Lefroy . . . by Abbot's route." At an altitude of about 10,000 feet, "Abbot had scanned the western side of Lefroy, now for the first time clearly revealed to us, and joyfully exclaimed: 'The peak is ours!' And surely his confidence seemed justified. From here an unobstructed way was seen leading up to the long summit arête, which still frowned nearly two thousand feet above the pass. The vast mountain side rose in a sloping wall, ice-clad for the greater part, yet with here and there long upward leads of rock that probably could be scaled . . . Assured of what it lay nearest to his heart to know, Abbot now turned his attention to the grand spectacle, and his enthusiasm found ample expression in that ever happy smile, his beaming eyes, and his quiet remark—and what was ever so convincing as that confident, almost childlike mental repose?—that nowhere had he ever seen that view surpassed for striking Alpine effects."

At an altitude of 11,300 feet, as Abbot, in the lead, was making his way around an immense bastion, his companions suddenly saw him "falling backward and head-foremost, saw him strike the upper margin of the ice slope within fifteen feet of us, turn completely over and instantly began rolling down its steep incline . . . How the terrible disaster occurred we shall never know. In all probability his foothold, or more likely his handhold, gave way . . . The autopsy revealed a fracture of the occipital and left parietal bones, with some depression of the former, which renders it practically certain that he was unconscious as he fell past us, and that he never regained consciousness."

This was "the saddest episode in the history of our Club . . . the first fatal accident in its twenty years of existence . . . But after duly weighing all that is urged against Alpine climbing, and while appreciating, none more profoundly, the value of the rare life that went out on Mt. Lefroy, we maintain that the gain therefrom for the general and the individual life in an age of growing carefulness for ease and luxury must be held to outweigh the deplorable losses, and that this casualty should not call a halt in American alpinism. That a man like Philip Abbot should love this form of recreation—and to him it was an education as well—argues for its nobility."

Fay includes part of a letter written by Philip Abbot's father: "The love of mountains had been with Philip almost a passion from early childhood. Wherever he was, he never lost an opportunity of ascending them. He had reached the extreme top of Popocatapetl in Mexico, and had spent nearly a month in ascending the peaks around Yosemite, before he was twenty years old. Afterwards he wandered over the mountains in Norway, and later spent two summers in Switzerland, in order, as he said, to study in the very university of mountaineering the scientific methods and experience of the masters of that art . . .

"Philip's mountaineering had grown from a delight into a steady purpose of exploration and study of our American Switzerland. These unexplored heights attracted him profoundly. He had learned to make reconnaissances after the methods of army engineers, to take barometric altitudes, to make maps and carry out geological research, and, in short, to spend his summers not only in recreation, but also in really useful scientific work. He had prepared himself for last summer's trip with the pains and skill of a thorough student, just as he entered upon it with the spirit of a brave man. He considered that mountaineering was the noblest form of athletic adventure which the opportunties of his day afforded"(*HGM*, 1896–97; 5 (December 1896): 275. Charles E. Fay, The Casualty on Mount Lefroy, *Appalachia*, 1896–1898; 8 (No. 2, November 1896): 133–153, illustrated.) See also 146n4 and **GHP**-32.

1896–97

GHP

Boxford Sept 22–26

Lucy Sprague with us this year, & Eric Lucy has N. E. front room, Eric ell next bathroom Eric enters college, Lucy special in Radcliffe**Note** 1–9

Room 16 University where I have taught some 15 years now turned into offices. I Sever 5.

Mrs. Sprague with us 1st fortnight

Oct 1 Georgianna & Amos White (negroes) as cook & servant

Nov. 27 Alice Palmer Herrick born at Chicago

" " A. B. Emery comes & gets place in Boston

Dec. 22–25 At Boxford. Cold weather in Emily's house Christmas at Freds

At this time give notice to A. E. B th. I sh'l now cease to contribute $680 annually to farm expenses at Boxford. Decide to buy my house**Note** 10

Jan. 28 Go today to Homoeopathic Hospital, E. Concord St Boston, to be operated on tomorrow for double inguinal hernia, which I have had 12 years I do so because I am in exceptionally good health Though the hernia is troubling me little at present I fear its disturbance in old age.

March 1 Pay A. E. B $1800 for his share in Boxford house & to Emily $900.00

Alices Lectures & Articles

Oct 8 Cambridgeport Xn Association Housekeeping	
Oct 9 Colleges & Prep Schools of N. E. — French Education	
Oct 12 Miss Boice Philadelphia Women in Professions	50.00
Oct 26 Dorchester Womans Club, Foreign Education	25.00
Oct 27 Boston Miss Emersons School Preparation f. Life Am. girls	25.00
Oct 22 A. M. A. Jubilee Boston	
Oct 29 Providence R I Institute Preparation f. t new demands	
Oct 30 A. C. A. Providence	
Nov. 12 Round Table Impressions of Foreign Education	
" 20 Education Assoc Bost. Univ. Womens Educ Abroad	
" 21 Wellesley College Universities of France & England	
" 23 Wilmington Del. " " " " "	50.00
" 24 Brooklyn Pratt Inst Bicycling Abroad**Note** 11	50.00
	200.00

My Lectures & Articles 1896–97

Oct. 12 Xn Association Radcliffe Welcome
" 21 Appalachia Club Philip Abbot
Nov. 7 Signet Dinner Tablets on Rooms
" 12 Xn Assoc Prayer f. Colleges College Sins
Nov. Number of Appalachia Article on P. S. Abbot [**GHP**-32]
" 18 Episc. Theol School Survey of Agencies of Reform
" 21 Girls College Club. Some Objections to Education for Women
Jan 4 Radcliffe Philos. Club. Society as an Organism
" 27 Brookline Education Society Profssn of t. Teacher 40.00
" " Article on Empedocles in "World's Best Reading"[**GHP-**33] 37.50
Apr 22 New Haven Teachers Assoc. Self Cultiv. in Eng. 50.00

Apr 23 Montclair N. J. Buddhism 75.00
May 8 Preach at Boxford on Geo. Herbert
June 3 Society for Home Study — Miss Tichnor
" 9 Wheaton Seminary Nature & Divis. of Philos. 25.00
" 19 Buddhism & Christianity The Outlook. [**GHP-**35]
40 copies & 10.00
" 21 Cambridge Latin School
" 28 Groton School
" 29 Class Supper Harvards Changes

Books Read 1896–97

Santayana Sense of Beauty
Harris, Moral Evolution
Watson, Hedonistic Theories
Francke, Social Forces in German Literature
Jewett, The Country of the Pointed Firs
Tarbell, History of Greek Art
Giddings Principles of Social Science
Schmidt Das Gewissein
F. B. Perkins France Under the Regency
Miss Sherwood A Puritan Bohemia
Kiplings Seven Seas
Bussell's School of Plato
Eliots Happy Life
Giles's Moral Pathology
Webers History of Philosophy
Gordons Immortality & the New Theodicy
Watsons Christianity & Idealism
Salmons Domestic Service
Warrens Buddhism in Translations
Percival Lowells Soul of the Far East
Dickinson's Greek View of Life
Herricks The Man Who Wins
Darcy's Short Study of Ethics
M. [?] Williams Buddhism
Sidis' Psychology of Suggestion
Rhys Davids Buddhism
Dugard La Societé Americaine
Augustine's City of God 2 vols

Hospital Experience

Jan 28 1897

1. The Operation. It was found impossible to give me ether on acc't of the choking it produced. Chloroform was therefore substituted after

I had fallen asleep at the 3d breath of ether. My heart as I went on to the table had not changed its normal beat This was at 10 A. M. & I waked at 2 P. M. Alice waiting downstairs all the time. There was no consciousness & both going to sleep & waking were easy & rapid.

The external cutting on the left side was three inches in length & the internal at the ring $1^{1/2}$. On this side there was no cutting of the peritoneal sack. The right side was much more serious. The doctors wondered I had had so little trouble & were sure I c'd not have gone on much longer without being disabled. The external cutting here was $4^{1/2}$ inches, the internal $2^{1/2}$, a portion of the sac was also removed & ligated. The tendon of the tail of kangeroo was used for the sewing. The spermatic chord was raised & the suture was carried around it. Yet less than a spoonful of blood was lost. Drs. Packard, Wesselhoeft, Winthrop Talbot, Bell & 4 others were present but the operation, though performed in the regular theatre, was not open to students or the public.

2. The pain from the wound after I awoke was slight. There was great stiffness & I was unable to move in bed, but the pain was of the nature of a dull soreness. The bandages however were tight around the waist, the bed was a thin mattrass on woven wire, there was no sleep for more than 24 hours, & there was mild pain in the whole length of the spine. This was reduced by giving me another mattrass & by Alice's bringing a soft thick pillow from home. The chloroform did not get out of my lungs for a day & produced throughout that time a feeling of nausea. I c'd not cough or blow my nose but had hardly more headache than is usual at home. On the 2nd day a little food was given every two hours & on the 7th day I had my first enema. Throughout my whole stay at the hospital—including the operation—my variation of temperature was only 3 degrees, from 98 to 101, & that of the pulse was 58 to 70. On the 9th day the collodion seal ws taken from the wounds & both were found perfect & without discharge. Two days later in one of the stitch holes a slight watery non-purulent discharge began & continued in that single spot seven weeks until after I was at work again. After 10 days I took my usual food, 3 meals, & had a glycerine enema every 2 or 3 days. I usually had about 6 hours sleep each night, but not more than an hour at a stretch for a month. The days did not seem long. Alice was with me an hour after the operation & almost every day afterward though she was obliged to keep some lecture engagements & each day there were a couple of other callers. After a week I c'd

read for a few minutes at a time, but was not allowed to be propped up in bed. Digestion was throughout feeble.

3. My nurse was Miss Malcolm who attended me night & day with the utmost devotion & skill. She had a bed beside mine & was called once or twice in the night. She more than the doctors took charge of me & decided on my needs, doing all with delicacy but entire absence of squeamishness. On Feb 14--2 weeks & 3 days from the time of my going—I was put in an ambulance & brought home to bed, Miss Malcolm accompanying me and remaining till Feb. 19. On that day I sat up for the 1st time & even came downstairs. Feb 23 I went to Faculty Meeting, & on Feb 24 had 3 lectures & my full work began.
4. I agreed with Dr. Packard that the whole expense sh'd be $250, but I sent him a check for $200 though the other charges were $100 more. My room was $16 a week & my special nurse $21 more.

I gave some pus & Dr. Wesselhoeft visited me in Cambridge. It was about two months after the operation that I was entirely free fr. feeling in the parts. I began to ride my bicycle six weeks after the operation.

Notes 1896–97

1. Lucy Sprague and members of her family are named in more Chronicle entries — thirty-seven — than any family other than the Palmers and Freemans. The opening list of birth-death dates, otherwise including only Palmer-Freeman members, has the dates of Lucy Sprague's birth and marriage, the name of her husband, Wesley Clair Mitchell, and the date of their son's birth. An entry in 1878 gives her date of birth. From 1896–7 through 1903, there are twenty-seven such entries, and seven more until the last, in 1916. In addition, Lucy Sprague figures prominently in Alice Freeman Palmer's diary for March 1900 (chapter 4).

Two publications provide much additional information about the relationship of Lucy Sprague and her family with the Palmers, and about Lucy's later, outstanding career: (LSM) Lucy Sprague Mitchell, *Two Lives: The Story of Wesley Clair Mitchell and Myself*, New York, Simon and Schuster, 1953, 575 pages. (JA) Joyce Antler, *Lucy Sprague Mitchell: The Making of a Modern Woman*, New Haven, Yale University Press, 1987, 436 pages. Some highlights are presented in the following eight notes:

2. Lucy Sprague and Alice Freeman Palmer first met in 1892 when Mrs. Palmer went to Chicago to be Dean of Woman at the newly

opened University; Lucy was fourteen years old. Lucy's father, Otho S. A. Sprague, a wealthy business man and important civic figure, "regarded professors with a kind of reverence once accorded the clergy. He felt it a personal opportunity as well as a civic responsibility to open his home to the faculty members who were strangers in his city" (LSM, 72). Mrs. Palmer lived with the Spragues when she was in Chicago. "Even in those hectic days when she was organizing her work at the University she had time for a withdrawn, overwrought little fourteen-year-old girl. Her eager zest for life, her capacity to listen as wholeheartedly as she talked, her versatility, her light touch even in executive matters in which she was a master, made her literally unique in my experience" (LSM, 73).

3. In 1895 Lucy was living in southern California. She was nursing her father, who had severe pulmonary tuberculosis, and her mother, who was severely depressed. Also, she was attending a small private school, and had another year before graduation. Feeling rebellious, she began to think about college but wondered how she could leave her parents. Wanting help with this dilemma, she wrote "the most important letter of my life" to her older sister, Mary Miller, who was in Paris with her husband, Adolph, who had been on the Harvard faculty. Soon after the letter arrived, the Millers met the Palmers, who were on a sabbatical leave (see 62n1), and Mary read them the letter. Mrs. Palmer wrote to Lucy. "Would I come to Radcliffe and live with them? . . . Mrs. Palmer wrote Father and Mother, too. She would see that I didn't break down. I could enter as a special student without full work, if need be. That letter changed my life. The decision was up to me. And it was an agonizing decision to make. I took my life in my hands and said I wanted to go. Mother was glad. Father did not oppose my decision" (LSM, 115).

Lucy studied hard during the year before graduation, took the Harvard college examinations — used by Radcliffe — near San Francisco (see 67n1), and was accepted by Radcliffe. "I was delirious with happiness" (LSM, 115–116).

4. In September 1896, "When I walked into the Palmer's home at 11 Quincy Street, Cambridge, I walked into a new world . . . Yes, here I was, western all through, now installed in one of the three houses within the sacred Harvard Yard . . . It seemed strange to me to live in the Harvard Yard, but to Radcliffe [in the person of Dean Agnes Irwin] it seemed shocking. What made it even worse was that Mr. Palmer's nephew Eric, a Harvard freshman, was to live in the

same house with me . . . It was a rule, a law, that no Radcliffe student could live in a house with a Harvard student. Yet here I was. And here the Palmers determined I should stay . . . The two sides reached a compromise. Eric and I were to continue to live at the Palmers', but I was never to walk home through the Harvard Yard. For four years I walked down Massachusetts Avenue and up Quincy Street" (LSM, 117–118).

"They [the Palmers] became a part of me and I became a part of them. I was still shy with strangers and to an extent with the girls at college. But with the Palmers I was as free as anyone has a right to be — foolish or thoughtful, talkative or silent, as I felt inclined. They lived a rich intellectual life and a rich human life and they took me into both. I responded to both. I fairly sprouted. It was then that Mrs. Palmer began calling me, 'My only daughter'" (LSM, 121).

5. "In her own home, I found Mrs. Palmer even more enchanting, abler, more human than my memories of her in the old Chicago days when she stayed with us. She loved life — her profession and her home. She still kept Wellesley on her mind, and I heard her persuade Caroline Hazard to become Wellesley's president . . . Her schedule was crowded. Yet, if you came home worn out and said, 'Let's go on a spree !' somehow, she found the time. She lectured a great deal, with careful preparation but without notes. She was personal without being mawkish or sentimental. She wanted to look right when she spoke but had no great sense of clothes, and Mr. Palmer favored severe, handsome dresses for her" (LSM, 122).

6. "Two memories of the Palmers during my four years with them stand out above the many that crowd upon me. The first is reading poetry. At one end of Mr. Palmer's booklined study, a coal fire is burning and at the other end of the long room through the big windows, the Harvard Yard stretches dimly. Mrs. Palmer is lying with feet up on the sofa. I am sitting on the floor in front of the fire. Mr. Palmer, under the light of a single lamp in the dark room, is reading aloud. A wonderful, modulated voice that could make Milton sound like an organ, or could make Nash's 'Cuckoo, jug-jug, pu-wee, to-whitta-whoo' sound like birds in the early morning. He read once or twice every week. He loved English poetry almost as much as he loved Greek — he had completed his great translations of Homer before I knew him. He read sixteenth — and seventeenth-century poets, victorian poets, modern poets . . . And I sat in the firelight and listened. He was then working on the life of George

Herbert, for whom he had been named, and editing his poems. I became an erudite Herbert scholar. Indeed, I did the bulk of the cross-referencing in his three volumes of Herbert. [In his preface to **GHP**-50, volume 1, page xix, Palmer indicates his "obligations to Miss Lucy Sprague . . . who, in pursuance of studies in Herbert, subjected the whole body of my notes to a searching revision"] Mr. Palmer was at his best reading poetry. That is the way I like to think of him now" (LSM, 123–124).

7. "The other persistent memory of the Palmers . . . is of week ends and vacations at Boxford . . . Mrs. Palmer adopted Boxford as her own, and her personality flooded the sweet old farm-house set in meadows with a meandering brook . . . In the darkling woods was a sort of natural clearing surrounded by tall trees — the 'Fairy Ring.' This spot spelled romance to the Palmers — I knew this long before their love letters were published (**GHP**-109, **AFP**-20). They always held hands when we walked down to see the moon sail across the opening above the Fairy Ring" (LSM, 124).

8. The three years after Lucy graduated from Radcliffe in June 1900, were "filled with family illnesses, and, finally, my own . . . Then, once more the Palmers came to my rescue. They were going abroad on Mr. Palmer's sabbatical. Would I like to go with them? Thin, constantly nauseated and coughing, I went to Boston to join them. And once more I stepped into a new world." Lucy goes on to describe their trip before Mrs. Palmer's tragic death in Paris on December 6, 1903: on a cattle steamer to England, a voyage "filled with excitement — and health"; how they traced "every spot that George Herbert had ever stood on in England, yes, in Wales, too"; then, a "week in the English Lakes with Wordsworth" and two weeks in Oxford with the Cairds; to London's museums and book shops, and to Stonehenge; to Salisbury where "the young Herbert . . . had held services for the few brief years of his priesthood . . . and where he had written those poems I knew so intimately . . . sacred ground to Mr. Palmer and hardly less so to Mrs. Palmer and me"; then, to Paris, Mrs. Palmer's illness, and, as "she was carried downstairs on a litter, she waved to me gaily. 'Have a good dinner ready for me when I come home'"; and finally, as Lucy waited in the apartment, "at three one morning, Mr. Palmer returned and said she was dead. He told me her last conscious remark was 'Take care of Lucy'" (LSM, 127–132).

"We were in a Catholic country with strict funeral laws, and she lay still and white after I had braided her dark hair and wound it as a crown on her head . . . Death was so official, so public in France. Official doctors — a series of them, official undertakers — a series of them, each explaining a new law, a new kind of red tape, even for the simple service which was held in the Foreign Chapel . . . And finally the little wooden box of ashes was brought up the winding stairs, down which I had watched her carried the last time I heard her cheerful voice. Mr. Palmer bought a trunk. We put the little wooden box in it with the few clothes from Mrs. Palmer's closet and the many papers from her desk and fled to England. We arrived in London the week before Christmas. One of the cattle steamers for which we had tickets was due to sail in a few days. With our one trunk and few bags, Mr. Palmer and I went on board and sailed for Boston. We were the only passengers . . . So we came at last to the Boston pier and to the silent, weeping little group of friends" (LSM, 132–133).

9. From Lucy Sprague Mitchell's biographer: "Lucy Sprague Mitchell was by any measure a woman of achievement: a writer, teacher, administrator and social reformer; an amateur architect, poet, illustrator and geographer. Her primary claim to the attention of readers today is her distinction as a builder of experimental institutions and as a leader in the education of children . . . But for me, the deepest interest in this life story goes beyond Lucy Mitchell's record as a key figure in progressive education; it lies in a woman's creative struggle to resolve the conflict between demanding, innovative professional work and full engagement as a wife and mother" (JA, page xiii).

10. Starting in 1863, short, confusing entries in the Chronicles refer to various properties in Boxford. Professor Palmer writes: "Our farm in Boxford has never been owned by anybody but ourselves and the Indians. Captain John Peabody built his house here in 1660 . . . Until 1856 the farm continued in that single name. Then by the death of my grandfather it descended to my mother, Lucy Peabody, and has for the last fifty years been known as the Palmer farm. Of its hundred and twenty-five acres about half is woodland." Several entries indicate alterations on different structures. Palmer writes: "I have altered successfully five houses. I never planned one from the ground up. I need something to begin with and improve."

With regard to the Boxford home where he and Alice Freeman Palmer were so happy, Palmer writes: "Her home was not the old house of the first settler. This fell into decay in my childhood. Nor was it even the stately second house, built on the original farm in 1825 by my grandfather. During Mrs. Palmer's life this was occupied by my sister and half a dozen others who might by an affectionate arithmetic be counted members of the family. Her home was on an adjoining lot, a stone's throw distant but unparted by boundaries . . . Half a century ago it came into my family, but was then already a hundred and fifty years old" Boxford and its structures are now preserved as a Historic District, and this residence, on Main Street, known as the Alice Freeman Palmer House, once belonged to Parson Briggs, minister of the First Parish from 1808 to 1833. When Professor Palmer bought the house, "it once again returned to a succession of Peabody family ownership, it having once been part of the Peabody farm" (**GHP**-57, page 280–282. **GHP**-104, page 126. Historic District Study Committee Report, December 15, 1970—in Boxford Public Library).

11. The *Pratt Institute Monthly* (Volume 5, Number 4, January 1897, page 145), summarizes her talk on November 24, 1896: "More swiftly than wheels could have taken us, we were away in Normandy, riding along country roads, looking off from Mont St. Michel, or shut in by tranquil beauty. We wound through the Rhone and Rhine valleys, with olives and mulberries, roses and palms, everywhere. Between the sunny Mediterranean and its bordering red heights we raced, and won our way into the mountains of Austria.

"Perhaps better than our sightseeing were our (?) reflections by the way. We found in Normandy and Brittany the true strength of France; in little schools among the Austrian mountains our educational pride was humbled; we read the hearts of the people; and we took into our keeping a message for our own land.

"Altogether, we came back exhilarated in body and spirit; but — such is human nature — we were unwilling to come back at all !"

In **GHP**-57, page 201–202, Professor Palmer writes: "But our greatest novelty, and the one to which [Mrs. Palmer's] thoughts afterwards most often recurred, was our bicycling — a sport now almost exterminated by the exciting and lazy automobile. One year we carried our wheels from America and, starting from Rouen, rode through Normandy, Brittany, and parts of Picardy and Provence; then over the Cornich Road from Fréjus to Alassio; we crossed the three hundred and sixty miles of Styria and Carinthia lying between Venice and Vienna; rode through the Black Forest from Tübingen to

> Freiburg; and at the close took some stretches of central England. Altogether our cyclometers registered over fifteen hundred miles. When we left home [Mrs. Palmer] had sat on a bicycle only three times; but as she had the queer characteristic of doing excellently and at once whatever she did, on our first day in Normandy she rode eighteen miles with entire ease."

1897

Summer

GHP

Little house let to C. D. Palmer[Note 1]
Prof & Mrs Todd in Mary Ellen Perly's
Robt Herrick & baby came fr West & after a fortnight with us in Cambridge go to Chocorua with the Fletchers
Mary & Fred sail July 8-Sept. 13 for England
Eric spends summer at Dr. Talbot's camp in Holderness as Councillor then with us
In Early Spring we were in Boxford several times
First week of cold June Dr. Bakewell & I here
We come to Boxford permanently July 3-Sept 29
Fred & Mary take parish—Ashton on Mersey—in England this summer bicycling there & in France
Aug 23–26 we visit Kimballs at Profile House, N. H.
Alice speaks once in Aug at Old South Church - Whittier
" " " " Sept " Town Hall - Bicycling
" " Dedication of High School Upton Sept 23
I preach in June on G. Herbert, in Sept on the Death of Friends
Wrote small books for series of T. Y. Crowell & Co.
I on "Self Cultivation in English" [**GHP**-34]
Alice on "Why Go to College" [**AFP**-8]
Miss Allen spent summer with Emily
Also Aug Lilly Mrs. Wilkinson & the two children
We cut paths in School House Pasture fr. first bars over Sunset Rock to 2nd bars, then on to 3d in New Field

Books Read

Nash's Genesis of the Social Conscience
Hendersons Social Spirit in America
Külpe's Introduction to Philosophy
Garbe's Philosophy of Ancient India
Seneca's Moral Essays (Latin)
Abelard & Heloises Letters (Latin) & Sicto Te 4 [?]
Rémusat's Abelard (French)

M. Arnolds Letters 2 vols
Mrs. Todds Solar Eclipses
J. L. Allens Choir Invisible
Verse von Hugo Terberg (German)
Fraser's India
Thatchers Medieval Europe
Swinburnes Atalanta in Caledon
Baines Margaret Ogilvy
Outline of Church History - Sohm [?]
Wenleys Outline of Kants Critique

Boxford-Summer

Repairs on House
- Both sofas removed
- New Bay window & entry cushion covers
- New book case in Library Secretary in Dining Room
- 6 additional pictures hung
- Shades in Dressing Room
- Muslin Curtains in Dining Room & back chamber
- Folding chair in dining room — China Tea Set
- Clock for Library & 2 rugs — also 1 for Blue Rms
- Lantern for Entry — Country Rug for Dining Room

$155.50

Visitors
- Bruce Wyman
- Lewis K. Morse & Wife[Note 2]
- Pres. W. J. Tucker & Wife
- Prof W. G. Hale, Wife & Bobby
- Franklin Head, Chicago
- W. C. Lane & Gus Emery
- J. H. Woods
- Prof. Mrs. & Millicent Todd
- Prof Walter & Ella Willcox
- Eric for 3 weeks
- Fred & Mary
- Sunday Night Tea (15 at table)
- Prof & Mrs Clifford H. Moore
- Mrs. Otho Sprague with Lucy & Nancy
- Robert Herrick

Autumn Events

Sept. Jean Mills returns as 2nd girl & seamstress

Mrs Sprague brings Lucy & Nancy. Nancy shows signs of attack of insanity. They quickly return to Chicago

Oct. 1st interest ($1200) on E. H. A's Western RR Bonds
Oct. 25 T. Y. Crowell & Co publish Self Cultivation in English & a month later Alices Why go to College, 35 cts each we receiving 10 per ct royalty. [**GHP**-34, **AFP**-8] [see 142n4]
Oct 25-Nov 6 Alice in West & at Saginaw
" 5-Nov. 16 Mary at Adams Nervine Asylum[Note 3] By Feb. 1 she was entirely well
Nov. David Kimball, after trying theatrical life, returns to Cambridge & joins Law School
Nov. 21 Albert Sprague, discouraged in this his last half year, begins to take his meals with us, leaving us Feb 7, with his degree
Nov. 25, Thanksgiving in Andover at A. E. Bs Mary with us
Nov. 15 T. Y. Crowell publish A's "Why Go to College?" [**AFP**-8]
Dec. 1 My salary raised to $5000, with that of 10 others, in consequence of Peirce Bequest
Dec 1 Katy McLean becomes our cook
Dec 23 Our 10th anniversary. All family to dinner ex. Jule Jacob & Bertha. I give A. sapphire ring ($100)[Note 4] & desk ($38) & she me 2 Library Rugs $125 each

Notes 1897

1. Professor Palmer's entries indicate that "C. D. Palmer" or "Mr and Mrs C. D. Palmer" or "The C. D. Palmers" were in one of the Palmer houses in Boxford in the summers of 1897, 1898, 1899, 1901, and 1902. They were not related to George Herbert Palmer or his family (I am grateful to Margaret Lane for this information).

2. This naming of "Lewis K. Morse and Wife" as Visitors in 1897 to the Palmer's summer home in Boxford is the first of many entries about the Morse family, who became close friends of the Palmers. Mr. Morse, a young attorney, and Annie Hooker Capron had been married in April of that year. He was a graduate of Harvard College and Harvard Law School; she, a graduate of Wellesley College. The Morses were in Boxford each summer for a number of years and they bought their own summer home there in 1904. The Diaries for March 1900 (chapter 4), show that Mr. Morse also saw the Palmers socially in Cambridge, and that Professor Palmer consulted him about legal matters.

Lewis Kennedy Morse shared the Palmers' literary interests. "During his years at Harvard he had the good fortune to be one of a small group chosen by the several professors to read with them in the evening. They read Greek with Palmer, Emerson with Peabody, Browning with Royce, art with Norton, aesthetics with Santayana, and English with Barrett Wendell." Morse was particularly interested in poetry, and he helped George Herbert Palmer in the major study of George Herbert, which was published in 1905 (**GHP**-50). In his preface (volume 1, page xix), Professor Palmer notes: "In the ten years during which my book has been growing, friends have made generous gifts of suggestion and criticism Especially large are my obligations to Mr. Lewis Kennedy Morse of Boston, the best Herbert scholar of my acquaintance and my perpetually watchful helper . . ."

In 1910, a book for children and their teachers, by Mr. Morse, was published by Houghton Mifflin Company: *Melodies of English Verse: Selections for memorizing chosen and arranged by Lewis Kennedy Morse.* In his introduction, entitled The Training of the Ear, Morse extols the value of memorizing poetry: "Memory in a remarkable way shapes life to what it holds. Especially in early childhood, when impressions are persistent and strong, poetry once learned becomes a large factor in education. It works by an agency all its own and grows with the growth of him who has learned it . . . We need to be long in the company of beauty, to hold it within us, in order to be vitalized by it into creatures of nobler mould . . . The volume contains one hundred and six short selections, making a total body of less than eighteen hundred lines. Forty-nine poets are represented. The length of each selection, averaging about sixteen lines, is fixed with a view, not only to avoid taxing the mind, but also to persuade children to delight in repetition and teachers to encourage it." Mrs. Morse died in October 1909; the book is dedicated TO HER AND TO HER CHILDREN ANNA AND ARTHUR.

Over the years, the Palmers became very devoted to the two Morse children — Anna Hooker Morse, born in April 1899, and Arthur Webster Morse, born in March 1900. Harvard's President Eliot said of Alice Freeman Palmer, "her love of children was intense, and her disappointment that she had none of her own merely made her all the more eager to love and serve the children of others." Two examples of Mrs. Palmer's love for Anna Morse are presented in a poem to Anna (**AFP**-12), who was only about a year and nine months old, and a letter to Anna (**AFP**-13), written about one year later. Professor Palmer also loved Anna: soon after her ninth birthday and immediately after the publication of *The Life of Alice Freeman Palmer* (**GHP**-57), he presented her with a copy inscribed to "Anna Morse with the love of G. H. Palmer April 23, 1908"; and about seven years later, immediately after the publication of *A Marriage Cycle* (**AFP**-18), he inscribed a copy to "Anna Hooker Morse With the love of G. H. Palmer 11 Quincy St. November 4,

1915." In the Chronicles, George Herbert Palmer's last entry relating to the Morses, dated August 10, 1925, reads: "Anna H. Morse and Winthrop P. Haynes married in Boxford Church."

In 1902, Mr. Morse sailed to Europe with the Palmers when they started their sabbatical year. He had returned to Boston, however, before Mrs. Palmer died in Paris, and promptly arranged a memorial service (**aboutAFPann**-4). Later, after Mrs. Morse died in 1909, he and Anna lived with Professor Palmer, and in 1916, Palmer married Mr. Morse and his second wife, Ednah A. Rich.

Like George Herbert Palmer, Lewis Kennedy Morse was also devoted to Wellesley College; like her mother, Anna was an alumna. After Morse died in 1930, a Harvard College classmate wrote: "One of the outstanding achievements of Morse, and one which will be long remembered, was his service to Wellesley College as a trustee and treasurer. He was elected to the Board of that college in November 1912, became assistant bursar in 1913, and treasurer on January 1, 1914. This position he held until ill-health caused him to retire. When he became treasurer in 1914 the funds of the college were somewhat less than $1,500,000, and when he retired in 1928 the college fund amounted to about $8,500,000. During his service the college undertook three campaigns for funds in which he participated. [In **GHP**-77, Professor Palmer describes Morse's role in the campaign for the Restoration and Endowment Fund that ended successfully early in 1915] How ably Morse accomplished his task is shown by the statement of the auditors that on December 31, 1927, the market value of the securities held by the college exceeded their book value by approximately $1,500,000.

"His wife and daughter were Wellesley graduates, and this, together with his personal loyalty to both Professor Palmer and Mrs. Palmer, no doubt inspired him to give to the college services way beyond those of treasurer. He was able to introduce several innovations in college finance, such as the budget system and the setting up of reserves to meet depreciation on buildings, from which Wellesley is benefiting today. He has left an influence on the handling of the financial end of the college that will be felt for many years to come. This service was recognized and appreciated by those interested in the college during his lifetime" (Harvard College, class of 1891, *50th Anniversary Report* . Eliot's remark in **aboutAFPann**-4, page 77. Poem, letter, and presentation copies to Anna Morse, in AJL Collection).

3. Located on Centre Street, West Roxbury, this was a special hospital for "indigent, debilitated, and nervous persons of both sexes,

inhabitants of this Commonwealth, who are not insane. Paying patients also received" (Associated Charities, *A Directory of the Charitable and Beneficent Organizations of Boston,* A. Williams & Co., 1880, p. 40).

4. Elizabeth Novy Proulx, Alice Freeman Palmer's grandniece, writes: This sapphire ring "would have to be the one she [Alice Freeman Palmer] left my mother [Estelle Freeman Novy] who in turn gave it to me" (Elizabeth N. Proulx to A. J. Linenthal, July 29, 1993).

1897–98

GHP

Speeches & Articles

Oct. 25 Self Cultivation in English, T. Y. Crowell & Co [**GHP**-34. 142n4]
Oct. 4. Address in Memorial to Freshmen "Harv. Modes of Instruction"
Nov. 1 Episc. Matriculatn Dinner — "Cambridge for Theol Students"
" 13 Sat. Morning Club "George Herbert"
" 16 November Club, Andover — George Herbert 25.00
" 17 Wakefield Lect Course — Self Cultivation Eng — 50.00
" 22 Wellesley College — State as Organism — 25.00
Jan 19 Wheaton Sem Odyssey 25.00
" 31-Feb 7. Dartmouth Coll 1 lect on Odyssey 110.00
5 lects Eth & other Sciences
1 sermon on R yu able to drink
Feb. 9 Woman's Ed. Assoc. for Teachers Wordsworth 25.00
Mar 9 Wheaton Seminary, Herbert 25.00
" 23 Prospect Union[Note 1] Roumanian Folk Songs[Note 2]
" 30 Radcliffe English Club " " "
April 6 Haverhill Harvard Club
" 13 Andover Sem. Soc. [?]ng.
May 28 Club Boston Normal School Tennyson 25.00
June 22 Western Reserve Univ. Profession of Teacher 100.00

387.00

Books Read

Bosanquets Essentials of Logic
Selby Bigges English Moralists
Royce's Conception of God
Lewis' First Book in Writing English
Palgrave's Golden Treasury 2nd Series

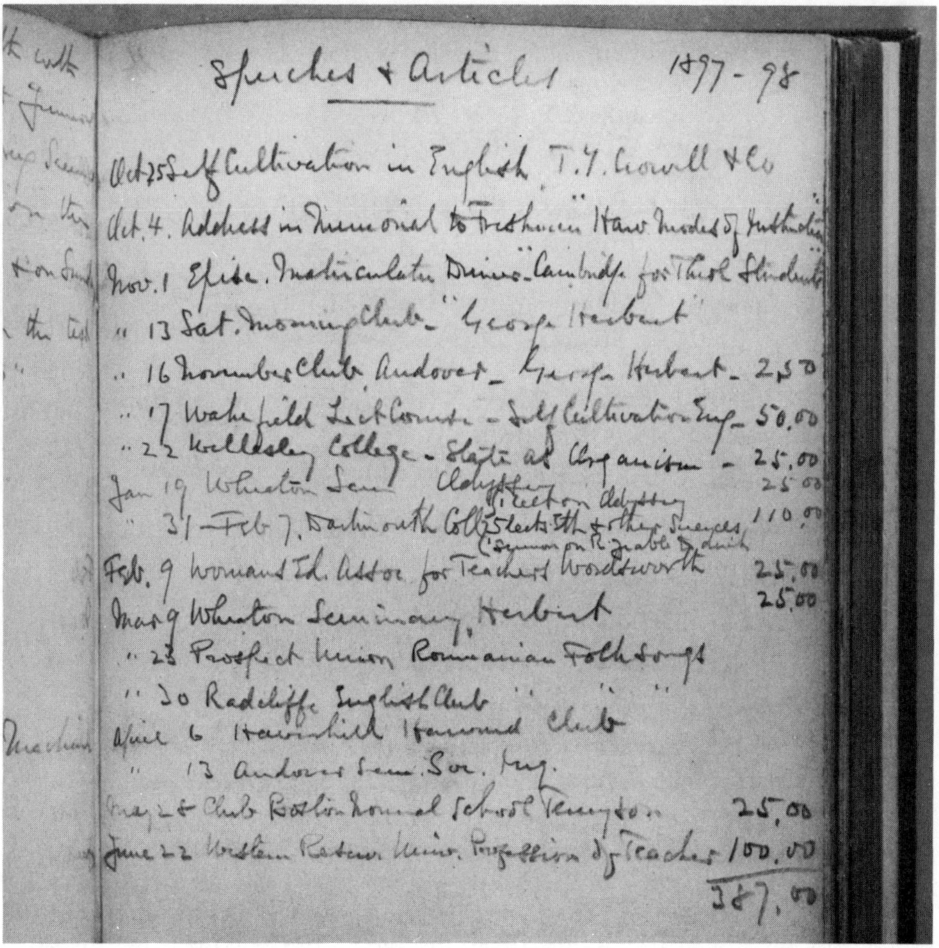

George Herbert Palmer's entries, 1897–98. (reduced size)

Flandran's Harvard Episodes
Hibben's Inductive Logic
Bosanquets Psychology of the Moral Self
Bosanquets Logic Vol II
LIfe of Tennyson 2 vols
Alice's Adventures in Wonderland
Kelley's Evolution & Effort
Hyde's Practical Idealism
Myes [?] Life of Wordsworth
Campbell & Abbots Life of B Jowett 2 vols
Jacobs The Skippers Wooing, & Many Cargoes
Pres Eliot's Report
Baldwins Mental Development Social & Eth Interpretations
Allens Christian Institutions
Carters Life of Nicholas Fenar
C. D. Warners Little Journey in World & Golden House
Van Dykes Tennyson Stefford [?] Brooks Tennyson
Douglas Ethics of J. S. Mills
Wundts Ethics 2 vols
Mallocks Aristocracy & Evolution
Herricks Gospel of Freedom

April 15 [1898] - For past three months there had appeared on the right side of my abdomen, above the place of the former incision, a projection which seemed like another rupture. At first the doctors thought it was not, but finally agreed it was a small protrusion. Dr Packard offer to conduct the operation on it freely & thought it so slight that it might be had at the house. My room was accordingly cleaned & its carpet removed & there on the morning of Apr 15 - just precedg the week of Spring Recess - I took a mixture of chloroform & Oxygen & was operated on. The incision was only a couple of inches long & did not extend into the cavity of the abdomen. There were but two layers of sewing. I was unconscious hardly an hour & had no disturbance from the gas afterwards. As before, the chief suffering was from collateral matters. For two days the spine was distressing, & it was found almost impossible to get discharges of the bowels by injections. Those of sweet oil & glycerine were the best; but there was so little result even from these that the attempt was abandoned & I went 7 days without a passage, although after the first 4 days I took the usual solid food of a healthy man.

After the first few days one part of the wound began to inflame, an abscess forming & for a while there was danger of peritonitis which was kept down only by ice bags & afterward flaxseed poultices. A steady discharge continued from the wound & did not altogether cease for more than a month; for shortly after the wound itself healed, a boil appeared half an inch away & broke into the wound. For this failure to heal as well as for the reappearance of the rupture, the doctors c'd find no reason. All the sewing of last years operation had held.

I got up for the first time on April 29, & went down stairs the next day, 3 weeks from the time of operation; but ws then so weak that I continued my nurse till May 7, & not lecturing till May 9. The lectures of the last fortnight Royce took.

I sent Dr Packard $100 - voluntarily, & paid the nurse 75.00. She was excellent Miss Vibber My head was clear throughout. & was able to hear reading & to do much reading myself But my wound was weak for more than two months.

[Tipped between the pages, a chart shows daily morning and evening temperatures and pulse counts from April 15 to May 5. From April 18 to 28 the temperature rose every day, from 98 degrees in the morning, occasionally to as high as 101 in the evening.]

Notes 1897–98

1. The Prospect Union, started in 1889, was an association of Harvard students and working men of Cambridgeport "for mutual helpfulness." In classes, five evenings a week, graduate students taught such subjects as the "history of political economy," and every Wednesday evening a member of the Harvard faculty lectured (*HGM,* 1892–1893; 1 (April 1893): 461–2).

2. For the same topic, Romanian Folk Songs, in subsequent entries (in 1907, 1908, 1909, 1920, and 1925) Professor Palmer writes "Dimbovitza." The city of Bucharest is on the Dimbovitza river in southern Romania.

In the Palmer poetry collection, Dimbovitza identifies six volumes published from 1889 to 1908 (**GHP**-93). Four of the volumes have the English title, *The Bard of the Dimbovitza: Roumania Folk-Songs;* one volume has the same title in German, the other, in French. Five of these books were "presented by Rev. and Mrs. Frederic Palmer" [the bookplate of Frederic Palmer described in 227n1, is from one of these books]. The songs were collected from the peasants by Hélene Vacaresco (1868–1947), a member of a family of famous poets. They were translated by Carmen Sylva and Alma Strettell. Carmen Sylva was the pseudonym of Queen Elizabeth

(1843–1916), the wife of Charles I, King of Romania from 1866 to 1881.

From Carmen Sylva's Introduction to the new and enlarged edition of *The Bard of the Dimbovitza,* in 1908: "The strange and beautiful songs, of which the following are a selection, seem to me a real treasure-trove, a valuable addition to the literature of the world. They are peculiar to a certain district of Roumania, and that a district in which the mysterious grandeur of mountains has combined with the melancholy and subtle beauty of vast plains, in influencing its people. The young poetess to whom we owe the discovery of these songs spent four years in collecting them among the peasants on her father's estate; and even though her family had for centuries been known and honoured by this race, yet she encountered many difficulties in trying to induce the peasants to repeat their songs for her. She was forced to affect a desire to learn spinning, that she might join the girls at their spinning-parties, and so overhear their songs more easily; she hid in the tall maize to hear the reapers crooning them; she caught them from the lips of peasant-women, of lute-players . . . of gipsies and fortune-tellers; she listened for them by death-beds, by cradles, at the dance and in the tavern, with inexhaustible patience. They are worthy to rank with the best national songs that India, Arabia, and the far North have given us; and are truly noble in their childlike purity, and simple treatment of, and sympathy with, every phase of natural human experience. They are mostly unrhymed — the gipsies using rhymes occasionally — and they depend more for rhythm on the long, musical cadence of each phrase, than on any definite poetical form; they are sung to a monotonous chant, and not accompanied by an instrument, except in the case of the Cobzar (so called from the name of their instrument, a 'cobzar' or lute), who sings to his lute. Most of them are improvisations. They usually begin and end with a refrain, which seems to have been suggested to the singer by something in his surroundings, and to have struck him as fitting in with the mood of the song, although it has not always any immediate connection with it . . . "

1898

GHP

Jan 31-Feb. 7 I spent at Dartmouth with the Tuckers lecturing to Seniors & Juniors the first five days on Eth. & t. neighboring Sciences on Saturday speakg to the Freshmen on the Sources of interest in the Odyssey & on Sunday preaching in the village Church on the text "Are you able to drink of my cup?"

This spring bought a Singer Sewing Machine
June 1. 98 A visit of about a week fr Dr. Freeman A. returning to Saginaw with him, speeches on the way
Mary Miller here at the same time, alarmed over Lucy
June 22 Litt. D. Degree given me by Western Resrv Univ.**Note** [1]

<u>Boxford, Summer</u>

Repairs
Magee Cooking stove $30.00
Picture Spring in Entry
Small old fashioned clock in A's room
China clock for piazza
Blue kitchen china (4.00)
Arbor over well
total 84.60
permanent additions
Blue Room bed spring
Pink " " " & mattrass made over
23.50

<u>Visitors</u>
Lucy Sprague for month of August
Mary & Fred last week of August
Bertha for 3 or 4 days in Sept
Mary Miller & Lucy Sprague, early June
Pres & Mrs Tucker 2 days
Mr & Mrs H. E. Scudder
Mr. & Mrs E. H. Abbot
Marian Talbot 3 days
Robt Herrick 3 times
Prof Tarbell
Prof & Mrs Todd
Millicent Todd 3 days
Gus Emery
Wm Lane
Mrs W. G Hale
Mary Gaw 5 days
Miss Bently a week (Dressmaker)

<u>Guests at meals</u>
Rev & Mrs Bradford & Ruth
Mr & Mrs L. K. Morse
Mr Moon & Bessie
Fred Mary & Eric
Aug Em & Miss Allen

Charley Wellman
Rev J. E. Frame
Mr & Mrs A A Sprage, Mr & Mrs Walker
Prof & Mrs S. E. Myes

Absences

Sunday in July Mrs Whitin in Whitinsville
Alice two lectures (July & August)
I twice to Boston
A. in Sept has operation on nose, & often [unfinished entry]
A. E. B. & Lily to White Mts last of Aug.

Families here

C. D. Palmer in Farm House
Mary & Fred during July with Em
L. K. Morse takes Miss Allens House & takes Mrs Loomis, Mrs Todds mother, to board
At Ems A. E. B., Lily Mrs Wilkinson, 2 children
Miss Allen with Em after Aug 1.

Events

Came July 2 - Sept 28 went
July 4 Fire Works front of Morses house
Gave 7 Tennyson Readings in Vestry, Aug & Sept
Preached Sept 25 & Oct 16
Aunt Anne Palmer died Sept 10
Leander Bachelder died early Sept
Rev. Mr Bradford broke down, & was sent to Clifton Springs for 2 months by subscription

AFP

I taught Sunday School class through Aug. & Sept.
Spoke in the Chapel Sunday evening on the Study of the Bible to Y.P.A.C.Y.

GHP

Rbt. & Harriet Herrick came East. She sick in Bost. Hospital

Occupations

Write Review of Wundts Ethics for Psych Rev [**GHP**-36]
A. writes Wh can women do for Prf Schools Independent [**AFP**-9]
Read MacMillan Ms of Prof Myes Ethics
Write translation of Antigone based on my old Ms [**GHP**-37]
Rest of time given to study of Fichte
Made 175 Jars jelly — 9 kinds
" 132 pints preserves — 9 kinds
" 15 pints of grape juice
Cleared up Brook Path & Round Point

Laid logs at Bathing Place, Bog near Plymouth Rock & over bog of the run near cave

Health

I weak early — strong later — no headaches

A. generally well — after nose in Sept, poorly

Weather

Cool July — hot & extremely damp Aug & Sept

No frosts — few storms — constant showers

Run full most of August — Full foliage

Largest hay crop in years

Note 1898

1. President Charles F. Thwing conferred the degree: "George Herbert Palmer, a man of great intellect and learning, dedicated to the study of philosophy, has — by his teaching — educated many young men in the path of virtue. For his splendid translation of Homer into the vernacular he deserves especial praise. For these reasons he is being awarded an honorary L. H. D. degree." (I am grateful to Nicholas Poole-Wilson for this translation from the Latin).

1898–9

GHP

October Mr & Mrs Sprague from California visit us & leave Nancy with Fred for winter

Alices sitting room repainted & papered

October 11 I appointed Chairman Phil Dept in place of Royce**Note** 1

" 30 Miss Abby Slute [?] E. H. A's sister, died in Cambridge

Nov 1 Appointed member of Committee on Fellowships

" 9 Alice's accident [see page 139]

Dec 15 Rev E. L. Bradford returns from two months at Clifton Springs where he had a serious operation.

Dec 25 Christmas at Freds in Andover

Jan 2 Lucy Sprague returns from her recess in Andover with grip — 3 weeks

In December Aunt Angeline dies at Compton**Note** 2

This winter the Talmages — who last spring abandoned Methodism & joined the Congregationalists — have lived in Cambridge with the Wrights waiting for a parish

March We take A B. Emery for Edisons & send him back to Scientific School

April Caroline Hazard chosen President of Wellesley**Note** 3

Spring recess at Boxford

May 1 The Hundred Shares of Stock (par value $100 each) which Edwin Abbot gave me thirteen years ago in the railroad from Milwaukee to Chicago have up to last year had no value. A year ago in Feb. $1200 of interest on them was paid. Now in the reorganization of the whole Wisconsin Central System this stock was redeemed in cash & we received $10,220, which was added to what we already have with E. H. Abbot making in all $20,000 at 5 per ct

May Outside house painted one coat by College

June 7 Katy McLean (our cook) married by me in our library to David McPherson of Bath, Me.

June 9 We move to Boxford for summer taking Lucy for fortnight

" 1 I appointed 1st Noble Lecturer at Harvard for 1899–1900 [see 211n2]

Aug Ceiling painted by College & furnaces renewed

The Talmages take our house for summer Mrs Freeman visits them

Articles & Addresses

Sept. Meyes Ms read for MacMillan	25.00
" 30 Harv. Xn Assoc. Unity o Relig Life	
Oct. 8 Boston College Club Homer	
" 16 Boxford Pulpit — Xn Simplification o Duties	
" 12 MacMillan Ms (A. K. Rogers, 5558 Drexel Ave Chicago) An Introduction to Philosophy	25.00
Nov. 12 Wheaton Seminary Club — Vendome — Homer	25.00
" 15 Eliz. Whittier Club, Amesbury — Homer	25.00
Dec 7 Wheaton Sem. Tennyson as a National Poet	25.00
" 23 Chelsea Womans Club — Homer	25.00
Jan 18 Read Antigone at Harvard in Greek 11 & at Radcliffe	
" 21 Crowells check for my two books[Note 4]	68.00
Feb 28 Jamaica Plain Womans Club Homer	25.00
Mar. 16 Charlestown Municipal Lecture Tennyson National	10.00
" 17 Cantabridgia Teachers & Mothers	25.00
May 1 Bridgewater Womans Club Herbert	27.00
" 17 Wheaton Seminary Antigone	25.00
April Radcliffe Phil. Club Criticism	150.00
" 28 Antigone Houghton Mifflin & Co [**GHP**-37]	
May 15 Harvard Mod. Lang. Conference Herbert	
June 2 Bost Normal School Gymnastics Profssn of Teacher	50.00
Jan 30 Amherst College Profssn of Teacher	50.00
" 31 " " Morning Prayers College Templative	
Feb 3 Cleveland Teachers Associatn Profssn of Teacher	50.00
Feb 1–8 Lectures at Adelbert College (6) Field of Ethics	200.00
" 2 Central High School Difficulties of Going to College	50.00

Feb 4 Womans College Read Antigone
" 5 Goodrich House Odyssey 19th Bk
" 8 Miss Shenens [?] School Odyssey 6 Bk
" 7 University School Hints on Going to College
June 23 Foxborough Maturity 17.00
" 17 Dummer Academy "
" 24 Thayer Academy Quincy Maturity

925.00

Alices Accident

Nov. 9 1.30 P.M. As Alice was returning from errands in Boston she stepped off the electric car by the doorway of Beck Hall [at corner of Massachusetts Avenue and Harvard Street, across from Quincy Street]. At this point there is a space between the car & curb stone of only about 12 feet. Into this space ran at the same moment on his bicycle T. W. Clark, 1898 Sci. Sch. of 48 Garden St Cambridge. He was on the wrong side of the street but was riding at no great pace. Seeing a collision to be inevitable, he threw his bicycle over & saved her from the concussion. But he was himself thrown over the handle bar, his head struck her head with a loud noise, she was driven violently to the ground, with her head against a stone, & lay senseless. Clark — who was uninjured — & W. S. Clough Harv. 1900, of Lynn, picked her up & assisted by two ladies on the sidewalk carried her into No 1 Beck Hall, a room occupied by F. M. Alger [class of 1899], who was at the time absent in Washington.

Clark called in Dr Henshaw & at 2 o'clock summoned me. She was still unconscious & remained substantially so until the following morning. We put her in a chair, brought her over & laid her in her own bed, I sending our man for Dr Wesselhoeft, who came immediately & telegraphed for Miss Vibber to come as nurse. The doctors found fracture of the skull & injury to the brain. There was continual nausea, no food even the slightest could be retained, & there was heavy hemorrhage. This the doctor subsequently believed to have come from the back of the nose.

On the following morning she recalled, as a dream, the whole accident up to the time of the blow. Nothing beyond. For a week, during which the nurse was with her day & night, she had violent pains in both sides of the head — the blow & swelling was on the right side — & shooting pain throughout the body. Neuritis set in & was very troublesome. The right thigh & shoulder were bruised but not seriously. She was in bed three weeks & a day, I taking charge of her at night during the last fortnight. She felt a good deal of weakness after recovery & was obliged to be very careful. She came down stairs for the first time to Thanksgiving dinner, at which were present — beside she & I — our three servants.

Julius' Death

In the early Autumn, partly in consequence of more stringent laws recently passed against usury, Julius closed his money lending business & retired to Wellfleet where for some four years he had greatly enjoyed his farm house at Gull Pond. He did not abandon his rooms at 10 Broad St, but closed them & paid half rent returning from time to time for a few days.

In this way he was in Boston for nearly a week Dec 29-Jan 4, Friday afternoon, Dec 30, he came to Quincy St by appointment & took his usual walk to Boston with me. At my house he also saw Alice & Mary. He said he had recently gained 3 lbs & had never in his life been so well. He had taken his bath out of doors every morning. He certainly looked in superb health. He had many calls to make about Boston during his stay & suffered much from overheated rooms. He also had some perplexing business, remaking his will with Albert Poor, his lawyer. There was much grip prevailing in Boston. I did not see him after Friday.

He returned to Wellfleet on Wednesday Jan 4, with a little cold but went to his own house. The Tubmans, calling on him Sunday night, saw that he did not look well & tried to persuade him to go home with them. He w'd not but records in his Journal that he felt decidedly ill on Monday. On Tuesday morning he hoisted his signal for his man Mr Eaton — who lived a mile away — to come. He intended to be carried to the train for Boston & to go to the Homoeopathic Hospital there. But his signal was not seen till noon, too late for the train. When his man came he ordered him to take him to the Holbrook House in the village. This was shut at the time, but the Holbrooks generously took him into their own home & gave him their daughters room. They and his friends the Tubmans, then gave him every care.

But the doctor whom they called at once told them it was so violent a case of pneumonia as to allow no hope. They telegraphed to Fred who took the first train which arrived at 8 P.M. on Wed, 3/4 hour after Julius had died Jan 11 That morning he said he shd die at night & repeated the statement several times during the day. After he learned that they had telegraphed Fred he watched the clock much & seemed to be looking for the train. He was conscious to the last but could talk but little. He was as brave & clear sighted as ever.

Fred returned to Cambridge Thursday night having arranged all for his funeral which was held at the Church of the Immaculate Conception in Boston on Saturday at 11.30. He was buried at Holyhood Cemetary in Brookline. Em, Fred & Mary, Frank Palmer & Mary Peabody attended the funeral, & there were some 200 others, all sorrowing. I did not learn of his illness until after his death, Mary mentioning it casually in a letter to Alice on Thurs. morning & Mr Poor writing me of it definitely Thursday afternoon

Capt Julius A. Palmer, Jr[Note 5]
Born March 1, 1842; Died Jan 11, 1899
Merchant Seaman Linguist Author
Explorer in Science
Defender of the Weak
Independent Fearless Solitary Genial Devout

Notes 1898–9

1. Palmer describes one of the "ethical features" in the organization of the Department of Philosophy: "The former controlling Head of the Department was abandoned. A Chairman took his place. This officer called our meetings, presided at them, and was our medium of communication with the President. Every few years he was changed. In the course of time most of our Professors served in this way and so became acquainted with administrative as well as teaching duties. Occasionally even an Assistant Professor was Chairman. But neither he nor any other Professor had authority over the rest. All were equal and independent . . . The fact that no Professor of ours was a subordinate gave dignity to the position and enabled us to call men of superior grade. I never knew any one invited to join our staff who refused. This organization . . . is now, I believe, employed in many Departments at Harvard" (**GHP**-104, pages 50–51).

2. George Herbert Palmer's entries also note the deaths of three other aunts: "Aunt Lucy" in 1869, "Aunt Margaret" in 1892, and "Aunt Anne Palmer" in 1898. I could find the family relationship of only Aunt Angeline (see Biographical Summaries).

3. From Miss Hazard's remarks in **aboutAFPann**-5: "As I rise in this Chapel of Harvard University, the fact comes over me with overwhelming force that if it had not been for the dear friend we are gathered to honor to-day, in all human probability I should not be here to add my word of grateful recognition and reverent praise; for it was she who first spoke to me of the possibility of coming to Wellesley, finding an opportunity in what to any one else would

have been the hopeless confusion of a crowded reception. Never shall I forget her contagious enthusiasm, to which my own responded; and though weeks elapsed before a final decision was reached, my heart had capitulated long before my mind was convinced."

4. Statements from T. Y. Crowell & Co., dated January 1, 1899, show the total number of copies printed, the number that had been sold from August 1898 to January 1, 1899, and the royalty for Palmer @ 3.5 cents per copy (10% of the 35 cent price): for *The Glory of the Imperfect*, 3090 printed, 1023 sold, and $35.80 (1023x3.5); for *Self-Cultivation in English*, 4092, 915, and $32.03. A check for $67.83 was enclosed (Wellesley College Archives, Box 2BI, folder 2I. See also table on page 480).

5. The inscription on his tombstone in the Holyhood Cemetery (lot 562) is slightly different:

Captain Julius A. Palmer, Jr.
Born March 1, 1840
Died January 11, 1899
Seaman, Merchant, Linguist, Author
Lover of Nature,
Defender of the Weak
Independent, Exact, Solitary, Genial, Devout

The adjacent tombstone has this inscription:

Sacred
To The
Memory of
Effie Wood
Wife of
Julius A. Palmer,
Died
May 10
1893

His publications reflect Captain Palmer's versatility: *Again in Hawaii*, articles written from Honolulu to the "Evening Post" [N.Y.] as special correspondent; *Memories of Hawaii*, articles written from Honolulu to the "Evening Transript" [Boston] as special correspondent; *About Mushrooms*, contributions, popular and scientific; *Mushrooms of America*, esculent and poisonous; *One Voyage and its Consequences, a romance of social life on shipboard (from a list in Julius A. Palmer, Jr., Again in Hawaii*, Boston, Lee and Shepard, 1895).

1899

GHP

Boxford

At Ems - She, Miss Allen, Aug, Lilly, Mrs Wilkinson, 2 Girls, Fred & Mary during July, then 6 weeks at Wellfleet

Farm House - Mr & Mrs C. D. Palmer

Miss Allens House - L. K. Morse

Jean Mills & her niece Jeannie our servants

June 9 We move bringing Lucy Sprague for fortnight Later Nancy Sprague spends week here Then both girls to Lake Forest to family

I at once begin work on my edition of G. Herbert Whole summer spent on it

June 24 Lottie Matthews marries Dr Perley in church

July 13 Read Antigone in Chapel 3–5 Thursday

" 19, 20, 21 Ethics & Religion Summer Sch Theol Cambridge 75.00

" 13 Alice visits Aunts & Mother at Old Farm N. Y. bringing her mother back to Cambridge, July 18

" 22 Mrs Freeman at Boxford

" 24–31 Alice & I visit Pres Eliot at Mt Desert Stopping at Castine for Herricks & home Aug 2

Aug. 3 Begin Shakspere readings with Tempest Henry V, Macbeth, Merch. Ven. Tennyson Review

Sept 24 Preached on Lords Prayer

Aug 18–23 Visit Wellfleet[Note 1]

Lucy Sprague with us last week in Boxford, which we left Sept 26

Sept 1 I had Ellens body removed from the tomb in the Old Cambridge Burying Ground where it had lain for twenty years to her family lot in Forest Hills — fulfilling my promise to her. [see 56n1]

This summer 11 Quincy St occupied by the Talmages

Closed Hotel Placidia & drove Mr Bodge from Boxford for liquor selling

Path made from cave thro Blackberry Orchard

Aneroid & Large Thermometer
Encyclopedia Britannica
Book Shelves over Fire Place
Kerosene Stove
Servants Bed Spring & Mattrass
Green Table Cover
Brass Lamp all $60

Cambridge

Sept. Alice has lace curtains in sitting room Large portable range in kitchen Ceilings of most rooms repainted

Oct 10 Inauguration of Miss Hazard at Wellesley

" 17 News of Frank Palmer marriage to Dr May McKinney

Christmas at Andover with Fred & week at Boxford

Feb 6–15 Alice visits Saginaw, I at Dartmouth

March 6 My Williams Ms of Herbert arrives £ 3.11 [see diary entry, March 11, 1900]

March 1 I pay the 2nd half of the annuity begun Sept. 1 of $150 payable 10 years to Emily J. Palmer Alice F. Palmer & to George H. Palmer, successively in this order About $1400 out of its $1700 was left me by Julius

April recess at Boxford (14–23) with Lucy Sprague

23 Eric put on probation for tardiness after Recess

May 21 Alices Bee spent day at Boxford [see 260n1]

April1 Sunday. I with 6 others visited and reproved Mrs Tidd**Note** 2

Throughout the year the furnishing of the Brooks House has gone on & my preparation of the Tablets. Correspondence with Shephard & Mrs Noble.**Note** 3, 4

Charles H. Talmage has been living in Cambridge seeking his M. A. degree while Ella spends the year in Saginaw In June he takes this degree Eric & Lucy taking B. A. magna cum laude Eric having honorable mention in Philosophy & Physics, Lucy Honors in Philosophy

We pay half the expenses of Elinor Wellman at the Hyannis Normal School & also support Ida Grillette [?] at Univ of Iowa.

June 2 A. B. E. was arrested & bailed $500. I spoke with him June 6 (Shaler having told me) He pled guilty June 11, sentence deferred to June 26 Defaulted Sat June 23 Mason & Proctor

Wellesley offered $100000 by Rockefeller on condition of clearing its debt of 110,000 9725 remaining 4 days before Commencement. E. H. A & we guaranteed it, ultimately paying**Note** 5

April Lottie Matthews Perleys 1st child daughter

June 18 Radcliffe girls give concert in Boxford

Notes 1899

1. Also, late in August 1899, Professor Palmer corresponded with Harry Linenthal, a senior in Harvard College, class of 1900, who had done most of his college work in philosophy and psychology, and who had just decided to go to medical school. On August 21, responding to Linenthal's request about serving as an assistant in one

of the courses, Professor Palmer wrote that an undergraduate could not be appointed to such an important position. At the same time, Palmer said he "knew [Linenthal's] work well," thought that "it [was] of remarkable quality," and offered him $100 or $150, "which may be counted as a gift or a loan as you please." [The annual tuition at the college was $150.] Palmer also advised him not to confine himself exclusively to philosophy because "you will need more material for your mind to work upon," and warned him that if he planned to teach philosophy such positions were "few and exceedingly difficult to obtain . . . [and] you will have a catastrophe." When Palmer learned, however, that Linenthal planned to study medicine, he wrote [on August 25] "You are quite right and altogether wise in devoting a large part of your time to Philosophy for such a purpose. I congratulate you for having aimed so clear."

In 1900, Linenthal asked Professor Palmer to support his request for scholarship help in Harvard Medical School, class of 1904. Palmer wrote that Harry Linenthal "ought to receive the very best aids which the medical school has in its power to give," and added "[h]e was one of my very highest scholars distinguishing himself not merely by diligence and accuracy but by the intelligence and originality of his work. I came to know him personally and greatly prize the energy, truthfulness and refinement of his nature" (Arthur J. Linenthal, *First A Dream: The History of Boston's Jewish Hospitals, 1896–1928*, Boston, Beth Israel Hospital and Countway Library, 1990, page 343–344. See also **aboutGHPann**-17 for a description of how Professor Palmer provided financial help "Whenever he learned of a superior boy or girl who was without funds.").

2. This is the visit to Boxford mentioned by Professor Palmer in his diary entries for March 22 and 31, 1900 (chapter 4). These entries for March 1900 also include references to the tablets for Phillips Brooks House.

3. As they record throughout their diaries for March 1900 (chapter 4), the Palmers were both much involved in the newly opened Phillips Brooks House in Harvard Yard, dedicated on January 23, 1900. Professor Palmer summarizes his involvement (page 197) as one of his "chief occupations" of the month. And after the last Friday afternoon tea of the season, attended by 175 people, Mrs. Palmer notes: "We all feel these afternoons have begun with astonishing success, and have formed a new source of good and pleasure in Harvard life" (page 196).

Activities at Phillips Brooks House began to fill an important, and heretofore, unmet need at Harvard. "The little College has been transformed into the Great University. Centrifugal forces have begun to operate there among the individual atoms, just as the old neighborly spirit of the village life ceases to exist in the great city. Athletics have become almost the only common topic possible in general college talk, and students who receive the same degree do not necessarily possess similar grounds of intellectual acquirement and taste. If Harvard is to preserve among its students that spirit of common loyalty and companionship which should draw University men together, it must provide a central place of intercourse and restore and develop centripetal attractions. No house in Cambridge can contain a college class of the present day."

In 1890, Phillips Brooks, class of 1855, and the other college preachers, aware of this problem, recommended the erection of a building in the college yard, which "should be generously used for all the various public interests of University life, and should unite and strengthen many undertakings which now rather tend to divide the forces which make for good among the students." Phillips Brooks, who had been particularly interested in such a building, died on January 23, 1893. A few days later, Philip S. Abbot [see 113n2], class of 1890 and a senior at the Law School, wrote in the *Harvard Crimson,* that "there certainly has been no one within our memory whom the whole body of undergraduates have felt as they have toward him . . . Cannot the proposed religious building . . . be made a memorial to Bishop Brooks? . . . If he stood for anything, it was for unity of the positive kind: the sinking of minor differences in hard work for the fundamental aims which belong to all the denominations in common." Many people in the United States and abroad sent subscriptions to help erect the building (Edwin H. Abbot, *HGM*, 1892–93; 2 (September 1893): 63–70. P. S. Abbot, Communication, *Harvard Crimson*, January 26, 1893).

4. Professor Palmer wrote the inscriptions for the seven bronze, memorial tablets in the entrance hall of Phillips Brooks House (see his diary for March 1900). Three, on the large side wall, are placed around a bust of Phillips Brooks which rests on a 55-inch pedestal. One tablet (39 inches wide and 20 inches high) is above the bust:

THIS HOUSE
IS DEDICATED TO
PIETY CHARITY HOSPITALITY

IN GRATEFUL MEMORY OF
PHILLIPS BROOKS

Two tablets (each 50 inches wide and 35 inches high) flank the bust:

BORN IN BOSTON DECEMBER 13 1835
AB HARVARD 1855 VIRGINIA THEOLOGICAL SEMINARY 1859
RECTOR CHURCH OF THE ADVENT PHILADELPHIA 1859–1861
CHURCH OF THE HOLY TRINITY PHILADELPHIA 1862–1869
TRINITY CHURCH BOSTON 1869–1891
BISHOP OF THE PROTESTANT EPISCOPAL CHURCH
IN MASSACHUSETTS 1891–1893
OVERSEER OF HARVARD COLLEGE 1870–1882 1883–1889
PREACHER TO HARVARD UNIVERSITY 1886–1891
DD UNION 1870 HARVARD 1877 OXFORD 1885 COLUMBIA 1887
DIED IN BOSTON JANUARY 23 1893

A PREACHER
OF RIGHTEOUSNESS AND HOPE
MAJESTIC IN STATURE IMPETUOUS IN UTTERANCE
UNHAMPERED BY BONDS OF CHURCH OR STATION
HE BROUGHT BY HIS LIFE AND DOCTRINE
FRESH FAITH TO A PEOPLE
FRESH MEANING TO ANCIENT CREEDS
TO THIS UNIVERSITY
HE GAVE
CONSTANT LOVE LARGE SERVICE HIGH EXAMPLE

Two tablets (each 35 inches wide and 53 inches high) flank the hall's rear door (regarding Philip Stanley Abbot, see 113n2):

PHILIP STANLEY ABBOT
BORN 1867 DIED 1896
HARVARD A.B. 1890 A.M. LL.B. 1893
ALWAYS A LEADER
HE ON JANUARY 23, 1893
STIRRED HIS FELLOW-STUDENTS
TO UNDERTAKE THIS MEMORIAL BUILDING
BUT BEFORE ITS COMPLETION WAS KILLED
IN CLIMBING MOUNT LEFROY

RICH IN NATURE FRIENDS FORTUNE
HE ADDED
WHATEVER TOIL AND CHARACTER CAN GIVE
TO MAKE SHORT LIFE COMPLETE

RALPH HAMILTON SHEPARD
BORN 1867 HARVARD A B 1892
ONE OF HARVARD'S YOUNGEST BENEFACTORS
STUDIOUS EARNEST DEVOUT
MEMBER OF
THE CHRISTIAN ASSOCIATION
THE RELIGIOUS UNION
THE SAINT PAUL'S SOCIETY
DYING IN 1894
HE GAVE FIVE THOUSAND DOLLARS
TO PROMOTE CHRISTIAN WORK
AT HARVARD COLLEGE

One tablet (41 inches wide and 51 inches high) is at the rear corner of the side wall:

BELINDA LULL RANDALL
BORN 1816 DIED 1897
WHO THROUGH THE TRUSTEES OF HER ESTATE
MADE PROVISION
WITHIN THE PHILLIPS BROOKS HOUSE
FOR THE ADMINISTRATION OF CHARITY
BY THE STUDENTS OF THIS UNIVERSITY
JOHN WITT RANDALL
BROTHER OF BELINDA BORN 1813 DIED 1892
A.B. HARVARD 1834 M.D. 1839
WHOSE NAME SHE WISHED
TO BE ASSOCIATED WITH HERS
IN THE MANY AND GREAT BENEFACTIONS
LOVELY AND PLEASANT IN THEIR LIVES
AND IN THEIR DEATHS THEY WERE NOT DIVIDED

And one tablet (29 inches wide and 47 inches high) is to the left of the front door (see 211n2):

WILLIAM BELDEN NOBLE
BORN 1860 DIED 1896

HARVARD A B 1885
ARDENT JOYOUS GENEROUS
YEARNING FOR KNOWLEDGE
IMPASSIONED FOR HOLINESS
HE SOUGHT TO BE A MINISTER
AFTER THE PATTERN OF
PHILLIPS BROOKS
BUT DIED BEFORE ORDINATION
MINDFUL OF HIS UNFINISHED AIMS
HIS WIFE ESTABLISHED
THE NOBLE LECTURES
IN 1898

5. In her diary entry for Saturday, March 17, 1900, Mrs. Palmer records that she heard from Wellesley's President Hazard the "great news" about Mr. Rockefeller's offer as soon as the college's debt was cleared. She also notes the determination to raise the necessary money soon so that the gift could be announced at Wellesley's twenty-fifth commencement in June [June 26th]. A week later, on March 24, she notes that "There will be no rest [in fund raising] until Mr. Rockefeller's gift is secured!"

Caroline Hazard continues the story: "At the last meeting of the Trustees there was still a considerable sum to raise. It was then beyond the middle of June. Between ten and twelve thousand dollars was lacking, and there was not very much prospect of its coming. It would have been a very great misfortune for the College to go on another year laboring under the debt. It had been definitely said that the debt should be paid in that year, and I think Mrs. Palmer felt this necessity more keenly than I. We came out of the meeting together and parted at the foot of Park Street, she to go to Cambridge, and I turning this way. Her last words were words of encouragement, that I must not be troubled, that something would be done.

"The very next morning came a brief note saying, 'Do not be troubled. It is sure to go through, and will go through at Commencement Day. You need not speak of it, but this is for your own private encouragement.' That lifted a great burden, though I did not know what she had done. She had many friends to whom she could appeal. I supposed she had found some one who would make good the amount. After many months I learned that she, with Professor Palmer's approval, had taken their savings-bank books and deposited them with the Treasurer of the College, saying that that sum was to be made good; the debt must be paid. She would give what was necessary. It was the savings of a lifetime she thus pledged. I am happy to say this large sum was not called for; the friends of the college responded, and the amount which she finally contributed was a comparatively small one. But she was willing to give the whole of her savings that Wellesley's debt might be paid" (**about-AFPann**-4, pages 24–25).

1899–1900

GHP

Lectures

Lecture	Fee
Sept. 29 Harv. Xn Association	
Oct 10. Inauguration of Miss Hazard , after dinner[Note 1]	
" 13. Reading Womans Club Teachers & Mothers	25.00
Nov. 20 Andover Womans Club Antigone	10.00
" 28 Dorchester Womans " Teachers & Mothers	25.00
Jan 26 Storrs Agricultural College Wordsworth	50.00
" 27 Lawrenceville School N. J. Homer	50.00
" 29- Feb 3 Western Reserve 6 Lectures on Nat of Goodness	250.00
Feb. 3 Youngstown Ohio Teachg as Profession	50.00
Jan 30 Cleaveland Teachers Assoc School as Eth Instruct	50.00
" 31 " High School Dif. bet. Man & Boy	
Feb. 1 " Harvard Club	
" 6–15 Dartmouth College 8 Lectures on Goodness	200.00
" 4 Hanover Sermon on Forgiveness	
Mar 7 & 5 folly Wednesdays Noble Lectures [see 211n2 and diaries]	600.00
May 2 Andover Theol Sem Shakesperes Sonnets	
" 9 Brown Univ. Philos. Society Law & Ethics	
" 16 Harvard Xn Association New Opportunities in Brooks House	
Mar. 16 Bridgewater Homer	25.00
June 5 Stamford Ct Miss Lows School On Growing up	50.00
" 6 Miss Gilmans School, Boston " " "	50.00
14 Brattleboro High School " " "	25.00
20 Manchester " " "	25.00
23 Gloucester " " "	25.00
10 Wheaton " " "	25.00
25 Boston Normal Qualification of the Teacher	
" Westfield " " " " "	25.00
26 Worcester " " " " "	20.00
29 Providence " " " " "	25
26 Class Supper Cubans	1700.00

Summer

At Emilys A. E. B. wife children & Mrs Wilkinson & Miss Allen Farm House Vacant

Morses in Herrick House, Homers in Allen

We arrive June 30

Church undergoing extensive repairs. We pay for taking out side pews $76.00 & subscribe $60.00 besides to fund**Note** 2

This summer 1260 Cuban Teachers are guests of Harvard, $70,000 needing to be raised**Note** 3 I engage in soliciting & we give up our house to Mrs Gulick for this use**Note** 4

Ella Talmage again takes City Mission work She & Charlie living at our house with Mrs Gulick

July 19 Begin readings on American Poets 3.30–5.00 Bryant & Poe - Longfellow-Lowell-Emerson-Whittier-Holmes-Romeo & Juliet

Aug 5 Preached at Boxford - Incarnation

Aug 4–11 Alice at Winsor N. Y.**Note** 5

Aug 13–18 I visit Fred at Wellfleet

Aug 23 Article in Congregationalist Non Decadent Country Town [**GHP**-39]

Sept 23 Preach on Forgiveness

Sept 25 Jeanies Law Suit lost

Oct 22 Moved to Cambridge

Notes 1899–1900

1. Harvard's president, Charles W. Eliot, one of the speakers at the inauguration exercise, said that "The work to which President Hazard this day puts her hand is novel and experimental in the highest degree: it still has all the fascination of pioneering. To be sure, Wellesley College has twenty-four good years behind it; but that period is a brief one in the life of an institution of education; and the College, like the entire group of women's colleges in this country, really stands at the very threshold of its work . . . It remains to prove that the higher education of women, wisely conducted, will be as profitable to society as the higher education of men" (*A Record of the Exercises Attending the Inauguration of Caroline Hazard, Litt. D., as President of Wellesley College III October MDCCCXCIX,* Cambridge, Riverside Press, 1899, page 16).

2. Professor Palmer describes the Boxford church and its congregation in 1900 (**GHP**-39): "Though during the past ten years the church has lost a third by death or removal, its total membership has increased. The average attendance at the Sunday school has nearly

doubled. A debt of $500 on the church, which had been allowed to accumulate, has been paid. Not less than $700 have been spent for repairing the parsonage, $1,500 in the building of a chapel, and we are just completing the renovation and refurnishing of the church itself at an expense of $1,000."

3. Starting in January 1899, Cuba was under United States military rule for three years, with Major-General Leonard Wood as the military governor. Cuba had been ravaged for years by civil wars, by Spanish troops, and then by the Spanish-American war in 1898. Much needed to be done for "public works, sanitation, and the reform of administration, civil service, and education."

Alexis Everett Frye, superintendent of schools in Cuba, and Ernest Lee Conant of Havana "suggested to President Eliot that much good might be done if a considerable number of Cuban teachers could attend the Harvard Summer School." Eliot was enthusiastic: "I believe that the shortest way of advancing the life, the character, and the institutions of any people is to work through the children . . . It is the children that are to be worked out for the growth of the future, for the increase of liberty, for the increase of happiness and joy. And how can we work on the Cuban children better than through the Cuban teachers?" He and Harvard's Fellows voted unanimously to guarantee $70,000 to welcome 1450 Cuban teachers, an estimate of about $45 per person. There was a public appeal for funds and, in addition, the United States government, the University, and large numbers of people in Cambridge provided gratuitous service.

This Summer School for six and a half weeks, with 1283 Cubans — about equal numbers of women and men —, was a project of great magnitude: five government transports brought the Cubans to Boston early in July; housing was arranged in college dormitories and in private homes in Cambridge; instructors in various fields from Harvard and many other schools and colleges conducted small classes and lectured; instructors, interpreters, and guides conducted frequent excursions to points of interest; and there were weekly receptions and concerts in honor of the Cubans.

"The Cubans are an appreciative people, and they feel grateful for the many favors that have been done for them. It is unfortunately true that the Cuban people, as a whole, have come to consider the 'Yankee' as rude and inconsiderate of others. This opinion of Americans, so far as it was held by the Cuban teachers, has been entirely changed as a result of their brief visit to the United States, and the Cubans at Cambridge speak admiringly of 'Yankee' courtesy and refinement. This one result is well worth the cost of the 'expedition'" (The Coming of the Cuban Teachers, *HGM*, 1899–1900; 8 (June 1900): 506–509. E. C. Hills, The Cuban Summer School, *HGM*, 1900–1901; 9 (September 1900): 37–41).

From the Dean of Barnard College: "The northern trip of the Cuban teachers in 1900 is, and will in all probability remain, unique in the history of international courtesies . . . The permanent result of this novel expedition of 1900 must be politically the existence of centers of friendly feeling and confidence which will affect whole communities . . . It was the first general association and organization of the teachers of the Cuban nation. It was a romantic awakening of a depressed people to higher ideals. It was an exchange of true sentiment, graciously expressed and intuitively fathomed as sincere. It was a glimpse into the promised land of peace and prosperity. What years of struggle and defeats and victories may precede the final entering in, we cannot lift the veil of the future to know. But all those who sincerely care for Cuba's future must rejoice in this disinterested international courtesy. It was conceived in its final proportions by Mr. Frye's idealistic nature, responded to by President Eliot's high appreciation of the fundamental need of any self-governing people, executed with the finish of Harvard traditions, and appreciated by as courteous and gratefuly responsive a people as the world knows (Laura D. Gill, The Northern Trip of the Cuban Teachers, *Association of Collegiate Alumnae Magazine*, 1902, February; series III, No. 5: 1–14).

4. In 1871, soon after she married William Hooker Gulick, the American Board of Commissioners for Foreign Missions (A.B.C.F.M.) sent Alice Gordon Gulick and her husband as the board's first missionaries to Spain. "Mrs. Gulick became convinced that her greatest service to Spain lay in the educational field. In 1877, with support from her sponsoring body in America, the Woman's Board of Missions of the A.B.C.F.M., she opened a small boarding school with five young women . . . Encouraged by . . . her students and by the cooperation of Spanish parents and educators, Mrs. Gulick determined on a more ambitious project, a nondenominational institution for the higher education of girls, to be modeled after such American colleges as Mount Holyoke and Wellesley . . . In the United States it was the period of the devel-

opment of women's colleges, and there was a ready response on the part of these institutions to Mrs. Gulick's appeal. In 1892 a corporation was chartered by the Commonwealth of Massachusetts to establish the International Institute for Girls in Spain" (*Notable American Women*).

For the Cuban Summer School (see Note 3 above), Mrs. Gulick was in charge of a large group who organized social activities for the Cuban women.

Alice Freeman Palmer, for many years, was "one of the two hundred and fifty corporate members of the [A.B.C.F.M.] in company with only six other women. Soon after she came to Cambridge, she was made President of the Woman's Home Missionary Association and found in its wide affairs a happy blending of her religious, charitable, patriotic, and educational aims" (**GHP**-57, page 250). In several entries in her diary for March 1900, Mrs. Palmer describes her own involvement in sending out 500 invitations to a fund-raising event for the school in Spain on April 6. On March 29 she writes (page 194): "If the wealth and fashion of Boston and vicinity do not turn out to help the Women and girls of Spain to an education next week, we can do no more." Later, she became president of the International Institute for Girls in Spain.

5. Her attendance at this reunion of Academy alumni, at age forty-five, twenty-eight years after she graduated, was Mrs. Palmer's last visit to Windsor; she died two years and four months later. The *Echo,* the alumni publication (December 1900, BCHSoc.) reported her address "to a large gathering of students of the old Academy and of the new . . . :

"[A]llow me to tell [the younger graduates] that you have the nicest place in the world; at least it seems to me so; it seemed to me so when I left the little village in the valley to go out into another world to attend college; to another world, another field . . . [M]any of . . . our old classmates, our friends and leaders, owe a great deal to the good instruction, the well laid foundation of a good education and the careful training received in the old Academy of Windsor . . .

"The impression of the village upon the mind of the boy or girl going out into the world is not soon forgotten—the little village in the valley of the Susquehanna. I am proud to say that I was the daughter of a farmer in the valley of the Susquehanna . . . Words cannot describe what the little place to me was when, a girl, I left it for other scenes and other duties. When in 1872 I graduated, who had never been away from the valley, and went a thousand miles to the west to a university to college, I well remember the desription I gave of the beautiful valley of the Susquehanna; I well remember during the years between '72 and '76 while in a town in Michigan in college—and by the way on the banks of a very respectable little river, so those who lived there thought—I well remember that the best, the first, and the only river to me was the Susquehanna; I used to tell of its enormous width, of the strong currents, the terrible freshets. It did not take a back seat for the Mississippi . . . There were no such hills as those along the Susquehanna, and well I remember when a school mate came home with me in vacation how, with reproachful eyes, she said to me, 'I thought you said it was larger than the Mississippi.' But to me there was no such place as Windsor, no valley, hills or river quite so nice It was not the fault of my geography teachers — I know some of them are here tonight . . . [**GHP**-57, between page 32 and 33, has a picture of the Susquehanna valley as seen from the Freeman house in Windsor]

"And so, Mr. Chairman, I want to give thanks to the Academy, and I know I may do it in the name of the old and the new students; words do not properly express the thanks which we owe to the teachers who taught us—not mathematics, French, Latin and Greek for we have forgotten that or a great deal of it; but who taught us truthfulness, to be honorable and upright, and who enthused us with that feeling which went with us as we went out into other scenes and to other duties which made of us men and women. Perhaps you younger members had just as good teachers, I don't like to say you didn't, I hope you did, but when we were taught by Miss Eastman and her brothers, and others, many of whom I have not seen since the days of 1865 when I went to the old Academy, I know you cannot have had any better teachers. Here we formed our first loves, our first hopes, our first ambitions, our first dreams, and some of us met our first disappointments. I hope, young people, with the new large buildings, new chances, new books, and new methods, it will be your good fortune to gain the enthusiasm and faith to go out into the public world with the same earnest desire to be men and women that we obtained from the old Academy, and I hope that all the new surroundings may be of the same aid to you, as the old to us, and even more."

Alice Freeman Palmer ca. 1900.

Chapter 4

Diaries for March 1900

GHP=*George Herbert Palmer*
AFP=*Alice Freeman Palmer*

Thursday, March 1, 1900

GHP

Breakfast at 8. To prayers at 8.45, a voluntary exercise of 15 minutes, conducted by Rev. Endicott Peabody, Head Master of Groton School. The order of exercises is responsive reading of a psalm, anthem by the choir, reading of Scripture by minister, with 5 minute sermon, prayer by minister, & Lord's prayer by all, hymn, benediction. On my way home I stop at the bank to cash the check for my quarter's salary, $1062.25. My whole salary is $5000, but $750.00 is deducted for rent of my house, 11 Quincy St - the low rental being due to the fact that six years ago I spent $3000.00 in repairs. I prepare a lecture on the religious character of the Renaissance in the introductory course on the History of Philosophy which is delivered at 11 A.M. at Radcliffe College to 30 girls, & at 1.30 also to 120 Harvard students. Between these lectures I lunch at 1, & from 12–1 attend a meeting of the Committee on the management of the Phillips Brooks House (Profs Peabody, Palmer, Sabine, Ropes, & Mr Gardiner) where we decide to buy a rug for the Randall room, another for the committee room, & to have the Brooks Parlor opened during the spring months from 1 to 6 o'clock as a waiting room for ladies.

At lunch I find my sister Emily, who has come fom our country place Boxford to spend a few days with me. I walk for an hour after lecture, with errands. Study till dinner time at 6.30, also reading the evening Transcript with its account of the Relief of Ladysmith [a South African town, scene of a long siege during the Boer War], & the passage by the House of the bill imposing a tarif on Porto Rico. Just before dinner appears L. K. Morse who last summer, living in Boxford, joined me in closing a place for selling liquor there. He wished to hear the letter I have just written to the Boxford town meeting, warning the Selectmen to let all intending liquor dealers know that they will be similarly treated. Mrs Mabel Loomis Todd comes in from a lecture she has just delivered in the neighborhood. He & she remain to dinner. After this the rest of the household go to the concert in Sanders Theatre given by the Boston Symphony Orchestra. I remain at home and write 11 letters. To bed at 10 o'clock.

From 3.30 to 4.30 there was held in my Library a committee meeting of the Division of Philosophy, of which I am Chairman. This is the second held since the return of Prof. Royce from Scotland, where he gave the second course of his Gifford Lectures. The object of this meeting was to draw up the list of courses to be offered in Philosophy for the coming year.

My lecture work for the present Half-Year is comparatively light Phil.1$^{\underline{b}}$ The History of Modern Philosophy Tues. Th. Sat. 130, & in Radcliffe Tu. Th. Sat. at 11. Phil 20$^{\underline{d}}$ The Ethics of Kant & Hegel, a seminary of 10 graduate students, meeting in my Library from 4 to 6 on Mondays. During the preceding Half Year I also gave a course on Kants Critique of Pure Reason, 3 hours a week. This month too I am doing less work because during the preceding period of Mid Year Examinations I gave a course of 6 Lectures at Western Reserve University (with 4 others at various places en route) & afterwards 8 Lectures at Dartmouth College, the whole period covered being 3 weeks & I receiving $650.00 in payment. The Dartmouth arrangement was an exchange with Pres. Tucker, he having agreed to come upon our Board of Preachers the present year on condition that I would give these lectures there. At Dartmouth I also preached on Sunday morning, though announcing that I was only a layman. During these journeyings I became somewhat fatigued & am trying now to loaf a little.

AFP

Last night's report is true, and Ladysmith is relieved. I woke early and ran down stairs for the paper, and read it in bed. This gave me only time to write Mrs. Whitman that Edwin Abbot promises to join the Archaeological Institute and that I cannot be at the meeting of the Committee on Membership, before Mrs. Pearmain came out from Boston at 9 o'clock to discuss the enquiry into the health and conditions of the 12000 women graduates of the Colleges and Universities in the Collegiate Alumnae Association. About 5000 answers to our questions have been received in the last three weeks, and we went in together to the State House, where the results are to be tabulated by the Mass. Bureau of Statistics.

Went to the monthly meeting of the State Board of Education at 10.30, after seeing Mr. Morse and finding that the case to protect Jeanie

Mills, a little Scotch servant, would probably come up next week. He will take charge of the case for us.

Pres. Carter of Williams College presided at the Board meeting where the chief discussion was on the position the Board should take about building dormitories at the Normal Schools in cities. Thus far we have provided them only for the Normal Schools in country places, and at large added cost to the State. But North Adams urges the need of one there. If that is granted Fitchburg, Salem and Lowell will immediately follow. Pres. Carter, Mr. Conley, Mrs. Wells and I are a committee to investigate the needs more fully. Afterward Pres. Carter and I had a long talk on the defects of young college teachers, apropos of one we are both interested in, a capital teacher, a fine scholar, hesitating as to leaving teaching for the ministry, — and yet deserting three important classes to go to a football game! Mr. Carter thinks lawlessness and "lack of loyalty to the organization" are increasing.

Came home to find that Emily arrived from Boxford in the pouring rain for a two days' visit. This is Julius Palmer's birthday — 60 years, if he had lived one year longer than he did ! and she clings more and more to the brothers she has left, and wishes to be with them on the family day. I sent in word that I would not come in town to the N. E. Woman's Club reception to Miss Evans, Dean in Carleton College, and took Emily and Lucy Sprague to a lecture on "Liberty and Equality" by W. D. Howells in aid of the Prospect Union, at Fogg Art Museum. The hall was full in spite of the rain to hear the delicious English, and the noble and great-hearted ideals Mr. Howells gave us. Prof. Norton came smiling to me, saying "The spirit is so beautiful we forget the faulty logic," and the Longfellows and Merrimans agreed that as long as he would talk like that it mattered little what he said.

After some talk in the informal reception he held among his old friends, Mr. Morse joined us for half an hour of M. de Reguier's first lecture in Sanders Theatre. None of the rest understood his French, for he sits and reads after the French fashion even in a great hall, so we went at 5 o'clock to Vespers in Appleton Chapel, and heard Endicott Peabody's impassioned cry for righteousness. No day anywhere could give three greater contrasts than Howells, de Reguier, & Peabody, with their pleas for Utopian equality, for literary prettinesses, and for stern and splendid self-sacrifice.

Mr. Morse came home to dinner and to talk Boxford, and Mrs. Todd joined us, coming down from her lecture in Arlington more brilliant, sparkling and witty than usual, but over-tired with too many lectures and too much society. It is fortunate that she sails in a month to join Prof. Todd in the eclipse expedition in Algiers. We finished dinner only in time to go to the Symphony concert, the best of the winter, ending in Beethoven's eighth symphony.

Friday, March 2, 1900

GHP

To Prayers, then to the furniture dealer's, where I made a contract for the construction of seven large chairs to stand in the Committee Room at the Phillips Brooks House. Reaching home, a man was awaiting me who had brought a beautiful Collie dog which I had sent for as a gift to my sister. She liked him, & I paid $20.00 for him. The remainder of the morning & the early afternoon was spent in study. At 3 P.M. I took my walk, stopping at the Market in Cambridgeport to order supplies for the next three days. From 4 to 6 I was at the Brooks House, where this winter a Committee of Faculty wives are holding afternoon Teas once a week for Professors & students. More than 60 students were there & 40 other persons, among the latter Mrs Brooks, who has just given to the House a pair of andirons & a large rug, formerly in the Library of Phillips Brooks. Callers & seven letters — four of them on business of the Department — fill the rest of the day.

AFP

Went to Mrs. Shaler's at 8.30 to arrange about the flowers for the tea this afternoon in the Phillips Brooks House, and found her in bed with the grip. At 9 o'clock the beautiful collie came which we had bought for Emily's birthday present, and charmed her as much as the rest of us. After arranging for his going to Boxford tomorrow I went to Miss Borden's in Boston to plan a meeting in April for the Institute for Girls in Spain; then at 10.30 to the hearing before the Legislative Com. on Labor at the State House, in behalf of a bill limiting women's work in mercantile establishments to fifty eight hours a week; — a large hearing attended by many influential women. Promised to go again next Tuesday and speak. Gave up the Cantabrigia Club meeting and went early to the Brooks House to receive all the afternoon. One hundred came, sixty one of them students. Dean Briggs met them all at the door, and they enjoyed especially meeting Mrs. Arthur Brooks, Mrs. Whitelaw Reid, Miss Alice Longfellow, and Endicott Peabody.

Mrs. Fiske Warren had sent word that Mr. Spencer Pratt had been sent abroad again by Pres. McKinley, so he would not be at her house to tell his experiences with Aguinaldo, and Emily had been in town all day and did not care to go to the Radcliffe play. so we got an evening to talk and to sew. I began a new dozen napkins for Boxford, and Emily and Lucy embroidered and made pillow cases.

I called on Mrs. Farlow for the first time since her romantic marriage. [See **AFP**-10 for Mrs. Palmer's rollicking poem in November 1899, about the engagement of Miss Horsford to Professor Farlow.]

Saturday, March 3, 1900

GHP

Prayers, followed by a consultation with Prof Peabody, my colleague on the Brooks House Committee. Then calls on Professors Royce & Münsterberg to settle the perplexing question how many hours a week of teaching can fairly be exacted from members of the Department of Philosophy. We agree that not less than two courses & a half ($7^{1/2}$ hours) should be given. And as Chairman of the Dep't I am instructed to call Prof. Santayana's attention to the fact that his work proposed for next year falls below this.

My Radcliffe Lecture follows at 11, study & writing from 12 to 1, Harvard Lecture at 1.30, after which I go with my wife to see a pretty dramatization of Miss Alcotts Little Women played by friends of ours at Brattle Hall. Lucy Sprague, a Radcliffe Senior, the daughter of a dear Chicago friend, who has lived with us the past four years, goes to Andover for the night. Her sister Nancy is living this year with my brother Rev. Frederic Palmer, the Episcopal Rector there. My evening is given to the newspaper, to writing & study. Three letters today & as many persons calling on me.

AFP

Emily Palmer, after banking and errands, went to Boxford, and Lucy Sprague to Andover to see her sick sister Nancy. Then I spent the morning housekeeping, marketing, and paying the February bills. This is the most interesting time because the most expensive half year — from September to March — is over. and my (family personals for both) accounts are now made up:-

Income, Sept. 1,1899 to March 1,1900		
Salary in hand		675.00
Six months salary		1312.50
" " books, lectures etc	1011.61	
Year's Board of Radclife student		600.00
Interest, dividends		529.30.
House Rent. +		4128.91 [*sic*]

Expenses, Sept 1,1899 to March 1,1900.
First Quarter 1908.97
Second " 1594.84.
3503.81
Chief expenses have been, gifts, charities etc 959.04
Traveling and correspondence 266.10; Provisions 572.34
Boxford,178.50; Taxes, fuel & light, 297.80;
Furnishings & repairs, 365.54; Service, 301.90;
Clothing, shoes etc 251.00; Books etc 113.10;
Amusements, 30.15; Personal, 48.35.

All this fairly corresponds to the same six months for the last three years, since I began this plan of keeping classified expenses, except that I have generally earned about two hundred dollars a month by lecturing, and this year am doing practically no speaking, hoping to fully recover from an accident last year. [See page 139]

Charles Talmage came in for a talk about his work for the M.A. degree, and his plans for getting a church next year. and Augustus Emery to discuss his sister Florence, and whether she should be prepared for College or study music only next year. He will bring her to see me soon.

I had planned to go to Wellesley for this afternoon and evening, but instead George and I went to the play "Little Women" given in behalf of the Woman's Industrial & Educational Union, in Brattle Hall. — the first time this year that we have taken a Saturday afternoon off together. It was admirably done, chiefly by Harvard and Radcliffe students we know, and brought back my childhood delight in the book. We went with the Lanes and had good talk with them and Col. Higginson who is full of the new Authors' Club, and has made me reconsider and join, and go on the Membership Committee.

Good byes to Dr. and Mrs. Lyman Abbott who leave after the Lowell Institute Lectures and the Edwin Abbots who go south today for a month, — with much talk of the miserable Porto Rican bills in Congress. I promised Lyman Abbott help in the Outlook's fight against false temperance teaching, and got Mr. Dutton of Brookline to see him. Mrs. Stevenson, Pres. of the Mass. W.C.T.U. promises to join us on the Board of Education in opposing the bill now before the House changing the temperance instruction laws.— a great result of our long Conferences this fall in harmonizing the educational and temperance reform forces !

The evening to letters, making arrangements for Education Association meetings, Wellesley reports, sending names for the George Junior Republic supporters, writing for sustaining members for Atlanta University, and planning for missionary meetings in New York in April.

Sunday, March 4, 1900

GHP

A restful Sunday - only one guest at dinner, two others calling, five letters written, four hours of study, a bicycle ride, quiet talks with my wife, & evening service at the College Chapel where Endicott Peabody preaches.

AFP

I have had no time for writing for a week because the early part was so crowded. Monday morning was full of appointments to see Wellesley teachers; at one o'clock I was at the Hotel Thorndike in Boston for Mrs. Kate Upson Clark's luncheon to eighteen ladies; reached home at 4 o'clock for the Ethical Seminary, and Anna Boynton Thompson's second Monday with them, she leading the discussion on Fichte; at 6.30 we had the second diner for the Seminary and Miss Thompson. On each Monday — and at 8 o'clock came the Radcliffe Philosophy Club. Forty two were present in the library, and Miss Puffer read an able attack on Mr. Santayana's "Sense of Beauty." He replied, and a good discussion followed until 10 o'clock when they had a hot, stand-up supper in the dining room.

Tuesday morning I hurried in to the State House to see Mr. Wadlin about the statistics of College women. The bureau will devote March to tabulating them, and they will be in time for the Paris Exposition. The Wellesley Exhibit has already gone; at 10.30 went to the second hearing before the joint Com. on Education, on the two reform bills for the Boston School administration. No more important educational measures have come up for years; the Boston school Committee has sunk to the lowest level it has ever reached, but if it were free from politics it could not do effective service under its present organization, yet the committee from the Legislature to whom we must look for relief is under an illiterate chairman, and has a majority of insolent, ignorant young men whose speech and manners disgrace their respectable colleagues. The House chairman on the Com. came to me after the hearing to "express his regret that we must see our own State shamed by having the dregs of the House on her educational Committee." It is a complete contrast to last year's Com. under Senator Parsons, and is a sad commentary on the results of a good man's over-anxiety to be speaker of the House, and "having debts to pay," which is the excuse made by Mr. Myers' friends. themselves such "good republicans" that they did not uphold Mr. Parsons' noble independence.

All this made me reach home to find Mrs. Todd already here to luncheon, full of talk about the Astronomical Expedition to Algiers, & of her last two weeks in Washington, — and while we talked my "at home" reception began, the day being chiefly given up to relatives and Boxford summer people.

Wednesday was given up to showing a party of New York ladies the University, to a long meeting of the Wellesley Executive Board, and another of the Archaeological Society. This report shows how the rest of the week has gone.

Sunday is always kept for family and intimate friends and students. The dinner table is set for from six to ten, and those half dozen students related to us or dependent upon us, or specially needing friendliness come then. It is the day for "talking things over," for making plans with them; and helping them if we can. This year we are responsible for seeing five through College; one will take his M.A. with honor in June; one his B.A. creditably; one is a Junior; one a Freshman; and one preparing to be a teacher, a Junior. All this costs us about $1500. a year, beside what friends do to help, — which of course we could not do if we were fortunate enough to have children of our own. With beautiful Lucy Sprague in the house, and these coming and going with their friends, full of eager "schemes,"— and all doing well — some brilliantly — life in the College Yard is the most interesting thing in the world.

We have just come in from the service in Appleton Chapel, where we always go Sunday evenings, and where Endicott Peabody preached the plainest sermon I ever heard to young men on their special temptations.

Mr. Robinson, a young instructor, came in, and sat long talking of the characteristics of the Harvard Faculty, their frankness of speech, their loyalty to each other, their freedom from pettiness and jealousy, their splendid power of differing profoundly in opinion, while loving and standing by each other personally, the kindness of the older to the younger, — and most of all the great qualities of the President.

So ends the quietest Sunday in a long time.

Monday, March 5, 1900

GHP

To Boston on business for the Brooks House Then a call from Prof Santayana, & afterwards from Prof Münsterberg, in regard to the announcement of their courses for the coming year. Endicott Peabody came in to lunch. I had three or four hours of study, & my seminary met in my Library at 4 P.M. with a paper from Carson on Hegel's Rechtsphilosophie. To dinner came Rev. E. L. Bradford our minister from Boxford, reporting the results of the Boxford town meeting. My letter had been read warning the selectmen to be more careful in future to state to all intending liquor-dealers that they would probably be prosecuted. He remained an hour after dinner, consulting me about other town & parish matters. Just after his departure came in Rev T. C. Williams who is just establishing the Hackley School at Tarrytown on the Hudson. He wished to talk of his plans & of possible teachers & remained over night.

AFP

I took two hours this morning for writing and then had long interviews with Mrs. Eliot on the management of the Brooks House afternoon teas and the buying of linen and silver for them; — and then with Mrs. Farlow on Wellesley appointments, chiefly on the Bible Department and the filling of Miss Woolley's place when she takes the Presidency of Mt. Holyoke.

Rev. Endicott Peabody came to luncheon, and we had interesting talk of Groton School, of Harvard life, — of girls' education also. He is deeply stirred by the need of a higher moral tone in Society, and is coming to feel that less is done for the girls than the boys, — that rich men's daughters have a much harder time than their brothers in making anything worthy out of their lives.

At 3 o'clock I went to the Boston Young Women's Christian Association's annual meeting. The Director showed me all the departments, especially in domestic science, — never doing so well as now. The girls looked fresh and happy, and stronger than usual.

At 4 o'clock went to Judge Robert Grant's room in the Probate Court to the meeting of the Membership Committee in the new Authors' Club. Judge Grant, Col. Higginson and Mr. Clement, Editor of the Transcript were also there, and we spent two hours in discussing the future of the Club, and in admitting thirteen new members —making the number now eighty two.

Upon reaching home at seven o'clock I found Mr. Bradford, our minister from Boxford, just arrived fresh from the Town Meeting with news of the annual votes: no-license carried, vote of one to three only against; the better of the two candidates chosen to the School Com.—yet only by a majority of one; and George's letter well received and promising good results in increasing a law-abiding spirit. Yesterday six joined the village church, five of them young people, and Mr. Bradford is much encouraged. He and his wife go tomorrow to New York for their first visit there.

Lucy Sprague and I went at 8 o'clock to Mr. Thomas Osborne's illustrated lecture on Shubert, but the Fogg Museum was so crowded that even standing was difficult in the crush, and the air grew so bad that we came away after half an hour,—very sorry, for he was original and spirited, and personally most refreshingly frank and sensible. If only all musicians were like him ! All this time, the dinner table talk of Boxford had gone steadily on with Mr. Bradford, for he wanted to make plans to repair the inside of the Church very fully this year. But at half past nine Theodore Williams surprised us by appearing for twenty four hours' visit & search for teachers for his new school for boys at Tarrytown-on-the-Hudson. I gladly gave up going into the Art Students' Association's opening reception for the McCormick Pictures, at Copley Hall, and we heard of all Theodore's experiences and plans until 11 o'clock.

Tuesday, March 6, 1900

GHP

To Prayers with Mr Williams, leaving him with Pres. Eliot & Endicott Peabody. I come home to work & to Radcliffe Lecture at 11. Letters written from 12 to 1. Harvard Lecture at 1.30. Then to Boston on more Brooks House business, coming out to Faculty Meeting 4 to 6. Evening tired, but write & study till bed time. My nephew, Eric Palmer, a senior, calls. I explain what I have heard about possible places where he may teach next year.

AFP

Yesterday morning there was snow on the ground, and this morning it was falling fast. All day the storm has gone on turning to rain, and making Mr. Williams' appointments hard to keep. But he has had a good morning among the men, and we had another cheerful luncheon and an hour's talk afterward. He is full of boyish enthusiasm, and turns from a minister to a school master with a young poet's gladness and ease.

All my morning has been spent in Legislative Committees, first speaking before the Com. on Labor for the 58 hour law for women; then a long time before the Education Committee to oppose some bills bought in by faddists.—1. to establish a new Normal School at Lawrence; 2. to make the Board of Education a bureau for getting teachers places; 3. establishing directorships (state) in Music, etc. I had not spoken to the Education Com before this year, and they took the occasion to ask opinions about the bills that had already come before them, but fortunately the storm (?) kept the most disagreeable members away, and we got through comfortably. We shall be thankful if we get through the year with no seriously bad legislation, even though we must postpone much good work.

Few callers came this "at home" afternoon in the storm. Miss Allen to talk over the Vacation Schools problems; Miss Wheelright and Miss Peabody from Boston to discuss a possible Art meeting in April; a student or two; but between times I have written letters, and sent Gov. Claflin a telegram of love and congratulations on his eighty-first birthday,—shut up by long illness under "The Old Elm" in Newtonville. I found time to write a resolution at the request of the Wellesley Trustees to go on the records, on the resignation of Miss Woolley, Prof. of Biblical History to accept the Presidency of Mt. Holyoke College next summer.

At 8 o'clock went down to City Hall where the Aldermen and Council were to have a joint session, and give a hearing to the petitioners that the City should vote $2000. to maintain Vacation Schools next summer. A few women;—Mrs. Adams and I speaking for them at this hearing,—have raised from $600. to $1500. a year for four years and supported schools for both boys and girls six weeks in the summer. Now we ask the city to take charge of them. J. G. Thorp—whose wife is on our Committee conducted our case admirably, and Sec. Hill of the State Board of Education, Judge Almy, Supt. of Schools Coggeswell, also spoke very well. But it was a most extraordinary sight, for the Council chambers, the galleries and halls were packed with men who had come to hear the defense of a policeman under charges, and a row of policemen made a path for us through this excited, smoking throng. For more than an hour they had to wait through our hearing, but they all listened with complete silence and respect to all we said.—perhaps learning something about the needs of their children, and what is being done for them, by private efforts as well as by the City.

Came home at 10 o'clock to find Lucy Sprague's Tuesday evening callers still here.

Wednesday, March 7, 1900

GHP

All day given to my first Noble Lecture, which is delivered in the evening in Peabody Hall, Brooks House. Mrs. W'm Belden Noble gave $20,000 for a course of annual lectures in memory of her husband. Last year 6 ministers preached a sermon apiece on this foundation. But my own lectures constitute the first continuous course. I was appointed last spring, am to give six lectures, to receive $600.00, the plates of my book to be issued in the Fall are to be paid for, & I am to own the copyright. I have taken as my subject "Ethics, in relation to the neighboring Sciences," & discuss in the first lecture "The Descriptive Sciences." In the morning after Prayers I must see that the Hall is arranged, must engage my ushers, & make two calls on other business. The rest of the day— apart from two letters written & three calls received— is given to preparation. Every seat in the hall was filled &, as usual, I spoke without notes. I had a stenographer report the lecture & shall work over the whole in the next Summer vacation.

AFP

Mrs. Murman, Supt. of Norumbega, in Wellesley, came this morning to talk over many Wellesley affairs, and I worked on my two dozen new napkins while we discussed college housekeeping. Afterward I worked on Wellesley reports, saw Mrs. Farlow about the Music department, and was just leaving for Boston when Mr. Wiggin of Saginaw, Mich. came. He is my brother's wife's father, and had much family news to give, and also many stories to tell of his explorations in the Nova Scotia forests, where he is now engaged in great lumber operations.

We went into Boston together finally for the 3 o'clock meeting of the Wellesley Executive committee. Only Mr. Scudder, Mrs. Durant, Pres. Hazard and I were there, and the other three men who were expected were all sick. We did a large amount of important business: chiefly on financial matters and faculty appointments, discussed many questions of policy, and made a start on the pension system. Miss Hazard contributed $1200 for a beginning of a fund for pensions, and we voted to retire Miss Clarke after twenty five years of devoted service, on $200. a year. We all propose to work toward increasing this fund, and founding a regular system upon which the Faculty can rely.

After the meeting I walked with Miss Hazard to Mrs. Whitman's where she is to dine and spend the night, going on to Bryn Mawr in the morning. There they give her a great reception. She is a glorious type of woman, and it is good for any girl to know her. She told me the amusing things of her late appearances before "Clubs" and "Unions," and from Beacon Hill we saw a superb sunset over the Charles, across the snow, beyond trees and church spire. This morning a pair of flickers has been about the house attracting much attention from the passers by. They are probably among the ones that have spent the winter in Cambridge,—but the sky has the spring blue in it, though the sharp air and the snow are still with us.

This evening was given to the first Noble lecture. The hall was crowded, and the beginning was prosperous, though the lecturer came away utterly dissatisfied, but as humble and philosophical as ever.

Thursday, March 8, 1900

GHP

This morning comes a letter offering my nephew Eric, who graduates from Harvard this year, a position as teacher of mathematics & Science in a boys school just starting at Asheville So. Carolina. He is to receive all his living & $1000 salary. The heads of the new school are two men whom I met on my recent lecture tour to Cleveland. They have had the charge of the University School there & are about to remove to Asheville. To them I recommended Eric, & they take him without personal acquaintance. After Prayers I call at his room in Hollis & report his fortune. He has already had (through me) partial proposals from Rev. T. C. Williams of Tarrytown. Each school has its advantages. After my lecture at Radcliffe, lunch, & then the Harvard lecture, I take train to Andover at 3.30 to consult Eric's father, Episcopal minister there. Reach home at 7.15 & spend evening over letters in regard to Eric's school & in a long interview with him.

AFP

At breakfast the great news came of Eric's appointment to teach Science and Mathematics next year in Asheville, at $1000. and his living. This is the greatest joy and relief to us for it insures him a field for which he is specially fitted, and gives him so good a salary that he can soon save enough to come back and work for his higher degree, or can study medicine, as he finally shall decide.

At noon came word from Dr. Allen that he wished my sister again this summer to take charge of the Vacation Schools and play grounds and soccer under the Episcopal City Mission in Boston. She did it all last summer with the greatest enthusiasm in every phase of it, and this will make her delighted.

The morning has been long and fatiguing. I had been summoned for three hearings at the State House; — before the Labor Com. on the protection of women and minors in manufactures from night work and overtime work; — before the Com on Prisons in behalf of a new reformatory for boys over fifteen who must now be sent to Concord with hardened criminals; and before the Com. on Education in behalf of a bill to make supervision of schools compulsory, — a measure the Board has very much at heart, to help the country schools, in the more backward places, where the schools are now much behind the others, and the children neglected. The Education Com. reports today against the bill to force more so-called "scientific temperance teaching" upon the schools; against several other bad measures, so I came down Beacon street as cheerful as the fine sunshine.

It is so warm that the pots of spring flowers had been set out on the side walks in front of the flower shops, and Mr. Leason, who told me about all the flowers when we were in the White Mountains, looked as happy as if he were not a Railroad Commissioner on his way to a fight over the Fitchburg lease question. He walked along the Common telling me of his son Robert's beginning in manufacture as gaily as by the Profile Lake [in New Hampshire, near Profile Mountain with its natural profile called the Old Man of the Mountains]. If it were only always spring !

Went to 83 Beacon St. to engage the Ruby Parlors for April 6, and Mrs. Gulick's meeting for the College for Girls in Spain. Then to Mrs. Merriman's to make plans for the meeting, and calls in Irving St. until M. de Reguier's lecture; from that to Vespers where the Chapel was packed with young people. Prof. Peabody reports that the Brooks parlor's first afternoon as a place for the students to take their friends was a great success. Mrs. Eliot came in to send messages to the Bee tomorrow and make plans for the faculty teas, and a student came to dinner. Then I went down to the Young Woman's Christian Association, and gave them a public lecture in their Entertainment Course, "Bicycle Journeys in Europe." A reception followed. Home at 10 o'clock to write letters, as I always do in all the odds and ends of time, and then I never catch up and have a free desk !

Friday, March 9, 1900

GHP

After Prayers comes by appointment Professor Whitman from Western Reserve College, Cleveland, O. The University School of Cleveland, having lost its head, I was consulted about a suitable successor when I was lecturing there a month ago. I recommended Gregg of Newport or Rieber, now a candidate for Ph.D. here. Prof. Whitman has been sent on to examine these & other candidates, & spends the day & night with me. I talk with him an hour, then take him to the Psychological Laboratory & introduce him to Rieber. Come home & write six letters, among them a long one to Mrs Noble informing her about the starting of the Noble Lectures & about the ways of carrying out her desire to do something for the Noble rooms in the Brooks House. Whitman returns to lunch. Afterwards I go again to Boston on business of the Brooks House & coming home have calls from two students. The evening is given to discussing with Whitman his experiences of the day.

AFP

This morning has gone in interview with the principal of a colored school in S. C. and her plans for raising $4000; with a Salvation Army

Captain and her "Self denial week" subscription; with the President of the new Equal Suffrage League among College women, and I let her have my name; in banking business for the Woman's Table in the Zoölogical Station at Naples, of which I am Treasurer; and with Prof. Whitman of Western Reserve University in Cleveland who came this morning, and will stay with us two or three days looking for teachers for the University and also for a large boy's school there.

Today I have promised to go to New York the last week in April as delegate to The Ecumenical Council, and preside at the educational meeting; address the public school association in New Haven on the way, and make a few speeches in New York and Brooklyn. I haven't been there since last year and I shall combine a good many things in one week.

After luncheon went to the Bee, a sewing circle for the poor, at Mrs. Horace Scudder's, where we worked for a child we have just adopted to clothe, until 5 o'clock, when I took Prof. Whitman to the Brooks House tea. Over ninety were there, having a delightful time. Dean Briggs is absolutely wonderful in his management of introducing the men. This evening we gave to Prof. Whitman, his friends & his affairs.

Saturday, March 10, 1900

GHP

Took Whitman to Prayers, introducing him to Pres. Eliot. Study until lecture time, 11 o'clock Coming home from Lecture found Mr Wiggin of Saginaw here. Spent the hour in showing him about the College grounds and buildings. He and Prof Whitman & Mr Talmage at lunch. I go from the table to lecture, afterwards walking with Mr Talmage to Cambridgeport Market. After an hour of study, Mrs Palmer & I go to hear Reguier give a lecture in French in Sanders Theatre on the French Symbolic Poets. Newspaper till dinner, a game of dominoes afterwards & letters till bed time.

Two students have called on me today & I have read the Doctoral Thesis of one of them. Before breakfast one called, Dr Savery one of my Assistants in Philosophy & asked me to write him a recomendation to the President of Fairmount College, Kansas, whom he was to meet in Boston. He comes in again this evening to say his interview was satisfactory. I must write two more letters in his behalf.

AFP

After getting Prof. Whitman started on his many appointments after prayers, and arranging for a luncheon for men, I went into Boston for a 10 o'clock meeting of the directors of the Woman's Education Assoc. of which I am President, and got back for a part of the annual meeting of The Harvard Teachers' Assoc. in Sanders Theatre, where I saw many of the leaders of secondary education in this part of N. E. They were discussing requirements for College again. Principal Baldwin of the Hyannis Normal School came on important business, as I am one of the two State Visitors having the school in charge.

Mr. Wiggin came out to see the College and take luncheon. Prof. Whitman left this afternoon. Mr. Wiggin went back to Nova Scotia. For Charles Talmage, who lunched here also, I have been writing letters to Detroit and elsewhere about getting him a church next year, when he wishes to preach again.

Today we uncovered all our flower beds, and let the poor pale sprouts into the sunshine. After that I was so sleepy I lay down. There is so much to talk of with my husband, and no time except late at nights and early in the mornings that I am far behind in sleep, and I have promised to do so much after this month that I shall not catch up then !

Annual meeting of the College Club to elect next year's officers. I have said nothing of this Club of four hundred college graduates (women) of which I accepted the presidency two years ago, and again last year, but now I have had to resign, in spite of all my interest in it, and fondness for it, on account of my accident, — so less work. I have them all here to a reception in April when Pres. and Mrs. Tucker will be staying with us ten days. George and I went together to M. de Reguier's French lecture, the first one he has heard. It was painfully dull. The large audience would never bear a second hour of such talk if it were in English. Boston friends sat near us and we came out together and took them to the car in the soft air and spring sunset.

Then the Transcript and dinner full of talk of the Peace proposals in South Africa. After dinner George, Lucy and I played our Saturday night game of dominoes and Lucy won. I wrote letters all the evening, and went to bed early.

Sunday, March 11, 1900

GHP

Sunday morning. Breakfast later & no haste in beginning the day. The morning paper on Sundays is abominably long, over 40 pps. One must take time to extract the news. Then on Sundays we have no house-to-house delivery of mail but I must go to the Post Office for it between 9.15 & 10.15. I do odd jobs in the morning & write nine letters, five of them to colleges where I hope to secure positions for my students who will take their degrees in June. We have dinner at noon on Sunday. To it come four of the students who are more closely connected with us. After it comes in the student who is reporting stenographically my Noble Lectures & brings his first report. I then ride for an hour on my bicycle & spend another hour over the sketch of the Thesis which one of my students is preparing for his Doctor's Degree. He wishes to be advised whether he is on the right track.

I indulge myself for an hour over a manuscript of George Herberts Poems which I have had copied in the Williams Library in London. It has been sent me this week by the professional copyist who has worked upon it under the supervision of our Professor Gross. To her I paid £3.11 for her work & find it very satisfactory. Last summer I began the preparation of a Critical Edition of George Herbert — for whom I was named — & I expect to push it on to completion next Summer. During Term time I am kept so busy that I can obtain little or no leisure for literary work. After supper I go to the College Chapel & hear Rev. Paul Revere Frothingham preach. He now comes into residence for 3 weeks as one of our preachers. A little reading afterwards & to bed.

AFP

This morning Col. Higginson came before I was dressed to talk of The Authors' Club and new members. I was able to tell him that my husband would join, that Mrs. Whitman would accept an invitation, and I am authorized to propose the matter to Profs. Royce, Münsterberg and Santayana, whose poems and books he carried off to read.

A special delivery letter came from Mr. Morse saying a boy had been born to them, and I wrote them at once, and also to Prof. Todd on the Riviera, before he goes over to Africa. His birthday and Mr. Palmers are the same, the 19th. Miss Bakewell of California called for an hour to tell me of her brother Charles' wedding, and their life at Bryn Mawr where he is teaching Philosophy, and then came the students to dinner, — four young men today, with much talk afterward about positions for next year, about examinations, about the measles, which Roderic Wellman has had, about the D.U. [Delta Upsilon] for which Ned Abbot is running under Eric's commands —they sat opposite each other !— about the Lampoon to which Roderic aspires, about Sheldon's conducting a daily paper this week in Kansas "as Jesus would," about a great swindle in selling "lucky boxes" in Boston, and a hundred other things. Boys are the most interesting beings in the world except girls — and they go very well together.

After they went Lucy and I had a long talk about her family matters, and her plans for next year, when she longs to study architecture. She is a glorious girl, so wise, so generous, so sensible, so farseeing;

knowing that to make her invalid family happy she must herself have a strong useful life.

This evening it was so cold that I did not face the fierce wind with my cough, and go in to the great meeting in behalf of Atlanta University at Trinity Church as I had planned — I am a Vice President of the Boston Organization — but went with George to Appleton Chapel Paul Revere Frothingham is in residence as Preacher now, a Unitarian minister who writes original and able sermons, but tries to read them eloquently & to be impressive in manner. — More letters and reading The Outlook, The Nation & Spectator.

Monday, March 12, 1900

GHP

Walk to Prayers with Pres. Eliot, calling his attention to two Spanish teachers for the Summer School. Carry my Williams Ms. to the book binder & attend to a table for the Brooks House. Give the morning to an Article for the Boston Transcript, recommending as a situation for intended new building, The Harvard Union, the lot between Cambridge St. & Broadway, behind the old Gymnasium. For two months past the proper site for this building has been much discussed among our students.

To lunch comes Professor Wilcox from Wellesley with a message from her father about a Western College to which I have been recommending one of my graduate students. Study, a walk, & a student caller, occupy my time till my Seminary on Ethics 4–6, at which 12 men were present, discussing the Introduction to Hegel's Rechtslehre. Before dinner I walk with one of them to make suggestions to him about changes in his Thesis for the Doctor's Degree, I having in the last two days gone over his first Sketch of this Thesis. In the evening Dr Folsom of Boston calls to prescribe for the cold our Radcliffe Senior, Lucy Sprague, caught in the cold wind of yesterday. Then I write a letter of recommendation for one of my students to help him obtain a place in a Western College, & after a little study to bed.

AFP

Housekeeping, letters, and Lucy Sprague sick with a cold from her ten mile walk in the high wind yesterday,—so the early half of the morning went. Then Mrs. Eliot came, and as she went from talk about the smoking passion among the students, and the bad manners that resulted in public, a lady came to consult about the choice of a college for her twin daughters, and an hour went between "co-education and women's colleges," between "the east and the west."

Prof. Willcox of Wellesley came to luncheon, and afterward I went in town to see Dr. Folsom about Lucy, and do a little shopping before

29

Monday. March 12. Housekeeping, letters and Lucy Sprague sick with a cold from her ten mile walk in the high wind yesterday, so the early half of the morning went. Then Mrs. Ellis came, and we had some talk about the smoking passion among the students, and the bad manners that results in public. a lady came to consult about the choice of a College for her twin daughters, and an hour went between "co-education and women's Colleges", between "the east and the west." Prof. Willcox of Wellesley came to luncheon, and afterward I went in town to see Dr. Folsom about Lucy, and do a little shopping before the College Club reception to Miss Woolley. All the Brown University, Mt. Holyoke and Wellesley people were there, with a large company besides, and it was an unusually delightful afternoon. Judson Smith, Pres. of Mt. Holyoke trustees, asked for help in finding a Dean of Women at Oberlin College, to whose President I had already written. Tonight Dr. Folsom came out, and ordered Lucy to stay in bed, for he has fears of the grip. Students and letters finished the evening.

Alice Freeman Palmer's diary entry for March 12, 1900. The photograph does not show the horizontal lines nor the margin line for the date column which is one and three-eighths inches wide in the original diary.

the College Club reception to Miss Woolley. All the Brown University, Mt. Holyoke and Wellesley people were there with a large company besides, and it was an unusually delightful afternoon. Judson Smith, Pres. of Mt. Holyoke Trustees, asked for help in finding a Dean of Women at Oberlin College, to whose President I had already written. Tonight Dr. Folsom came out, and ordered Lucy to stay in bed, for he has fears of the grip. Students and letters finished the evening.

Tuesday, March 13, 1900

GHP

Before going to bed last night I went in to Pres. Eliots (he lives in the house next mine) to learn the result of the Corporation Meeting. This year Professor W. James is absent on his Sabbatical Year & he expected to deliver the first course of his Gifford Lectures at Edinburg. He has been so ill with complications of heart trouble that he has obtained leave of absence for a second year & his lectures have been postponed until that time. Dr. D. S. Miller has been hired as an Instructor to do his work here. But the Department at its last meeting requested the Corporation also to appoint for the coming year some man of eminent name to give a single course as an attraction for graduate students. They named Prof. J. Mark Baldwin of Princeton or Pres. G. Stanley Hall of Clark University. The Corporation answers us that they are unwilling to spend the money to call either of these gentlemen.

After Prayers I learn from Pres. Eliot the name of the new President of the University of Cincinnati & write to inquire if he will not take one of my graduate students as a teacher of Philosophy. A call from L. K. Morse tells of a son just born & also of his preparation of the case of our servant Jean which he is soon to try. Two years ago Jean was knocked down by her employer & badly damaged. She has brought suit. I study & then to lecture at 11 and again at 1.30. After lecture I go to Boston & see A. W. Longfellow, the architect of the Brooks House, about preparing the memorial tablets in the entrance hall whose inscriptions I am to write. I walk out. There are two young ladies & a student with us at dinner. I have two long calls from students in the evening, write 8 letters.

AFP

Lucy Sprague was so ill this morning that I did not go in Boston to the hearings at the State House. To the one on Vivisection I was particularly anxious to go. Pres. Eliot, Bishop Lawrence and distinguished physicians defended Science against the efforts to stop experiments.

Pres. Eliot told us of it at luncheon at his house where I went to meet Mr. and Mrs. Frothingham and Dr. Hall, and had much interesting discussion.

I came home to find my callers already arriving, and the afternoon has been full of visitors from Boston, Cambridge and Brookline. Four young people were invited to dinner, and Florence Emery to stay over night. They have been having music all the evening. while Lucy's fever all day has made me anxious, and I telephoned at 8 o'clock for the doctor to come again.

Mr. Morse came this morning to plan for Jean's case which may come on at any time. Both the servants are therefore very nervous over it, as nothing except a hospital could frighten them more than a law court. Called on the Münsterbergs this morning to invite him to join the Authors' Club.

Wednesday, March 14, 1900

GHP

The day chiefly given to preparation for my Noble Lecture on the Relations of Ethics & The Law. These lectures I deliver without notes, have a stenographer report them, & then am to rewrite & publish them next summer. I have five calls today, make one also myself on Prof Royce, & write half a dozen letters. A girl and a student are here at lunch & my sister-in-law at dinner. She comes from Andover to attend the lecture. At the lecture 8–9 every seat is taken. I thought the first lecture was wretched, but this went better.

AFP

Had little sleep last night. Lucy was so ill. This morning her fever is much reduced, and pneumonia is averted ! I gave up all engagements for ~~this morning~~ today, and have withdrawn the invitations I had out for a dinner of young people. Left Lucy for two hours this morning to take Florence Emery about the College buildings, and to see a cousin — and for the afternoon to do Florence's shopping in Boston, and send her back to Andover at five o'clock. She is an interesting girl of quick mind and great intelligence, and only needs good training, and new ambitions, and interests of a worthy sort to make a fine woman.

This evening was the second Noble lecture, much better than the first, and with the same fine audience. This time many young lawyers came, some from Boston; and neighboring ministers, some from New Hampshire, to hear "Ethics & The Law." Gus Emery has taken his meals here with his sister yesterday and today, and tonight came

Mary Palmer from Andover to dinner and to the lecture, returning afterward. & Eric too came to talk of his summer plans.

Thursday, March 15, 1900

GHP

Prayers, study, lecture, a bicycle ride this morning. In the afternoon a lecture, a Department Committee meeting, & four calls from students. In the evening Symphony Concert at Sanders Theatre — last of the season.

AFP

Lucy slowly improves, but still has fever and a tearing cough.

The program for today was — more hearings at the State House on Charities and reforms this morning; presiding at the Woman's Education Assoc. Boston March meeting in the afternoon; speaking at a great meeting of the Boston Teachers' Club and parents of the public school children in the Church of The Disciples in the evening, and afterward to the meeting of The Round Table Club.

Many letters are coming in now for speeches at Commencements in June, for annual meetings of Societies, for every kind of Charity. An interesting interview from an agent of Fisk University to get me to speak at a public meeting for them in April, and help them raise money. What can we do with so many appeals every day, all of them for good causes, from the children in the slums to the support of Colleges in the south and west, and maintaining fellowships, for foreign study ! And the poor country places needing books and pictures and music to break their monotony !

The meeting this afternoon was large and the speeches were full of hope — Dr. Hill, Sec. of the Board of Education on "What the State is doing for teachers"; Prof. Hanus of Harvard on "What the Universities and Colleges are doing," and Supt. Dutton of Brookline on "The City experiments." It is clear that the interest of women whose children are in private schools is growing more practical in public education which is Boston's hope now. Tonight's movement of bringing parents and teachers together is more full of promise than anything else, except the reorganization of school management, and that being a reform which affects politics must be a losing reform.

Friday, March 16, 1900

GHP

A morning spent in study & letter writing. Committee Meeting of the Brooks House at 3 P.M. & I take the train from Boston at 5 for

Bridgewater, where I lecture this evening before the Normal School. They pay me $25.00 & expenses.

AFP

A violent snow storm came on in the night turning to rain in the early morning, and at ten o'clock the mercury had risen to 57 degrees. Miss Hazard had telegraphed me to come to Wellesley, but the storm was too serious to allow it. However Mlle. Schaeys, the chief French teacher there, came over here and kept me three hours with her wishes, her fears, her jealousies of other people, her ambitions. She proudly acknowledges that French people are "sensitive," but fails to understand why their peculiarities and bad temper make it unusually unwise to place them at the head of a department where others must work under them and with them.

In the rain came again my new acquaintance, the mother of twin daughters, who cannot decide "between co-education and the woman's colleges." I am afraid I was rather sharp and finally had to say that if she had brought up her children well, they were at nineteen capable of making a success of either.

Immediately after lunch I went to the Board meeting of the Cantabrigia Club, where I promised, as Vice-President, to preside at a musicale April 6. At three o'clock Mr. Dutton read his paper before the whole Club on "By-products in Education," and afterward we had the usual reception. Then I went into Boston to see Mrs. J. L. Bremer on the Spanish Institute business, and came home just in time to have dinner with Lucy Sprague up stairs, as Mr. Palmer is lecturing at Bridgewater, and she sits up for the first time this week.

Then I dressed and went to the Reception at the opening of The Photographic Club's Annual Exhibition. A great company and a remarkable collection of pictures. Miss Devens' and Mrs. Russell's were so astonishing that I must really go again to see them, but all were so good that any other year would have distinguished them. I had half an hour with Mr. Fitzgerald, the famous engineer, who told me of the Thursday Club's discussions, and many amusing tales of "Boston's brains."

Saturday, March 17, 1900

GHP

Return from Bridgewater at 8. Study & Lecture occupy the morning till 12, when I go to the storage warehouse in Boston with a Committee to inspect some paintings which have been offered as decorations of the Brooks House. We select eight. Lecture at 1.30, after which I go with my wife to Boston to a reception at the house of

Mrs Julia Ward Howe of the Authors Club, which has recently been established to include 100 of the writers in & about Boston. Mrs Palmer and I have joined. We go out to dinner at the house of Prof. J. B. Ames with the Eliots Münsterbergs & Brandeis. Three calls of students today.

AFP

I hurried off to Wellesley early this morning — to get the great news from Miss Hazard that her brother Roland sends word that Mr. Rockefeller will give Wellesley $100 000.00, as soon as our debt is paid ! his gift to be kept intact forever, never to be borrowed from; and the income to be used for educational purposes only. We have already, within a year, got $60000. pledged toward freeing the college from debt, and have $50000 more to get. Now we <u>must</u> raise this to announce at Commencement in June when the College will be twenty five years old. All else is going well too, and I got the noon train and was just in time to join Prof. Wendell at the Colonial Club, where I had promised to help him entertain an English lord and his bride, going from their estate in Jamaica to England. They were an agreeable pair of young radicals, who wanted to know all about Colleges for girls, and heard with joy of Wellesley and the others.

After luncheon we took them to the library, faculty room and Memorial Hall, where I had to leave them to go with George to the Authors' Club at Mrs. Julia Ward Howe's. Nearly all the Club, now of eighty members, was there, and the getting acquainted was very interesting. We had to come away early but not until Judge Grant had rejoiced me in a corner, with his witty talk, trying various verses on me. "She has forgotten my verses, and I cannot think of her name" and an attempt to imitate Whitman -"Whoever she is, I will kiss the mud from her rubbers." Mrs. Howe was in one of her gayest moods, and a more beautiful and fascinating woman of more than eighty could not be found.

At 7 o'clock we dined with Prof. & Mrs. J. B. Ames. He is the Dean of the Law School, and they had Pres. & Mrs. Eliot, Prof. & Mrs. Münsterberg, and Mr. & Mrs Brandeis, the latter a great lawyer in Boston, beside whom I sat and had most interesting accounts of his office, and the nine women he employs there. He chooses them instead of men as his confidential clerks, and has never known one to prove untrustworthy. They are more loyal, more conscientious, "never go on a spree," can be absolutely relied on — But in ten years no one has married, though they are able, intelligent, attractive. Mr. Brandeis thinks that very sad.— "The one drawback to such a life for women." They seem so happy, busy and contented that they go on from year to year. —They see in the office very superior men, and outside they doubtless know few men who interest them.

Mrs. Howe promises to speak in my place for Fisk Univ.

Sunday, March 18, 1900

GHP

Sunday - The long newpaper. Then to Post Office before it closes at 10.15. At 10 comes R. B. Perry for whom I obtained a place to teach in Philosophy at Williams last year. He has been teaching well, but has failed to identify himself well with the interests of the College & is not to be employed next year. I spend an hour over his plans. A little reading & writing & then with my wife to lunch at the house of W. P. P. Longfellow, 478 Broadway —a dinner a little awkward. Last night I published in the Boston Transcript a letter advising as a site for the new Harvard Union the ground immediately adjoining Mr Longfellow's house. He was, however, very kind and conciliatory.

On leaving there, I went to see an exhibition of amateur photographs in Brown & Nichols School, & on coming home found waiting for me a father from Chicago who has a son in College. When he had gone I set to work on letters & wrote eight, among them a long one to Prof W. James, now sick abroad. To evening service at the College Chapel where Rev. P. R. Frothingham preached.

AFP

It is very cold and windy again, with clouds of dust blowing through the streets. I staid with Lucy all the morning, and Miss Coes, Radcliffe's Secretary, came in to go over the applications for Fellowships. We have two of five hundred dollars each for study in Europe open to women college graduates, one given by the Education Assoc. of Boston, and the other by the Collegiate Alumnae Assoc. The Com. on award has been coming in all the week to study the applications which are here.

We made a great exception and went out to dinner today with Mr. and Mrs. Longfellow. They live in the house in which we spent the first six months of our married life. He is an architect, and they have been adding to it in a charming fashion, and they took us all over it, from the cellar and kitchen up.

We had hardly come home when Mr. Blackwelder of Chicago came with his son Paul who is a Senior, a fine student from a genuine western home. This evening Mr. Frothingham preached a really remarkable sermon in Appleton Chapel, and Prof. Peabody afterward spoke of it with deep feeling to me; but I had to talk to Pres. Eliot on Wellesley business and our department of Music and could not see the minister to tell him how good he had been.

I had an hour afterward working on the Fellowship papers.

Monday, March 19, 1900

GHP

Prayers. Then to Secretary's Office to see about students for whom I have been finding places. Forenoon given to study. Two visitors come in from the West.

It being my birth day today & I becoming 58, my sister Emily comes from Boxford & is with us at luncheon & dinner. After luncheon I go to Boston for some errands, reaching home by 4 o'clock when my seminary on Hegel is held in my library. I become much tired in the long debate which goes on till much after 6 o'clock. After dinner the ladies go out to a public meeting, while I rest at home with newspapers, study, & letter writing — five letters today & four calls.

AFP

This is my husband's birthday - fifty eight. He doesn't like a celebration, particularly as Monday is a busy day, but his sister Emily comes this morning to pass the day with him, he has had a great many flowers sent to him, the Lanes and Mr. Morse and his relatives in College to call, and the luncheon and dinner he likes best. What else can we do on Seminary day?

This morning I had for four hours the Committee on the award of the Fellowships. We have succeeded in reducing the number to three, among whom we must still decide. In the meantime I stopped for an interview with Miss Luce for whom I am trying to get a College position, and a delightful call from Mrs. Severance of St. Paul and her sister.

I took the 2 o'clock train for Wellesley with Mrs. Scudder where we were to pour the tea and coffee at a reception and art exhibition.— a great success. Miss Hazard announced the Rockefeller promise of $100 000 ! Reached home to find Mrs. Lane and Will here, and then the birthday dinner !

At 8 o'clock Emily, Mr. Morse and I went to the Atlanta University meeting at the Colonial Club, and heard Mr. Chesnutt read from his stories, and Robert Smith of Texas tell of his work among the negro farmers there. Dr. McKenzie, Dr. Bumstead, Prof. Cummings and I spoke for Atlanta, and refreshments and an hour's talk followed. an interesting meeting, and very full in spite of the rain. Mr. Smith spoke more effectively than any one else I ever heard on the southern question, and Mr. Chesnutt's stories, when he kept to the negro dialect, were perfect. He does not read well enough to make his regulation short story better than any others of white people — but his sense of humor is delicious as he reads.

Note

Atlanta University (in Atlanta, Georgia) was one of several schools started in the South soon after the Civil War to provide educational opportunities for "Negroes." This university opened in 1869 with the help of the American Missionary Association, the Congregational Church, and the Freedman's Bureau. The first four-year students from its College Department graduated, with B. A. degrees, in 1876.

Horace Bumstead, white, Yale class of 1863, joined the faculty in 1875. By the time he became the second president of Atlanta University in 1888, the "institution had gained academic respectability in educational circles." The university was threatened, however, by "extreme racism" in the South and by serious financial problems, so that Bumstead lectured widely in the North, seeking moral and financial support for the school. He was called the "Apostle of Higher Education of the Negro."

Bumstead argued that "since the North had been instrumental in emancipating the slaves and bestowing citizenship and the elective franchise upon them, it was the responsibility of the region to save the nation from the dangers of an illiterate and degraded vote in the South." But this responsibility, he went on, "was accompanied by a glorious opportunity. It is the privilege, as well as the duty of the North, to further the work of Southern education. Lawlessness, insecurity of life and property in the South, proceeding either directly or indirectly from the presence of an illiterate and degraded population, constitute just so much limitation on the possibilities of the profitable investment of capital which the North is ever seeking to enlarge. All these hindrances the North can largely remove,by judicious investments in the work of Southern education."

Atlanta University had many sympathizers in Boston and Cambridge. In 1890, for example, a committee of prominent citizens, headed by Phillips Brooks, Rector of Trinity Church, circulated a letter "to the Friends of Atlanta University." The letter, "which appeared in many newspapers in the North, explained the beneficent work whch the University had done and was doing, and that its acute financial crisis was largely due to its refusal to recognize the color line in the admission of students. An institution that was willing to stand on such a principle . . . deserved the most generous support."

Other meetings in Trinity Church in behalf of Atlanta University, were addressed by George Herbert Palmer in March 1894, and by Charles William Eliot and William DeWitt Hyde in February 1896. And at the university in Atlanta, in 1894, Julia Ward Howe addressed the students and told them "how she had written the *Battle Hymn of the Republic.*"

Alice Freeman Palmer was involved in various missionary activities in the 1890s. She was a member of the American Board of Commisioners for Foreign Missions and President of the Woman's Home Missionary Association. As her husband wrote, she found in this work "a happy blending of her religious, charitable, patriotic, and educational aims."

Regarding the question of the education of negroes in the South, Mrs. Palmer remarked that "some of the women of Boston should go without, if necessary, the next Easter Bonnet, and give the money for scholarship in Atlanta University." In April 1895, both she and her friend, Julia Ward Howe, became vice-presidents of the Atlanta University Alumni Association.

Even before the March 19, 1900, meeting at which she spoke in behalf of this university, several of her March diary entries related to missionary activities: "writing for sustaining members for Atlanta University and planning for missionary meetings in New York in April" (March 3); "interview with the principal of a colored school in S. C. and her plans for raising $4,000" (March 9); and "This evening it was so cold that I did not face the fierce wind with my cough, and go to the great meeting in behalf of Atlanta University at Trinity Church as I had planned — I am a Vice President of the Boston Organization" (March 11).

And three other diary entries related to Fisk University in Nashville, Tennessee, another school for negroes: "An interesting interview from an agent of Fisk University to get me to speak at a public meeting for them in April, and help them raise money" (March 15); "Mrs. Howe promises to speak in my place for Fisk Univ." (March 17); and "Another College President this morning, this time of Fisk University. The great meeting is well arranged for next Sunday night. It is fortunate that Mrs. Howe would speak instead of me, for we decide to go to Boxford Saturday to stay till Tuesday" (March 29).

Alexander McKenzie and Edward Cummings, both liberal clergymen, were interested in social problems. McKenzie was devoted to

Hampton Institute, an early college for negroes, in Hampton, Virginia. On yearly visits, he taught and preached at the school. In 1895 Atlanta University had consulted Cummings, who was also a sociologist, when it was planning a "systematic and thorough investigation of the conditions of living among the Negro population of cities."

Judging from Mrs. Palmer's comments about the meeting, Charles W. Chesnutt's stories counterpointed the more serious presentations. Age forty-one, a negro who was so light that he could have passed as white, largely self-educated, Chesnutt was a prominent author, educator, lawyer, and legal stenographer. He had learned that "the former slaves remained interesting subjects to people in the North." A recent (1993) editor of a volume of Chesnutt's stories, writes: "In the tradition of *Uncle Remus* the conjure tale listens in on a poor black southerner, who recounts in a strong dialect a local incident to a transplanted northerner for the northerner's enlightenment and edification. But in Chesnutt's hands the tradition is transformed. No longer a reactionary flight of nostalgia for the antebellum South, the stories . . . celebrate and at the same time question the folk culture they so pungently portray, ultimately conveying the pleasures and anxieties of a world in transition. Humorous, heart-breaking, lyrical, and wise, these stories make clear why the fiction of Charles W. Chesnutt has continued to captivate audiences for a century."

In 1929 the Atlanta University Affiliation was established, with Atlanta University for graduate studies, and Morehouse College and Spelman College for undergraduates.

Sources: Clarence A. Bacote, *The Story of Atlanta University, A Century of Service, 1865–1965* , Atlanta, Georgia, Atlanta University, 1969. **GHP**-57, page 250. Harvard University Archives, biographical files of McKenzie and Cummings. Frances Richardson Keller, *An American Crusade, The Life of Charles Waddell Chesnutt* , Provo, Utah, Brigham Young University Press, 1978. Charles W. Chesnutt, *The Conjure Woman and Other Conjure Tales* , Edited and with an Introduction by Richard H. Brodhead (Housum Professor of English at Yale University and Dean of Yale College), Durham, Duke University Press, 1993.

Tuesday, March 20, 1900

GHP

Prayers, Study, Lecture, errands, fill the morning. After lunch another lecture, then a long call from Amen, Principal of Exeter Academy, wanting advice about problems there. I afterwards call on Mrs Lane before Faculty Meeting 4–6.15. Then with my wife to Boston to dine at the Touraine with the Severances.

AFP

This is Pres. Eliot's sixty sixth birthday and the Crimson comes out with a special Eliot number in the preparation of which we have been much interested. I take it in to Mrs. Eliot after Emily Palmer went, and join her in plans for furnishing the Brooks House, and in talk of our husbands' birthdays. So the morning went with more calls, and flowers, and then I went to Mrs. Münsterberg's stately ladies' luncheon. The long table was laid in the library, and a very sumptuous luncheon was served. I had to leave on rising from three hours at the table, for my own "at home," which was very pleasant today as many kinds of agreeable people called, with many interests.

Then we went to dine at The Touraine with the Severances, and heard of the Washington situation from which they had just come. He is close to many public men, and reports an impossible condition of disruption over the Porto Rican bill. The whole northwest republican forces are in rebellion against McKinley's weakness, and there is good hope of saving the country from disgracing itself and breaking all our promises to Porto Rico,— in spite of the President and Ohio.

Wednesday, March 21, 1900

GHP

After Prayers morning given to business connected with Philosophy Department, with Brooks House, & to half a dozen letters. In the afternoon I make two calls & work on my evening Lecture. This comes at 8 PM in the Noble Course, on the relation of Ethics & the Fine Arts. Every thing in the room was occupied. I walked home with Pres. Eliot afterwards & found company awaiting me.

AFP

Letters, work for the Naples Table, talks with students who want positions took the morning. At 1 o'clock Mrs. William T. Sampson and I lunched with Mrs. Merriman to make final arrangements for the invitations to the Spanish meeting April 6th. Afterward went to Mrs. Pickering's reception at the Observatory, and Mrs. Agassiz's at Radcliffe, and made plans to take Mrs. Agassiz to the College Club to see the girls by themselves without other guests. She has been too ill to keep her engagements to go twice, but now is stronger. Made final plans for the meetings, speeches, etc in New York the last week in April.

Went to the third Noble lecture at the Brooks House; the audience larger than ever, and the lecture better. Half a dozen people from

Boston came home with us and sat awhile to talk. Then wrote letters about new Dean of Women at Brown whom I had urged for place.

Thursday, March 22, 1900

GHP

Morning given to Prayers study & lecture. E. L. Bradford my minister in Boxford called to tell me of perplexities in his parish caused by slanderous stories against himself, set in circulation by a woman of no character. I tell him that the church is too strongly attached to him to allow such stories to be reckoned of any consequence. He says half a dozen of the prominent men think they had better visit the woman & order her to stop, but they know they cannot talk. They have accordingly sent him to ask me to go with them & be their spokesman. I promise to go a week from Saturday.

Lecture in the afternoon, then I must call on Mr Rieber who, as I am informed by letter, has declined the Headship of the University School in Cleveland which for a month past I have been trying to secure for him. In an hour's talk I persuade him to go out & inspect the school before declining it.

On my return Prof Hanus comes in, feeling that his Department of Education has been slighted by the Department of Philosophy — a frequent trouble — & I must spend an hour in appeasing him & making the points of divergence clear. Then I dress & after dinner with my wife go to the German Play in Sanders Theatre. — Iphigenie in Aulis — & to the Reception at Pres. Eliots afterwards. Letters

AFP

Many letters, and business after breakfast! The W.C.T.U. of Somerville sent to have me come to talk at a public meeting in behalf of the Curfew Law, but I persuaded them to get lawyers and public men to speak, especially in regard to the results of lawlessness among the boys, and the causes.

Then I went to Boston to see Mrs. Roger Wolcott and interest her in Mrs. Gulick and Spain, finding her more kind and wise than usual, if that can be. Coming home I found our dear "little minister" from Boxford here to talk of the possibilities of raising the money to repair the village church, and we sent out for builders to come and consult for he is lame. He went at 3 o'clock and I read over Goethe's Iphigenie auf Tauris before hearing it, and worked on my address for tomorrow instead of going to the N. E. Woman's Club or to Miss Hazard's reception.

The German play this evening was unexpectedly strong and beautiful.

The setting admirable, and the acting fine. Iphigenie was noble and stately, and we went to the reception given by Pres. and Mrs. Eliot afterward in great spirits. All the invited guests were there, and I had good talks with Pres. Schurman of Cornell, with Mr. Hale [?] Scenary [?] of the Peace Conference at The Hague last summer, — and guests from other Colleges.

Friday, March 23, 1900

GHP

I rise early & catch the train leaving Boston at 7.30 & breakfast with my brother, Fred, in Andover. He has been sick with a cold this week. Reaching Cambridge again at 11.30 I call on Mr Rieber, & then write six letters, till lunch A student calls on me afterwards. I get a little study. Go to the regular Friday afternoon reception at the Brooks House. Pres. & Mrs D. S. Jordan of Leland Stanford University — dine with us & spend the evening. Two other calls.

AFP

Miss Borden came from Boston before breakfast with news from Mrs. Gulick and her efforts to raise money for the College in Spain. More than $70 000 is promised. Miss Hazard had been spending the night with Mrs. Agassiz and came from nine to ten o'clock on Wellesley matters and to say Good bye, as she leaves tomorrow on her tour through the Wellesley Clubs. Then orders for a dinner party, letters, three calls, and the noon train for Gloucester where I lectured at 2.30 to the teachers and parents of the City on "What shall we teach the children?" A little reception afterward, and the 4 o'clock train for Boston, reaching home at six.

Pres. and Mrs. Jordan of Leland Stanford Jr. University came at 6.30 to dinner, and we have had a most interesting and delightful evening with them, he so big and strong, and brave; she so dainty and exquisite and sweet.

Saturday, March 24, 1900

GHP

Prayers, a morning of study & lecture, & a call from President Jordan. After lecture in the afternoon I go to Boston to consult lawyer, L. K. Morse, about the case of Mr Bradford of Boxford. Mr Morse & I walk home to Cambridge. Evening given to drawing up list of courses in Philosophy for next year. These I send to the Chairman of the Committee of the Faculty at night.

AFP

I had to rise early to go to Mrs. Eliot's and Mrs. Merriman's to arrange finally for the list of patrons and patronesses for the big Spanish meeting in Boston, before seeing the printer at 9 o'clock. Then I called on Mrs. John Graham Brooks who has just returned from Chicago, where she has been ever since her splendid boy of fourteen died two months ago. She looks like a withered flower, and said "I have come back to try to make the house beautiful again for Mr. Brooks and Lawrence, but I don't know where to begin !"

Pres. Jordan came in with Clifford Moore, bringing pictures of Stanford,- full of talk, until he had to go in town to meet Miss Luce to whom I telegraphed. He thinks he may want her to come out to California to teach English.

As soon as he had gone I went to Mrs. Farlow's for a consultation on the Wellesley gymnasium which must be brought up to better condition immediately. This afternoon we have had another meeting here on the award of the European Fellowship having decided to give it to Miss Williams of Knox and Barnard Colleges now studying in Paris Romance languages; but there are so many good candidates that we are going to try to raise another Fellowship and send Miss Trueblood of Earlham and Michigan, in Mathematics.

I had so many letters waiting that I have given up other things to write to five College Presidents about teachers, and answer letters about lecturing during the spring. We have today sent $200 to the fund to pay the Wellesley debt, and the alumnae are begging us to ask others for money ! There will be no rest until Mr. Rockefeller's gift is secured !

Pres. Eliot came in this evening to talk of the Wellesley Prof. of Music whom we are trying to find. He offers to help in the Spanish meeting, and the Forestry speech.

Sunday, March 25, 1900

GHP

A large part of today I have been reading Spinoza's Ethics, which I had not read consecutively for many years. Three of our boys were here at dinner. I also wrote eight letters, had a bicycle ride, & went to the College Chapel in the evening, where Rabbi Hirsch preached.

Among my letters was one to Mr Gillis of Boxford, warning him that we proposed to investigate whether he is selling liquor contrary to law. Last summer we detected and drove out of town Mr Bodge of the Hotel Placidia, who had been keeping a bar in a town which had voted for no-licence.

AFP

I did not feel well this morning, and so have spent the day very quietly, and read Janice Meredith through,— a much talked of revolutionary novel, very good for taking up and going straight through on some off day, or a long journey. Four students came to dinner and the last left at four o'clock. Then more students and Mrs. Pickering to talk of the Friday Teas at the Brooks House for next year.

This evening we went to Appleton Chapel and heard Rabbi Hirsch of Chicago University, whom I knew there. The Chapel was crowded, chiefly by Jews — a most strange and foreign Harvard scene, — and the long sermon, over-rhetorical and eloquent, matched the company. But it was a Hebrew prophet's basis and appeal, and most characteristic and interesting. We had a pleasant talk with him afterward, and then I came home and finished my novel.

Monday, March 26, 1900

GHP

Prayers & then a morning of Study at the end of which I ride to Boston on my bicycle for a call. One of my former students calls to ask me to write a Preface to a new volume of his on philosophy. Another comes to report about a College which has offered him a place. Further study, then my Seminary 4–6. The Seminary today was visited by Mrs. Dr Fitz, one of my best students at Radcliffe four years ago. Evening study & two student callers.

AFP

A bleak day, with snow coming on in the middle of the afternoon. I went out only for marketing and errands, and have written hard all day except when called down stairs by business. Two callers about saving the White Mountains as a National Reservation, and three in regard to positions for next year. — College woman. Fortunately two are willing to go into secondary teaching.

Made up my report as Treasurer for the annual meeting of the Assoc. for maintaining a woman's table in Naples, which meets at Bryn Mawr April 11 & 12; wrote many letters, and addressed three hundred envelopes for the Spanish Girl's College meeting April 6th. The lists have to be made up as I go, from this whole vicinity, so I have taken it in hand personally, and laid everything else aside.

The stormy day and night made it easier to give up the College Club, and this evening's lecture on the Transvaal question. And Lucy Sprague is not strong yet, so I postpone the invitations for another week. But I must have extra entertaining in April and May, as soon as the extra work of the Noble lectures is over.

Tuesday, March 27, 1900

GHP

Study and lecture till 12 o'clock. Till lunch time busy with furnishings at the Brooks House. Lecture after lunch. Then a walk, study, & two

18

Placidia, who had been keeping a bar in a town
which had voted for no-licence.
26 Prayers + then a morning of Study at the end
of which I ride to Boston on my bicycle for a call.
One of my former students calls to ask me to
write a Preface to a new volume of his on
philosophy. Another comes to report about a
College which has offered him a place. Further
study, then my Seminary 4–6. The Seminary
today was visited by Mrs Dr Fitz, one of my best
students at Radcliffe four years ago. Evening
study + two student callers.
27 Study + lecture till 12 o'clock. Till lunch time
busy with furnishings at the Brooks House. Lecture
after lunch. Then a walk, study, + two calls—one
of them from Prof. Hanus who seems disposed to take
my advice about the counsel he is to announce. In
the evening I get a good deal of time for study, but a
student calls + then Prof Münsterberg to talk of students
coming up for their degrees.
28 After Prayers Pres. Morrison of Fairmount College,
Kansas, is at my house by appointment to see about
engaging Dr Sawey, one of my graduates, as an instructor
next year. He decides to appoint him. Then comes
Pres. Barrows of Oberlin College to see about finding a
Dean of his Women's Department. Much of my morning

George Herbert Palmer's diary entries for March 26, 27, and 28, 1900. The photograph does not show the horizontal lines nor the margin line for the date column which is one and three-eighths inches wide in the original diary.

calls — one of them from Prof. Hanus who seems disposed to take my advice about the courses he is to announce. In the evening I get a good deal of time for study, but a student calls & then Prof Münsterberg to talk of students coming up for their degrees.

AFP

We woke this morning in a fairy world; every twig was heavy with damp, clinging snow, which lay thick enough every where to transform every thing. The trees in the College Yard were exquisite, and the sun came up at eight o'clock. By noon it had all gone, like a mysterious dream.

Charles Talmage was shut up in his room all day yesterday with grip, but crept out and spent the morning here, staying to luncheon. These days seem to be given to students and teachers, and schools wanting teachers.

This afternoon and evening I was very busy with guests — "at home" day bringing them. Mrs. Kimball, our dear friend, has returned from the south, and came to stay all the afternoon. Other Boston friends came, and Mr. & Mrs. Frothingham of New Bedford. A good many students, and a fine college woman from the west. a Prof. of Mathematics. She wants a Fellowship to study in Göttingen, and a beautiful Radcliffe girl, wanting to teach in Boston instead of New York where I can find her a place !

Wednesday, March 28, 1900

GHP

After Prayers Pres. Morrison of Fairmount College, Kansas, is at my house by appointment to see about engaging Dr Savery, one of my graduates, as an instructor next year. He decides to appoint him. Then comes Pres. Barrows of Oberlin College to see about finding a Dean of his Womens Department. Much of my morning is taken by my list of Elective Studies which is returned to me by the Dean in proof & which is to be brought before the Faculty for approval on Tuesday. I am obliged to call on Professors Royce Münsterberg & Santayana & secure their approval of changes in it.

I get a few minutes for work on my evening lecture, (the Noble Series), on the relations of Ethics & Religion, when President Hyde of Bowdoin appears & stays to lunch. William Lane, our Harvard Librarian, also lunching with us. Hyde consults me about two books on which he is now engaged. The rest of the afternoon, after he goes, I get for work on my lecture. My sister-in-law from Andover comes to dinner, & my lecture — with a very full house — is at 8 o'clock. Several people walk home with me, my wife going for an hour to a

Reception of the Cantabrigia Club, while I get a little time for reading.

AFP

This has been College Presidents' Day ! At nine o'clock came Pres. Morison of Fairmount College in Kansas. While he talked in the library about getting Dr. Savery to go out to teach philosophy, I had Pres. Barrows of Oberlin, who had come at the same time, to talk of Miss Luce for Dean of Women there. He wants her very much, and Wellesley will lose another able teacher. After Dr. Barrows left I went to Mrs. Durant's in Boston to discuss this, and the raising of the Wellesley fund, reaching home only in time to meet Pres. Hyde of Bowdoin and Mr. Lane at luncheon. More books, new teachers at Bowdoin, new libraries, new theology, to be discussed. Alas ! the week is too full to hear Mr. Hyde's lectures on Browning !

Then letters to the Trustees of Wellesley on business and at 4 o'clock I went to town again to the Reception of Gen. & Mrs. Lorring in Otis Place. They have taken a little house on the water's edge, and rebuilt it until it is like a fairy's bower, with a marvellous view of the Charles and Corey Hill in the distance.

I got home to find Mary Palmer from Andover here to dinner. We talked afterward while I dressed for a reception. Covered up long red velvet and lace with a big cloak, and went together with four friends from Boston who joined us to the ~~sixth~~ fourth Noble lecture. The hall was more crowded than before, and it went very well. When Mrs. Noble comes on next week the course and the audience are sure to give her pleasure. After the lecture I spoke to many people, — Anson Phelps Stokes, Jr. our new Wellesley Trustee was especially warm about the lecture and several ministers thanked me ! and a Harvard Freshman said "Prof. Palmer's talk is like a music box." When I looked surprised, he said, "It's the perfect way he does it, and just as easy !"

I escaped after that, and took the car to the Newtowne Club in North Cambridge, where Cantabrigia was having her annual "Gentlemen's Night." Over six hundred were there, and the Pres. & two Vice-Presidents (I am one) stood in line, and shook hands, after the musicale, — just closing as I arrived at 9.30. Then supper and dancing followed, all very brilliant. I came home soon after eleven.

Thursday, March 29, 1900

GHP

A hard morning of study & lecture. At 1 o'clock comes Professor Marcou to see what we can do about raising a subscription to protect

Prof. Sanderson who has been getting deeply into debt & is now in danger of losing his home. I advise him to ascertain the facts more exactly & see if our efforts can be of permanent use. Then lecture, at the close of which one of my men (E. P. Carr) who is offering himself for a Ph.D. degree this June, call to tell me he is broken down & must withdraw, going to his home in the South. I am very sorry. I then call on Mr & Mrs Rieber, who have been hesitating about accepting the headship of the great Cleveland School & explain matters more fully to them. They agree that he shall visit the School next Tuesday. Dr. Savery, for whom I have been trying to secure a place at Fairmount College (he is one of my assistants this year) calls to tell me has had a formal offer & has accepted. He will marry & take his wife with him. Dr. Stoops, for whom I last year obtained a position in a small Ohio College, calls to tell me of his success there. I give the evening to seven letters & some other writing.

AFP

Charles Talmage was here again this morning and to luncheon. He is slowly growing better, but is blue because letters from home say that Ella is in bed with the grip. As practically everybody is, he must only be more courageous and busy.

Another College President this morning, this time of Fisk University [Erastus Milo Cravath, 1833–1900 (September)]. The great meeting is well arranged for next Sunday night. It is fortunate that Mrs. Howe would speak instead of me, for we decide to go to Boxford Saturday to stay till Tuesday. Those blissful days we shall have among the woods, planning the garden, trimming the vines and shrubs, and rejoicing in the first birds. At 2 o'clock Mrs. Merriman came and before five we had finished preparing five hundred invitations for the mail. I had them all addressed and stamped. If the wealth and fashion of Boston and vicinity do not turn out to help the Women and girls of Spain to an education next week, we can do no more. At 5 o'clock I went to Vespers, crowded full of young men and women. It is a splendid sight, and on the whole a reverent company, though some ill-bred couples always talk right through the superb music. Today Dr. McKenzie preached — more eloquent and sentimental than usual, but they listened perfectly.

I worked through the evening, promised to be patroness to three Society Plays — the Hasty Pudding, Pi Eta, and D.U. — so I am trying to dispose of tickets; wrote Mrs. Noble at length about the lectures and her visiting us next week. —had a long interview with Dr. Folsom about the health of Lucy and her invalid sister Nancy at Andover, and then wrote a long letter to the [Sprague] family in southern California; began the effort to raise another Fellowship for Miss Trueblood, wrote letters about admitting Mt. Holyoke, Brown and the Univ. of Illinois to the A. C. A. and then George and I carried our mail, and the five hundred invitations to the post office, and disposed of everything and had a walk in the mild spring night.

Friday, March 30, 1900

GHP

To Boston after Prayers, calling on Robt T. Paine to discuss with him the inscriptions I have written for the tablets to be set up in the Brooks House. Then to the office of Wadsworth Longfellow, the architect of Brooks House, to consult about the material & lettering of the tablets. Together we go to see some tablets & to see a maker of them.

Some study before lunch & after; then 3–4 Committee on the Brooks House meets; 4–6 my Seminary, brought forward from Monday afternoon when I am to be absent from Cambridge; 6–6.30 Professor Peabody gets me to walk with him for consultation on difficulties in the administration of Brooks House. In the evening I write four or five letters and draw up a paper for an hour examination in Phil. 1b. the History of Philosophy. Two calls from students.

AFP

This morning the thermometer was 38 while we were dressing, with no wind and a feeling of spring in the air. All ~~the~~ day the men in charge of the College grounds have been trimming our shrubs and trees, and carrying off great piles of rubbish. The flickers and robins are scolding about the house — and Boxford tomorrow !

The Chairman of our Vacation Schools Com. came to plan our closing report, for it is now decided that the City takes the schools and supports them. Then came the discussion on what colleges should next be considered for admission to the Alumnae Association. These committees and letters with calls from three students filled the morning.

I went to Mrs. Joseph Russells to luncheon in honor of her sister-in-law, Mrs. Gilpin of Wilmington Delware, whom I once visited. About twenty ladies were there, in the beautiful old house, and it was a delightful three hours. Mrs. Russell is charming, and I had good talk with Mrs. Vinton, the beautiful wife of the artist, Mrs. Harry Russell, and many others.

At 4 o'clock I came back to the Brooks House, where I promised to be again from 4 to 6 o'clock as this was the last Tea of this season. It was a very full day, one hundred and seventy five coming, and several notables among them. Ex. Gov. Wolcott and John Fiske were centers of attraction, and the Pres. was there all the afternoon. We all feel these afternoons have begun with astonishing success, and have formed a new source of good and pleasure in Harvard life. But it is exhausting work, and kept me away from the Archaeological meeting where I should have been in town this afternoon, and left me unwilling to go out again this evening to the Graduate Clubs of Radcliffe and Harvard, before whom Mrs. Julia Ward Howe spoke, and had a reception.

But there are so many different things I wished to do tonight that it is only left to decide to stay at home and work. Dean Briggs and Mr. Hurlburt walked home with me and rejoiced over the Teas, and confessed their anxiety over the Vesper services, or rather the careless manners that follow.

Saturday, March 31, 1900

GHP

Leave my examination paper at the printer's on my way from Prayers & find at home Pres. Morrison of Fairmount College waiting for me. He gets from me the names of some persons to whom he may apply for subscriptions in order to raise a salary for my boy Dr Savery. A student then calls to consult about his employment for the Summer. I then get to work on my 11 o'clock lecture, after which I give the dealer orders for a carpet at the Brooks House. Professor Hanus calls at lunch time to see about the mode of announcing his courses on Education.

Lecture at 1.30, & I catch the 3 o'clock train from Boston for Boxford. On board it are my wife, Lucy Sprague, & my two servants. We are to have two days at our happy country home, although bound on an unhappy errand. A woman in the parish has been circulating foul stories about our adored minister E. L. Bradford. Half a dozen leading men of the parish are to call on her Sunday afternoon & wish me as their spokesman. So we all go.

At the R. R. Station, 2 miles from our house, our carriage meets us. I however prefer to walk & on the way stop at Mr Bradford's house to learn where I am to meet the other men. Then I call on my sister, now living in the village, & see the beautiful dog I sent her on her birthday. Fires are burning everywhere in our house. Though the day is gloomy & cold, within all is warmth & cheer. I wind the clocks, put up the hangings, go to the well for fresh water, & after supper we three have a game of dominoes. Then warming the beds with a warming pan, we all go early to sleep.

[Sections on Boxford and 11 Quincy St., which appeared here in the Diary, are presented with his Autobiographical Sketch in chapter 1]

Business of the Month

My chief occupations in Cambridge this month, outside my regular work of lecturing, have been connected with the Brooks House, with my position as Chairman of the Division of Philosophy, & with the Noble Lectures. Of these last I have probably spoken sufficiently already. This is the first year in which a connected series has been given. I give six on successive Wednesday evenings, in the hall of Brooks House, on the general subject of "Ethics in its relations to the neighboring provinces."

The Phillips Brooks House has been put in charge of an Administrative Committee of five, of which I am one. The House has been opened this year & we are feeling our way along in furnishing it. To each member of the Committee certain portions are assigned. For these he orders the furniture, with frequent consultation of the taste of his colleagues. Besides other smaller matters, I have entire charge of the two Committee Rooms & of the tablets to be placed in the Entrance Hall. The inscriptions for nearly all these latter must be written by me. Nearly every week our Committee must meet & report progress. There are many puzzling questions connected with the use of the building — what societies shall meet there & what shall be the nature of their rights. I have approved of allowing no smoking in the building, in order to mark off the contrast between it & the proposed new Club Building — The Union. I want to keep this House for the higher, the more domestic, sorts of hospitality — that where woman's presence would be appropriate — leaving the more familiar & less ennobling forms of comradeship to find a lodgment at the Club. This is also the view of the majority of the Committee. One member has very violently advocated the cause of the smokers.

As Chairman of the Division of Philosophy, much work falls on me, in finding positions where my graduate students who ~~have just~~ are about to take their higher degrees may begin to teach. The number of possible positions in Philosophy is small. But last spring I found places for eight men. Much correspondence is necessary, & the heaviest part of the work comes at this season of the year. At this season comes too the preparation of the program of courses of study, which is announced in June for the following year. My own Department, though made up of men singularly unlike in temperament & character, is a very harmonious one. We are all friends. Yet it is inevitable that there should be some difference of judgment about the policy of the Department. Traces of such differences will be found in my record. But they are friendly differences & take away more of the Chairman's time than of his temper. One of our Department, Professor W'm James, is now on his Sabbatical Year of absence in Europe. He was intending to give this Spring his first course of Gifford Lectures at Edinburg University. But he has been ill & will be unable to undertake it till a year hence. He is therefore to have another year of absence. Professor J. Royce was absent six weeks in order to give his second course of Gifford Lectures at Aberdeen. That University has announced that it will confer on him the Degree of LL.D. in June.

AFP

To our horror it was snowing when we opened our window blinds this morning, but we refused to give up Boxford, and were rewarded in seeing the clouds and snow disappear by noon.

All the morning was very busy. Pres. Morison of Fairmount College came again to have us help him in raising money and we gave him names. Miss Hopkins of Brookline called to place articles on Girls' Education in Spain for next week in the papers. I saw Mrs. Eliot about the monthly Teas of the Faculty wives which I must miss today; Mrs. Farlow about a great meeting in May in behalf of money for the Students Aid Society of Wellesley; Mrs. Merriman on the Spanish meeting, and speakers for the meeting to preserve the White Mountains from the lumbermen and their waste of the forests; several students came, and a dozen letters and notes had to be written, but we got off at 2 o'clock and reached this blessed haven of peace at 4.15.

The day had grown mild, but there is little sign of spring in the grass or trees. A few big brown butterflies have come out in the sun, and robins, bluebirds, song sparrows, chickadees, crows, and winter birds of other kinds can be seen and heard. The run and brooks are very full of shining amber-colored water, the wind is out of the west, the sky is spring blue, and a tiny calf is in the barn. "I rose and looked out of my window, and Lo ! it was spring !"

We stopped to see Emily Palmer and Miss Allen on the way through the village, and rejoiced with them over their Collie, already learning new tricks, and a charming companion. The rest of the daylight went in investigations of the whole place inside and out, and after supper we three played two games of dominoes, and so felt the full joy of idleness, far-away-ness from work and Boxford leisure. Then we pushed the warming-pan through the beds, and are put into them at 9 o'clock for twelve hours of solid sleep, knowing that we have two whole days of woods and silence ahead !

Chapter 5

The Chronicles

from March 1900, annotated

1900

GHP

<u>Additions to Boxford</u>

Muslin Curtains for Library Spare Room & A's room
Spare room bed redressed
Preserve Closet built in back shed
Pink & Blue Bed Spreads
Pearsons Field ($500) Fencing, Stepping Stone, & Bars ($40)
Made Cathedral or Lion Path & cleaned all old ones
Coal stove for Library air tight for Chamber
Stone underpinning of S. E. corner of house relaid
New sill for this part of house
New Platform in front of dining room windows
New Flower Box over Porch
Pearson's & our walls relaid, stiles, bars filled ($18.00)
Dec. coal stove for blue chamber

Permanent Additions
65.45

Oct. Charles & Ella Talmage settle at Barre, Mass. $1200, without house

Eric Palmer goes to Ashville School as Teacher of Math & Physics [see pages 166, 169] he having during past summer taken [long blank space] as pupil ($300) to New Brunswick & New Foundland

Nov 27–Dec 3 Boxford Thanksgiving

Dec 21–Jan 3 " Christmas Recess At Fred's in Andover on Xmas Day[Note 1]

Dec Fred Freeman has daughter, Estelle

Note 1900

1. During this Christmas Recess, Mrs. Palmer wrote a poem to 21-month old Anna Morse (**AFP**-12). On Christmas Day, either before or after their visit to Andover (about 7 miles from Boxford), Professor Palmer wrote to Professor William James who had begun to talk about retirement from teaching:

"Dear James, —

. . . My thoughts go back over the long years of our association — twenty-five years I think they must be — and I recall the first time I ever saw you, as you entered the railroad car somewhere near Beverly, accompanied by a dog or two. I did not then know your name, but was introduced to you shortly after. Then came my fight with Bowen over your proposal to offer a course on Spencer. And soon your marriage and my first sight of lovely Mrs. James, sitting on a low stool in the window of your rooms on Harvard Street, when I made my wedding call. These were the days when you used to visit my course on Locke, the days when you encouraged my Readings in Homer, the many hours of comradeship and difference in Department meetings, chance walks, calls at each other's house. We began at opposite poles, you in anatomy [William James graduated from the Harvard Medical School in 1869], I in divinity. Perhaps in that early time each was narrow. I know I distrusted you and thought you ought to dislike me. But how steady the growth of confidence and affection has been! Hardly anybody in Harvard has given me so much as you. . . "

James replied from Rome on February 1, 1901:

"Dear Palmer, —

Your letter written from Boxford on Christmas Day was one of the pleasantest things I ever received, coming as it did from an eye as unused to flow (at least in outward show of lachrimosity) and a tongue as sincere as yours; and speaking of the past in a way that made of it a gold framed picture; and emblazoning my character as 'twere a figure on historic tapestry; and treating my lack of training for my profession as if so chosen, by a deliberate stroke of genius; but above all, dear Palmer, by its straight words of recognition of me as a valued co-worker and of affection from your heart. From a man as critical minded as yourself and as absolutely frank when truths are bitter, such expressions have more significance to a fellow than you yourself can probably comprehend, and your letter will surely form one of the brightest features in the 'archives' to be handed as a legacy to my children. . . " (Ralph Barton Perry, *The*

Thought and Character of William James, Briefer Version, New York, Harper & Rowe, 1964: page 323-324).

1900-01

GHP

Lectures

Oct 28 Preach at Wellesley Forgiveness

" 26 Worcester Teachers Association Qual. of Teacher 50.00

Nov. 10 Margarets School Waterbury Ct
Miss Hillend " " " 50.00

" 14 Medford Teachers Institute School as Eth. Instr. 20.00

" 16 Wellesley Phil. Club — Henry Sidgwick

" 20 Boston Kindergarten Assoc Qual of Teacher 25.00

Dec 14 New Bedford Normal School " " " 25.00

Jan 5, 12, 19, 26, Feb 2, 9, 16, 23 (Saturdays, 11 A. M. & conference from 12-12.30) University Lectures under charge of Education Department Twentieth Century Club at Lorimer Hall Tremont Temple on The Nature of Goodness [The stenographer's reports of the last five lectures are in the AJL Collection] 400.00

Same Dates, course repeated in afternoons at State Normal School Providence R. I. 350.00

Mar. 2, 9, 16, 23, 30, Apr 6, 13, repeated at State Normal School Fitchburg, 7 Lectures 2.45 PM 250.00

Feb 1 Harvard Chapel Forgiveness

Feb.12, Radcliffe English Club — Church of Brou Arnolds[Note 1]

Jan. 26. Preach in Appleton Chapel — Forgiveness 50.00

Feb. 19. Mod Lang. Conference, Harvard, Church of Brou

Mar 24 Preach Dartmouth Incarnation 40.00

Apr 8 Harv. Relig. Union — Shaksperes Sonnets

" 23 Jamaica Plain Womans Club — Herbert 30.00

" 26 Vassar Founders Day Teaching 100.00

" 30 Newburyport Womans Club — Homer 25.00

" " & May 7 Abbot Academy — Ideals of Conduct 50.00

May 14 Wheaton Sem. Divisions of Philosophy 25.00

" 22 Harvard Xn Assoc. Jones Very

June 5 Rye Seminary — Patience 50.00

" 6 Hackley School — College Ideals[Note 2]

" 21 Mansfield High School, Self Cultivation in Eng Poetry 50.00

" 24 Hyannis Normal School — Teaching 50.00

" 25 Bridgewater " " " 50.00

" " Class Supper

" 27 Φ.B.K. Impromptu Harvard Expansion

July 2, 3 & 5 Harvard Summer Schol Theology — Agencies of Redemption 75.00

1800.00

Sept 15 Boxford Pulpit Holy — [?]

Jan. 15 — Jacob P. Palmer dies in New York at the Hotel Chelsea, 222 W 23 St He being the head of the diamond department of Tiffany & Co's store. The funeral was at Boxford on Jan. 17. conducted by Fred & me.

Jan. 17 Alice goes to N. E. Hospital for Women & Children, Dimock St., Roxbury, & is operated on for hemorrhoids, remaining there till Jan. 29, then having nurse at home for a week.

Jan 23 Emily & Miss Allen take apartment in Andover

Mar 19 Eleanor Wellman goes to Adams Nervine after six weeks stay at Andover

Mar. 22 Send accounts to C. Sidney Shepard of my work in spending $1500 given me by him for furnishing rooms in Brooks House [see his diary, pages 195, 197]

Apr 13–22 April Recess at Boxford. Plant 19 trees & shrubs 4 vines. Put down new straw matting in Dining room Library Porch & Blue.

May 24–June 3 At Boxford

June 12–29 Alice goes to 10th Anniversary of Chicago Univ 25th of graduation at Ann Arbor[Note 3] & visits Saginaw

June 29 Move to Boxford

Notes 1900–01

1. This French church is in the Burgundy region, near the east-central border of France, 45 miles west of Geneva, Switzerland. "The monastery of Brou, near the gates of the town of Bourg, is a magnificent example of the transition from the Flamboyant to the Renaissance style . . . the richness, dynamism and exuberance of its design and its sculpture cannot fail to excite the enthusiasm of connoisseurs of the style. Its sculptors seem to have defied the laws of matter and gravity by blending sculptures in the round, high- and low relief with unequalled audacity. The church and its treasures are the result of a vow made by Marguerite de Bourbon [1457–1482] and accomplished by her daughter-in-law, Margaret of Austria [1480–1530]. Magnificent white limestone façade, a luminous nave, stone rood-screen, seventy-four oak choir-stalls (1532) and three tombs of which the most beautiful. . . is that of Margaret of Austria, white marble retable of the Annunication in the chapel of

Sainte-Marguerite. and stained-glass windows in the chapel, are among the treasures of the church. The regional museum of the Ain department has been installed nearby in the monastery buildings, which have a fine cloister dating from 1506. The whole of the architecture here is of the 16th century, without a single exception" (Pierre Tisné and Laurent Tisné, trans. by Raymond Pudorff, *Guide to the Art Treasures of France*, New York, E. P. Dutton and Co., 1966: 316).

Palmer also identifies talks about the Church of Brou on February 19, 1901, November 18, 1901, and May 6, 1915.

The mention of "Arnolds" in this February 12, 1901 entry suggests that the Palmers were familiar with the long poem by Matthew Arnold (1822–1888), entitled The Church of Brou, and that Professor Palmer's presentation included his reading aloud from this poem. He was known for such poetry readings (121n6, 247n2, 255n1), and at least once he entered in the Chronicles that he had read from Arnold (225, July 21–Sept 1). Their library included volumes of Arnold's poems; the catalogue of the collection that he gave to Wellesley College lists 12 such volumes (**GHP**-93). Professor and Mrs. Palmer probably visited this church, a tourist attraction, during their 1895-1896 sabbatical when they bicycled in France (124n11).

Matthew Arnold's narrative poem, The Church of Brou, published in 1853, has three parts: The Castle, with 112 lines; The Church, with 40 lines; and The Tomb, with 46 lines (C. B. Tinker and H. F. Lowry, eds., *The Poetical Works of Matthew Arnold*, London, Oxford University Press, 1950). The first seven stanzas of The Castle help one appreciate how forceful a reading by Palmer might be:

> Down the Savoy valleys sounding,
> Echoing round this castle old,
> 'Mid the distant mountain-chalets
> Hark! what bell for church is toll'd?
>
> In the bright October morning
> Savoy's Duke had left his bride.
> From the castle, past the drawbridge,
> Flow'd the hunters' merry tide.
>
> Steeds are neighing, gallants glittering;
> Gay, her smiling lord to greet,
> From her mullion'd chamber-casement
> Smiles the Duchess Marguerite.
> From Vienna, by the Danube,

Here she came, a bride, in spring.
Now the autumn crisps the forest;
Hunters gather, bugles ring.

Hounds are pulling, prickers swearing,
Horses fret, and boar-spears glance,
Off! — They sweep the marshy forests,
Westward, on the side of France.

Hark! the game's on foot; they scatter! —
Down the forest-ridings lone,
Furious, single horsemen gallop —
Hark! a shout — a crash — a groan!

Pale and breathless, came the hunters;
On the turf dead lies the boar —
God! the Duke lies stretch'd beside him,
Senseless, weltering in his gore.

2. Professor Palmer's friend, Theodore C. Williams, was headmaster of the Hackley School. In **GHP**-82 (pages 15–16), Palmer writes: ". . . His scholarship, his interest in education and his influence over young men had always been so marked that when in 1899 it was proposed to found an important fitting-school for boys at Tarrytown on the Hudson, he was asked to take charge. In five years he built Hackley School from its foundations, acquiring land, constructing its beautiful quadrangle, filling it with students, and establishing such traditions of scholarship, manliness and simplicity as have not been surpassed by the oldest schools in the country. Pupils, teachers and parents joined in admiration and affection for him. But such work cannot be done without friction and fatigue. In 1905 he. . . laid down his work and took two years of recuperation in Europe." In her diary for March 5th and 6th (pages 165, 166), as Mrs. Palmer describes a visit from Williams, she writes, "He is full of boyish enthusiasm, and turns from a minister to a school master with a young poet's gladness and ease."

3. From the address by James Burrill Angell, President of the University of Michigan, at the memorial service for Alice Freeman Palmer: "I am glad to say that she ever manifested the most loving fealty to her Alma Mater. At our invitation she came repeatedly to deliver addresses to our students, and always to their edification and delight. Her last visit was at Commencement in 1901, when her

class celebrated its twenty-fifth anniversary. No one of the class entered with greater zest into the spirit of the occasion. I never saw her more buoyant and joyful. She was a girl again, the life and inspiration of the class. They selected her to respond for them to my call at the Commencement dinner. How I wish I had a copy of her speech to read to you here ! I never heard her speak more charmingly and pathetically. Wit, humor, reminiscence, affection for her classmates, gratitude to her Alma Mater, — all were there. Her voice was tremulous with emotion. Never have I seen her audience more completely swayed by her. . . " (**aboutAFPann**-5, page 40–41).

1901

GHP

In Boxford this summer were at Emily's Aug & Lily, Mrs. Wilkinson Katherine & Barbara Bertha with Mrs Thomson Alice Cheney & Henry for servants

In the Farm House C. D. Palmer

In the Allen House Th [?] Homer

In the Herrick House L. K. Morse

Fred & Mary were at Wellfleet for two months

Mr. Bradford attends Summer School in Cambridge sleeping at our house where were also Charles & Ella Talmage (he in Harv. Sch of Theol. she in in Boston Mission work) Eric in summer school, & Bertha there too, though going & coming

July 18 Our Boxford house struck by lightning in the ell & North room.[Note 1] $15 damage, paid by Insurance Co. We all in S. W. room unhurt

July 9 Began systematic writing on Noble Lectures [see 211n2]

" 25 Browning Readings in Chapel Th $3^{1/2}$-5 seven given

Sept. 9 Handed Ms of Noble Lectures to Houghton Mifflin [see 211n2]

Aug. 6 Shaved off side whiskers, worn for 25 years[Note 2]

Aug 26-Sept 9 Alice in N. E. Hospital for Women & Children, Roxbury, for second operation[Note 3, 4]

Sept 5 Trenched gravelled & ploughed meadow in my front field $260.00

Sept 6 Pres. McKinley shot

This summer made path from our stepping stones to Coles bars & cleared crosspath

<u>Additions to Boxford</u>

Matting on Lower Floor & spare room

Stoves Library spare Room & Back Room

Chair fr. Cambridge Library & Rocking covered

Old Chamber arm chairs covered
Hall papered
Back Entry & Servants & East Room pain'ed
Kitchen & Pantry painted
Vase for Entry & 2 Library Vases
Pillows for piazza & 1 for Lounge in Ding Room
7 pictures & frames
Rag Rugs (6) & Rug for Library fr Cambridge
Lamp for piazza
Umbrella stand
Repairs & Kitchen Utensils
Tablecloth for Alices Chamber

Total Additions
334.70

Oct 22. Moved fr. Boxford. Up to this date I went to & Fro
Nov 2–4 Boxford Sunday with Morse photographing
" 23 Saturday in Boxford cutting trees

Notes 1901

1. A hymn written by Mrs. Palmer has these lines: "Though the thunders roam at large, Though the lightning round me plays, Like a child I lay my head In sweet sleep upon my bed." The hymn appears on page 60, **AFP**-18, as The Tempest, and on page 9, **aboutAFPann**-5, Professor Palmer describes the circumstances related to this hymn:

"As she [AFP] lay ill at Boxford, lightning struck the house and destroyed the chamber adjoining her own. She seemed much interested in the novel event, as if it were something contrived for her entertainment. It did not apparently disturb her. No one knew that she had written about it, or indeed that she was in the practice of writing verse. After her death, among many other poems, this hymn was found with the date attached."

Palmer records [page 231] that lightning struck the house again early in July 1905, and "the cook was instantly killed in her chamber."

2. See the photograph on page 38. And Dorothy Elia Howells, *A Century to Celebrate*, Radcliffe College, 1879–1979, Cambridge, Radcliffe College, 1978, page 42, has a photograph of George Herbert Palmer, about 45 years of age, that shows clearly an extensive band of side whiskers and a bushy moustache.

3. In his preface to *A Marriage Cycle* (**AFP**-18), in which he publish-

ed forty-eight poems by Alice Freeman Palmer, George Herbert Palmer writes: ". . . [H]er longest periods of leisure came in two serious illnesses, greatly prized by her as opportunities for quiet, for study, and for writing. . . "

A small blue notebook, labeled No. 3, in the Wellesley College Archives (Alice Freeman Palmer: Poems 1900–1901), includes nine poems that she wrote during this hospitalization. She dated them and sometimes included the day of the week and another notation: August 26 (Monday, N. E. Hospital), 28 (In the Hospital), 29, 30 (Last Friday of Summer), 31 (Last day of Summer, N. E. Hospital), September 1 (Communion Sunday), 2 (Monday), 4 (Wednesday, Sunset), and 6 (Friday, In the N. E. Hospital).

Professor Palmer included two of these poems, with titles that he wrote, in *A Marriage Cycle*: The Poets (August 31) and The Present Heaven (September 4).

THE POETS

These are he poems he loves,
    These are the books he has read;
I turn them over and over,
    I lay them under my head.

Poems of love and of sorrow,
    Of hope, of parting, of pain,
But of love that knew no measure;
    I read them again and again.

Ah dear, if I were a poet,
    I would show you a woman's heart;
And you should be king in a country
    Where lovers never can part.

THE PRESENT HEAVEN

I lie and watch the great white clouds drift by.
As far above the earth as Heaven is high.
        "How far is Heaven?" I cry.

"As far as east is from the west, so far
Hath he removed" —Can any sun or star
        Measure that space afar?
But I know well that Heaven is near today,

And all the world is fair and fresh as May.
My heart's a child at play.

For love floods all my life, like a great sea.
Dear God, does Heaven hold more than this for
me,
Peace deeper, joy more free?

4. Alice Freeman Palmer was an early president of the Boston Society for the Protection of Italian Immigrants, organized in 1901.

"Agents meet all steamers both incoming and outgoing, bearing Italian immigrants, supervise the interests of the newly arrived at dock and railroad stations, investigate cases of detention, and help immigrants to find their friends. A woman agent accompanies to the church all immigrant girls who come to this country to be married, witnesses the marriage ceremony and files certificates with U. S. Commissioner of Immigration; also files certificates, duly viséd by the Italian counsul, in the native villages of the contracting parties, thus legalizing the marriage in Italy.

"The society secures, through the Italian counsul, transportation to Italy at a nominal sum for indigent Italians [who are denied admission to the United States], secures birth certificates for Italian minors for the purpose of registration in school or as a requirement for obtaining an employment certificate, recommends evening and continuation schools to newly arrived immigrants, works in co-operation with Boston Juvenile Court in the interest of Italian girls, and co-operates with various public and private organizations in the interest of Italians."

This society was incorporated in 1903, and in 1907 changed its name to the Boston Italian Immigrant Society.

In his *Life of Alice Freeman Palmer* (**GHP**-57), Professor Palmer remarks that she was known "to have uncommon adminstrative talents and entire readiness to place them at the service of whoever needed them. . . " As an example of how he learned about one such acitivity, he describes an incident when he was "in Venice in the summer of 1905. I needed help in a little Italian business. Learning that a certain lady might furnish it, I applied to her. She doubted if she had the necessary time. I pressed. Though she spoke no English, she said she had some acquaintance with America and began to inquire who I was. I reported myself a Harvard professor, but she remained obstinate. Incidentally I mentioned that my wife was formerly president of Wellesley College. Then all barriers went down. Was I the husband of Alice Freeman Palmer? She was adored in Italy. Poor Italians coming to America had been badly plundered. Attempts had been made in several cities to start a society for their protection, but with little success, until in Boston it had been suggested that Mrs. Palmer should head the movement. Then difficulties disappeared.

"I was obliged to say that I knew nothing of all this. Only two incidents connected with it could I subsequently recall. One day, in the year when she went abroad for the last time [1902], I picked up from her desk a circular appealing for the protection of Italian immigrants. Making some slurring remark about the absurdity of sending such things to an educational expert, I tossed the paper down. She was silent. A little later a letter came, addressed to her as president of the league for the protection of Italian immigrants. Then I broke into hot remonstrance. Was she, when already strained by. . . much else, so reckless as to go outside her province and take up something for which she had no special knowledge or fitness? She glanced up from her writing and gently said that I was taking things quite too seriously. She did not usually travel far from her own field, nor had she any idea now of giving important time to outside affairs. These people certainly were in a pitiful case, and some of her friends had asked her to lend her name for their aid. That was all. She might preside at a public meeting or two, but could give little attention to the matter. She never mentioned the subject again. How much she may have done I do not know today [this biography of Mrs. Palmer was published in 1908]. But three years after she had left our earth [December 6, 1902] I came on the tracks of her quiet good deeds in far-away Venice."

(Letterhead of Boston Society for the Protection of Italian Immigrants, that identifies Mrs. Alice Freeman Palmer, President; the back of this sheet was used by Gerge Herbert Palmer as a worksheet, in a volume entitled Notes on Herbert's Poems, in the Boxford Historical Document Center. *A Directory of the Charitable and Beneficent Organizations of Boston*, compiled by The Associated Charities of Boston, 6th edition, Boston, Old Corner Bookstore, 1914, page 46–47. **GHP**-57, page 254–255.)

1901–1902

GHP

Lectures & Articles

Nov. 11	Harvard Religious Union — Dogma	
" 16	Amherst College pulpit — Forgiveness	50.00

" 18 Prospect Union — Church of Brou
" 25 Brockton Teachers Assoc — Qual of Teacher 50.00
Dec 7 Milwaukee Harvard Club — Student opportunities for society [?] w Professors
" " " " Dinner — Power & Scholarly success of Harvard
" 6 Chicago ΦBK — The Glory of the Scholars Life
" 9 " Prayers — The aim at distinction
" " " Reception — George Herbert
" 10 " Philos Grad Students — Difficulties in early teaching of Philosophy
Jan 23-Feb 1 Bangor Theol Sem, 9 Lectures on Nat of Goodness 250.00
" 26 Central Ch Bangor Sermon on Forgiveness
Feb 8 Lasell Seminary Auburndale — Teaching 50.00
" 12 Wheaton Seminary Homer 25.00
" 16 Wellesley College Sermon Incarnation 20.00
" 14 Mrs Bullards Boston — Emerson Hall
Mar 23 Preached at Yale (Forgiveness) & Sheff Xn Assoc X-type o College 50.00
" 27 Harvard Vespers — Xs Youth & College Youths 25.00
Apr 11 Ohio State Univ. Columbus Large & small colleges
" " Columbus Harvard Club
" 12 Cincinnati Optimist Club College as assisting success
" 12 Harvard Club
May 5-10 (6 days) Conduct Prayers in Appleton Chapel
May 18 Dartmouth — 3 youthful aims in X's life (sermon)
May 25 Read Herbert & Vaughan at Wellesley
June 4 Brooklyn Heights Seminary — Maturity 50.00
" 10 Miss Mittleburgers School Cleveland English Poetry Study 50.00
" 11 Womans College Cleveland Objectns to Womans Education 100.00
" 18 Mt Holyoke College — Teaching 50.00
" 19 New Haven Normal Training School — Teaching 50.00
" " Naugatuck High School — Maturity 50.00
" 20 Worcester High School — Objections to going to College 50.00
" 23 Springfield High School " " " " " 50.00
" 26 Harvard ΦBK — Self Sacrifice[Note 1] [**GHP**-42]
July 1 & 2 " School of Theology — Defence of Dogma 50.00
1120.00

" 2 East Weymouth — Charge to E. L. Bradford
June 24 Class Supper on Eliot & Briggs
July 26 Midsummer Nights Dream read in Town Hall

" 27 Preach Boxford on 3 aims of X's growth
Harvard Union opened
Oct 6 Robert Herrick's baby Harriet dies
Nov. 1 This winter Emily & Miss Allen take the Marland house in Andover corner Chestnut & Central Sts
Nov 1 C. H. Talmage resigns church in Barre [Massachusetts] (one year) & takes church in Taunton [Massachusetts]
Nov. 17 Field of Ethics published [**GHP**-40][Note 2]
Dec. 3-13 Edwin Abbot Alice & I go to Milwaukee to attend Federation of Harvard Clubs.[Note 3] Stop also in Chicago & Saginaw. A remaining here a week
Dec 23 Give Alice amethyst pin
" 25 To Jean Mills Diamond ring — Jeannie gold watch
Feb. [1902] Agitation abt building Emerson Hall[Note 4]
Mar 14–17 In Boxford photographing
March 19 My 60th Birthday — Dept dines with me[Note 5]
Apr. 10 I go to Columbus & Cincinnati Harvard Clubs. Receiving there telegram fr. Alice th. she has started for Saginaw, her father being very ill. I meet her in Detroit & remain with her in Saginaw returning to Cambridge Apr 18. She remaining there till Apr 29 We thus lose Spring Recess at Boxford
May 22 Silver Wedding at Andover of Fred & Mary Palmer
May 26-June 3 At Boxford
June 15 Emery L Bradford leaves Boxford Parish for E. Weymouth

Notes 1901–1902

1. From Caroline Hazard: "I shall never forget one of the last occasions that I had the happiness to be in her house — the day when Professor Palmer delivered the Phi Beta Kappa Oration in Cambridge. Mrs Palmer had asked to lunch with her a company of friends, all of whom were her friends and Mr. Palmer's, but many of whom were quite unknown to each other, so that they instinctively formed little groups. The charming way with which Mrs. Palmer looked after each individual in that company was never more deeply impressed on me, drawing just the right people together and securing the pleasure of all her guests" (Personal Recollections of Alice Freeman Palmer, in Caroline Hazard, *From College Gates*, Boston, Houghton Mifflin Co., 1925, page 201).

2. As a memorial to the late William Belden Noble of Washington, D. C. (Harvard, 1885), in January 1898, Mrs. Noble gave Harvard University $20,000 to endow "The William Belden Noble Lectureship." [146n4] The terms of the annual lectureship required that

each lecturer deliver six to twelve lectures and that they be published. The lectures could include "philosophy, literature, art, poetry, the natural sciences, political economy, sociology, ethics, history, both civil and ecclesiastical, as well as theology and the more direct interests of the religious life." To choose the lecturers, Mrs. Noble selected Charles W. Eliot, William Lawrence, Alexander McKenzie, George Hodges, Francis G. Peabody, George A. Gordon, and Alexander V. G. Allen (*HGM*, 1897–98; 6 (March, 1898): 456–457).

In The Chronicles Palmer has five related entries: on June 1, 1899, he was notified of his appointment as the first lecturer, for 1899–1900; he delivered six lectures, on successive Wednesdays starting on March 7, 1900 [see numerous comments about these lectures in the diaries of the Palmers in chapter 4], and received a stipend of $600.00; on July 9, 1901, he began systematic writing of the lectures, presumably working with a stenographer's transcription; he handed the manuscript to the publisher, Houghton Mifflin Company, on September 9, 1901; and the book, titled *The Field of Ethics* (**GHP**-40), was published on November 17, 1901.

3. This was the fifth annual meeting of the Associated Harvard Clubs. At the end of the afternoon session, Professor Palmer, present as a guest, "complimented the delegates on their enthusiastic loyalty to the University, and gave an instructive account of the birth of the Harvard Union, its purposes, and its promises of usefulness. At the close of his talk three times three cheers were given for him, and three times three for Harvard."

In the evening he was a guest of honor, and his after-dinner speech was received with loud applause. He "spoke of the wonderful spread of Harvard influence throughout the land. He cited facts illustrating the great antiquity of the University, and then characterized it as the youngest of all our institutions, for none has the spirit of the modern age in a greater degree. He said he did not mean that Harvard had got quickly at the current fashions, but that she had made them, and had shown what are the new modes of advancement. It had set itself under matchless leadership, at the head of all educational movements in this country. He spoke also of the new building era at the University, pointing out the fact that the number of buildings added this year practically equaled the total equipment of an average sized college.

"The increasing interest in study among the students he instanced by some personal experiences of men who had arranged their courses without regard to the covenience of the hours. He defended the so-called 'snap courses' by saying they are as a rule the most valuable in the curriculum, being taught by men of genius, who are able themselves to impart so much that there is little left for students to obtain from text-books. Still he believed that students choose their courses by the question of how interesting they are, and not how easy they are, just as they choose their sports. The severest courses often have the greatest attendance, and from all classes of students.

"After touching on several other topics, he spoke in conclusion of a proposed memorial to Emerson in the form of a hall for the Department of Philosophy" (*HGM*, 1901–1902; 10 (March, 1902): 424–427).

4. "To supplement the work of philosophical instruction there had long existed at Harvard a demand for a separate hall exclusively devoted to philosophy. The actual movement for the attainment of this project began on the 23d of February, 1901, under the chairmanship of Hugo Münsterberg. It took its official inception in a letter of the Philosophical Division addressed to the visiting committee for philosophy and psychology appointed by the Overseers of the University. The committee members furthered the plan of the department for the building with zeal and devotion. It was the suggestion of Professor George Herbert Palmer in this undertaking that there should be associated with the proposed edifice the name of Ralph Waldo Emerson. After five years of effort the erection of such a hall, properly equipped at a cost of over $200,000, became fully realized. This noble structure, probably the earliest on record to be built solely for philosophical instruction, was opened at Harvard University on the 27th December, 1905, and bears the name of Emerson Hall" (Benjamin Rand, Philosophical instruction in Harvard University from 1636 to 1906, III, *HGM*, 1928–29; 37 (March 1929): 310).

Münsterberg's letter to the visiting committee, dated March 20, 1901, has this final paragraph: "We have sought whose name might give symbolic expression to this underlying sentiment of idealism and might thus properly be connected with the whole building. It cannot be a technical philosopher. Such a name would indicate a prejudice for a special system of philosophy while we want above all freedom of thought. It ought to be an American, to remind the younger generation that they do not live up to the hopes of [Harvard's] School of Philosophy if they simply learn thoughts imported from other parts of the world but that they themselves as young

Americans ought to help the growth of philosophical thought. It ought to be a Harvard man — a man whose memory deserves that his name be daily on the lips of our students, and whose character and whose writing will remain a fountain of inspiration. Only one man fulfills all these demands perfectly: Ralph Waldo Emerson. It is our wish and hope that the new, dignified, beautiful home of philosophy may soon rise as the moral and intellectual center of Harvard University and that over its doors we shall see the name: Emerson Hall—School of Philosophy" (Margaret Münsterberg, *Hugo Münsterberg: His Life and Work*, New York, D. Appleton and Co., 1922: 72-73. In her acknowledgment, the author of this book, Hugo Münsterberg's daughter, expresses "her thanks to Professor George Herbert Palmer for his inspiration, encouragement and suggestions,. . . " And Professor Münsterberg dedicated a book — **dedctdGHPann**-2 — to George Herbert Palmer).

Ralph Waldo Emerson (1803–1882): A.B., ΦBK, 1821; A.M., 1827; LL.D. (honorary), 1866; overseer, 1867–1879; lecturer on philosophy, 1869–1870; lecturer on the natural history of the intellect, 1870–1871.

5. On March 20, Palmer wrote: "Dear Dr. Münsterberg: . . . I was so overwhelmed last night with what you brought me that I am sure I did not adequately express my sense of gratitude for the thought and labor that brought it all about. It must have been an enormous task to communicate so suddenly with all my graduate students, to arrange for obtaining their photographs, and to present the results in such exquisite form. Nothing could please me more. And I am especially thankful that no gift from you, my colleagues, was attempted. And yet it makes me sore to think that this work should have fallen on you, just when you should have been resting yourself after the toils undertaken in another public interest [As chairman of the Philosophy Department, Professor Münsterberg led the movement for a building to house the Philosophy Department — Emerson Hall; see Note 4 above]. If I did not know how natural kindness is to you and how much refreshment you always seem to derive from it I should condemn Mrs. Palmer's exposure of my advancing years as a cruel mistake. But I have no heart for condemnation after so much enjoyment. I can only feel a tightening of ties that always have been dear and a desire to be more like the person my friends generously imagined me to be. 'You flatter me. But please continue' said the French lady. So I will say. Sincerely and gratefully yours, G. H. Palmer" (Münsterberg, *Hugo Münsterberg*, pages 78–79).

1902

GHP

May 23 Rex died, the Collie dog who has been with us since 1889[Note 1]

June 1 Removed Observatory fr 11 Quincy St

Commencement [President] Roosevelt visits Harvard[Note 2]

July 4 Moved to Boxford, letting Cambridge house, Sept 1, 1902–Sept 1, 1903 [when the Palmers planned to be away on sabbatical] to Edward Nixdorff & his mother for $1000, they to pay taxes & water rates

At Boxford this summer our two families are unchanged Alice & I, Jean Mills & Margaret Gaw (in place of Jeannie)

Emily, Miss Allen, Aug, Lilly, Mrs Wilkinson, Katherine Barbara Bertha & the dog Max

We have no man. Aug. has given the farm house to William & we hire him & his horse

The C. D. Palmers are in my old rooms
" L. K. Morses board with Mrs Magoun
Miss Allens house is let to the Davis family
Herricks " " " " " Baldwin "

Hospital

July 29–Aug. 15. My two previous operations for hernia were not successful so far as the right side was concerned. This healed only after long suppuration & remained weak. Last winter I concluded I had better have another operation before going to Europe, though I was advised that danger was unlikely for a year or two. As soon therefore as I was rested from the fatigue of the closing Term I went again to the Mass. Homœopathic Hospital, E. Concord St. Boston & was operated on by Dr Horace Packard, he coming from his vacation in Maine to attend to me. I was then put in charge of Dr Briggs, my chief nurse being Mrs Bertha Pinney [?]. I was weak when I went to the Hospital & weighed only 124 lbs, but everything turned out as well as possible. I suffered hardly at all, no pain in back or head. The wound was nearly four inches long & contained over 40 stitches of silver wire. But in just one week it was completely healed. My first movement of the bowels was on the tenth day by oil enema which took thirty hours to work.

During all but the first three days I was able to read & on the whole I did about as much literary work at the hospital as I usually do at home. Chiefly James' book on Religion [*The Varieties of Religious Experience*, published in 1902] & writing on Herbert. A fortnight from the day of the operation, I got out of bed & could at once walk across without a cane. Three days later I came back to Boxford with Alice, very comfortably, finding my strength but little impaired. I had actually gained 1/2 lb in weight. For five weeks afterward I gained a pound a week, although there was a steady sense of discomfort from the wire in the wound Dr Packard refused all pay. I gave $50 to the other assistants & for expenses. My Hospital expenses were also $50.00

Sept. 23 Anna Cleaveland marries Charles Loring

Sept 24 We sail from Boston on Leyland Steamer Victorian with Lucy Sprague & L. K. Morse

Dec. 6 Alice dies in Paris, being taken from 69 (now 67) Avenue Marceau where we had been keeping house to the private Hospital 23 Rue Bizet where she was operated on by Dr Henri Hartmann for intussusception of the intestine. This occurred on Wednesday noon. She died at 630 Saturday morning.[**Note** 3,4]

Dec. 20 Lucy Sprague & I sail for home from Liverpool on Leyland Steamer Armenian arriving Dec. 31. We go directly to Andover which becomes the home of us both until we begin work in Cambridge, Lucy on Feb. 2 I on Feb. 9 Lucy in the meanwhile spent a week in Chicago & I Dec 16–19 in Saginaw. Lucy in Office at Radcliffe.

Dec. 31 — Harvard Memorial service for A. F. P.

Feb. 4 [1903] — Natalie & Edward Nixdorff (mother & son) give me my Library, wash room, Lucys chamber & my meals, I paying $100 a month.

Notes 1902

1. Professor Horsford gave the dog to Alice Freeman, and the philosophy department at Harvard named the dog Rex (Jean Glasscock,*Wellesley College: A Century of Women*, Wellesley College, 1975, page 29. Page 478 has a picture of Rex).

Professor Palmer wrote about Rex: "I had a magnificent dog named Rex, who used to lie in front of the door & wait until I came out of the lecture room. He was most watchful, and never would he strike up an acquaintance with any one unless that person had been in my house & known me for over a year. As is the custom when a professor concludes a course, the students have a manner of applauding to show the teacher that they wish to acknowledge in a small way, his labor. They did this the last day. My dog, Rex, on guard outside, heard the uproar & thought something was happening to me, so as soon as the door was opened he dashed in, leaped upon the platform and put his paws here on my shoulders. And that didn't quiet the room in the least" (Wellesley College Archives box 2B1, from *New York Times*, June 24, 1932).

2. The citation for his honorary degree, LL.D., on June 25, 1902: "Theodore Roosevelt, President of the United States, from his youth a member of this society of scholars, now in his prime a true type of the sturdy gentleman, and the high-minded public servant in a democracy" (*HGM*, 1902–1903; 11 (September 1902): 82).

3. Scattered details in Chapter 14, entitled Death, in *The Life of Alice Freeman Palmer* (**GHP**-57), provide this description of her final illness:

"About the first of November" the Palmers left London and "crossed to Paris. During much of that month she was not ill, but was merely ailing. From time to time she was able to go about freely. . . between the attacks of seeming indigestion. . . " Three weeks before her death she went out for the last time [Saturday, November 15], "for an address at a girls' school [where] she was never more delightful."

"There followed. . . a week [November 15–22] under the doctor's charge with apparent cure; another [November 22–29] of fresh outbreak and of consultation with three eminent physicians, all perplexed. . . During her last fortnight [November 22–December 6] she lay most of the time, patient and interested, in the library, and had me read her two books which had just been sent. . . and when the Boston papers arrived, I must quickly discover the home news. . . A spasm of pain would overwhelm her, leaving her for a moment unconscious; then the eyes would unclose and she would say, 'There, that is gone, and what did they do on the School Board". . . To the last she did not lose that mental eagerness.

"On Wednesday of the last week [December 3] the doubtful doctors came early, and after consultation ordered an operation for that noon; they did not conceal from her that it would probably be fatal. . . " On Thursday morning, "her face was all aglow. . . [and] She reminded me of her two previous hospital experiences [see entries: Jan. 17, 1901, and Aug 26–Sept 9, 1901], but neither so satisfactory as this. . . With a gay smile [she said] that together we had pulled ourselves through many tight places, and we really might cheat the doctors yet." Then, "early on Saturday morning [December 6] the breath quietly stopped. . . "

"She died of a rare disease, intus-susception of the intestine ["the slipping of a length of intestine into an adjacent portion, usually causing obstruction"], a disease against which no precautions are possible. Its causes are totally unknown. Many physicians believe it to be congenital, and all those consulted agreed that nothing which she had done or left undone could in any way have hastened it. Of the many experienced surgeons summoned for diagnosis not one suspected danger till five days before she died. . . Yet even then so hardy was she that she came through one of the severest operations known to surgery [the surgeons probably established the diagnosis during the operation], lay painless and peaceful for three days [this suggests that her condition continued to be satisfactory on Friday, December 5], and would probably have survived had nature endowed her at birth with a full pulse [this statement is confusing and suggests that the immediate cause of death was some circulatory problem]."

4. From Paris, on December 12, 1902, only six days after Alice Freeman Palmer died, George Herbert Palmer wrote the following letter to Swinburne Hale, known as "Bobby" (copy of typescript, 2 pages, Houghton Library, bMS AM 1629–246). His parents and the Palmers were close friends; his father, William Gardner Hale, formerly at Harvard, was a professor at the University of Chicago. In the summer of 1897, Bobby and his parents had visited the Palmers in Boxford (Chronicle entry, page 126). At the time of this letter he was eighteen years old, a sophomore in Harvard College, class of 1905. As a student, he had undoubtedly enjoyed a close relationship with Mrs. Palmer, such as she described with other students in her diary for March 1900 (chapter 4).

"Dear Bob:

You will have heard the sad news. Within a month I shall be in America and can tell you all about it. You will want to know now that nothing more could have been done to save her. She had every care, and I looking back over the terrible course of affairs I can discover no point at which we might wisely have done differently. So there are no regrets. The disease — Intersusception of the small intestine — is excessively rare in adults, has little connection with previous conditions of health, its causes are quite unknown, and the chances of escape from death of anyone on whom it falls are very small. She went through the necessary operation well at the hospital, but two days afterwards the heart gave out and she was gone — gone with no pain and with entire peace, the sweetness and the courage that were always hers were with her to the last. And I sat beside her, holding her hand.

"But it is not for the sake of these useless details that I write.

Hereafter you shall learn from me whatever of them you care to know. But you loved her, and she loved you dearly. As she left the house for the Hospital, not expecting to return, she said 'Bobby will miss me.' Indeed I know you will. Probably this is the first great sorrow you have ever known. I want it to be a strengthening and not a crushing sorrow. Wordsworth writes after the death of his brother, 'A deep distress has humanized my soul.' And your own Arnold speaks of being 'ennobled by a vast regret.' Better still, Jesus tells his disciples, 'It is expedient for you that I go away.' So she wished that her departure should come to you with blessing, making your life not blasted but the more mature. Henceforth a charge is laid on you. You are endowed more richly than other men and cannot permit yourself to be unfaithful to her trust. That is the way I shall try to live, and I know you will join me in such honor to the one we love.

"For I am sure you feel as I do that any gloom or lassitude, any mere brooding over our own loss, would be to put ourselves quite away from her. She stood for gladness, energy, wide human sympathy, quick helpfulness, clear intelligence, sunny enjoyment of every moment, — no matter what it brought — for merriment even. We who are now called on to follow her, to express her spirit, and to carry forward the life that was so sadly brief in her, must — however sharp the pang of her absence — set to work to be cheerful, strong, widely helpful beings that she showed us how to be. Anything else would be an insult to her memory. She has given to us enormously. Let us think of that and not of what she cannot now give. We can live in her spirit and so do her honor. Whenever you fall into gloomy and brooding ineffectiveness, I want you to remember you are being unfaithful to her. Whenever on the contrary you tackle life energetically and heartily enjoy yourself in any worthy way, then you are loyal to her, her spirit is with you, and that blessing of God on you for which she ever prayed is becoming yours. Let thoughts of her steadily make you glad, gentle and strong.

Always affectionately
G. H. Palmer"

1903

GHP

Addresses & Articles

Dec. 20 Preached at Saginaw — Forgiveness
Feb. 22 " " Taunton — Childhood of X
" 24 Course on Nat. of Goodness begun at Wellesley
" 24, 25 Take charge of Prayers — Tones & Parables
March 29, Yale — Childhood of X, Sheff. Repentance (Shef) 50.00

May 3, Bradford Acad Vespers — Forgiveness**Note** 1
May 12, Andover Harvard Club Dinner
May 24, Reading of Comus at Norumbega, Wellesley
May I elected President Harvard Memorial Society [see entry 1905–6, May 29]
Lucy Sprague is living with Evelyn Livermore Prescott [a Radcliffe classmate] at 613 Riverbank Court the great hotel on the Charles River, Cambridgeport She is working in the Office at Radcliffe all the morning. On Feb 7 she began to take her luncheons here at the Nixdorffs.
March 22 James H. Lee dies in Rome of pneumonia**Note** 2
" Hedge at 11 Quincy St dies & is cut down
April 18–25 Fred, Mary, Lucy & I at Wellfleet
April 12 — Memorial volume published [**aboutAFPann**-5] Lucy & I at Boxford
May 10 Evening at Riverbank Court
May 12 Bertha Palmer marries Wm C. Lane Fred & Mr Smith performing service in Fred's Church Andover & I giving her away
May 13 — Lucy goes West
May 17 — I spend Sunday at Boxford, 1st nights alone there
May 28 — Move from Cambridge for a few weeks writing on Nat. of Goodness at Boxford Leave there June 9 for Cambridge
June 13, Sat. Take So. Pacific for Pasadena, stopping on way at Chicago & Grand Canon arriving 20. That day ride in the Arroya — Sun, Church & Georgie Caswell — Mon. books & Angel Church — Tues. Books & San Gabriella — Wed. Mt Lowe — Thurs. Los Angeles — Fri. Barrels, Sierra Madre 4 — Sat L's books, Eagle Rock — leave 6.45 A.M. Sun. night in San Francisco, Berkeley 9 a.m. Mon. Lecture 10
June 29-July 31 Lecture at Summer School Univ of California receiving $750 5 Lectures a week, besides 2 hours of questions a course of 6 Lectures on Freedom, a Greek Reading & an address to teachers, Harv. & Univ. Clubs 2 Lectures to Bakewells course
Aug. 21 Address before Phil Union on The Heart of Ethics (Self Sacrifice) [**GHP**-45] $250 for expenses
July 5–8 Sun.–Wed. Lucy in Berkeley Ride round mountain
" 25 At Monterey
Aug. 1–17 Prof & Mrs Bakewell Lucy & I to Alaska I paying Prof. B's passage in return for my summer board. We go by rail to Tacoma & there take Steamer Spokane $100 fare on steamer, 50 on rail
Aug 1 Lv. Berkeley 8 P. M. — 3. Portland 8 AM–3 PM — Tacoma 8 PM 4. Seattle 7 AM — 830 Sail, Victoria 3 PM — 6. Ketchikan 8 PM 7. Wrangel 7–830 AM, Tonka [?] Cannery 11, Juneau 8 P.M.

8. Skagway, 11–4. Haines Landing 5 PM, Davidson Glacier 7–10 P.M.
9. Glacier Bay too foggy, Hoonan Indian Village, Killesnoo 4–6 PM
10. Sitka 8–4 — 11 Treadwell mine, Juneau again Taku Glacier, Potlatch Indian Village, Fishing
12. Old Kazaan, Ketchikan again, Mittakalla [probably Metlakatla] 6–9 PM
14. Vancouver — 15. Seattle 7–9.30, Tacoma 11–3,[Note 3] Portland 9
17. Berkeley 9.30 AM — 19–25 at A. C. Miller's

Aug 25 10 AM Leave Berkeley — Saginaw 29-31 — Cambridge Sept 1

Sept 2 — At Boxford with Fred Mary & Eric, I writing on Nature of Goodness, Fred on X'n Church

Lucy Sprague at Univ. of Cal. Ass't in Economics & studying

Nov. 14 Nature of Goodness published by H M & Co [**GHP**-46]

Notes 1903

1. Bradford Academy, an advanced school for girls, founded in 1804, was in Bradford, Massachusetts, about seven miles from Boxford. With his talk there on Forgiveness (**GHP**-96), in May 1903, five months after his wife died (December 1902), and with his appointment as a trustee of the school from 1903 to 1924, George Herbert Palmer was continuing her important contributions to the Academy.

After many successful years, the general state of the school had declined as it had not adjusted to "modern conditions." By 1900, Bradford faced a crisis. In September 1901, Laura A. Knott, who had received the degree of Master of Arts at Radcliffe in 1897, became principal. While in Cambridge, Miss Knott had studied ethics with Professor Palmer and had developed "an enduring friendship" with Alice Freeman Palmer. Also in September 1901, Mrs. Palmer accepted an appointment to the board of trustees, although, at first, "some of the other members thought her well-known progressiveness dangerous."

Professor Palmer summarizes Mrs. Palmer's contribution to Bradford Academy during the year when it was "one of her principal cares": "During this time it passed from obscurity to a degree of public favor as great as it had ever known. Able men and women joined its board of trustees; its methods of study were modernized; its teachers were increased and their salaries raised; its debt was checked; it attracted as many students as its rooms could hold; and a way was prepared for the enlargement which has gone on since her death. In this case, as in many others, the remarkable results cannot be called hers. Many earnest men and women joined in producing them [for example, Lewis Kennedy Morse, the Palmers' close friend and the treasurer of Wellesley College, was treasurer of Bradford Academy from 1901 to 1918]. But wherever she came, earnest men and women were pretty sure to appear and to find such success in their undertakings as they had previously believed impossible [for example, from 1906 to 1910, the Reverend Frederic Palmer offered instruction in the Bible]."

Other entries indicate Professor Palmer's continuing interest in the Academy: on June 15, 1904; March 6, 1910; April 16, 1911; and May 6, 1915. Finally, he "gave a kind of valedictory, closing his trusteeship, at the Commencement of 1924. This was a short talk about Mrs. Palmer's own triumphs over hardships and about the help she had been able to offer the girls of the next generation."

(Bradford Academy is now Bradford College. Jean S. Pond, *Bradford: A New England School*, revised by Dale Mitchell, Portland, Maine, Anthoensen Press, 1954: pages 214, 236, 237. **GHP**-57, pages 252-254. Lewis Kennedy Morse, see 127n2. Reverend Frederic Palmer, see 71n1).

2. George Herbert Palmer and James Hattrick Lee, the one a graduate of Harvard in 1864, the other a graduate of Amherst in the same year, both interested in philosophy, first met when they matriculated at the Andover Theological Seminary in 1865. Lee, Palmer writes, "had just returned from the war with tastes similar to mine." "Theology and Philosophy were pretty closely identified. . . [and] the best opportunity for continuous study of Philosophy was in a Divinity School." They "formed a studious alliance [and] read Philosophy three hours a day." After graduation in 1867, Palmer and Lee were "lifelong friends."

Palmer has only a few scattered entries regarding Lee in the Chronicles: about their trip to Germany together to study philosophy in Tübingen and Lee's return in 1868; about Lee's son William rooming with the Palmers as a freshman in Harvard College, 1890–1891; about Lee's move to Hilliard Street in Cambridge, not far from the Palmers, in 1892; and about Lee's death in March 1903.

After he returned from Germany, Lee attended the Episcopal Theological School in Cambridge from 1868 to 1869, married the daughter of Amherst's President W. A. Stearns in 1869, and was ordained in the Protestant Episcopal church in 1870. Then he was away from Boston and Cambridge until 1892: from 1870 to 1884, as rector of three churches, seriatim; and from 1884 to 1892, as schoolmaster of a boy's school in New York state. From 1892, when he moved to Cambridge, he was principal of Milton Academy near Boston until the summer of 1902, when he "went abroad for rest and travel, and died of pneumonia in Rome, Italy, March 23, 1903."

Professor Palmer wrote this eulogy: "Throughout the nearly forty years during which I enjoyed Mr. Lee's friendship I found him steadily high-minded, unassuming and original. An unusual group of conflicting interests met in him, interests scientific, literary, artistic, religious and humane. He was as devoted to Homer as to physics, to wood-carving as to offering friendly help to awkward and tempted boys. He loved his pipe and his church, was as mirthful as he was serious. He had an old-fashioned way of counting his own advantage of little consequence compared with obligations of honor. His learning was certainly large, his industry extreme, his dignity impressive, and his power to manage and incite others remarkable. For all these qualities he was justly admired, as other teachers have been. What was rare was to find a man arousing such general admiration for his talents, and even a certain respectful awe for his person, who was at the same time so widely and profoundly loved" (**GHP**-104, page 20–21. Amherst College: Biographical Record, page 110; J. H. Lee's biographical file which includes Palmer's eulogy).

3. During this twelve-day cruise from Tacoma (August 3 to 15) the steamer sailed along the southeast Panhandle of Alaska, through the sheltered Inner Passage among the islands of the Alexander Archipelago. It reached Ketchikan, the nearest city in Alaska, on August 6, and Skagway, the farthest city, 1,000 miles from Seattle, on August 8.

In 1867 the United States had purchased Alaska from Russia for $7,200,000, and a boundary dispute with British Columbia was arbitrated in favor of the United States in October 1903, two months after Palmer's trip. The discovery of gold in the region of Canada's Klondike River late in 1897 led to the Gold Rush which was still going on in 1903; thousands of prospectors sailed up the coast from Seattle, landed at Skagway, and then made their way into Canada. U. S. territorial status and then statehood were in Alaska's future; in 1912 and 1959, respectively.

Today, in 1994, ninety years after Professor Palmer's trip, similar cruises through the waters off Alaska's Panhandle are popular in the summer. Tourists are attracted by "an unparalleled view of the terrain and wildlife. . . In an almost endless display, whales sound, porpoises frolic, and eagles soar. Mountain ranges draped with Sitka spruce, western hemlock, and yellow cedar jut thousand of feet above salt water; huge grumbling glaciers course back to the sea, where they calve icebergs of monumental proportions and bizarre shapes." From a naturalist with the U. S. Forest Service: "Almost everything in this part of Alaska was formed by glaciation. Some 10,000 years ago a massive ice sheet more than a mile thick blanketed all of the Southeast. As it advanced, it cut and gouged the land, forming the distinctive islands and canals, fiords and inlets that we see today. Right now we're in the midst of a 'little ice age' which began about 4,000 years ago. That's when the Juneau Icefield and the current glaciers began to be created. The Juneau Icefield and its glaciers form an expanse of ice nearly 2,000 square miles in extent. Thirty-five glaciers plow down from an elevation of about 5,000 feet, and some don't stop until they reach salt water; we call these tidewater glaciers"(Robert L. Breeden, ed., *Alaska: High Roads to Adventure,* Washington, D.C., Special Publications Division, National Geographic Society, 1976, pages 44, 48).

Numerous ten to fourteen-night cruises are available for the summer of 1993; rates range from about $1,300 to $6,000 per person (The Sophisticated Traveler. Ruth Rendell, *A Voyage among Misty Isles: Through Alaska's Inside Passage, with Binoculars. Bears, Sea Otters and Rare Lillies Abound.* The New York Times Magazine, part 2, May 16, 1993, page 96).

1904

GHP

Jan 16 Outlook article on A's Poems written Dec 4–11 [**GHP**-47]
Feb 3–10 Eric in Chicago
" 12–22 Journey to Chicago Lincoln Kansas City Saginaw
Apr 17–24 At Wellfleet with Fred Mary Eric Will & Bertha
Feb 11–May Silence
July 1 Move to Boxford with Fred & Mary Servants — Mrs Westcott & Mabel Morse in Farm House. Emily & Miss Allen in Miss Allen's House. Emily's house let to Roberts family
Fred Mary & I spend a week of July at Wellfleet. They another with Fraziers at Mt Desert & still another with the Tyers at Rockport I work all summer finishing Herbert & Fred also on his book We clear the Old Cellar & lay bridges on Brook Path
I get sofa, table & Riviese [?] for dining room also green table cloth & refrigerator
I have house shingled, East End clapboarded
East piazza shingled new closets upstairs

Front stair carpet — $10 kitchen supplies
Piazza beams strengthened.
July 21–Sept 1 Seven Readings on the Later Victorian Poets in Chapel on Thursdays at 330–near 5. Clough Arnold Morris 2 Rossettis Swinburne Patmore & in group Omar Henley & Kipling
Aug. 1 Mr Snell resigns Pastorate
L. K. Morse buys Pierson place
Sept. 22 Augustus E. Bachelder died in Andover — Sarcoma & heart disease
Sept. 19–27 Visit to St Louis World's Fair[Note 1] & Saginaw
Oct. 11 I appointed President Boxford Public Library
Dec. 24 Rev. J. [?] H. Willcox of Malden dies
Jan. 6 [1905] Gov. Wm Claflin dies
" 14 Put in telephone at 11 Quincy St
" 12 Jean Mills marries

<u>Lectures & Articles 1903–4</u>

Harv. Xn Association — Bible study — Oct 7
Wellesley College — X's Youth — Oct 11
Nov. 10 — Radcliffe English Club — Th. Traherne
" 14 — Nature of Goodness published — H. M. & Co [**GHP**-46]
Jan 16 — Outlook Alices Poems 50.00 [**GHP**-47]
Feb. 15 — Univ. of Nebraska Lincoln — Teaching — 150.00
" 16 — Kansas City — Harv. Club
" 21 — Saginaw Sermon — Incarnation
" 28 — Union Theol Sem — Church & Individual 50.00
Mar 2 — 20th Cent Club — Gifts to Colleges 50.00
Feb. 28 — Hackley School
May 2 — Emmanuel Ch. Girl students Youth of X 50.00
" 17 & 19 — In Phil V (Peabody sick) Social Organism
June 10 Haverford Coll. Herberts Love Lyrics ΦΒΚ 25.00
" 11 Hackley School Meeting Disappointment
" 15 Bradford Academy — Alice 50.00
Ï 26 Kings Chapel Incarnation 30.00
" 22 Danvers Normal School Teaching 25.00
" 28 Wellesley Commencement Alice[Note 2] <u>50.00</u>
" " Class Supper 430.00

President Harvard Memorial Society 1904–07 Set Stone Plan of Yard, Tablets on Hollis Stoughton & Holworthy, & put records of occupants in Hollis Stoughton & Holworthy

Notes 1904

1. Professor Münsterberg, a major participant in planning the Fair, had suggested that an international congress of scholars be included "as the living accompaniments to the material exhibitions." This suggestion was adopted with the theme of "The Progress of Man since the Louisiana Purchase" [by the United States from France on April 30, 1803]. "Many of the scholars. . . were quite absorbed in work and so contentedly settled that a long journey to the heat and swarm of St. Louis. . . would be a formidable prospect unless they were convinced that the undertaking was undoubtedly worth while. . . the 150 personal invitations presented in the summer of 1903 were rewarded by 117 acceptances for lectures in 128 sections of the program. . . The academic work of the Congress was accompanied by brilliant festivities that had for a background the magnificent buildings of the World's Fair" (Münsterberg, *Hugo Münsterberg*, pages 94–117).

2. This was also the twentieth reunion for the class of 1884, of which Alice Freeman Palmer was an honorary member. Professor Palmer spoke twice on Commencement Day: in the morning, "a sketch of the life and character of Mrs. Palmer"; in the afternoon, "again [he] spoke of Mrs. Palmer, more intimately and touchingly than it is possible to realize unless one could listen" (Wellesley College Archives: 6C/1884 class of 1884; Alumnae, badges, reunions (1885–1909)).

1904–5

GHP

<u>Lectures & Articles 1904–5</u>

Sept. 20 Indianapolis Teachers on Teaching	50.00
Oct. 11 Atlantic accepts Herbert as Religious Poet (Feb) [**GHP**-49]	120.00
Nov. 13 Weston Unit Church — Evil	25.00
Jan 10 Mod Lang Confer Harvard Herberts Technique	
Dec 24 Address on Dr Willcox at funeral [**GHP**-54]	
Feb. 2 Herberts Technique in Gayby's Seminary	
" 10 " Religious Verse Cong Lecture Course	100.00
" 13 Pacific Theol Sem — Cong Standpoint	
Mar. 13 Lowell Womans Club, Self Sacrifice	25.00
" 26 Andover Theol Sem Forgiveness, X's Temptation	50.00
Apr 2 Freds Ch. Andover — Teaching	
" 9 Old South Ch Boston Phil & Religion	100.00
May 7 Wellesley Chapel Are yu able to drink	25.00

" 9 Miss D L[?] Cafields School Evil
" 11 Dartmouth — School as Eth Instrument 35.00

May — Book plate drawn by Bruce Rogers ($25.00) & engraved by J Winfred Spencely $35.00[Note 1]
September Nellie Dougherty comes as servant

Note 1904–5

1. In **GHP**-79, page 19, Professor Palmer writes: "I have had my book-plate made small so as to fit books of even 32mo size" (see a photograph of this bookplate on page 229, and see page 454 for reference to its inclusion in an exhibit of work by Bruce Rogers). It is decorated with a scallop shell and two crossed branches of palm leaves. A letter is visible at the lower end of each branch; on the left, H, on the right, U, presumably indicating Harvard University. The Greek words mean 'I yearn for my country' (I am grateful to Nicholas Poole-Wilson for this translation from the Greek).

The bookplate of Frederic Palmer, Professor Palmer's brother, has similar decorations: two scallop shells and four pairs of branches with palm leaves (see illustration on page 229. This bookplate was found in a volume in Wellesley College, Special Collections — Hélene Vacaresco, *The Bard of the Dimbovitza.*) The fact that a "palmer" wears two crossed palm leaves or a scallop shell as a sign of pilgrimage or crusade to the Holy Land could explain the decorations on the bookplates of the two Palmers (Christopher Hohler, The Badge of St James, in Ian Cox, ed., *The Scallop Shell: Studies of a Shell and its Influence on Mankind*, London, 'Shell' Transport and Trading Co., 1957, page 49–70. Michael Mitchiner, *Medieval Pilgrim and Secular Badges*, London, Hawkins Publ., 1986, pages 41, 152, 271.)

"The legend surrounding [scallop shells] dates to the 10th century when a local [Spanish] knight who was fighting the Moors was forced to flee across a river. When he emerged, his body was covered with scallop shells. From then on, they became the symbol of the pilgrim. And, to this day in France, they are called coquilles St. Jacques — St. James's scallops" (Alan Riding, Spain's Saintly City of Pilgrims, Santiago de Compostela honors an apostle, *New York Times*, July 25, 1993, section 5, pages 1, 8, 9).

Scallop shells can also be seen on buildings at Wellesley College, and a 1875 sermon by Henry Fowle Durant is relevant. He viewed the Wellesley College plan as "a revolt against the slavery in which women are held by the customs of society — the broken health, the aimless lives, the subordinate position, the helpless dependence, the dishonesties and shams of so-called education. The Higher Education of Women is one of the great world battle cries for freedom; for right against might. . . It is the assertion of absolute equality. The war is sacred, because it is the war of Christ against the principalities and powers of sin, against spiritual wickedness in high places." Surely the scallop shell was an appropriate symbol of "this new crusade against darkness, chaos, and old night" (Florence Morse Kingsley, *Henry Fowle Durant Founder of Wellesley College*, New York, Century Co., page 238–241).

I found scallop shells at four Wellesley College sites:

1. Carved in stone over the north entrance to the old Music Hall (given by Mr. Durant and dedicated in 1880), now part of the Schneider Center.
2. Carved in stone over the windows to the right of the main entrance to Billings Hall, now also part of the Schneider Center. In an address at the opening of Billings Hall, on October 14, 1904, Caroline Hazard, president of Wellesley College, said: "High upon its eastern wall looking toward the morning sun is placed a cross-crosslet, the Jerusalem cross, [which is also visible high up near the south side of the back wall of the Schneider Center] and on its west front is carved the Palmer's shell. The mediaeval symbols have their significance to-day. Our ancestors left their homes to seek the earthly Jerusalem, the holy city. We seek it no less, not in some remote region of the word; but here and now we seek a better country even an heavenly [one], and we seek to plant it here where we are (Caroline Hazard, *From College Gates*, Boston, Houghton Mifflin Co., page 317–318).

   Three other volumes by Miss Hazard each have a large scallop shell stamped in gold under the title on the front cover: *A Scallop Shell of Quiet* (1907) and *The Yosemite and Other Verse* (1917). In the third volume, *A Brief Pilgrimage to the Holy Land* (1909), she writes: "So we landed under the shadow of Mt. Carmel, as some of my ancestors must have done, for the Crusaders' shell is the crest of my father's family."

   And Miss Hazard's own bookplate features a large scallop shell (see illustration of this bookplate in Glasscock, *Wellesley College, 1875–1975*, page 121).
3. Prominently displayed on a large bronze tablet just inside the Central Street entrance to the Hazard Quadrangle. As shown

Bookplates, actual size (see 227n1): Upper, the line border is used here only to show the all-white bookplate; lower, picture of Christ Church, Andover, Massachusetts (see 71n1).

on the tablet, the four dormitories were built during Miss Hazard's presidency (1899–1910): Pomeroy Hall, 1904; Cazenove Hall, 1905; Beebe Hall, 1908; and Shafer Hall, 1909.

4. Fourteen large scallop shells decorate the edge of the roof of the marble Whitin Observatory, also opened during Miss Hazard's presidency, in 1900 (see picture in Glasscock, *Wellesley College*, page 391).

In addition, Miss Hazard "built Oakwoods as her residence, and especially in it the design [that is, the scallop shell] was employed frequently — as Mrs. Ilchman [Dean of the College], her husband, and their two children who live there now [in 1975], have discovered with great delight" (Glasscock, *Wellesley College*, fn page 121).

In 1994 I can see no scallop shells on the outside of Oakwoods, and the current resident [Dean of Students] reports that none can be seen inside.

A relevant poem, entitled The Passionate Man's Pilgrimage, by Sir Walter Ralegh (or Raleigh), sixteenth century English poet, has been called to my attention by Minda Kutz and by Nicholas Poole-Wilson. The first stanza appears just before the Prelude in Miss Hazard's *A Scallop Shell of Quiet:*

Give me my scallop-shell of quiet,
My staff of faith to walk upon,
My scrip of joy, immortal diet,
My bottle of salvation,
My gown of glory, hope's true gage,
And thus I'll take my pilgrimage.

Blood must be my body's balmer,
No other balm will there be given,
While my soul like a white palmer
Travels to the land of heaven,. . .

1905

GHP

Jan. 25 Up to this date I have given all my time this year to putting my Herbert through the Press. It is now all printed in page proofs. I hand in Vol I for electrotyping take Vols II & III with me for final revision & set off California where at Berkeley Mrs C. H. Rieber is at work on a bust of Alice. I go by Overland Limited returning by Santa Fe. Reaching Berkeley Jan 30, I reach home Feb. 19 having had

16 days there. Lucy is keeping house at 1506 Euclid Avenue I have apartment at [Hotel] Cloyne Court $2 a day.

April 7 Margaret Lane born

May 17 D. C. French brings model for Alice's monument [see 244n5]

Mrs. Rieber sends her bust of Alice

June 6–Sept 26 In Europe with Fred Mary & Eric I to England & after a week there have a week in Paris with them, then three days with Fred on the Loire, a week in Geneva, 10 days in reaching Venice through Zermatt the Simpton Pass & Milan A fortnight in Venice, a week in Fiesole, when Fred Eric & I take a week for Rome Assisi & Perugia,when after a day or two more in Fiesole we join the Williams at Lucerne & go with them after a few days to Lymdelwald [?] Then after a fortnight Eric leaves for Spain & the Eclipse, Fred & Mary for Venice. A week later I go to Tübingen for 4 days when Williams join me at Huditburg [?] & after stopping at Cologne Ghent & Bruges we spend a fortnight together in London. Cairds too at Oxford.

1905–6

GHP

This summer $2400000 Fund for Professors at Wellesley raised

[undoubtedly, this entry refers to a "Teachers' Endowment Fund of over two million dollars," not at Wellesley but at Harvard, subscribed by graduates to make up a deficit (Samuel E. Morison, *Three Centuries of Harvard, 1636–1936*, Cambridge, Harvard University Press, 1937, page 365).]

My salary raised $500

Bertha & Will Lane take my Boxford house for July & August, the Morses having it during May & June while they are rebuilding theirs (Piersons) In early July it was again struck by lightning & the cook was instantly killed in her chamber [see 206n1]

The Nixdorffs continue with me this year

Emily & Miss Allen go in early October to Freds

Nov 3-6 I spend Sunday with Eric at Haverford & Monday with Bakewells at Yale where they have just come

This autumn Barbara French enters Waltham School for Nurses, instead of returning for last year & a half at Vassar. Katherine who graduated in June remains in Andover this year.

Christmas — I put $1000 in Savings Bank & give book to Bertha for Margaret Lanes Wellesley expenses

Feb 4-8 Journey to Saginaw

Put in Steam heat in Boxford 450.00 & refit the Library & dining room $600.00 Warren Cranston

April 10 Prof N. S. Shaler dies**Note 1** — J. M. Peirce 3 weeks earlier [see Note 3 below]
" 18 Great San Francisco Fire & Earthquake
May 29 Resigned Presidency of Harv. Memorial Society During my Presidency (3 years) we put up Diagram of Yard $650.00 tablets on Holworthy & Stoughton, Lists of rooms in Holworthy, Hollis & Stoughton
July 9 To Boxford with Fred & Mary writing Alices Life [see 237n3]

Lectures & Articles

Oct. 18 — George Herbert 3 vols Houghton Mifflin & Co [**GHP**-50]
" 16 & 23 Young Mens Hebrew Association E Concord St Introduction to Philosophy

Nov. 12 Wellesley The Lords Prayer		20.00
" 17 Hyannis Teachers	"School as Eth Inst"	40.00
" 20 Waltham School Committee	" " " "	25.00
Jan 26–Feb 3 — 7 Lectures at Yale on The Conscience**Note 2**		250.00
Feb 4 — Union Theol Sem N. Y. Faith & Ethics		50.00
" 21 — Christian Assoc. Dinner		
Mar 3 — Taunton Teachers on Qualif. of Teacher		
" 4 — " Preach Lords Prayer		
" 18 — Yale — Lords Prayer		50.00
" 28 — Miss Sanborns Somerville Read Herbert		
Apr. 10 & 12 Harvard, English 15, Lectures on Herbert		
May 13 Dartmouth Church Lords Prayer		25.00
" 14 " Philosophy Class Objections to Philosophy		
" 15 Wheaton Seminary Homers Odyssey		25.00
" 30 Memorial Day Two Speeches		50.00
June 3 Amherst Pulpit — Lords Prayer		50.00
" 2 Mt Holyoke ΦBK — Criticism		
" 10 Wellesley Vespers — Praise & Blessing		
" 20 Oberlin A Fortunate Life (Alice) [**GHP**-53]		100.00
" " Dinner Duty of Graduates		
" 24 Kings Chapel — Lords Prayer		30.00
" 26 Salem Normal Sch. Moral Teaching		50.00
" " Melrose High " Boy & Man		50.00
" 27 Harv. Commencement The 3 Dead Professors**Note 3**		
July 1 Saginaw Church Lords Prayer		
" 2–5 Three Addresses Agencies of Redemption		
Ypsilanti Normal College School as Eth Inst		200.00
		1015

Sept 16 Boxford Pulpit — Lords Prayer

Notes 1905–6

1. "This volume" (Nathaniel Southgate Shaler, *The Autobiography of Nathaniel Southgate Shaler*, with a Supplementary Memoir by his wife, Boston, Houghton Mifflin Co., 1909), Mrs. Shaler writes "can draw no more fitly to its close than with a paragraph [page 445] from a letter from Professor George Herbert Palmer, Mr. Shaler's neighbor and intimate friend for many years":

"Thank you for this delightful volume. All of Mr. Shaler's writing is highly characteristic. In every sentence of his one hears his voice. But I think he has nowhere more completely expressed himself than in this book. Here is his chivalry, his adventure, his public spirit, his perpetual humor, his wide sympathy, his profound religiousness. Through his escapade with Elizabeth, too, he has acquired ease in blank verse. So that he seems himself to be muttering these tales and setting his lips hard together after the climactic passages. How many such yarns has he spun to me in equally picturesque prose! Some of these poems, too, I had already seen. He brought them to me in manuscript, and in my ruthlessly critical way I pulled them to pieces and told him to go to work at them longer. Now they are precious. I long to tell him so and to say over the love and admiration which then seemed unnecessary. Fortunately he was big enough not to need our approval. I think he knew how many of us loved him, and deep within was glad. But the great powerful creature strode along his noble and independent path while we little fellows scrambled after, hardly near enough to make our delight in him audible. How large your companionship with him was your words in this volume, and elsewhere, show. Happy woman to have been so blest, and happy we who were allowed to know you both!"

2. "It was in the foregoing autumn that the Corporation of Yale University resolved to invite some Harvard professors every winter to speak at Yale 'to cement the friendship between the two oldest universities in the country.' President Eliot had made the opening address, [and] Professor Palmer had then held a series of lectures. . ." (Münsterberg, *Hugo Münsterberg*, page 135).

3. On Commencement morning Professor Palmer received the honorary degree, Doctor of Law. "There was less interest than usual in the conferring of the honorary degrees, for the reason that many of the recipients were almost unknown to the audience. The greatest enthusiasm was shown at the announcement of Prof. Palmer's name." President Eliot conferred the degree: "George Herbert Pal-

mer, for thirty years a Harvard teacher of ethics whose example has illustrated his teaching; a master of accurate and elegant style in both prose and verse, ennobled by intimate companionship with finest spirits." (*HGM*, 1906-07; 15 (September 1906): 54).

In the afternoon Palmer addressed the Alumni Association in Memorial Hall:

"Through you I may thank the University for its surprising and disproportionate honor conferred upon me to-day. I should like to tell you of the extreme happiness that comes to a professor. It seems to me it is one of the most delightful callings to which a man may turn, and I should like to explain it to you in detail, but the hour is already past for our closing. It is no time for a speech, yet I cannot leave, and I think you would not be willing to leave, without the mention of three beloved names who are henceforth to be but memories, Peirce [James Mills Peirce, Professor of Mathematics], Paine [John Knowles Paine, Professor of Music], Shaler [Nathaniel Southgate Shaler, Professor of Geology]. The year has been one unexampled in loss. Our President has rightly recounted to you all the great gains. These are severe offsetting losses, and yet in the career of these men I think we must see a type set to which professors hereafter should conform.

"It is often remarked that there is something injurious in a university atmosphere. There is a kind of intellectual terrorism there, for every one of us knows that at our elbow is somebody who understands a lttle more about any subject of which we treat than we ourselves do. That is not an atmosphere favorable for creative work; not an atmosphere favorable, it would seem, for originality.

"Now I think the career of these three men ought to be a mighty encouragement to all those who are pressing up into the glorious ranks of professors. These three were men of width. While admirable specialists in their field, they were men who looked far and wide and honored that field out of gains brought from every side. They were men of the world. Further than this, they were men who dared to express what they loved. They had eager interests, and those interests they were not ashamed of, and by directly moving along unconventional lines they have enriched this University, enriched the lives of hundreds of youths; in short, these men showed originality, and originality pays. It was because of their intrepidity in taking lines of scholarship that were unusual that they were carried to their high endings. In their departure, therefore, they have left a type and stimulus to all young men who are pressing on into these ranks" (page 70 in the source above).

1906–7

GHP

This year I teach each Monday Yale Seminary [see 233n2]

This winter Eric has leave of absence fr. Haverford & lives with me, hall bed room & Alices room

I am assigned seat of honor in Harv. Faculty — J. M. Peirce's [October 11]**Note 1**

Nov. 26 Eric becomes engaged to Helen Wallace**Note 2**

" 29 Thanksgiving at 11 Quincy without Em & Lily

Christmas at The Rectory — Helen Wallace with us

Jan 21–31 Course of Lectures at Kansas University

Visit Saginaw. Talk of Alice Freeman Palmer Homer

Feb. 11–13 Five Lectures Bangor Theol Sem

Feb 17 Emily J. Palmer died at the Rectory, Andover

" 22 Rosamond Lane Born

May 11 Quincy St painted in Colonial Style

June 4 Mrs Nixdorff & Edward go to Europe

June 19 Eric Palmer marries Helen Wallace in St Matthews Church W 84 St New York her mother there in an apartment 117 W. 79 St. he, his father, mother, & I spending the previous night at Manhattan Square Hotel W. 77 St They are to occupy 11 Quincy St this summer Eric going on with his Laboratory & Helen in Summer School

June 28 I move to Boxford, Mrs Jones & Mae in kitchen

Will & Bertha take Emily's house & build piazza

Fred & Mary with me for summer

I shingle & paint piazza. I finish Alice's Life**Note 3**

Buy fr Will & Bertha for $100 all land on East of Run My front boundry md [?] to move fr S. E corner S. to Cross path

Sept. Mary Moriarty comes as servant

<u>Lectures & Articles</u>

Nov. 18 Andover Seminary Lord's Prayer	
" " " Vespers Aim at Distinction	[for both] 50.00
Dec 30 Montclair Lords Prayer	50.00
Jan. 20 Atlantic article on Teaching [**GHP**-55]	150.00
" 21–31 Six Lectures Kansas Theories of Ethics Also Lds Prayer, College Temptations Odyssey Harvard & 4 miscellaneous talks	250.00
Feb. 11–13 Bangor 5 Lectures on Poetry & Life Attitudes twd Nat. of Homer Dimbovitza Barnes Keats Herbert with 3 additional speeches	125.00
" 24 Mt Holyoke College Lords Prayer	25.00

Mar 6	Mod Lang & Classical Clubs	Dimbovitza	
″ 20	Newburyport Womans Club	Arnold Ch of Brou	50.00
Apr 22	Jamaica Plain Womans Club	″ ″ ″ ″	40.00
″ 28	Yale Chapel	Death of Friends	50.00
May 19	Wellesley Chapel	″ ″	20.00
″ 26	Harvard ″	Lds Prayer	50.00
June 11	Ogonty [?]	On Growing up	100.00
″ 13	Harvard Seminary	Growing Up	50.00
″ 19	Miss Porter's Springfield	″ ″	50.00
″ 21	Willimantic Normal School	as Eth Instr	~~50.00~~
″ 23	Kings Chapel	Loss of Friends	30.00
			1090.00
	Yale Seminary in Ethics		1200.00
			2290.00

Notes 1906–7

1. Early in this academic year, Wallace Clement Sabine, Professor of Physics, was appointed Dean of a planned Graduate School of Applied Science at Harvard. "Professor George H. Palmer, diametrically opposed to many of Sabine's academic ideas, sent him these enthusiastic lines (October 11, 1906): 'My paper has just brought the announcement of this splendid appointment, and I am rejoicing, as all friends of the Scientific School must. What an array of qualifications you bring! — the highest scientific standing, administrative ability, interest in human beings, and acquaintance with schools. And what a delight to exercise such powers in constructing a vast, beneficent engine in a vacant field! To few men does such an opportunity ever come, and none of our colleagues could awaken such a confident assurance of success. I congratulate you, the School, and the public. Don't answer this, but excuse it as a burst of delight.'

"The Sabine family were perhaps as intimate with the George H. Palmers as with any friends, yet one of Sabine's closest associates in his college work expressed absolute incredulity when some one thus referred to their relations. Mrs. Palmer used to telephone Mrs. Sabine that her husband had 'stood it as long as he could without seeing Mr. Sabine,' and would invite them to dine at the Palmer house in Cambridge, or to spend the week end at Boxford. Teaching widely differing subjects, and viewing life from the standpoint of different generations [Palmer was 26 years older than Sabine], Palmer and Sabine rarely agreed on any subject. Mrs. Palmer once said laughingly that she believed they 'always sat in Faculty meetings holding hands and voting opposite!' As Professor Palmer himself expressed it, 'I, having been drawn to him on many important occasions, came away with a sense of permanent love'" (William Dana Orcutt, *Wallace Clement Sabine: A Study in Achievement*, privately printed, 1933, pages 164, 77–78).

2. Eric (Frederic Palmer, Jr.) and Helen Wallace were married on June 19, 1907. Frederic Palmer dedicated to them a humorous collection that he wrote for "The Christmas Festival 1907" (*The Ring and the Book*, privately printed, hardback, 35 pages, 1908; from a copy in the Boxford Public Library). In the poetic prologue, as the young couple are asking permission to marry, Reverend Palmer writes:

> Even Don Giorgio nods his "Yes, you may."
> "Who's he?" Well, well, my country friend! you have
> Still some o' the hayseed sticking in your hair.
> This Giorgio's Don, Chief, Head-man, what you will,
> Great Mumbo Jumbo of the Palmer Clan;
> Nay more, Floor-walker to the Universe,
> Whose each transaction must be first approved,
> Stamped, validated, by his signature.
> Things cannot happen till he gives the word.
> An Adam he, to whom the animals
> Must come — ox, fox, cock, seal o' the rocks -
> And whatsoe'er he calls it, that's its name.
> So when he said, "You may," the two breathed free,
> Jumped up and laughed and clapped their little hands,
> And straight gave orders for the wedding cake.

3. His manuscript of *The Life of Alice Freeman Palmer* (**GHP**-57) is in the Wellesley College Archives. He wrote in pencil on one side of $6x8^{1/2}$ inch paper with lines 1/2 inch apart. There are numerous changes. The sheets are in two volumes, bound in full leather. Stamped at the bottom of each spine: Written at Boxford 1905–1906. An undated, laid-in card reads "Christmas Greetings to Uncle George from Milton & Rosamond" [his grandniece Rosamond Lane Lord and her husband].

1907–8

GHP

April 1 [1908] Mrs Rieber brings Alices Portrait East & paints my portrait

" 15 My Life of Mrs Palmer published**Note 1** [**GHP**-57]

" 21 Mrs Nixdorff goes to Europe & Edward enters a New York Law office. Our Cambridge Connection Ends

May 12 Frederic Palmer 3d born at Andover
June 9 Chime of bells dedicated at Univ of Chicago to memory of Alice**Note** 2
" 20 I go to The Newton Hospital & am operated on for hernia on the right side — 4th time
July 9 Fred & Mary sail for five months in Europe taking with them the two Miss Williams
" 15 I leave hospital for Boxford where Theodore & Velma Williams spend summer with me, he engaged on his Aeneid, she on Italian Art, I on book of educational essays [**GHP**-65]. My house had previously been occupied for three weeks by Mrs Walmsley [?]. Bertha & family in Emily's Mr Morses closed, he in California. This summer A. V. G. Allen & Louis Dyer die
Eric & Helen at Andover, he working in Harvard Laboratory He appointed Dean of Haverford for coming year

Notes 1907–8

1. On April 20, 1908, Professor Palmer wrote to Anne Whitney, the sculptress, who had been a good friend of the Palmers (see 109n3): ". . . I am glad you like the book & find elusive Alice there. She is such a difficult creature to catch & imprison between two covers! And how angry she would be at my attempt! But if I can make more people love her, I shall not mind her wrath" (3P, Anne Whitney Papers, Wellesley College Archives).

2. The Alice Freeman Palmer Chimes were installed in the Mitchell Tower, which was modeled after the famous Magdalen Tower of Oxford. John J. Mitchell's contribution of $50,000 was used to build the tower. John D. Rockefeller's gifts to the University of Chicago included $5,000 for the chimes; his gifts totaled $34,702,375.28. "[I]t was arranged that every night, at five minutes after ten o'clock, the chimes should send out over the quadrangles the pleasing melody of the Alma Mater, indicating that the day was ended and the hour for rest had come."

Professor Palmer suggested the inscription for the tablet in the entry to the tower:

Joyfully to recall
ALICE FREEMAN PALMER
— Dean of Women —
In this University 1892–1895
These Bells make music

He also wrote an inscription for each of the ten bells (which ranged in weight and diameter from 600 pounds and 24 inches to 2,212 pounds and 51 inches; BCHSoc.): 1. A gracious woman retaining honor. 2. Rooted and grounded in love. 3. Easy to be entreated. 4. Fervent in spirit. 5. Always rejoicing. 6. Given to hospitality. 7. Making the lame to walk, the blind to see. 8. The sweetness of her lips increasing learning. 9. Great in counsel and mighty in work. 10. In God's law meditating day and night.

During the installation ceremony, Palmer read his wife's hymn, The Tempest, and music was then played on the bells. (Thomas Wakefield Goodspeed, *A History of the University of Chicago, Founded by John D. Rockefeller: The First Quarter Century,* Chicago, University of Chicago, 1916, pages 345–346, 497–498. Wellesley College Archives, Box 1DD2. See also **aboutAFPann**-16).

Walter Van Dyke Bingham, who had studied at Harvard and became an admirer of George Herbert Palmer, was receiving his doctorate from the University of Chicago at this time. He had an unusual role in the ceremony. "The Alice Freeman Palmer chimes in the tower not far from the assembly hall had been recently installed. Just as the great audience was assembling it was discovered that the organ was out of order. Walter was standing in the academic procession about to move toward the stage when the secretary of the president hurried up to him and whispered, 'Can you play the Convocation hymn on the chimes?' 'Never have,' said Walter. 'Do you think you could?' 'I could try,' he said. In a piece of speedy organization which could only be called sleight of hand, a relay of scouts was stationed at intervals from the hall to within sight of Walter who had scurried up to the top of the bell tower. At the proper instant the signal was passed along, the audience awaiting the opening notes of the hymn rose to sing, but instead of the customary peal of the organ the melody rang out from the newly christened chimes. The audience caught its breath as the eerie beauty of the familiar tune resounded from the unfamiliar quarter. It is said to have given an original and memorable touch to that ceremony" (Millicent Todd Bingham, Beyond Psychology, in *Homo Sapiens Auduboniensis, A Tribute to Walter Van Dyke Bingham,* New York, National Audubon Society, 1953; from a copy in the Boxford Historic Document Center).

1908

GHP

Lectures & Articles

Oct 2 [1907] — Xn Association Dinner
" 3 — Graduate Reception Specialization

" 8 — Malden Womans Club (Barnes)	35.00
Nov 3 — Princeton College Lds Prayer	50.00
" 7 — Coll. Alumnae Assoc — Alices Hopes[Note 1]	
Jan 17– Harvard Divinity Club — Jones Very	
Dec 1 Hackley School Going to College — & at Prayers	20.00
Apr. 4 Exeter X's Youth	
" " " Morning Prayers Maturity	
" 12 Jamaica Plain, Dole's, Can yu drink	30.00
" " Kings Chapel Can you drink	40.00
" 19 Mt Holyoke Loss of Friends	25.00
May 8 Hartford Teachers Schol as Eth Inst	50.00
" 9 Ann Arbor ΦBK Specialization	50.00
" 23 Bowdoin Coll (3) Art of Being Happy	157.00
" 28 Miss Dean [?] & Haskells School Marlboro St Maturity	
" " Harvard Xn Assoc. Temptations	
June 3 Miss Elys School Cincinnati Maturity	100.00
" 6 Kirkland Lecture, Chicago, Dimbovitza	100.00
" 9 Convocation Univ Chicago Specialization	100.00
" 17 Waterbury Normal School, School as Ethical	50.00

Note 1908

1. Alice Freeman Palmer's husband, "Professor George Herbert Palmer, told the Association [organized on January 14, 1882] at its twenty-fifth anniversary, in speaking of the fellowship established as a memorial to his wife, that she believed the Association should exist and be fostered for the sake of society, for the sake of knowledge, and for the sake of the individual members themselves. She thought it was important that women who had gone to college should carry the college idea far and wide in the community and make it a rightly valued thing for a girl to go to college. She desired to set up a standard for the higher training of women, to insist that it be held there, and she thought it important that those young women who go out from the colleges into different occupations should feel the helpful influence of an unseen but guardian company close around them. Professor Palmer said that she had rejoiced when steadily she saw these aims being realized" (Marion Talbot and Lois Kimbal Mathews Rosenberry, *The History of the American Association of University Women, 1881–1931*, Boston, Houghton Mifflin Co., 1931, page 11).

1908–9

GHP

Sept. Sold Lot at Mt Auburn to L. K. Morse $225.00 & moved family to Boxford buying 4 new stones [Harriet A. Palmer and Julius A.

Palmer, Sr., died in 1872; Lucy Palmer Bachelder, died in 1880; and Julia A. Palmer, died in 1881]

Katherine French comes to live with me

I pay Mrs Nixdorff $500.00 for her belongings here

Oct. 23 Funeral of C. E. Norton

Oct 7 Begin Evening Course (Half Year) Wed & Fri. at Medical School, repeating for Lowell Institute[Note 1] Phil A

Nov. 14 The Teacher appears [**GHP**-65] & also Williams' Aeneid [**GHP**-66]

Dec 25 Fred & Mary arrive from Egypt

This Half Year I give Introd Course in Greek Philos at Lowell Institute Evenings

In November Pres Eliot resigns & in January Lawrence Lowell is elected

Feb. 1 I give Fred & Mary $2250 to be joined with 2000 from Emily for annuity of 300 a year

March O. S. A. Sprague dies at Pasadena

May 3 Dr. J. W. Freeman dies at Saginaw

June 27 Dartmouth give me LL.D.[Note 2]

July 1 to Boxford where the Williamses are with me through July, Fred & Mary afterwards

" 27 Mrs C. E. Severance of St Paul sends me a Collie dog Rex, four months old

June 13 Boston Post publishes report of my engagement which I deny in Congregationalist July 3[Note 3]

" 20 It prints purported interview with me on Flirtation about which I write letter to The Outlook Aug. 14 [**GHP**-67]

" Eric appointed Asst Professor at Haverford

Lectures & Articles

Oct 27 Wheaton Seminary — Homer	25.00
" 5 Address new students at Union — Morning Prayers	
Dec Yale Sermon Are yu able to drink	50.00
Nov. 21 Outlook Review of T. C. W. Aeneid [**GHP**-66]	10.00
Feb 28., Doles Church — (Forgiveness)	30.00
Mar. 7, Princeton (Forgiveness)	50.00
" 11 Newton Centre (Dimbovitza)	25.00
Oct–Feb Lowell Institute Evening Cours Phil A	500.00
Feb. 16–Mar. 12 Lowell Lectures Freedom & Deter	1200.00
Apr. 7. Harv. Coll. Library Herbert Bibliography	
Apr 15, Dinner to Rev. G. A. Gordon Boston[Note 4]	
May 18, Faculty Address of Farewell to Pres Eliot	
June 7 A. F. P. Memorial Statue, Wellesley Chapel[Note 5]	

" 10 Wilson College Objections to Girls Education 100.00
" 12 Hotchkiss School Lakeville Going to College 62.00
" 16 Simmons College — Objections to Girls Education 100.00
" 27 Dartmouth Baccalaureate & Dinner 100.00
Aug 6-27, 4 Readings fr. Milton, Boxford, Fri, 3.30
" 14 Letter to Outlook on Newspapers [**GHP**-67] 25.00

This year I plow the Fairy Ring & rebuild my front wall

Notes 1908–9

1. Boston's Lowell Institute: an educational foundation which supported public lectures in the evening, often as university extension courses.

In 1909 Palmer's course on the history of ancient philosophy had 372 students, one of whom recorded this description: "At the stroke of eight every lecture evening, notebooks were spread and until nine o'clock not a glance wandered to the clock nor was there any sign of wavering interest. The students were all voluntary seekers of knowledge who elected philosophy as an aid in constructive thinking. Young and old, black and white, artisans and teachers, men and women — who had questioned the meaning of life and the universe and were eager to compare their thoughts with the questioners of all time. It was an audience to challenge any professor's attention and respect, as it did that of Professor Palmer" (Harvard University Extension, 75 Years of Community and Classroom, *Harvard University Gazette*, April 26, 1985, page 3).

2. Professor J. K. Lord, acting president, conferred the degree: "George Herbert Palmer, whom men call philosopher, teacher, and friend, because while you transmit and interpret the inspiration of ancient life to the present, you expound in simple but illuminating words the essentials of philosophy and religion, adding to public speech the personal counsel that reaches the heart, upon you, in no vain repetition of academic honors already bestowed upon you, but in recognition of your continuing and increasing service to your generation, I confer the honorary degree of Doctor of Laws" (*Dartmouth Alumni Magazine*, June 1909, pages 284–285).

3. The article on the front page of the *Boston Post* for Saturday, June 12, 1909, was headed Cupid Stirs Two Colleges, Professor Palmer's Engagement Arouses Harvard and Wellesley:

"A report that Professor George Herbert Palmer, Alford professor of religion and the oldest member of the faculty at Harvard, is soon to take a bride from Wellesley, has caused a stir in college circles at Cambridge and Wellesley and much speculation as to who the intended bride will prove to be. Professor Palmer is 67 years of age and a widower, having lost his wife, who was Alice Freeman Palmer, president of Wellesley College from 1881 to 1887. He had previously married Ellen Margaret Wellman of Brookline, who died in 1879.

"Professor Palmer was in Lakeville, Connecticut, last night, and when asked over the telephone whether or not the report of his intended marriage was true refused to affirm or deny the rumor. The woman in the case, who refuses the use of her name, is supposed to be a Wellesley woman and a friend of Professor Palmer's former wife. The officers of Wellesley, when seen yesterday by a reporter, admitted that they had heard the report but refused to name the person.

"Among the students the report is accepted as a certainty. With true feminine interest, they are quite solicitous in regard to the affair of the heart of the venerable professor, who is well known to many of them through the prominent part which he took at the unveiling of the memorial tablet in honor of his wife in Houghton Memorial Chapel last Monday [June 7, 1909; see Note 5 below]. At that time he spoke feelingly of his late wife who had been president of the college."

On June 26, 1909, the *Congregationalist* (volume 94, No. 26, page 852) printed this short paragraph among various items under the heading, Editorial in Brief: "'Marrying is the most precious thing in life," said Prof. George H. Palmer of Harvard to the graduates of Simmons College last week' [see entry for June 16]. He has twice proved his statement by his experience, and it is rumored that he will soon do it again. His biography of his second wife, Alice Freeman Palmer, will long remain a classic in the literature of marriage."

Two days later, on June 28, Professor Palmer sent a letter to the editor of the *Congregationalist* which was published on July 3, 1909: "In your issue of June 26 I see you have been misled into accepting as true a story recently started by a Boston daily paper in regard to a person so unimportant as myself. Let me give you the facts.

"At the Hotchkiss School in Lakeville, on June 12, I was about to deliver a Commencement address when I was called to the telephone and told that the Boston *Post* desired an interview.

"'What about?' I asked.

"'Wait a minute,' was the answer.

"'But I cannot wait,' I replied, 'and I have no interest in an interview with the Post.' That was all I said or heard. The next day the paper announced that it had reported to me a rumor that I was engaged to be married, and I had refused to deny or confirm it.

"I suppose the only defense one has against such outrages is the public reprobation of those who commit them. This reprobation you will feel and you will be glad to publish the letter as soon as you are acquainted with the facts. Let me say then as unequivocally as possible that the original rumor is as baseless as the asserted reticence on my part, invented to give color to the tale. One might imagine a more appropriate time for launching such a story than the very week when I was taking part in a memorial service over my dead wife at Wellesley [see Note 5 below]. But one does not demand delicacies of the *Post* ."

4. Dinner given by the Old South Club at Hotel Somerset. Professor Palmer spoke in response to Reverend George A. Gordon: ". . . We should not feel that this occasion was properly organized," he told the members and guests, "were it not possible for some representative of Harvard to appear here and say that our great university is as truly the debtor to your minister as are you, yourselves." Both the church and Harvard "think of him as a scholar. . . as a preacher . . . [and] as a master of men."

Palmer described Reverend Gordon's associations with Harvard: as recipient of a bachelor's degree in 1881; only five years later, as a member of the first Board of preachers; and as one of the governors of the College, a member of the Board of Overseers. (*Twenty-Fifth Anniversary: Record of the Celebration by The Old South Church and Society of the Twenty-Fifth Anniversary of the Installation as Minister of The Old South Church of Reverend George A. Gordon, D. D., April, MCMIX*, University Press, p. 119–125).

5. Alice Freeman Palmer was cremated in Paris; her husband was also cremated and his ashes, too, were placed here three days after he died, in a ceremony presided over by Willard L. Sperry, dean of the Harvard Theological School (*Boston Evening Globe*, May 10, 1933). Above the base, the memorial is $6^{1/2}$ feet high and $4^{1/4}$ feet wide (see the frontispiece). The base has a medallion face of Alice Freeman Palmer and, underneath, these inscriptions:

HERE REST THE ASHES OF
ALICE FREEMAN PALMER
IN THE HEART OF THE COLLEGE SHE LOVED
1855–1902
GEORGE HERBERT PALMER
1842–1933

Samuel B. Capen, president of the trustees of Wellesley College, described the unveiling exercise:

"On the afternoon of June 7 there was unveiled in the chapel at Wellesley College a memorial to Alice Freeman Palmer, its president from 1882 to 1887. The service was simple and dignified, befitting the occasion. After a few well-chosen words, President Hazard introduced Rev. Dr. William F. Warren, the oldest trustee, who led the devotional service. The College is indebted to another of its trustees, Edwin Hale Abbot, for the beautiful memorial. A neighbor and intimate friend of Mrs. Palmer's, it has been in Mr. Abbot's mind ever since her death in December, 1902, to provide some memorial worthy of her. Most wisely he committed his dream to Daniel Chester French, and after six years of thought this beautiful memorial is the result. In tender words, Mr. Abbot told not only the meaning of the statue in the conception of the artist, but also that the most permanent place to perpetuate a memorial was in connection with a college or a university. No other institution is so nearly immortal as are these, as is illustrated by the great universities of Europe which have lived on through changing dynasties. Professor Palmer followed in an address which interpreted to us anew the meaning of the wonderful life of Alice Freeman Palmer.

"The memorial itself is a relief in the purest marble. At one side is an altar with its flame, from which a young girl has just lighted a lamp. The central figure is a beautiful feminine form who, resting one hand upon the girl's shoulder, with the other is directing her out into the world. It is a fitting representation of Mrs. Palmer's life-work, lovingly and yet earnestly putting courage and hope into the lives of all whom she touched, as she pointed them to a life of service. It was a favorite habit of Mrs. Palmer's with intimate friends, to put her hand gently upon them and then pour out her thoughts in words which were irresistible. The artist could not have conceived a more fitting attitude to illustrate her life. Her overflowing love was at the service of each individual however obscure. She made the timid soul brave and filled the discouraged with hope.

"President Eliot has placed Mrs. Palmer in the front rank of American women. Gentle, brave, patient, untiring, self-forgetful, she gave her life for the world. Her power to inspire others was matchless, firing them with something of her own enthusiasm and conviction. It is fitting, therefore, that this memorial should be placed in the chapel, the heart of the College, to inspire Wellesley students in the generations to come to nobler and higher service" (Samuel B. Capen, Wellesley's Memorial to Alice Freeman Palmer, *Congregationalist*, July 3, 1909, page 15).

A picture of this bas-relief is the frontispiece of this compilation.

1909–10

GHP

During Summer 1909 I had bath room put in my Cambridg. Chamber & hard floors on upper Entry

Oct. Barbara French graduates fr. Waltham Training School

Oct 31 Mrs Lewis Kennedy Morse dies in Boston

Dec 7 Lily Bachelder goes to Homœopathic hospital in Boston & has internal tumor removed

" 21 Lily W. Bachelder dies in Boston at the Homœopathic Hospital after removal of an internal tumor

Jan 22 [1910] Helen Palmer, daughter of Eric & Helen born

" 25 President Lowell offers me the Lectureship for next year either in Berlin or Paris. I decline on grounds of age [he was almost 68] & aversion to the Kaiser[Note 1]

May Katherine French graduates fr Medical School

June Fred receives D. D. fr Cambridge Episc School for his book just published Winning of Immortality [**dedctdGHPann**-3]

" This spring I put hard wood floors in 2nd Story electric lighting, & bath rooms in 2 South rooms

" I Chaplain for Harvard Class Day

July 2 Move to Boxford, leaving Nellie to take care of Eric & Helen who occupy my Cambridge house this summer. Fred & Mary with me at Boxford The Lanes during July & Aug at Mt Desert

For remaining hard wood floors, bath rooms & electric lighting of 11 Quincy St I paid $750 the College paying as much more

Addresses & Articles

Sept. 29 Waltham Training School — Nursing
Oct. 1. P. Brooks House Reception to Freshman
Dec 20 Theodore Williams House Read Herbert
Jan 23 R. C. Cabots " " " " **Note 2**
" 18 Wm James Dinner Speech
Mar 6 Bradford Righteous Anger

" 13 Princeton " "	50.00
April 11 English Club Samson Agonistes	
May 1 Wheaton Herber	25.00
" 8 Kings Chapel (Anger)	50.00
Feb 12–Mar 26, White Lectures Lawrence, Browning & Tennyson	600.00
May 31, Morristown School, Maturity	64.00
June 8, De Paw Univ., Gains & Losses of College	150.00

" 12 Yale (Anger)
" 20 Wellesley Library Dedication[Note 3, 4, 5]
" 22 Troy High School (Maturity) 100.00
" 23 Danbury Normal (Confessions of Teacher) 50.00
" 25 Chaplain Class Day — College Abstractions
" 28 Class Supper
June 29 Browning Course at Boxford (5)

This year C. H. Moore sold Boxford house & moved to England

Notes 1909–10

1. Starting in 1902, Professor Münsterberg and others at Harvard began "definite discussions. . . about the advisability of a professorial exchange between Harvard and Berlin Universities. . . President Eliot approved of the plan, as it was afterward carried out, of sending an eminent professor from Harvard to Berlin University for an academic half-year, and a professor from a German university to Harvard for the same length of time. . . At Berlin the visiting guest was considered, more or less, the guest of the state, entertained by high officials of the state as well as of the University, [and] was given guest privileges at the royal opera and theater. . . (Münsterberg, *Hugo Münsterberg*, pages 118–119).

2. A few years later, on the occasion of Professor Palmer's retirement, Dr. Cabot commented on Palmer's "favorite art of reading aloud. That surely was and is recreation to him, and now that he has finished teaching all who have heard him read his translations of Homer, seen him smile over English dialect poems as he rolled them out and enjoyed his expressive rendering of George Herbert's poems must hope that he will continue to read aloud and allow more of us to hear him" (Richard C. Cabot, George Herbert Palmer: The retiring and much beloved Harvard teacher, as his pupils regard him, *Boston Evening Transcript*, January 25, 1913. See also **aboutGHPann**-3).

And Professor Hocking (in **aboutGHPann**-15, page 63) addressed "Professor Palmer's art of reading poetry. As a self-contained person, averse to emotionality, sober in manner, and preferring a kind of gritty literalness of statement, his person suggested nothing so little as an actor. But his reading of poetry, in those intimate groups at his home on Sunday evenings, was a revelation of another self, a self of marked dramatic power. At the beginning, and perhaps also at the close, of the season's series of readings, a play of Shakespere was in order; and this was commonly read by Professor Palmer, *taking all the parts* ! He often read poetry in dialect, and enjoyed characterization such as one finds in Masefield's "The Widow in the Bye Street." Nothing was foreign to him as reader, however foreign to his conventional appearance, — ribaldry, buffoonery, war-fury, madness, romance, convivial nonsense: the poised precision of his voice became at will gruff, appealing, coarse, feminine, tender, tremendous. Poetry opened to him the universe of man's emotional experience."

And from **aboutGHPann**-17, page 70: "He and Alice Freeman Palmer had established the practice of reading poetry with a few friends on Sunday evening. Doing that was much better than frittering away the time even in the pleasantest matters. So in all his years of solitude he had continued the practice himself. Dr. Richard Cabot and his wife, Professor Ernest Hocking and his wife, Dean Willard Sperry and his wife, and enough others to make up a dozen or more still came in the middle 1920's. When all were present and seated in the long library, the lights were turned off save for a perfectly concealed desk light, and in the solitude afforded by darkness we heard him read from Homer, from George Herbert, from anyone in the entire range of poetry. If he sometimes found the readings too much of a chore, he drafted some of the others of us to read, so that the hour of calm and enrichment might not be lost."

And see comment by Lucy Sprague in 121n6.

3. In her remarks at the dedication, President Hazard pointed out that the "shield of the college, over the fireplace in the main room, is flanked on the left and right by the shields of Emmanuel and Christ Colleges, Cambridge. This signifies the descent of the college, for Wellesley was founded by Mr. Durant, a Harvard graduate, Harvard having been founded in 1636 by a graduate of Emmanuel College [John Harvard]. This, in its turn, was founded in 1584 by a graduate of Christ's College [Sir Walter Mildmay], which was founded by a woman [Lady Margaret Beaufort] in 1505 (The Dedication of the New Library, *College News*, vol. 9 (No. 32), June 15, 1910, page 1. The last two bracketed names are from Caroline Hazard, The Illuminators, [a poem] read at the installation of the Eta Chapter of Phi Beta Kappa Society in Massachusetts, at Wellesley College, January 17, 1905; in Hazard, *From College Gates*, page 325fn).

4. At the dedication, "Professor Palmer. . . spoke of the peculiar uses to which the library and its collections would be put. He emphasized Wellesley's rare good fortune in having for its founder

a man who insisted on the necessity of an efficient library, and who himself was a devout lover of books. Mr. Durant, with his initial gift of ten thousand volumes, and his friend, Mr. Horsford, gave us the foundation of our present collection. Professor Palmer also recognized a possible danger of the library checking the incentive for personal possession of books, and pointed out the value of owning consulting books of all kinds, from dictionaries to Wordsworth" (The Dedication of the New Library. See also **GHP**-17).

5. Both George Herbert Palmer and Alice Freeman Palmer had long been interested in poetry. Entries in the Chronicles show that he often lectured on poets and poetry, and Note 2 above describes him reading poetry. Together, the Palmers collected first editions of English poets.

After Mrs. Palmer died, in 1902, Professor Palmer decided to give their English poetry collection to Wellesley College as a memorial to his wife. "The Browning Collection, consisting of first and other rare editions of the works of Robert and Elizabeth Barrett Browning. . . was only the first installment of this gift." On the day of the presentation in College Hall, February 21, 1911, Alice Freeman Palmer would have been fifty-six years old. Palmer "stated that the gift was mainly due to Wellesley's interest in the Brownings stimulated by Mr. Durant who considered Mrs. Browning the ideal wife, the intellectual comrade of her husband, and furnished the Browning Room in College Hall as a memorial to her. . . Professor Palmer read from the poems in College Hall Chapel and talked for a few moments on the character of Robert Browning. Then followed the installation of the books in the Browning Room. A procession was formed of 'Alices,' some of them alumnae who had known President Freeman, and headed by Professor Palmer they bore the books in state from the Horsford Parlor to the Browning Room where they were locked in the case provided for them. There they remained till the time of the fire [see 272n1], but the case with its valuable contents was removed in safety and brought to the library." These book are now part of the English Poetry Collection in the Margaret Clapp Library's Special Collections (Ethel Dane Roberts, *A Brief History of the Wellesley College Library*, pamphlet, 46 pages; page 11).

During the next twenty-two years, until he died in 1933, George Herbert Palmer gave the remainder of the poetry collection — with the exception of his books on George Herbert, which he gave to Harvard (entry, page 254) and which are shelved in the rotunda of the Houghton Library — and other gifts to the Wellesley College library. Also, from 1911 to 1923, he had two publications related to the collection and six related to poetry. In her introduction to the Hall of Fame edition of *The Life of Alice Freeman Palmer* (**GHP**-59), Katharine Lee Bates writes: "That Professor Palmer has donated the royalties of this Hall of Fame edition to Wellesley's Semi-Centennial Endowment Fund is characteristic. Ever since the day when he won away her president he has been making to the College continual restitution."

There are numerous examples of his interest in poets and poetry, and of his devotion to the Wellesley College Library:

- On December 23, 1912, his "silver wedding" (he had married Alice E. Freeman on December 23, 1887), he sent "40 volumes of books on Homer to Wellesley Library." In the preface to his first publication of *The Odyssey* (**GHP**-1), "To aid those who may wish to enter on a more elaborate study of the Odyssey," he lists more than 40 "of the most serviceable books."
- Published in February 1911: *A Herbert Bibliogaphy* Being a Catalogue of Books related to George Herbert gathered by George Herbert Palmer (**GHP**-68).
- Published in November 1912, Harvard's Ingersoll Lecture on the Immortality of Man: *Intimations of Immortality in the Sonnets of Shakspere* (**GHP**-72).
- At Boxford, in the summer of 1914, he wrote *Notes on a Collection of English Poetry* Intended for Wellesley College with Instructions for its Proper Care. In February 1915, he read these notes to 30 Wellesley teachers, and the book was published in June 1915 (**GHP**-79).
- Also in June 1915, he gave the library a portrait of Robert Browning by William Fisher (Roberts, *Brief History*, page 15).
- He arranged for the publication, in October 1915, of Alice Freeman Pamer's poems: *A Marriage Cycle* (**GHP**-81).
- Published in 1916: *The English Poems of George Herbert newly arranged in relation to his life* (**GHP**-84).
- On January 31, 1917, he "deeded" his library to Wellesley College.
- "At Commencement time in 1918 Professor Palmer presented to the library his collection of the works of Tennyson, containing besides a complete collection of first editions much valuable collateral material. On the day preceding Commencement he formally presented the books, talking to a small gathering in the Treasure Room of his aim in presenting the collection of English

poets to the college, the care of the books and the uses they might serve" (Roberts, *Brief History*, page 11–12).

- Published in April 1918: The Monologue of Browning (**GHP**-87).
- Published in November 1918, the Earl Lectures of 1917, delivered before the Pacific Theological Seminary in Berkeley, California: *Formative Types in English Poetry* (**GHP**-88).
- Professor Palmer's entry on August 6, 1921: "I turn over $15000 to Wellesley for endowment of my library, they to pay annuity of $100 a month to Fred & Mary [his brother and sister-in-law] during their lives, or to me in case of their death." Frederic Palmer died in 1932, Professor Palmer in 1933, and Mary Palmer in 1936. Accordingly, this George Herbert Palmer Fund became available to the college in 1936, [to be used, as Palmer provided in his will] "for the preservation of the Library of English Poetry. . . I wish the income to be applied to keeping worn bindings in order and to the increase of the collection by the purchase of other rare volumes of English Poetry. If, as I hope, a special curator of the Collection is appointed, I am willing to have $200 a year,— not more,— withdrawn from the Fund for her salary, but other natural expenses of the Collection, such as shelving, heating, lighting, etc., shall not be charged to the account" (Record of the Trust Funds of Wellesley College, June 1940. page 81. Wellesley College Archives, 8D).
- Published in December 1923: *A Catalogue of Early and Rare Editions of English Poetry* presented to Wellesley College by George Herbert Palmer with additions from other sources (**GHP**-93).
- On February 21, 1924, Mrs. Palmer's birthday, Professor Palmer brought the remainder of the collection to the college. "Then for several weeks he was an almost daily visitor at the Library, working up in the Treasure Room at the task of arranging the books in their places" (Professor Palmer's Books, *The Wellesley Alumnae Quarterly*, 1924; 8 (May): 161–165).
- On March 19, 1924, Professor Palmer's eighty-second birthday, "a small group, consisting of trustees, member of the faculty, the library staff and gradate students of the English Literature Department, gathered in the Treasure Room for the formal presentation of his entire collection of first and rare editions of the English poets from Chaucer to Masefield. . . His speech on that occasion dealt with the history of the collection and with his hope for its use by Wellesley. The collection was begun by Mrs. Palmer and himself and after her death he continued to add to

it, always intending it for Wellesley and using the royalties which he received from the sale of the *Life of Alice Freeman Palmer* [and of the *Odyssey*] to build up the collection. As time went on he interested other friends in adding to it rare editions that were beyond his own means to purchase" (Roberts, *Brief History*, page 12).

- On Baccalaureate Sunday, 1930, Wellesley's former president, Miss Caroline Hazard, presented to the college "the original love letters of Robert and Elizabeth Browning, still in the caskets in which the recipients had carefully preserved them." Miss Hazard had learned from Professor Palmer that these letters were for sale; the price was $80,000. He considered this "the crowning gift to the Browning Collection" (Roberts, *Brief History*, page 12–13. Frank Herrmann, Sotheby's *Portrait of an Auction House*, London, 1980, page 131fn1).
- In the autumn of 1931, Professor Palmer "presented to the Collection eleven morocco bound volumes of holograph letters of Elizabeth Barrett Browning, most of them unpublished and of great interest." This gift made "the Wellesley collection of Browning manuscripts, first editions, and personalia, one of the most distinguished and valuable in the world" (Roberts, *Brief History*, page 13. Valuable Acquisition, *Wellesley Magazine*, 1931; 15 (February): 157).
- After George Herbert Palmer died in 1933, May 7th, "it was found that his will provided that the royalties from the sale of his *Life of Alice Freeman Palmer* and *A Marriage Cycle* . . . were to be used for the increase and upkeep of the English Poetry Collection, and that the income from another fund bequeathed to the college [see the George Herbert Palmer Fund above] was eventually to be applied to the same purpose" (Roberts, *Brief History*, page 13).

1910–11

GHP

July 21, To Mt Desert to visit Pres. Eliot

Aug 5. Lilys Birth Day, Fred & I scatter her ashes on Augustus' grave, as she desired

Sept. Katherine French enters Homœopathic Hospital as intern

" L. K. Morse & Anna come to live with me

Dec. 7 Barbara French sails for Naples in company with Miss Mills of Andover

Dec. 23–Jan 2 Portrait painted by Charles Hopkinson for Harvard College on subscription by my students from all over the country[Note 1]

Nov. 28 — Annuity of $333.33 purchased for 4659.43 for self, Mary & Fred — to be continued on my & Freds birth days.
" " Swinburne Hale & new wife visit me
Feb. 4 Nellie Donohue marries Mr Casey, $5^{1/2}$ years with me Norah Moriarty Taking her place
Jan 27–Feb 6 Mr Morse & I visit Washington & Baltimore
Feb 21 — I present 1st editions of Mr & Mrs Browning 82 vols, to Browning Room, Wellesley, & read [see 249n5]
" 12 Meet Lucy Sprague in N. Y. after $3^{1/2}$ years absence
" 25 Dinner 40 guests at Union for presentation of my portrait to Harvard. Speeches by Hyde, presiding, Royce Rand Baker Ross Eliot Lowell & self[Note 1]
Apr 17–22 Wellfleet — Eric & Helen Fred Mary & I Cold
Erics family with Ella Talmage in my Cambridge house
Summer at Boxford with Fred & Mary I finishing Freedom [**GHP**-71]
Sent Bertha & Will to California ($250)
This summer I complete joint annuity

<u>Speeches</u>

Oct 2 Harvard Xn Assoc, Puritan Home	
Nov. 13 Dole's Church — Death of Friends	30.00
" 20 Crothers' Club Herbert	
Jan 22 Crothers Club, Cambridge Death of Friends	35.00
" 16 Shakspere Societ — Shakspere Sonnets	
" 23 Brooks House — P. Brooks Ideals	
Feb. 10 Herbert Bibliography published [**GHP**-68]	
" 21 Wellesley Presentation of Browning [see 249n5]	
" 24 Presentation of my Portrait to Harvard	
Mar 10 Dobbs Ferry School — Herbert	50.00
" 12 Princeton — Death of Friends	50.00
April 9 Kings Chapel — Forgiveness	30.00
" 16 Bradford — Death of Friends	
" 25 Xn Assoc. Dinner	
May 20 Haverford Teachers. 3 Aspects o Teacers Life	70.00
June 7 Newton Theol. Inst, Puritan Home	50.00
" 22 Class Day Chaplain X 3 Tests or Temptations	
Aug. 4 Readings from Wordsworth in Boxford Chapel	

Note 1910–11

1. "At a banquest held in the Trophy Room of the Union, on Feb. 25, an oil portrait of Prof. George Herbert Palmer, '64, was presented to the University. Last June, when Prof. Palmer had been a teacher at Harvard for 40 years, a committee of 27 of his former pupils, of

which Prof. C. M. Bakewell, of Yale, was chairman, decided to have the portrait painted as a token of their deep appreciation of his work. The portrait was painted by Charles Hopkinson, '91. [In August 1993, this portrait was hanging in Emerson Hall's Bechtel Room.] The banquet at which the picture was presented was attended by over 40 of Prof. Palmer's friends and close asociates — members of the University Faculty and men who were formerly his students. Prof. R. B. Perry, '97, of the Department of Philosophy, presided. Addresses were delivered by Pres. Eliot, Prof. J. Royce [see **aboutGHPann**-2], Prof. E. K. Rand, '94, Dr. D. W. Ross, '75, Prof. George P. Baker, '87, Pres. Hyde of Bowdoin, Pres. Lowell, and Prof. Palmer" (*HGM*, 1910–1911; 19 (June, 1911), page 575fn).

1911–12

GHP

Oct. Mr Morse returns to me fr. West, Anna fr. Europe

Barbara French returns fr 8 months abroad & soon falls ill at hospital, Katherine still there

Nov I go to New York to see Lucy Sprague

Dec Lucy spends evening here & takes A. F. Ps vases

Feb [1912] I accept Chairmanship of Department for Half Year Royce has slight stroke of apoplexy

Mar. 7 Mrs Lane has stroke of paralysis [mother of William C. Lane]

Mar. 23 Cambridge subway opens

Mar. 19 On this my 70th birthday I give my Collection of books on Herbert (168 vols) to the Harvard Library. Printed invitations were issued by the Library & a hundred or more of my colleagues & their wives came. Mr. Lane spoke, then I, then Pres Lowell. A key was given me of the closet where the collection is kept.

In the evening Mr & Mrs Theodore Williams gave me a reception at 99 Mt Vernon St Boston. About 100 personal friends, to who I read Blakes Infinit Sorrow Spensers Minopolinos, Whittiers Rose, A. F. P's Spring journey & myself**Note** 1 Shakspere's Phinx [Phœnix] & [the] Turtle, Vaughans Joy of my Life, Watts True Riches, Wordsworths Personal Talk, Barnes- [?] Friends -[?], Watsons World Strangeness, Emersons Terminus, Herberts Gratefulness & Love

Speeches

Oct	1	Baptist Social Union, Puritan Home—	50.00
"	16	Radcliffe " "	
"	28	Episc Theol School — Relations to Harvard	

Nov. 4 Ganer's Ch. Worcester — Lords Prayer 30.00
" 18 The Problem of Freedom [**GHP**-71]
Dec 11 ΦBK Dinner — Scholarship
" 17 Worcester Church — Forgiveness 30.00
Feb. 4 Bowdoin College Lords Prayer 50.00
" 5–7 Bangor — Shakespere Pope Wordsworth Tennyson Lords Prayer (5) also Dinner & Conference 200.00
March 17–23 Preach & conduct prayers at Harvard 110.00
Apr. 30 Williams College G. Herbert 15
May 19 Wellesley Temptation of X 20
June 9 Simmons Coll Reunion (3d Year)
" 17 Class Day Prayers
" 19 Class Day Supper

Mar 19 Forty eight letters, 6 telegrams, & 18 flowers were sent
May 8, Lucy Sprague marries Prof Wesley Clair Mitchell at Berkeley
" 11 President Hibben inaugurated at Princeton University
" 17 Elected Fellow American Academy of Arts & Sciences
June 11 Doctor of Letters Princeton [tipped in page with citation] with Howells-AM CH Butler D.D. G.P. Pierson, LLD A Reed J. A. Stewart James Ford Rhodes [Note 2]
" 28 In Boxford this summer Theodore & Velma Williams with me 10 days then Fred & Mary. Bertha & children not arriving till Aug. 21 on account of illness of Mrs Lane Mr Morse's house closed, he in Alaska children in Switzerland
I give 5 readings on the Fridays of August, 330 P.M. on Keats & Shelley
Aug. 6 I arrange with H. M. & Co for publishing F & M's Poems [**dedctdGHPann**-4]
" 20 Finish writing Ingersoll Lecture [**GHP**-72]
Sept 1 Widener Library given Harvard[Note 3]
Nellie Fitzgerald my cook at Boxford
Cambridge Subway opened

Notes 1911–1912

1. Not until three and one-half years later, thirteen years after Alice Freeman Palmer died, did Professor Palmer publish a collection of her poems (**AFP**-18). In 1912, he was still interested in his friends' opinions about the propriety of publishing such intimate poems. The two that he read at this reception were later published in the same sequence, in a group entitled Together.

A Spring Journey

We journeyed through broad woodland ways,
My Love and I.
The maples set the shining fields ablaze.
The blue May sky
Brought to us its great Spring surprise;
While we saw all things through each other's eyes.

And sometimes from a steep hillside
Shone fair and bright
The shadbush, like a young June bride,
Fresh clothed in white.
Sometimes came glimpses glad of the blue sea;
But I smiled only on my Love; he smiled on me.

The violets made a field one mass of blue—
Even bluer than the sky;
The little brook took on that color too,
And sang more merrily.
"Your dress is blue" he laughing said. "Your eyes,"
My heart sang, "sweeter than the bending skies."

We spoke of poets dead so long ago,
And their wise words;
We glanced at apple trees, like drifted snow;
We watched the nesting birds,—
Only a moment! Ah, how short the day!
Yet all the winters cannot blow its sweetness quite away.

Myself

Oh, to be alone!
To escape from the work, the play,
The talking every day!
To escape from all I have done
And all that remains to do!
To escape, —yes, even from you,
My only Love,—and be
Alone and free!

Could I only stand
Beneath pale moon and gray sky,
Where the winds and the sea-gulls cry,

And no man is at hand,
And feel the free air blow
On my rain-wet face, and know
I am free,—not yours, but my own,—
Free and alone!

For the soft firelight
And the home of your heart, my dear
They hurt, being always here.
I want to stand upright
And to cool my eyes in the air,
And to see how my back can bear
Burdens,—to try, to know,
To learn, to grow.

I am only you.
I am yours, part of you, your wife,
And I have no other life.
I cannot think, cannot do;
I cannot breathe, cannot see;
There is "us," but there is not "me."
And worst, at your touch I grow
Contented so!

2. President John Grier Hibben conferred the degree: "L.H.D. George Herbert Palmer, Professor of philosophy in Harvard University, a teacher who holds his students by scholarship of living power, a thinker of calm meditative tone, a student of ethics with a deep grasp on that theistic truth which underlies all righteousness, a literary artist — fit editor of the poems of his spiritual ancestor, George Herbert; his refinement in style, whether in philosophy or literature, being no mere fastidiousness but the reflex of refined thought, a philosopher in the original sense, widely influential for good and imbued with a tranquil enthusiasm for truth which gives substance and worth to all his work."

The other honorees: "A.M.—Charles Henry Butler, a writer of authority on the treaty-making power of the United States. . . D.D.—George Peck Pierson . . . author of [a] commentary in Japanese on the New Testament. . . L.H.D.—William Dean Howells, President of the American Academy of Arts and Letters. . . LL.D.—Alfred Reed. . . Justice of the Supreme Court of New Jersey. . . LL.D.—James Ford Rhodes, our first living American political historian. . . LL.D.—John Aikman Stewart, the venerable retiring

President *pro tempore* of Princeton University" (*Princeton Alumni Quarterly*, June 12, 1912, pages 599–601).

3. In the vestibule to the main lobby of the Harry Elkins Widener Memorial Library, two marble tablets have this bronze script:

HARRY ELKINS WIDENER
A GRADUATE OF
THIS UNIVERSITY
BORN JANUARY 3 1885
DIED AT SEA APRIL 15 1912
UPON THE FOUNDERING
OF THE STEAMSHIP
TITANIC

THIS LIBRARY
ERECTED
IN LOVING MEMORY OF
HARRY ELKINS WIDENER
BY HIS MOTHER
ELEANOR ELKINS WIDENER
DEDICATED
JUNE 24 1915

Harry Elkins Widener, Harvard, A.B.,1907, and his parents, members of a wealthy Philadelphia family, were all serious book collectors. Before they sailed from England on the Titanic's maiden voyage, they had been in London. Soon before sailing, Harry bought from Alfred Quaritch, London bookseller, a "tiny duodecimo second edition of Bacon's *Essayes*. His farewell words to Quaritch were, 'I think I'll take that little Bacon with me in my pocket, and if I'm shipwrecked it will go down with me.'" Harry and his father "saw Mrs. Widener and her maid into one of the [life]boats"; the women were two of the 711 survivors. Harry and his father were two of the 1,513 people who died (Edwin Wolf, 2nd., John F. Fleming, *Rosenbach*: *A Biography*, Cleveland, World Publishing Co., 1960, page 76).

Another tablet is in the lobby of the library:

HARRY ELKINS WIDENER
A B 1907
LOVED THE BOOKS

WHICH HE HAD COLLECTED
AND THE COLLEGE
TO WHICH HE BEQUEATHED THEM
"HE LABOURED
NOT FOR HIMSELF ONLY
BUT FOR ALL THOSE
WHO SEEK LEARNING"
THIS MEMORIAL
HAS BEEN PLACED HERE BY HIS CLASSMATES

In the two Harry Elkins Widener Memorial Rooms, a Rotunda leads to a Library which houses his collection — "comprising rare and early editions of English literature, association books, authors' manuscripts, extra-illustrated books, and color prints" — with additions purchased by his mother after the tragedy (Samuel Eliot Morison, *The Development of Harvard University since the Inauguration of President Eliot, 1869–1929*, Cambridge, Harvard University Press, 1930, page 623. Wolf, *Rosenbach*, page 78).

1912–13

GHP

September. I agree with Newton Theological Institution to give a course of 20 lectures on Ethics for $600 beginning Oct 1

Sept. Katherine French established as Doctor with the Dewings 469 Broadway

Sept. Eric Helen & the two children established in Prof. Morse's house 1 Langdon Square he having Sabbatical Year for Ph. D. I give him $500

Nov. 19 Father of Katherine & Barbara dies in N. Y.

" 20 Fred & Marys Poems published [**dedctdGHPann**-4]

" " Mills College negotiates through Mrs Cleveland with Eric to become its President, Rejecting him because Episcopalian

Dec 6 Decennial of Alice's death, The Bee held at 11 Quincy St & I read her poems[Note 1]

" 24 Dedication Reception at Pres Lowells new house

" 23 My silver wedding I send 40 volumes of books on Homer to Wellesley Library [see 249n5]

Jan Fred proposed as President of Hobart College but rejected on account of age [64 years]

April 3 Freds 25th anniversary of settlement in Andover

" 29 Fred called to Harv Div School & editor Theol Rev

May 4 " resigns parish at Andover

Lectures

Oct. 1, First lecture at Newton Theol Institution
Sept 25, Conduct Morning Prayers (Concentration) 10.00
Oct 5 Princeton Sermon Concentration 50.00
" 9 Ingersoll Lecture, Shakespere Sonnets
Nov 9 " " Published [**GHP**-72]
" 12 Wordsworth, Wellesley & Harvard Seminaries
Dec 9 Appleton Chapel On Freshmen going to Prayers
Oct 1–Dec 14, 20 Lectures Newton Theol Sem 600.00
Jan 2 — Newton Theol Chapel — Conditions o th Ministry
" 6 — Faculty Meeting Comptrollers Circular
" 10 — Reception to Prof Eucken, Phil. Club
" 22 — Presentation Pres Lowells new house[Note 2]
" 29 — Start for Colorado & 4 months in the West
June 2 Return 162 Lectures 60 Dinners 24 Receptions 17 weeks Colorado Grinnell Beloit Knox 1 month each Carleton a week Rockford Milwaukee Iowa & Wis. a day Loving Cup given me by Beloit[Note 3]
" 12 Middlesex School Concord 50.00
17 25 Anniversary Wellesley 1888 Address on Alice[Note 4]
Class day Harvard Morning Prayers
18 Harvard Class Supper
24 Installation of E. L. Bradford Boxford Charg. to Pastor
27 Pittsburgh Normal College (Confessions) 135
20 Harvard ΦBK Speak on Western trip & Harv Leadership
Sept 7 Mt Desert Church Lords Prayer 20.00
" 14 Boxford " " "

Notes 1912–13

1. Started in 1861 by Cambridge girls who sewed articles of clothing for Union Army soldiers, the activity continued as the Cambridge Bee, a group of about 24 women who combined sewing and social activities. Alice Freeman Palmer had been an enthusiatic member who entertained the Bee in Cambridge and in Boxford (see Chronicle entry for May 21, 1899, and **AFP**-10). A copy (in AJL Collection) of *Poems* by Frederic and Mary Palmer (Boston, Houghton Mifflin Co., 1912) is inscribed: "From your fellow-Bee Mary Palmer and from G. H. and F. P. Eleven Quincy Street December sixth 1912." It is likely that each member received a similar memento of the special occasion.

In 1924, Mary Palmer's book, *The Story of the Bee* (Cambridge, Riverside Press, 108 pages; a copy is in Special Collections at

Wellesley College) was published. She and her husband were living with George Herbert Palmer at 11 Quincy Street, and she was hostess there for meetings of the Bee. In her book, she describes one such gathering:

"At one of my Bees in this house full of memories, the members found at dinner, at each place, a volume of Alice's poems [**AFP**-18, *A Marriage Cycle*]. The volumes were gifts from Professor Palmer. They were bound in white [rather than the dark cloth of the regular edition] and on the back of each a little golden bee testified that they had been made expressly for us [the bee is centered in a gold circle, diameter 3 cm.; the same gold stamping is seen on the front cover of *The Story of the Bee.* In a letter to Houghton Mifflin Co. on September 13, 1915, Palmer suggested the special volume bound in white; see page 472]. That evening after dinner Professor Palmer was allowed to join our group and he read to us from the little volume." One of these volumes (in the AJL Collection) is inscribed "To Her Fellow-Bee Helen A. Brooks From G. H. Palmer." Helen Appleton Brooks was the wife of John Graham Brooks, a sociologist and widely known lecturer. A similar volume, in the Wellesley College Archives, is inscribed to another "Fellow-Bee," Grace Eliot, the wife of Harvard's president.

2. An open house was arranged at President Lowell's new, brick house on Quincy Street, between the old president's house and Emerson Hall. "All the members of the various Faculties and of the Governing Boards, with their families, were invited, and the house, spacious as it is, was thronged. During the evening a silver bowl, from members of the Faculty of Arts and Sciences, was presented to President and Mrs. Lowell. Professor Palmer spoke as follows:

"'As senior member of the Harvard Faculty, I am instructed by my colleagues to offer to Mrs. Lowell and yourself this piece of silver. We gladly seize the occasion of your entrance into this new home to express our warm regard for you and our sense of that public spirit which has marked your conduct of affairs here, even such affairs as might naturally be reserved for your personal pleasure.

'This house itself is no ordinary home. While admirably contrived for domestic convenience and comfort, much more has entered into its design. It has evidently been conceived as a place of kindness, a centre of hospitality, a refuge for easing the solitude of students, a means of entertaining with suitable stateliness guests of the University. For this blending of your own interests with those of Harvard we desire to thank you. It is a fresh illustration of the genial and generous disposition you have steadily shown since you first came among us, a disposition which obliges us to think of you rather as the friend than the official, and makes us glad, through this shining bowl, to occupy a quiet corner in one of these hospitable rooms'" (*HGM*, 1912–13; 21 (March 1913): 580).

3. In the spring of 1911, the authorities of four western colleges — Beloit (Wisconsin), Colorado, Grinnell (Iowa), and Knox (Illinois) — proposed an exchange to which Harvard agreed: that Harvard send a professor to them for part of each year, and that each of the four colleges send a teacher each year to assist in one of the larger courses at Harvard. The colleges thought that Harvard "of all the larger Eastern institutions, could be of most service to them." Albert Bushnell Hart, Eaton Professor of the Science of Government, had been Harvard's first such exchange professor, in the 1911–1912 academic year; George Herbert Palmer was the second, in 1912–1913.

Professor Palmer's basic activities were quite similar at each of the colleges that he visited: on Monday, Wednesday, and Friday, a series of lectures on The Problem of Duty; on Tuesday and Thursday, a series of public lectures on English poetry — Chaucer and Spenser, George Herbert, Alexander Pope, William Wordsworth, Alfred Tennyson, and Robert Browning (see **GHP**-88); readings to large and small groups, from his translation of *The Odyssey of Homer* or *The Antigone of Sophocles* (see **GHP**-2 or 37); speeches at Chapel services; and speeches, such as, a scholarly analysis of the Lord's Prayer (see **GHP**-90), at Sunday Vespers. In addition, there were dinners, receptions, and meetings with students.

At Beloit, students in the first year course in Rhetoric were required to read his *Life of Alice Freeman Palmer* (**GHP**-57), and *Self-Cultivation in English* (**GHP**-63) was used as a text in the Rhetoric Department. At the end of his visit, *The Beloit Record*, published by a journalism class, noted: "Dr. Palmer has brought us more than Ethics or Poetry, he has brought us a new chapel service. He has shown us that a short talk to the point on some vital subject of college interest can replace the reading of a lengthy Bible quotation. . . we could say goodbye to Prof. Palmer with less sorrow when he leaves us next week, if we knew that some of his personality were to remain, stamped in the innovation he has made in the service of our noonday hour of devotion." And the student newspaper, *The Round Table* said: "Dr. Palmer is no ordinary man. His quiet, unassuming presence on the campus connoted that steady, patient study that probes intellectual problems to their essence, that weighs these problems during years of contemplation, and publishes the results of this work only with the conviction that the book may be a step toward truth. He impressed us as a scholar of wide interests and achievements, and a gentleman possessed of the culture and refinement of noble thoughts and high ideals. . . We are proud that he is now part of us; we regret only that his stay was so short and that each one of us did not have the privilege of closer touch with his personality. Our hope is that the Harvard Exchange Professorship may bring us more men like Dr. Palmer."

At Grinnell, he spoke at a banquet of the Harvard Club of Iowa, and he traveled to Iowa State University to speak at the annual Phi Beta Kappa banquet and, on the next day, at Sunday Vespers. While at Beloit, he went to Madison to address the Harvard Club of Wisconsin, and, through the courtesy of the president of Beloit, he spent one week at Carleton College in Minnesota. For the next year, the exchange program would include Carleton.

Reactions to his visits were uniformly enthusiastic. From Carleton, for example: "It is not likely that the inspiration which Dr. Palmer brought to us for study along the lines of philosophy and literature will soon pass, and yet we should all begin immediately to take advantage of it. As he told us in his lectures on 'The Problem of Duty,' he did not solve for us the problems in this branch of learning; he merely presented them to us in the hope that we would try to think them out for ourselves. In the literary work, too, if we are to make the most of our opportunity we must put into practice the valuable suggestions which he made."

At the end of each visit, Professor Palmer complimented the college. At Carleton, for example, he "expressed himself as much pleased with the democratic spirit of the college. . . The fact that the college is co-educational gives it a different atmosphere from most of the eastern schools. As a rule these are not co-educational although I would be glad to see them so. I can see no reason why boys and girls should not study together, be at church together, and even eat together as they do here." On at least one occasion, as he was leaving Grinnell College, he left, as a parting gift, a large photograph of the Alice Freeman Palmer Memorial in the Wellesley College Chapel (see frontispiece).

Beloit's professor of philosophy in 1913, Karl Tinsley Waugh, with a Ph.D. degree in philosophy from Harvard in 1906, pointed out that Palmer's "lectures are 'easy to take.' There are not many lecturers at Harvard whose lectures are so clear, so full of simple illustrations, and so thoroughly systematized. Even the novice in note-taking goes away from the lecture feeling that the outline of the subject has become his own." In his graduate study, Waugh took Philosophy 4,

Palmer's course on Ethics, "one of the most famous and popular courses in Harvard College" (Morison, *Development*, page 20), which included the lectures on The Problem of Duty. A summary of these lectures delivered by Professor Palmer at Carleton College follows:

"In presenting the claims of society upon the individual, Dr. Palmer said, in summarizing his lectures, 'The call of the whole to the parts is a call to all to preserve, to embody, and better to render adjusted, those relations and institutions which will give the individual the opportunity for the fullest life. . . No institution of society can improve itself. It must be watched and readjusted by individuals so as to meet the needs of the times.'

"Dr. Palmer gave a brief statement of some of the fundamental definitions of ethics in beginning his course of lectures. Duty, he said, is what we do with reference to other people. Goodness is concerned with what we do for ourselves. We alone are subject to our own arbitrary choices. Kant said that the starry heavens were the most majestic thing of which he knew because they showed complete conformity to law. But duty never arises except where disobedience is possible. There is no sign of duty beyond human beings.

"Every time duty appears it is in objective form. It is something not within us. It is not derived from our own subjectivity. Nobody chooses his duty. It is created for us. Duty calls for universality of action. By our acts we should express what we think should be the conduct of every one. Not to make ourselves an exception in what we do is an important part of duty.

"Duty is authoritative in character. A little girl once defined the sense of duty as 'something inside of us we can't do as we please with.' Duty is the law which should control the action of the parts of society, or the individuals which make up the society. The authority of duty is the call of the whole to the parts.

"Dr. Palmer then discussed the ten commandments from an ethical standpoint in a very interesting way. According to [him] these commandments do not mention all of our duties, and are not all of equal importance as some duties are superior to others. He stated that the Golden Rule was not intended as a piece of a system of ethics, but as a rule to help us in our daily life. It is a device to help us stand the strains of life.

"In Plato's Republic he presents the Greek code of duties. Justice is the supreme virtue which is a combination of temperance, courage and wisdom. According to Plato virtue is an instinctive tendency to bring about results which are for man's good. Virtue is of little value until it has become instinctive. You must not need to meditate about these things, you must have an instinct to do them, as for example to tell the truth. . . All our passions should be so disciplined by instinct. Until this tendency has become such not much has been accomplished.

"The Greek idea was that temperance, courage and wisdom were included in justice. But this conception was distorted by Cicero who introduced some of the Greek philosophy into Italy. He studied for a while in Greece, got his note-book full, and a few ideas penetrated into his head. But in some way he failed to get the point of this part of Plato's teaching, and thought he meant that there were four necessary virtues instead of three; while the Greek philosopher taught that justice, instead of being a separate virture, was really made up of the other three."

Sources for this note: *HGM*,1910-11;19 (June 1911): 636-637. 1913-14; 22 (September 1913): 76, 138. From Beloit: *The Beloit Record*, April 24, 1913. *The Round Table,* January 31, February 7, March 21, April 4, April 11, April 18, April 25, May 2,1913. From Carleton: *The Carletonia*, April 8, April 22, May 6, 1913. From Grinnell: *The Scarlet and Black*, January 29, March 1, March 12, March 15, March 22, March 29, 1913. From Knox: *Republican Register*, May (before 12), May 12, May 13, 1913; a copy of Professor Palmer's resumé; a copy of Josiah Royce's article, In Honor of Professor Palmer (**aboutGHPann**-5); a photograph of George Herbert Palmer; and a list of The Harvard Lectures 1912–13.

4. Professor Palmer was an honorary member of Wellesley's class of 1888 (see 64n1), which celebrated its 25th anniversary. In a copy of the "fourth impression" of the *Life of Alice Freeman Palmer* (**GHP**-57; in the AJL Collection), pasted on the mid-left margin of the right front endpaper, is a white sheet, approximately 3x5 inches, with this printing:

with
The Good Wishes of
GEORGE HERBERT PALMER
of
The Class of 1888

1913–1914

GHP

July 1 Eric has operation for appendicitis

May 25 Morse & his 2 chidren sail for Spain. He leaves them in

Switzerland for the year. He inspects mines & factories in Germany, & returns on [blank space] His Boxford house closed

" Charles H. Talmage's long illness

June 19 Commencement at Harvard I resign & am elected Overseer[Note 1]

" 30 To Wellfleet for a fortnight

July 14 To Boxford with Fred & Mary

Eric & family at Quincy St. Lanes in Boxford

Aug. 6 I assign to Fred & Mary the 2/3 of my annuity which fall on their birth days.

September — Fred & Mary move to Cambridge settling with me in Quincy St Fred also takes a Study in Divinity Hall

Jan 26 [1914] Start with Morse for West & visit for Wellesley Fund N.Y Philad. Rochester Cleveland Chicago St Louis

We then part, I going to Grand Canyon Santa Barbara Cal. for a week with Theodore Williams who very ill & on Feb. 16 to Claremont Pomona College for four weeks lectures, 3 hours each week Ethics, 2 on Literature I make about 5 addresses each week in addition, receiving $600.00 for the service[Note 2]

Then back to Santa Barbara & to Berkeley where, during a week Mrs Rieber paints my portrait.[Note 3] From there I return with the Williamses in $3^{3/4}$ days — April 1

March 17 College Hall Wellesley burns

I Chairman of Committee to raise $2 500 000 [**GHP**-77]

This spring Robert Herrick & Harriet separate

Lectures 1913–1914

Sept 24 Harvard Prayers David	10.00
Oct 22. 9 Lowell Lectures [see 242n1], Wed 5 P. M.	
Some Types of English Poetry	800.00

Nov. 21 Harv. Phil Dinner

Dec. 8. Freshman Prayer Service

" 29 Welcome to Philol. & Classical Associations

Nov. Grinnell Alumni's Gathering

Dec. 29 Receive for Pres Lowell Mod. Lang. Assoc.

Feb 4 Wellesley Club St Louis

" 5 Mary Institute " "

Mar 18 Ednah Richs Normal Training College

Mar. 28 Harvard Club lunch San Francisco

June 5 Detroit, Liggett School Blunder

" 16 Class Day Prayers

" ~~17 Class Supper~~

" 18 Commencement Fiftieth Anniversary[Note 4]

1913–1914

1. Dean Briggs spoke at the afternoon exercises: "The coming year will bring many gains and not a few losses, — certainly not a few losses to the Faculty of Arts and Sciences. As a teacher in active service Prof. George Herbert Palmer has taught his last class in the College that without him can never be the same. More than 40 years ago we found him here, a young tutor in prescribed — unescapable — Greek, and a young tutor whom no pupil can forget, for he made crude Freshmen feel, as he felt, the fascination and the glory of that literature which nowadays it is the fashion to desert for economics. It was a blow to Greek at Harvard when he ceased to teach Greek. It is a blow to philosophy in Harvard College when he ceases to teach philosophy. No subject can afford to lose him, for his is the highest calling of the supreme teacher" (*HGM,* 1913–14; 22 (September 1913): 82).

For the election of overseers, first by postal ballots and then by votes at commencement, the committee presented 19 nominations for 5 vacancies. The total vote was 6279: 4853, postal; 1426, at commencement. Professor Palmer received the largest number of votes, 4075 (3065, postal; 1010, at commencement), 65% of the total and 833 more than the second place man (*HGM,* 1912–13; 21 (June 1913): 794–795. 1913–14; 22 (September 1913): 91).

2. Professor Palmer's program at Pomona College was similar to the one for his long western trip in 1913 (see 262n3).

"From no single point of view can a fair appreciation of Professor Palmer's visit be had. Naturally one finds in the marvelous courses of lectures upon Duty and Poetry the largest contribution to our community life. And yet so much beyond these was given, without stint, in the way of occasional address, lecture, sermon or informal remark, that the latter with their more personal touch seem almost to outweigh the former in influence. The great lectures accomplished their purpose of illumination and inspiration; their impress is indelibly upon every hearer. The occasional address came with the force of a personal utterance and bound one to the speaker as a friend. As a member of the Faculty for the time being, Professor Palmer in his turn conducted Chapel service. Surely no student listening to his words, so sensible of the student's difficulties and so rich in suggestions of possible growth and enlargement, felt that a stranger was addressing him. The words became to him, as of one who had long been among us, even as the other members of the Faculty.

"In the more intimate address of smaller assemblies this feeling was intensified, as at the meeting of the folk-moot in the College Commons when serious problems of college life were under discussion and in the gathering of the women in Sumner Hall to listen to the sympathetic portrayal of the life of Alice Freeman Palmer, and at the reading in Rembrandt Hall of the Nausicaa episode from Professor Palmer's translation of the Odyssey. . .

"The revival of an ancient order was the folk-moot assembly of faculty and students at the Commons. The remark of a student to a faculty member that outside activities were so absorbing as to leave no time for concentration upon college work, led to the calling of the meeting for a frank discussion of the subject of 'Concentration in College.' The prevailing sentiment was opposed to any attempt at legislation to regulate the number of an individual's activities, as well as any attempt to hold men by appeal to college loyalty to outside activities which were detrimental to their special interests in scholarship lines. . .

"Professor Palmer's contribution to faculty discussions had the double value of an inside as well as an outside point of view. His intimate knowledge of his own university and his life-long observations of colleges the country over enabled him to shed light upon many of our problems. Especially were his full outline of the administration of Harvard in all departments and his characterization of its undergraduate life of value in correcting impressions drawn from general and often misleading sources. His discriminating recognition of the excellences of Pomona College and his candid criticism, when invited, of our deficiencies were alike appreciated.

"To the writer, Professor Palmer's interpretative powers found their most fitting and adequate play in the themes presented in the pulpit of the Claremont church. His sermon upon the Lord's Prayer and the Temptations in the Wilderness will not be forgotten by those who heard them. One thinks with longing of the change that would come over the face of the church and society if such simple, natural, rational views of the Founder of Christianity could be made prevalent."

During his four weeks at Pomona, Palmer also delivered the Phi Beta Kappa oration at the founding of Gamma of California Chapter at Pomona College (**GHP**-73), addressed the "ceremony of matriculation," and spoke at a banquet for the faculty and trustees (*Pomona College Quarterly Magazine*, June 1914, pages 117–119).

3. Charles Rieber and his wife were living in California where he was teaching.

Pomona College, 1914. *Left,* James Arnold Blaisdell, *right,* George Herbert Palmer.

4. At the exercises George Herbert Palmer spoke for the Class of 1864 (**GHP**-74).

1914

GHP

May. Fred has an automobile given him by Mr Wood

June 23 I sail on the Laconia with Katherine French & Mr Morse

From Liverpool in five days go through English Lakes to Edinburgh Melrose Dryburgh, Abbotsford, Durham York Somersby, Lincoln, Boston Peterborough, Cambridge In London Mr Morse left us for Switzerland & his children. We settled at Hotel Victoria where remained a fortnight, with Excursions to Stratford Warwick Leamington — Winchester Bemerton, & a night with Moore at Hartley Wintury I was buying books — Barnes, Toltils Miscellany Spenser, Googe, Omar Khayyam, Phair &c spending for them $1700. We had ten days in Paris at Hotel International, Avenue d'Jena, where joined by Morses Excursions to Versailles St Germaine Chartres. We sailed fr Boulogne July 30 on Cincinnati Hamburg American Line & landed Aug 8. being chased by English cruisers, & moving each night without lights & through fog[Note 1]

—I go immediately to Boxford with Fred Mary & my cook Mary. Mr Morse & his children to his house. Eric & Helen in Wm's house — Will & Bertha still at Mt Desert. We use at Boxford the Ford automobile which Mr Wood gave Fred in June

At Boxford wrote Article on Wellesley books [**GHP**-79]

Oct. 5 Norah Moriarty leave us & Nellie Fitzgerald becomes our cook

A year ago this month the Wellesley Trustees decided to raise $1000000 Endowment Fund. The times being bad, little was done in winter. I was appointed Chairman of Committee. In June I went abroad with Mr Morse the Treasurer. March 17 fire destroyed College Hall & on Aug. 1 the great war broke out. We received $950000 from two Rockefeller Boards on condition that we raise by Jan 1 1915 $2,430,000. This we did receiving 50,000 over, also paying College debt of 42,000 & obtaining $560,000 of Insurance. Graduates had already raised $60,000 for an Alumnae Building [see **GHP**-77]

Note 1914

1. In **GHP**-96, page 474, Palmer says: "I was in Paris just as the war was breaking out. On every hand I heard astonishment expressed that so hideous a thing should happen, and a belief that even at the last moment some way would be found to prevent it."

During the tense days just before Britain and Germany were at war, English warships would certainly have followed a German steamer in the English Channel: "In the event of war the British fleet, upon which an island nation depended for its life, had to establish and maintain mastery of the ocean trade routes; it had to protect the British Isles from invasion; it had to protect the Channel and the French coasts in fulfillment of the pact with France; it had to keep concentrated in sufficient strength to win any engagement if the German fleet sought battle; and above all it had to guard itself against that new and menacing weapon of unknown potential, the torpedo. The fear of a sudden, undeclared torpedo attack haunted the Admiralty" (Barbara Tuchman, *The Guns of August*, New York, Macmillan, 1962, page 93).

1914–1915

GHP

Lectures

Oct. 1 Morning Prayers — Anger 10.00
" 22 Univ State of N. Y. Albany Convocation Prfssion 150.00
Nov. Liggett School Detroit Alice
Dec. 24 Trades & Professions H. M. & Co published [**GHP**-76]
Jan 5–28 Two Lectures a week at Union Coll. 600.00
" 15 Wellesley Completion of Fund[Note 1]
Dec 26 Trades & Professions Published [**GHP**-76]
Jan 28 Prayer for Colleges, Union College
Feb. 7. Graduate Y. M. C. A. Harv. Puritan Home
" 6 Paper on Books read to 30 Wellesley Teachers [see 249n5]
" 16 Begin 2 lectures each week at Princeton, with Seminary
To May 19
May 1 Club of Odd Volumes meets at my Library
" 6 Bradford Church of Brou 50.00
June 3 Buffalo Seminary 3 Tests of School 100.00
" " " Harvard Club Lunch
" 10 Harvard Dames Puritan Home
" 14 Notes on a Collection of English Poetry published [**GHP**-79]
" 16 Wheaton College Anger 50.00
" 22 Class Day Prayers
" " Lowell Normal School Confessions
" 23 Class Supper
Sept 29 Morning Prayers 10.00
Oct 7 Smith College, 4 weeks. Two lectures each week on American Poetry, Two on Shakspere. Public on Puritan Home[Note 2] 600.00
Nov. 11 Newton Womans Club Browning 50.00

Dec. 5 N. Y. ΦBK — Philos affecting War	100.00
	1670.00

Notes 1914–1915

1. After the fire on March 17, 1914, destroyed College Hall, the cornerstone of this building, laid in 1871, was recovered from the ruins, and, in a simple ceremony on January 15, 1915, was laid as the cornerstone of a new residence hall, Tower Court, on College Hall Hill. After this ceremony, a meeting was held in the college chapel to celebrate the completion of the Restoration and Endowment Fund. At this meeting, Professor Palmer, who was chairman of the trustees' Committee on Restoration and Endowment, described the successful campaign in some detail (**GHP**-77).

2. From an editorial in *The Smith College Monthly*, November,1915, pages 103–104: ". . . Concerning our most recent distinguished guest, Mr. George Herbert Palmer, Emeritus Professor of Philosophy of Harvard University, it may be said that the impression which he left is almost unique in the annals of the college. Indeed the term 'guest' cannot be correctly applied to him. For four weeks he was, technically, a member of the faculty of instruction, and in that period of time, he succeeded in identifying himself with the life of the college to an extraordinary degree. He fitted himself into the well-worn grooves of our academic routine with an easy naturalness that often takes one years to acquire.

"The mere fact of his daily presence on the platform at chapel seems to us most significant. The morning service is one of our most intimate institutions. We have so many diverse interests, our days are so chopped up by the necessity of doing a great many things in a very short space of time, and each has so much to do in her own individual way, that we frequently lose sight of the fact that we are after all, a real and organic community. With the rapid increase in the numbers of the college, this lack of structural unity has grown more pronounced, until now, it is only at our chapel exercises, that we come together as an institution. The spirit in which we meet then is not one of mere enthusiastic college loyalty: it is rather a keen sense of communion or fellowship with Christian members of a Christian organization.

". . . The most precious of the gifts which Mr. Palmer has left to us is the lavish gift of his own personality. We have been stirred to an indefinable longing to at least follow by the side of the path he has trodden. We have been stimulated with a desire to think more seriously; to find a deeper, truer meaning of the life around us; to discern, in the sonnets of Shakespeare, something more than the beauty of the lines or their very apparent meaning. We have seen that, even in this iconoclastic age, there are persons who have some sort of spiritual life and we have been spurred on to a hope of our own future by this knowledge.

"The modern college student is such a material realist. Romance, of course, is not entirely dead for us but we think of it as existing only in the shadowy world of books. We seldom stop to think that these books were created in the same real world in which we live; that their authors were men and women more real and human perhaps than ourselves. When we are reminded of this as we were by Mr. Palmer's reminiscences of writers whom he had known, we regard our books from a new point of view — as expressive glimpses of real personalities. It thrills us, too, to know that the fascinating realm where authors live, has a tangible existence, and some of us are daring to dream delightful dreams in which we are allowed to pass inside of its sacred portals."

1915

GHP

May 6 Theodore C Williams died
June 8 Gave Portrait of Browning to Wellesley
" Dudley Gate erected & Fence before my house
Dec. 2 Bought from E. D. Brooks of Minneapolis a 3d Folio Shakspere giving him a Shelley letter for which I paid $100.00 & $1600 additional

Lectures

Oct. 1 Morning Prayers 10.00
" 5 Freshman Reception
" 7–28 (4 weeks) Smith College Shakespere & American Literature with public address on Puritan Home 600.00
Nov. 3 A Marriage Cycle published [**AFP**-18]
" 11 Newton Center Club Browning 50.00
Dec 6 At Miss Calkins Lecture
" 9 N. Y. ΦBK Philos. of War
" 11 Edith Cavell Meeting presided

Salary		
1870	Tutor in Greek	1000
1871	"	1000 + Curatorship 500
1872	" " Philosophy	1000 " " " + Forensics 500
1873	Asst Prof	2000 " " " " " "

1876	Resigned Curatorship		
1878	Asst Prof	2500	〃 〃 〃
1880	Resigned Forensics		
1883	Professor	3000	
1886	〃	3500	
1888	〃	4000	
1892	〃	4500	
1897	〃	5000	
1906	〃	5500	
		Last	

Tutor	1870–73	3000
Curator	1872–76	2000
Asst Prof	1873–78	10000
〃	1878–83	12500
Forensics	1873–80	3500
Prof.	1883–86	9000
〃	1886–88	7000
〃	1888–92	16000
〃	1892–95	13500
		76500

For conditions of retiring allowance see Pres' Reports
1898–9 p 12 & 307
Early proposal 1879–80 p. 20 & 139
20/60 at 60, now [?] 40/60
My pension: 3666

Mary Moriaty

1915–16

GHP

Dec 28 Leave Cambridge for Berkeley Stopping at Colorado & Pomona Colleges & Santa Barbara Settle there at Cloyne Court. Have at my table Prof Everett & daughter Helen of Brown Univ. then Prof Bach[?] of Pacific Seminary. J. M. Pierce & wife keep the house**Note** 1

May 16 Join Fred & Mary at Merced. They have visited Grand Canyon & Riverside, Fred San Diego We have $3^{1/2}$ days in Yosemite, 10 at Berkeley 3 days 20 hours on Overland home. They my guests $700.00. Arrive home May 28

During this time Lewis Morse becomes engaged to Ednah A. Rich of Santa Barbara Apr 15 They dine with me & go to Greek Theatre

Evening Julius Caesar. I promise to marry them as my wedding present

August — Barbara French breaks skull

June 23 — with Lewis Morse start again for San Francisco — Denver & Rio Grande & Western Pacific, stopping Colorado Springs & Salt Lake City — arriving June 29 July 1 in forenoon I marry them in company with Mr Weld, and at noon we all take train for Seattle — they to Alaska, I home by Canadian Pacific

July 10 I reach New York where I remain till Sat. 15, Mrs Rieber painting two portraits of me at t house of Lucy Mitchell in Washington Square. At Boxford on 17th

This Summer Bertha let her house till Sept 1 to Rev. Mr Roberts & family. Mr Morse's was closed, & Eric & family at Katy's

I wrote a review of Harpers Wordsworth for Harv. Theol. Rev. [**GHP**-85] Fred & I cleared all the paths through the woods & cut the largest lot of wood we ever accomplished [see picture on page 438]

August & September were given up to boring an artesian well & putting in a bath room. Three unsuccessful borings were made & the work was not ended when we returned to Cambridge, Oct. 2 Throughout I had Louis Pariot[?] take general oversight of all

September — Both Wellfleet & 11 Quincy St were broken into by boys, little taken

Sept 14 Josiah Royce dies aged 61

Dec 16 Hugo Munsterberg died aged 53[Note 2]

Notes 1915–16

1. The city of Berkeley, California, was named after George Berkeley, the Irish philosopher, who was made bishop of Cloyne in 1734. James M. Pierce was manager of Hotel Cloyne Court, at Ridge Road and Le Roy Avenue (from letterhead on which Palmer wrote to Houghton Mifflin Co., chapter 10).

2. Professor Münsterberg dropped dead as he was beginning a lecture at Radcliffe Colllege. From home ". . . he put on his fur coat and overshoes and walked out into the snow and wind, for the students at Radcliffe were waiting for the professor. The gale was strong and sharp—deadly sharp. He struggled against it and reached the College, exhausted. Yet, after a short rest, he entered the lecture room and mounted the platform. He began to lecture, but, with the words of instruction on his lips, he fell to the floor" (Münsterberg, *Hugo Münsterberg*, page 302).

The war in Europe started in August, 1914; the United States did not join the alliance against Germany until April 1917. At Harvard, "[t]he first issue raised by the war was that of Professor Münsterberg, one of the most eminent and popular Harvard professors. He had served the community well through his researches in psychology, and had performed innumerable acts of kindness to individuals. But all this availed him nothing when, as a loyal German subject, he undertook (completely within his rights in a supposedly neutral country) to present the German case to the American public; and this he did with dignity and good taste. . . The public left Münsterberg alone, but old friends and [some] colleagues would no longer speak to him, and a vociferous minority of alumni demanded that he be dismissed, as a poisonous pro-German influence on the students. This the Corporation steadfastly declined to do. . . " (Samuel Eliot Morison, *Three Centuries of Harvard: 1636–1936*, Cambridge, Harvard University Press, 1937, page 453).

1916

GHP

Lectures

Jan 5 — April 28 Univ of California
3 Lectures a week, 2 Seminary, Ethics 3000.00
Jan 29 Collegiate Alumnae Lunch
Feb 7 Mrs Hooker Conference
" 25 Talk to Divinity School
Mar 10 Wellesley Club Browning (328.00)
" 14 Fraternity Talk
" 15 Episc Div. School Herbert
Jan 21 Gymnasium Harv. & California
Mar 31 Phil Union Puritan Home
Apr 1 Wellesley Lunch, Alice
" 9 Cong Church Lords Prayer
" 19 Greek Club Odyssey
" 27 Pacific Sem Graduates Dogma 25.00
" " Dinner Ministers Difficulties
June 20 Harv. Class Day Prayers

1916–17

GHP

Lectures

Sept 28 Morning Prayers — Over & Above 10.00
Oct 1 Philos Graduates (Hocking) Royce
Nov 23 Palmer Mem. Inst[Note 1] — Crothers Vestry

Dec 25 Phillips Brooks House — Myths
Dec 1, Royce in Harv Grad. Magazine [**GHP**-83]
Jan. 1, Review of Wordsworth Harv. Theol Rev [**GHP**-85] 12.00
Dec. 3 Preface to Self Cultivation, Riverside Series
Jan 19 Münsterberg — Phil Graduates
Feb 20–21 Pomona, Harvard Univ. 50.00
" 23 Santa Barbara — Alice & Ednah
Feb. 26–Mar 29. Pacific Seminary Types of Poetry 1200.00
Mar 26 Berkeley Charter Day Bp Berkeley [**GHP**-86] 250.00
Apr 2–30 Duty & Types of Poetry 600.00
" " " Sermons Lds Prayer & Death of Friends
" " " Homer, Alice (2), Philosophers, Germany
June 12 Abbot Academy Puritan Home 50.00
" 19 Wellesley Commencement Prayer
Aug 4. Eliot Hubberd Wedding
" 12 Mrs Rich, Funeral

Jan 31 — Today I deeded my Library to Wellesley College [see 249n5] —Subject to recall— in a sealed document deposited with the Treasurer, Lewis K. Morse

Feb. 7. Leave Cambridge for West Three days in N. Y. sitting for my portrait, four in Washington with Fred & Mary. Go through New Orleans (15th) & Pomona College (19-21) & Santa Barbara (23) to Cloyne Court, Berkeley (24) where at Pacific Theol Sem I give 8 lectures beginning Feb 26 Mon. & Thursday I take Lowells place as Orator in Greek Theatre on Charter Day, Mar 26, on Bp Berkeley [**GHP-86**] & leave on Mar 31 for Reed College, Portland where for 4 weeks I lecture 3 times a week on Ethics & 2ce [=twice] on Poetry. I return to Berkeley May 1, receive LL.D. from Univ. of California[**Note** 2] on May 16, leave that afternoon & after a day & night in New York arrive in Cambridge May 21. Ednah is with me when I receive the degree, & the week before Sadie Matthews died. Eleanor Rowland marries Henry Wembridge May 31.

In March my accident of falling from a table to the floor lames me permanently

Pres. W. D. Hyde of Bowdoin College dies June 30, 1917[**Note** 3]

June 30 Addelaide Allen dies

Notes 1916–17

1. Charlotte Hawkins, later Charlotte Hawkins Brown, a young girl from North Carolina, had gone to grammar school and high school in Cambridge. Then, Alice Freeman Palmer helped her attend the

Teachers' College in Salem, Massachusetts. Miss Hawkins returned to North Carolina and accepted a teaching position in a small school in Sedalia, which was directed by the American Missionary Association. A year later, when the Association withdrew its support, Miss Hawkins continued the work, and a gift of land enabled her to expand the size of the school. After Alice Freeman Palmer died, in 1902, Professor Palmer agreed to Miss Hawkins' request that she name the school after his wife — the Palmer Memorial Institute. Palmer visited the school in 1920, and spoke at the dedication of the Alice Freeman Palmer Building in April 1922. As the most distinguished private boarding school for blacks in the nation, the Institute, with an enrollment of about 180 students, provided college preparatory training at junior and senior high school levels. The school closed in 1971, after desegregation changed the educational situation in the South (Typescript about Charlotte Hawkins and the school, 4 pages, and typescript of Palmer's 1922 talk, 15 pages, both at Schlesinger Library, Radcliffe College; additional information, folder in box 1DD2, Wellesley College Archives).

2. President Benjamin Ide Wheeler conferred the degree: "By authority of the University of California, I confer upon you, George Herbert Palmer, the symbolic degree of Doctor of Laws and admit you to spiritual fellowship with this community of scholars. In eminent degree your life among men has represented, as for yourself, the refining of knowledge into wisdom and the refining of judgment into taste and as toward others clarifying instruction on the simplicity of truth and inspiring counsel in ways of righteousness."

3. Hyde was 58 years old. He and the Palmers had been close friends for many years; in 1887 he named his son George Palmer Hyde. Hyde's biographer (Charles T. Burnett, *Hyde of Bowdoin: A Biography of William DeWitt Hyde*, Boston, Houghton Mifflin Co., 1931) writes in the preface: "In criticism of the manuscript I have been much aided. . . by Professor George H. Palmer, also, a severe, just, and kindly critic, who urged the preparation of this biography, who has written the introduction, and now moves through the events of the narrative like the chorus in Greek drama [scattered through the book are numerous letters and quotations from Palmer]."

From the Introduction (page xv–xvii) by George Herbert Palmer, dated September 1, 1930 (Palmer was 88 years old): "With Hyde I had no intimate acquaintance till 1881. He had been one of my many students at Harvard and, probably enough, I had advised him to go to Andover. . . In my time I find three presidents, and only three, who were as truly presidents of all other colleges as of their own. In this I do not refer to their standing and influence. Several have overtopped them here; one for example at Columbia, two at least at Harvard. But the position of W. D. Hyde, W. G. Tucker [Dartmouth College], and Mark Hopkins [Williams College] was unique. They entered the lives of all other colleges in the same way and at the same time as they entered that of their own. And their stamp remains.

"I have said nothing of Hyde as a teacher. It is hardly necessary to speak of it. Of course he endeared himself to his students and them to Philosophy. He did not inform them, but he set them to thinking and questioning. And something of the same sort may be said of his many books; only that here his simple language and quiet utterance are better preserved. . . The last book Mrs. Palmer had me read to her was one of Hyde's ["Jesus' Way" **GHP**-57, page 324].

"Good-bye, dear friend! You will never pass from my life."

1917–18

GHP

Oct 2 — Helen Everett comes to live with us

Dec. Millicent Todd joins us for several weeks, after building a house at Amherst, & then decides to go to France for Y. M. C. A. work [the United States entered the European war in April 1917]

This summer & autumn I am occupied with writing out my lectures on English Poetry [**GHP**-88]

Feb. 4 Leave Cambridge to give a course of Lectures on Ethics at Haverford each week Mon. Tu. Wed. & at Union Theol Sem Th & Fri for three months, receiving for each $1500.00. I live at the Seminary N. Y. & with Professor Grant at Haverford

Lectures & Articles

Sept 27 Prayers Think on these things	10.00
Feb–May 3 Haverford College (3)	1500.00
" " Union Theol Sem (2)	1500.00
Apr 4–26 Ely Lectures " " (2) [**GHP**-89]	1000.00
June 1 — I marry Margaret F. Williston to Capt. Chester B. McLaughlin Jr in Appelton Chapel	20.00

1918–19

GHP

This summer I lend Quincy St to Ella & Charlie, he having just been operated on for hernia. They remain till October

Eric takes up war work at Newport little Eric going to a summer camp & Helen & little Helen coming to Quincy St. Eric falls sick of grippe & is brought to Cambridge, afterwards to Boxford & Wellfleet

I spend summer at Boxford writing out my literature lectures & also my Ely Ethics lectures. There visited by Helen Everett. On Freds 70th birthday I offer him a portrait of himself & Mrs Rieber spends 10 days with us painting it

Bertha & the children are in their house most of the summer. Mr Morse's home closed. Katie Matthews confined to her bed. Joe & Edith in my -[?] We carry much wood to Cambridge by automobile

Dec 17 News of engagement of Millicent Todd to Joseph Thomas
Helen Everett with us only intermittently
Her father marries Clara Comstock Dec. 11

Eric & Helen in house 50 Shepard St. he teaching in Physics Dep't
Fred takes room in Widener Library
Last of Nov. my Formative Types published [**GHP**-88]
This summer Mr Winship & Mrs Livingston began cataloguing my library. They making but slow progress with the early poetry, on Jan 13 I began on those after 1800
Nov. 15 Formative Types in English Poetry published [**GHP**-88]
February — Altruism published [**GHP**-89]
May 15 Norumbega on A. F. P.
" 25 Wellesley teachers on Miss Balch[Note 1]

Note 1918–19

1. "Emily G. Balch began her teaching in the Department of Economics [at Wellesley College] in 1896. She was an authority on questions of immigration and author of *Our Slavic Citizens* (1910). An ardent pacifist, in 1915 she went with Jane Addams and other American women to the International Congress of Women at the Hague, and in 1916 she was in Stockholm as a member of Henry Ford's Neutral Conference on Continuous Mediation. After two leaves of absence extending from 1916 to 1918, one of her terms as professor expired in 1918. At this time the question of her reappointment came before the Trustees who, after long deliberations which extended until April 1919, decided not to reappoint her. It was a close vote and President Pendleton was one who voted in favor of reappointment. In the absence of detailed minutes we do not know whether this action was taken because of Miss Balch's activity as a pacifist when the United States was engaged in the First World War, or because of her long absences from the College to attend her outside interests. After leaving Wellesley she continued to work for

peace, chiefly through the Women's International League for Peace and Freedom, and was honored in 1946 when she received the Nobel Peace Prize, having been recommended for this honor by [Wellesley's] President Horton" (Ella Keats Whiting, The Faculty, in Glasscock, *Wellesley College, 1875–1975*, page 100).

[some discontinuity of yearly dates follows]

1920

GHP

Jan 23 At the corner of Garden & Waterhouse Sts I was run down by an automobile, bruising me considerably & giving my leg a bad sprain It was just before the time for lighting the lamps & in the thick fog nothing could be seen.

Jan 29–April 15 I give 10 lectures at Boston University on Conscience receiving $350.00

This spring I founded a Fellowship in History at Michigan University in Memory of Alice. It will form an annuity of $100.00 a month while Ella Talmage & I live. Afterwards the income goes to some girl student of History.

1919

GHP

This spring Mrs Rieber paints two portraits of me for Wellesley[Note 1] She & President Foster of Reed College occupy my house the first part of the summer & Mr & Mrs Ross the last part

Fred & Mary spend 10 weeks at Colorado Springs, he taking charge of Tafts Church

Eric & the two Helens join me at Boxford small Eric being at camp in New Hampshire. Bertha & children at Boxford continuously The Morse house closed

I had no book in writing, & no paper even the first summer vacation I had had for 20 years. Did much reading & wood cutting [see picture on page 438]

Millicent Todd returns from war work in mid summer & finds her lover Joe Thomas in consumption at a Denver hospital. She plans to spend a year at Chicago & to take her Doctors Degree there. On reflection she changes & decides to spend the year at Harvard & with us, Davis taking her as a private pupil

Paul Palmer enters Harvard & takes Divinity 29 as his room Fred returns to his old room Divinity-16

Note 1919

1. A portrait of Professor Palmer by Winifred Rieber hangs in Special Collections at Wellesley College.

1921

GHP

Sept 24 Prayers, Pharisaism in Study 10.00
Oct 18 Wellesley Teachers — Confessions 25.00
G-[?] in A's Life to teachers
Nov. 17 Exhibition & speech Herbert Grad English Club
" 20 Alice Woman's Educ. Soc. Everett Morse House
Dec 13 Womans City Club, Herbert
Feb 14 I give my 1st Editions of Philosophy to Harvard, making a display of them & a lecture
March 28 Union College Xs Youthful Ideals
Apr 1 Harv Theol Rev Lords Prayer [**GHP**-90] 16.00
Apr 1-27 Schenectady Conscience 8 Lectures 700.00
June 2 Edward Nixdorff marries Elizabeth Schroeder I going to New York & officiating
" Helen being ill, was brought on by Eric & placed in hospital here the week before Commencement, he Mary Fred & the children going to Wellfleet. We did not therefore reach Boxford till July 10 Helen recovered, Eric taught in Harv Summer School & had my home for six weeks Linette at Boxford small Eric in N. H. camp. After School ended the whole family with Fred & Mary went to Wellfleet for three weeks, I remaining in Boxford at work on the revision of my Odyssey. We cut this summer about three cords of wood & cleared out the Alice & Cellar paths & also the Cave & Western paths. Hilda Pakka & her baby were with us Mr Morse was in the West, his house closed. Bertha's family were in Boxford continuously. I bought a blue front stair carpet. We had much trouble with the Ford automobile & in October exchanged it for a new one, I contributing $400.00. I also gave Fred 500.00 on his birthday & again — 200.00 toward small Erics expenses at Ashville. I had brief visits from Millicent Todd [page starting here is dated 1920] & Helen Everett, the latter of whom then went to England for 2 years study
Nov. Festival Sunday at Poetry Club I announce that Alice has been elected to the Hall of Fame [see 286n1] & that Millicent Todd has become engaged to Walter V Bingham. The following day a letter from Bp Lawrence informs us that Fred has had a pension of $500 a

year granted him On Tues Nov 9 Mrs Lane [mother of William Coolidge Lane] died at 86 & was buried in Boxford Nov. 11.

Nov. 29–Dec. 9 Journey to Coconut Grove Florida to marry Millicent Todd to Walter V Bingham, Stopping on the way at Palmer Institute, Haverford & New York

Dec 4 I marry Millicent Todd to W. V. Bingham in CocoaNut Grove Flr

Aug. 1921 Shingle barn & East piazza

Aug 27–Sept 17 Visit in Boxford from Maud Mason

Sept Ellen Scott Davison dies in Portland

<u>Lectures & Articles</u> 1920–21

Harv Theol Rev Lords Prayer [**GHP**-90] Reprinted in the Churchman
Harv. Grad Magazine W. James Sept. 1 [**GHP**-91]
Sept. 29 Prayers David pourng out water 10.00
Oct. 28 Harvard Dames Dimbovitza
Dec. 22 Mt Vernon Church Puritan Home
" 25 Brooks House Angel's Song
Jan 19 Sedalia Harvard Music Hall
May 26 Presentation of Nortons Portrait
" 21 Tablet in Hall of Fame A. F. P. [see 286n1]
June 16 Mrs Kimball, Bertram Hall
" 19 Boxford Wellesley Girls AFP.
" 21 Class Day Prayers
Aug 21 Puritan Home to Atlantic [**GHP**-92] 200.00

1921

GHP

Eric teaches in summer school & takes Quincy St. Fred, Mary & I go to Boxford. Will & Bertha here all summer. Mr Morse takes Anna to Oxford with Arthur, he returning in late Aug Our servant little Marie & her baby. I busy first half of summer on My Puritan Home. [**GHP**-92] Aug. 18 Katie Matthews dies after four years in bed

Aug. 6. I turn over $15000 to Wellesley for endowment of my library, they to pay annuity of $100 a month to Fred & Mary during their lives, or to me in case of their death. [see 249n5]

Our reading aloud was in Stracheys Victoria Hawthorne & George Eliot

Aug 26–Sept 17 Maude Mason spends three weeks with me while F. & M at Wellfleet She spends the winter at Ware Hall Cambridge

Nov. 6 Begin Sunday Evening Readings

1921–2

GHP

Lectures & Articles

Oct 25 — Wellesley Tablets Mrs Kimball & Gould
Nov. 1 Puritan Home Atlantic [**GHP**-92] 200.00
" 5 Michigan Alumnae Charlestown
Dec. 2 Harvard Dames Life as Game
" 13 Grad Philos Students — History of Dept
" 25 Angels Song Brooks House
Mar 8 Beria College
" 25 Department Dinner
June 1 Framingham Normal Confessons of Teacher

The ΦBK Orator this year was Vachel Lindsay who spent Commencement week with us. Mrs Dargan was also with us

July 6. We settle in Boxford, Bertha & her children being already in her house Our two girls were Marie & Louise, both servants Mr Bradford had broken down & was given a long vacation. After a week here Fred & Mary went to Wellfleet to join their children. Velma Williams comes.

July 15–Aug 12 Velma Williams visits me in absence of Fred & Mary at Wellfleet This summer we have for servants Marie Alden with her baby Ralph & Louise

Professor Bingham & Millicent occupied 11 Quincy St in July & August

1922–23

GHP

Sept 11 Eric enters Phillips Academy with a room at the Williams House, & Margaret Lane enters Wellesley

Sept. 18 I move to Cambridge

In October Nellie Boland becomes our cook bringing her daughter Anna (4 years) Three weeks later came her sister Delia Sharkey as house maid

Lectures & Articles

Nov. 14 — Authors Club — Herbert
Feb 13 — Homer — Literature Course
" 23 — Forgiveness, Graduates Club
Mar. 11 " Wellesley College
" 17 Boston Poetry Association Preside
May 22 Episc School, Forgiveness
" 8 Colby College Teaching & Philosophy

June 11 Prof Winters 25th — Harv. Dinner
" 16 Wellesley, Dr. Abbot & Class Supper

1923

GHP

April 9 Fred goes to Brooks Hospital, Corey Hill, for operation on bladder

I am examined by Dr Pratt & pronounced perfect

1923–4

GHP

Nov. 5 Bp Slattery engaged to Sarah Lawrence

Dec. After two years & a month of labor my Bibliography of Poetry appears [**GHP**-93] I paid H. M. Co $1000.00 at the start & agreed to take $400.00 worth of copies 200 copies were printed at 25.00 each I received 18 and am allowed more at $20.00 [see table on page 480 and 249n5]

May 13 [1924] Alice's bust installed in Hall of Fame with 9 others. Address by Pres Angell of Yale**Note 1**

June 21 Resigned Chairmanship of the Literary committee of the ΦBK Society — Deferred

April 21 Poetry Collection carried to Wellesley [see 249n5]

March 19 Wellesley Festival over Poetry with Speeches [see 249n5]
" 20 Pres Eliots 90th Birth Day celebrated

Aug 13 A sudden stoppage of urine which a katheter could not relieve obliged me to be taken at night to Dr Jenkins in Topsfield & then, when he found he could not help it, to the Beverly Hospital, where I remained a week having a tube inserted in my bladder, & after a talk with Dr Packard at the Homœopathic Hospital in Boston, I returned to Quincy St. Aug 22

Sept 13 Helen & Linette Palmer sail for Europe

Oct 22 Resigned Chairmanship of ΦBK

Lectures

Nov. 4 Brooks Grad Club, Liberalism
Dec 3. Grad Throwgs[?], Professional Questions
" 25 Christmas Reading & Talk
Jan 22 Lewis Seminary Egoism & Altruism
Dec 20 Cabots House — Department
" Bibliography of Poetry
Feb 4 Fred's Virgin Birth [published]

Mar 19 Wellesley Book Collection [see 249n5]
Apr 22 B. U. Kant Centenary [**GHP**-95]
" 26 Herbert Reading for Michigan
May 27 Memorial Society at Harv. Club
Aug 10 Boxford Macbeth
This summer the Binghams in 11 Quincy St then resign Pittsburgh & go to New York

Note 1923–4

1. Alice Freeman Palmer was elected to the Hall of Fame for Great Americans in November 1920. Of the seven people elected then, she was the only woman. Her installation into the Hall, located on the University Heights campus of New York University, began in May, 1921. On the 20th, in New York's Brick Church, Caroline Hazard, Wellesley's former president, delivered a commemorative address on Alice Freeman Palmer (**aboutAFPann**-21). On the 21st, Professor Palmer unveiled a tablet inscribed, as was the usual procedure, with a sentence written by the honoree. The inscription is from *Why Go To College* [**AFP**-8]:

> The smallest village, the
> plainest home, gives ample
> space for the resources of the
> trained college woman.

Three years later, in another ceremony, on May 13, 1924, a bust of Alice Freeman Palmer by the sculptress Evelyn Longman was presented by Wellesley's President Ellen Fitz Pendleton and unveiled by Professor Palmer (a copy of the bust is in the Special Collections of the Wellesley College Library). Then, President James Roland Angell of Yale University (the son of Mrs. Palmer's mentor and friend, James Burrill Angell, President of the University of Michigan, who died in 1916), delivered an address (I have been unable to find a copy of this address. Wellesley College Archives, Box 1DD2. The Hall of Fame is now part of Bronx Community College; A Scenic Overlook on Great Americans, *New York Times*, January 27, 1991, page 34).

1924–5

GHP

On Freds birthday, Aug 6, the entire family was at Wellfleet, where Fred & Mary had been for several weeks with Erics family, I alone at Boxford. They returned with me to Boxford. At midnight of Aug 11 I had such an obstruction of urine as obliged me to call Fred to take me to Dr. Jenkins at Topsfield. He too unable to draw the water took me to the Beverly Hospital where a tube was put into the bladder Until this was healed on Aug 20 I staid at the Hospital. Then was taken to the Homœopathic Hospital for consultation with Dr Packard. He assured me that the prostate gland would now steadily enlarge & should be removed. I remained there but two days, then to Quincy St joining the Binghams, & two days later consulting Dr Chute who a year & a half earlier had operated most successfully on Fred. I asked him if I might not wait safely till early October & was told that I might & that this would be a more convenient time for him.

During this interval I obtained from Edwin Abbot the $50000 which I had gradually saved & loaned to him at 5 per ct & opened a correspondence with the Univ. of Michigan by which this fund was turned over to them, they paying me 8 per ct annuity during my life & those of Fred & Mary, and after our deaths they establishing a Professorship of History in Alice's name to be held by a woman at full salary.

This was completed before I went to the Hospital, and also a visit from Prof & Mrs Myers, psychologist from Cambridge, England. He was with us four days.

This time Fred & Mary spent at Wellfleet but returned the 1st of October

On October 3 Fred took me to the Brooks Hospital in Brookline, I being in perfect health. The following day Dr. Chute inserted a tube into the bladder & began his water treatment. For the operation cocaine was used to cover the abdomen. 10 days later this tube was removed as too large & a smaller one was inserted, & this was done again a week later, these two later operations being much more painful than the first. A glass of water was to be drunk every hour, day & night & was followed by an excruciating spasm. The pain of the whole affair was more intense & continuous than I had ever before known.

Nov. 24 the second operation occurred & the prostate was taken out, I having no ether. For three or four days all went well, then came leakage which so delayed the healing that I was not allowed to go home till Dec 13 — 10 weeks

Apr. 2 Charles Talmage dies suddenly — heart
May 19 Authors Club elects me Honorary Member
June 28 E. L. Bradford's last sermon at Boxford
Aug. 7 Eric & family return fr summer abroad
" 10 [1925] Anna H. Morse & Winthrop P. Haynes married in Boxford Church

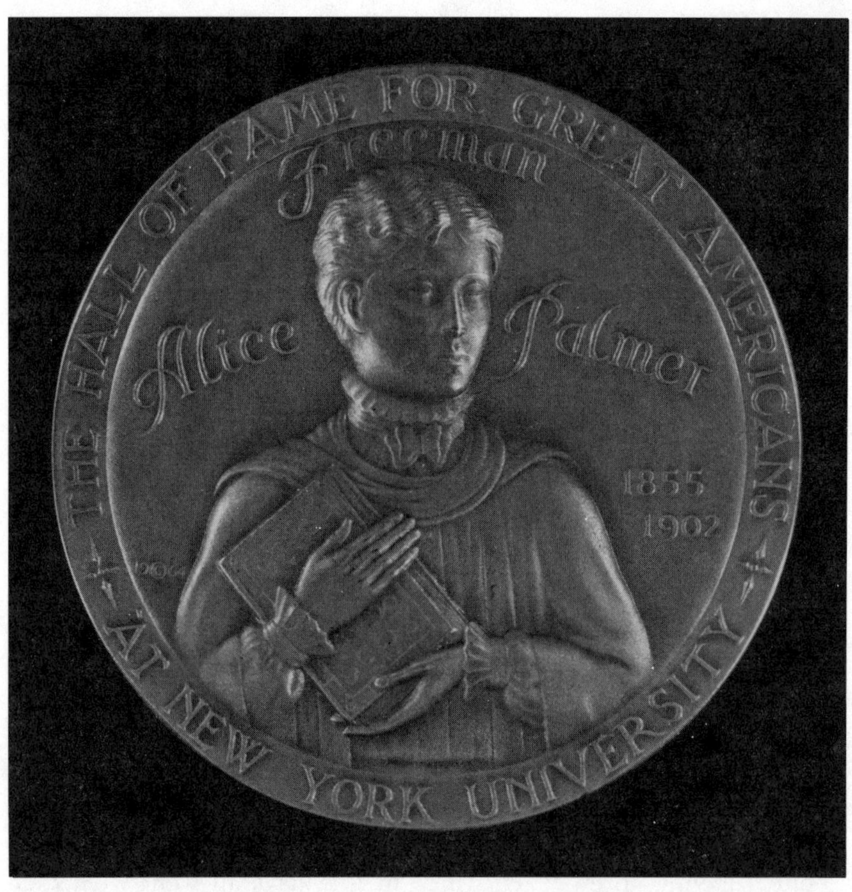

The Alice Freeman Palmer Medal, sculptured by Thomas G. Lo Medico, on the occasion of her election to The Hall of Fame for Great Americans (see 286n1). Original diameter, $1^{11/16}$ inches. *Above,* the front of the medal; *on the opposite page,* the reverse.

Alice Freeman Palmer's credo, "'The smallest village, the plainest home, give ample space for the resources of the college trained woman,' is the theme for the reverse of the medal. The design depicts, Motherhood, woman's role in the home, her participation in the arts, the natural urge to teach and to learn, and her role in science and industry. In general, her contribution to progress and development for the benefit of mankind."

1925

GHP

<u>Lectures</u>

April 20, To Department on Committee Room
May 7 Harvard Dames Odyssey
April 23 New York Shakspere Club
May 19 Boston Authors Club Dimbovitza
" 22 Dinner to K. L. Bates Wellesley[Note 1, 2]
June 26 Address on Mr & Mrs Bradford

Sept. I turn over to Ella Talmage $100 a month for the rest of her life, from her & my joint annuity at Michigan University

Christmas — I put away $2400.00, 12 paid up shares in the Wellesley Cooperative Bank to pay the College expenses of Anna Boland, she being now 8 years old At 17 it would be about $3500 & stands under the Trusteeship of Nellie Boland & Delia Sharkey. It may be used at any college, but I have expressed my preference for Wellesley.

Notes 1925

1. On Friday evening, May 22, the Department of English Literature gave a dinner in honor of Miss Bates who was to retire at the close of the school year. Professor Palmer, age 83, the first of several speakers, "spoke chiefly of the beauty and power of her poetry and of her character as exemplifying that poetry" (Miss Bates, Soon to Retire, Honored at Dinner at Agora, *Wellesley College News*, May 28, 1925, page 5).

2. At the Semi-Centenial celebration on May 29, 1925, one week after the dinner for Katharine Lee Bates (see Note 1 above), William Allan Neilson, President of Smith College was one of the speakers: ". . . Wellesley and Smith began together with a common aim. They have pursued common methods and they have arrived beyond the wont of academic institutions, in a common understanding. You may have, Madam President [Pendleton], more eloquent congratulations than I can bring you from Smith, but I know there is no representative of any organization, learned or unlearned, here who can come to Wellesley knowing what this moment means more than we do, and bring you congratulations more heartfelt.

"When I thought that I was really going to make a speech here today, I thought of one element in the institutions seldom dealt with. The official founders, officers, and great alumnae are honored, but every college has one or two people who occupy none of these positions, yet who do as much as any one for the prosperity and development and for the individuality of the institution. Every college has some private friends, and it happens that some of the most important of the private friends of Wellesley I have been proud to call my own friends.

"I am thinking especially today of a friend of thirty years at Harvard, Mr. George Herbert Palmer [eighty-three years old]. Mr. Palmer's relation to Wellesley is a unique one. Before an audience of Wellesley people, I need not elaborate what it was, what it is, what it will continue to be through the permanent contribution he made to your life and culture. My own relations with him have been of a peculiar nature. Twice in my life I have resorted to Professor Palmer for advice and he has allowed himself to be treated as an adviser ought to allow himself to be treated and seldom does. On one occasion, I asked him whether I should stay on at Harvard or whether I should go. He said, 'Go. You will do better if you go.' So I stayed. At a later time I asked him if I should go away from Harvard to Smith and he said, 'No, stay.' So I went. On both occasions he took it like a man. He was, I think, more easily reconciled to my disregard of his advice than a physician. He understands that the function of an adviser is to stimulate thought in the advisee, not to dictate. So long as he stimulates thought we know that he has fulfilled his function. I am sure that is the way he has acted toward Wellesley College and I have ventured here to put in my word to the name because I knew that he was not to be on the program" (*The Wellesley Alumnae Magazine*, Semi-Centennial Issue, June 1925, page 234).

Neilson's biographer quotes from this letter, starting with "Twice in my life I have resorted to Professor Palmer for advice. . . ," and describes how other important Harvard figures — Charles W. Eliot, George Lyman Kittredge, Bliss Perry, and F. N. Robinson — also advised Neilson not to leave Harvard to go to Smith College (Margaret Farrand Thorp, *Neilson of Smith*, New York, Oxford University Press, 1956, pages 151–158).

1925–1926

GHP

June 1. Put in Socony Oil Heating

" Dan V. Thompson secures position in Yale Art School, 2 years at 2500 a year & becomes engaged to Cecile

June 9 — Alexander Meiklejon & Helen Everett are married in the Old South Church by Dr. G. A. Gordon & myself

June 8. Put in Socony Oil Heating Plant
Mary's long illness
I alone at Boxford writng on my growth in Philos return to Cambridge August 31
Sept 13-18 International Congress o Philos
Oct. 9 I resign the Kimball Fund & leave Prof. C. I. Lewis appointed for four years
Dec 25 Galen L. Stone dies

<u>Lectures & Articles</u> 1925–1926

Late Oct. Forgiveness — Atlantic for April [**GHP**-96] $150.00
Dec. 28 Riverside Pamphlet on Mr Bradford [**GHP**-94] cost 50.00
Jan. 11 Psychical Society, Hodgson's 2 methods
Nov. 15. Brooks House — Religion & Ethics — Proof Jan 13
Feb 10 Emerson Hall — Homer (Storm) [?]
Mar 10 Dana Hall "
May 10 Harte Dinner — Grounds of Happiness here
June 9 I marry Meiklejohn & Helen Everett
Sept. 13 Preside & speak at section on Ethics

1927

GHP

May 22 F. & M Golden Wedding I give $1000.00
Go late to Boxford
On account ot Delia's illness returning Sept 16 — Bixby bringing us all with luggage for $10.00
Mary recovering from her years illness stays with Fred & children at Wellfleet Eric in Labrador with Dr Grenfell.

<u>Lectures & Articles</u>

April 1. The Junior College, Atlantic [**GHP**-99] 1.50
May 19 Dana Hall My Religious Beliefs

1928 Dec 17 My toe cut off by [incomplete entry]
1929 June 24 Moved to Boxford
This summer G. A. Parkhurst thoroughly repaired the old house at an expense of $100.00 & Edith Matthews put new muslin curtains throughout at expense of 30.00
Mr Bixby brought us back to Cambridge Sept. 12
This year t Federal Govt threatened suits for taxes which would have ruined us all We received an entire & official acquttance came Aug 5 1929

H. M. Co.
March 1890

Field Ethics	38
Formative	11
Glory Impf	9
Life of A. F. P.	530
Marriage Cyl	5
Nat. Goodness	51
Odys Wyeth	706
" regular	96
Self Cult	159
Shakspere	3
Trades & Prof	2
Antigone	29
Eth & Moral	28
Freedom	75

[This table is not clear. For each book listed, it might present the number sold in March 1890, but, except for the regular Odyssey, they were all published *after* that date.]

1929

GHP
Oct 21 On Growing Old [**GHP**-105]

California

GHP
June 1885 Sent by Harvard for Examinations in San Francisco
June–Sept California Summer School & Alaska
Jan 25–Feb 17 — Berkeley with Mrs. Rieber
Feb 12–Apr 1 — Claremont, Sta Barbara & Berkeley

Voyages to Europe

GHP
Nov.–May, 1857. To Egypt & Sicily on Wild Gazelle with Jule
May 1867 To Germany with Lee, he returning 1868, I in June 1869
June–Sept. Nell & I at St Germains France
May 31–July 11, 1878, I in Glasgow with E. Caird
June–Sept. 1879 with Cairds at Dingwall, Scotland
June-Sept. 1880 " " " Borrowdale England

Aug 1884 — Six weeks with Edwin & Philip Abbot in England
June 1888–Sept 1889 Sabbatical Year in Europe with Alice
Aug 1895–Sept., 1896 " " Bicycling " " " "
Sept 24–Dec 31 Half Sabbatical. Alice dies in Paris
June–Sept — Europe with Fred Mary & Eric
June 23–Aug 8. England & France w. Mr Morse & Katharine French

Publications

Introduction

Publications

Publications related to George Herbert Palmer are identified as follows: those by him (chapter 6) as **GHP**-number; the annotations (chapter 7) as **GHPann** with corresponding numbers; those about him (chapter 8) as **aboutGHPann**-number; and those dedicated to him (chapter 9) as **dedctdGHPann**-number. Similar identification, with the prefix **AFP,** is used for publications by and about Alice Freeman Palmer.

I have tried to develop complete bibliographies by the Palmers. Chapter 6 lists 109 publications by George Herbert Palmer; I have found all except **GHP**-23 and 33. Entries in the Chronicles helped to identify numerous publications, including unsigned book reviews. A "letter to the editor" by him may appear in this list or in a note to the Chronicles. Despite his prolificacy as a writer, when Professor Palmer mentions his publications in chapter 1 (page 10), he says: "But I have made it my ambition to be a teacher rather than a writer, & I count it my most gratifying success to have deeply influenced many subsequently powerful lives."

The quality of Professor Palmer's speaking and writing is specifically addressed in the citations for three of his honorary degrees: ". . . a master of accurate and elegant style in both prose and verse . . ." (233n3); ". . . you expound in simple but illuminating words . . ." (242n2); and ". . . his refinement in style, whether in philosophy or literature, being no mere fastidiousness, but the reflex of refined thought . . ." (257n2).

Chapter 11 lists 20 publications by Alice Freeman Palmer; I have found all. The list also includes two pieces — **AFP**-12 and 13 — that are published here for the first time.

In 1908, six years after his wife died, Professor Palmer regretted that she had written so little for publication: "While Mrs. Palmer always avoided writing, and thought — generous prodigal ! — that her work was best accomplished by spoken words, her complying spirit could not always resist the appeals of magazine editors. I could wish now that their requests had been even more urgent. And I believe that those who read these pages will regret that one possessed of such breadth of view, clearness, charm and cogency of style should have left a literary record so meagre . . ." (**GHP**-65, page 311).

Caroline Hazard, president of Wellesley College from 1899 to 1910, also noted that Mrs. Palmer "did not leave many written discourses. The effect of personality on personality was the instrument which she used; so that in some sense her fame and influence may be ephemeral, and yet in another sense it will truly live in the minds of all who knew her and all who felt the power of her life" (**aboutAFPann**-8: Hazard, *From College Gates*, page 207).

And James B. Angell, Mrs. Palmer's friend and mentor, said that "few speakers have in so large a measure as she that magnetic unanalyzable power, divinely given now and then to some fortunate man or woman, of captivating and charming and holding complete possession of assemblies from the first to the last utterance" (**GHP**-57, page 258).

The annotations in chapters 7 and 12 are not reviews by the compiler; rather they present the very language of the Palmers. Depending on the nature of the particular publication, the selection is from a preface or a text.

Similarly, in chapters 8, 9, and 13, the annotations present the language of the authors. So much has been written about the Palmers, that these lists are undoubtedly incomplete.

A large collection of material by and about Alice Freeman Palmer, described in the Chronicles' note 2 on page 32, was obtained from the Broome County Historical Society and the Windsor Central School District. When used elsewhere in the compilation, items from this collection are identified as BCHSoc.

Chapter 6

Publications by George Herbert Palmer

identified as **GHP**-number

For an explanation of the *net* price, see pages 471–72. The inclusion of such prices (from *Publishers Weekly*) in this list may be incomplete.

1 *The Odyssey of Homer: Books I.-XII., The Text and an English Version in Rhythmic Prose*, Boston, Houghton, Mifflin and Co., 1884. Copyright, 1884, by G. H. Palmer. 433 pages, 6x8$^{3/4}$ inches. $2.50, *net*

2 *The Odyssey of Homer*, translated by George Herbert Palmer, Boston, Houghton, Mifflin and Co., 1891. Copyright, 1891, by G. H. Palmer. 387 pages, about 5$^{1/4}$x8 inches. $1.50.

3 *The Odyssey of Homer*, School Edition, Boston, Houghton, Mifflin and Co. Copyright, 1891, by G. H. Palmer. xxxvi+394 pages, 5$^{1/4}$x8 inches. $1.00, *net.*

4 *The Odyssey of Homer*, Abridged School Edition, Boston, The Riverside Literature Series, Houghton Mifflin Co. Copyright, 1891, by G. H. Palmer. 410 pages, 4$^{3/4}$ x7$^{1/8}$ inches.

5 *The Odyssey of Homer*, Boston, The Riverside Literature Series, Houghton Mifflin Co. Copyright, 1884, 1912, 1921 by George Herbert Palmer. 400 pages, 4$^{1/2}$x6$^{3/4}$ inches.

6 *The Odyssey of Homer*, with [16] Illustrations by N. C. Wyeth, Boston, Houghton Mifflin Co., 1929. Copyright, 1884, 1891, and 1912, by George H. Palmer Copyright, 1929, by Houghton Mifflin Co. 314 pages, 7$^{3/4}$x10$^{3/8}$ inches. $5.00.

7 *The Odyssey of Homer*, with [16] Illustrations by N. C. Wyeth,

Boston, Houghton Mifflin Co., 1929. Copyright, 1884, 1891, and 1912, by George H. Palmer Copyright, 1929, by Houghton Mifflin Co. 314 pages, $7^{3/4}$x$10^{3/8}$ inches. $25.00 A deluxe edition of **GHP**-6.

8 *The Odyssey of Homer*, Boston, The Riverside Literature Series, Houghton Mifflin Co. Copyright, 1949, by Frederic Palmer, Copyright, 1884, 1912, 1921 by George Herbert Palmer. 402 pages, $4^{3/4}$x7 inches.

9 *The Odyssey Homer*, trans. George Herbert Palmer, ed. Howard Porter, New York, Bantam Books, 1971. Copyright 1962 by Bantam Books, Inc.

10 The New Education, *Andover Review*, 1885; 4 (November): 393–407. Also published in **GHP-**13 and **GHP**-65.

11 Possible Limitations of the Elective System I, *Andover Review*, 1886; 6 (December): 569–590. Also published in **GHP**-13 and, entitled Erroneous Limitations of the Elective System, in **GHP**-65.

12 Possible Limitations of the Elective System II, *Andover Review*, 1887; 7 (January): 1–18. Also published in **GHP**-13 and, entitled Necessary Limitations of the Elective System, in **GHP-**65.

13 *The New Education, Three Papers*, Boston, Little, Brown, & Co., 1887. Copyright, 1887, by George Herbert Palmer. 154 pages, $4^{3/4}$x$7^{1/8}$ inches.

14 *Expenses at Harvard*, An address by Professor George Herbert Palmer before Harvard graduates, Commencement Day, 1887. Paper cover, Cambridge, John Wilson and Son, 1887. 22 pages, about 6x9 inches. Also published, entitled College Expenses, in **GHP**-65.

15 Hexameters and Rhythmic Prose, *Atlantic Monthly*, 1890; 66 (October): 526–534.

16 Reminiscences of Professor Sophocles, *Atlantic Monthly*, 1891; 67 (June): 779–788. Also published, entitled A Teacher of the Olden Time, in **GHP**-65.

17 Ownership of Books, *Christian Union*, 1891; July 11: 78–79.

18 *The Glory of the Imperfect*, An address given at the first com-

mencement of the Woman's College of Western Reserve University, Cleveland, Ohio, 1891. Pamphlet, Boston, D. C. Heath & Co., 1891. Copyright, 1891, by D. C. Heath & Co. 29 pages, 5x7 inches.

19 *The Glory of the Imperfect*, a revised edition published by Thomas Y. Crowell Co., Boston, in 1898. Copyright, 1898, by Thomas Y. Crowell & Co.

20 Barnes's Rural Poems, *Christian Union*, 1891; December 26: 1270–1271.

21 Manliness of Boyhood, *Congregationalist*, 1892; February 18: 54.

22 Doubts about University Extension, *Atlantic Monthly*, 1892; 69 (March): 367–374.

23 Public Support of College Vices, *McClure*: not found.

24 The Cultivation of Tact, *The Sibyl* (Elmira College News and Literary Magazine), 1892; 21 (No.4, July): 78–82.

25 Book review. B. Jowett, M. A., *The Dialogues of Plato*, translated into English, with analyses and introductions. Third edition. 5 vols. Macmillan, 1892. *The Nation*, 1892; 55 (July 7): 15.

26 Philosophy in the Colleges, *Independent* (New York), 1892; August 4: 3.

27 Book review. J. Burnet, M. A., *Early Greek Philosophy*, Edinburgh: Adam & Charles Black; New York: Macmillan, 1892. Pp. 378. *Nation*, 1892; 55 (August 11): 113.

28 Book Review. William DeWitt Hyde, *Practical Ethics*, New York, Henry Holt & Co. 1892. Pp. 208. *Christian Union*, 1892; October 22: 744.

29 Can Moral Conduct be Taught in Schools?, *Forum*, 1893; 14 (January): 673–685. Also published, entitled Ethical Instruction in the Schools, in **GHP**-65, and as a Riverside Educational Monograph entitled Ethical and Moral Instruction in Schools (**GHP**-76).

30 The Ethical Doctrine of Pleasure, *Chautauqua Assembly Herald*, July 24, 1893, page 5.

31 Harvard University, in *Johnson's Universal Cyclopædia*, new ed., 8 vols., prepared by a corps of thirty-six editors assisted by eminent European and American specialists, under the direction of Charles K. Adams, LL.D., editor-in-chief, president of the University of Wisconsin, vol. 4, 1894, page 163–164.

32 Philip Stanley Abbot, *Appalachia* (Journal of the Appalachian Mountain Club), 1896–1898; 8 (No. 2, November 1896): 153–156.

33 Empedocles, *World's Best Reading*, January 27, 1897: not found.

34 *Self-Cultivation in English*, New York, T. Y. Crowell & Co., 1897. Copyright, 1897, by T. Y. Crowell & Co. Crowell also published *Self-Cultivation in English* and *The Glory of the Imperfect* (**GHP**-18) together in a large type edition, Copyright, 1897 & 1898. (see titles with **GHP**-76)

35 Similarities and Contrasts of Christianity and Buddhism, *Outlook*, 1897; 56 (June 19): 443–450.

36 Book review. Wilhelm Wundt, *Ethics*, translated by Edward Bradford Titchener, Julia Henrietta Gulliver, and Margaret Floy Washburn. Volume 1, Introduction: The Facts of the Moral Life. Volume 2, Ethical Systems. *Psychological Review,* 1898; 5: 513–518.

37 *The Antigone of Sophocles*, Translated with Introduction and Notes, Boston, Houghton Mifflin Co., April 1899. Copyright, 1899, by George Herbert Palmer; another printing is Copyright, 1899 and 1927, by George Herbert Palmer. 100 pages, about $5x7^{1/2}$ inches. 75 cents.

38 The Harvard Union Site, Letter to the Editor, *Boston Evening Transcript*, March 17, 1900.

39 A Non-Decadent Country Town, *Congregationalist*, 1900; August 23: 256.

40 *The Field of Ethics*, Being the William Belden Noble Lectures for 1899, Boston, Houghton Mifflin and Co., November 1901. Copyright, 1901, by George Herbert Palmer. 213 pages, about $5x7^{1/2}$ inches. $1.10, *net*. Postpaid, $1.21.

41 *The Field of Ethics*, translated into Japanese by Shinko Imaizumi.

42 A Study of Self-Sacrifice. *Harvard Graduates' Magazine,* 1902–1903; 11 (September 1902): 12–27.

43 Book review. William James, *Varieties of Religious Experience,* (Gifford Lectures, Third Series), New York, Longmans, Green & Co., 1902. *Outlook,* 1902; 72 (December 27): 991–995.

44 *A Service in Memory of Alice Freeman Palmer.* See **about-AFPann**-5.

45 The Heart of Ethics, Pamphlet, Berkeley, The University Press, 1903. 20 pages. Reprinted from the *University Chronicle,* November 1903.

46 *The Nature of Goodness,* Boston, Houghton Mifflin Co., November 1903. Copyright, 1903, by George Herbert Palmer. 248 pages, about 5x7$^{1/2}$ inches. $1.10, *net.* Postpaid, $1.21.

47 Some Religious Verse of Alice Freeman Palmer. See **AFP**-16.

48 *Twenty-Five Portraits of Alice Freeman Palmer.* See **about-AFPann**-7.

49 George Herbert as a Religious Poet, *Atlantic Monthly,* 1905; 95 (February): 194–205.

50 *The English Works of George Herbert newly arranged and annotated and considered in relation to his life,* 3 volumes: 1. Essays and Prose, 429 pages. 2. Cambridge Poems, 443 pages. 3. Bemerton Poems, 455 pages. Illustrated. Boston, Houghton Mifflin and Co., October 1905. Each volume 5$^{3/4}$x8$^{1/2}$ inches. $6.00.

51 *The English Works of George Herbert newly arranged and annotated and considered in relation to his life,* Large-paper edition, six volumes, limited to 150 numbered copies. 1. Essays, 191 pages. 2. Prose, 233 pages. 3 and 4. Cambridge Poems, 219, 208 pages. 5 and 6. Bemerton Poems, 239, 211 pages. Illustrated. Boston, Houghton Mifflin and Co., 1905. Each volume 6x8$^{3/4}$ inches. $20.00.

52 *The English Works of George Herbert newly arranged and annotated and considered in relation to his life,* Second edition, 3 volumes. 1. 443 pages. 2. 437 pages, 3. 485 pages. Illustrated. Boston, Houghton Mifflin and Co., 1907. Each volume about 5$^{1/2}$x8 inches. $6.00, *net.*

53 Alice Freeman Palmer. See **aboutAFPann**-9.

54 *William Henry Willcox: A sketch by his children wih an address by George Herbert Palmer*, Cambridge, Riverside Press, 1906. 66 pages. $5^{1/4}$x8 inches.

55 The Ideal Teacher, *Atlantic Monthly*, 1907; 99 (April): 433–442. Also published in **GHP**-65 and as a Riverside Educational Monograph (see titles with **GHP**-76).

56 For Professor Norton's Eightieth Birthday, *Harvard Graduates' Magazine*, 1907–1908; 16 (December 1907): 226–228.

57 *The Life of Alice Freeman Palmer*, Boston and New York, Houghton, Mifflin & Co., The Riverside Press, Cambridge, [April] 1908. frontispiece and 9 illustrations. [xii], 354, [ii]. $5^{3/8}$x $7^{7/8}$ inches. cloth. $1.50, *net*. Postpaid, $1.65. See **aboutAFPann**-10.

58 *The Life of Alice Freeman Palmer*, edition for the blind, Louisville, Kentucky, American Printing House for the Blind, 1910, 2 vols, folio. See **aboutAFPann**-11.

59 *The Life of Alice Freeman Palmer*, Hall of Fame edition, Boston, Houghton Mifflin & Co., 1908. Copyright 1908 by George Herbert Palmer. Illustrated. 349 pages, $4^{3/4}$x$7^{1/4}$ inches. See **aboutAFPann**-12.

60 *The Life of Alice Freeman Palmer*, tranlated into Japanese by Katsuji Sugimoto, 1923. See **aboutAFPann**-13.

61 *The Life of Alice Freeman Palmer*, New Edition with Appendix, Boston, Houghton Mifflin & Co., 1924. Copyright, 1908 and 1924, by George Herbert Palmer. Illustrated. 363 pages, about $5^{1/2}$x8 inches. See **aboutAFPann**-14.

62 *The Life of Alice Freeman Palmer*, Boston, Houghton Mifflin & Co., 1908. Copyright 1908 and 1924 by George Herbert Palmer and Copyright 1936 by Frederic Palmer, Jr. Illustrated. 363 pages, about $5^{1/2}$x$8^{1/4}$ inches. See **aboutAFPann**-15.

63 *Self-Cultivation in English*, Boston, Houghton Mifflin Co., 1908, Copyright, 1908, by George Herbert Palmer, and Copyright, 1909, by Houghton Mifflin Co. 50 cents. See **GHPann**-34. Also published in **GHP**-65 and as a Riverside Educational Monograph (see titles with **GHP**-76).

64 Specialization. *The University Record* (University of Chicago), 1908; 13 (No. 1, July): 1–8. Also published in **GHP**-65.

65 *The Teacher: Essays and Addresses on Education*, by George Herbert Palmer and Alice Freeman Palmer, Boston, Houghton Mifflin Co., November 1908. Copyright, 1908, by George Herbert Palmer. 395 pages, $5^{3/8}$x8 inches. $1.50, *net*. Postpaid, $1.65. See also **AFP**-17.

66 Book review. Theodore C. Williams, translation of *The Æneid of Virgil,* Boston, Houghton Mifflin Co. $1. *Outlook*, 1909; 91 (January 2): 24.

67 Gossip and the Newspapers, Letter to the Editor, *Outlook*, 1909; 92 (August 14): 876–878.

68 *A Herbert Bibliography*, Being a Catalogue of a Collection of Books Relating to George Herbert Gathered by George Herbert Palmer. Bibliographical Contributions of the Library of Harvard University, No. 59. paperback. 19 pages, about 7x10 inches. Cambridge, Issued by the Library of Harvard University, 1911.

69 *A Herbert Bibliography*. A hardcover edition of **GHP**-68, with the same dimensions and the identical text.

70 *A Herbert Bibliography*, Privately printed, February 1911. hardcover. 61 pages, about $5^{1/2}$x8 inches.

71 *The Problem of Freedom*, Boston, Houghton Mifflin Co., November 1911. Copyright, 1911, by George Herbert Palmer. ix+211 pages, 5x$7^{1/2}$ inches. Reprinted by AMS Press, New York, in 1971.

72 *Intimations of Immortality in the Sonnets of Shakspere*, Boston, Houghton Mifflin Co., November 1912. Copyright, 1912, by George Herbert Palmer. vii+57 pages, $4^{3/4}$x$7^{1/8}$ inches.

73 Phi Beta Kappa Oration, *Pomona College Quarterly Magazine*, 1914; 2 (No. 3, March): 81–92.

74 Across Fifty Years: 1864–1914. *Harvard Graduates' Magazine*, 1914–1915; 23 (September 1914); 33–36.

75 What is a Profession? *Journal of Education*, 1914; 80 (No. 2, December 3): 537–539.

76 *Trades and Professions*, Riverside Educational Monograph,

Boston, Houghton Mifflin Co., 1914 (December 24). Copyright, 1914, by George Herbert Palmer. Edited, with Editor's Introduction (v-xii), by Henry Suzzallo, professor of the philosophy of education, Teachers College, Columbia University. 36 pages. $4^{3/4}$x7 inches. 35 cents. The 40 titles in the series of monographs also include *The Ideal Teacher* (**GHP**-55), *Ethical and Moral Instruction in Schools* (**GHP**-29), *The Glory of the Imperfect* (**GHP**-18), and *Self-Cultivation in English* (**GHP**-63).

77 Address (pages 14–24) in *Wellesley College: Restoration and Endowment Fund*, Record of a Meeting in Celebration of its Completion Held January 15 1915, published by Wellesley College, 1915. 35 pages, $5^{1/2}$x$8^{3/8}$ inches.

78 Riverside Uplift Series, Boston, Houghton Mifflin Co., Copyright, 1914, by George Herbert Palmer: *The Glory of the Imperfect* (**GHP**-18), *Self-Cultivation in English* (**GHP**-63), and *Trades and Professions* (**GHP**-76). Each $4^{3/4}$x7 inches. 50 cents, *net.*

79 *Notes on a Collection of English Poetry intended for Wellesley College with instructions for its proper care.* Thirty copies printed at the Riverside Press, Cambridge, June 1915. 36 pages, $5^{3/4}$x$7^{7/8}$ inches.

80 Editorial. The College and the Student, *Outlook*, 1915; 110 (July 28): 702–703.

81 *A Marriage Cycle*, by Alice Freeman Palmer with a preface by George Herbert Palmer, Boston, Houghton Mifflin Co., October 1915. Copyright, 1915, by George Herbert Palmer. xvii+71 pages, $5^{1/2}$x8 inches. See **AFP**-18.

82 Introduction (page 3–19) to T. C. Williams, translation of *The Georgics and Eclogues of Virgil*, Cambridge, Harvard University Press, 1915. 166 pages, $5^{1/4}$x$8^{1/4}$ inches.

83 Josiah Royce, *Harvard Graduates' Magazine*, 1916–1917; 25 (December 1916): 165–170. Also published with minor changes in *The Development of Harvard University* [**GHP**-102] and in *Contemporary Idealism in America* [**GHP**-107].

84 *The English Poems of George Herbert newly arranged in relation to his life*, Boston, Houghton Mifflin Co., 1916. Copyright 1905 and 1916 by George Herbert Palmer. xv+427 pages, $4^{1/2}$x$6^{3/4}$ inches.

85 Book review. George McLean Harper, *William Wordsworth: His Life, Works, and Influence*, Scribner's, 1916. 2 Vols. Vol. I, pp. xvi, 441; Vol. II, pp. 451. $6.50. *Harvard Theological Review*, 1917; 10: 84–89.

86 Bishop Berkeley, Pamphlet, 22 pages. Reprinted from the University of California *Chronicle*, Vol. XIX, No. 3.

87 The Monologue of Browning, *Harvard Theological Review*, 1918; 11 (April): 121–144. Also published, entitled Robert Browning, as chapter 8 in **GHP**-88.

88 *Formative Types in English Poetry*, The Earl Lectures of 1917, Boston, Houghton Mifflin Co., November 1918. Copyright, 1918, by George Herbert Palmer. x+311 pages, 5x7$^{1/2}$ inches. $1.50. Reprinted by Books for Libraries Press, Essay Index Reprint Series, Freeport, New York, in 1968.

89 *Altruism: Its Nature and Varieties*, The Ely Lectures for 1917–18, New York, Scribner's, 1920, Copyright, 1919, by Charles Scribner's Sons. viii+138 pages, 5x7$^{5/8}$ inches. $1.25. Reprinted by Greenwood Press, Westport, Connecticut, in 1970.

90 The Lord's Prayer, *Harvard Theological Review*, 1920; 13 (No. 3): 124–135. Also published as **GHP**-108.

91 William James, *Harvard Graduates' Magazine*, 1920–21; 29 (September 1920): 29–34. Also published with minor changes in *The Development of Harvard University (**GHP**-102)*.

92 The Puritan Home, *Atlantic Monthly*, 1921; 128 (November): 589–598.

93 *A Catalogue of Early and Rare Editions of English Poetry Collected and Presented to Wellesley College*, Boston, Houghton Mifflin Co., November 1923. Copyright, 1923, by George Herbert Palmer. xii+613 pages, 6x8$^{3/4}$ inches.

94 *Emery Lucius Bradford: A Sketch*, Privately printed, Riverside Press, 1925. 15 pages.

95 Introductory (page 1–15) to E. C. Wilm, ed., *Immanuel Kant, 1724–1924*, New Haven, Yale University Press, 1925. 88 pages. 6$^{1/2}$x9 inches. Reprinted by Folcroft Library Editions in 1978.

96 Forgiveness, *Atlantic Monthly*, 1926; 137 (April): 469–475.

97 Commencement Day Speech to Trustees and Alumnae, *Wellesley Magazine*, 1926; 10: 311–312.

98 Foreword, xi-xii, to Constance Grosvenor Alexander, *Francesca Alexander: A "Hidden Servant,"* Amore e cor gentil sono una cosa — Vita Nuova XX.3, Memories garnered by one who loved her dearly. Cambridge, Harvard University Press, 1927, xii+233 pages, 8x10$^{3/4}$ inches.

99 The Junior College, *Atlantic Monthly*, 1927; 139 (April): 497–501.

100 The Junior College Again, *Atlantic Monthly*, 1927; 140 (December): 828–830.

101 College Expenses, *Harvard Graduates' Magazine*, 1929–30; 38 (September 1929): 12–13.

102 Department of Philosophy at Harvard, 1870–1929: Personnel, Organization, in Samuel E. Morison, *The Development of Harvard University Since the Inauguration of President Eliot, 1869–1929*, Cambridge, Harvard University Press, 1930, xc+660 pages.

103 Introduction (volume 1, pages 13, 17–62) to George P. Adams, Wm. Peperell Montague, eds., *Contemporary American Philosophy: Personal Statements*, 2 vols, New York, Macmillan Co., 1930. vol I, 450 pages; vol II, 447 pages. 5$^{1/2}$x8$^{1/2}$ inches. This Introduction was also published as **GHP**-104.

104 *The Autobiography of a Philosopher*, Boston, Houghton Mifflin Co., 1930. Copyright, 1930, by George Herbert Palmer. vii+138 pages, 5$^{3/8}$x8 inches. $2.00 Reprinted by Greenwood Press, New York, in 1968, and by Johnson Reprint Corporation, New York, in 1969.

105 On Growing Old, *Atlantic Monthly*, 1930; 145 (March): 319–321.

106 Introduction (xv-xvii, September 1, 1930) to Charles T. Burnett, *Hyde of Bowdoin: A Biography of William DeWitt Hyde*, Boston, Houghton Mifflin Co., 1931.

107 In Dedication: Josiah Royce, in C. Barrett, *Contemporary Idealism in America*, New York, Macmillan Co., October 1932.

108 *The Lord's Prayer*, Boston, Pilgrim Press, 1932. Copyright 1932 by Sidney A. Weston. 24 pages, $4^{1/2}$x7 inches.

George Herbert Palmer died on May 7, 1933.

109 *An Academic Courtship*: *Letters of Alice Freeman and George Herbert Palmer, 1886–1887*, Cambridge, Harvard Unversity Press, 1940, 259 pages. See also **AFP**-20.

Chapter 7

Publications by George Herbert Palmer, annotated

identified as **GHPann**-number (corresponding to chapter 6)

1 *The Odyssey of Homer: Books I.–XII.*
(See correspondence between George Herbert Palmer and Houghton Mifflin Company, pages 455–463)

On opposite pages, Professor Palmer presents the Greek text on the left and his translation on the right. He dates the preface from Boxford, April 2, 1884; this would have been the forty-ninth birthday of Ellen Wellman Palmer, his first wife. They were married on June 15, 1871; she died on February 10, 1879. He attributes this publication to her urging (**GHP**-104, page 39) and dedicates it to her: "I present this tribute to you above all who gave me [the opportunity] to see Nausicaä, the beautiful Helen, and Penelope." (I am grateful to Nicholas Poole-Wilson for this translation from the Greek.) Palmer repeats this dedication in his later publications of the Odyssey.

In the preface Palmer states ". . . I print these twelve Books (I have no intention of publishing more) in the hope of stimulating some one more skilful and scholarly than I to try what may be done here." He goes on to describe the background of this volume:

> "My work was begun twelve years ago, with no thought of publication. For two years I had been teaching Greek at Harvard College, and I was discouraged to find that my pupils had but a feeble conception of the Odyssey as a piece of literature. It is easy, all teachers know, to

> convince students that the Greeks devised a highly ingenious grammar; to show how rightly they understood the springs of human life is a harder matter. Few authors, however, in any language, will bear to be read at the rate of three pages a day.
>
> "To supplement the classroom drill and give a broader outlook, I proposed to read a Book of the Odyssey at a sitting; I translating into the simplest possible language, and my pupils following me, text in hand. The plan proved so useful and attractive that it has since been adopted at Harvard for other authors and languages, and a series of such readings is now regularly given during the winter evenings to all, students or civilians, who may care to attend.
>
> "In the ten years during which have I have taught philosophy [he was appointed Assistant Professor of Philosophy in 1873] I have read the Odyssey through several times to these little companies . . . ."

Also in the preface Palmer lists twenty translations of the Odyssey; from 1615—"George Chapman, five iambics, couplet rhyme"—to 1880—"Avia, six anapaests, couplet rhyme." He acknowledges his "large indebtedness to previous translators," and hopes that he has "gathered every choice expression which the translators of the past have discovered." He wishes that translators of Homer would develop the same spirit as that set by translators of the English Bible: "They acknowledged allegiance only to the text before them. To elucidate this they used the labors of other men as freely as if they were their own . . . Who first hit upon a rendering must cease to be an important question . . . One sort of originality alone should be prized—the originality of a fresh spirit." In addition, "To aid those who may wish to enter on a more elaborate study of the Odyssey," Palmer presents an annotated list of twenty-one of "the most serviceable books."

Wellesley College's Special Collections has Palmer's working copy with his marginal notes and corrections penciled on almost every page, and a copy of this book inscribed "to Alice E. Freeman, Sept. 3, 1886 Best wishes of GH Palmer." Miss Freeman was president of Wellesley College when she and Professor Palmer first met, in December 1884; she resigned when they were married in December 1887.

2 *The Odyssey of Homer.*

Along with the dedication of the book to his late, first wife, Ellen Wellman Palmer, Professor Palmer dates the preface February 21, 1891, the thirty-sixth birthday of his second wife, Alice Freeman Palmer.

"In this [complete] translation of the Odyssey [he writes in the preface] I have had the following aims":

> "To give to the thought of Homer a more direct and simple expression than has hitherto been judged admissible; to be at once minutely faithful to the Greek original and to keep out of sight the fact that either an original or a translator exists; to present especially the objective, unreflective, realistic, and non-literary features of the primitive story; to report in all their delicacy the events which Homer reports, to exhibit his attitude of mind toward them, and to produce again the impression produced by him that things did happen just so; in the wording, to discard originality and to make free use of the fortunate phrases of preceding translators; but to employ persistently the veracious language, the language of prose, rather than the dream language, the language of poetry; and still to confess that the story, unlike a bare record of fact, is throughout, like poetry, illuminated with an underglow of joy; to mark gently this permeating joy by a simple rhythm, a rhythm so unobtrusive and so free from systematic arrangement that no one need turn from the matter to mark the movement; above all, to discharge a debt of gratitude to the great friend who for twenty-five years has been showing me the beauty of himself and of the world; and finally, to make it plain that I cannot attain these aims, and to commend them to others as alluring and impossible."

In his autobiography, published in 1930 when he was eighty-eight years old (**GHP**-104), Palmer identifies his 'Homer' as one of "my books of affection and gratitude . . . [which] may live for half a century." The others are 'George Herbert' (**GHP**-50) and the 'Life of Mrs. Palmer' (**GHP**-57). "I tried to restore [the Odyssey] to nature and redeem [it] from artificial 'Classicism'. The sales of my translation . . . have increased in each of the thirty-odd years since it was published, during the last three being over forty thousand a year."

A copy from a used bookshop in Boston has an inscription

to "C. C. Everett, with warm regards of The Translator," and a tipped-in letter from 3 Mason Street, Cambridge, dated April 11, [1891]: "Dear Dr Everett: Let me bring you my book myself, instead of trusting longer to disobedient publishers. You will see that it has little to do with mental matters — your perplexities and mine. Perhaps on that account it may refresh the more, as if it had the power to transport you to some open spot of summer country & give you a day in the Maine woods, or at Cortina, or Capri. I hope so, at least. I should like to bring you some such helpful impetus as you have been imparting to me ever since I knew you. Sincerely, yours, G. H. Palmer" (AJL Collection).

3 *The Odyssey of Homer*, School Edition.

Palmer starts a long Introduction (vii-xxvi) with a discussion of three general matters: "Date [which begins] When the poems of Homer were written, no man knows"; "Material [which begins] Moreover, the question When and by whom was the Odyssey written? is not so simple as it sounds; and "Authorship [which begins] To what extent this accumulated material was already shaped before its appearance here we cannot say."

He then goes on to "The Tale of Troy, The Island of Ithaca, The Theme of the Odyssey" and to the two main parts of the poem, "The Homeward Voyage [and] The Recovery of the Kingdom." The twenty-four Books of the Odyssey "group themselves in sets of four, each little group having its distinctive theme, and making its needful contribution to the common plot." Professor Palmer carefully summarizes the story of each group. Then he writes about "The Division by Days, The Scenery, The Characters, The Style, [and] Books relating to the Odyssey."

Finally in the last section, entitled "Translations," after stating that there were "twenty-three English translations of the Odyssey," Palmer predicts that "Some such activity of translation we may expect for the future": "A world's book like the Odyssey cannot be exhausted, nor can any one person completely report it. It has as many aspects as it has translators. Hobbes commended it to his readers as a series of lessons in morals; to Worsley it was the world's great fairy tale; to Butcher and Lang it is an archaic 'historical document.' Others have found in it a philological interest, a mythological, a grammatical. However broad-minded a student may be, his sympathies are sure to reach a limit somewhere short of the compass of Homer. I have approached the Odyssey from the philosophic and poetic side, delighting in Homer's unique mental attitude. Notwithstanding his extraordinary powers of observation and utterance, he seems to me to confront the world like a child. Turning to him, I escape from our complicated and introspective world, and am refreshed."

Other features of this edition are a map of Homer's world to show the "Wanderings of Ulysses and Aeneas," and, at the very end, a "Pronouncing Vocabulary of Proper Names."

4 *The Odyssey of Homer,* Abridged School Edition.

Occasional lines are deleted, such as:

- "Her equally with his faithful wife he honored at the palace, but he never sought her bed, avoiding a wife's anger." (Book I, lines 431–433)
- "Hard are you gods and envious beyond all, to grudge the goddesses their meeting men in open wedlock, when one makes the man she loves her husband. So when rosy-fingered Dawn had chosen Orion, you gods that live at ease grudged him to her, till in Ortygia chaste gold-throned Artemis attacked and slew him with her gentle arrows. When, too, fair-haired Demeter, following her heart, lay with Iasion in the thrice-ploughed field, not long was Zeus unmindful; for he slew him, hurling his gleaming bolt." (Book V, 119–128)
- "Meanwhile, Eurynome and the nurse prepared their bed with clothing soft, under the light of blazing torches. And after they had spread the comfortable bed, with busy speed, the old woman departed to her room to rest; while the chamber-servant, Eurynome, with torch in hand, walked on before, as they two came to bed. She brought them to their chamber, and then she went her way. So they came gladly to their old bed's rites. And now, Telemachus, the neatherd and the swineherd stayed their feet from dancing, and bade the women stay, and all betook themselves to rest throughout the dusky halls. So when the pair had joined in happy love, they joyed in talking too, . . ." (Book XXIII, 287–302).

Besides the introduction, map, and pronouncing vocabulary, this edition has a section titled "Outline, Questions, and Suggestions" by Clarence E. Ackley, Instructor in English, Manual

Training High School, Louisville, Ky. Copyright, 1914, by Clarence E. Ackley.

5 *The Odyssey of Homer.*

The introduction, previously undated, is now from "Harvard University July 16, 1897," and is followed by A Retrospect (xxvii–xxxi) from "Boxford, July 29, 1920." A colored picture from a painting by N. C. Wyeth — The Trial of the Bow — follows the retrospect; the map is not included.

"Many years have passed since this novel interpretation of Homer was offered to an uncertain public," begins the Retrospect:

> "In 1884 twelve Books appeared, accompanied by the Greek text; in 1891, twelve Books more, the earlier being revised and the Greek omitted. At intervals later, to meet the supposed needs of schools, additions have been made: by myself, a long historical and critical Introduction; by the publishers, a Pronouncing Vocabulary of Proper Names, a series of Questions calculated to stimulate the pupil to think about what he had read, and a mythical Map of the Wanderings of Odysseus, to curb thought and give school-teachers the comfort of certainty on matters about which the rest of the world is content to remain in romantic ignorance. During these thirty-six years 200,000 copies have been sold, the plates have become worn, and a fresh setting of type is now demanded. The happy crisis brings me an opportunity for a thorough revision of the text, for adding a frontispiece, and for reconsidering in this note the principles of my translation.
>
> The general plan of that translation — whether as regards the characteristics of Homer there emphasized or the rhythmic medium chosen for their presentation — I do not desire to change. The astonishing popular acceptance of the book warns me away from fundamental alteration, while increasing my annoyance over the many defects in the early workmanship. Seldom in later years have I turned the pages of the book without lighting on some ungainly sentence which I could hardly believe my own . . . I originally wrote my entire translation eleven times from cover to cover; but I have still been obliged in this revision to introduce a multitude of small changes in order to make the narrative run smooth . . .

> "[I]t seemed to me that Homer might best be interpreted by a rhythmic prose which should keep something of the swiftness of the ancient hexameter, its variety, its capacity for taking on the color of a purposed emotion, while still retaining that power which prose alone seems to possess, the power of impressing on us its statements as facts. Time has confirmed this early judgment, the wide acceptance of my book bringing an assurance which I am little disposed to question. I can only hope that some translator hereafter who uses my methods may possess an ampler poetic endowment than I and so be able to impart to his rhythms a significant diversity not to be found here."

6 *The Odyssey of Homer*, with Illustrations by N. C. Wyeth.

This special edition has A Note by the Artist, a short preface (the paragraph quoted in **GHPann**-2 that describes George Herbert Palmer's aims in translating the Odyssey), the complete introduction, and sixteen colored illustration by Wyeth, each $5^{1/8}$x $6^{5/8}$ inches.

A Note by the Artist:

> "One of the great joys of this story by Homer is its magnificent fexibility and freedom from rigid consistency in presenting incidents and details. The mood is invariably subjective, which permits the imagination to interpret the thrilling pageant of the Odyssey as it occurs under particular emotional stress or by dramatic contrast . . .
>
> "The pictorial designs contained in this edition of the Odyssey present a group of selected dramatic events, each one less a literal translation of a certain moment, but more the embracing and moving impression of an episode."

7 *The Odyssey of Homer*, with Illustrations by N. C. Wyeth.

A delux edition of **GHP**-6: pigskin spine; "limited to five hundred and fifty numbered copies, of which five hundred are for sale"; signed by George H. Palmer and N. C. Wyeth; illustrations as mounted plates; a separate set of plates available; and a facsimile of a full-page, handwritten letter to Houghton Mifflin Company [for the text of this letter, see page 463. Professor Palmer was 87 years old].

8 *The Odyssey of Homer.*

The picture of a second painting by N. C. Wyeth — The Raft of Odysseus — is the only difference from **GHP**-5.

9 *The Odyssey Homer.*

Edited by Howard N. Porter, Professor of Greek and Latin at Columbia University, this edition presents Palmer's translation, complete and unabridged. In addition to an Introduction, Synopsis, Glossary, and annotated Bibliography, Porter includes A Note on the Translation:

"In this edition of the *Odyssey* the famous Palmer translation, through which millions of Americans have been introduced to the world of Homer, is reprinted." He goes on: "In the preface to the first edition the translator wrote that his aim was: 'To give to the thought of Homer a more direct and simple expression than has hitherto been judged admissible; to be at once minutely faithful to the Greek original and to keep out of sight the fact that either an original or a translator exists . . . ' Palmer was in healthy reaction to the elaborately archaizing style of his time. His 'direct and simple expression' was revolutionary. He was perhaps more successful in being 'minutely faithful to the Greek original' than in keeping 'out of sight the fact that . . . a translator exists,' for he translates word for word, retaining even the Greek word-order wherever possible. As this word-order is different from that which we would normally expect in idiomatic English, there is a constant slight tug, as it were, against our expectation, but this very tension contributes greatly to the vigor of the style — as in the King James Bible, a translation based on the same principle. Today it is a fashion in some quarters to translate ancient poetry so that it reads like modern colloquial prose fiction — a serious distortion.

"There have been a few changes made in the text. Some of them were cases where it was thought possible to translate even more directly and accurately. In other instances words that were current in Palmer's day seventy years ago but are now somewhat archaic were changed — this entirely within the spirit of Palmer's enterprise."

10 The New Education.

Professor Palmer describes the development of the "elective system" in Harvard College. In contrast to the time when all courses were prescribed, students now were able to choose most of their courses. This change started in 1825, progressed slowly, and in the year 1884–1885, all classes chose a majority of their studies. At first Palmer "distrusted the more extreme developments" of this system. As his opinion slowly changed, however, he characterizes himself as "that desirable persuader, the man who has himself been persuaded. The misconceptions through which I passed, I am sure beset others. I want to clear them away, and to present some of the reasons which have turned me from an adherent of the old to an apostle of the new faith."

After an extensive analysis of the new system, Palmer concludes: "there is a method which we and many other colleges in different degrees have adopted, which is demonstrably a sound method. Its soundness should by this time be generally ackowledged, and criticism should now turn to the important work of bettering its details of operation. May what I have written encourage such criticism and help to make it wise, penetrative, and friendly."

11 Possible Limitations of the Elective System I.

After a brief statement of the new educational principle stated in **GHP**-10, Professor Palmer goes on: "Over what I wrote an eager controversy has arisen, a controversy which must have proved instructive to those who need instruction most. In the last resort questions of education are decided by educators, as those of sanitation by sanitary engineers; but in both cases the decision has reference to public needs, and people require to be instructed in the working of appliances which are designed for no other end than their comfort. There is danger that such instruction may not be given. Professional men become absorbed in their art and content themselves with reticence, leaving the public ignorant of the devices by which its health is to be preserved. A great opportunity, therefore, comes to the common householder when these professional men fall foul of one another. In pressing arguments home they frequently take to ordinary speech, and anybody who then lends an ear learns of the mysteries. The present discussion, I am sure, has brought this informatory gain to every parent who reads the 'Andover Review' and has a studious boy. The gain will have been greater because of the candor and courtesy with which the attacking party has delivered its assault. The contest has been earnest. Its issues have been rightly judged momentous. For good or for ill, the choice youth of the land are to be shaped by whatever educational policy finally wins. Yet, so far as I recall, no unkind word has slipped from the pen of one of my stout opponents; no disparagement of man or college has mixed with the energetic advocacy of principle. The discussion has set in well toward things. I cannot call this remarkable. Of course it is not easy to be fair and strong at once. Sweetness and light are often parted. Yet we rightly expect the scholar's life to civilize him who pursues it, and we anticipate from books a refinement of the spirit and the manners as well as the understanding. My opponents have been scholars, and have spoken as scholars speak. It is a pleasure to linger in their kindly contentious company. So I gladly accept the invitation of the editors of the 'Review' to sum up our discussion and to add some explanatory last words.

"The papers which have appeared fall into two easily distinguishable classes, — the descriptive and the critical. To the former I devote but a brief space, so much more direct is the bearing of the latter on the main topic of debate, the question, namely, what course the higher education can and what it cannot now take. Yet the descriptive papers perform a service and deserve a welcome word. Suspecting that I was showing off Harvard rather favorably, professors planted elsewhere have attempted to make an equally favorable exhibit of their own colleges. In my manifesto they have seen 'a coveted opportunity to bring forward corresponding statistics which have not been formed under the Harvard method.' Perhaps this was to mistake my aim a little. I did intend to advance my college in public esteem; she deserves that of me in everything I write. But primarily I thought of myself as the expounder of an important policy, which happens to have been longer perceived and more elaborately studied at Harvard than elsewhere. I hope I did not imply that Harvard, having this excellence, has all others. She has many weaknesses, which should not be shielded from discerning discussion. Nor did I intend to commit the injustice to Harvard — an injustice as gross as it is frequent — of treating her as a mere embodiment of the elective system. Harvard is a complex and august institution, possessed of all the attractions which can be lent by age, tradition, learning, continually renewed resources, fortunate situation, widespread clientage, enthusiastic loyalty, and forceful guidance. She is the intellectual mother of us all, honored certainly by me, and I believe by thousand of others, for a multiplicity of subtle influences which stretch far outside her special modes of instruction. But for the last half century Harvard has been developing a new and important policy of education. Coincident with this development she has attained enormous popular esteem and internal power. The value and limits of this policy, the sources of this esteem and power, I wish everybody, colleges and populace, to scrutinize. To make these things understood is to help the higher education everywhere."

In the body of this long paper, Professor Palmer presents and discusses in great detail the numerous "critical" responses that he received.

In **GHP**-12, the third paper in this trilogy, Palmer starts with this summary of **GHP**-11: "The preceding paper has sufficiently discussed the impossible limitations of the elective system, and has shown with some minuteness the grounds of their impossibility. The methods there examined are the only ones suggested by my critics. They all agree in this, that they seek to narrow the scope of choice. They try to combine with it a hostile factor, and they differ merely in their mode of combination. The first puts a restraining check before election; the second puts one by its side; the third makes the two inseparable by allowing nothing to be chosen which is not first prescribed. The general purpose of all these methods is mine also. Election must be limited. Unchartered choice is licentious and self-destructive. I quarrel with them only because the modes of effecting their purpose tend to produce results of a transient and inappropriate sort. The aim of education, as I conceive it, is to spiritualize the largest possible number of persons, that is, to teach them how to do their own thinking and willing, and to do it well. But these methods effect something widely different. They either aristocratize where they should democratize, or they belittle where they should mature, or else they professionalize where they should humanize. A common trouble besets them all: the limiting authority is placed in external and arbitrary juxtaposition to the personal initiative which it professes to support. It should grow out of this initiative and be its interpreter and realization. By limitation of choice the proposers of these schemes appear to mean making choice less. I mean fortifying it, keeping it true to itself, making it more. Control that diminishes the quantity of choice is one thing; control that raises the quality, quite another. How important is this distinction and how frequently it is forgotten! Words like 'limitation,' 'control,' 'authority,' 'obedience,' are words of majesty, but words of doubtful import. They carry a freight of wisdom or of folly, according to the end towards which they steer. In order to sanction or discard limitations which induce obedience, we must bear that end in mind . . ."

12 Possible Limitations of the Elective System II.

The opening page has a footnote from the editor: "This article closes the discussion introduced by Professor Palmer in the November number (1885) of the *Review*) [**GHP**-10], and is the final answer of the author to his critics."

After his opening summary of **GHP**-11 (see above), Palmer identifies and discusses some necessary limitations of the elective system: "Old educational systems are often said to have erred by excess of authority. I could not say so . . . More accurately we say that their authority was of a wrong sort . . . There are two kinds of authority, — the authority of moral guidance, and the authority of repressive control . . . This moral authority is what the new education seeks . . . Men [in the colleges of today] are striving to bring about a germane and ethical authority in the room of the baser mechanical authorities of the past . . . As the elective principle is essentially ethical, its limitations, if helpfully congruous, must be ethical too . . . Moral guidance is a delicate affair. Its spirit is more important than its procedure . . . Experiments now in progress at Harvard and elsewhere must discriminate safe from unsafe limitations . . .

"That intentionality should be cultivated, I need not spend many words in explaining. All acknowledge that without a certain degree of it choice is impossible . . . Suitable subjects, attractively taught, awake lethargic intention as nothing else can . . . A boy dropped into the middle of a large college must not be lost to sight. He must be looked after. To allow the teacher's work of instruction to become divorced from his pastoral, his priestly, function is to cheapen and externalize education. I would have every student in college supplied with somebody who might serve as a discretionary friend: and I should not think it a disadvantage that such an expectation of friendship would be as apt to better the instructor as the student . . .

"A second class of limitations of the elective system . . . spring from the need of furnishing the young elector ample information about that which he is to choose . . . [A] student must know when he chooses, what he chooses. He must be able to estimate whether the choice of Greek 5 will further his designs better than the choice of Greek 8 . . .

"[W]e must have a third class of helpful limitations . . . the most important and complex of all. To yield a paying return, study must be stuck to . . . Self-direction implies such patient continuance in well-doing that only after persistence has become somewhat habitual can choice be called mature . . .

"Originally a doubter, I have come to regard the elective system, that is election under such limitations as I have described, as the safest — indeed as the only possible — course which education can now take . . . I proclaim it . . . not as a popular cry nor as an educational panacea, but as a sober opportunity for moral and intellectual training . . ."

13 *The New Education, Three Papers.*
(See correspondence between George Herbert Palmer and Houghton Mifflin Company, page 463)

The papers are **GHP**-10, 11, and 12. The preface is dated February 21, 1887, Alice Freeman's thirty-second birthday and the day that they became engaged.

Professor Palmer writes in his preface: ". . . I have attempted to explain to non-professional people some recent tendencies in education which have been much misunderstood. A mode of college discipline which, when rightly employed, proves a powerful engine for maturing the character of students has been supposed, both by advocates and opponents, to be a contrivance for letting boys do as they please . . . I have exhibited here in some detail the safeguards which a well-contrived elective system throws around its students. I have tried to show the ethical principles on which wise election rests; and I have drawn attention to the special conditions of our time which at present render some sort of elective system a necessity. I hope such a survey will throw light on the question how a young student may encounter most safely the risks which his transformation into manhood involves. The dangers of the evolutionary period are great. We are not likely to guard against them adequately till we see that the opportunity of personal choice is a necessary part of the cure, as it unquestionably is the cause, of our perplexities. . . . I believe there is a tolerably well determined ideal of educated manhood toward which most of our colleges are moving. . . . To point out what this ideal is, and so to purify and strengthen its influence, is the object of my writing."

Twenty-one years later, in **GHP**-65 (page 171), Professor Palmer comments on these three papers: "Time has changed most of the facts recorded in these papers, and the University is now a different place from the one depicted here. An educational revolution was then in progress, more influential than any which has ever visited our country before or since. Harvard was its leader, and had consequently become an object of suspicion through wide sections of the land. I was one of those who sought to allay those suspicions and to clear up some of the mental confusions in which they arose. Today Harvard's cause is won. *All courses leading to the Bachelor's degree throughout the country now recognize the importance of personal choice* (AJL's italics). But the history of the struggle exhibits with peculiar distinctness a conflict which perpetually goes on between two currents of human progress, a conflict whose opposing ideals are almost equally necessary and whose champions never fail alike to awaken sympathy. As a result of this struggle our children enjoy an ampler heritage than was open to us their fathers. Do they comprehend their added wealth and turn it to the high uses for which it was designed? In good measure they do."

14 *Expenses at Harvard.*

This address, delivered at the Commencement dinner in Memorial Hall on June 29, 1887, is based on data obtained from a questionnaire sent to the two hundred and thirty-five members of the graduating class. Two hundred and nineteen (93%) responded. The pamphlet includes an "Appendix of Correspondence." From an analysis of the replies, Professor Palmer concludes that, contrary to popular impressions, "a soberly sensible average of expense prevails at Harvard."

A small committee of graduates obtained a corrected copy of the speech from Palmer and distributed it "in the hope that its figures, if widely known, may do something to ease the way of poor boys ambitious of a Harvard training, and that they may also rectify some features in that popular portrait of a Harvard student which has about the same relation to the living reality as the stage Yankee has to the average citizen of Boston."

15 Hexameters and Rhythmic Prose.

Palmer discusses the prosodic considerations as he developed a new method for translating *The Odyssey* — "an iambic *recitative,* or free unmetred rhythm, whose cadences wait upon the pauses of the thought rather than upon those of any prearranged system" — and used it for the first twelve books (**GHP**-1). As "a specimen of [this] recent experiment . . . in rhythmic prose," the paper includes his translation of the twenty-third book of *The Odyssey.*

16 Reminiscences of Professor Sophocles.
(See correspondence between George Herbert Palmer and Houghton Mifflin Company, page 464)

Since his Junior year in college (1862–1863) George Herbert Palmer had known Evangelinus Apostolides Sophocles — Professor of Ancient, Byzantine, and Modern Greek — who had been teaching at Harvard since 1842, the year that Palmer was born. Harvard students — "probably as large a number as ever sat under an American professor — have been introduced by him to the poets and history of Greece." Sophocles died on February 14, 1883. Eight years later, a "decent interval after death," Palmer thought it "ungrateful to allow one formerly so stimulating and talked about to go out in silence . . ."

In this long, affectionate essay, Professor Palmer records numerous stories about Sophocles that ". . . reflect some of those rugged, paradoxical, witty, and benignant aspects of his nature which marked him off from the humdrum herd of men."

His head was "a magnificent subject for painting," but Sophocles "would never allow a portrait of himself to be drawn." "Several admirable photographs of him exist," however, and Palmer's striking description of "the elementary features of shape, hair and eyes" can readily be appreciated in the photograph of Sophocles that faces page 38 in *The Development of Harvard University* (see **GHP-**102).

17 Ownership of Books.

The entire article is presented here:

"The growth of public libraries, the multiplication of paper-bound books, the increase in the number of well-written weekly journals, bring nowadays to a man of moderate means a mass of good literature which twenty-five years ago was accessible only to the wealthy. Everybody can now have a book, and a good book; and nobody need deprive himself of other things in order to get it. A resident of almost any large city, and of many subordinate towns, can count with tolerable certainty on reading, without expense and within a short time of its publication, every important book published in America and England. To readers of German and French a fair selection of books in those languages is pretty generally open. So cheaply, too, are the great books now published that for five or ten dollars one may possess himself of about all the books of our race which can fairly be called universal; books, that is, whose worth is not restricted to any single age. At the same time, in the journals of the week, and in an increasing number of those of the day, excellent brief discussions of political, social, literary, and religious questions are to be had at a trifling cost. Through one or the other of these agencies a larger amount of high-grade literature is probably accessible to an average American than has ever before been offered at so small expense to the inhabitant of any country on earth.

"This prevalence of literature has produced prevalence of reading. Everybody now reads. In the cars, at the restaurant, over the noon dinner-pail, at the public library hall, by the Rochester lamp in the poor home, by the electric light in the rich, reading is perpetual. Young and old engage in it; and though many sensational papers and many non-natural novels are absorbed, it is doubtful whether the consumption of feeble and vicious literature has increased more rapidly than that of the virile, the lucid, and the nutritious. In any case, whether for good or ill, throughout our country the reading habit has been formed. Handling books, criticising the worth of what is written, has among us ceased to be the occupation of a class. It has become one of the regular occupations of John, Henry, and Susan.

"In this great democratizing of the conditions of literature, when so much reading matter is furnished by the corporate organizations of society at little individual cost, the question arises whether the private ownership of books — of books that will last — might not well be abandoned. Why should I buy a book when it can be read for nothing at the public library? Why store a book which will be sold me any day for twenty-five cents at the railroad stand? Why accumulate a library when newspapers may occupy agreeably and instructively all my leisure time? The book-case was a great enrichment of our boyhood home. Is it in future to disappear, destroyed by the very ease and currency of reading? Is society to become the owner of our books as of our railroads, and we withering individuals to content ourselves merely with their use? I hope we may not be so Bellamized [see biographical summary of Edward Bellamy]. There is much to make it probable that we need not be. Abandon to public instrumentalities all the books that can be read, and there will still remain enough to fill our private shelves.

"For there are the dictionaries. The State cannot advantageously take these away. We cannot economically run to the public hall whenever we need to turn to Worcester and Webster. And, the principle once admitted, it is evident that the atlas, the gazetteer, the biographical dictionary, will be better used if on our own shelf. It should be noticed, too, that as the reading habit increases, so does the habit of consultation. More encyclopædias have appeared in the last twenty years than in the previous two hundred; a fact which means that ten times more people now want swift access to solid, if fragmentary, information than formerly. The dictionary-makers have found this out, and are breaking down the line of separation between encyclopædia and dictionary. The line was always an artificial one. Why should not all books of reference be counted as dictionaries? If so, in saying that dictionaries can be owned more profitably than they can be borrowed, we have already made pretty good provision for the domestic book-case. Fill it exclusively with dictionaries, but give the word all the meaning it will carry. Books of physical science are dictionaries. They are not written for reading, but for consultation. And why not also call books of poetry dictionaries? Browning no less than Bancroft is most helpful when taken at intervals and in small doses. Imagine a man drawing Wordsworth from the public library and reading him through in the prescribed week! Nobody can know a poet without owning him; owning first his book, and then, through repeated approaches in many moods, coming to own the thought and style. It is a dangerous error to suppose the best books are written to be read. They are written to furnish power, and all the dictionary class — books of poetry included — will furnish power only if they are examined to-day and then laid by till a month, a year hence, when the occasion once more calls. For this sort of use, private ownership is necessary. What does Hooker say in that passage which so much affected me a few years ago? If I have the 'Ecclesiastical Polity' at hand I shall find out; if it is in the next street I shall not.

"The objection, then, against buying more books, that we

probably have not read all we now own, is thus seen to rest on a misconception. It is the office of a book not only to be gone through, but to be at hand as a prompter, a corrector, an inspiration. The book which supplants our own observation, our own growing minds, injures; it helps when it supplies what we from moment to moment need. The true reader is he who through the means of books masters a subject, not he who passes from cover to cover of many volumes. And to become a master of any subject, or even intelligently to deal with any practical department of modern life, one must be able to consult conveniently the best judgments of many minds. If this business use of books were better understood, there would be no fear for the future of private libraries. No busy carpenter will consent to keep his tools at the City Hall, and to run thither whenever he requires hammer and saw. A man who has learned to use books wisely may make the rule to buy only dictionaries and to borrow every book whose virtue can be taken out of it by a single reading. But if he purchases substantial copies of the books which will lend power through occasional approach, he has still material for a pretty extensive library.

"And now we are prepared to press a step beyond this point, and to say, further, that, little as loan collections and paper issues can supply us with dictionaries, just as little can they furnish us with books that will be our friends. If we cannot become acquainted with Wordsworth by reading him through, still less can we in that way learn to love him and to live as he lived. The work of the friend is accomplished by recurrence. To get a friendship we must give our own. We must be willing to open ourselves to unhurried influences, and to let the friend come near whenever the haste of life may pause. At first we understand the friendly book superficially; it must touch us again and again. But a book which has the capacity of becoming a friend will ultimately disclose a tremendous shaping power. I know a man who for many years read nothing but Aristotle and Hegel; another who for hardly less time read Ruskin and Swedenborg; both became accomplished men, welcomed everywhere because of their rounded knowledge. They could not have reached their beautiful culture on borrowed book or destructible copies. The training of one whom I knew began with Shelley; of another, with J. S. Mill; of another, with Newman. These were their favorite and formative authors. They owned them; read and re-read them; then passed on to know the influences which had gone to their growth; acquired the works of the masters of these masters; and, familiarizing themselves thus with a slowly widening circle, became intimate and kinsmen of the great. Had not a place by the fireside been reserved for these noblemen of letters, they would hardly have allowed their readers their friendship.

"Such, then, are the reasons for hoping that the purchase of good editions of good books will continue. They are wanted as dictionaries and as friends. The library in the little back room must remain as our tool-box and our place of spiritual communion. Both represent needs of the individual life. It will be a misfortune if either is crowded out. The spirituality and efficiency of the community will be endangered if churches come to supersede private meditation and prayer. They will be endangered no less truly if the value of the public and temporary book obscures that of the private and permanent one. By incidental supply we may become a nation of readers; we shall not so become scholars or book-lovers."

18 *The Glory of the Imperfect.*

From the outside of the back cover: "Western Reserve University. Cleveland College for Women. Cleveland College for Women was opened in 1888, under the direction of the trustees of Western Reserve University and of the Faculty of Adelbert College. Its purpose is to offer to young women advantages equal to those which the older colleges offer to young man."

19 *The Glory of the Imperfect.*

Professor Palmer points out that "The following address was delivered at the first Commencement of the Woman's College of Western Reserve University, at Cleveland, and was then printed by the University from stenographer's notes. As it is now to assume permanent form, it has been revised and in some parts rewritten."

As part of a long opening section, Palmer points out that "It was the office of that astonishing people, the Greeks, to teach us to honor completeness, the majesty of the rounded whole. We see this in every department of their marvellous life . . .

"And yet this beautiful Greek work shows only one aspect of the world. It omitted one little fact, it omitted formative life. Joy in birth, delight in beginnings, interest in origins, — these things did not belong to the Greeks; they came in with Christianity. It is Jesus Christ who turns our attention toward growth, and so teaches us to delight in the imperfect rather than in the perfect . . . And he teaches us that this delight in progress, in growth, in aspiration, in completing, may rightly be greater than our exaltation in completeness. In his view the joy of perfecting is beyond the joy of perfection.

"Now I want to be sure that you young students, who are preparing yourselves for larger life and are soon to emerge into the perplexing world, go forth with clear and Christian purpose . . . Will you demand that the things about you should already possess their perfection? Will you ask from life that it be completed, finished, beautiful? If so, you are doomed to dreary days. Or are you to get your intellectual eyes open, see beauty in the making, and come to rejoice in it there rather than after it is made? That is the question I wish to present to-day . . .

"I can direct your attention to certain modes by which you may instruct yourselves how to take an interest in the imperfect thing . . . In my judgment, then, your first care should be to learn to observe . . . There is no object so remote from human life that when we come to study it we may not detect within its narrow compass illuminating and therefore interesting matter . . . Observe, observe, observe in every direction! Keep your eyes open. Go forward, understanding that the world was made for your knowledge, that you have the right to enter into and possess it.

"And then besides, you need to train yourselves to sympathize with that which lies beyond you . . . When we observe, the object we observe is alien to us; when we sympathize, we identify ourselves with it . . . Do not then, stand apart from the movements of the country, — the political, charitable, religious, scientific, literary movements — however distastefully they may strike you. Identify yourself with them, sympathize with them. They all have a noble side; seek it out and claim it as your own . . . But I am afraid it would be impossible for you thus to observe, thus to sympathize, unless you bring within your imperfect self just grounds of self-respect. You must contribute to things if you would draw from things. You must already have acquired some sort of excellence in order to detect larger excellence elsewhere . . . You should be training yourself to do something well, it really does not matter what."

And Professor Palmer presents a challenge to the graduating class: ". . . it seems to me if ever a people were called on to understand this glory of the imperfect, it is we of America, it is you of the Middle West; it is especially you who are undertaking here the experiment of a woman's college."

Palmer refers to this paper in his autobiography (**GHP**-104, page 125–126): "The wisdom of life is to accept whatever comes and extract power from it . . . Criticism became my sacred word . . . Its simplest definition is the sense of inadequacy. Slightly modified as the Glory of the Imperfect, it appeared as the title of one of my earliest papers. Combined with appreciation of beauty — beauty in poetry, pictures, architecture, or landscape — it becomes a mighty engine, successively revealing what is adequate or harmonious and teasing us to bring this perfection to birth . . . I need something to begin with and improve. This ethical sense of a better in alliance with its twin sister, the æsthetic, trains practical judgment and makes one a generally useful person, resorted to by many for advice . . ."

20 Barnes's Rural Poems.

William Barnes (1801–1886) was an English poet, philologist, and clergyman. In his catalogue of English poetry for Wellesley College (**GHP**-93), Professor Palmer lists eight volumes by Barnes. One of these volumes, *Poems in the Dorset Dialect*, has the autograph of "Alice E. Freeman, July 1886." She and Palmer had first met in December 1884, and were married in December 1887. In their correspondence (*An Academic Courtship*, **GHP**-109, **AFP**-20), in July 1886, they mention Barnes: as Miss Freeman invites Professor Palmer to Wellesley — "Can you not come next Wednesday morning? I think you can get the 9:15 train from Boston — or the 10 o'clock certainly. And bring Barnes? I must have more of him . . . If Wednesday is not convenient, any following day will find me." Palmer replies from Boxford the next day — "Barnes and I will take the 10 o'clock train on Thursday." Later, in December 1886, Palmer quotes from Barnes: "[W]e two may together make up one more righteous person than either could be alone. I ask you merely

> To help me and shear all my lot
> And in faithvulness keep all your life by my zide
> Tho the way mid be happy or not."

Professor Palmer starts his *Christian Union* article: "William Barnes has been deeply loved by scholars and by farmers.

Few other people know him. Five years ago he died, an old and revered man, in the peaceful county of Dorset, England, where he was also born. An Oxford graduate, an ardent student of English literature, the author of many more or less whimsical works on philology and of one or two on mathematics, a country clergyman for more than forty years, he was all his life the maker of exquisite little poems which say what never has been said so well before . . . May one who is nothing of a farmer and but little of a scholar tell why he thinks these peasant poems remarkable; why he believes that here for the first time the life of the fields finds its beautiful expression?

"Rural life is peculiarly unapproachable by poetry . . . The facts are not inaccessible. But the report of facts becomes poetry only when they are shown in human terms, colored by expression of the spiritual life which goes on among them . . . The uncorrupted countryman, whose emotional experience makes the matter of rural poetry, is an inarticulate being. He cannot voice himself. Perhaps he cannot quite perceive himself. His thoughts and feelings are not merely not uttered; they are not formed with precision . . . This is the fundamental obstacle to the rise of rural poetry . . .

"It is simply necessary . . . [for rural life] that its poetic reporters should come from outside itself. Their report need not, however, be bare, external, or simply descriptive. It may be — it must be, if it is to be poetry at all — rich, internal, and dramatic; for drama is but the sympathetic temporary identification of a trained observer with his alien characters.

"That is what William Barnes has done. Living long among his simple friends, he has noted their lives, has identified himself with their conditions, and has employed his own acuteness, learning, rich imagination, and delicate art for presenting what is blunted, lumpish, and all but half aware of itself. The result is unique and exquisite; astonishing, one would call it, were not all pitched in so gentle a key that one is never startled. But certainly it is marvelous . . .

"The dialect in which these vivid verses appear belongs to them. It is not a bit of outward clothing. No other form of speech would serve so well. It connects itself with their very substance. Its homeliness is needful to shape as well as dress the homely thought beneath . . . His stock of poetic agencies is admirably fitted to its work. Everywhere he uses strongly marked rhythm, abundant rhyme, much assonance and alliteration, frequent refrains; in short, he gives that frank prominence to the elementary principles of verse which pleases the unrefined ear. The refined ear, too, it must please, so congruent is all — thought and diction and artistic resource . . ."

21 Manliness of Boyhood.

Professor Palmer begins: "Every boy wants to stop being a boy. A man thinks of his boyhood as a period of romance, and often clumsily attempts to be a boy again. He longs for the irresponsibility, the nimble interests, the headlong passions, the confident hopes, the exuberant health of boyhood. But the boy looks at boyhood in a different light. To him it is a time to get out of. He sees manhood right ahead and he longs to be in it. He reaches, he aspires. No wish is more constant in noble boys than the wish to be a man. It is not a wish to be laughed at. Of course it is comic to see [boys of] sixteen years adopting the cane and cigarette, to hear opinions on politics, literature, the mechanic arts and theology as confidently vented as if they sprang from the experience of maturity. But, after all, a boy incapable of such offenses would be doubtfully worth bringing up, for these are the extravagant exhibits of that highest of the desires — the desire to be more than one is, the desire to grow, to be complete, to be a man. Pitiable the boy who does not perpetually assume the way he thinks manly.

"But if the boy's secret wish to be manly is nothing to be ashamed of may not we who are of riper growth talk openly with him about it and show him how he may wisely obtain his desire? For there are silly ways and sound ways of putting off childish things . . . [T]here is the solid and beautiful way where something manly is discovered within the nature of boyhood itself and this, respected and cultivated, is allowed to grow into the power and complexity of a man's life. Abundant elements there are in the youth which need nothing but expression to render them honorable. I select only one, truthfulness. And I mean to show that the boy who sticks to this single principle and is ready to follow wherever it leads is quickly recognized as a manly boy and is sure every day to grow into a more and more manly man.

"Perhaps the easiest form of this truthful manliness is hatred of humbug. And how splendidly common the aggressive virtue is! In every company of boys there is sure to be one or more who puts on airs and gives himself out as a superior person . . . To the standing honor of average boyhood be it said that the lives of these top-lofty little humbugs are rendered perpetually miserable . . . May the day be distant when conceit, affectation, priggishness, sanctimoniousness, find any mercy among our healthy boys . . . Among boys claims to superiority are not lightly admitted. They are scrutinized suspiciously and criticized with great freedom. If unreal, they are called rubbish, if real, they are as frankly honored. Nothing is cared for that is untrue. In this detestation of falsehood is found the first solid basis of a boy's manliness.

"Unhappily it is easier to hate humbug in another than in one's self. It seems so easy for anybody else to drop affectation and appear as just that which he really is . . . But when we ourselves try to be clean of pretense we find we have undertaken a different task. Readiness to attack this task marks a higher stage of truthfulness in manly boys . . . For he who within is truthful will recognize where his knowledge stops and will decline to hold beliefs or make statements beyond that limit, and this is what we mean by culture and scientific spirit. He will do his work in the most direct way, with the least fuss and unnecessary clamor, and that is what we call efficiency and skill . . . [L]et the boy not flinch from truthfulness when it costs him persistent and unseen effort, and [there] is no species of excellence on which he will not in this degree have entered. He will have no need to wait for years to crown him with manliness. He has ceased to be a boy. He is a man already.

". . . [T]he fullness of these powers does not appear without adhesion to a truthfulness more comprehensive still . . . To be fully truthful I must not be contented with my defects but energetic to remove them. For these very defects are liable to become pretenses . . . So to enlarge my knowledge as to be able to perceive and sanction what is implied in my conduct, thoughts and even my feelings is necessary, if the full stature of manly truthfulness is to be reached . . . [T]his is a task which will more than fill a lifetime . . . Anyone who undertakes it in earnest will soon detect how little he is and how small is thc compass of his individual powers. Thus, in his very force, feeling his own dependence, he will be led to that last exquisite glory of manliness — humility and quiet reverence . . ."

22 Doubts about University Extension.

Professor Palmer describes a university "extension movement" in England, which has been so successful that its introduction into the United States is being proposed. English universities, "discontented with their isolation," started this movement of "popularized education . . . [for] the common man . . . Far and wide, throughout England, an enthusiastic band of young teachers, under the guidance of officers of the universities, have been giving instruction . . . to companies in which social grades are for the first time forgotten." Palmer points out that the name "university extension . . . [is] largely misleading; since neither the agencies for extending, nor indeed, for the most part, the studies extended, are found at the universities at all." The movement, he says, is "as much social as scholarly, and accompanies a general democratic upheaval of an aristocratic nation . . ."

In America, Palmer recognizes, "[n]ot every man is free to seek a systematic training [in the] four hundred colleges . . . Multitudes are tied to daily toil, and only in the evening can they consider their own enlargement." He identifies some "earnest efforts to surmount [this] serious limitation in our educational scheme": public libraries; Chautauqua (82n5); "endowed courses of higher instruction," such as the Lowell Institute where Palmer had lectured (242n1); and other presentations by college teachers to popular audiences, such as Palmer's numerous lectures. Worthwhile as these efforts may be, however, Palmer points out that they are "deficient in guiding power. Most persons, especially if novices, work best when under inspection . . . To learners teachers are generally important." And, although he thinks that the aims of the English system are excellent, he has "doubts of three sorts" about whether the system would be practicable in this country: "those [doubts] which suspect a fundamental difference in the two countries which try the experiment; those which are incredulous about the permanent response which our people will make to the education offered; and [most importantly] those which question the possibility of securing a stable body of extension teachers."

"There seems to be still a place in our well-supplied country," Professor Palmer thinks, " for an organization which shall arouse a more general desire for knowledge which shall stand ready to satisfy this desire more cheaply, with less interruption to daily occupation, and consequently, in ways more fragmentary than the college can; and yet one which shall not leave its pupils alone with books, but shall supply them with the impulse of the living word, and, through writing, discussion, and directed reading, shall economize and render effective the costly hours of learning . . . Let the extension leaders give up all thought of doing here what has been done in England . . . If, however, university extension can keep itself clearly detached from other educational agencies and make a quiet offer of humble yet serviceable instruction, there is a fair prospect that, by somewhat slow degrees, a permanent new power may be added to the appliances for rendering busy Americans intelligent."

23 Public Support of College Vices. (not found)

24 The Cultivation of Tact.

On June 16, 1892, the day after the thirty-seventh commencement of Elmira College, the *Elmira Daily Advertiser* noted that President Charles Van Norden had introduced "the orator of the occasion, Professor George H. Palmer of Massachusetts . . . This address was a special feature of the exercises. It was a departure from the established method and had been anticipated wih considerable interest. Professor Palmer is a fluent speaker and his address was given more especially to the graduates [eleven women comprised the graduating class] and in the style of a class room lecture. He was thoroughly master of his subject and elaborated the various points with considerable skill . . ."

The Sibyl, in its next issue, presented the text of the address: ". . . As I recall my own graduating day [in 1864], it seems to me to have been a season of fear. I stood with the riches that I hardly thought I should have attained, and as I stood the question arose in my mind, what shall I do with them in the world? Shall I succeed, shall I be as successful as I have sometimes dreamed? . . . I can not increase your stock of knowledge, but can I not say a word which will aid you in the use of it, or which will save you from disappointment . . . I am to speak to you today on the 'Cultivation of Tact' because without it you will not be sure of success . . . Tact, touch. You must have a sense of touch. Are you in doubt about anything, you can learn something of it by the sense of touch . . . What takes place in regard to the physical objects that are around us, also takes place when spirit meets spirit. You approach a multitude of persons no two of whom are alike . . . I must approach an individual as an individual; a single being with his own particular surroundings in the world. The tactful man is careful to understand all this . . . He goes forth from himself and lives in the lives of those without. I must not only be concerned with my own thought, but with the thoughts of other men . . . We are continually full of ourselves and answering our emotions when really we should be going abroad and into the lives of those around us. And for that you need imagination . . .

"I have called this a fine art . . . I say therefore use this fine art; this ability to use the lives of those with whom you come in contact, but do not use it selfishly, because without it you cannot hope to control men; without it, it is impossible for you to serve your fellow-men . . . This fine art is but the development of the great law of Christian service, 'not to be ministered unto, but to minister' [the Wellesley College motto — Non Ministrari sed Ministrare — from Mark 10:45] . . .

"When you do not succeed in life you will be very apt to repine and possibly to blame the world. There is a certain mode of dealing with failure. Instead of blaming the world take it back to yourselves, and say, is it not possible that I have been a little lacking in tact? Have I not been thinking of my own knowledge rather than the modes of impartation? The very lack of success may be made the means of cultivation of tact to you. Therefore refuse to accept any failure in life as an evil. Take it as a good; take it as a means of instruction in this fine art. In this way all things might work together for your good."

25 Book review. B. Jowett, *The Dialogues of Plato*, translated into English.

George Herbert Palmer wrote an unsigned, fairly long review — approximately 740 words — of this "monumental work" by Benjamin Jowett [who held the Greek professorship at Oxford University]. The first third of the review deals with additions and alterations that had been made since the second edition, particularly in the design of the pages.

The remainder of the review deals with the translation itself. "In 1871 [when the first edition was published] Prof. Jowett was no tyro [Palmer points out] . . . But being, like his master, an artist; he has never ceased to study neatness, simplicity, adaptation to the reader, subtle textual accord . . . [and] it would be hard to find half-a-dozen consecutive lines in the entire work which have altogether escaped alteration . . . Prof. Jowett himself has said, that 'translation is dependent for its effect on very minute touches,' [and] most readers will agree that on the whole each page, while making a closer approach to the Greek, conveys more than ever to both ear and mind the impression of a piece of masterly English."

Palmer goes on: "Commonly the translator who seeks to reproduce beauty fails because he has not the resources of his own tongue at command. For purposes of translation, scholarship is more important as regards the language into which, than as regards that out of which, the rendering is made. Defects in the latter can largely be made up at the moment from books; for the former a man must rely on himself."

In conclusion, Palmer says, "No other English translation from the Greek, except our English Bible, has brought over so fully the riches of its original."

26 Philosophy in the Colleges.

"Of late years [Professor Palmer begins] there has come about a great change in the method and aim of college instruction in philosophy. The persons who teach it are not the same as formerly. Ten years ago it was customary for the minister-president to take charge of the entire subject. In my time at Harvard [1860–1864], Professor Bowen [whom Palmer succeeded as Alford Professor of Natural Religion, Moral Philosophy, and Civil Polity, in 1889] was one of the three or four professors of it to be found in the entire country; and he gave but a single course, and coupled with his teaching of philosophy that of political economy. In 1870, when I went to Harvard as his assistant, I believe that there was no other assistant teacher of philosophy in any college in the land, unless we count those cases where the philosophy-teaching president, finding his work too heavy, had called another man to his aid. The rule was one man for philosophy, and that the president; the occasional luxury, a professor exclusively devoted to the subject; Harvard was so extravagant as to employ two. At present Harvard has five professors, two assistant professors, two assistants, and an instructor. A staff similar, if smaller, is maintained at Cornell, Yale, Columbia, Princeton, Michigan, Pennsylvania, Oberlin. In nearly all the New England colleges, and in something like half of those of the West, the teaching of philosophy has passed away from the president and has come into the hands of a professor.

"This change in the persons teaching has been accompanied and largely caused by an equally great change in the subjects taught. The only course formerly offered was in the senior year, and was made up in about equal parts of psychology, logic and ethics. The first was taught without experiment; the second without exercises; and the third without observation . . . [I]n all cases a text-book was used, a lesson was set, and he was generally counted the best scholar who could most nearly give back to his teacher the words of his author. Lectures were few; discussions, unless the teacher were a Hopkins or a Seelye, were infrequent; and investigation, or even collateral reading, did not exist.

"With the wide growth of elective methods [see **GHP**-13], this simplicity has passed away. At each of half a dozen colleges as many as a dozen courses in philosophy are simultaneously offered. At Harvard there are eighteen, besides a dozen more, philosophical in substance, but taught by instructors outside the philosophical department. And the gain in scope is no less remarkable than the gain in number. Besides the introductory course — which offers the outlines of logic, psychology, and history of philosophy — Harvard offers seven historical courses, seven theoretic or systematic, and four seminaries for advanced research . . . The professor no longer hides behind a text-book, but ventures forth and enunciates his own systematized doctrine of psychology, cosmology, esthetics, ethics, sociology, pedagogics or religion. The subjects which our advanced students a few years ago could not investigate without a voyage to Europe, are now taught at our own doors . . .

"Philosophy is philosophizing; it needs to be done, and not learned. To lecture on it to a young man day after day, and expect him to grow wise through listening, is to cut him off from philosophy altogether. That was the strong point in the old recitation system; it presented something for each student to do. But so do the new schemes. The professor's lectures are but guides to the student's private work; and the results of this private work are shown in carefully prepared papers presented from month to month . . . Living personal interest has taken the place of ancient mechanic dullness.

"If such are the contrasts in methods of teaching, what are the contrasts in aim? . . . Philosophy was at that time conceived not as a body of knowledge, but as a certain mode of life. The Senior Year introduced the student to such a mode of life . . . Each individual was encouraged to acquire the habit of performing his tasks with consideration, interest, and a sense of responsibility. To many a young man the course in philosophy was the beginning of a higher life.

"In the new order of things these ennobling aims have not disappeared . . . But they have now become the subordinate, and no longer the principal aim . . . Philosophy is now studied with the same aim as biology or astronomy. The aim of knowledge itself, psychology, ethics, the theory of knowledge, of Nature, of society, are explored with the dispassionate minuteness, often with the observational and even laboratory methods, which are the accredited modes of approach to the other sciences. The old dogmatism has, accordingly disappeared. The pupil has become a fellow-investigator, and has acquired the independence and dignity which investigation brings . . ."

Palmer goes on to point out that "large numbers of [Harvard] graduates — this year sixty-seven — are pursuing advanced philosophical studies . . . I asked twenty or thirty of them why they had turned to philosophy. Nearly half answered that they hoped for light on a religious perplexity. Others had met some difficuty in mathematics, physics, literary criticism, or the care of the poor, which, when followed up, became a philosophical problem . . . [I]n general, Aristotle's observation was verified, that philosophy begins in wonder and aims at the solution of a difficulty . . .

"All over the land there is going on a great philosophic, I had almost said a great religious, revival. More patiently men are asking searching questions about themselves and the world they live in, than ever they asked them before. A company of experts are growing up, determined to push inquiries in this field as seriously as the last generation pushed them in physical science. Philosophy bids fair to become not merely a way of life, but an organized body of knowledge to which successive generations may add."

"Boxford, Mass." appears at the end of the article.

A century later: ". . . Now, a handful of philosophers are beginning to show how the biology of the brain can illuminate some of the issues that have vexed scholars for centuries. Questions such as the nature of mind, the structure of knowledge and the puzzle of consciousness are being tackled by philosophers who are as likely to be found outfitted in white coats and toiling in neurobiology labs as sitting contemplatively in leather-padded chairs. 'In the past, philosophers thought they could answer the important questions without knowing anything about neuroscience,' says [University of Iowa Professor Patricia] Churchland, one of the leading scholars in this new movement. 'That's not enough any more — you have to look at the brain itself'" (William F. Allman, Biology of the mind, Philosophers are moving out of the ivory tower and into the laboratory, *U. S. News and World Report*, December 14, 1992, pages 66, 93, 94).

27 Book review. John Burnet, *Early Greek Philosophy*.

George Herbert Palmer starts this unsigned, long review (approximately 980 words) of the book by Burnet (Scottish classical scholar): "The modern interest in origins is continually shifting the centres of consequence in history and transforming unimportant tracts of human experience into important. This book deals with the first 175 years of Greek speculation, from about 600 B. C. to the Peloponnesian War . . . [The] book is based on an independent study of the sources, and enjoys the distinction of being at once a solid piece of scholarship and the only volume written in English which considers exlusively this first division of Greek philosophy."

Professor Palmer includes an extensive analysis of Burnet's thoughts about numerous men who gave "a distinct character . . . [to] one of the most constructive portions of Greek philosophy . . ." Then, in conclusion, Palmer says that Burnet "has subjected to fresh criticism an enormous mass of historical material, and he has produced a weighty and intensely interesting book with which every student of Greek philosophy hereafter must reckon."

28 Book Review. William Dewitt Hyde, *Practical Ethics*.

William Dewitt Hyde was president and professor of philosophy at Bowdoin College when this book was published. At Harvard he had studied philosophy with Professor Palmer, both as an undergraduate (class of 1879) and in a postgraduate seminar. From this seminar a close relationship developed, and he and the Palmers became intimate friends. In 1930, Professor Palmer wrote the introduction to a biography of Hyde who died in 1917 (**GHP**-106); in this introduction, he writes that "the last book Mrs. Palmer had me read to her [before she died in Paris] was one of Hyde's."

Years later, in a 1927 volume (**aboutGHPann**-6, page 317–318), their mutual friend, Charles F. Thwing, writes: "In Hyde's method of reasoning and in his style of writing, it is easy to detect the influence of his early teacher and constant friend, George Herbert Palmer. In the fullness and detail of analysis, and in the greater gift and achievement of synthesis and of proportion, one hears Palmer still speaking. In simplicity of interpretation and of statement, a simplicity liable to blind one to the statement's depth and significance, Palmer's voice is still heard. In the lucidity of argument and of method, a method at once Greek and French, Palmer is still recognized. In the persuasiveness of sentence and paragraph, a persuasiveness whose conclusiveness is inevitable, Palmer's power is still regnant. Here are found the sweetness and light of Matthew Arnold and of Palmer, which are touched with a genuine eloquence which neither the Oxford professor of poetry nor the Harvard professor of philosophy were accustomed to use."

At the beginning of this unsigned review, Professor Palmer says that President Hyde devotes the book to "discussing what the nature of morality is . . . what it is that moral judgment as such expresses . . . [T]he necessary assumptions in regard to the nature of morality are briefly summarized . . . [I]nnumerable as are the varieties of human endeavor, for scientific purposes they can readily be reduced to *aims* connected with twenty-three classes of *objects* [AJL's italics]; that between each of these objects and ourselves many possible relations exist; that in reference to each object we may stand in a relation which shall at the same time promote the development of ourselves and preserve the object's proper worth; that since life consists in the maintenance of relations, the maintenance of this best relation of complete union of self and object is our duty in regard to that object . . . A table, prefixed to the book, names in its left column the twenty-three kinds of Objects which condition our lives, while in the following six columns stand the corresponding Virtues, Rewards, Temptations, Vices of Defect, Vices of Excess, and Penalties . . . Such is the ingenious yet simple scheme according to which the complex facts of man's moral nature are grouped for convenient survey . . .

"For example, taking Time as one of the objects by which every life is conditioned, it is shown that our duty will be to express through conduct the unity of ourself, and also the separated sequence of the onward-flowing moments; and this is co-ordination, or the organization of a future as part of a present. Practice in considering present conduct with reference to future welfare breeds the virtue of prudence, and brings into the life of the prudent man the reward of harmonious wholeness. But there is a perpetual temptation to lay too little or too great stress on the fact of futurity. In the one case we procrastinate; in the other we are anxious. For while prudence co-ordinates present and future in a consistent whole, procrastination sacrifices the future to the present, and anxiety sacrifices the present to the future. In either case we incur the penalty of discord. Life is at issue with itself . . .

"His work is observation and classification, not analysis. He studies duties, not duty. An admitted principle of righteousness when handed over to conduct takes on amazing ramifications, subtly diversifies itself with reference to everything it touches, until the multitude of resulting forms is more likely to suggest willful and oppressive chaos than helpful and inevitable order. These perplexing ramifications of duty which practice breeds, it is the business of this book to trace out. It is a work seldom attempted. The writer of this notice does not recall a book in which the diversities of righteousness are catalogued with such minute exhaustiveness . . . Probably its condensed and systematic character renders it less suitable for a young student's reading, but makes it also the richer thesaurus for the teacher and for the student of older growth . . ."

Palmer then points out that the "President of Bowdoin, as all who are acquainted with his other writings know, possesses the calm power of saying a plain things plainly. But he possesses other powers as well as powers of fresh and daring observation, of neatness, pungency, humor, rememberable cast of phrase. All these powers appear abundantly in these pages, and gladden the serious discussion with pleasant epigrams:

"'Like milk which is allowed to stand, the spirit of man or woman, if left unoccupied, turns sour' . . . 'Cheating is very common, and one is tempted to do a little cheating himself in order to keep even with the rest' . . . 'A good liar must have a long memory. Having no recognized standard to go by, he cannot remember whether he said one thing or another about a given fact' . . . 'Kindness is the recognition that a feeling of another being is of just as much consequence as a feeling of my own' [and] 'We must remember that the quality of an act determines the worth of the pleasure, and that the amount of pleasure does not determine the quality of the act.'"

"Scientific as the aim of the book really is, strange indeed would be the young man to whom such ethics did not appear decidedly practical."

29 Can Moral Conduct be Taught in Schools?

This essay was prompted by "a strong demand [that] had arisen for ethical teaching in the schools." The demand, Professor Palmer points out, occurred because "[t]he ancient and accredited means of training youth in goodness, [namely] the clergy . . . and the home . . ., are becoming enfeebled and distrusted."

[One hundred years later, in 1994, the compiler-annotator can not refrain from pointing out that the next paragraph is particularly relevant today!]

Palmer describes how "[t]he home . . . which has hitherto been the fundamental agency for fostering morality in the young, is just now in sore need of repair. We can no longer depend upon it alone for moral guardianship. It must be supplemented, possibly reconstructed. New dangers to it have arisen. In the complex civilization of city life, in the huge influx of untutored foreigners, in the substitution of the apartment for the house, in the greater ease of divorce, in the larger freedom now given to children, to women, in the breaking down of class distinctions and the readier accessibility of man to man, there are perils for boy and girl which did not exist before. And while these changes in the outward form of domestic life are advancing, certain protections against moral peril which the home formerly afforded have decayed. It would be curious to ascertain in how many families of our immediate time daily prayers are used, and to compare the number with that of those in which the holy practice was common fifty years ago. It would be interesting to know how frequently parents to-day converse with their children on subjects serious, pious, or personal. The hurry of modern life has swept away many uplifting intimacies. Even in families which prize them most, a few minutes only can be had each day for such fortifying things. Domestic training has shrunk, while the training of haphazard companions, the training of the streets, the training of the newspapers, have acquired a potency hitherto unknown."

Although the "popular discussion [concerned] itself chiefly with the methods by which ethics may be taught," Palmer goes "behind this controversy . . . to raise the . . . question whether ethics should be taught to boys and girls at all." He distinguishes between ethics and morals: "ethics, as was long ago remarked, is related to morals as geometry to carpentry: the one is a science, the other its practical embodiment. In the former, consciousness is a prime factor; from the latter it is often absent altogether." Teachers are asked to direct the study "of the principles of right conduct, that we awaken [the pupils'] consciousness about their [own] modes of life, and so by degrees impart to them a science of righteousness. This is theory, ethics; not morals, practice; . . . [and] Many matters do not take their rise in knowledge at all. Morality does not." In a lengthy analysis, he presents an "inexpugnable objection to the ethical instruction of children": it can be unwholesome and dangerous to stimulate self-criticism in the child, and furthermore "the end sought is performance, not knowledge, and we cannot by supplying the latter induce the former."

"The college, not the school," Palmer goes on, "is the place for the study [of ethics] . . . It is a sound principle of modern education that questions should not be answered before they are asked; and many of the evils that I have thus far traced are brought about by projecting upon a young mind problems which it had not yet encountered in itself. Such problems abound in the later teens and twenties, and then is the time to set about their discussion." Even in college, Palmer thought, the study of ethics should be elective, "the student should be informed at the outset that the aim of the course is knowledge, not the endeavor to make better men," and "the students themselves [should] do the ethicizing . . . trace the logic of their own beliefs and . . . not rest in dogmatic statement."

Finally, in a positive note, on the last three pages of the essay, Professor Palmer presents some ideas as to how both school and college can act as "moral guardians" and "can surround those committed to their charge with the unnoticed pressure of a moral world."

In *The Teacher* (**GHP**-65) and as a Riverside Educational Monograph (**GHP**-76), most of this essay was published, entitled Ethical Instruction in Schools; the final three-page section was expanded and published, entitled Moral Instruction in Schools, in **GHP**-65.

30 The Ethical Doctrine of Pleasure.

The *Chautauqua Assembly Herald* printed a long "Synopsis of a Course of Six Lectures Delivered in the Hall of Philosophy, July17–22 [Monday-Saturday], 1893, by Professor George H. Palmer, of Harvard University." (See also 82n5)

Palmer begins the series: "You will doubtless think it very strange that I should have chosen Pleasure for my subject, because it is such a familiar thing. But we philosophers like best to explain the things which we know best, from the fact that just because the subject is very near to us, it may be very far from us . . . The nature of pleasure is a section of the large subject of ethics, which deals with human conduct, with persons who can act. Because it deals with you, you probably know least about it. It is the king of sciences, and to its assessments all other subjects must come. I have thought it wiser to select but a single central doctrine of the science. I shall endeavor to reveal yourself to yourself."

Palmer proceeds in the first lecture to ". . . attempt to make out the nature of pleasure. To the question, 'What is meant by pleasure?' we instinctively answer, 'It's what we like.' What more is there to be said? We have said about all that can be said in defining it . . . [Pleasure] has a double aspect, — a positive and a negative aspect . . . The positive aspect of pleasure is known to us all. We are pleased with beauty, and the thousand and one things about us. No sense is incapable of pleasure . . . The negative aspect of pleasure may be described as the absence of pain . . . pleasure and pain seem to be twins. They are always together, and we must estimate the character of one by reference to the other . . . Thus we see there is much which casts a melancholy shade on our pleasure. It is transient, limited, and is absence of pain . . ."

In his second lecture, Professor Palmer addresses the question, "Can Pleasure Be an Aim of Life?" He concludes this analysis: "There are few willing to acknowledge that they live for pleasure. They preach to others that pleasure is by no means a reputable thing, yet in their lives they secretly aim at it. Practice and principle are not in harmony here. If pleasure is the only rational aim in life, why this shame?"

He goes on in the third lecture to consider "what other aims we may take in place of pleasure . . . One of these aims is action. We aim at action for itself, and not for the pleasure it yields. An illustration is the mountain-climber . . . Another aim is that of knowledge . . . We must sacrifice ourselves in the interest of knowledge or we will get neither pleasure nor knowledge. This aim at knowledge comes mainly in the form of interests. We may define an interest as the marking out of a certain sphere, within which we will know all that can be known . . ."

As he continues this analysis in the fourth lecture, Palmer says: "Action and knowledge are the most fundamental aims of life, but they are both aims for ourself. If we would stop here we would leave morality out of account . . . There is a class of aims besides aims relating only to ourselves and to others. There is a class of ideal aims. We are slaves of ideas or ideals. Men enlist in the service of some law, and occupy themselves in bringing it to light and embodying it in the world. The scientific man illustrates this aim. This must be specified as the last and, on the whole, the highest aim to be taken in life. It is possible to follow any one of these aims without regard to pleasure. But it is not possible to have pleasure not attend them . . . The proper ethical aim in life *is life,* and life is the conjunction of all these aims . . ."

"The Place of Pleasure in Life," is the title of the fifth lecture. "It is valuable as a sign, as a function, and as an end in itself. As a sign it is valuable as indicating that our various functions are fulfilling their respective aims. When we are not cheerful it is a pretty good sign that something is wrong about our machinery . . . Pleasure is [also] valuable as a function, in that it produces something else than itself. It is the oil of life which takes off the friction from the other functions. It is an exhileration, a stimulus to life. Pleasure is worthy as an end in itself. It is no sin to aim at it . . . We ought to expect pleasure and should demand it of life. If we don't have it, we are going to work wrong, and should work some other way. We should not be ashamed of trivial pleasures, on the contrary we should be proud of them. They are the keenest and purest pleasures, for in trivial things alone, the aim of pleasure predominates. The little, trivial pleasures tone our lives and are greatly to be desired when they don't interfere with the workings of more important functions . . ."

In the sixth and last lecture in the course, Palmer gave "The Rules for Attaining Pleasure . . . [that is] to construct an art of pleasure. Before giving the rules of our art we must determine the principles of the art. The general law of the art will be to find the conditions which will least interfere with the exercise of our powers, and when these conditions are found, to exercise our powers on objects as durable as possible . . . We may say that the conditions are property, society, home, health, freedom, knowledge and habits. The positive conditions are all-important . . . they are courage, self-forgetfulness, and devotion to perpetual things. Courage is used in the sense of making ourselves look always at the bright side of life."

On the day after the last lecture, at the Vesper service, Professor Palmer "made a brief address in which he spoke feelingly of the mystery of pain. Pain exists in the world. It is a necessary element in every human life, the unwelcome visitor at every fireside. In my lectures of the past week I have given pleasure so much prominence that I am afraid that you who have found life principally sorrow and disappointment will think me the apostle of a very wrong philosophy. But I do not forget pain . . . There is a great deal, in fact, a preponderance of the tragic in life. No poem or work of fiction is great and admirable which fails to give pain and pleasure each a place. Pleasure, however, is the natural, the wholesome, the complete side of life. Pain is unnatural, unwholesome and incomplete. Joy is the symbol of perfection, the outward sign of of the fitness of function . . . Pain is unavoidable but it should be remembered that it is indicative of the presence of evil . . . Happiness would not be happiness if pain did not exist to furnish a contrast. Pain is the portal to the palace of pleasure. We should conquer it with the forces of our manhood and thus make it minister to our truest self-hood. We can make it enhance our lives and characters. Pain, I am aware, is closely connected with the Christian religion. Sorrow is a large element in it . . . Christ died to lift the sorrows of men. He takes away the sting of pain. He brings glad tidings of great joy" (The

Vesper Hour Yesterday, *Chautauqua Assembly Herald*, July 24, 1893).

31 Harvard University.

This long piece is presented in its entirety because the source is very difficult to find, the content is quite different from that of George Herbert Palmer's other writings, and he provides a profile of Harvard University 100 years ago when the university was already about two and one-half centuries old.

"**Harvard University:** the oldest and largest institution of learning in the U. S. It had its beginning in 1636 in a vote of the general court of Massachusetts Bay, which in September of that year agreed to give £400 toward its foundation. The following year the proposed college was ordered to be at Newtown or Cambridge (as in remembrance of the English university town, it then began to be called), at a spot 3 miles distant from the present Boston Statehouse. No students, however, had been received in 1638, when John Harvard, a young minister of Charlestown, who had been in the colony but a year, died and left half his property and his entire library to the hardly existent college. His gift amounted to nearly £400, with 260 volumes. The general court immediately ordered 'that the college agreed upon formerly to be built at Cambridge shall be called Harvard College.' The first class was formed in the same year, and graduated, nine in number, in 1642. About the same number appear in the other classes of the seventeenth century, except that in 1644, 1648, 1672, 1682, and 1688 there were no graduating classes. These are the only empty years in the entire history of the college. Through the eighteenth century the annual number of graduates was between twenty and forty; during the first half of the nineteenth century between fifty and seventy. The class of 1860 first crossed the line of 100; 1883, that of 200; 1893, that of 300. The quinquennial catalogue of 1890 contains the names of 16,390 graduates of Harvard University, more than half of whom were then living. In the year 1893–94 [when this article was written] there were 3,156 students in attendance, of whom 2,188 were in the charge of the faculty of arts and sciences. The professors and other instructors number 322, an average of more than one teacher to each ten students.

"By the circumstances of its foundation Harvard unites the

characteristics of the three types of college prevalent in the U. S. — the sect college, the State college, and the college of individual benefaction. Its charter declares its aims to be 'the education of the English and Indian youth of the country in knowledge and godliness.' Its first board of overseers were charged with 'furthering the college in piety, morality, and learning.' Its two mottos, *Veritas* and *Christo et Ecclesiœ*, have a similar signifance. During the first century of its existence half its graduates entered the pulpit of Puritanism, and few colleges even now send more men into the ministry than Harvard. Yet it has from the first stood for the humane rather than the rigid spirit in religion. Into none even among its earliest constitutions does a word of dogmatic restriction enter. Its Divinity School is forbidden to exact 'assent to the peculiarities of any denomination of Christians' from either instructors or students. Until 1870 it was mainly a Unitarian college, but it is now managed in the interest of no single sect. All its faculties and all its governing boards include men of diverse religious beliefs. Its chapel exercises — daily morning prayers, Sunday preaching, and Thursday vesper services — are voluntary. The board of six preachers in charge of these services has had ministers of six denominations among its members. The president, who until 1829 had, with a single exception, been a minister, has since that date generally been a layman. The university, in short, while under strong religious influence, is thoroughly unsectarian.

"The relations of the university to the State have been no less peculiar. The general court at first intrusted the government of the college to a board of overseers; but in 1650 a charter was granted, by which the college was made a corporation, consisting of the president, five fellows, and a treasurer, to be known as 'the president and fellows of Harvard College.' This corporation had power to fill vacancies in its numbers, with the approval of the overseers, and continues in its original form as 'the corporation,' acting under the charter first issued in 1650, and with its rights and privileges confirmed by a special section in the constitution of the Commonwealth of Massachusetts, framed in 1780. The State government retained control of the board of overseers until 1865, when all official connection between the college and the State was broken by the passage of a legislative act directing that vacancies occurring in the board of overseers thereafter should be filled by the alumni of the college 'voting on commencement-day in the city of Cambridge.' Instructors are allowed neither to vote nor to become overseers. The corporation holds and manages the property of the university, the overseers have ordinarily no voice in the investment or other disposition of university funds. But in all matters relating to statutes and regulations, the appointment of professors and other instructors, and in general the internal administration of university affairs, the consent of the overseers is necessary. That board consists of the president and treasurer, *ex officio*, and of thirty other persons elected for terms of six years, five retiring each year. All indications of State control have disappeared, except that the governor is still escorted to commencement by his bodyguard, and that the assembly there gathered is called to order by the county sheriff.

"From the beginning, Harvard has derived its chief support from private benefactions. The exemption of its property from taxation is a continual and weighty public gift, but the university has received no other subsidy from the State since 1814. Throughout its entire history government grants seem never to have discouraged individual bounty; since 1870 the gifts from private sources have amounted to $350,000 a year. Its property at present consists of $8,000,000 of interest-bearing funds, of nearly 700 acres of land, and of more than 60 buildings occupied by the university. To these should be added the immense collections of its museums, and its library of 430,000 volumes and 400,000 pamphlets, a library increasing at the rate of 13,000 volumes a year. In round numbers $1,000,000 is received and expended annually for university purposes. As the majority of the students are poor or in moderate circumstances, $90,000 is appropriated each year to fellowships, scholarships. and other forms of aid. In the public dining-halls, 1,500 persons are boarded at a charge of $3 to $4 a week, but the college dormitories are sufficient to lodge hardly more than a third of the students in residence.

"The name Harvard University designates the entire complex institution; its central portion is the college. In this the degree of A. B. is given to students of four years' standing who have completed satisfactorily eighteen courses, sixteen of them elective. By a course is understood a single line of study in which three hours a week of instruction are given throughout a year. Each student chooses four such courses at the beginning of the year from a list printed by the faculty of arts and sciences. The courses offered for election number 349. The plan of the elective system, gradually matured at Harvard during half a century, is to fix the quantity and quality of study, but to leave the choice of topic to the individual student. Accordingly, it may in a sense be said that members of the three upper classes are free to choose any studies they desire; but as the advanced and technical courses of each department presuppose careful elementary training, the choice is in practice much restricted. During his brief college life a student is able to pursue only about one-thirteenth of the instruction offered.

"Each department of the university has its own dean and faculty, but the College, the Graduate School, and the Lawrence Scientific School have also a faculty in common, called the faculty of arts and sciences. The Graduate School, giving the degrees of A. M., Ph. D., and S. D., has this year (1893–94) 252 students; the Scientific School (1847), giving the degree of S. B., has 280. In Cambridge, too, though governed by independent faculties, are the Divinity School (1819), with its 36 undergraduates and 11 graduate students, which requires of candidates for its degree of D. B. that they shall also possess the degree of A. B.; and the Law School (1817), whose course is three years and whose students number 353. The other departments of the university are not in Cambridge. In Boston are the Medical School (1783), containing 446 students and 81 instructors, and requiring a four years' course of study; the Dental School (1867) and the School of Veterinary Medicine (1882), each giving its degree after a graded course of three years. The School of Agriculture and Horticulture, known as the Bussey Institution (1861), is in Jamaica Plain, within the limits of Boston. The beautiful Arnold Arboretum occupies 120 acres of the Bussey estate. The library (1839–77), observatory (1846), botanic gardens (1805), university (1852–89) and Peabody museums (1876–89), memorial hall (1870–76), the gymnasiums (1879 and 1890), boat-houses (1870 and 1890), and athletic-grounds are all in Cambridge. To students in one department of the university instruction in all others is open without additional charge. Summer school courses, yielding no degree, and mainly in science, history, language, and physical training, are offered in Cambridge during six weeks of July and August for a small fee, and are attended by large numbers of teachers and other students. The annual fee in most of the departments of the university is $150, but that of the Divinity School is $50, and that of the Medical School $200.

"*Radcliffe College.* — In 1878 a company of men and women of Cambridge and Boston were organized under the title of 'A Society for the Collegiate Instruction of Women.' This society, quickly known to popular speech as 'The Harvard Annex,' employed such teachers of Harvard College as were willing to undertake the labor of giving to young women the instruction already given in the college to young men. Its building, overshadowed by the Washington elm, is known as Fay House. In 1893 application was made to the Legislature for a charter and for the right to grant degrees. Prior to that date it had given only certificates of study. The institution is now called Radcliffe College, in memory of Anne Radcliffe, Lady Moulson, the founder of the first scholarship in Harvard College; its board of visitors (without whose consent no instructor can be appointed) is the corporation of Harvard College; its degrees will be signed by Harvard's president; but its property is held by an independent board. Radcliffe College started with an enrollment of 250 students.

"The following are the names of the presidents of Harvard University: Henry Dunster, 1640–54; Charles Chauncy, 1654–72; Leonard Hoar, 1672–75; Uriah Oakes, 1675–81; John Rogers, 1682–84; Increase Mather, 1685–1701; Samuel Willard, 1700-07; John Leverett, 1707–24; Benjamin Wadsworth, 1725–37; Edward Holyoke, 1737–69; Samuel Locke, 1770–73; Samuel Langdon, 1774–80; Joseph Willard, 1781–1804; Samuel Webber, 1806–10; John Thornton Kirkland, 1810–28; Josiah Quincy, 1829–45; Edward Everett, 1846–49; Jared Sparks, 1849–53; James Walker, 1853–60; Cornelius Conway Felton, 1860–62; Thomas Hill, 1862–68; Charles William Eliot, elected in 1869.

> "Quincy's *History of Harvard University* (Cambridge, 2 vols., 1840) gives the fullest account of the college. W. Thayer's *Historical Sketch of Harvard University*, in the *History of Middlesex County* (Boston, 1890), is compact and interesting. *The Harvard Graduates' Magazine*, a quarterly journal begun in 1892, contains a careful record of whatever concerns the university. The annual reports of the president and treasurer are sent free on application, as are all pamphlets descriptive of each of the departments and of the conditions of admission."

32 Philip Stanley Abbot.

On October 21, 1896, at the Appalachian Mountain Club's memorial meeting to Philip Stanley Abbot, with 140 people present, Professor Palmer eulogized him with this "sketch of [his] life and character." The Palmers and the Abbot family were close friends. The Chronicles include numerous entries about Edwin Hale Abbot, and Professor Palmer enters in 1884 that he went "with Edwin and Philip Abbot [Edwin's son] to England for six weeks." In her diary entry for Sunday, March 11, 1900, Mrs. Palmer names Ned Abbot [Edwin Hale Abbot, Jr.] as one of the students having dinner at 11 Quincy Street. And Edwin Hale Abbot, also a trustee of Wellesley College, provided the memorial to Alice Freeman Palmer in the college chapel (See 113n2, frontispiece, and 244n5).

Palmer's eulogy: "[I]t was an unusual man who died on the peak of Mt. Lefroy. Fortunate as I was in knowing him for twenty-five years, I can perhaps cheer many who miss him by recalling to them anew the facts of his life and the impression of power and beauty which he so singularly gave."

Professor Palmer then presented some basic information about Philip Abbot: Born on September 1, 1867. Harvard College, class of 1890. Harvard Law School, class of 1893. "Both in college and the Law School he led his class in scholarship, while he also managed the 'Harvard Monthly' and the 'Law Review,' was Secretary of the Cambridge Civil Service Association . . . and carried on regular charity work among the poor of Boston." After law school "he entered at once the law-office of Warren & Brandeis in Boston [Samuel Dennis Warren, Jr. and Louis Dembitz Brandeis graduated from Harvard Law School in 1877 and started this practice in 1879]. Here he had a year of general practice, and then began to devote himself to the legal affairs of the Wisconsin Central Railroad, with which he was connected at the time of his death."

". . . Of all who have gone forth from Harvard during the twenty-six years of my connection with it, none has more impressed me as the all-accomplished person, disciplined for leadership." Palmer listed Abbot's many and varied accomplishments, such as: "He knew the chief English poets before he could comprehend their meaning. He had read more Greek and Latin at entering college than all but a few have read at graduation . . . French, German, and some Spanish were also at his command. He took high rank in History and Economics . . . [T]wo important professorships of law were offered him. But his interests were not confined to books; he was a wholesome and out-of-door person . . . Later in life he enjoyed nothing so much as the visits to an ancestral New Hampshire farm, of which he undertook the management. To make the list of his accomplishments less incomplete, it should be added that he handled a boat well, was an unwearied walker, a forceful and luminous writer, a companion excellently gay or serious . . .

"[H]is large endowments of mind and body were matched by an elevated character, a character simple in outline and in some respects old-fashioned, yet possessing a subtlety, sweetness, originality, an odd conjunction of seemingly opposed virtues which confound the describer. Remembering that winning face and sturdy form, and thinking of the high nature which shone through them, it is difficult to keep the just measure of praise. Dutiful he was, unsolicited by vagrant pleasures; public-minded, brave; considerately but pertinaciously truthful; ingenious in kindness; tender to the aged, the weak, the obtuse; swift of sympathy, a capital listener; dull at noticing slights to himself, unsuspicious, dispassionate in regard to his own mistakes; loyal, unstinting, having a veritable genius for friendship, sonship, brotherhood; forward in accepting responsibilities; cautious, forecasting, decisive; mannerly; abhorring cant and pretence; profoundly and continually religious, buoyant accordingly, and not distrustful of natural impulse; capable of outbursts of anger or of play; having the confidence of women; pure and clean, not for any squaring with decency but because dirt was repulsive; so regardful of the fair and fit that he made all whom he came near feel righteousness easy and best. He brought out the genuine and fragrant side of everybody, and everybody gave him back an admiring love. He took the love and was careless of the admiration . . .

"Studious though he was, he was attracted by risk and rejoiced in daring wherever difficulties were to be found. In study, in business, or on the mountains, he was continually laying sagacious plans for battling with obstacles. Had fears or considerations of ease interested him, even without a fall from a precipice Philip Abbot would have ceased to be Philip Abbot. Lesser man may be mourned, for when they die they disappear. But his few years and gallant death, illuminated as they were by well doing and Christian hope, must always be to his friends a source of gladness."

33 Empedocles. (not found)

34 *Self-Cultivation in English.*

This essay was the Commencement Oration at the University of Michigan on June 28, 1894.

"English study has four aims [Palmer begins]:

> the mastery of our language as a science, as a history, as a joy, and as a tool. I am concerned with but one, the mastery of it as a tool . . . Every hour our language is an engine for communicating with others, every instant for fashioning the thoughts of our own minds. I want to call attention to the means of mastering this curious and essential tool, and to lead every one who hears me to become discontented with his employment of it . . . It is as certain as anything can be [he concludes] that faithful endeavor will bring expertness in the use of English. If we are watchful of our speech, making our words continually more minutely true, free, and resourceful; if we look upon our occasions of writing as opportunities for the deliberate work of unified construction; if in all our utterances we think of him who hears as well as of him who speaks; and above all, if we fix the attention of ourselves and our hearers on the matter we talk about and so let ourselves be supported by our subject, — we shall make a daily advance not only in English study, but in personal power, in general serviceableness, and in consequent delight."

This essay, one of Professor Palmer's most popular publications, can be fully appreciated only in its entirety. See 142n4 and 262n3.

As a "model of exposition" — that is, the explanation of "a term or a set of facts" — part of this essay is reprinted in Charles R. Nutter, F. W. C. Hersey, and Chester N. Greenough, *Specimens of Prose Composition*, Boston, Ginn & Co., 1906, page 23–32. And the notes (page 467–468) present some "comments which have been useful [for teachers] in class-room practice . . . It will repay careful analysis for the means by which Unity, Coherence, and Emphasis are obtained in the whole composition and in the paragraphs . . . The [verbal] illustrations and figures of speech are particularly effective because they deal with familiar things . . . The quotations from Ben Jonson, Henry Ward Beecher, Thomas Jefferson, etc., add to clearness and to force, and contribute liveliness to the style."

And Charles S. Thomas recommends Palmer's piece as an example for "the teaching of the essay" in *The Teaching of English in the Secondary School,* Boston, Houghton Mifflin Co., 1917, pages 117, 129, 226.

35 Similarities and Contrasts of Christianity and Buddhism.

In a footnote at the beginning of this article, the editors of the *Outlook* state that it is based on an address — stenographically recorded and then revised by Professor Palmer — before the Outlook Club in Montclair, New Jersey. Palmer's list of Books Read 1896–97 (page 117) includes three on Buddhism; Warren's book — *Buddhism in Translations,* the third volume of the Harvard Oriental Series, — Palmer says, contains the original text on which he has based his remarks.

The same issue of the *Outlook* (page 435–436) has this editorial: "The keyote to Professor Palmer's remarkable address . . . may be found in his quotation from Leibnitz: 'Every denial is false; every affirmation is true.' Professor Palmer shows clearly that the affirmations of Buddhism are all more clearly and vitally affirmed by Christianity, while its denials are equally repugnant to the teaching of Christ, of philosophy, and of the highest life. The explanation of *the curious though very limited passion for Buddhism which has shown itself recently in certain circles in America* [AJL's italics] is to be found in ignorance either of what Buddhism is or of what Christianity is. For the first the enthusiast has gone to such poetical portrayals as 'The Light of Asia'; for the second, not to the teachings of Jesus Christ or the interpretations of his immediate Apostles, but to ecclesiastical misinterpretations, in which mediæval paganism and primitive Christianity are intermingled, and from which they have generally selected, for a comparison with Buddhism, the elements contributed to Christian doctrine by mediæval paganism, not those contributed by primitive Christianity.

"Let us add that Professor Palmer's article affords a splendid illustration of the light which can be thrown on a perplexing subject by a mind furnished by large scholarship and trained to select the essential and vital elements from amidst a mass of heterogeneous matter, mated to a spirit whose faith is at once so clear and so vital that it can neither be obscured nor shaken, and so irenic that no controversy or antagonisn can either embitter or ruffle its calm confidence in the truth. This paper . . . is a noble example of what all theological discussion should be: namely, never controversial but always truth-seeking; never an attack on supposed falsehood, but always an exposition of the truth."

Professor Palmer opens this long essay: "Glad though I am to fulfill my appointed task tonight, I feel that it is an ungracious one, for I seem to be set in antagonism to my admired friend [from the footnote: "Professor Palmer's address followed one by the well-known Oriental scholar, Mr. Dharmapala"], who has stirred me as deeply as he has stirred you. And yet the fundamental comparison of ideas need not involve hostility. It is necessary for me to place Christianity in a certain sense in contrast with Buddhism, but I hope the contrast may only bring out more sharply the excellencies of both."

Palmer concludes: "In my judgment, during the next fifty years, both in philosophy and in religion, there is sure to come a struggle between the large faiths, and what I call the partial faiths, between the East and the West. Up to fifty years ago, as Mr. Dharmapala pointed out to you, the East and the West had not discovered one another. We professed to live upon a globe, we were living upon a hemisphere. Now we must address ourselves to the entire earth, and my impression is that before long there will come a clinch and a struggle between the religious ideals of its two sides. Let us only ask that in that struggle all that is precious in belief may survive; that from each of those faiths which we cannot substitute for our own there may come to us so beautiful a teacher as we have with us tonight."

The *New York Times* on October, 11, 1991, has a long article that begins: "There may be few things as incompatible as Manhattan and Buddhism. One means competition, self-fulfillment and the fast track; the other means contemplation, self-abnegation and savoring the moment. But all around Manhattan these days are little oases of Buddhism, part of a celebration of religion and culture called the Year of Tibet. The Dalai Lama arrived earlier this week to take part" (Ari L.

Goldman, Buddhism and Manhattan: An Unlikely Joining Together, page B1, B4).

And in December 1992, "The Harvard Buddhist Studies Forum . . . received a grant from Koji Ihara, CEO of the Mind Culture Group of Tokyo — an amount large enough to maintain the Forum's public lecture series over the next six years and intended to develop ino a permanent endowment . . . The grant's purpose is to promote a better understanding of Buddhism in all its different contexts, both in this country and in other parts of the world" (*Harvard University Gazette*, December 11, 1992: 3, 18).

36 Book Review. Wilhelm Wundt, *Ethics*.

To open this review, Palmer points out that "[s]ince its first appearance in 1886, Wundt's Ethics has had an eminence in Germany accorded to few other books on its subject . . . Wundt will be made at home among us, and in the stylish garb given him by these two skillful ladies will not appear a foreigner. Yet widely as the book is likely to be read, both on account of its intrinsic merits and because of the great service its author is known to have rendered in a neighboring field [psychology], it will hardly be admitted by English readers to that small group of epoch-making books produced in a single quarter century by Mill, Spencer, Sidgwick, Bradley, Green and Martineau . . . Wundt does not offer such spiritual sustenance, nor any such body of minute and scholarly matter, as our half dozen greatest ethical writers present."

For volume 1, Facts of the Moral Life, Palmer confines his review to "a single question . . . I wish to set forth more precisely than the author has seen fit to do the reasons why this portion of the work has been given its present position. These reasons are not at once apparent to the hasty reader, and the purpose of the volume may in consequence easily be misconceived." During his lengthy analyses of many aspects of Wundt's presentation, Palmer points out that "[e]thics is a systematic assessment of the relative values of human conduct. Its chief problem is, accordingly, the establishment of a standard by which these values may be tested. No accumulation of facts can erect such a standard. Judgment of values and description of facts are disparate processes, and can never grow from a common root. Ethics, strictly speaking, is not concerned with facts."

With regard to volume 2, Ethical Systems, "a history of ethics from Socrates to Spencer . . . ," Professor Palmer states that this "section of the work cannot be said to have any large value . . . It was unfortunate that the demands of a systematic plan . . . should have induced the author to interpolate into an important book a section of such cramped and inferior merit."

37 *The Antigone of Sophocles*, Translated with Introduction and Notes.

Palmer dedicates the translation of this play by the Greek dramatic playwright "To you who as a young girl rejoiced to make a fair beginning of these things [that is, Greek studies] and who as my wife has now been persuaded to join me in my love of them" (I am grateful to Nicholas Poole-Wilson for this translation from the Greek). His wife, Alice Freeman Palmer, had studied Greek literature in college, and had declined an invitation in 1878 to teach Greek at Wellesley College.

"In putting forth this ancient masterpiece in an English dress, [the introduction begins] I wish to assert for my rendering the least possible originality.

> Sophocles I hope has furnished all its ideas, and a large part of its language has been borrowed from previous workmen. The piece has been loved for ages, and every illumination which affection, learning, and ingenious phrase can give has long been bestowed upon it. The new translator, unless he cares for himself more than for the heroic maid [Antigone], must make it his chief business to sort the stores already accumulated. He should remember, however, that good literary sorting can be performed in no mechanical fashion. It is constructive work and calls for creative imagination. Situations must be felt, characters conceived, the mode of utterance which suits the individual persons, and suits their passing feelings, be delicately measured, before any selection of verbal material, whether furnished by one's own mind or that of others, can be sanctioned. This need is apt to be overlooked, even by many who are not so ready as I to indulge in plagiarism. The translator of the Antigone is the manager of a dramatic action. If he cannot make the appealing play appeal, it is inapposite to say that his words fit much else in the Greek text. In the mind of Sophocles all else

existed for the sake of presenting human character; and when this all-controlling interest is omitted, the ministering niceties of language become pedantic monstrosities . . .

"The medium employed is that which I used many years ago in rendering the Odyssey, — an unobtrusive iambic rhythm, not broken by measure. I thought it suited Homer well, but I fear it is too simple a contrivance to express the full and complex mind of Sophocles. But since fulness has not been my principal aim, the enginery to which my mind is already accustomed may be permissible."

38 The Harvard Union Site.

"After the announcement . . . that Major H. L. Higginson, ['55], had given $150,000 to erect a University Club, to be known as the Harvard Union," a committee "welcomed . . . all expressions of interest from graduates and undergraduates." The *Crimson* insisted that the Warren estate, at the corner of Quincy and Harvard Streets, was too far from the social centre . . . a [student] vote . . . brought out 650 votes in favor of the Quincy Street site, and 450 against it . . ." (*HGM*, 1900–1901; 9 (September 1900): 25; 1899–1900; 8 (March 1900): 428).

In his Diary entry for Sunday, March 18, 1900 (page 181), Professor Palmer mentions his letter that appeared on the previous evening:

To the Editor of the Transcript:

"For the past two months an animated discussion has been carried on among Harvard students in regard to the site of the new Union, the latest gift of our frequent benefactor, Major Higginson. The Union will be the great social Club, or meeting place for graduates and every species of undergraduate, which Harvard has long desired. Here will be assembled all those interests of the collective 'College Life' which in the judgment of some persons outweigh in importance the studious occupations of our little community. It is no easy matter to choose a wise site for such a building. The points to be studied are three: accessibility, dignity, and adaptation to the future growth of the university. But of these three the first is the only one which the not very long-sighted student mind has thus far taken at all seriously. Each particular group of students is inclined to think that the proper site is the one which is most accessible to its own lodging. The Warren lot, on the corner of Quincy and Harvard streets, was at first proposed, a lot not five minutes distant from any college building. But it met with furious opposition from the little group of club men who haunt Mt. Auburn street, and from the many dwellers in the half dozen sumptuous dormitories of that and the connecting streets — dormitories not owned by Harvard — who wish to make this hitherto neglected quarter of the city a controlling factor in Harvard life [see the map and its legend, pages 512 & 513].

"Possibly the discussion has now reached a point where the broader judgment of our graduates may well be appealed to. In the interest of a symmetrical development of the college grounds, I should like to suggest the following plan to the many Harvard graduates who read the Transcript. Let the site be the lot on which Professor Wright's house stands, opposite the old gymnasium, on Quincy street. This old gymnasium, never a costly building, is now outworn and unsightly. Occupied at present by the engineers, it will be vacated when the new Engineering Building is erected next year. The corporation might then be induced to remove it altogether and to turn its pleasing little plot of ground into an enclosed common, with perhaps eventually a statue in its centre. The whole square, with this bit of green in the middle, would then become one of the most notable in this part of the country — its base occupied by the Union, one of its sides by Memorial Hall, the other by the Art Museum and the splendid Architectural Building which is to be erected on the corner of Quincy street and Broadway this coming year.

"While the objection to the Warren lot — that it 'is out of the way' — seems to me a pretty lazy one, I feel that the site I here propose has superior recommendations in its dignity and in the fact that 2000 students necessarily pass it three times a day. Twelve hundred men board at Memorial, 800 at Randall. A meal well taken disposes one to social intercourse. I should even fear that a location so convenient might lead to more loafing than is well. Certainly there could be no danger that on so populous a spot the club would be unsuccessful. Study, athletics and eating are among our chief employments. Since the building must inevitably be remote from our athletic field, it may well be placed in the path of the studious and the hungry. A line of cars on each side of it gives the desirable connection with Boston.

"It must not be forgotten that in choosing a site adjustment to the future is more important than present convenience. We are arranging for coming centuries. The selection should be a part of a broad plan and be intimately related to the permanent well-being of Harvard. This seems to me the serious objection to the Warren lot. It is demonstrable that the growth of the university must be away from that corner. It must be to the north, over Holmes and Jarvis Fields, since that is the only unoccupied ground remaining in our possession. My proposal creates an open square as a magnificent Harvard centre, having nearly equal portions of grounds and buildings to the north and south. By the adoption of the Warren lot the value of our northern property would be diminished; by my plan it would be increased.

"If as time goes on the Wright lot proves too small for the expanding purposes of the Union, the two wooden houses in its rear might be bought and the whole block — bounded by Quincy, Broadway, Prescott and Cambridge street — be devoted to this single use."

G. H. Palmer

The committee decided to build on the Warren lot and presented a statement which included these remarks: "In the first place, the corner of Quincy and Harvard Streets is not distant from any part of the University, and it is close to the car lines. Although at present it may seem to be a little out of the track of students, there is no certainty about the direction of the University's future growth. It is likely to render Quincy Square more central in the course of another generation. This is an important consideration, as the Union will be part of student life for many generations to come" (*HGM*, 1900–1901; 9 (September 1900): 25–26).

39 A Non-Decadent Country Town.

This piece of about 1100 words by Professor Palmer appeared in a section headed "Life and Work of the Churches." The town is Boxford where the Palmers spent so much time.

"The problem of the country town has been much discussed of late. New England, we are told, is decaying. Our soil at best is thin and yields but a scanty support. Our impoverished farmers are niggardly and lacking in public spirit. In their isolated homes they become ignorant, morose and inclined to sour gossip. The vigorous young of both sexes soon depart. The few who remain turn to cider-drinking and other cheap and uninventive vices. Against the prevalent evil and despondency churches are impotent, being so much occupied with theological uncharitableness and sectarian rivalry. In short, the religious basis of the old New England country life is gone, and the dignity, content, intelligence and piety which once distinguished our little corner of the globe are things of the past . . .

"But good people still remain good. Courage, energy, and ability to look on the bright side are not yet altogether discredited virtues. Under their vivifying influence many a village is kept sweet and wholesome. One of these I want to describe, partly because I love and honor the little town, partly to report facts unlike the depressing ones which commonly get into print.

"Boxford is twenty-five miles from Boston, at about the center of Essex County, in that picturesque and unfruitful region where rocks, gravel, brooks, ponds and woods take the place of soil. Corn and potatoes, a slender crop of hay, apples and the domestic virtues are its chief products. It is an extensive township, with two villages — Boxford and West Boxford. I speak only of the one I know, Boxford proper. Its total population is 314 — less than twenty-five years ago, much less than a hundred years ago. It has one church, one store, two district schools, no hotel, no factory, no lawyer, no doctor. Its railroad station is a mile from the village. It contains hardly any poor people, no man of wealth, no foreigners, few summer residents. The majority of its families have been here for many generations, my own for more than 200 years . . .

"It is an average country town. But let us see what man has done here to make life worth living during the last ten years. Roads have been kept in good order, there has been fair attention to shade trees, and almost every house has presented an appearance of neatness and unobtrusive dignity. [See 59n1 for the development of a public library; 86n1 for the building and maintenance of a Town Hall.] . . . While neither the property nor the population of the town is sufficient to maintain schools of a high grade, any child is allowed to attend the high school of the neighboring towns without expense for tuition.

"But the center of the New England country town has always been the church. We are proud of the fact that we have only one. It is, of course, Congregational, but we welcome to it every species of pious soul and are pretty regardless of speculative niceties. A few attempts have been made to organize a separate society, but thus far the friendliness of Boxford has thwarted divisive Satan. [See 151n2 for details about the church] . . .

"Two great influences . . . have been at work which are not found everywhere — a high average character and enlightened leadership. The old New England stock is vigorous here. Everybody desires to keep himself intelligent, kind and God-fearing. These are men and women of pronounced individuality, not indisposed to opinions of their own. But instead of quarreling, they tell each other plainly what they think without losing their sense of comradeship. And this general friendliness has been fostered by a noble line of ministers. For thirty years [1838–1868] Dr. William S. Coggin sweetened and refined every home in the parish. He is our saint, fragrant and influential in memory. Three devoted men followed him in pastorates of worthy length [S. L. Gammell, 1868–1880; Alcott, 1880–1883; Kendall, 1883–1892]. For the past eight years a young man in his first settlement has been our leader [Emery Lucius Bradford]. The remarkable development of the church here described is chiefly his work. During the early years of his ministry Dr. Coggin was still living, and became his example and adviser . . . Exchanging infrequently, he has preached Sunday after Sunday quiet sermons marked by a spiritual insight and a simple beauty of language rare in any pulpit [Palmer had studied at Andover Theological Seminary, and he often preached in the Boxford church]. Any minister who can preach, who can be the dear and trusted friend of all, who can forget personal claims and bodily infirmity [in early life Bradford lost his left leg] in the service of his Master, and, while showing in himself the beauty of holiness, can on a small salary tactfully advise, encourage, instruct his people, is an enormous social power in any community. Decay is not easy in his neighborhood [See **GHP**-94 for Palmer's sketch of Bradford twenty-five years later]. The problem of the country town would largely disappear if such leadership could be multiplied. Where material conditions are unfavorable, strong personalities are doubly important and valued."

40 *The Field of Ethics.*

(See correspondence between George Herbert Palmer and Houghton Mifflin Company, page 465)

On June 1, 1899, Professor Palmer was notified of his appointment to be the first Noble lecturer to give a continuous course of lectures at Harvard, for 1899–1900; he gave the lectures on six successive Wednesday starting on March 7, 1900, and a stenographer reported them (the four lectures in March are mentioned in the Diaries for that month, in chapter 4). Publication of each course of lectures was required, and on July 9, 1901, he began to rewrite the stenographer's reports into a final manuscript. He delivered the manuscript to Houghton Mifflin Company on September 9, 1901; the book, *The Field of Ethics,* was published on November 17, 1901. He was paid $600 for the lectures, the plates of the book were paid for, and he owned the copyright of the book (These details are from the Chronicles, the Diaries, and the terms of the lectureship).

The six chapters of Palmer's book, "not divided precisely as were the original six lectures" (footnote, page 205), are entitled: 1. Ethics and the descriptive sciences. 2. Ethics and the law. 3. Ethics and æsthetics. 4. Ethics and religion — affinities. 5. Ethics and religion — divergencies. 6. Conclusion. Chapters 1, 2, 3, and 5 each end with a list of references for further reading.

A contemporary reviewer wrote: "Those who listened to the William Noble Lectures for 1899 by Prof. Palmer will be glad to review them in their present form, while others interested in the subject should not fail to acquaint themselves with this fresh, clear, and suggestive presentation of an important subject" (*HGM,* 1901–1902; 10 (March 1902): 479–480).

41 *The Field of Ethics,* translated into Japanese.

42 A Study of Self Sacrifice.

This publication was based on an "Oration delivered in Sanders Theatre, before the Harvard Chapter of Phi Beta Kappa, Thursday, June 26, 1902." Professor Palmer revised the stenographer's report. (See also **GHP**-45 and 46.)

After some general opening remarks, Palmer says: "I shall speak to you to-day about the nature and limits of self-sacrifice. Often have I discussed the subject before; again and again must I discuss it hereafter, for it is the central theme of ethics. He who has mastered self-sacrifice has comprehended all righteousness, human and divine. But it is not easy to comprehend, for it is full of seeming contradictions. To know it truly one must be patient of refinements, accessible to qualification, and ever ready to admit the opposite of what he has laboriously established. Each year as I go over the ground with my classes and try to trace the plan of this labyrinth, I end with dissatisfaction. Some clue has been missed which might have led to larger reality. I will try once more. I will call on older and more experienced men to help me unravel the tangled skein."

After his lengthy analysis, Palmer concludes: "Gentlemen, I have tried to mark you out a clear path through this ethical jungle, overgrown as it is with the exuberance of human life. I have not succeeded, and perhaps it is impossible to succeed. In the subject itself there is paradox. We all desire by study to win a swift simplicity. But nature abhors simplicity. She complicates. She forces us who would know to take pains, to proceed cautiously, and to feel our way along from point to point. In tracking shy truth we must content ourselves with verifiable and not always reconcilable fragments. We are not allowed to grasp the easy totalities of concrete experience. Such are the limitations of critical scholarship. But fortunately scholarship is not all. It is supplemented by art, which deals with wholes all saturated with human life."

43 Book review. William James, *Varieties of Religious Experience.*

This volume, Professor Palmer writes at the beginning of his long, unsigned review, "is remarkable alike for the purpose of the author and the manner in which he has executed it. That purpose is to subject religious experience to a scientific scrutiny, and it is only very recently that this has been attempted." Palmer highlights his detailed analysis with laudatory comments: "It is not only in his perfectly frank examination of these phenomena that Professor James's book is remarkable if not absolutely unique; it is no less so in the manner in which this examination is conducted. This is, indeed, much more than a manner; the catholicity is that of large-mindedness as well as of large scholarship; the dispassionateness is that of a supreme love of truth, not merely that of an omnivorous curiosity; and the dramatic perception is much more than that of a great artist — it is that of one possessed of a great sympathy with his kind . . . It is this passionate devotion to and sympathy with men in their highest life which gives to his volume its fascinating dramatic quality . . . [and] As the critic reads these lectures, the charm of which no . . . chance quotations are adequate to illustrate, he envies the happy students who heard them delivered with the personality of the speaker pervading them and speaking in them."

44 *A Service in Memory of Alice Freeman Palmer.*
See **aboutAFPann**-5.

45 *The Heart of Ethics.*
This was the annual public address before the Philosophical Union of the University of California at Berkeley, on August 21, 1903. This Union was organized in 1889 by "graduates and other members of the Department of Philosophy . . . [who were] convinced of the supreme interest and import of philosophical studies for human life in all its aspects, individual or social, private or public; and [who desired] . . . to promote them among ourselves and among others, especially in the communities on the Pacific Coast . . ." (Preamble of the Constitution of the Union). Previous lecturer from Harvard had been Josiah Royce in 1895 and William James in 1898

Professor Palmer opens his address: "I cannot begin my address this evening without expressing my pleasure that you exist and that you have been kind enough to allow me to come before you. So far as I know you are unique, the only case of yourselves which the development of philosophy in our country can show. It is certainly desirable that philosophy should be accounted no mere academic interest, but the concern of all human beings. Yet no other American university has been fortunate enough to secure a company of competent men and women pledged to follow up these grave inquiries and supplement the work of the class room . . ."

Palmer then addresses "the problem of self-sacrifice . . . which seems to me to conduct us farthest into the heart of ethics." His detailed analysis and discussion is similar to that in his Phi Beta Kappa address at Harvard about a year before (**GHP**-42) and many long passages are identical in the two presentations.

He concludes his address: "It is to a company of . . . scholars that I speak tonight. Many among you have undertaken the task of tracking shy truth. Setting aside beliefs to which as isolated individuals you may well be attached, you seek after that possible harmony of all minds to which we give the name of right reason. Justly therefore it may be said of you that you try not to think your own thoughts nor to speak your own words. In such service of the absolute is found the highest expression of self-sacrifice, of social service, of self-realization. The doctrine that through union with a reason and righteousness not exclusively our own each of us may hourly be renewed is the very heart of ethics."

46 *The Nature of Goodness.*

(See correspondence between George Herbert Palmer and Houghton Mifflin Company, page 465)

Palmer dedicates this book to "A. F. P. loved by many for her exceptional goodness, distinguished for the elegance of her literary judgment, and recently snatched from my joyous home" (I am grateful to Nicholas Poole-Wilson for this translation from the Latin). Alice Freeman Palmer, his wife, died on December 6, 1902.

The Preface: "The substance of these [eight] chapters was delivered as a course of lectures at Harvard University, Dartmouth and Wellesley Colleges, Western Reserve University, the University of California, and the Twentieth Century Club of Boston. A part of the sixth chapter ["Self-Sacrifice"] was used as an address before the Phi Beta Kappa Society of Harvard [**GHP**-42], and another part before the Philosophical Union of Berkeley, California [**GHP**-45]. Several of these audiences have materially aided my work by their searching criticisms, and all have helped to clear my thought and simplify its expression. Since discussions necessarily so severe have been felt as vital by companies so diverse, I venture to offer them here to a wider audience. [From Chronicle entries: In 1900, in payment for these lectures, he received $250 at Western Reserve, and $200 at Dartmouth; in 1901, $400 at the Twentieth Century Club of Boston, $350 at the State Normal School in Providence, and $250 at the State Normal School at Fitchburg. His salary from Harvard in each of these years was $5,000.]

"Previously, in 'The Field of Ethics' [**GHP**-40], I marked out the place which ethics occupies among the sciences. In this book the first problem of ethics is examined. The two volumes will form, I hope, an easy yet serious introduction to this gravest and most perpetual of studies."

The Nature of Goodness has eight chapters: 1. The double aspect of goodness. 2. Misconceptions of goodness. 3. Self-consciousness. 4. Self-direction. 5. Self-development. 6. Self-sacrifice. 7. Nature and spirit. and 8. The three stages of goodness. Each chapter ends with a list of references for further reading.

A contemporary reviewer writes: "We think the two volumes constitute more than an introduction . . . One who has no intention of pursuing any further the study of moral philosophy will find in these two volumes luminous and inspiring reading . . . We wish both volumes, especially this second one might be introduced as a text-book for study by adult classes in our Sunday-schools, if not in our high schools" (*Outlook*, 1903; 75 (December 12): 913).

(I am grateful to the late G. William Patten and to Arnold P. Silverman for the gift of five, typed, stenographic reports of Palmer's lectures — numbers 4, 5, 6, 7, and 8, totaling 143 pages — on The Nature of Goodness before the Twentieth Century Club in January and February 1901. Scattered through the reports are Professor Palmer's penciled changes.)

47 Some Religious Verse of Alice Freeman Palmer.
See **AFPann**-16.

48 *Twenty-Five Portraits of Alice Freeman Palmer.*
See **aboutAFPann**-7.

49 George Herbert as a Religious Poet.

This paper, the first of Professor Palmer's several publications on George Herbert, also appears with a few minor changes in volume 1 of **GHP**-50, 51, and 52, as Introductory Essay III, The Type of Religious Poetry, pages 85–120.

In his autobiography (**GHP**-104, page 5), Palmer explains his great interest in this English poet (1593–1633): "An uncle of mine, a professor of Latin in Amherst College [William Augustus Peabody] had loved the old English poet, George Herbert, and suggested to my mother to give me his name 'so that I might always have a friend.' A rich endowment indeed!"

"To English poetry George Herbert made a notable contribution, [Professor Palmer begins] — he devised the religious love-lyric. This forms his substantial claim to originality. To state, illustrate, and qualify that claim is the object of this paper." Palmer himself provides a summary of this paper in **GHP**-88, pages 112–115: Based on his extensive familiarity with English poetry, Professor Palmer identifies a group of men who contributed to the development of the religious love-lyric a "new type of poetry, a poetry of the inner life, veracious, intellectual, individualistic, energetic." He selected Herbert as his representative of this type: "In one respect he differs from all the other members of his group. He is a conscious artist and has a strong sense of orderly poetic form. His small body of verse he revised continually, in order to bring it to that beauty which he loved and which he felt its subject to demand." With the other members of the group he shared "their aggressive intellectualism, their audacity of diction, their absorption in the inner life, thorough-going individualism, wide-ranging allusion, candor, exactitude, and tenderness." When we open a volume of Herbert's verse, Palmer says, "we should at once recognize the master's guiding hand."

50 *The English Works of George Herbert.*

In his diary for March 1900 (page 173), Professor Palmer describes the background as he began work on this project. In his autobiography (**GHP**-104, pages 137–138), he lists this publication as the first of his three "books of affection and gratitude [which] may live for half a century"; the others are **GHP**-2 and 57. His 'George Herbert,' he says, "was not intended for wide circulation, but was an appeal to scholars in behalf of a much misunderstood poet. The London 'Times' gave it two strongly commendatory articles and declared that whoever dealt with Herbert hereafter must take this book into account."

In the preface, dated March 19, 1905 (his sixty-third birthday), Palmer describes the book as "a Variorum Edition, I have gathered into it whatever of importance has been proposed by previous commentators, and I have myself steadily turned toward fulness of comment . . . Let there be applied to Herbert those comparative and encyclopædic methods which have already been accorded to Chaucer, Shakespeare, Milton, Pope, Byron, Wordsworth, Shelley, Tennyson, and Browning . . . I am attempting a kind of critical dictionary of Herbert, in which his meaning may be systematically fixed with reference to the text itself, to the facts of the author's life, and to the literary conditions under which his poetry arose."

At the end of the preface, Professor Palmer identifies numerous "friends [who] have made generous gifts of suggestion and criticism . . . [i]n the ten years during which my book has been growing [see 121n6 for role of Lucy Sprague, 127n2 for role of Lewis Kennedy Morse] . . . All this aid, however, is insignificant compared with that furnished by my wife, Alice Freeman Palmer. In reality the book is only half mine. It was begun at her instance, enriched by her daily contributions, sustained through difficulties by her resourceful courage, the tedium of its mechanical part lightened by her ever ready fingers. When she was dying she asked for its speedy publication [in **GHP**-57, page 325, as Palmer describes his wife's preparations to go to the hospital in Paris where she died, he mentions, among her instructions, that ". . . I must not allow anything to intervene till our Herbert was published."]. Alas, that she should not see what through more than half her married life she eagerly foresaw, and that the book must miss that ultimate perfection which her full coöperation might have secured!" The publication has no formal dedication page.

From a review: ". . . It was to have been expected from the author that his research would go as deep as the inmost spring of the poet's life. There is here also a rich combination of author and subject, for Mr. Palmer has put himself into the work. Everywhere is visible the hand of the accomplished translator of the Odyssey [**GHP**-2] and of the Antigone [**GHP**-37], the subtle and profound critic, the incessant student and observer of the ways of man in the world. No man, poet or other, could have been more fortunate than Herbert has been in meeting with such a mind whose gifts have been concentrated in one supreme effort to know and to make known (A. V. G. Allen, Palmer's Herbert, *Atlantic Monthly*, 1906; 97 (No. 1): 90–100).

And another contemporary reviewer writes: "These volumes are in all repects a delight. In size, in paper, in illustrations, in simplicity and elegance of form, they come so near perfection . . . and all this at a low cost . . . But this is only the body of the work: the heart and soul of it, whether by that we mean Herbert's text or Prof. Palmer's essays and comment, are equally rare, equally satisfying . . . Prof. Palmer arranges the poems in a new order, placing his notes on the page facing the text. For pictorial illustrations he gives portraits, views of scenes and buildings connected with Herbert, facsimiles of manuscripts and reproductions of title-pages. The result is as nearly perfect a book — in which, author, editor, critic, and publisher unite to do their best — as we are likely to see. It is the definitive edition of George Herbert: a delight for every lover of fine bookmaking; and it may serve as a model of the way in which poets can (and therefore should) be edited" (*HGM*, 1905-06, 14 (December 1905): 247–249).

51 *The English Works of George Herbert*, Large-paper edition.

The publisher's impressive, illustrated prospectus (AJL Collection) describes some features of these volumes which were designed by Bruce Rogers (Frederic Warde, *Bruce Rogers: Designer of Books*, Cambridge, Harvard University Press, 1926, page 56, #59): "Printed at the Riverside Press, directly from type, on a paper of high quality with uncut edges, and bound in boards with buckram back and leather label. With 29 photogravure and half-tone illustrations. Octavo. $20.00 net. Postpaid."

The prospectus goes on: "Professor Palmer has made this the most complete, and, critically speaking, the final edition of Herbert's work. It is the result of the labor of a life-time, a labor of love, and is perhaps the most thoroughly edited edition of an English poet in existence. It is very fitting that Herbert, in whose work the purest poetry and the most devoted piety are mingled, should have been treated with such fidelity and taste. Without question it is the most beautiful edition that has yet appeared. The poems are printed on the right-hand page and the notes face them on the left, a novel and interesting method. In the volume of prose [Volume II], the notes are placed at the end. These notes are as copious as they are critically valuable . . . This limited large paper edition is a noble monument to the poet and a treasure to the book-lover and collector."

The title page of each volume has the Herbert family coat of arms, copied from the family monument in the parish church at Montgomery, in North Wales where George Herbert was born (**GHP**-52, note to List of Illustrations, Volume III). The frontispiece in Volume IV of this large-print edition is a picture of this monument with the prominent coat of arms, and the same picture faces page 200 in volume II of **GHP**-52.

52 *The English Works of George Herbert*, Second edition.

Palmer's prefatory Note To The Second Edition is dated April 3, 1907: "In this edition, called for unexpectedly soon, many small changes have been made, a few errors corrected, two title-pages added, — completing the list of the original title-pages of Herbert's English works, — two indexes changed in position, and two new ones introduced. One of these indexes, placed at the end of the first volume, catalogues Herbert's biblical allusions; the other, for which I am indebted to Mrs. Grace R. Walden, at the end of the third volume, gives access to the extensive notes, essays, and prefaces."

Tooled, linear, geometric designs on the covers frame the gold stamping of the title of each volume on the front and of the Herbert family coat of arms on the back. As in the first edition [**GHP**-50], a formée cross appears on each title page.

53 Alice Freeman Palmer.
See **aboutAFPann**-9.

54 *William Henry Willcox.*
Like **aboutAFPann**-5, this volume was probably also designed by Bruce Rogers; the two books differ in size but are identical in details of the design.

Willcox (1821–1904) had been a trustee of Wellesley College since 1878 and chairman of the executive committee of the board since 1884. Professor Palmer had known him for twenty years, since about the time when Palmer met Miss Freeman, who had become Wellesley's president in 1882. Palmer's eulogy in this volume (page 57–65) includes a tribute to Willcox's close association with Alice Freeman:

"In the early years when Miss Freeman was president of Wellesley, the number of persons engaged in the conduct of that important college who were acquainted with education was much smaller than at present. Dr. Willcox had large experience in education matters, and Miss Freeman turned to him continually, and more and more leaned on his sagacious counsel. He thought of her apparently as if she were his own daughter [Willcox was thirty-four years older then Alice Freeman]; I well knew she looked up to him as a second father; and few were the visits more welcome to our home than those in which he came and sat down by our fireside and talked of Wellesley's affairs as if there were nothing more important to him in the world" (pages 61–62).

55 The Ideal Teacher.
Professor Palmer addresses this essay on "the profession of teaching" to "those . . . who are drawn to teaching by the love of it, . . . [and] intend to give their lives to mastering its

subtleties . . . He distinguishes a trade [which] aims primarily at personal gain . . . [from] a profession [which aims] at the exercise of powers beneficial to mankind." Based on his experiences in "teaching thirty-seven years in Harvard College," [his first appointment, as Tutor of Greek, was in 1870] he presents as "the roots of success . . . four fundamental characteristics which every teacher must possess." The first characteristic is an "aptitude for vicariousness . . . The teacher's task is not primarily the acquisition of knowledge, but the impartation of it . . . We teachers are forever taking thoughts out of our minds and putting them elsewhere. So long as we are content to keep them in our possession, we are not teachers at all." An important aid is "imagination, the sympathetic creation in ourselves of conditions which belong to others . . . [so that we] understand how [the] subject should appear to the meagre mind of [the student who is] glancing at it for the first time." Palmer emphasizes that this vicariousness must "become as nearly as possible an instinct. Until it is rendered instinctive and passes beyond conscious direction, it will be of little worth."

The "ideal teacher will [also] need . . . an already accumulated wealth" of knowledge and must "prepare more matter than can be used." Palmer says "I cannot teach right up to the edge of my knowledge without a fear of falling off. My pupils discover this fear and my words are ineffective. They feel the influence of what I do not say. One cannot precisely explain it; but when I move freely across my subject as if it mattered little on what part of it I rest, they get a sense of assured power which is compulsive and fructifying." Furthermore, Palmer thinks that "[t]o be a great teacher one must be a great personality, and without ardent and individual tastes the roots of our being are not fed. For developing personal power it is well . . . for each teacher to cultivate interests unconnected with his official work. Let the mathematician turn to the English poets, the teacher of classics to the study of birds and flowers, and each will gain a lightness, a freedom from exhaustion, a mental hospitality, which can only be acquired in some disinterested pursuit."

The successful teacher also needs "a third something, the power to invigorate life through learning . . . Truth . . . being impersonal, seems untrue, abstract, and insignificant. It needs to shine through a human being before it can exert its vital force on a young student. Quite as much for vital transmission as for intellectual elucidation, is a teacher employed . . . If he is a scholar, there will appear in him an augustness, accuracy, fullness of knowledge, a buoyant enthusiasm even in drudgery, and an unshakable confidence that others must soon see and enjoy what has enriched himself; and all this will quickly convey itself to his students and create attention in his classroom . . ."

And, finally, Palmer says, "a teacher must have a readiness to be forgotten . . . the teacher must keep himself entirely out of the way, fixing young attention on the proffered knowledge and not on anything so small as the one who brings it. Only then can he be vicarious, whole-hearted in invigorating the lives committed to his charge . . ."

56 For Professor Norton's Eightieth Birthday [November 16, 1907].

The editors of the *Harvard Graduates' Magazine* invited Professor Palmer and several other individuals "to set down briefly some estimate of the value of Mr. Norton's sevices in many fields, and to express the personal gratitude and admiration which many thousands feel for him."

From Professor Palmer: ". . . In the College Faculty Mr. Norton stood as our great humanist. Though easily confused with dilettantism, and then justly laughed at, humanism when solidly grounded begets a kind of awe . . . He was a welcome member of a company of scholars who almost from childhood had been so charged with responsibility for single subjects that the relations of these to man's interests as a whole had been often overlooked. A representative of that wholeness Mr. Norton became. To the anxious debates of the Faculty, through which the modern Harvard has been gradually evolved, he brought the steadying influence of a mind free from provinciality, an acquaintance with the best the world elsewhere has known, a spirit averse to mechanical methods, a loyalty to high ideals, and a disposition ever to make the moral being of the students his prime care . . . To him many a young instructor has turned in a literary or personal exigency and found in his disciplined judgment and sympathetic heart help of incalculable worth . . .

"Over the student body his influence has been of the same nature as that felt by the Faculty; for he is made all of a piece.

His personal kindnesses have been innumerable and untraceable . . . The methods of Mr. Norton were superbly out of date in our specialistic time. He saw in the Fine Arts the embodiment of man's deepest and more durable ideals; and with almost a religious fervor he brought these to bear on every aspect of the petty and careless life around him. He has been a preacher of reverence to a headlong age. And if sometimes a despairing note has been heard in his voice, it has been perhaps a necessary corrective of overconfident America.

"Both for Faculty and Students Mr. Norton himself has been more important than what he has said. Through him all have come in contact with the literary leaders of the last generation; with most that is notable in the circles of literature, politics, and the Fine Arts abroad; with whatever forces have worked for beauty and dignity in every age. He has been an epitome of the world's best thought, brought to our own doors and opened for our daily use . . ."

57 *The Life of Alice Freeman Palmer.*
See **aboutAFPann**-10.

58–62 *The Life of Alice Freeman Palmer.*
See **aboutAFPann**-11 to 15.

63 *Self-Cultivation in English.*
See **GHPann**-34.

64 Specialization.

Professor Palmer delivered this lecture in the afternoon on Tuesday, June 9, 1908, at the Convocation Exercises of the University of Chicago. In the morning he took part there in the dedication of the Alice Freeman Palmer Chimes (238n2).

Palmer begins the address: "Ladies and gentleman, and particularly you members of the graduating class, it is to you I would speak. This afternoon is yours. In the moving exercises of the morning you had but a slender share. Probably not half a dozen of you ever saw her who, once seen, was loved with romantic ardor, though many of you are undoubtedly different from what you would have been had she not lived, and lived here; for her ennobling influence so passed into the structure of this University that she will shape successive generations of you for a long time to come. But enough of her. Let us dismiss her from our thoughts. Too much praise we have already lavished on one who was ever simple and self-forgetting. She would chide our profusion. If we would think as she would wish us to think, let us turn rather to the common matters of the day, reflecting on those joys and perplexities which have attended you throughout these formative years. One especially of these perplexities, perhaps the greatest of all, I would invite you to consider now. Let me set it clearly before you."

Palmer then describes the University of Chicago "as a great specializing machine," and introduces his analysis of specialization: "So long as we are simply learning that which is set before us, taking the routine mass of academic subjects, we may be faithful students, but we are not scholars. No, it is when with a free heart we give ourselves to a subject and say, 'Take all of me you demand — rather this I would do than anything else, for this expresses my personal desires' — then it is that a quickening education begins. But this is specialization."

He identifies "three roots of specialization . . . it is grounded in the very nature of the knowing process; it is grounded in the needs of ourselves as individuals, in order that we may attain our maximum efficiency; it is grounded in the needs of society, because only so can society reach that fulness of knowledge from which it is richly fed."

Palmer goes on to describe some dangers of specialization and to suggest ways to reduce them to a minimum. "[I]f we are fully alive to the great danger that in specializing we are cutting off a large part of the universe, we shall be wise in gathering eagerly whatever additional knowledge we may, outside our specialty . . . [W]e must be careful to conceive our specialty broadly enough. There lies our chief danger. There are two types of specialists. There is the man who regards his specialty as a door into which he goes and by which he shuts the world out, hiding himself with his own little interests . . . But there is an entirely different sort of specialist from that; it is the man who regards his specialty as *a window out of which he may peer upon all the world* [annotator's italics]. His specialty is merely a point of view from which everything may be regarded. Consequently without departing from our specialty each of us may escape narrowness."

A few years earlier, Palmer had eulogized three Harvard Professors who had died recently: ". . . These three were men of width. While admirable specialists in their field, they were men who looked far and wide and honored that field out of gains brought from every side. They were men of the world . . ." (see 233n3).

And one is reminded of lines from the poet, William Blake (J. Bartlett, *Familiar Quotations*, 14th ed., page 490a):

> "To see the world in a grain of sand,
> And a heaven in a wild flower."

Many years later, George Wald, Harvard physiology professor, commented on his own specialization. In 1967 he won a Nobel Prize in Medicine and Physiology "for working out the chemical reactions that light sets off in the receptors of the eye." Professor Wald "once wrote that he used to worry about being overspecialized — studying not vision, not the eye, not the whole retina, not even the receptor cells, but just the reactions and nature of the pigments they contain. But, he said, 'it is as though this were a very narrow window through which at a distance one can see only a crack of light. As one comes closer, the view grows wider and wider, until finally through this same window one is looking at the universe. I think this is the way it always goes in science, because science is all one. It hardly matters where one enters, provided one can come closer . . .'" (George Wald delivers final Nat. Sci. 5 Lecture, *Harvard University Gazette*, May 27, 1977).

65 *The Teacher*.

(See correspondence between George Herbert Palmer and Houghton Mifflin Company, page 467)

The papers in the first section, entitled Problems of School and College, all by Professor Palmer, "deal [he says] with questions about which we teachers, eager about our immeasurable art beyond most professional persons, never cease to wonder and debate: What is teaching? How far may it influence character? Can it be practiced on persons too busy or too poor to come to our class-rooms? To subjects of what scope should it be applied? And how shall we content ourselves with its necessary limitations? Under these diverse headings a kind of philosophy of education is outlined . . ."

There are seven chapters in this section: I. The Ideal Teacher (**GHP**-55). II. Ethical Instruction in Schools (**GHP**-29, in part). III. Moral Instruction in Schools (see below). IV. Self-Cultivation in English (**GHP**-34). V. Doubts About University Extension (**GHP**-22). VI. Specialization (**GHP**-64). VII. The Glory of the Imperfect (**GHP**-19).

Chapter III, previously unpublished, is an expansion of the final section of **GHP**-29. Having shown, in **GHP**-29, "how a theoretic knowledge of good conduct had better not be given to children . . ." in this essay Professor Palmer develops the view that "[s]o conditioned on morality is the process of knowing, so inwrought is it in the very structure of the school, that a school might well be called an ethical instrument and its daily sessions hours for the manufacture of character. Only the species of character manufactured will largely depend on the teacher's acquaintance with the instrument he is using. To increase that acqaintance and give greater deftness in the use of so exquisite an instrument is the object of this paper . . ."

Palmer goes on: "It will be easiest to point out the kind of moral instruction a school is fitted to give, if we distinguish . . . its several lines of activity. A school is primarily a place of learning; it is unavoidably a social unit, and it is incidentally a dependent fellowship. No one of these aspects is ever absent from it. Each affords its own opportunity for moral training . . ." Professor Palmer then discusses each aspect in detail and emphasizes the important role of the teacher in the whole process. "Without turning aside in the slightest from their proper aim of imparting knowledge, teachers are able, — almost compelled — to supply their pupils with an intellectual, social, and personal righteousness. . . . That school where neatness, courtesy, simplicity, obtain; where enthusiasm goes with mental exactitude, thoroughness of work with interest, and absence of artificiality with refinement; where sneaks, liars, loafers, pretenders, rough persons are despised, while teachers who refuse to be mechanical hold sway — that school is engaged in moral training all day long."

The chapters in the second section, entitled Harvard Papers, all by Professor Palmer and all previously published "relate primarily to Harvard University and are chiefly of historic interest. But since out of that centre of investigation and criticism has come a large part of what is significant in American education, the story of its experiences will be found pretty generally instructive for whoever would teach or learn."

This section has five chapters: VIII. The New Education (**GHP**-10). IX. Erroneous Limitations of the Elective System

(**GHP**-11). X. Necessary Limitations of the Elective System (**GHP**-12). XI. College Expenses (**GHP**-14). XII. A Teacher of the Olden Time (**GHP**-16).

As indicated in **AFPann**-17, the third section has four publications by Alice Freeman Palmer: **AFP**-4, 11, 6, and 8.

66 Book review. T. C. Williams, translation of *The Æneid of Virgil.*

The translator, Theodore Chickering Williams, was Palmer's close friend who dedicated this book to both Virgil and George Herbert Palmer (**dedctGHPann**-1). As noted in the Chronicles, Williams worked on this translation while he and his wife spent the month of July 1908, in Boxford with Palmer, who was working on *The Teacher* (**GHP**-65). Both volumes were published on November 14, 1908.

Williams, Palmer writes in this unsigned review, "has been able to reach astonishing success in turning the Æneid into English blank verse. Here is a translation of exceptional force, grace, accuracy, and readability. . . . Virgil's matter has been passed through a poetic mind, and freshly minted into current coin; but no alloy has been added, nor has any of the original disappeared. . . . Being already a successful poet, schoolmaster, and user of delicate speech, Mr. Williams is in condition to respond to rather conflicting claims of his exacting author. The publishers have done their work well, giving a simple and beautiful setting to a book which has evidently been a labor of love, and one which is likely to remain for a long time a standard rendering of the Æneid."

Six years later, in his introduction to Williams's translation into English verse of *The Georgics and Eclogues of Virgil* (**GHP**-82), Palmer also addresses this translation of the *Æneid*: "To this august and elusive poet he was early drawn, perhaps by a certain kinship of nature. In every time of fatigue, anxiety or affliction — and such times befell this eager and joyous spirit by no means rarely — Virgil became his refuge and solace. Turning a few pages of his sensitive Latin into his own hardly less sensitive English freed him from annoyance. In the Virgil classes of his two schools [Hackley School in Tarrytown on the Hudson, New York, and Roxbury Latin School in Boston, Massachusetts] he had the opportunity to try the effects of his work on young and groping minds. Accordingly, when . . . he published through Houghton Mifflin Company his version of the *Aeneid*, it was at once acclaimed as an extraordinary performance. In a greater degree than any other translation of Virgil it harmonizes the conflicting claims of poetry and scholarship. One reads it as an English poem, heedless of a constraining original; yet the many shades of that original are reflected here with a fullness and accuracy unequalled even in prose . . ."

67 Gossip and the Newspapers.

The editor introduces the letter as one "which so clearly and delightfully exposes one of the wretchedest evils of 'modern' daily journalism in this country that we are glad to print it here as an expression of our editorial views . . ." He goes on to introduce Palmer as the author of the Life of Alice Freeman Palmer [**GHP**-57] and adds that "[n]o one who has read it can for a moment be in doubt as to [Palmer's] views regarding refinement of manners and spirit in the education of women."

According to Professor Palmer himself, the "facts are these . . . On [Wednesday] June 16, [1909,] I delivered a Commencement address at a girls' college in Boston [Simmons College], taking for my subject the common objections to the higher education of women, objections generally rather felt than formulated by hesitating mothers. Five were mentioned: the danger to health, to manners, to marriage, to religion, and to companionship with parents in the home. These I described from the parents' point of view, and then pointed out the misconceptions on which I believed them to rest. In speaking of manners, I said that a mother often fears that attention to study may make her daughter awkward, keep her unfamiliar with the general world, and leave her unfit for mixed society. To which I replied that in the rare cases where intellectual interests do for a time overshadow the social, we may well bear in mind the relative difficulties of subsequent repair. A girl who has had only social interests before twenty-one does not usually gain intellectual ones afterwards; while the ways of the world are rapidly acquired by any young woman of brains.

"To illustrate, I told of a strong student of Radcliffe who had lived much withdrawn during her course there, alarming her uncollegiate parents by her slender interest in social functions. At graduation they pressed her to devote a year to balls and dinners and to mastering what they regarded as the occult art of manners. She came to me for counsel, and I advised her to accede to their wishes. 'Flirt hard, M.,' said I, 'and show that a college girl is equal to whatever is required of her.' This was the only allusion to the naughty topic which my speech, an hour in length, contained.

"That evening one of the 'yellowest' of the Boston papers [the *Boston Post*] printed a report of my 'Address on Flirtation,' and the next day a reporter came from the same paper requesting an interview. The interview I refused, saying that I had given no such address and I wished my name kept altogether out of print. The following Sunday, however, the bubble was fully blown, the paper printing a column of pretended interview, generously adorned with headlines and quotation marks, setting forth in gay colors my 'advocacy of flirtation.'

"And now the dirty bubble began to float. Not being a constant reader of this particular paper, I knew nothing of its mischief until a week had gone by. Then remonstrances began to be sent to me from all parts of the country, denouncing my hoary frivolity. From half the States of the Union they came, and in such numbers that few days of the past month have been free from a morning insult. My mail has been crowded with solemn, or derisive editorials, with distressed letters, abusive postal cards, and occasionally the leaflet of some society for the prevention of vice, its significant passages marked."

Palmer continued in his letter to the editor: "During all this hullabaloo I have been silent. The story was already widespread when my attention was first called to it. It struck me then as merely a gigantic piece of summer silliness, arguing emptiness of the editorial mind. I felt, too, how easily a man makes himself ridiculous in attempting to prove that he is not a fit subject for ridicule, and how in the long run character is its own best vindication. I should accordingly prefer to remain silent still."

Then he explained why he had decided to write about the episode: "But the story, like all that touches on questions of sex, has shown a strange persistency. My friends are disquieted. Harvard is defamed. Reports of my depravity have lately been sent to me from English and French papers, and in a recent number of Life I appear in a capital cartoon, my utterance being reckoned as one of the principal incidents of the month. Perhaps, then, it is as well to say that no such incident has occurred, and that now, when all of us have had our laugh, the racket has better cease . . ."

Professor Palmer went on to discuss some "defects in our newspapers, and especially in the attitude of our people toward them . . . [T]he plan of reporting practiced here is a mistaken one . . . [o]ur papers rarely try to give an ordered outline of an address . . . Of the indifference to truth in the lower class of our papers, their vulgarity, intrusions into private life, and eagerness at all hazards to print something startling, I say little, because these characteristics are widely known and deplored . . . The line which parts lightness from reality is becoming blurred. My lively remark has served as the subject for portentous sermonizing, while the earnest appeal made later in my address to look upon marriage seriously, as that which gives life its best meaning, has been either passed by in silence or mentioned as giving additional point to my nonsense . . . The part of the affair, however, which should give us gravest concern is the lazy credulity of the public. They know the recklessness of journalism as clearly as do I, on whom its dirty water has been poured. Yet readers trust, and journals copy journals, as securely as if the authorities were quite above suspicion . . . Nothing in all this curious business has surprised me more than the ease with which the American people can be hoaxed . . ."

68 *A Herbert Bibliography.*

The preface, dated December 6, 1910, the eighth anniversary of Alice Freeman Palmer's death, refers to 141 titles and 158 volumes, grouped under nine headings: I. Biographies of George Herbert. II. Manuscripts of Herbert's writings. III. Herbert's writings, other than The Temple. IV. The fourteen editions of the Temple published during the first century after Herbert's death. V. Modern editions of The Temple. VI. Writings of Herbert's brothers. VII. Books relating to Nicholas Ferrar and Little Gidding. VIII. Other books associated with George Herbert. and IX. Desiderata, which Palmer explains:

> "But since unhappily, a collection can never be complete, I mention in a final Group four books [the first on the list is a first edition of The Synagoguc] which the watchful pursuit of many years has not yet brought me. May some reader of this Bibliography know where they are hiding and bless me by disclosing them!"

69 *A Herbert Bibliography.*

The title page, now undated, identifies William Coolidge Lane, librarian, as editor of the Bibliographical Contributions, and indicates that the volume was "Printed at the expense of the Richard Manning Hodges Fund." The verso of this page now has information about other Contributions and lists the Herbert Bibliography as the first Contribution in Volume V.

70 *A Herbert Bibliography.*

The covers have the same tooled, linear, geometric design as **GHP**-52, which frames the gold stamping of the title on the front and the Herbert family coat of arms on the back. The preface now refers to 142 titles and 159 volumes, an additional title and volume having been added to group VII.

Soon after publication, Palmer inscribed a copy to "Bertram Dobell With regards of G. H. Palmer Harvard University February 14, 1911." Dobell, a London bookseller and man of letters, died in December 1914, and the business was continued by his sons, Percy John and Eustace Arthur. This volume, part of the Dobell residue when the business closed, was acquired by the booksellers Hofmann and Freeman, who gave it to me in April 1990. Tipped inside the back cover is this letter from Palmer, handwritten on his personal stationery from his home at 11 Quincy Street, Cambridge, five days before his 88th birthday:

> Dear Mr. Dobell, [probably Percy John]
>
> I thank you most warmly for sending me The Synagogue. It fills the single gap in my collection. I have never seen another first edition, & have hunted for one for these many years. For my purposes this is entirely good. I gladly enclose the small price you charge.
>
> Gratefully yours,
>
> March 14- G. H. Palmer
> 1930

(I am grateful to Theodore Hofmann and Richard A. Linenthal, of Bernard Quaritch, Ltd., London, England, for this association copy and for information about the Dobells.)

71 *The Problem of Freedom.*

"The following chapters [Palmer writes in the preface] are the substance of a course of lectures delivered in 1909 before the Lowell Institute of Boston [see 242n1]. Delivered without notes, they were carefully reported and subsequently much revised.

"The circumstances of their delivery were, I feel sure, favorable to certain good habits which I have tried to retain. My hearers, though exceptionally intelligent and critical, were for the most part untrained in the subject. Being hearers too and not readers, they constantly forced me, if I would be understood, to turn away from technicalities toward naturalness of speech; they led me to emphasize crucial points in the argument; and then by short sentences, easy transitions, and homely illustrations, to make the necessarily close attention rewarding and agreeable. These are useful habits for any one who undertakes to treat contentious topics.

"Nor do I see that such adjustments unfit a discussion for consideration by specialists. Such men, it is true, rightly lay stress on fullness of knowledge, fresh points of view, candor in observation, and a scientific spirit. But lucidity is not unfriendly to these worthy qualities. Bishop Berkeley bids us 'to think with the learned and speak with the vulgar.' I wish I were able to conform myself to the precept of this profound and limpid writer. But at least I will offer here a fairly intelligible, systematic, and in some respects not unoriginal survey of an intricate, ancient, and ever-present problem."

72 *Intimations of Immortality in the Sonnets of Shakspere.*

Professor Palmer delivered Harvard's thirteenth annual "Ingersoll lecture on the Immortality of Man" on October 9, 1912. He finished writing this lecture on August 20, and the book was published on November 9, 1912.

"In view . . . of the already large body of writing [by others] in which my own beliefs are admirably set forth [Palmer writes], I abandon the theoretic discussion of immortality and turn to examine an instance which long ago struck me in English literature, where the massive truth naïvely discloses its varied meanings and practical import . . . My subject, 'Intimations of Immortality in the Sonnets of Shakspere,' blends with the central religious theme interests of an ethical, historical, and literary nature.

"But since the extraordinary literary merits of the Sonnets must here be unduly subordinated to certain hitherto unconsidered ethical aspects, I wish to pause a moment and interject a paragraph of homage to the Sonnets as pure poetry. My personal debt to them in this regard is large. In my early manhood a friend lived with me who was as greedy as I of sweet sounds and delicate diction. We made a compact that each of us should repeat one of these Sonnets each morning at breakfast, explaining what he had found in it worthy of remark. We chose them merely in the order of our liking. In this way, during the otherwise unprofitable moments of dressing, I committed eighty to memory and my friend no fewer. Many years afterwards he told me that he believed himself to have derived more benefit from this exercise than from any two years of his college course. Certainly in my opinion no other body of poetry in the language is so precious for internal possession . . ."

In his analysis of the Sonnets, Palmer holds "that they have a common theme and are not a miscellaneous lot of verses . . . Of course that theme is love . . . The significant question is what aspect of it is here presented? . . . I understand it to be the transitoriness of love . . . The loved object, so prized for what he is to-day, to-morrow is changed . . . The hostile force of oncoming time unceasingly intervenes and brings us alteration. Throughout the Sonnets Shakspere is represented as engrossed with this pathetic transitoriness of love, as seeking for means to overcome it and give perpetuity to that which is so precious and so frail. Rightly does the mysterious dedication name the dominant motive of the Sonnets as a 'promised eternitie.'"

73 Phi Beta Kappa Oration (Pomona College).

Professor Palmer delivered this address "at the founding of Gamma of California Chapter at Pomona College, March 7, 1914. Printed from stenographic report with consent of the author." See 267n2 for a description of his visit at Pomona. On March 17, while Palmer was still in California, College Hall at Wellesley College burned to the ground (272n1).

". . . Twenty years ago this spring [Pomona's] first class was graduated. Two or three of those who assisted in that graduation are here today. It is due to their efforts largely that the College was at that time facing in the right direction. But slight resources did they at that time have for maintaining the standards they desired . . . But at any rate for many years they have known that they were doing with their means all that could be done; and now they have subjected themselves to independent judgment.

"There is one supreme court of scholarship in this country. It is the organization of Phi Beta Kappa; a democratic court indeed. No single judges decide this matter. The guardians of scholarship all over the country sit in watchful suspicion. They must maintain the standard high, and not let it down in consideration of some college with which they sympathize. This degree is not given as a bait to lure men on, but a stamp on that which has already been attained. Pomona has submitted herself to this high court, and today we have received our judgment. Hereafter this college stands side by side with all those who are recognized as leaders. A proud day indeed, when we may congratulate ourselves on all the hard work of the past. But it is also a day when we must feel afresh all our responsibilities. We are now to maintain this standard, to become a judge of others who are pressing in the same direction. Here, therefore, we stand, accepting this large responsibility, and so we will allow nothing to come into this college that will in any wise detract from that confidence that the colleges of high standing throughout the country have reposed in this admirable institution.

"But after all, this is not an occasion of rejoicing which is merely an individual affair. Every individual good must be social before we can have any real satisfaction in it . . . [The leaders] all know that in the attainment of this high standing they are blessing every college in California . . . The time was, not so many years ago, when each college thought of itself as a competitor in the field for students. I well remember when I was in California, just as Stanford was being founded. I was at Berkeley, and the leaders there were full of sorrow. They said here was another college arising at their doors to cut off their resources. 'But,' I said, 'is it not possible that there will be enough for you both?' They said, 'Impossible! We shall lose our students and our standing. The Rockies are a barrier between us and the East. Our field is limited. There is no room here for two universities.' But what has happened? Berkeley has about quadrupled its numbers, while Stanford has nearly as many. Each is rejoicing. It is just so with the colleges. They are all platoons in a great army. Every one of them is strong, and every advance on the part of one is a new stimulus to all the others . . .

"[N]ot only does Pomona rejoice today; not only may all her sister colleges rejoice in that which she has attained. The state of California may rejoice. This is a blessing to it, far and wide. For how often has it been imagined, where ignorance prevailed, in other parts of the country, that respect for learning stops at the Rocky Mountains, except as there is great wealth, except as there is some single great giver, or except as the state has put itself behind the university and insists that the standard be maintained high. How many people have been prevented from coming to this country by the fear that their children will be unable to get a respectable education in a small college on the Pacific Coast. Today it is proclaimed that this is an entire delusion. The college here is the same as the college elsewhere. It has the same standards. It will bear the most careful scrutiny. And the honor is the higher in that it is received not by Pomona and her sister colleges merely, but by the whole of this exultant land . . .

"Last year I visited nine of the colleges in the central West [see 262n3]. I have been visiting colleges all my life. I find very marked distinctions among colleges. Some have merely carried on those school ideas. They tell their boys and girls to learn their lessons, and often they are very diligent; but never have they come in sight of education yet. A man is not educated until he begins to question for himself. The Greek word for 'teach' is 'didasko'; the Greek word for 'learn' is 'didaskomai,' 'I teach myself . . . '

"The real work of the college should be the training of leaders. That is the great need of the democracy everywhere. The democracy needs some one who shall carefully think out the end toward which their work is tending. It is desirable, therefore, if we would make democracy strong in this country, that we have clear thinking leaders, who have been willing to spend years in earnest study while they were preparing themselves for their place in life. It is to this service that your college devotes herself. Students of Pomona, help her in this! Show her that you are worthy to receive this noble charter today."

74 Across Fifty Years: 1864–1914.

In this address at Harvard's Commencement Exercises on June 18, 1914, George Herbert Palmer, as speaker for the Fiftieth Reunion Class of 1864, presented some historical highlights.

"The glory of the Class of 1864 lies in its usualness. It represents the regular product of Harvard fifty years ago . . .

Harvard was not then training experts, yet then as always was sending out groups of strong, quiet, trustworthy men to refine and ennoble all varieties of American life. Entering 143 members, we graduated 99, more than a third of whom are still living . . . Yet '64 has one real preëminence, one shared by only a single other class. It and '65 experienced the Civil War throughout their entire college course . . . Early in our Freshman year we gave our six Southern classmates a dinner and sent them the next day from Cambridge to the Confederate camps . . . Thirty-five members of the class served in the Northern army or navy, most of them enlisting as privates . . . During our college course we had three presidencies [at Harvard — Felton, Peabody, Hill] . . . Harvard University, when our class entered it, was an advanced High School, with only 896 students and forty teachers in all its departments. Excepting a single study in the Junior and another in the Senior year, all our work was prescribed and therefore elementary."

Professor Palmer then addressed some changes during the fifty years since the class graduated: "We all know what happened when a rather vigorous young man [Charles W. Eliot], chosen President at thirty-five [in 1869], broke into these absurdities. The transformation of Harvard from a School to a University, and the consequent vitalizing of education throughout the country, is one of the notable events of our half century. For its cautious introduction of the Elective System Harvard was for many years denounced; then, as students and riches flowed in, envied and covertly admired; and at last, so far as the resources of other colleges allowed, universally imitated and honored."

Finally, Palmer presented a challenge: "By its very eminence Harvard has ceased to be a rival of any other institution, and has become the strong support of all. Its office is to be a much needed setter of standard time. In behalf of American education it seeks to assemble in a single spot the best expert scholarship in every field of knowledge and then disinterestedly to disseminate it . . . As leaders we must endeavor to be strong rather than big . . . Excellence we covet for ourselves in order that the country at large may share. May the coming half century conduct us again as far toward that excellence as we have already advanced since the primitive but happy days of 1864."

75 What is a Profession?

This article, like the monograph, **GHP**-76, is based on Professor Palmer's address before the University of the State of New York at its fiftieth annual convocation on October 22, 1914. The material for the article appears to have been selected from the stenographer's report, which was carefully edited for the monograph.

Some material in both presentations is of interest in the light of William Rainey Harper's 1893 report on "The Pay of American College Professors" (see 93n1).

From the article: "As I look over the ranks of teachers, it seems to me that they are all working on a scale of salary which is uneconomical for the community, which depresses their freedom, their efficiency, and their dignity. A year or more ago I visited nine of the colleges of the West and took a small part in their instruction, so that I became rather well acquainted (262n3). In very few of them did I find the salary of the full professor as high as two thousand dollars. In several of them I found the salary of the president only twenty-five hundred dollars, and in one I found that the president received a salary of twenty-five hundred dollars but had to pay back to the trustees six-hundred dollars for the house that he lived in, which was owned by the college.

"I hold that this is not the scale on which the best work can be done by teachers. We expect — I think we properly expect, and ought to be content to expect — that our life will always be just above the level of want. We can not carry it beyond that. I do not think any of us teachers ought to go into the work with any other expectation than that we shall always be living just above, or slightly above, the level of want. But I believe we may rightly claim, in the interest of the community, as well as in our own interest, that our salaries rise at least up to the edge of want and somewhat exceed it . . ."

76 *Trades and Professions.*

(See correspondence between George Herbert Palmer and Houghton Mifflin Company, pages 468–471; **GHPann**-75)

This address was delivered on October 22, 1914, at the fiftieth annual convocation of the University of the State of New York in Albany. The book was published on December 24.

From the Editor's Introduction: "The teachers of the public schools perform their work with high-minded intention . . . Yet in spite of our ungrudging praise of the idealism of teachers, the public is not completely pleased with the schools and their products . . . In such a situation, the need is for a body of guiding principles . . . There are some particular things that are of special pertinence to our present educational situation . . . It would also be a considerable gain if all educational officials could really be convinced that there is coincidence of interest among all human factors working in the school situation . . . Finally, it will be a great advantage to teachers if they will realize how impotent they are when working in isolation from all their profession knows and does from day to day . . . Many of the difficulties which now confront the teaching profession arise from the fact that the specialized functionaries of the schools have little appreciation of each other and therefore offer little mutual support . . . The educational profession as a whole must soon grasp the principle that coöperation is increasingly necessary as the tasks within schools become more specialized . . . [A]n aggregation of fine-souled teachers does not make a profession, — at least not a profession adequate to meet current responsibilities. In a sense the most important and inclusive truth presented in the masterly essay which follows is the one which insists that we shall find the 'superiority to our own detached selves, which comes only through whole-hearted loyalty to a profession.'"

Palmer starts his address with a question: "What is a profession and how does it differ from a trade? We teachers pride ourselves on being professional people and altogether repudiate the notion that we are mere tradesmen. But do we quite understand what we mean by the distinction? It is important we should. A clear understanding of it will, I believe, deliver us from some of the petty hardships of our work or even carry us on through these to discover its exceeding glory."

After a lengthy analysis of trades and professions, Palmer writes: "On the whole, then, I am obliged to conclude that the kind of work we do does not make us professional men, but the spirit in which we do it. There is no fixed number of professions. One may be found anywhere, for professionalism is an attitude of mind. Wherever, outrunning the desire for personal profit, we find joy in work, eagerness for service, and a readiness for cooperative progress, there trade has been left behind and a profession entered.

"We teachers should count ourselves more favorably circumstanced than most workers for acquiring this life-giving professional spirit . . . So distinct . . . is our business, so sharply separating us from those for whom we work, and even from the rest of the community, that the sense of belonging to a consecrated brotherhood comes to us almost as a matter of course. Such an attitude of mind is no doubt more difficult for those who work confusedly in the miscellaneous world. Yet may we not believe that our profession is prophetic and presents a type toward which all organized society moves? . . . In those happy days we shall esteem all men of good will as our professional brothers, regardless of whether they are teachers, lawyers, scientists, or business men . . .

"Believing as I do that teaching is a profession which thus illuminates all life, training us to sound method whatever we do, I warmly congratulate the members of this assembly on having found entrance to an occupation so glorious."

77 *Wellesley College: Restoration and Endowment Fund.*

From the Introduction: "At the meeting of the Board of Trustees on January 1, 1915, the treasurer [Lewis Kennedy Morse, see 127n2] announced that the Two Million [Dollar] Restoration and Endowment Fund was complete. It was then decided that as soon as an audited report of the fund could be presented, there should be a public meeting at the College in celebration of the completion of this fund. The date of this meeting [in the chapel] was later fixed for January 15. Happily it was found possible to lay the cornerstone of the new residence hall on College Hall Hill on the same day . . ."

Wellesley's President Pendleton introduced "Professor George Herbert Palmer, the Chairman of the Committee of the Trustees on Restoration and Endowment, . . . our next speaker [after Bishop Lawrence]. Professor Palmer has given himself unsparingly to work for the fund. In its interests he has travelled literally from the Atlantic to the Pacific. *We are grateful to him and to her whom we know to be the inspiration of his zeal for the College* [annotator's italics]. Professor Palmer will tell us something of the story of the campaign."

Professor Palmer: "Students and Friends of Wellesley: A

miracle has happened. None of us quite believes it yet. We seem to be in a glorious dream. We are only sure that what has occurred is not due to any one of us, nor to any single group. It seems to have come about almost by magic, or rather by divine appointment. At a time when business conditions are probably more uncertain than they have been since the Civil War, the public has been ready to count the needs of Wellesley urgent, and to increase its resources by an amount larger than was ever raised by subscription for a college before. An event so marvellous must make this day a memorable epoch in the history of Wellesley so long as this College, loved as few colleges ever have been loved, endures . . .

"The first suggestion in regard to the whole affair came, as you might imagine, from Miss Pendleton. More than two years ago she stated to the trustees that the funds of Wellesley were altogether inadequate for its work. In spite of increased charges for residence, in spite, too, of the many gifts we had received, we were in urgent need of larger endowment. She thought, I believe rightly, that Wellesley had in the past been too modest. For all the other women's colleges large funds have been raised. We have never had a general campaign. She believed it was time to start one . . .

"[S]everal of the trustees pointed out how dangerous were the times for such an effort, and how serious failure would be. A new administration had come in at Washington [a Democrat, Woodrow Wilson, was president, and the Democrats controlled both Houses of Congress], revolutionary tariff and currency bills had just been passed [Federal Reserve Act, Federal Trade Commission Act, Clayton Antitrust Act] and all trade stood waiting, uncertain of its future. A more unfavorable season for launching such an undertaking could hardly be found . . . A perfect time would never come. We must accept risk, and bank on the confidence of the community in the value of the work Wellesley had already done . . . [The trustees] appointed a Committee, charging it to raise an endowment fund of a million dollars.

"The Committee had several meetings for consultation about best methods of setting to work . . . Personal approaches require maturity, tact, and inquiry. Accordingly we instructed the Wellesley Clubs, and other groups of graduates throughout the country, to gather all the information they could about important persons of their neighborhood and report it to us.

Their lists were then subjected to careful analysis and criticism . . . [T]he actual work of canvassing fell for the most part into the hands of the President of the Trustees [Bishop William Lawrence], the Chairman of the Committee [George Herbert Palmer], and the Treasurer of the College [Lewis Kennedy Morse]. The three together represented the religious, academic, and financial interests which meet in the College. More than to any one else — I had almost said more than to all else combined, — the success of the undertaking has been due to our Treasurer, whose labors have been incessant and almost overwhelming . . ."

Palmer then mentions: "the General Education Board . . . promised two hundred thousand dollars if we should succeed in raising a million by July 1, 1915. Two anonymous gifts of a hundred thousand each and thirty thousand dollars raised in small gifts carried the fund to four hundred and thirty thousand, when fire destroyed College Hall and laid . . . the burden of restoration as well as endowment . . . The Rockefeller Foundation offered us seven hundred and fifty thousand dollars on condition of our raising [an additional] two million by the first of January [1915] . . . [an] unnamed friend of the College offered to build a large dormitory on College Hall Hill . . . meanwhile a world war broke out [in August 1914] and doubled difficulties which were disheartening already . . ."

Active campaigning began in September 1914. "The Committee, one or two at a time, travelled repeatedly through the West, going as far as the Pacific, besides canvassing cities nearer at hand . . . we had three great assets on which to base our appeal . . . [1] In calling on the West for aid, we pointed out that Wellesley is not an eastern college . . . only thirty-seven per cent of our students coming from New England. Whereas, in my own University, Harvard, sixty per cent come from within a hundred miles of Harvard . . . [2] Wherever we came, we found people already knew how, when the great hall burned, our girls refused to be saved alone and, unexcited by smoke, roar, or the hasty summons, waited till assurance could be had that all might be saved together. Such coolness and nobility, demonstrating how deeply the motto of our College [Non-ministrari Sed-ministrare] had affected the character of its students, was a second and powerful means of stirring the generosity of the country . . . [3] a third sort of help . . . perhaps the most influential of all . . . was the spirit of self-sacrifice among our graduates . . . They all insisted on giving, and giving up to the very limit of their ability . . . Deducting the Rockefeller gifts, more than half of our money and pledges came from women scattered all over the country, and to a large extent from women having no connection with Wellesley . . .

"The total result . . . may be summed up as follows: $430,000 raised before the fire, $2,092,000 since. To this should be added $560,000 of insurance money; and . . . just before this movement started nearly $60,000 had been raised for an alumnae building. Perhaps I should state that the Committee's total expense for collecting the Restoration and Endowment Fund, including secretaries, stenographers, and travelling expenses was less than $4000. For the new Wellesley there is therefore now in hand or in pledges $3,142,000 . . . A year ago Wellesley was the third in equipment among the colleges for women. It is now the best endowed of all."

[*Wellesley*, Spring 1992, page 46, reports completion of a campaign that raised $168 million, "a new national record for campaign giving by a liberal arts college."]

78 Riverside Uplift Series.

79 *Notes on a Collection of English Poetry.*

This small volume, a publication of only thirty copies, from the Riverside Press, has special design features that suggest the influence of Bruce Rogers (regarding Bruce Rogers, see page 453 in this compilation). It was clearly meant to be a companion to Palmer's later publication, *A Catalogue of Early and Rare Editions of English Poetry Collected and Presented to Wellesley College* (**GHP**-93), and much of his Introduction to the *Notes* is repeated in his Preface to the *Catalogue* .

Professor Palmer introduces the *Notes*: "My entire library at Cambridge, consisting of some five thousand volumes, I gratefully bequeath to Wellesley College. Its working books need not be kept together, but should be treated precisely like those derived from other sources, that is, be distributed on the shelves according to subject, be put at the service of all students whether experts or amateurs, and be sold or exchanged whenever such course is thought desirable. But about a quarter of the library is made up of what may be called rare books in contrast with working books. They cover the fields of English Poetry and Philosophy and are so unlike my other books, or indeed those now owned by Wellesley, that they should be kept apart as special collections . . . [In February 1921, he gave his 1st Editions of Philosophy to Harvard.]

"The prime impulse to form these collections came from my absorbing interest in their twin subjects. But midway in my life [he was forty-five years old when he married Alice Elvira Freeman] this impulse became reinforced and sanctioned. Mrs. Palmer too, even before I knew her, was a devoted student of English poetry. Her work as a teacher began in this subject, and she soon had a wider and more accurate knowledge of it than is common with persons of her years [see 247n2]. Being poor, the books she bought were for the most part cheap, small, and unimportant. But she always loved choice books, especially those which through some association might be regarded as more than mere books . . . After our marriage these poetic tastes in us both were more indulged and deepened. Together we were constantly tracing the byeways of English poetry, and an original edition which the poet himself might have looked on acquired a kind of sanctity in our eyes. Whenever opportunity and our purse permitted, we put one of these sacred volumes on our shelves.

"After Mrs. Palmer's death, when I asked myself *what memorial of her I might ultimately leave to Wellesley in thanksgiving for what that college had brought me* [annotator's italics] none seemed so fitting as the systematic building up of our collection of first editions of the poets . . . An unexpectedly large sale of Mrs. Palmer's *Life* [**GHP**-57] furnished the means [see table on page 480]. All income from that book has been applied to this purpose, and to Wellesley I now leave its copyright for the further increase of the collection . . ."

Palmer continued: "For common use early editions are not best editions. Their shape is often unhandy, their type and paper poor, they usually abound in typographical errors, and they are not supplied with such notes and introductions as aid a reader to stand where the writer stood . . . Accordingly ordinary students should not be given access to original editions nor ordinary funds be spent in obtaining them. Yet college libraries lack something so long as they meet merely ordinary needs. As they grow strong they should offer temptation to higher scholarship and stimulate their students, especially in literature, to go behind current texts and make acquaintance with the sources from which these are derived. That is the fundamental importance of first editions . . . the presence of the poet is there as it cannot be in later issues . . .

"Wellesley itself can never spend the time, knowledge, or funds which such collections demand . . . rare books cannot be had by an order at the neighboring book-shop. They must be hunted. There are books in my library which have cost me a ten years' search, though almost every day I have read a bookseller's catalogue . . . The cost of such books is very great and it constantly and rapidly rises. A narrowing supply makes this inevitable . . . Watching and waiting, I have generally bought at exceptionally low rates; yet I calculate that something like a quarter of my books have cost me $25.00 each, half that number $50.00, half of the rest have gone to $100.00, and a large group beyond $300.00 . . .

"The condition of a book greatly affects its price. It should be clean, unstained, without worm-holes, patches, writing, or tampering with the text; it should have all the subsidiary parts — portrait, half-title, licence-leaf, errata, advertisements; should have wide margins, being 'uncut,' i.e., with rough outer edges; or even 'unopened,' i.e., untouched by the paper cutter. It is all the better if it bears a book-plate, important autograph, is a presentation copy, or has some association connected with it. The original binding is usually prized more than a later, even though the later is much handsomer . . ."

Palmer goes on to address various related matters, such as, rebinding, "the cases that best preserve books," the way in which a book should be handled because "[a]n ignorant person can in a few minutes take half the value from a book by careless handling," how his collection should be arranged on the library shelves, and suggestions of some books "with which a collector of poetry needs to familiarize himself . . ."

In giving this collection to Wellesley, Professor Palmer states clearly his "threefold aim: to raise the repute of the College Library throughout the community, through its possession of a costly class of books which in time will surely be expected there; to impart added dignity to the English Literature Department in the eyes of all its students and instructors; and then — an aim still dearer — to entice from time to time small groups of specially prepared girls to that first-hand, exact, vivid, even romantic intimacy with the bards of passion and of mirth which has blessed the joint life of myself and Alice Freeman."

A. Edward Newton (1863–1940), an American bibliophile, writes: "My visit to Professor Palmer will ever be remembered: he is a past master in the art of book-collecting, and has since my first visit to him given his fine collection of first editions of English poetry to Wellesley College in memory of his wife, the late Alice Freeman Palmer. He accompanied his gift with an excellent catalogue — a large volume, well printed, and substantially bound [**GHP**-93], — and he has also printed a slender little volume, *Notes on a Collection of English Poetry*, of which he had thirty copies struck off at the Riverside Press at Cambridge, one of which is before me. Immediately following the title-page is a quotation from the famous translation of *The Ship of Fooles*, reading, —

> For this is my minde, this one pleasure have I,
> Of books to have great plentie,
> and more to the same effect"

(This Book-Collecting Game, *Atlantic Monthly*, 1926; 138: 750. See also **aboutGHPann**-7).

I am grateful to Arthur Freeman, of Bernard Quaritch, Ltd., London, England, for a set of the three unbound signatures of this publication, inscribed to "P. J. [Percy John] Dobell with kind regards of G. H. Palmer" (AJL Collection. See also **GHPann**-70).

80 The College and the Student.

This unsigned editorial by Professor Palmer was in response to an unsigned article in the same issue of the *Outlook*, entitled The Confessions of An Undergraduate (*Outlook*, 1915; 110 (July 28): 711–714). The writer was very critical of his experiences during four years at an unnamed college. In summary, he wrote: "These two things, then, I have found that the college works to give her undergraduates: an inability to work, due to four years of pleasant idleness, and a habit of thinking — nay, a desire to think — as the rest think and do as the rest do. A college training tends to destroy industry and independence. The two causes which make for these results are the lack of discipline in the curriculum and the competitive social system. From the point of view of one undergraduate about to be thrust forth upon the world to earn his living, it does not seem that the college has performed its duty of preparing him to lead a useful life . . ."

The editors of the *Outlook* introduced this article with some questions: "Was the trouble with this undergraduate in himself, or in the college system, or in the social environment? Is his view of college life exaggerated, or pessimistic, or simply incomplete? Does his 'confession' suggest practical means of improvement and phases that ought to have more consideration?"

Professor Palmer addresses the many questions raised by these "confessions," which, he writes, "must be read as confessions and not as mature criticism. They must be read, too, as the reaction of one particular college upon one particular student. Yet in so revealing the attitude of one student mind they also bring out some of the natural failures of our colleges to solve the problems of the reluctant scholar . . . The faculty, however devoted and educated to their work, cannot do that work without the aid of the students. Nor can that work be made wholly agreeable, since one of its chief ends is by discipline to train the mind to concentration, steadiness, and persistence. Underlying these confessions there is the feeling on the part of the student that things ought to be made pleasant for him; and that, if he is not interested, he is absolved from attention . . . A distinguished educator has commented on the extraordinary ability of the American undergraduate to resist the introduction of knowledge."

Palmer went on to describe another side to this matter: "The college, like the school, suffers from the absence of any real moral education in hosts of American homes. The freshman arrives without having had any training in self-denial, self-control, and self-direction; he has no habits of work; and he regards any endeavor to teach him to work and to hold him to tasks as essentially undemocratic in a free country . . . The 'Confessions of an Undergraduate' will be read with interest . . . because of the revelation they make of an attitude of mind which involves permanent loss to a great body of young men and the most penetrating criticism of the homes from which they come."

81 *A Marriage Cycle.*
See **AFPann**-18.

82 Introduction to T. C. Williams, translation of *The Georgics and Eclogues of Virgil.*

As indicated by numerous entries in the Chronicles, Thomas Chickering Williams and his wife, Velma, were among George Herbert Palmer's close friends. Williams died on May 6, 1915.

Palmer begins his seventeen page introduction, dated September, 1, 1915: "A peculiar pathos attaches to artistic work interrupted by death. Three weeks before Mr. Williams died he said to me joyfully, 'I have reached the end of my '*Georgics* and *Eclogues*. Of course all needs revision, and to that I shall at once address myself. But I wrote the last line today.' It was too true. He never wrote another. His twenty years' companionship with Virgil was ended . . .

"Receiving his papers I have merely attempted to set them in order for the press. After correcting the usual copyist's errors, I have chosen among the multitude of alternative readings those which seemed best to accord with Williams' mind, regardless of my own. His and my methods of composition are so unlike that I soon found it useless to attempt such a revision as he himself had planned. The taste of one writer cannot wisely be superposed on that of another. I am no Latinist, and patching such artistry at any one spot involved operations too wide either for my powers or my sense of rightful ownership. I have left the work, therefore, substantially as I found it."

As "an appropriate introduction to the present volume," Professor Palmer then summarizes, on eight pages, an unpublished paper in which Williams gives "[h]is fullest comment on the *Georgics* and *Eclogues*, and his indication of their place in the total scheme of Virgil's life . . ."

Then, Palmer writes, "I cannot be discharged until I have stated the leading facts of [Williams'] life and sketched, at least in outline, a character which in its full charm was indescribable." He ends with a five and one-half page biographical piece.

From 1883 to 1896, Williams was the minister at All Souls Unitarian Church in New York City, and from 1907 to 1909, he was headmaster of the Roxbury Latin School in Boston, Massachusetts, where he had prepared for college. In an article about Williams, the school's newsletter presents George Herbert Palmer's biographical piece from the introduction to the *Georgics and Eclogues of Virgil*, and also includes pictures of an oil painting and a bas-relief of Williams in New York's All Souls Unitarian Church (Walter H. Marx, class of 1957, Theodore Chickering Williams, Class of 1872, Headmaster 1907–1909, *Roxbury Latin Newsletter*, volume 58, number 2, pages 10–11, January 1985).

83 Josiah Royce.

Josiah Royce, professor of philosophy, at Harvard since 1882, 61 years old, died on September 14, 1916. George Herbert Palmer ends his long profile of Royce: "That elvish figure with the unconventional dress and slouching step, that face which blended the infant and the sage, that total personality, as amused, amusing, and intent on righteousness as Socrates himself — happy the University that had for a long time so vitalizing a presence!"

Palmer begins this piece: "A picturesque figure has left us, a prodigious scholar, a stimulating teacher, a heroic character, a playful and widely loved friend. He was one of the glories of three universities — California, Johns Hopkins, Harvard — and was almost as well known in England, France, and Germany as here. His thought is already absorbed into the mind of the race. To depict the great philosopher in due proportions will be the work of another time, place, and writer. The present paper has a narrower and more personal aim. We teachers work in a way unlike the members of other professions. We constitute a family, which meets each week, and feels its mutual dependence; our successes and failures are interlocked, ourselves enriched by the supplemental traits of one another. When one of us dies, his colleagues mourn, not for the public loss alone, but for their own much more, each sharing with each such bits of remembrance as illustrate the beauty and excellence of the absent friend. In the family journal of Harvard I would record in this fragmentary and intimate way the affection which thirty-four years have bred in me for Josiah Royce."

84 *The English Poems of George Herbert newly arranged in relation to his life.*

Palmer begins this volume with a general preface: "For poems so few as those of George Herbert, and of so intimate a nature, a small book is fitting. I once gave them enormous bulk. Bearing Herbert's name and studying him for half a lifetime, in 1905 I devoted thirteen hundred pages to telling the world what I thought of him [*The English Works of George*

Herbert, **GHP**-50] . . . But the elaborateness of that book brought me a certain discontent. I revealed the new Herbert to scholars but hid him from the general public to whom I also wish him known . . . But most friends of the spirit speak from a pocket volume. My god-father shall have one which will allow him to appeal, in all his complexity, across the centuries to us."

85 Book review. George McLean Harper, *William Wordsworth.*

"This is a solid, engaging, and much-needed book, [Palmer begins,] of a type commoner in England than in America, commoner in France than in either. It shows a German acquaintance with the enormous biographic material, a material probably more extensive than illustrates the life of any other English poet. But Professor Harper [1863–1947; professor of English Literature at Princeton University] has such easy mastery of his sources, such ability to tell a story, such charm of style, and such attractiveness in his own personality, as to make it difficult to break off reading at the close of any chapter. Here we follow Wordsworth with eager interest through all his eighty years [1770–1850], attending him not merely from month to month, but from week to week, and at important periods from day to day. We watch the development of a human being much as if we were meeting him in the pages of a modern novel. Through letters he talks with us, his biographer supplying delightful comment. It is a piece of imaginative portraiture which will form a veritable epoch in Wordsworth study."

As a final paragraph in his long review, Professor Palmer writes: "I have developed here my divergencies from Professor Harper rather than my agreements and large indebtedness. A book is good as it forces us to rethink its subject and to adjust our minds to its fresh material. Such a stimulating book is this, and I bring it my tribute of grateful criticism. In scope, seriousness, and minute knowledge, it takes rank with Masson's Milton, Elwin's Pope, and Dowden's Shelley, having besides its own special distinction. Its rich scholarship never clogs its literary ease. In every chapter one lingers over passages of penetrative insight and felicitous expression. Professor Harper agrees with Matthew Arnold in counting Wordsworth the most significant force in English poetry since Milton. Most readers of this book will accept that judgment."

86 Bishop Berkeley.

In the Chronicles, Palmer enters as "Bp Berkeley," this address, delivered at the Charter Day Exercises of the University of California in Berkeley, on March 23, 1917. See **about GHPann**-4

The university's President Benjamin I. Wheeler introduced Professor Palmer: "I introduce to you as the speaker of the day a man who for many years has been, in a rather unique way, but in a quiet and inconspicuous way, after his sort, a friend of this university. His inherent sense for order has given him always in life a peculiar delight in seeing the right man put in the right place, and this fact, coupled with his rare judgment as to men, has caused him to be consulted by men and universities. Notably has he been consulted over and over again by this university, and we do not forget that early gift of his to us which came by his recommendation of the late head of the Department of Philosophy [George Holmes Howison, 1834–1916, lectured at Harvard on ethics from 1879 to 1880]. I introduce to you as the speaker, then, a man whose sense of fitness has made him for a long time your friend. His sense of order has made him master of the beauty of the spoken word beyond the ordinary, has made him a historian of letters and a man of letters himself. But that sense for form, the native craving in his heart for the simplicity of fundamental things, has made him a philosopher, a philosopher in the largest and purest sense of the word. Philosopher, man of letters, counsellor, friend, the Alford Professor of Natural Religion, Moral Philosophy, and Civil Polity in Harvard University, George Herbert Palmer."

Professor Palmer substituted for Harvard's president, A. Lawrence Lowell, who, because of "a sense of public duty," was not able to attend. [Eleven days later, on April 6, the United States declared war on Germany.] Palmer had been lecturing in California since late in February; from February 26 to March 29, he delivered the series of Earl Lectures before the Pacific Theological Seminary in Berkeley (see **GHPann**-88).

"My subject [Palmer said] must be one of common interest to you and to myself — one, too, in which, through previous acquaintance, I shall not be unduly disturbed by the absence of books and papers. Such a subject I seem to myself to have found in him who stands as the patron saint of your city and at the same time as one of the supporters of my own philosophic studies, George Berkeley [Irish philosopher, 1685–1753].

"When the trustees of the College of California decided to move their little institution from Oakland to a more permanent and ample site on these wooded hills [in 1853], they rightly anticipated that before long a large city would grow up around them. How should it be called? Many proposals were made . . . none of them satisfactory, until . . . a leader among the trustees, proposed the name of Berkeley. It was at once seen that this name precisely expressed the ideals which they desired for their new city. They meant that this place should be a place consecrated to thoughtful study, to public spirit, to the enthusiasm of humanity; and where else could so admirable a defender of these things be found as in the great English idealist? On the whole their forecasts have been justified. Berkeley has been true to these lofty aims. But how often have you connected these matters with him in whom they originally appeared? How many are there in this audience who could state with any fullness the events of that picturesque career? It is well that they should be recalled, that you should from time to time freshen the inspiration and pride which you have in a godfather so august. Instead, then, of presenting to you today an abstract and argumentative oration, I will briefly recount the life of George Berkeley."

After a long presentation about Berkeley, Palmer concluded: "Are not the splendid enthusiasms of this man, and at the same time his desire for accurate thought, precisely what should inspire you? Long may he remain as a power in the consciousness of the University of California!"

87 The Monologue of Browning.

Palmer introduces this long piece: "Hardly another poet in the whole course of English literature has met with such violent and continuous partisanship as Robert Browning. When Wordsworth put forth his epoch-making little volume of *Lyrical Ballads*, he too met with derision, but it lasted only twenty years. By the time he reached middle age his position as a master was assured, and his limitations were well understood. Over Browning disputation has continued longer. Throughout his life [1812–1889] and during the quarter-century since his death he has had ardent assailants and just as ardent defenders. Persons of standing declare the man a barbarian, who broke into the fair fields of verse with poetry cacophonous in sound, obscure in expression, and shocking in subject. On the other hand, there are those who regard Browning as half divine. He is a prophet, they say, and has so disclosed to them the significance of their personal lives that they cannot hear any criticism of him without a shiver. Sometimes Browning is set up in laudatory antagonism to Tennyson [1809–1892], or Tennyson in antagonism to Browning; and certainly these poets do differ fundamentally. But are their differences disparaging or supplemental? I believe I shall find the safest approach to my heated subject if, without praise or blame, I coolly note some of the points of contrast between the two."

After some comparison of the two poets, Palmer proceeds to a lengthy presentation of the personal life and poetry of Robert Browning. At the end, he writes: "We may say that Tennyson and Browning summarize the imaginative life of their century. Browning shows the beginning of that Naturalism which henceforth, for good or ill, was to flood our poetry. Tennyson sings regretfully the shimmering charm, the ideal beauty, the refinement, the wistfulness, which were soon to pass away."

88 *Formative Types in English Poetry.*

Professor Palmer opens the preface: "The substance of this book was delivered as a series of lectures on the Earl Foundation before the Pacific Theological Seminary in Berkeley, California during the spring of 1917. The subject was one which had long interested me. I had spoken on it before the Lowell Institute in Boston in 1913 and subsequently on several occasions had found for it eager auditors and critics among college students. This frequent traversing of the same ground has helped me to perceive more plainly the path to be followed and has controlled the inclination to turn to this side or that in search of better prospects . . .

"In my judgment the English understanding of poetry has unfolded itself slowly, passing through certain well-marked crises of epochs at each of which has stood a revolter from past practice who, setting up antagonistic, yet really supplemental, conceptions of poetry has thrown open tracts of emotions which our beautiful art had not previously touched. Of course minor changes of this sort occur continually. I have wished to fix attention on the half-dozen fundamental, logical and productive crises which have brought us the rich poetry we now possess and may yet bring us richer still."

Palmer lectured on seven poets in the following sequence: Geoffrey Chaucer (1340–1400), Edmund Spenser (1552–1599), George Herbert (1593–1633), Alexander Pope (1688–1744), William Wordsworth (1770–1850), Alfred Tennyson (1809–1889), and Robert Browning (1812–1889). He had already published the pieces on George Herbert (**GHP**-50) and Robert Browning (**GHP**-87). "For one huge omission . . . [he adds] I have little excuse beside incompetence. Milton was too big for me . . ."

"At the close of each of these lectures, as originally delivered, [Palmer says,] I read for half an hour from the poet discussed. Criticism, taken apart from that which is discussed, is arid and blinding stuff. I accordingly at first thought of printing after each lecture a selection of 'illustrative material.' But seeing that this would double the size of my book, and possibly render it less attractive to those who found there poetry already pretty familiar, I abandoned the plan and have substituted brief lists, sufficient, however, to enable the novice to bring my judgments to the test.

"Perhaps a word of apology is needed for here venturing outside my province. My professional work has been in Philosophy. To the poets I have listened only as an amateur. Yet every one is wise, whatever his occupation, in cherishing some collateral interest which produces nothing for the market, is amenable to no social standard, and is valued simply for sweetening his own life. Such an unpaid invigorator has poetry been to me during a long life. On nearing the close [Palmer was then seventy-six years old; he lived for fifteen more years!] I am glad to give it publicity and commend it as a privy councillor to others."

A contemporary reviewer writes that "[n]o more appropriate moment could have been chosen for the publication of Professor Palmer's 'Formative Types in English Poetry' . . . Never has there been greater interest in poetry than now. Two American magazines of verse have survived the war [the war in Europe ended on November 11, 1918; the book was published on November 15], and within the past four years many new names have come to be associated with the writing of verse.

Amid the present universal expectancy, there is the feeling that poetry, since it, too, belongs to the world of reconstruction, will be changed with our thoughts and institutions" (Norreys Jephson O'Conor, *HGM,* 1918–1919; 27 (March 1919): 436–7).

89 *Altruism.*

Professor Palmer begins the preface, dated October 21, 1918: "I here present the substance of eight Ely Lectures delivered in the spring of 1918 [April 4–26] at Union Theological Seminary in New York. They were spoken without manuscript. In writing them out from the stenographer's notes I have condensed them considerably. In these belligerent days [the war in Europe did not end until November 1918] publishers are disposed to economize paper and print, and readers to prize brevity in everything except newspapers. Such restrictions force on us loquacious book-makers greater regard for compactness and lucidity, and are thus not altogether an injury.

"The book seeks to call attention to a section of ethics in regard to which the public mind greatly needs clarifying. Altruism and egoism, socialism and individualism, are in our time sentimentally arrayed against one another as independent and antagonistic agencies, each having its partisans. A careful examination will show, I think, that the one has meaning only when in company with its supposed rival. I have thought to make this clearest by tracing three stages through which the altruistic impulse passes in every-day life, exhibiting their varying degrees of dignity and the helpful presence in all of them of egoistic balance. If through my notion of a conjunct self I have made this curious partnership plain I shall count it no mean contribution to our generous, sacrificial, self-assertive, and perplexed time."

Francis G. Peabody (Harvard's Plummer Professor of Christian Morals, First Chairman of the Board of Preachers, and Dean of the Faculty of Divinity) reviewed the book: "This little book is Professor Palmer at his best. One is justified in saying it *is* Professor Palmer; for it is in reality not a book, but a wise man teaching, a great teacher reflecting, a subtle thinker setting forth his ideas. It is in its form, not so much instruction as consultation. The teacher is sitting at his desk with a group of young men about him, and reporting to them in the most intimate fashion his experience of life. 'I have been moving about lately through the country,' he begins; 'When a plate of apples is passed and I pick out the best one,' he goes on; 'A stranger hands me a five dollar bill'; 'A man I knew broke his leg' — how elementary and unsophisticated such teachings appear! One might even suspect that they were mere autobiography. The fact is, however, that the profoundest antinomies of conduct are approached through these trivial incidents, and that, in purporting to narrate the experience of the teacher, they in reality illustrate the most serious problems of ethics. The great guns of philosophical discussion are disguised by this ingenious camoflage of simplicity . . ." (*Harvard Theological Review*, 1920; 13: 79–81).

90 The Lord's Prayer.

Professor Palmer proposes in this paper "to hold up the Lord's Prayer to the light and let the sunshine shimmer through it. Let us discern what lies hidden here. Let us, with no irreverent hand, dissect, analyze, become distinctly conscious of the beauty and power of blessing which the Prayer contains. Often has something like this been attempted before . . . Though deriving much from the strong scholars and fervent devotees who have preceded me in telling what they have found in the Prayer . . . [m]y aim is somewhat peculiar. I approach the Prayer as a lover of psychology and poetry no less than of religion, and would fix attention on some of its less noticed perfections as a work of art. In my judgment it is a masterpiece of literature, whose quality our translators have astonishingly preserved . . . In making a literary survey of the Lord's Prayer we must . . . ask how normal and formative are the desires here engaged, how exactly and simply are they reported, and how well do they come together to form a thing of beauty, good for contemplation, good for stimulus."

Palmer then proceeds with his long and detailed survey.

91 William James.

Palmer gives the background for this presentation in 1920, about William James who died in 1910: "In view of the publication of the letters of William James [edited by his son, Henry James], I am asked to state how he appeared to his colleagues in the daily course of his work as a Harvard professor.

"In brief he showed among us the same surprising, rich, brilliant, and profitable variety of speech and act which appeared in his home, his books, and his championship of an unpopular cause. His nature was so abundant and original that it never became standardized or usual. We, who met him most intimately, found in him every day something fresh to wonder at and admire. I might then properly enough decline the work of description and say that James was indescribable. But I cannot content myself so. I loved the man, and far away I hear his prompting voice. When Professor Bowen died [Francis Bowen died in January 1890], I, as his successor [Palmer succeeded Bowen as the Alford Professor in December 1889], was called on to prepare a minute on him for the Faculty Record. As James and I came out together from the meeting where this had been read, he turned to me with one of his sudden bursts, 'Palmer, I mean to die before you, so that you can operate on me too.' Alas! he had his cruel wish, and I drew up his official minute. But such a man claims something more personal. I will set down a few random recollections of such sayings and incidents, slight in themselves, as bear his mark. The connected history of his life, discussion of his philosophy, and criticism of his many books, I leave to others. Mine is the pleasanter, if harder, task of setting forth an exceptionally engaging personality."

Palmer ends his affectionate piece: "Perhaps the grounds of endearment, and its long reach beyond admiration, must always remain unstateable. They certainly appear but slenderly in this meagre sketch. I can only say that we, who for more than thirty years were blest with James's presence, loved him with increasing fervor. We found in him a masterful type of human being, developed almost to perfection. We found an ever fresh and genial companion, of whom we could say with Chaucer that 'dulnesse was of him y-drad.' We found the tenderest of friends, who was at our side in every affliction, great or small. We found a noble soul, high-bred and democratically minded, incapable of doing anything to be seen of men [*sic*], but who, perceiving that our age stands in extreme need of patient thought and lucid speech, earned the gratitude of two continents by what he gave. Who that came close to such a being could fail to love? In him there was nothing to excuse."

92 The Puritan Home.

Professor Palmer opens this largely autobiographical piece: "This year we are celebrating the third centennial of the landing of the Pilgrims, and our people are making an effort gratefully to recall the tremendous event. To do so requires considerable effort; for to any but themselves Puritans have generally been a distasteful folk. Especially was the last century for them a time of bitter and almost continuous attack, caricature, and denunciation. Now, however, when the gaunt figures no longer walk our streets, feeling has grown kinder and aversions less clamorous. Not unwelcome now will be a dispassionate estimate of what the Puritan actually was . . .

"I was brought up in it [the Puritan home], am profoundly grateful for its discipline, and feel that I owe to it more than half of all that has made my life beautiful and rewarding. Today I would come forward as its eulogist. And while not blind to its defects, — aware indeed that its sudden passing has been inevitable, — I would insist that American civilization will have a hard task to find a source from which to draw an inspiration so bounteous and so constructive.

"To fix the worth of the Puritan home I shall endeavor first to give a clear account of the facts usually found in such homes . . . To be of any worth, this depictive side of my subject should be minute and well authenticated. I will base it on a description of my own childhood, and thus will show in some detail what were the assumptions, the practices, and the ideals of a typical Puritan home."

Palmer describes some features of the home: "all was plain and solid. There was no luxury . . . on all that we possessed and did religion set its mark . . . To the family tie the Puritans gave great prominence . . . there was the insistence on learning, fostered by the presence of abundant books, by the studies around the centre table in the evening, by the reading aloud that went on wherever three or four could be gathered together . . . several of the Fine Arts, notably poetry and music, were cultivated with an ardor and general approval infrequent to-day . . . In almost every family there were seasons of song in which all were expected to join . . . Puritans were strong in the arts of design . . . I would put forward prominently the literary power its training gave . . . Puritan children, we have seen, were likely to read or hear six passages of the English Bible every day. That book, without regard to its religious value, is acknowledged to be the consummate masterpiece of our language."

With regard to Puritan religious conceptions, Palmer pointed out that "there was much diversity among the Puritans, and never any such thing as a Puritan Church or creed. Each little group of believers had an independent existence, and formulated for itself its understanding or creed about things divine and human, changing this whenever it could be brought into closer conformity with the mind of the majority. During my life my country church has rewritten its entire creed three times."

As he discusses in detail the reasons for the "decay" of Puritanism, Palmer stresses that "[i]t fitted its followers to fight Indians, endure the hardships of New England, found a democracy, and send forth throughout the land a sturdier folk than any other single stock can boast."

93 *A Catalogue of Early and Rare Editions of English Poetry.*

The front cover has the same tooled, linear, geometric design as **GHP**-52 and **GHP**-70, which frames here, in gold stamping, A Catalogue of English Poetry.

Professor Palmer begins the preface: "This collection of English poetry, extending from Chaucer to Masefield, has been gathered under the stimulus of three converging interests, interests personal, affectional, institutional. Its basis was laid in the enthusiasm of boyhood, when George Herbert took me in charge, and by fixing my attention for a long time on his small plot of poetic ground taught me to feel the significance of poetry in general. By degrees he freed me from himself. His exquisite accomplishment excited curiosity about his ancestors and descendants. Acquaintance, too, with him and a few others begot a longing to possess some day the books in which their genius first declared itself, and even to trace its unfolding through successive volumes. Soon similar desires sprang up toward inferior and more accessible writers. Better than the pioneers small men reveal the temper of a time, and not seldom each endears himself by flashes of individual insight. I began to extend my grasp and to lay hold of poets genuine though humble. The continuity of English poetry fascinated me. An insatiable passion for completeness seized and still holds me. With old age, too [the preface is dated, August 3, 1923; Palmer was eighty-one years old], the hobby of collecting grows stronger. Until I possess a first edition of every piece of English verse that once had influence, I cannot be at ease. Need I say that I am far from easy yet?

"This personal inclination to treat poetry as a serious and cumulative affair, after running through half my life, received a powerful reinforcement through the similar tastes of my wife, Alice Freeman Palmer . . ."

Much of the remaining preface is included in the earlier publication, *Notes on a Collection of English Poetry* (**GHPann-**79), but Palmer gives the preface to the Catalogue a different ending: "Beautiful Wellesley has long been known as a special home of the Muses. Admirable verse has been written there by a group of teachers, and its powerful department of literature has trained an exceptional number of brilliant students. These idealistic influences Mrs. Palmer and I would honor and foster. Particularly does that task belong to me who for fifteen years had as my comrade *her who in an extraordinary degree embodied a radiant idealism, and who since her death has become a kind of patron saint of college girls*" (annotator's italics).

In 1933, after Palmer died, Ethel Dane Roberts, the Wellesley College librarian, described A Morning in Professor Palmer's Library: "More than a year before Professor Palmer brought his priceless collection of English poets to Wellesley and placed them with his own hands on the shelves of the Treasure Room, he asked me to come to his house in Cambridge to see the books on the shelves of his own library, and the morning I spent with him there will always be one of my most vivid and cherished memories. When I returned to Wellesley with the experience fresh in my mind, I wrote down at once, and as nearly as possible in his own words, what I remembered of his running comment on the treasures he showed me. Afterward I told him I had done so and he said, 'You may publish it after I am gone'" (*Wellesley Magazine*, October 1933).

Professor Palmer brought the books to the college library on February 21, 1924, Alice Freeman Palmer's birthday. "It has long been his custom to celebrate this day by making Wellesley a present of some rare book from the collection which he and his wife started together. This year he brought the whole library. Then for several weeks he was an almost daily visitor at the Library, working up in the Treasure Room at the task of arranging the books in their places. By the time his own birthday came, the task was finished, and on March 19 [he was eighty-two years old] at a reception in the Treasure Room, where trustees, officers, and professors of the college gathered, he gave over to the college the custody of the books" (Professor Palmer's Books, *The Wellesley Alumnae Quarterly*, 1924; 8 (No. 3, May): 161–165).

94 *Emery Lucius Bradford.*

In the Chronicles Professor Palmer has numerous entries about Reverend Bradford, starting in 1892 when Bradford settled in Boxford and was married, and ending in 1925 when he delivered his last sermon. In addition, Palmer mentions Bradford in the March 1900 diary and in **GHP**-39.

This pamphlet was privately printed at the Riverside Press, and, according to a Chronicle entry, "cost $50.00." An inside heading identifies the text as a "Memorandum for the Church Records on the ministry of E. L. Bradford."

Palmer gives numerous details of Bradford's personal life and his service in Boxford for twenty-two years. Professor Palmer also emphasizes Bradford's "excellence as a preacher" and the "tenderness and wisdom" that he showed when he visited members of the church in their homes. "Of course it was natural with such a minister that the Boxford parish should know nothing of cliques and factions and should experience no need of more churches then one. In towns not far away there have been frequent ecclesiastical quarrels, resulting in short pastorates and in several meagerly equipped churches. We have followed the better tradition of harmony, welcoming to our communion persons of widely different beliefs who were at one in their desire to serve a common Master . . .

"Mr. and Mrs. Bradford have been so united that it is impossible to think of one apart from the other. It is a joint service to the town which they have liberally rendered, and our gratitude goes forth to the pair as to a single benefactor." They were married in 1892, soon after he came to Boxford, and their daughter, Ruth, was born in 1893. (Ruth Bradford graduated from Wellesley College in 1915.)

95 Introductory to *Immanuel Kant, 1724–1924.*

On April 22, 1924, in Boston University's Jacob Sleeper Hall, to celebrate the two-hundredth anniversary of the birth of Immanuel Kant, eight speakers address various aspects of Kant's life and work.

In the "Opening Words" of this exercise, Professor Palmer

addresses some "facts of [Kant's] life and the traits of his simple but massive character. By circumstance and disposition the quiet scholar whom I have called an Earth-shaker seems peculiarly unfitted for such a role: From the beginning of his life in 1724 to its end in 1804 he was encompassed with such restrictions as would have cut off anyone but himself from public notice. These hindering restrictions were of four sorts — local, monetary, bodily, and professional."

After his analysis of each of these restrictions, Palmer ends: "[T]he majority of us are probably different from what we should be had Kant not been born, so pervasive has his influence been even over those who never heard his name. I owe him a deep personal debt. After struggling for many years with the arbitrary limitations of English Empiricism, I found in him my liberator. I never became a Kantian. Few are that. But I gained an idealistic method, I learned the primacy of the Practical Reason, and I acquired a lifelong admiration for the man 'who broke the bands of circumstance and grappled with his evil star.'"

96 Forgiveness.

Professor Palmer's entries in the Chronicles show that he lectured on Forgiveness thirteen times from 1900 to 1911. This paper appeared eight years after the war in Europe ended with the defeat of Germany. Here, in addition to his discussion of the "perplexities of private forgiveness — that between persons," Palmer addresses "the possibility of forgiveness between nations [which] has been the most debated form of our problem . . . in recent years.

"Many of us believe that a single nation sought to aggrandize itself at the cost of the rest of the world. To hold it in check took millions of lives and dollars, enough to leave half a dozen nations poor for a century. A crime so colossal was never before known. Ours was the victory. But what should be our attitude toward the conquered nation to-day? If we believe the Prussians as much at fault as is here assumed, shall we forgive them, find excuses for their conduct, and treat them as if nothing had happened? Would that be honest? Would it even be well for society?"

To bring "order and daylight into that which has always been obscurely familiar," Palmer discusses four varieties of forgiveness: "the Forgiveness of Superiority, the Forgiveness of

Oblivion, the Forgiveness of Excuse, and the Forgiveness of Faith." Then he asks, "can we honestly forgive the Germans, welcome them again to our friendship, and, . . . still have faith in their future and put them back into pretty much the place they had before? To all these questions I, an ardent pro-Ally, both formerly and at present, answer yes." And finally Palmer explains his answer by analyzing the German situation with reference to each variety of forgiveness.

97 Commencement Day Speech to Trustees and Alumnae.

Following the luncheon of trustees and alumnae, Professor Palmer, eighty-four years old, was the last speaker. According to the editor of the *Wellesley Magazine*, he "spoke for the trustees. Not only because he is so dear a friend to the college, a friend whose service and devotion go back almost to the beginnings of Wellesley, but also because the things he said are things which need to be said again and again, things without which no Commencement at Wellesley would be complete, we give you here the substance of his speech."

Palmer began: "After all your speaking, your excellent speaking, I do not know that there can be much left for me to say, and yet I am anxious that, going out from Wellesley's great day, you should carry some deep impression of what Wellesley has meant. As one of the older members of the Trustees, perhaps I can bring it home to you by turning our thoughts for a few moments to the three persons of genius who have invented Wellesley, and who stamped Wellesley's spirit so deeply on this place that it has spread over the entire country . . ."

First he addressed "Mr. Durant [whom] I never saw. I speak therefore, in regard to him by reputation, and especially by seeing his work. Miss Freeman, when she came to me, brought with her a very great love for this man. She always had his picture on her chamber shelf, and was continually talking of him, so that I seem to have acquired a certain acquaintance with him. A masterly man! A sensitive man! One who had the courage of his convictions everywhere . . . One who was capable of transforming his personal affliction into a public benefit. When his only child [a son] died, he dedicated his own life to the memory of that child. One might have expected, therefore, that he would have founded a men's college; but he did not lose his sound judgment. 'Men have had a great deal done for them; the needy ones now are women.' While he had

had very little experience of education, he had a singular foresight of what the needs of education were . . . To make independent minds was always his aim . . . He gathered beautiful pictures; he had music here; he was a devotee of poetry. His own library was superb, and indeed for that matter it is — it is still in your possession."

Next Professor Palmer addressed Mrs. Durant. "When her husband died [in 1881, six years after Wellesley College opened] he left this college in her trust . . . She showed . . . absolute loyalty to her husband and her own desires and at the same time entire respect for her voting colleagues [on the Board of Trustees]."

And then he turned to the third person, Alice Freeman. "I hardly need to remind you of the stamp which she set on this college, coming in its charge when she was twenty-five and leaving it at the time when most people were beginning their life work, at thirty-two . . . She had a fervor as deeply religious as that of Mr. Durant, and with it a loving heart. Her religion was always manifested to her on the positive side, not as restriction, but as an opportunity. As a student she was a modernist before modernism was heard of. I sometimes feel that you may have lost her. The country has taken her up and considers that it owns her. I find some memorial of her wherever I go — photographs of her in every college. She is claimed as the patron saint of college girls, and she belongs to you.

"To these three I then commend you. They have set their stamp of moral ideals on the college."

98 Foreword to C. G. Alexander, *Francesca Alexander*.

Constance G. Alexander introduces these memories of her cousin, Francesca Alexander (1837–1917), "garnered by one who loved her dearly . . . Though to Boston people of fifty years ago, she of whom I write here was a familiar household name, and though in England and Italy, as well as in America, there are still so many who remember her vividly, yet there are, of course, many more who never heard of Ruskin's [John Ruskin, 1819–1900, English art critic and sociological writer] friend 'Francesca', never read her exquisite transcription of the life and legends of the Tuscan peasantry. Because, as she says in her 'Story of Ida,' 'her life has left a great peacefulness in mine, like the light which remains long after sunset on a summer's day, and while I am yet, as it were, within her influence, I have wished to write down a little of what I (and others of her friends) remember of her, that so beautiful a life and death may not be quite forgotten.' Perhaps, too, some who first read of her here may be moved to seek in libraries for her books, and so discover a new and rare delight."

Constance G. Alexander (head of the English Department at Pine Manor Junior College in Brookline, Massachusetts) and George Herbert Palmer were close friends. Her unpublished manuscript, entitled George Herbert Palmer, Counsellor and Friend, in the Wellesley College Archives, directed me to several of Palmer's periodical publications.

In his Foreword Palmer writes: "A new type of biography has come into being since Boswell's [James Boswell, 1740–1795, *Life of Samuel Johnson*] immortal book. It aims primarily at presenting a character not to be imitated, but to be understood. Acts and sayings are recorded because, however strange, they have the tang of individuality. Whatever is done or said we are made to feel proceeds from just this person and no other. Indeed, it furnishes better material for literature if another person of this particular type never existed. Such a character lives in this book and is presented in essentially the modern way . . .

"An intimate acquaintance with so rare a person enriches our own life. I have said that the governing motive of modern portraiture is not moral instruction. Yet how can we come in contact with one built so four-square without thereafter becoming ourselves more stable in the midst of a bustling world? Such a benignant effect will be more natural too because of the simplicity with which Francesca's cousin here records her life. She knows that life at every period of its gentle flow. Ardently she loves both the girl and the woman. That love refreshingly permeates her book, and often makes its pages seem a poetic meditation designed to ease the author's own heart rather than a set piece of writing prepared for a reader. The fact that it differs widely from most books of today will lend it distinction and commend it to the little company of those who, oppressed by a garish literature, have kept their taste for homely events, beautiful characters, and a diction showing everywhere acquaintance with those who in former times knew how to use our English speech."

99 The Junior College.

Palmer begins with a description of a recent, popular movement in secondary education in the United States: "Our academies, seminaries, and even our high schools have been offering their graduates an additional two years of study of college grade, enabling them to enter college as juniors instead of as freshmen. This advance work, known as the Junior College course, is optional . . . Nothing is more striking in this movement than its escape from criticism. I at least have heard no word of doubt. Such silence alarms me. I want to hear discussion."

He goes on to say that "In my judgment it is more likely to bring disaster than anything which has happened in our world of education during the last fifty years. I call on the public to see whether there is still time to lessen this damage and I acknowledge my own fault in not having protested before. Perhaps some excuse may be found for a very old man [age 85 years] already burdened with other heavy cares . . . Almost certainly the Junior College will in the long run blot out what I regard as the precious distinction of the American university in contrast to the European . . . Wherever Junior Colleges are strong, colleges will drop their first two years and will add two graduate years, chiefly of professional study. The unique intermediate culture college of America will disappear, and with it the great troop of men and women who, having had contact with scholarship, have become leaders in idealism and centres of civilization for our waste [*sic*] places. The financial backing of these persons, the main support of our colleges hitherto, now ceasing, we must, like the universities of Europe, come into dependence on the State and let our politicians refuse money if we teach such science as they do not like . . .

"My only desire is to awaken thought. This paper is an impassioned cry to superintendents to mind what they are doing, to regard ultimate consequences rather than attractive immediate issues. Whoever will show that I am unduly alarmed and that it is wise to break down the distinction between American and European education will earn my gratitude. I don't want to think as I do, but I can't help it."

100 The Junior College Again.

In response to his attack on the Junior College (**GHP**-99), Professor Palmer says, "A multitude of letters have come to me from persons whom I do not know and from nearly every state in the Union. Almost uniformly they tell of the harm done them or their children by a Junior College and express gratitude that someone has at last spoken out and bidden our educators stop and think about ultimate consequences. I shall not attempt to summarize their stories. Too few years are left me for other work I mean to do. But one of their requests is altogether courteous and fair. They ask, What can we do about it? What means have we for checking its wider spread? . . ."

After detailing six suggestions, Palmer concludes: "In defense of the magnificent American experiment of democracy I felt called on to stir up criticism over the Junior College. The unpleasant task is ended, and with a quieter conscience I may now return to my library."

101 College Expenses.

"The World War [Professor Palmer begins] has heightened the estimate of College education. Business men were formerly fond of saying that four years of study took all practical pep out of a youngster. But during the war College men and women were everywhere leaders. One College man, it was jestingly said, was worth three or four out of the shops. Naturally then when the war ended our Colleges were filled as they never had been before. Several new ones were founded to catch the overflow and many established a rigid limit beyond which no more students would be accepted, however well prepared. My impression is that the disturbance due to this cause has been unduly exaggerated. Some of it is inevitable, apart from the war. In twenty years our population increases by at least a quarter. We must be prepared for about that amount of permanent increase, war or no war.

"To meet the rise in cost produced by this continual increase in numbers College Presidents feel themselves compelled to seek from their constituents continually increasing funds. More teachers are needed, more buildings, ampler grounds for exercise. Sometimes a drive is launched for a specific object; sometimes an annual or graduating subscription is called for to furnish free funds. There is something pathetic in the frequency of these appeals, something astonishing in their success. Our great universities accumulate princely fortunes and are never satisfied . . . In the last five years the property of Yale has increased twenty millions, and Yale is still poor. Columbia follows hard after Yale in both wealth and poverty. Harvard's annual increase is not less than five millions . . .

"Now it is the purpose of this paper to show that in order

to meet the annual increase of expense College Presidents need not correspondingly increase their property. There is another way, a more productive way. Let them cut down their expenses. At present education is looked upon as a costly luxury not made for common folk, but the badge of a class, something in which only the fixedly rich can indulge. It is becoming therefore divisive, splitting the community into two contrasted classes. Against this I would protest.

"My plan for relief is a simple one. At the end of the junior year let every one who has not attained some sort of honorable rank be dropped without degree or certificate. Something like a quarter of the cost of that year, and of each succeeding year, would be saved. Probably, too, among those thus dropped there would be a goodly proportion of the dullards, the indolent, and the vicious . . .

After mentioning some problems with his plan, Palmer says in conclusion: "I put forth the scheme tentatively, as a basis for discussion. The only part of it I feel sure of is that the cost of college education should be much reduced and the solicitation of funds become less frequent."

102 Department of Philosophy at Harvard, 1870–1929.

Personnel (pages 3–20)

Palmer, a member from 1872 until his retirement in 1913, declared that the department had "the first well-rounded staff for teaching philosophy organized in this country . . . made up of extraordinary men, too eminent for praise. In this section I attempt to describe the impression their diverse characters made."

For William James and Josiah Royce, he presents, with very minor changes, the texts from **GHP**-91 and **GHP**-83, respectively.

"George Santayana [he says] is unique in a variety of ways. In the philosophical menagerie which made up our department he stood somewhat aloof, and was valued the more on that account. When on several occasions he wished to resign and devote himself to writing, it was our urgency which kept him in his chair. I shall expound him best by enumerating successively the points of his uniqueness which most impressed us in daily intercourse . . .

"Hugo Münsterberg was confessed by all to be one of the most brilliant Harvard professors of his time. Yet he had quite as many foes as friends, and these two groups were about equally ardent. They agreed, however, in calling him puzzling. Most of us are that, and about in proportion to our greatness. Or is it that the ordinary man is puzzling too but is of too little consequence to repay the effort to understand? We leave him unexplained. Münsterberg had too wide and deep an influence to be left so. I shall endeavor to tell how he seemed to me to be put together . . ."

Of the last of the five men, Palmer writes: "Ralph Barton Perry is fortunately still in active service. It would then be unbecoming to analyze his character as I have analyzed our absent colleagues . . ." (see Palmer's diary entry for March 18, 1900, page 181).

Finally Palmer identifies "Dr. Benjamin Rand [who] has been associated with us almost from the beginning as our Librarian, an erudite aid in philosophic research . . ."

Facing page 21 is a photograph of the Hopkinson portrait of Palmer which hangs in the Bechtel Room at Emerson Hall (see 253n1).

Organization (page 24–26)

Palmer begins: "My colleagues were all men of genius who independently would have had a deep influence anywhere. But I believe that influence was doubled by certain ethical features of our organization. As these features have attracted little notice, though in my judgment well worth reproducing elsewhere [see **GHP**-103 and 104], I name them here."

Excerpts give some idea of the text: "The former controlling headship of the Department was abandoned. A chairman took the place. This officer called our meetings, presided at them, and was our medium of communication with the President. He was changed every few years. In the course of time most of the professors served in this way and so became acquainted with administrative as well as teaching duties . . . We avoided 'breeding in' and directly aimed at diversity in our staff. When a new member was proposed we at once asked whether he had not the same mental attitude as someone we had already. If so, we did not want him. There is therefore no Harvard 'school' of philosophy . . . The differences of opinion in our staff were always openly acknowledged. In our lectures we were accustomed to attack each other by name . . . Our students were not misled by these our attacks on each other. They knew that we were all warm friends. But truth was sacred; and criticism, the surest way of approaching it, was a friendly not a hostile process . . . James has admirably defined philosophy as the obstinate attempt to think clearly; and nowhere is such obstinacy more needed than for purging one's judgment from personal bias . . ."

Palmer adds a final personal note: "What I have described is merely the Department of which I was once a member. Sixteen years have passed since then [he resigned in 1913 and the period of this book ends in 1929], probably as eventful as any of the forty preceding. Those managing the Department have been altogether worthy of its traditions. Yet I say nothing of these years or men. Since the beginning of the war I have had little connection with the organization which was once my life. Its staff and I have the friendliest relations, but personal ones only. For I hold that when an officer's corporate responsibility ceases, interference, advice, even detailed knowledge, should also cease. While then I rejoicingly perceive the great influence in the University and beyond it of the present Harvard Department of Philosophy, I am incompetent to be its historian."

103 Introduction to *Contemporary American Philosophy.*

A 1977 publication "charts the history of philosophic thinking in the United States as dominated by Harvard from 1860 to 1930 . . . 1860 produced a report on the moribund state of Harvard philosophy while 1930 produced a book [*Contemporary American Philosophy*] testifying to its potency . . . The three divisions of the American Philosophical Association — Eastern, Western, and Pacific — had each conducted a referendum of its members to select the thirty-four American philosophers whose 'personal statements' would represent the state of American thought; the presidents of the three divisions edited the book. All three editors had received their Ph.D.s from Harvard. The professors from across the country had dedicated the book to another Harvard-trained philosopher who had taught at the university for over forty years [**dedctdGHPann**-6]. Sixteen of the thirty-four contributors had received their highest degrees at Harvard, fourteen of them the doctorate . . ." (Bruce Kuklick, *The Rise of American Philosophy: Cambridge, Massachusetts, 1860–1930,* New Haven, Yale University Press, 1977, pages xvi-xvii).

In their preface the editors characterize this collection of "philosophical autobiographies . . . Each contributor was requested to state his principal philosophic beliefs, the reasons supporting them, and the manner in which he had reached them." Volume 1 has fifteen such personal statements, in addition to Palmer's Introduction; volume 2 has eighteen.

Professor Palmer introduces his formal Introduction: "The American Philosophy Association dedicates its new volume of discussions to me and asks me to write the introductory paper. I am somewhat puzzled by the honour. It cannot be due to any signal contribution on my part to philosophical doctrine, such as has been made by several of my colleagues, by James, Royce, Münsterberg, Santayana, Perry, McDougall. My name is connected with none of the many fighting faiths which have enriched American thought during the eighty-seven years of my life. There is no distinctively Palmerian philosophy. But I have viewed the whole marvellous expansion of thought which has gone on from the the restricted outlook of Hopkins, Porter, Bowen, and McCosh to the wide horizons of Dewey, Montague, Hocking, and Whitehead.

"What, then, is the mental condition of one who has seen it all, seen it too instructed by a pretty wide acquaintance with the general history of philosophy? This may well be the question I am asked to answer. Of argumentation over single problems enough will be offered by other contributors to these volumes. They are still in the field of conflict. Something more personal I can supply. By making my paper largely biographic I can treat myself as a kind of representative of the philosophic young men of my time. I can tell of the haphazards, discouragements, helps, and changes of public opinion through which they have forced their way from the stagnation of early thought into the tumultuous activity of the present time, and beyond this into individual careers and positive personal beliefs. Of course each of us is unique. No man is completely typical. Yet there are sufficient resemblances among the buffetings which we all have had to encounter to make a single candid story of them interesting and instructive. The plot of the story may fit us all, even if the incidents vary. So I shall try to set down here an old man's memories of the struggles through which he has passed in reaching the criticized convictions about ultimate things on which he now relies."

This short statement is followed by Palmer's long, autobiographical piece; the text is identical with that in **GHP**-104. At the end, he presents a NOTE:

"Perhaps I should say that this Anatomy of myself is not intended as a complete autobiography. Being addressed to those who, for the most part, are teachers and writers, I sketch only those traits which directly concern their work. Several, even more fundamental, I have not mentioned. For example, I have inherited the Puritan distaste for ornament and prize simplicity. With this goes a passion for order that almost amounts to a disease. If anything is a little out of adjustment, I am as uncomfortable as a musical ear that hears a wrong note struck. While these traits have their worthy side, they sometimes lead me to harsh judgments."

Palmer is mentioned by other contributors to the volumes. W. E. Hocking (Harvard): "George Herbert Palmer was teaching the history of philosophy and ethics as few men have ever taught them. In teaching them he conveyed his own metaphysics, largely through occasional and unforgettable sentences, which as someone well put it, 'continued to glow in the dark of the mind.'" Wm. Pepperell Montague (Barnard College): "Palmer's lectures were incomparably the most finished, both as to content and to form, of all that I have ever heard; and whether because of, or in spite of, their literary perfection, their pedagogical effectiveness was extraordinary. I had the good luck to be his assistant or reader, and so had an opportunity to see the progress in philosophic comprehension made by the large group of undergraduates in his course, each of whom was required to submit four papers during the year." Ralph Barton Perry (Harvard): "Palmer taught us ethics, and by his example taught us how to teach." George Santayana (Harvard): "There was one lesson . . . which I [learned] from Professor Palmer . . . — I refer to the historical spirit of the nineteenth century, and to that splendid panorama of nations and religions, literatures and arts, which it unrolled before the imagination. These picturesque vistas into the past came to fill in circumstantially that geographical and moral vastness to which my imagination was already accustomed. Professor Palmer was especially skilful in bending the mind to a suave and sympathetic participation in the views of all philosophers in turn: were they not all great men, and must not the aspects of things which seemed persuasive to them be really persuasive?"

104 *The Autobiography of a Philosopher.*

The preface to this volume consists of Palmer's introduction to his long piece in **GHPann**-103 with four changes: the opening sentence now reads, "In 1930 the American Philosophy Association dedicated its new volume of discussions to me and asked me to write the introductory paper"; he gives his age as eighty-six years rather than eighty-seven; he omits the NOTE; and he adds this final sentence - "In short, through following the instructions given me at starting I have been led into what closely resembles an autobiography."

The main text is identical in both publications.

A contemporary review of this book is entitled George Herbert Palmer in the Evening of His Years: "The main concern of the book is such a frank baring of a soul as only one of such limpid clearness of days [*sic*] as Professor Palmer could give to his fellow-man. Indeed, so delicate in its texture is this short narrative a reviewer is hesitant lest he mar so fine a web. The work 'poetic' is not too strong to be used here. The reader who does not feel on putting the book aside that he has somehow been in touch with the poetic will have missed the rare quality of its modest, something [*sic*] too modest, pages . . ." (Percy Hutchison, *New York Times*, March 29, 1931, section IV, page 9).

105 On Growing Old.

When he was eighty-eight years old, three years before he died, Professor Palmer published this paper.

"I lately gave a lecture at Harvard on growing old, [he begins] explaining minutely how it is accomplished and tracing the steps through which I have passed in reaching a great age. But growing old is not confined to Harvard. We are all busied with it. Accordingly I here print what I there said, including even its personal and intimate details. It may all be summed up in a single warning precept. Old age is no bit of good luck. It comes only as the result of effort . . .

"I hold . . . that we construct old age in precisely the same way as we build a barn. We merely need knowledge and persistent effort. Combined they will carry us through anything.

I have undergone six surgical operations and am now — except for a lameness induced by that early folly [walking too soon on a sprained leg] — in perfect health and enjoyment. To enable others to find a course which may be equally serviceable for themselves I here trace in detail and entire frankness six definite stages of my progress as relates to Food, Sleep, Exercise, Clothing, Moods, [and] Religion."

106 Introduction to C. T. Burnett, *Hyde of Bowdoin*.
See 278n3.

107 In Dedication: Josiah Royce.
With minor changes this is the same as **GHP**-83.

108 The Lord's Prayer.
The text is identical with that in **GHP**-90.

George Herbert Palmer died on May 7, 1933.

109 *An Academic Courtship: The Letters of Alice Freeman and George Herbert Palmer, 1886–1887*.
See **AFPann**-20.

Chapter 8

Publications about George Herbert Palmer, annotated

identified as **aboutGHPann**-number

So much has been written about George Herbert Palmer that this list is undoubtedly incomplete.

1 Frederic Palmer, The Ring and the Book, Written for The Christmas Festival, 1907, privately printed, 1908 (from a copy in the Boxford Public Library).
See 237n2.

2 Josiah Royce, In Honor of Professor Palmer, *Harvard Graduates' Magazine*, 1910–1911; 19 (June 1911): 575–579.
(The circumstances of this presentation are described in 253n1)

The opening paragraph of Royce's long address: "Professor Palmer in his own work, both as a teacher and as a writer, has very highly developed and has beautifully applied the art of characterizing men. Few teachers of philosophy have used that art more skilfully as an aid to the exposition of the doctrines of philosophers. And Professor Palmer in his published works has also employed his art of personal characterization for purposes far more intimate and more beautiful still than are those which can be expressed by any classroom teaching. I am now called upon to take my little part, upon the present occasion, in the grateful, but vastly difficult task of saying something that may in a measure serve towards characterizing our guest himself. We should all be glad indeed if in a few words any of us could portray him as a philosopher. We should rejoice still more if we too could succeed in the more intimate and beautiful office of portraying him as a friend."

Continuing with paragraph openings: "But in order to accomplish either of these tasks, I myself feel that I should need, if that were conceivable, to be able to borrow for this evening his own literary style, — a style without which his art of personal characterization could not be imagined . . . Since I myself am an officer, I must first speak of how I have known him as an organizer, and in many respects as the creator of our philosophical department . . . Now the 'union of opposites,' the 'synthesis of conflicts,' is, as you know, the art to which those philosophers aspire with whom Professor Palmer, in his own independently thoughtful way, has always expressed a certain very deep sympathy. I wish to point out that upon this art the very existence of our department has depended . . . But our guest is not only leader in our common department work. He is also philosopher . . ."

And Professor Royce ends his presentation: "I have been priviliged to be a fellow laborer in his company. I deeply regret that I was not in the ordinary sense his pupil. You who have been his pupils know that herein I have lost much. But this I know, that we can none of us ever lose him or his influence so long as we continue either to reflect or to love."

Immediately after Royce's article is a short poem in Greek by Professor Rand, entitled "To George Herbert Palmer," with Rand's English translation:

> Hail, wise in counsel! Over many seas
> Of thought thou ridest, and shalt ride, at ease.
> Modern and ancient thou, for whom agree
> The imperfect glory and fair symmetry.

3 Dr. Richard C. Cabot, George Herbert Palmer: The retiring and much beloved Harvard teacher, as his pupils regard him. *Boston Evening Transcript*, January 25, 1913, page 2. (Professor Palmer was to retire from his professorship in June 1913)

As a student at Harvard College, Cabot majored in philosophy and he continued his close association with the philosophy department. In 1901 he was a member of the visiting committee for philosophy and psychology appointed by the overseers of the university, and in 1903–1904 he lectured in Royce's course in Logic (*HGM*, 1928–29; 37 (March 1929): 310. *New England Journal of Medicine*, 1939; 220: 1049–52).

"In my college days ('85-'89) [Dr. Cabot begins] Professor Palmer was one of the few men engaged in teaching at Harvard, who knew how to teach, or had given thought and pains to the subject. As a notably good teacher he stood out preëminent among the group of learned professors, who could write and investigate, but had never been required to think about the art of developing a student's mind or to practise and study that art. Professor Palmer has been first of all a teacher. Study, research and writing he thought should be secondary to the business of imparting truth and stimulating the student's mind to receive it. No one could write truly about him without putting first and foremost among his characteristics this wonderful teaching art to which he devoted himself. He has taught Greek and English, as well as philosophy, during his long service at Harvard, and by those who have watched his teaching in all three subjects, I have been told that his mastery has been notable in them all."

In view of Dr. Cabot's remarks about the art of teaching, it should be noted that he himself was highly regarded as a teacher of medicine at the Harvard Medical School and the Massachusetts General Hospital when he wrote this tribute to Professor Palmer. See 247n2, and **aboutAFPann**-5 for two of the several other vignettes in Cabot's long, perceptive piece.

4 John Wright Buckham, George Herbert Palmer, Ideal Teacher: An appreciation of a beloved personality who has enriched human thought with the great doctrine of mutuality, *Christian Register*, 1920; March 18: 279–280.

Buckham, from the Pacific School of Religion, starts his piece: "A writer in the *Nation* has divided the educated public of America into two classes, 'both large, — those who have studied under Mr. Palmer and those who have not.' Not only the first of these classes but very many in the second would unite in saying of Professor Palmer that he fulfills pre-eminently two ideals, — the ideal of the American scholar and that of the American teacher . . .

"The kind of scholar whom Mr. Palmer represents is not the technical scholar, although he is such in his own field, but the all-around, informed scholar, the man of large culture, with due appreciation of the realm of knowledge as a whole, in close touch with literature and art and all wide human interests . . . He is thinker, philosopher, critic, and constructor of truth . . . Moreover, his philosophy is no detached or cloud-built pile, remote from life and conduct, for it lies in the world of morals, which is with us day and night . . .

"Yet even more than the scholar and philosopher, Professor Palmer is the *teacher,* — born teacher, trained teacher, trainer of teachers, 'Dean of American teachers,' he was well termed when presented for his latest doctorate, at the University of California in 1917 [for the citation with this honorary degree, see 278n2] . . . No teacher can read that unconscious revelation of his aims, 'The Ideal Teacher,' [**GHP**-55] — the final word upon this high theme — without gratitude mingled with deep heart-searching . . .

"The most characteristic achievement of Mr. Palmer as a teacher seems to me to be his power to introduce the atmosphere and spirit of mutuality into a crowded class-room. With a small class it is comparatively easy to secure contact, interchange of mental movement between teacher and students. But how accomplish this with a class of two hundred or more? Professor Palmer has discovered the secret. By a subtle, vicarious apprehension and sympathy he manages to discern, to objectify, to interpret, the working of the pupil-mind, to anticipate its questions and objections and then to state and meet them with a lucidity that removes all confusion and a comradeship that gives the sense of a great common discovery . . . In that great out-of-door auditorium, the Greek theatre at Berkeley, where he delivered the Charter Day address of the University of California in 1917 upon 'Bishop Berkeley,' [**GHP**-86] he held a popular audience of upward of six thousand while he expounded, without a note, yet with perfect accuracy of phrase and sustained power of interest, the life and principles of the supreme idealist of the English race . . .

"His wisdom and art — his very method itself — has happily passed over into his published writings and will remain as a permanent enrichment to both education and literature . . .

"It is a perilous thing to be scholar, teacher, author, — say nothing of all three, — lest any one of these high vocations absorb and extinguish the man. Professor Palmer, constantly threatened by this peril, has escaped with more than ordinary success. He has remained inalienably human, — a considerate companion, an honest observer, a humble spirit, an unspoiled human being . . . In keeping him true to the steady normalities of life, one event in his life has been of exceptional influence, — his marriage in 1887 to Miss Alice Freeman, at that time president of Wellesley College. The comradeship thus formed enriched his as well as her personal life and in consequence greatly enhanced his power to understand and interpret the finer and deeper side of personal relationships.

"The story of this romance, as he has related it in his Life of Mrs. Palmer, who died in 1902 [**GHP**-57], has purified and deepened the meaning of the marriage tie for thousands. It is not only a skilful portraiture of one of the most beloved and influential women of her time in America, but it has also come to be recognized as a rare representation of ideal womanhood as it finds its fruition through a happy home in the service of others . . . It broke through the long-cherished but unreasonable reserves of New England without invading the sanctities of personality. This was done with a frankness and fulness that disarmed criticism and with a vividness that encircled it with fascination . . .

"Another service which this wise man has rendered is to impart to all with whom he has come in contact the *spirit of catholicity*. The catholicity of his mind, together with a deeper sense of the beauty and nobility of catholicity itself, came very forcibly to me in connection with his Earl lecture on English poets, since published under the title, 'Formative Types of English Poetry' [**GHP**-88] . . . Professor Palmer's knowledge of and love for poetry is itself a mark of his catholicity. He is *par excellence* the philosopher-interpreter of poetry, and although he terms himself an 'amateur,' brings to the understanding of poetry an acumen and breadth of outlook as well as a sympathy and reverence which render his contribution to the appreciation of poetry unique . . .

"Perhaps the most characteristic contribution to spiritual truth which Professor Palmer has made appears in his recent book, 'Altruism' [**GHP**-89] . . . [H]is definition . . . 'By mutuality . . . I mean the recognition of another and myself as inseparable elements of one another, each being essential to the welfare of each . . . '"

5 William Ernest Hocking, Professor Palmer at Eighty, *Harvard Graduates' Magazine*, 1921–1922; 30 (June 1922): 516–522. (Hocking had been a student at Harvard College, class of 1901.)

"On March 19th, Professor Palmer passed his eightieth birthday. Fifty-two years ago he began his teaching in Harvard College. And although the fifteen thousand men who have been in his classes make a fair circle of friends, they are but a fraction of the actual circle; for by far the greater number of all men who have studied in Harvard from 1870 to this day have heard his voice and are familiar with his presence. Nine years ago he retired from active lecturing in the College; but he is still of the College, living within the Yard, concerned in all that passes there, an untitled officer — one might almost say — of every class. Large as our numbers have grown, they have not outgrown the knowledge of this one man, slight of figure, with the silent, occupied manner of one who would avoid notice, whose eyes when they seek one out seize the body vaguely, but grapple with the soul."

Paragraph openings give the sense of the remainder of this long tribute: "Hence it is that we seldom think of him as one who has come down to us from a former generation . . . I speak as if Mr. Palmer had been made by an institution: such an assumption is strangely out of keeping with the impression of ruggedly independent personal power which he gives . . . Mr. Palmer's personal force, devoid as it is of self-assertion and bluster, a force wholly sublimated into power of thought and will, is neither overbearing nor overpersuading . . . The suggestion of finality in Mr. Palmer's speech is conveyed in part by perfection of form . . . To my mind, however, the great quality of Mr. Palmer's language is not its fitness nor its fluency, but its honorableness . . . It is this respect for precision which gave his lectures their memorable march, their absence of repetition, their freedom from the need of the clumsy draftsman to overlay one stroke with another for mutual correction . . . Yet it was Palmer who showed us James, securing his attachment to the philosophical staff at Harvard . . . This connoisseurship of life is in all of Mr. Palmer's deeds . . . What that [philosophical] position is, his students could not help sensing as a whole, for the order and system of his discourse left a mental initiation in its wake . . . One of these phrases which has become common coin, 'the glory of the imperfect,' epitomizes the central thought in Palmer's system . . . This philosophy Professor Palmer both believes and lives . . . It is commonly supposed that originality in philosophy implies the inauguration of a 'movement' or the founding of a 'school.' Mr. Palmer did neither of these things . . . Mr. Palmer's effect as a person and a teacher has been shaped by a deep trace of reticence . . . And in his teaching of ethics itself, this characteristic restraint has been always evident . . . So much, then, I dare say, Mr. Palmer has in common with the mystics, that he prefers to reveal indirectly rather than expressly the sources of his own strength . . . But there can be no doubt what those ultimate sources are . . . This may be due in part to the fact that our training is fragmentary — however the fragments may be distributed and balanced, the thing lacks wholeness . . . But Mr. Palmer remains the great teacher also in this, that he utters no complaints or despairing notes about this age. He see the possible glories of its imperfections, perhaps because he is consantly the giver, imputing everywhere something of his own nobility."

6 Charles Franklin Thwing, *Guides, Philosophers and Friends: Studies of College Men*, New York, Macmillan Co., 1927, 476 pages. Chapter XXII, George Herbert Palmer: Scholar, Teacher, Author, Interpreter of Homer.

Thwing, president emeritus of Western Reserve University and Adelbert College, writes in the preface that "each one of the twenty-two men considered I number among my personal friends. For them . . . I have a heart overflowing with fragrant and grateful memory. For them, if they still continue here, and only one does [George Herbert Palmer] my heart is a loving heart . . ." Each chapter is devoted to a college man, twelve of whom were college presidents. The "sketches . . . are concerned with the personal character and services of the subjects themselves. Yet, I venture to believe that they also may serve a bit to present some of the educational movements, to interpret some of the educational facts, and to intimate a few of the many educational problems, of the last half-century."

George Herbert Palmer was the only subject still living in 1927; the book is dedicated to him (**dedctdGHPann**-5), and the last and by far the longest chapter is about him (page 415–461). Near the end of the chapter, having quoted extensively from Professor Palmer's publications, Thwing writes that he "comes to certain conclusions which are indicated in various *dicta obiter* which are found scattered in [Palmer's] volumes. I am picking up some of these nuggets broken off from their surrounding mass. For they are, in their singleness even, weighty and precious in substance as they are discriminating and delicate in form [as seen in this selection of "nuggets"]:

> "Instruction must go all through. We are obliged to treat each little human being as a whole if we would have our treatment wholesome . . .
>
> "It is safest not to meddle much with the insides of our pupils. An occasional weighty word is more compulsive than frequent talk . . .
>
> "Something like what we mean must never be counted equivalent to what we mean. And if we are not sure of our meaning or of our word, we must pause until we are sure. Accuracy does not come of itself . . .
>
> "What stamps a man as great is not freedom from faults, but abundance of powers . . .
>
> "Let us make ourselves as large as possible, in order that we may contribute our little something to that to which all others are contributing . . .
>
> "The joy of perfecting is beyond the joy of perfection . . .
>
> "Where little money is, there often appears a kind of compensatory devotion . . .
>
> "Civilization rests upon dedicated lives, lives which acknowledge obligation not to themselves or to other single persons, but to the community, to science, to art, to a cause . . .
>
> "Delight in discovering difficulties is a good preservative against error.
>
> "Richness of character is as important as correctness. The world's benefactors have often been onesided and faulty men. None of us can be complete; and we had better not be much disturbed over the fact, but rather set ourselves to grow strong enough to carry off our defects."

7 A. Edward Newton, This Book-Collecting Game, *Atlantic Monthly*, 1926; 138 (December): 742–754.

See also **GHPann**-79

Newton describes an evening in Boston at the home of Miss

Amy Lowell when Professor Palmer was also a dinner guest: "That evening when Miss Lowell's motor called for us we found Professor Palmer ensconced therein, and I soon discovered that a fine bibliographical evening was in contemplation; for the dear old man had with him a green baize bag, such as Philadelphia lawyers used to carry, full of rare books to show to Miss Lowell, in exchange for which she was to show him her wonderful Keats collection, which is now one of the treasures of Harvard. There is a fine spirit of rivalry among collectors . . .

"Out of Mr. Palmer's green bag came one rare volume after another: Herrick, and Herbert, and Blake, and Milton; giants, housed in tiny volumes, one after another, all to be matched by Miss Lowell . . . Finally I said to Mr. Palmer, 'Let us see your [Richard] Lovelace *Lucasta* ; mine is in old sheep.' Out of the bag it came, but, unluckily, in a modern binding. 'I have you both there' said Miss Lowell, displaying, with glee, her copy of the rare little volume; 'look at the title-page.' We looked, and found thereon the inscription, 'Ex dono authoris .' It was as pretty a game of 'authors' as I have ever seen played, and the sport continued till after midnight, at which time it was agreed that I should witness a game of what might be called 'solitaire' as played by Mr. Palmer in his library next morning . . ." Newton goes on to describe his subsequent visit to Professor Palmer, "a past master in the art of book-collecting."

8 Ralph Barton Perry, *Palmer* (part of chapter 1, Philosophy, 1870–1929), in Samuel Eliot Morison, ed., *The Development of Harvard University: Since the Inauguration of President Eliot 1869–1929*, Cambridge, Harvard University Press, 1930, page 20–21 with a picture of George Herbert Palmer (a photograph of the Hopkinson portrait; 253n1).

Perry's whole piece is presented here: "The retirement of Gerge Herbert Palmer in 1913 was a serious loss to the Department. He was its senior member, most skilful teacher, and wisest counsellor. He had always taken a peculiar interest in the academic side of his vocation, in his relations with colleages and students, in the relations of the Department to the Faculty and Governing Boards, and in questions of policy within the Department itself. He felt a peculiar responsibility for the Department, nursed it during its infancy and growth, expected great things of it, and thought nothing too good for it. His teaching was remarkable, the more so in view of his physical disabilities. Always frail, he felt obliged to sit during his lectures; and being near-sighted, he could not recognize his students beyond the first few rows of the classroom. Philosophy 4, the course on Ethics which he gave from 1884 until the year of his retirement, was one of the most famous and popular courses in Harvard College. He was no less successful with his introductory course on the History of Philosophy, in which his remarkable lucidity of exposition and vividness of characterization held the attention of several hundred students.

"Although so largely absorbed in the life of Harvard College, Palmer exercised a wide influence throughout the country by his frequent visits to other colleges and his writings on educational subjects. In the early years of Eliot's administration he took a prominent part in the public controversy over the elective system [**GHP**-10 to 13]. Owing to his association with Alice Freeman Palmer he has always felt a special interest in Wellesley College and in the education of women. His essay on 'Self-cultivation in English' [**GHP**-34, 63] has become a classic among teachers and students of composition. His personal influence upon his colleagues and more advanced students has been due to his remarkable self-mastery, to the definiteness and consistency of his judgments, to the clarity and aptness of his speech — and to the range and balance of his culture. Translator of Homer [**GHP**-1 to 9] and Sophocles [**GHP**-37]; writer on Shakspere [**GHP**-72] and George Herbert [**GHP**-49 to 52, 68 to 70]; collector, lover, and reader of the English classics; he has known as have few men of his time how to temper learning with sensibility."

As an "advanced student" at Harvard, Perry himself had been helped by Professor Palmer (see page 181).

9 W. A. Macdonald, George Herbert Palmer at 90, Reminiscences of a great Harvard teacher, writer and philosopher — as some of his students recall him on this, his birthday, *Boston Transcript*, March 19, 1932.

The opening paragraph: "A fragile old man in overshoes and tightly buttoned overcoat came along Harvard Square to the corner of Massachusetts avenue and Holyoke street. As he paused on the icy footing the automobiles rushed by with hardly a break that would allow a young man time to get across the avenue. From behind the old man came an arm in blue, a traffic officer; it took the arm of George Herbert Palmer; the big young man and the small old one went forth into the avenue; the drivers of all cars paid heed, and the Alford professor of natural religion, moral philosophy and civil polity, emeritus, was safe on the Yard side and headed toward his home at 11 Quincy street.

"That was last week. Professor Palmer is ninety years old today. This week he has been seen ascending the rise of the Yard that leads to his house, walking alone. He often walks out that way, and only a little warmth of weather and he walks without the overcoat. Sometimes he is with his brother, Frederic. He walks slowly and uncertainly, blue eyes under heavy brows looking straight ahead, ragged moustache drooping. And one sometimes has the feeling that one knows him and should bow with a lift of the hat. For those ninety years stand for a strength that is greater than any man; they are a little part of an ideal that may yet transform the world."

The body of this long, newspaper piece is devoted to a review of Palmer's life, teaching, and writings.

Then, the final paragraph: "Thus he wrote. And one, passing him on the incline as he plods slowly and uncertainly up the slope under the weight of his ninety years is impelled to think of his full mind, his full life. And if a stranger, thus observing, is never seen to make a slight bow with lifted hat, it does not mean that the stranger has not that thought in mind."

10 Selma [Mrs. Hugo] Münsterberg, Old Memories, *Harvard Graduates' Magazine*, 1931–1932; 40 (June 1932): 331–344.

Mrs. Münsterberg recalls (page 339–340) how she and her husband "spent a never-forgotten happy day at George Herbert Palmer's summer home in Boxford. An early train brought us to the next station, either Salem or Danvers, I have forgotten which. There was our dear philosopher waiting, a perfect country gentleman, driving his little carriage. We drove through shady lanes, bordered by feathery elm trees, to his home, where Mrs. Palmer in a white-flowered dress looking like a flower herself, led us to a homelike guest room, to 'rest a little and shed the dust of the journey.' Then all of us meandered through

The Wood Choppers. Boxford, August 1921. *left*, Frederic Palmer, 73 years old; *right*, George Herbert Palmer, 79 years old.

fields and woods, Professor Palmer pointing here and there to irregular piles of cut wood explaining: 'That I cut yesterday. My brother and I will make a neat pile of it today!' It was a new experience to us: this frail, scholarly, philosopher turning an expert wood-cutter! But there he was, happy and smiling, the same Palmer as in Cambridge.

"After luncheon and coffee I had another surprise: 'I want to show you what my summer occupation is, as I do not chop wood,' said Mrs. Palmer, and she opened the door of a sunshiny pantry full of shelves with rows and rows and rows of jams and jellies, neatly labeled and fairly sparkling — 'This is my own *Handarbeit*.' The President of Wellesley, the director of so many young lives, busy with nation-wide problems — turning an efficient house-wife and cook in the given moment, and with such grace! How much our so-called '*gute Deutsche Hausfrau*' could learn from such an example."

11 Grace Hollingsworth Tucker, The Gods Serve Hebe, *Harvard Graduates' Magazine*, 1932–1933; 41 (June 1933): 207–229.

Tucker, Radcliffe College class of 1903, reminisces (page 223–225): "When a questionnaire asks, 'What course in college most influenced you?' I answer without hesitation, 'Philosophy 4,' which can mean to me only Professor George Herbert Palmer . . . No one may know him as we knew him. Truly our day was the day of intellectual gods at Harvard. We who should have borne the cup were guests at the unsparing feast they set before us.

"Philosophy 4 — Ethics — The study of right and wrong — was constructed with us. How well I recall the first lecture, our introduction to Professor Palmer and through him to the challenge of life. He was unfaltering in his creed, unflinching in his denouncements, unconquerable in his faith. His ethical code had the finality and the soundness of The Sermon on the Mount . . .

". . . Professor Palmer loved to read to us the simple goodness and rightness of George Herbert. But gently, surely, inevitably, by his vision of eternal verities, we wrote our own course, and with it moulded our own lives. The milestones he helped us to set along the road are still in our minds and hearts. The moral cross-roads are still marked for us. If we take the wrong turn now, we cannot plead a fog of uncertainty. He began his moral road-map with a very human preamble. He told us of the letters he received each year from mothers throughout the country, mothers whose boys were 'signed up' for Philosophy 4. Philosophy of any sort was to them a menace to religious faith. Had they not read of science laying bare the facts of things, stripping the veil from religion, calling it superstition? Could they, indeed, think with equanimity of the son who, followed by their prayers, would now become too wise, too cynical to pray?

"To each pleading mother Professor Palmer sent the same answer: 'I have for many years been a student and teacher of philosophy. I am not only a Churchman, I am a Trinitarian. My faith stands unshaken, secure, abiding.' Science annihilate religion? 'Said the wind to the moon, 'I will blow you out.'"

George Herbert Palmer died at home on May 7, 1933.

He had attended the chapel service on the previous Sunday, suffered a heart attack on Wednesday, and was then unconscious for the three days until his death at 12:30 A. M. on Sunday. Relatives were present when he died. As he had requested, he was cremated and his ashes were placed with those of his wife in the Alice Freeman Palmer Memorial in the Chapel at Wellesley College (Newspaper clipping, Wellesley College Archives. See 244n5 and frontispiece).

12 Robert Herrick, Death of a Puritan, *Nation*, 1933; 136 (May 31): 612–613.

See 97n4 for Herrick's relations with the Palmers, and see Palmer's article entitled The Puritan Home (**GHP**-92).

Herrick begins: "On the seventh of this May an old man died in Cambridge, Massachusetts, who was perhaps the last of his kind. A small company of grave elderly folk gathered in the big imitation of the New England meeting house that has replaced Appleton Chapel to honor this colleague, who more than anyone now living symbolized what Harvard College once was and no longer is, what New England and America once venerated and today jeer at — the Puritan. The entire life of this old man, whose years ran into the nineties, had been centered in Harvard College — as student, tutor, professor, overseer, and professor emeritus. The last third of his long life had been lived within the precincts of the Yard in an old wooden house that had formerly been the home of another Harvard worthy. During half a century his slight, drab person might have been seen any morning of the college year going across the college Yard to chapel. The Sunday before he died he attended morning service. After that day he never rose again from his bed, and thus completed the lifelong worship of his God."

Then the paragraph openings: "Education — of himself and of others — was to George Herbert Palmer the one supremely worth-while human function . . . So many foolish and defamatory and ignorant things have been said latterly about the Puritans that it is necessary to reiterate those traits of the real Puritan that characterized George Herbert Palmer . . . He loved travel and from his boyhood made many long journeys to different parts of the world, not solely for professional advantage but for culture in the older sense of the word . . .

And finally: "His vacation periods were passed on the place that his ancestors had reclaimed from the New England wilderness. There he would sit long laborious days at his table in the bare outdoors room where he worked, meditating the felicitously exact phrases that after much toil and revision composed his books, occasionally raising his shortsighted eyes to gaze over a green meadow to the fringes of pines beyond which rose the white steeple of the village meeting-house where his forefathers had worshiped, where he himself at times conducted the service. From work he might turn to reading aloud from some well-remembered classic — Homer, Sophocles, Milton, Browning, Shakespeare, Wordsworth, his own George Herbert. His taste in letters was catholic but aristocratic. Even when the blurred eyes no longer distinguished the printed symbols he would still hold a book and turn its pages, whose record echoed familiarly in his well-stored mind. All in all, there was a harmony, a serenity, a unity, in the life of this ancient Puritan that few in these days ever attain."

13 Margaret Sherwood, George Herbert Palmer, *Wellesley Magazine,* 1933; 17 (No. 5, June): 427–428.

Sherwood, Professor of English Literature at Wellesley College, begins: "For years since his presentation of his priceless collection of books illustrating the development of English Poetry to the Treasure Room of Wellesley College [**GHP**-79 and 93], Professor Palmer, as his loyal helper and custodian of the collection, Miss Lilla Weed, tells us, has been in the habit of slipping over from time to time from Cambridge, taking some rare book from his pocket to add to the gift. Then he would steal away as quietly to walk alone, despite his swiftly advancing years, across the back meadow to the station, as dignified, alert, as firm of step and of feature, as much a master of himself and of life as ever. Now his ashes have come to rest with those of his wife in an urn back of the Alice Freeman Palmer Memorial Relief in the Chapel" (see 244n5 and frontispiece).

Miss Sherwood goes on to describe many details of Palmer's life, his teaching, and his writings.

14 R. B. Perry, W. E. Hocking, C. I. Lewis, committee. The following minute on the life and services of Professor George Herbert Palmer, Alford Professor of Natural Religion, Moral Philosophy, and Civil Polity, *Emeritus*, was placed upon the records of the Faculty of Arts and Sciences, October 3, 1933. *Harvard University Gazette,* October 21, 1933, page 17–18.

"George Herbert Palmer died May 7, 1933, having passed by two months his ninety-first birthday. He had long been the oldest in years and in academic seniority on the list of Harvard officers of instruction. He retired from active instruction in 1913, twenty years ago, but he remained a familiar figure, continuing his residence in the Harvard Yard, and feeling a strong and hospitable interest in the ever-changing University at his door. He maintained close relations with the Department of Philosophy and Psychology, both as a representative of its legendary and heroic past and as a present counsellor and benefactor. After his retirement he served as Overseer for six years, and many successive Senior Classes chose him as leader of their final chapel service on Class Day . . .

"He was deeply concerned with the lives and careers of his students. Prevented by defective vision from recognizing them easily except at close range, he was led to emphasize such qualities as appeared in conversation and writing. These personal interests were never indiscriminate or democratic; his search was for quality of mind and character. The friendship he offered was never genial, easy, or profuse, but, while warm, observant and enduring, held its own dignity and reserve. Few have been so gifted in the capacity of reaching objective estimates of personal ability, including his own. It was a part of his rigorous self-discipline to maintain an element of realism in his judgments, and in view of his own belief that the imperfect had its peculiar glory, he was never inclined to ignore the defects and paradoxes of the character with which he dealt. It was in part owing to this relentless objectivity that he was so widely sought for as a counsellor in the placing of men. Toward himself he was equally rigorous; indeed it is in no small degree a secret of his success that he knew and respected his own limitations . . .

"He was not a lover of debate, in the form of conversational sparring, nor yet of learned controversy. He took no part in the American Philosophical Association. But he appreciated divergences of judgment, both in the constitution of the Harvard Department — it was his ideal that it should never become a 'school' — and in the minds of his own students . . .

Fifteen thousand Harvard students have passed through his classes, receiving the impact of his quietly energetic personality, with its distinguished human achievement of serenity, courtesy, self-control and inner force. Many of these students have carried away phrases and sentences of condensed wisdom — words which, as President Hyde of Bowdoin put it, 'continued to glow in the dark of the mind.' Though he had many readers and distant admirers, and was for many years a national figure, his fame was essentially a light which radiated from his study and his class-room. He was widely known and widely honored as one who exercised his own proper vocation with undeviating loyalty and rare perfection."

15 *George Herbert Palmer, 1842–1933: Memorial Addresses*, Cambridge, Harvard University Press, 1935, 80 pages.

Preface: "On December seventh, 1933, in the afternoon, a meeting in memory of Professor George Herbert Palmer was held in Room D of Emerson Hall under the auspices of the Department of Philosophy of Harvard University. For forty years (1872–1913) Professor Palmer had been connected with this Department as one of its creators. Emerson Hall itself, built to house the activties in philosophy, psychology, and social ethics, was largely due to his imagination and energy.

"At this meeting Professor Ralph Barton Perry, chairman of the Division of Philosophy and Psychology, presided. Addresses were given by Professor Charles M. Bakewell of Yale University [page 3–43, on Palmer's philosophy] and Professor William Ernest Hocking of Harvard University [page 47–65, on Palmer's personal traits]. These addresses are here reprinted, together with the Faculty Minute on the Life and Services of Professor Palmer [**aboutGHPann**-14]."

16 Frances Lee Panchaud, *George Herbert Palmer*, Thesis submitted in partial fulfillment of the requirements for the degree of Doctor of Philosophy in the School of Education of New York University, 1936, 117 pages, illustrated.

(Facsimile from a microfilm copy of the original dissertation, 73–3349 by Xerox University Microfilms, Ann Arbor, Michigan.)

Frances Lee Panchaud (1889–1962) prepared for Wellesley College at Westfield High School, Westfield, New Jersey, and received the B. A. degree with the class of 1909. After graduation she was a school teacher and principal, married Charles A. Panchaud in 1919, and received the M. A. degree in the Philosophy of Education from New York University in 1932 (Wellesley College Archives, 7B Alumnae Biographical Files).

The foreword: "Many years ago [1905], the writer entered Wellesley College as a freshman. In those days, the college was deeply imbued with the spirit of its former well-beloved president, Alice Freeman Palmer, who had recently died in Europe. The beautiful Daniel Chester French memorial tablet had been placed upon the chapel wall, and faced the transept in which sat the young freshman during morning devotion [244n5 and frontispiece]. Perhaps freshmen were more impressionable in those days, for the daily sight of that young, gracious figure leading her girls onward to new fields of learning and service was an inspiration that has lasted through the long years . . .

"Nowadays Alice Freeman is a memory to be proud of; but in our days she was a living spirit watching over her girls and loving them as always. She was as real to us as her actual presence could have been, with the additional lustrous patina given to a figure by time and tradition . . ."

Many years later "the same girl . . . doing graduate work at another university . . . turned to CONTEMPORARY AMERICAN PHILOSOSPHY [**GHP**-103] for a record of the life and work of Ernest Hocking. . . . there on the very first page was a dedication to George Herbert Palmer by his contemporary philosophers [**dedctdGHPann**-6], and farther on a picture of Professor Palmer himself. It was an interesting face, keen, intellectual and with a look of honest searching under heavy brows. The Wellesley woman exclaimed: 'Why, that's Alice Freeman's husband.' And from that moment she decided to find out just who George Herbert Palmer was and what he had accomplished since the days when he had gone out to Wellesley and taken away its president to grace his own home at Harvard."

Panchaud began with a preliminary study "to find out just what [Palmer's] position in the world of education was and to find out whether it justified intensive research . . . [She concluded] that Professor George Palmer was a sincere philosopher who lived his philosophy and taught it to others in so far as they were teachable . . . our research will be to find out what that philosophy was . . .

"Our conclusion [page 108] is that the world would be a better place if we developed more men of the Palmer type in it. Men who have a definite goal in mind, who are not swerved from the path by disappointments, who are willing to work hard to achieve their chosen ends. We need to train children to discipline themselves as Palmer disciplined himself. We must teach them that hard work is the secret to any real success and that the only prizes worth while are the things we have honestly earned by our own efforts. Too much emphasis is put upon material possessions today. We could all be happier with much less. Too much is done for young people today. They have none of the fun of simple things.

"As Palmer noted years ago, the break-up of the American home is responsible for much of the discontent and unrest in the world today. Quiet home amusements seem dull to the modern child. He must always be dashing about the country with other young things of like tastes. We might well revive interest in our homes and try to recapture its prestige as an amusement center. Family life is still the best stabilizer for growing youth."

On page 110, Panchaud presents her sonnet to George Herbert Palmer.

17 Rollo Walter Brown, *Harvard Yard in the Golden Age*, New York, Current Books, Inc., 1948, 208 pages.

Page 48–49: "George Herbert Palmer's repute among students just at that time was based even less [than that of William James] on circumstances related to systematic philosophies. He, a middle-aged professor at Harvard, and for many years a widower, had bravely penetrated the sylvan fastnesses of the Wellesley campus and captured the young president and brought her to Cambridge and the Harvard Yard for keeps. To Harvard undergraduates there was something unbelievably poetic about a woman's giving up the presidency of Wellesley in order to become the wife of a professor at Harvard. And now after she had endeared herself to three or four college generations at Harvard, just as she had endeared herself to the girls at Wellesley, and after she had in many ways outshone her distinguished husband in the brilliance of her achievements — always much to his delight — she had suddenly died. Students who had gone to the spreading yellow house on Quincy Street therefore were inclined to make understated references to him as a romantic variant in the academic life.

"He was a queer little figure as he crossed the Yard, his great mustache too heavy for the size of his face, his friendly but tired-looking eyes peering from deep beneath shaggy brows, a suggestion of his fine forehead showing beneath his anomalous little hat. But students smiled appreciatively when he spoke to them — as was his wont — and were glad that he was around."

Section entitled Philosophic Lover (page 67–74). Brown's recollections of Professor Palmer are "touched by a very personal relation . . . [C]ircumstances [he says] led me for the rest of his life to look upon him as a kind of benevolent third grandfather." Some excerpts follow:

> "On a pleasant side piazza [in Boxford] where there was a writer's table with some sheets of paper on it, he told me once again what he had often told me before — that he did not like to write, but felt that he must, since he had something he wished to say. He went into great detail. 'I have never overstated the case when I have said that I always hated to face a sheet of white paper. Right here at this table I have had the experience hundreds of times. But I have a pretty well-disciplined mind, and after I have driven myself through the first page I am quite content to go along until I have done my stint for the morning.'
>
> "Over one fireplace there was a bust of Alice Freeman Palmer; and not far away, a tablet bearing some lines of hers. In the pew of the village church where we sat with

> him on Sunday, there was another tiny tablet. He saw that I had noticed these evidences of great devotion everywhere, and said, smiling profoundly, 'You see, we made our contribution to solving the divorce problem . . . '
>
> "Scores of boys and girls of slender means — or of none at all — owe their college education to Professor Palmer. He had a list of men and women of financial standing who did not wish to be pursued by the hired representatives of causes, yet who were generous. Whenever he learned of a superior boy or girl who was without funds, he turned to one of the men or women in his list, and the problem was solved [see 144n1] . . .
>
> "As he kept adding years and years to his life, he became a familiar — yet often unknown — figure in the region of Harvard Square. Sometimes he became a matter of serious concern. 'That damned old bird,' said the policeman at the Square one morning when Professor Palmer was pushing through the traffic, 'makes more trouble for me than any twenty people who cross the Square.' At times, some former student walked protectingly with him . . ."

And Brown ends his piece: "When he was the last of his generation — thirty years after the death of Alice Freeman Palmer — he sat in the spreading yellow house on Quincy Street and reread books that had unfailing value. When he could no longer read he had the nurse read to him. 'Let's have some more of *The Odyssey*,' and he would tell her just where in his translation. 'Read that.' He listened, his face alight, his great shaggy brows standing high. 'That's good! That's good! Read that again!' Who had anything to propose that was better than keeping in the presence of the great?"

18 Walter I. Trattner, *Homer Folks* [1867–1963]*: Pioneer in Social Welfare*, New York, Columbia University Press, 1968, page 13.

"George Herbert Palmer, professor of philosophy at Harvard, was another long-lasting, constructive influence. Palmer's course on ethics, known at Philosophy 4, was officially announced as 'A Theory of Ethics Considered Constructively-Lectures, Theses, and Private Reading.' This course, which Palmer taught to Harvard students for more than twenty-five years, was devoted not to metaphysics and epistemology, but to a critical analysis of human conduct. Palmer, who liked to refer to himself as a 'moderate idealist,' taught that morality had no meaning apart from society, a society whose claims were paramount. Man is essentially a social being and a single isolated individual is an empty fiction, wholly abstract and unreal. The real man is only he who stands in living relationship with his fellows. Self-sacrifice, then, for Palmer, was simply the effective affirmation of the supreme worth of selfhood, and was, therefore, the highest form of rationality. Service to the social and infinite self became, by definition, virtue. It was also the supreme principle of rationality in the realm of deeds, for it brought order out of the chaos of conflicting aims. At his death it was agreed that 'Palmer's chief contributions were written in the souls of men, wrought in the lives of the thousands of students whose eyes he opened to the meaning and the possibilities of life.' George Herbert Palmer could, without doubt, list Folks as one among those thousands."

Chapter 9

Books dedicated to George Herbert Palmer, annotated

identified as **dedctdGHPann**-number

1 Theodore C. Williams, *The Æneid of Virgil* (**GHP**-66)

To George Herbert Palmer

I hear thy accent when I read
The change-and-time-defying creed
of Shakespeare's youth; or when divine
Odysseus pleads in words of thine;
Through thee our England's laureled choir
Breathed o'er my youth their generous fire:
And now these strains of Virgil's song
Not less to thee than him belong.

2 Hugo Münsterberg, *Psychology and the Teacher*, New York, D. Appelton & Co., 1909.

To
George Herbert Palmer
In Gratitude

Professor Palmer gave Wellesley College Special Collections a presentation copy of this book, inscribed under the dedication: Hugo Münsterberg Harvard University October 15, 1909.

3 Frederic Palmer, *The Winning of Immortality*, New York, Thomas Y. Crowell & Co., 1910.

To
G. H. P.
Who Has
Interpreted, Endowed, Irradiated,
Ennobled Life,
This Study of Life is Dedicated

4 Frederic Palmer and Mary Palmer, *Poems*, Boston, Houghton Mifflin Co., 1912.

To George Herbert Palmer

Ever the Leader ! since we pushed from shore
In daring voyage across the Boxford Pond,
And I looked up, and thought what lay beyond
Your vast omniscience God still held in store.

I heard, through Poetry's Garden led by you,
The clash of Arthur's knights; the dreary call
Of curlews flying over Locksley Hall,
And the cold silence of the Church of Brou.

And as we walked where men of Thought had trod,
You cleared the way; and lo ! beneath my feet
The ground grew firm, and I pressed on to greet,
Confident, unabashed, the face of God.

So close we dwelt, we hardly stood apart.
Before one spoke, subtly the other heard,
As hand serves hand without the need of word
In quick response, as pulse keeps touch with heart.

Now at the restful gate of Age you stand.
Shall I, outstripping you for once, press past,
And so become the leader at the last,
And turn and thence reach back to you a hand?

Or shall you still be foremost? in the throng
Of swift-winged angels speeding far and near
On God's bright ministrations, there as here
Still foremost, guiding, loving, generous strong !

Frederic Palmer died first, twenty years later, on July 4, 1932, at the age of 83 years. George Herbert Palmer died on May 7, 1933, age 91.

5 Charles F. Thwing, *Guides, Philosophers and Friends, Studies of College Men*, (**aboutGHPann**-6)

To
George Herbert Palmer
Scholar, Teacher, Author,
Interpreter of Homer,
This Volume is Dedicated
in Gratitude and Affection

6 *Contemporary American Philosophy* (**GHP**-103)

These Essays are
Affectionately Dedicated to
George Herbert Palmer
The Friend and Teacher
Of So Many American Philosophers

Professor Palmer's portrait is the frontispiece for volume I.

Introduction

George Herbert Palmer and Houghton Mifflin Company

For forty-seven years, most of George Herbert Palmer's books and articles were published by Houghton Mifflin Company in Boston, Massachusetts, and were printed at its Riverside Press. His first publication was a book, *The Odyssey of Homer*, in 1884 when he was forty-two years old; the last, an article, On Growing Old, in 1931 when he was eighty-nine.

There were twenty-five books and fourteen articles. Three books were published in more than one edition: *The Odyssey of Homer*, *The English Works of George Herbert*, and *The Life of Alice Freeman Palmer*. Some of the books were included in special series: the Riverside Literature Series, Riverside Education Monographs, and the Riverside Uplift Series. Others were privately printed by the Riverside Press, and Professor Palmer, not Houghton Mifflin Company, arranged the payment.

The articles appeared in three periodicals published by Houghton Mifflin: ten in *The Atlantic Monthly*; three in *The Andover Review*; and one in *Appalachia*, the Journal of the Appalachian Mountain Club.

In 1905–1906, *A Portrait Catalogue* of Houghton, Mifflin and Company included a picture and autograph of George Herbert Palmer.

A number of Palmer's books are examples of fine bookmaking. At least three were designed by Bruce Rogers (1870–1957), a "typographic genius of his time," who worked at the Riverside Press from 1895 to 1911. Two of the three were included in an exhibition of Rogers' work: *A Memorial Service for Alice Freeman Palmer* (**GHP-**44) and the large-paper edition of the *English Works of George Herbert* (**GHP**-51). The third is *The Life of Alice Freeman Palmer* (**GHP**-57); in the numerous printings of the original edition, the Houghton Mifflin emblem on the title page includes a drawing of Rogers' distinctive mark, a thistle. The exhibit also showed the bookplate that Rogers drew for George Herbert Palmer in 1904.

(Sources: *The Work of Bruce Rogers Jack of All Trades: Master of One*. A catalogue of an exhibition arranged by the American Institute of Graphic Arts and the Grolier Club of New York. New York, Oxford University Press, 1939, #98, #125, #465. Ellen B. Ballou, *The Building of the House: Houghton Mifflin's Formative Years*, Boston, Houghton Mifflin Co., 1970, page 528–538. Thistle: Bruce Rogers et al, *BR Marks & Remarks,* New York, The Typophiles, 1946. Bookplate: entry on page 227; 227n1; and picture on page 229).

The compiler selected and transcribed, in whole or in part, seventy-six letters from a collection of correspondence between George Herbert Palmer and Houghton Mifflin Company, at Harvard University in the Houghton Library (bMS AM 1925–1356). Twelve folders hold 136 letters [**GHP**], handwritten between 1884 and 1928, from Palmer to Houghton Mifflin, and 132 letters [**HMCo.**], largely in the form of carbon copies between 1914 and 1928, from Houghton Mifflin to him. Misspellings, such as "questionaire," have been left unchanged. Professor Palmer often wrote on letterheads, such as, "11 Quincy Street Cambridge," his home; "Gull Pond Wellfleet" on Cape Cod, where he often visited a family cottage; and "Hotel Cloyne Court" where he stayed on his trips to Berkeley, California.

Horace Elisha Scudder, whose name appears in the correspondence, was editor of the *Atlantic Monthly* from 1890 to 1897, an early member of the publishing firm, and an active member of Houghton Mifflin's editorial department until his death in 1902 (*A Portrait Catalogue*, page xiii).

Chapter 10

George Herbert Palmer and Houghton Mifflin Company

The Odyssey of Homer
GHP-1 to 8

Professor Palmer's first book, published in 1884 by Houghton Mifflin Company, was his translation of Books 1–12 of the Odyssey, with the Greek text and his English version on facing pages.

May 30, [ca.1890] GHP to H. E. Scudder (folder 1 in Collected Letters)

"Would Houghton Mifflin & Co be disposed to complete my Odyssey?

"At the time when my first volume was issued I did not intend to publish more. But this year I have read to College Classes B'ks 19–24, and the Greek Department now press me so strongly to read the remaining six B'ks 13–18, that I have consented to do so next year. I shall accordingly have a manuscript of the whole last half of the Odyssey, & prepared with such care that it could go into print with half the care we were obliged to exercise in our previous venture. There w'd be no need now of sending proofs to critics. I could submit all my copy in type writer's print, & the resulting text would vary but little from my copy. One third of the alterations we had before I am sure would be quite sufficient.

"My proposition w'd be this:— that your house sometime within a year sh'd issue volume two in precisely the same style as vol. one, gaining for yourselves by that means a fresh opportunity to work off copies of the old volume; that then, after that year or two of sale in which the book will probably run its course, you sh'd reissue the whole text in a single small volume without the Greek text, allowing me to revise the two parts so as to bring them into closer accord. Naturally my recent work shows considerable improvement on my earlier in point of style, & the two c'd scarcely be printed in the same volume without readjustment.

"This is the plan I like best. It is obviously best for me, & I sh'd suppose it best for you. Any other w'd sacrifice at once the plates you now own. But if you do not care to be at the expense of setting up a new volume of Greek type in order to make a sale of the old, I will propose another plan, a second best.

"If you will reset the English type of my first volume, & so give me the opportunity of revising it throughout, we will issue a single volume of English text alone, convenient in size for either literary or school use. That such a book w'd sell well seems to me evident from the success of Butcher & Lang's version, a book harsh & repellent in literary ways, but the only prose translation besides my own now in the market.

"The sale of mine must have been greatly hindered by the fact that it is only half a book. Either of these plans I propose will turn it into a whole one."

After a decision to implement Palmer's "second best" plan, letters to Houghton Mifflin Company on January 22 and 26, 1891, deal with corrections for the "galley slips." (folder 1)

February 1, 1891 GHP to HMCo. (folder 1)

The book is now in page proofs and he would like to change a phrase that appears on pages 223, line 1 and 305, line 9: from "serve a different" to "support man after." He points out that the number of letters would be the same. Then he writes: "If the plate can be amended at an expense of not more than $1.00, I should be glad to have the form I now propose inserted in both texts. But if change would cost more than this, let both pages remain as at present."

The final pages include the change.

February 15, 1891 GHP to HMCo. (folder 1)

"Within a few days the last proof of my Odyssey will reach me, & I must then decide what to do in regard to a Preface. The natural thing to do would be to recast the Preface to my former volume; since that contains a history of the growth of my ideas & a full discussion of my peculiar purposes. That the reviewers should understand these easily, seems essential if the hurried writers of book notices are to treat my translation as that which I conceive it to be — a piece of literature — and not as a school book. There is, however, one objection to repeating that Preface: to do so might damage the integrity of the former volume & perhaps check its sale. I should be glad to keep the two books independent, & so let any success of the one assist that of the other.

"Might not some such arrangement as this be judicious? Supposing I write a new brief Preface for the new book, would you be willing to strike off copies of the old Preface & send them out with the volumes given to reviewers; accompanying them with a brief note, saying that in this Preface to a former volume (full title and date given) I had discussed at length the history principles & methods of my work? Reviewers would then be instructed what to say; both the old & the new book would receive an inexpensive advertisement; each would remain complete in itself; & in each might afterwards be placed a fly-leaf announcing the other as prepared by the same author.

"As soon as convenient I should like to learn your views in regard to this matter. If the plan commends itself to you, I will at once prepare a brief & pointed Preface to the new book, for appeal to the general public; leaving you to supply the more detailed explanation to the reviewers."

The preface to the new volume (**GHP**-2) is slightly more than one page long; that of the first volume (**GHP**-1), fourteen pages.

July 12, 1891 GHP to HMCo. (folder 1)

"If you think it wise, I am entirely willing to have the School Edition of my Odyssey (**GHP**-3) delayed for a year in the hope of extending the sale of the one already issued. Of course the book can never compete favorably with Butcher & Lang until it is sold at the same price; but perhaps special efforts in advertisement may overcome this hindrance for a time. At any rate, I shall accept your judgment in the matter, & shall be glad to see your circular to teachers."

In 1888 the Butcher and Lang translation sold for $1.50 (I am grateful to Richard A. Linenthal for this information from Macmillan, London). Palmer's 1891 publication also sold for $1.50.

October 21, 1914 HMCo. to GHP. (folder 8)

"We are sending you a pamphlet containing questions on your translation of the Odyssey. The author of this pamphlet who is an instructor in English in the Helena Montana High School has asked us to consider publishing the pamphlet. Before giving our decision, we should appreciate very much having your opinion of the quality of the work in this pamphlet. We, of course, should not wish to publish it if it is not an entirely creditable aid to the teaching of the book. Whereas, if, in your judgment, it is sufficiently well done to assist teachers without training and experience to use the book with more satisfactory results in their classes, it may be well for us to consider making it available.

"We hope that we shall not be imposing upon you too heavy a burden in making this request."

October 24, 1914 GHP to HMCo. (folder 2)

"The questionaire on the Odyssey strikes me as exceptionally good. It is of course addressed to young persons, but there are comparatively few questions in it which would not command the respect of grown persons. Managed by a judicious teacher, it would give the pupil a sensible & exact knowledge of the Odyssey such as few readers gain.

"I do not think it would be wise to print these questions at the close of my book. They would make it too exclusively a school book. But it would be well to print them as an accompanying pamphlet, particularly if this would be furnished free to schools in which the book is used. Many teachers would feel these questions to be such an advantage that the book would gain entrance to schools which it would otherwise miss. They might be a make-weight in deciding between my translation & Butcher & Lang's.

"But I am sure these considerations have occurred to you. I can only say that if questions are to be prepared, they can hardly be better done."

October 26, 1914 HMCo. to GHP. (folder 8)

" . . . Referring to the question of using the questionaire on the Odyssey let me say that we did not have it in mind to include this in the regular $1.00 Edition of the Odyssey, which sells to the general trade, but only in the exclusively school-book edition in the Riverside Literature series. As we now have two editions so nearly equal in price, we do not think that there is much demand for the Riverside Literature outside of the schools and we believe that if the questionaire is to be used, it ought to be found in the book, itself. In reconsidering the matter, we think that you will agree with us. We should like to have your confirmation of this before we go ahead. Will you also kindly return the pamphlet, as we have no other copy of it."

The editions in the Riverside Literature Series (**GHP**-4 and 5) have a fourteen page section entitled Outline, Questions, and Suggestions, by Clarence E. Ackley, Instructor in English, Manual Training High School, Louisville, Kentucky.

January 8, 1916 HMCo. to GHP. (folder 4)

An inconsistent spelling of a name in *The Odyssey* has been brought to their attention: Melanthius in some places, Melantheus in others. Webster's Collegiate Dictionary gives Melanthius. What does Professor Palmer think should be done?

January 18, 1916 GHP to HMCo. (folder 4)

"The twofold forms of this name in my Odyssey is not a typographical error but the result of a possibly unreasonable desire for accuracy. Homer himself has two forms, sometimes in successive lines. I followed him with precision. I am inclined to think, however, that such minuteness in a book intended for English readers is undesirable, especially in a book largely used by the young. I see no objection, therefore, to your printing 'Melanthius' everywhere — if you desire to do so."

January 24, 1916 HMCo. to GHP. (folder 9)

"Since you give us the authority of Homer's official stenographer (!) for the two spellings of 'Melanthius,' we are quite content to let it remain as it is in your 'Odyssey.' It has gone unquestioned for so long that it seems a pity to sacrifice your careful accuracy and patch our good plates to satisfy a modern zeal for standardization. We shall therefore make no change in the book."

April 8, 1916 GHP to HMCo. (folder 4)

"I have come across a curious misprint in my Odyssey. In the Introduction, p. xxvi, l. 13, 'Spencerian' should be 'Spenserian.' As it stands, Herbert Spencer would seem to have invented this stanza, not Edmund Spenser. How I could have passed by such a blunder so long is incomprehensible . . . "

The misprint appears in the 1884 publication (**GHP**-1). The regular 1891 edition (**GHP**-2) does not include the long Introduction, but the School Edition (**GHP**-3) does, and the misprint is still present. A copy of the Riverside Literature Series edition, copyrighted in 1921 (**GHP**-5), however, has the Introduction, now dated July 16, 1897, and the misprint has been corrected.

April 3, 1918 HMCo. to GHP. (folder 5)

High school teachers using the School edition of *The Odyssey* (**GHP**-3) would like to have some changes: "a compendium of mythological characters . . . further explanations of the hyphenated adjectives . . . [more adequate] notes on the classical illusions . . . [and] full notes on the Trojan War."

after April 3, 1918 GHP to HMCo. (folder 5)

"This is a project which has no interest for me. It is an example of that stupid mechanism that is the teacher's besetting sin. What does it matter what the dictionaries say about Hermes or Menelaus? Let the scholars learn about those gentlemen from the text. It is just because I have my translation a book of living interest & not an antiquarian document that it differs favorably from the other translations. I was annoyed when the teachers obliged me to put into it a list of pronunciations and a map of the wanderings of Odysseus. Further I will not go. My Introduction furnishes all that a sensible human being needs. I must retain a fragment of poetry & fairy-land."

In Boxford, on July 29, 1920, Professor Palmer wrote A Retrospect for an edition of *The Odyssey* in the Riverside Literature Series. About the changes that have been made over the years, he wrote: "At intervals . . . to meet the supposed needs of schools, additions have been made: by myself, a long historical and critical Introduction; by the publishers, a Pronouncing Vocabulary of Proper Names, a series of Questions calculated to stimulate the pupil to think about what he has read, and a mythical Map of the Wanderings of Odysseus, to curb thought and give school-teachers the comfort of certainty on matters about which the rest of the world is content to remain in romantic ignorance."

September 1923 GHP to HMCo. (folder 6)

"I shall be glad to see the illustrator of my Odyssey whenever now he is able to make an appointment with me.

"I must ask that this old text of my Odyssey be stopped from further circulation. It is exasperating to find that years after I spent a summer rewriting my translation at your request, that this inferior rendering is still circulated. I expressly struck out the words 'School Edition' & substituted 'Revised Edition,' because I wished no other to be on the market. If it is thought desirable to have a larger sized edition, & a somewhat handsomer one, on sale also, the new text can be used for it. The size of the text page is the same.

"But I cannot sanction any further printing of the old version."

The first sentence in Book 1 immediately distinguishes different versions. In the revised version: "Tell of the storm-tossed man, O Muse, who wandered long after he sacked the sacred citadel of Troy." The earlier, "old," version, however, was used for the Wyeth edition: "Speak to me, Muse, of the adventurous man who wandered long after he sacked the sacred citadel of Troy." And in Palmer's first published translation, in 1884: "Tell me, O Muse, of an adventurous man who wandered far, when he had overthrown the sacred hold of Troy."

September 21, 1923 HMCo. to GHP. (folder 10)

" . . . As you know, the General Department has been interested for several years in the prospect of issuing a beautifully illustrated edition of your translation of the ODYSSEY, the pictures to be drawn by Mr. Wyeth. We hope that something can be done this winter toward this project. We would like to bring you and Mr. Wyeth together for this purpose as soon as may be mutually convenient."

September 6, 1924 GHP to HMCo. (folder 6)

"I went round to the First National Bank & saw Mr Wyeth's spirited designs. They fit in with all that splendor admirably. The Clipper Ship — with which I was not familiar — pleased my especially.

"Would it not be well for him to offer his Odyssey series to one of the great Classical schools — Andover, Exeter, Lawrenceville Groton? These schools are always building & have many rich graduates ready to subscribe for anything that will bring honor to the happy place of their boyhood . . . "

June 1, 1925 HMCo. to GHP. (folder 11)

"Mr. Wyeth the artist, called to see me to-day and I think that before long he will probably start his work on THE ODYSSEY.

"It is clear that the expenses both of securing his drawings and later of reproducing them after they are finished will be very great. Would it be possible for us to have a talk sometime in regard to the financial aspects of this new edition so that we may know what your wishes are? . . . "

June 4, 1925 GHP to HMCo. (folder 6)

"My interest in the Wyeth Edition of my Odyssey is in its circulation rather than in any financial profit. I am anxious too to have Mr Wyeth derive from his venture a suitable compensation. So I will accept a royalty of ten and eight tenths cents on each copy of his book, the same as for the cloth bound Riverside Edition of my own . . . "

July 22, 1925 HMCo. to GHP. (folder 11)

"You will be interested to know that Mr. Wyeth has made a call on me . . . and that the arrangements and terms are practically settled with him, as with you, for the publication of the ODYSSEY.

"In his letter to me today he says 'I am enjoying the Odyssey with a new enthusiasm. The reading of it within earshot of the pounding seas is even more exciting than to listen to Dvorak's New World Symphony' . . . "

December 1927, GHP to HMCo. (folder 7)

"I am delighted that the artist is now giving himself steadily to his work. For me speed is a matter of importance. I am now in my 86th year & naturally can't go on more than a year of two longer. I ought to see & criticize these designs before they are published."

Professor Palmer lived until his 91st year; he died on May 7, 1933.

November 30, 1928 HMCo. to GHP. (folder 7)

"I think you will be interested in knowing we have just had a telegram from the artist, Wyeth, to the effect that he will start the illustrations for the ODYSSEY in a month's time with the expectation that the drawings will be ready so that the book may be published next fall."

December 1, 1928 GHP to HMCo. (folder 7)

"Amusing ! I believe this is the fourth time he was to begin his work in about a month."

May 1, 1929 GHP to HMCo. (copied from a facsimile in **GHP**-7)

"I am glad that you are publishing a quarto edition of the Odyssey, and especially that you are having it illustrated by Wyeth. No one has entered more deeply into the heart of the Odyssey than he.

"For forty years the Odyssey has been an important factor in my life. But in 1870, when I read it with a class, I was shocked to find them giving more attention to its words and its grammar than to its poetry. In 1875, therefore, I changed my plan. I asked as many as cared to come to meet me in Holden Chapel where I would supply them with the Greek texts and translate so simply that no one would have difficulty in following. To my surprise a roomful gathered and seemed to feel much of Homer's magic. On successive evenings I read them the entire story. Attempting in later years to simplify my rendering and rid it of unnatural language, I rewrote it from cover to cover thirteen times.

"Mr. Wyeth will have a surer means for conveying the enchanting legend to eager ears. Those who inspect his drawings will swiftly feel what words report more slowly."

The New Education, Three Papers
GHP-13

February 7, 1887 GHP to HMCo. (folder 1)

Professor Palmer is interested in publication of a book to combine his three papers on education that have appeared in the Andover Review. He proposes to add a preface and to "claim no royalty." He thinks that Houghton Mifflin, publisher of this periodical, has the papers printed in "small 8vo or 12mo" and that the collection would make a "little vol of, say, 100 pps."

Palmer goes on: "There are continually applications for them, & discussion is still going on in the public prints . . . Pres. Eliot . . . said to me it w'd be a great benefit to the University to have these in permanently accessible form. Mr Norton made the same remark today. Though in form the papers deal directly with the Harvard Education, the problems involved are those which almost every college in the country now finds itself obliged to grapple with. It seems to me that if the book c'd be put out this spring, it w'd find a ready sale now & during the summer vacation."

The abbreviations, 8vo and 12mo, refer to octavo and twelvemo sizes — 8 or 12 leaves, respectively, from one large sheet of paper. Octavo, that is 8vo, gives a book of about 6x9 inches; twelvemo, that is 12mo, of about 5x7 inches.

April 4, 1887 GHP to HMCo. (folder 1)

Palmer writes that the editors of the Andover Review have given permission to publish the three articles in book form, and he also needs permission from Houghton Mifflin Company.

The book of 154 pages was published by Little, Brown, and Company in the spring of 1887; the preface is dated February 21, 1887, the thirty-second birthday of Professor Palmer's fiancée, Alice Elvira Freeman, President of Wellesley College.

Reminiscences of Professor Sophocles
GHP-16

Near the beginning of this article in the *Atlantic Monthly*, Professor Palmer writes: "Now that the decent interval after death is passed [more than eight years], a memorial to this unusual man may be reverently set up. His likeness may be drawn by a fond, though faithful hand. Or at least such stories about him may be kindly put into the record of print as will reflect some of those rugged, paradoxical, witty, and benignant aspects of his nature which marked him off from the humdrum herd of men."

March 22, 1891 GHP to H. E. Scudder. (folder 1)

"I have the anecdote I was in search of; or rather I have found fragments of it in different places & these I have 'edited.' The sheet which I send will be interpolated into the vacant space left — I believe — on p. 13. I suppose it will be easier to set it up now for the galley-slip, rather than to let me keep it & see it first in type in the page-proof.

"I think it w'd be easy to add other excellent stories to those I have already told. If when your galley-proof is sent me I should read it to a little group of Sophocles connoisseurs I do not doubt that their many memories would be stirred & that I might add some treasures to my store. But they might not fit with my design; & you might not care to lengthen or disturb your present article."

Field of Ethics
GHP-40

January 2, 1902 GHP to HMCo. (folder 1)

"I am afraid there is no end to my blundering. On p. 196, l. 8 from the bottom, of my 'Field of Ethics' I find that 'Etrocles' has slipped in instead of 'Polynices.' The blunder is peculiarly bad since I had myself translated the Antigone. This too I will ask you to have corrected in the plate, at my expense. The name should read 'Polynices.'"

To illustrate a point in chapter 5, on Ethics and Religion, Professor Palmer uses a scene from The Antigone of Sophocles. The blunder is in this sentence: "King Creon has issued an edict that under penalty of death no one shall bury the traitor Etrocles who has fallen in an attack on his native city, Thebes." The traitor was not Etrocles but his brother, Polynices.

The Nature of Goodness
GHP-46

August 12, 1904 GHP to HMCo. (folder 1)

"I received an inquiry today from an English teacher asking where in London my 'Nature of Goodness' could be procured if it was wanted as a text book. What shall I tell him? Who is your London agent?"

Houghton Mifflin's *Portrait Catalogue* for 1905–1906 (page xiv) provides the answer: Messrs. Archibald Constable and Company Ltd.

The Life of Alice Freeman Palmer
GHP-57 to 62

April 11, 1908 GHP to HMCo. (folder 2)

"Would it be possible to use most of the copies of my book which have the illustrations wrongly placed for the English order?

"Persons in England are less likely to be acquainted with Mrs. Palmer than those here, & we should in this way avoid much of the confusion caused by divergent copies here."

The first edition has ten illustrations, with the "Last Portrait" of Alice Freeman Palmer as the frontispiece, and her "Portrait in 1892" near the end of the book. Starting with the second "impression" (i.e., printing), the positions of the two portraits are exchanged.

April 22, 1908 GHP to HMCo. (folder 2)

"Thank you for sending me these encouraging English accounts, & also the news of the book's progress in Boston. I am receiving a multitude of enthusiastic letters."

April 27, 1908 GHP to HMCo. (folder 2)

" . . . Just as I was leaving your office this morning something was said which has disturbed me all day. I hope I misunderstood, but it seemed to be stated that my book had been published as a 'Special.' That would mean that the ordinary book seller would not keep it in stock, & that only those persons who had definitely decided that they wished it & would take the trouble to wait [for] it on an order would obtain it. This, I see, is an altogether wise method of issuing a book of limited appeal. But it precisely defeats my purpose. I wrote the book for wide circulation; stripped it, accordingly, of the usual characteristics of the regular Life & Letters; turned it so far as possible into a work of literature, & studied how it could be made to appeal to all classes of the community alike. That even now, with this heavy handicap of not being found on the counters of the book shop, it will slowly make its way into steady sale I am inclined to believe; but it will not stand on the same footing with other books, nor have the same chance to win people's attention as they. In spite of my strong attachment to your house, I should have turned elsewhere if I had had any idea that this was the mode of publication intended. That I should naturally have been informed before so important a step was taken makes me still hope that I have been misinformed. If it has been taken, I must ascribe it to a fundamental difference in our views of the aim of the book. You might naturally enough have conceived it as having something of the character of a private memorial — for which such 'special' publication would be altogether appropriate; while I have been laboring to remove every suspicion of that character from the book. I cannot help feeling a sharp disappointment at not discovering in time that you thought it unwise to accept my aims."

October 21, 1918 GHP to HMCo. (folder 5)

"I sign and return this contract [for Formative Types in English Poetry, **GHP**-88], though I am not sure that the last line of the first page expresses our present practice. By a special arrangement the payment of royalty on my books is now not deferred till four months after the statement, but paid at once. At the time of the publication of Mrs Palmer's Life a letter was sent to me to this effect."

The Teacher
GHP-65

July 24, 1924 HMCo. to GHP. (folder 10)

"We have recently been considering the advisability of reprinting your volume entitled THE TEACHER [published in 1908], the stock of which is at present down to five copies. The record of our sale, and the high cost necessitated by the manufacture of a small edition have led us to the unfortunate decision that it would be inadvisable for us to do so.

"In looking at our record we find that the sales for the last three years are as follows:

1921–31
1922–33
1923–58

"It is customary for us to consider the average sale for the last three years as an indication of the probable demand for the coming year. In the case of this title, unfortunately, the number is so low that it does not seem wise for us to reprint.

"You probably know that the cost of printing small editions has increased very materially during the past few years and the minimum edition which it has been found possible to print is 270 copies. It has also been ascertained that it is unwise for a publishing house to provide in advance for more than three years' supply. In the case of THE TEACHER the average sale according to our statistics would be 40 copies whereas the sale should be 90 copies in order to give us a reasonable leeway.

"In addition to these points, the cost of printing and binding 270 copies of THE TEACHER would necessitate our raising the list price [from $1.50] to at least $2.50 which we feel is somewhat excessive considering the size of the book.

"Under these circumstances we are reluctantly forced to drop the title from our list as soon as the copies now in stock are sold."

Trades and Professions
GHP-76

On October 22, 1914, Professor Palmer delivered an address before the University of the State of New York at its 50th annual convocation in Albany. In the Chronicles (page 271) he entered the title of the address as "Prfssion."

October 26, 1914 HMCo. to GHP. (folder 8)

"One of our representatives who came into the office from New York on Saturday spoke enthusiastically of your address at the Convocation of the Regents of the University of the State of New York at Albany on 'Teaching as a Profession.' It occurred to us at once that this address might make another admirable volume in the series of the Riverside Educational Monographs, in which we already print your 'Self-Cutivation in English' and 'The Glory of the Imperfect.' It is, of course, possible that the substance of this address is already embodied in your addresses previously printed, but if, as we suppose, it contains new material, would you care to send it to us and let us consider it for this series? . . . "

November 8, 1914 GHP to HMCo. (folder 2)

"I have received President Finley's permission to give you my Albany address for the Riverside Series, but am afraid a week or two must pass before I can furnish the copy, as I am just leaving home for that time."

John Huston Finley (1863–1940) was Commissioner of Education of the State of New York. From 1903 to 1913, he had been President of City College of New York.

November 9, 1914 HMCo. to GHP. (folder 8)

"I was interested to get your letter of November 8th saying that you had President Finley's permission to include your address in the series of Riverside Educational Monographs. We have been over this address and believe that it will be very valuable for all teachers. It will make, however, a very slight book, as far as the number of words is concerned, and we wonder whether you would not like to select one of your essays, which is already in print but which has not been included in the Monographs, which we could join with the present address to increase the size of the book. It is suggested here that 'The Glory of the Imperfect' might be the best to include, but we should much rather have your suggestion than to make our own."

"We also believe that the title included in President Finley's Bulletin would not be the best one for the book. 'Teaching as a Profession' seems to us as the better one, but there are doubtless much better suggestions.

"There is no pressing haste in regard to supplying copy, but of course, we should be glad to have it when you can conveniently get it ready."

November 9, 1914 HMCo. to GHP. (folder 8)

"Dr. Finley has sent us two copies of the Bulletin, one of which I am enclosing herewith for you, although I presume that he has sent one to you direct."

December 10, 1914 HMCo. to GHP. (folder 8)

"We enclose our agreement in duplicate for the publication of your new monograph, 'Trades and Professions.' If you find it entirely satisfactory, will you kindly sign both copies and return one to us for our files.

"We expect to mail to you tonight all the proof for the book. The first half of it will be in pages and the second half in galleys. The press in order to save time started to make the book up in pages with the idea of sending you only page proof, but, after your call this morning, we asked them to send the part of the proof that wasn't then made up as galleys. You can feel free to make such changes as you find necessary both in the galley and in the page proofs."

December 11, 1914 GHP to HMCo. (folder 2)

"I return herewith the signed contract for the publication of my 'Trades and Professions.' You will notice that I have made two changes in it. The fifth article I strike out, being unwilling at my age [72 years] to pledge myself to further writing. If any changes are in future found wise — as is improbable — we shall no doubt be able to agree about them as we did in the case of my Odyssey.

"In section 2 I have also made a considerable alteration, in order that with this book the same practice of payment may obtain as with my others.

"If these changes are not approved by you, you will notify me & I will return my copy of the contract. If they are acceptable, you will keep the copy here enclosed."

December 14, 1914 HMCo. to GHP. (folder 8)

"We have received this morning the contract for 'Trades and Professions.'
The changes which you have made are entirely satisfactory, as you would, of course, know. We will file our copy of the contract and hope that you have made the same changes in the copy for your file."

December 14, 1914 GHP to HMCo. (folder 2)

"Your note is as generous as usual.
"I have made the corresponding changes in my copy of the contract & placed it on file."

December 17, 1914 HMCo. to GHP. (original, folder 2; carbon copy, folder 8)

"I tried to telephone you this morning to explain that we should be obliged to go to press with your monograph today in order to have copies ready by Christmas as you desired. This will make it impossible for us to send you Dr. Suzzallo's Introduction to read in proof. As I learned over the telephone that you were out of town, I am sure that you would not wish us to hold up the printing of the book in order that you might read Dr. Suzzallo's Introduction in proof. When the book appears, if there are any changes in the Introduction that you feel ought to be made, we will make them in the next printing."

December 18, 1914 GHP to HMCo. (folder 2)

"I think it just as well that I should not see the Introduction, & I agree with you in thinking that every day we gain is important."

December 24, 1914 GHP to HMCo. (folder 2)

"Let me thank you for sending me copies of my little book so promptly. The speed with which you have carried it through the press is truly remarkable.
"The only harm too I see from that haste is two small errors which can easily be changed in the plates. On p. 10 the Latin word sine seems to have as its final letter a c; and on p. 22, l.16 phase should be phrase.
"I saw only a single proof, & these errors escaped me. But they are of small consequence & easily corrected."

January 27, 1915 HMCo. to GHP. (folder 8)

"We are enclosing a little circular of those volumes of yours which we have reprinted in the Riverside Educational Monographs. We are sending this to a good many people and we thought you might be interested to see it. This series of monographs is becoming a very standard one, apparently.

"You will be interested to know that President Finley finally ordered ten thousand copies [compiler's underline] of 'Trades and Professions.' He insisted on having the pamphlet printed on very thin paper so that it could be enclosed with something else and it did not, therefore, make as attractive a book as we had hoped, not nearly as attractive as the dummy we originally sent him. We assumed, however, that he knew his requirements and furnished the book to suit him."

A Marriage Cycle
GHP-81

August 25, 1915 GHP to HMCo. (folder 3)

"Here are the verses of which we talked. In reading them will you please judge,

(1) the propriety of publishing,
(2) their literary value,
(3) whether some are so far inferior that they should be omitted,
(4) whether changes are desirable in any of the titles or the Preface.

"As I said to you, I have little power to improve their infirmities. We must let them go out substantially as they are, or else withhold them."

August 31, 1915 GHP to HMCo. (folder 3)

"I enclose a picture of Mrs. Palmer [very similar to her "Portrait in 1892"] to serve as the frontispiece to the book. It is the only copy I have, but I have the negative which can be used if this is too faint.

"I hope the type chosen will be the same as was used in my Life, Cazlin [Caslon] I believe. And I should be glad if the book could be issued with a regular trade discount & not 'net,' so that book sellers would be able to keep it in stock. 'Net' books are apt to remain pretty well unknown after the first few months."

The same type was used in both books.

Regular trade discounts to retailers were as high as 40 to 50 percent, and books were often sold "for less than the catalogue price. Only fools would pay more than $1.20 for a $1.50 book. Bargain hunters could secure a copy for less." "Net" pricing was designed by the American Publishers' Association and the American Booksellers' Association as "a system of pricing and discounts that would be universally observed . . . to maintain uniform prices throughout the country. No reduction in the publishers' announced 'net' or list price would be tolerated. Discounts on 'net' price books were to be limited to 25 percent on one copy, 30 percent on five, 40 percent on 250 or more" (Ballou, *The Building of the House*, page 518).

September 13, 1915 GHP to HMCo. (folder 3)

"On the whole I like the cover of the dummie less well than the other. That line of lettering at top and bottom gives a pleasing effect. The dummie will be so thin, while lettering lengthwise is disagreeable, that I don't see how you can manage a long word like 'marriage.' Perhaps it would be well to print 'Poems' on the back, reserving the full title for front cover & title page. Probably under the word 'Poems' you could print also 'A. F. Palmer.' Be sure the color of the cover precisely matches that of the Life. This does not.

"I like the type & paper, but there is too little space between the text and the running title, & I should prefer to have the page number in the upper corner as in the Life. With these changes the page will be very agreeable.

"When the paging is complete, I shall prepare an alphabetic Index to the poems, preceding it with the three titles of divisions in Capitals & spaced from the poem titles.

"Beside the regular edition it might be well to issue a special 'Wedding Edition' bound in white. But be sure to print a large enough regular edition for the Christmas sale."

The actual dimensions of the volume (except for the spine), the dark cloth cover, and the gold stamping on the cover are the same as for The Life of Alice Freeman Palmer. Across the top of the cover in large type, the one has A MARRIAGE CYCLE, the other, ALICE FREEMAN PALMER; only the former has lettering across the bottom, ALICE FREEMAN PALMER. As Professor Palmer preferred, the lettering on the thin spine is horizontal: POEMS and underneath in three lines of smaller type, ALICE FREEMAN PALMER.

A copy of the white cloth edition in the Wellesley College Archives shows the same gold stamping, and a variant is described in 260n1.

Instead of an index, the book has the Contents listed on three pages. Under three division titles — The Approach, Together, and The Parting — are the poem titles, arranged not alphabetically but in sequence, each with a page number. The front pages, including the Preface, are numbered in the upper corners, but only sixteen of the regular seventy-one pages have numbers.

September 15, 1915 GHP to HMCo. (folder 3)

"This is a beautiful little [title] page. I should be content with it as it stands. Perhaps it might be drawn into closer resemblance to the title of the Life if the Central stamp were — as in that case — oval. This triangular form was chosen, I suppose, to carry down the lines of the wording above. But I think this would be accomplished sufficiently by the oval form, & the present one seems to call attention to itself more. But I am uncertain. You shall judge."

"Central stamp" refers to the Houghton Mifflin emblem. This shows a piper and the motto which has long been in use by the firm, *Tout bien ou rien*, that is, "Do it well or not at all" (Title-Page Devices used by Houghton, Mifflin and Company, in *A Portrait Catalogue*, 245–246). The publisher retained the triangular emblem.

September 23, 1915 GHP to HMCo. (folder 4)

"I agree with you in thinking the triangular title [page emblem] the more graceful. I inclined to the oval merely because it appears in the Life. But I think your taste had better decide the matter, rather than my divided mind."

September 26, 1915 GHP to HMCo. (folder 4)

"I return a signed copy of the contract for 'A Marriage Cycle.' It should have been sent earlier had it not been following me in my somewhat irregular travel.

"I thought it proper to accept but 10 per cent on the first thousand in order to meet your necessary outlay. But I shall have such heavy expense myself in sending copies to her influential friends that I should be glad if you could assist me in this. Perhaps you would be willing to let me have 50 copies instead of the regular 12. Or is that too much? The copies I send out work to a considerable degree as advertisements. But I shall be content with whatever you decide."

September 28, 1915 HMCo. to GHP. (folder 9)

"We have your letter of September 26th returning the signed contract for 'A Marriage Cycle.'

"We should be glad to generously envisage the number of complimentary copies. Any copies that are sent out with a view to promoting the general publicity of the book can of course be charged to the advertising account. We shall be glad to allow you twenty-five free copies, and as many more as are specifically useful for publicity purposes wthout charge, and any others that you may desire at the wholesale rate."

September 29, 1915 GHP to HMCo. (folder 4)

"Let me thank you for your kind proposal in regard to complimetary copies of 'A Marriage Cycle.' Just before the book appears I will send you a list of those to whom I must send & see if you can relieve me of some of them."

October 13, 1915 GHP to HMCo. (folder 4)

"I carried to the Press today page proofs of the Marriage Cycle, so completing my work on the book.

"You will now announce & issue whenever you please. I strongly hope you will conclude to set the price at $1.00, rather than $1.25. The book will be small, only 71 pages."

October 14, 1915 HMCo. to GHP. (folder 9)

"We have your note of the 13th. Unfortunately, we have alredy printed our Holiday Bulletin in which the price for The Marriage Cycle is set for $1.25.

"Our belief is here that the higher price is reasonable, and that the average person who wishes to have the volume would pay the extra twenty-five cents without demur. This additional sum allows a certain lee way, both in the manufacture and advertising. As of course you realize, it is as expensive to launch a small book as a larger one, and the margin even at this higher price will not be excesssive."

November 18, 1915 GHP to HMCo. (folder 4)

"I wonder if you are making known sufficiently the publication of 'A Marriage Cycle'? It has not appeared on the counters of the Cambridge book stores, not even of the Cooperative Society. I have seen only two brief announcements of it in the papers, & have received letters inquiring whether & through whom such a book had been published. As the community holds something like 100000 persons who have read Mrs Palmer's Life, we have a prepared constituency whom it seems worthwhile to notify of the appearance of this sequel.

"I have just concluded a month of lecturing at Smith College. Are the book stores at Northampton supplied with copies? From January to May I am to be lecturing at the University of Berkeley, California. Probably sales can be made there both of this book & the Life."

November 20, 1915 HMCo. to GHP. (folder 9)

"We have your note in regard to both the selling and the advertising of 'The Marriage Cycle.' We had planned to do some special advertising as soon as substantial reviews had appeared. Announcements have already been arranged for in the papers, a list of which is enclosed.

"With regard to the sale, the advance orders aggregated about as many copies as the advance orders for the 'Life.' We are glad to know of your plans for lecturing, and will see that special emphasis is laid on this book in Northampton and elsewhere. We do not quite understand why you have been unable to find the book in Cambridge, as all the important book stores of this country have been supplied with a few copies. Later, when we have our report from the selling department, we will write you more fully in regard to this."

November 23, 1915 HMCo. to GHP. (folder 9)

"In further reply to your letter regarding 'The Marriage Cycle,' we find that the Harvard Cooperative bought ten copies of the book, and the other Cambridge stores five each on publication. Every store in Boston was supplied, the principal ones purchasing in lots of from ten to twenty-five.

"Bridgman and Lyman of Northampton never buy in large quantities, but we will lay special stress on this volume, and hope to interest them to the extent of a small order."

December 8, 1915 GHP to HMCo. (folder 4)

"A week ago I wrote that I had not seen a copy of the Marriage Cycle at any Cambridge book store. Ths morning I send you a Cooperative advertisement which seems to me significant. Under the heading 'New Poetry' eight titles are mentioned, several of books which have been out for many months, but the Marriage Cycle is not mentioned. During the past fortnight I have happened to see in the papers five lists of the recent publications of H. M. Co., & in only one of them was this book mentioned.

"I do not desire for it any expensive advertising. Descriptions or commendations are of no consequence. All that is wanted is that people shall know that the book exists. The 33000 who have found it worthwhile to buy Mrs Palmer's Life & the multitudes of others who have read it constitute a body of probable buyers to whom an appeal different from that for an ordinary book should be made. They only need an announcement not urgency. But they cannot buy until they see the title. I very much fear the book will merely be printed & remain unknown. And as I voluntarily gave up five per cent of my royalty on the first edition [see his letter of September 26,1915] to meet these very expenses of announcement, I am naturally disappointed. A little effort might secure a large sale among her thousands of friends, did they but know. Are they to be left in ignorance? Your and my interests are in this matter identical."

December 10, 1915 HMCo. to GHP. (folder 9)

" . . . Since the publication of The Marriage Cycle, we have inserted announcements of it in the following periodicals and newspapers": at least twice in The Bookman, Nation, The Outlook, and the Atlantic Monthly; in nine other periodicals; and in sixteen newspapers, in Boston, Cambridge, Chicago, New York, Philadelphia, St. Louis, and Springfield.

December 12, 1915 GHP to HMCo. (folder 4)

"Your kind letter much relieves my mind. The strange conduct of the Cooperative Society here in printing its list of recent poetry & omitting Mrs Palmer's showed that they hadn't taken the book seriously. If such silence were at all general, I knew the book was doomed. But you have evidently been pretty industrious, & I have given away 150 copies in influential quarters. Her many followers will therefore probably discover in time that she has been reincarnated."

January 31, 1916 HMCo. to GHP. (folder 9)

"We take pleasure in enclosing herewith a copyright statement showing the sales of your books to January 1st, 1916.

"The initial sale of 'A Marriage Cycle' i.e., between twelve and thirteen hundred copies, is a very good one indeed for a volume of verse in its first period. We trust it will show a continued vitality. Our check for $1118.62, being the balance due you, is being deposited to your credit in the Cambridge Trust Company."

November 22, 1916 GHP to HMCo. (folder 5)

"In a copy recently bought of Mrs Palmer's Life I looked in vain on the tablet for an anouncement of the Marriage Cycle. Ths is a strange omission. Persons who purchase the Life are the very ones most likely to wish the poems, & yet we tell them nothing about them. Is this good advertising? When the Poems were published I thought I asked to have them mentioned on the tablets of all my books."

April 1927 GHP to HMCo. (folder 6)

"On thinking the matter over I believe I made a mistake in suggesting that the Marriage Cycle might be incorporated with Mrs Palmer's Life. The book would have to be made over pretty fully. Already there are ten pages of verse in it, & these would all need to be rearranged. When a book has acquired so authorized a standing, with its more than 50000 copies, it isn't safe to meddle with it much. After my death these changes might be made, with a photograph of me & possibly a couple of pages of biography. But for the present we had better continue as at present, except that I abandon royalty."

April 29, 1927 GHP to HMCo. (folder 7)

"On careful reflection this is my proposal:-

"For the present you will go on printing the Marriage Cycle precisely as at present, except that I remit the royalty. At my death you announce a new edition of Mrs. Palmer's Life & Poetry, taking out a new copyright for my heirs, i.e. Wellesley College. The poetry will then be removed from the Life, the Cycle in its present order preceded by a photograph of me, which I will send you, & also by my Introduction, immediately following. The appendices will then be rearranged, the first being not over a couple of pages for the dates of my life, the others following in the present order.

"When completed in this form I should expect the book to find a considerable sale among those who already have the original volumes."

No such volumes were published.

Riverside Uplift Series
GHP-78

September 17, 1915 GHP to HMCo. (folder 4)

"Let me thank you for the pretty volumes of your Uplift series which have reached me today. The binding is charming, & I feel much honored in my associates.

"I think it would have been well if page numbers had been used in The Glory of the Imperfect, as in the others. And on p. 22, l.17 of Trades and Professions I am very sorry to see that 'phase' has not been corrected to 'phrase.' I gave notice of it as soon as the little book originally appeared but it must have been overlooked." [See his letter of December 24, 1914]

The series included three volumes by Palmer — *The Glory of the Imperfect, Self-Cultivation in English,* and *Trades and Professions* — and four others: *The Amateur Spirit* by Bliss Perry, *The Cultivated Man* by Charles W. Eliot, *Whither* anonymous, and *Calm Yourself* by George L. Walton.

General Correspondence

January 19, 1914 GHP to HMCo. (folder 2)

"A week from today I leave home for two or three months in California. I wonder if it would be feasible for you to settle my account before I start? My decision to go is so sudden, & the time allowed you is therefore so brief, that I fear you may not find it quite convenient to send my check before the first of February. If this is the case, you will not hesitate to tell me & I will leave my affairs here in the hands of a friend. But I should feel rather more secure if I could attend to a few matters before my departure."

January 20, 1914 HMCo. to GHP. (folder 8)

"In reply to your note of yesterday's date, our copyright man has run through the returns which would appear on the 1st of February, and as far as we can figure them out at the moment, $700. will be about the amount that will be payable then. Accordingly we take pleasure in handing you cheque herewith for $700., and we trust you will have a very agreeable soujourn in California."

February 11, 1914 (postcard from Santa Barbara, California) **GHP** to HMCo. (folder 2)

"Let me thank you for this large & welcome supplemental report."

January 31, 1917 HMCo. to GHP. (folder 9)

"We trust that you will be pleased and rejoiced by the copyright statement, with its accompanying check, that we have the pleasure of sending you.

"It is not often that commercial returns are made in accordance with character or quality of work. You seem to be the charmed exception to this general rule."

February 1, 1917 GHP to HMCo. (folder 5)

"Let me thank you for this enormous check, which I feel to be as much due to the ability & devotion of my publishers as to any merits in my books."

August 9, 1918 HMCo. to GHP. (folder 10)

" . . . The book [*Formative Types in English Poetry*, **GHP**-88] will come out all right in respect to thickness. We are lucky enough to have on hand at the moment some paper which is entirely opaque for printing on both sides, and which will not, at the same time, bulk the book unduly.

"We say we are fortunate to have it on hand, since with the present paper shortage and the Governmental restrictions [related to the war in Europe], it is not always possible to find the kind of paper for any given book that we would like to use."

January 31, 1919 HMCo. to GHP. (folder 10)

"We take pleasure in enclosing a copyright statement showing the sales of your books for the six months ending December 31, together with our check for $1119.45, to balance the account."

January 26, 1923 HMCo. to GHP. (folder 10)

"We take pleasure in enclosing herewith a copyright statement showing the sales of your books for the half year ending December 31st, 1922, together with our check for $1504.67 to balance the account."

Regarding Other Writers

March 1, 1887 GHP to H. E. Scudder. (folder 1)

"You will not be pleased to see this pile of Mss. It is a novel written by a friend of mine in a distant part of the country . . . You better than I can tell how it meets the trade standards. I sh'd say there was in it a note of distinction. But my ear is distorted by friendship."

January 5, 1902 GHP to HMCo. (folder 1)

"Miss [Ella Isabel] Harris writes me that she has sent you her completed translation of Seneca's Plays. I hope you will find it possible to publish them. Her work seems to me quite extraordinary in exactitude, naturalness, & literary power. While of course Seneca's Plays can never be made popular, I believe a complete English rendering of them will have a steady, if not a wide, sale among students of literature."

The Royalty Accounting Department at Houghton Mifflin Company provided the figures tabulated below (Barbara E. Amidon to the compiler, May 6, 1974; AJL Collection). From left to right, the columns indicate: the **GHP**-number, a short title, the period covered, the total number of printings, the total number of copies printed, and the notes to the table.

1	Odyssey	1884–1895	4	950	
2 to 5	Odyssey	1891–1927	35	25,830	n1
6 & 7	Odyssey	1929	1	525	
37	Antigone	1899–1937	15	4,898	
40	Field Ethics	1901–1930	15	5,700	
44	Service, AFP	1903–1909	2	1,150	
46	Goodness	1903–1929	17	6,414	n2
57	Life of AFP	1908–1922	36	46,115	n1,3
57	Life of AFP	1924–1936	6	10,000	
63	Self-Cult Engl	1909–1938	28	57,718	n4
65	Teacher	1908–1924	7	4,093	
71	Problem Freedom	1911–1928	2	2,270	
72	Immort Sonnets	1912	1	1,500	
76	Trades Profsns	1914	1	3,000	n5
76	Ethics Moral	1909–1927	7	6,344	
76	Ideal Teach	1910–1942	13	21,338	
78	Glory Imperf	1915	1	1,000	n4
81	Marriage Cyc	1915–1927	7	4,064	
88	Form Types Poet	1918–1928	4	2,520	
93	Catalog Engl Poet	1923	1	210	n6
104	Autobiog Philos	1930–1931	2	2,500	

Notes (n)

1. In his Retrospect (dated July 29, 1920) in **GHP**-5, Professor Palmer writes: "During these thirty-six years (from 1884 to 1920) 200,000 copies have been sold, the plates have become worn, and a fresh setting of type is now demanded."

A few years later, when Palmer brought the English poetry books to Wellesley (249n5), he described the background of the collection. He and Alice Freeman Palmer, he said, were both "lovers of poetry." "The last part of her life we began to talk seriously about Wellesley in this connection and wondered whether it would be possible for us to gather a library of poetry that would make it possible for the students here to get the same sort of pleasure that we were having. Books of this sort were very expensive, and I had only my salary, but from time to time we got a single precious volume, and when she left me and I asked what I could send to Wellesley, it seemed to me there was nothing on the whole so well within my power as the completion of this collection that we had both in mind, especially as then the means began to be furnished to my hands. My books began to pay. Her life [*The Life of Alice Freeman Palmer*, **GHP**-57] has sold just under 50,000 and my Homer up to 300,000. There was a gentle flow of money coming in, and whatever has come from my own books has been consecrated to this purpose" (Professor Palmer's Books, *Wellesley Alumnae Quarterly*, 1924; 8 (No. 3, May): 161–165).

2. In his diary for March 7, 1900 (page 167), the day of his first Noble Lecture, Professor Palmer writes: "I was appointed last spring, am to give six lectures, to receive $600.00, the plates of my book to be issued in the Fall are to be paid for, & I am to own the copyright."

3. From a history of Houghton Mifflin Company: "Much has been written about the novelists of the first two decades of this century . . . Less notice has been taken of the growth of a reading public for books of nonfiction . . . A sale of 2,000 qualified a book of this class as a success. If the figure passed 4,000, both publisher and author had reason to throw their caps in the air . . . George Herbert Palmer's *The Life of Alice Freeman Palmer* sold over 16,000 copies in its first year" (Ballou, *The Building of the House*, page 569).

4. See 142n4 for data regarding this title and *The Glory of the Imperfect* when they were published previously — **GHP**-19 and 34 — by T. Y. Crowell & Co.

5. On January 27, 1915, Houghton Mifflin Company wrote to Professor Palmer: "You will be interested to know that President Finley [formerly president of City College of New York; then, Commissioner of Education of the State of New York] finally ordered ten thousand copies of "Trades and Professions" (see letter on page 471).

6. For December 1923, Professor Palmer made this entry (see page 285): "After two years and a month of labor my Bibliography of Poetry appears I paid H. M. Co. $1000.00 at the start & agreed to take $400.00 worth of copies 200 copies were printed at 25.00 each I received 18 and am allowed more at $20.00"

Chapter 11

Publications by Alice Freeman Palmer

identified as **AFP**-number

1 Four Mottoes, *Lend A Hand: A Journal of Organized Philanthropy*, 1886; 1:182.

2 The Advantage of the Woman's College to the Women of America, *Christian Union*, 1890; May 15: 903–904.

3 Education is Life, *Chautauquan*, 1890; October: 66–70.

4 A Review of the Higher Education of Women, *Forum*, 1891; 12 (September): 28–40. Also published in **AFP**-17 as Three Types of Women's Colleges.

5 The Higher Education of Women, *Chautauqua Assembly Herald*, 1893; July 26: 5.

6 Some Lasting Results of the World's Fair, *Forum*, 1893; 16 (December): 517–523. Also published in **AFP**-17 as Women's Education at the World's Fair.

7 Introduction to Cordelia C. Nevers, *Wellesley Lyrics*, Poems Written by Students and Graduates of Wellesley College, Nevers, 1896. Copyright by C. C. Nevers. 159 pages, $5^{1/4}$x$6^{3/4}$ inches. $1.00.

8 *Why Go To College*, Boston, T. Y. Crowell & Co., 1897. Copyright, 1897, by T. Y. Crowell & Co. 32 pages, 5x$7^{1/4}$ inches. 35 cents. Also published in **AFP**-17.

9 What Women Can Do For The Public Schoools, *Independent* (New York), 1898; 50 (August 4): 301–304.

10 The History of the Case, November 3, 1899, On Lilian Horsford's Engagement to the Professor of Cryptogamic Botany, a poem, in Mary Towle Palmer, *The Story of the Bee*, Privately printed, Cambridge, Riverside Press, 1924: 89–94.

11 Women's Education in the Nineteenth Century.
The annotator has not seen the original publication; it was also published in **AFP**-17 (pages 337–350) with this footnote: "Published in *The New York Evening Post*, 1900."

12 An unpublished poem from Alice Freeman Palmer to Anna Hooker Morse (1 year and 9 months old), Christmas 1900.

13 An unpublished letter from Alice Freeman Palmer to Anna Hooker Morse (2 years and $9^{1/2}$ months old), January 18, 1902.

14 The Need of Well Educated Teachers and Adequate Salaries in the Elementary Grades of our Public Schools. II. The Practical Side of Adequate Salaries. *Association of Collegiate Alumnae Magazine*, Series III, 1902; No. 5 (February): 39–43.

15 Why I Am An Optimist, April 5, 1902. (Clipping, source unknown, in Wellesley College Archives, Alice Freeman Palmer Papers, general folder.)

Alice Freeman Palmer died on December 6, 1902

16 Some Religious Verse of Alice Freeman Palmer, *Outlook*, 1904; 76 (No. 3, January 16): 175–179. (also **GHP**-47)

17 *The Teacher: Essays and Addresses on Education*, by George Herbert Palmer and Alice Freeman Palmer, Boston, Houghton Mifflin Co., November 1908. Copyright, 1908, by George Herbert Palmer. 395 pages, $5^{3/8}$x8 inches. $1.50. (also **GHP**-65)

18 *A Marriage Cycle*, with a Preface by George Herbert Palmer, Boston, Houghton Mifflin Co., October 1915. Copyright, 1915, by George Herbert Palmer. xvii+71 pages, $5^{1/2}$x8 inches. (also **GHP**-81)

19 Meeting (a poem). Number 14 in Martha Hale Shackford, ed., *Wellesley Verse: 1875–1925*, Wellesley Semi-Centennial Series, New York, Oxford University Press, 1925: 13.

20 *An Academic Courtship: Letters of Alice Freeman and George Herbert Palmer, 1886–1887*, Cambridge, Harvard University Press, 1940. $5^{1/2}$x$8^{1/4}$ inches, 259 pages. (also **GHP**-109)

Chapter 12

Publications by Alice Freeman Palmer, annotated

identified as **AFPann**-number
(corresponding to chapter 11)

1 Four Mottoes

"Look up and not down, out and not in, forward and not backward, and lend a hand."— Harry Wadsworth.

"Look up and not down!" Do you mind how the tree-top
Rejoices in sunshine denied to its root?
And hear how the lark, gazing skyward, is flooding
All the earth with its song, while the ground bird is mute?

"Look out and not in!" See the sap rushing outward
In leaf, bud, and blossom. All winter it lay
Imprisoned, while earth wore a white desolation.
Now Nature is glad with the beauty of May.

"Look forward, not back!" 'Tis the chant of creation,
The chime of the seasons as onward they roll;
'Tis the pulse of the world, 'tis the hope of the ages,
This voice of the Lord in the depths of the soul.

"Lend a hand!" Like the sun that turns night into morning,
The moon that guides storm-driven sailors to land.
Ah! life were worth living with this for its watchword,
"Look up, out, and forward, and each lend a hand!"

A. E. F.

Wellesley College.

Edward Everett Hale's story, Ten Times One is Ten, with its four "wholesome mottoes . . . is a translation of the Christian Gospel into the language and habits of today" (G. L. Chaney, Edward Everett Hale, *Harvard Register*, 1881; 3 (January–July): 271).

Hale introduces the story in 1870: "I was simply trying in an 'invented example,' to show to young people the extent and the rapidity by which the effort of one man extends itself in larger and larger circles if he really looks out and not in and is determined to lend a hand . . . With no expectation of mine, the parable of the story took form immediately in actual life. Miss Ella Elizabeth Russell of New York, in the end of May 1870, read this story to a class of boys whom she met every Sunday, in a Sunday School. They were of different ages from thirteen to seventeen. She writes of them, 'they felt that they were too old to go to any Mission School, but the idea of a Club to meet Sunday afternoons seemed a more grown-up affair. I had read them the story of Harry Wadsworth [the name that Hale gave to the main character in the story] and as the class was ten in number, they decided to call themselves the Harry Wadsworth Helpers, to adopt the 'Four Mottoes' and to see what they could do to 'lend a hand'" (Hale, *Works*, Preface, pages vi, v).

A. E. F. (Alice Elvira Freeman, President of Wellesley College in 1886) starts each of her four verses with one of the four mottoes.

2 The Advantage of the Woman's College to the Women of America.

Wellesley College opened in 1875, and Alice E. Freeman became the second president, in 1882. She prepared this piece about two and one-half years after she married Professor Palmer and left the presidency. From her home in Cambridge, she continued and broadened her interest in the higher education of women.

"During the last quarter of a century the woman's college has opened a new world to American women. Since Vassar's first class entered in 1865, one great college foundation after another has been laid, until now hundreds of courses of study under excellent professors, valuable libraries, well equipped laboratories and museums, are at the service of young women in centers of learning already famous. One college — probably more than one — has received students from every State and Territory in the Union. Thousands of girls have returned from longer or shorter periods of college study, and have entered all the walks of life where cultivated women have a place. The home, the school, the hospital, the charitable organization, has taken them in and given them occupation. Their interests have largely centered, as all women's do — and the wisest women's most wisely — in improving the conditions of children's lives, and in lessening the sufferings, the poverty, and the vice of society. It is not too early, then, to point out the special service which the woman's college renders to women, and the manner in which the college has tried to train its students to meet the pressing demands of American life. Some of these demands are new. Let us see what they are.

"Women are no longer free fom public responsibility. In our new communities we have been forced to utilize all our material for society development . . . Through a combination of national characteristics with the complex conditions found in our rapidly growing societies, it has come about that women in America are being called to high positions of public trust in many departments of life more rapidly than they can qualify themselves to take them. Two-thirds of the teachers in the public schools are women . . . The great majority of the twelve million children in the public schools of America never pass beyond the country school or the grammar grade of the city. These children receive all the instruction they ever get exclusively from women. This state of things is by no means peculiar to the public schools. It is practically the same in the private . . . Nor is this all. The higher schools and academies are being turned over to women as fast as women can be equipped for their charge . . . Learning of a higher order than was ever before demanded of women is now sought in every department of instruction, and with this learning must be associated trained aptitudes, gracious manners, and acquaintance with business methods . . . As many of them as are needed cannot be found. Within a fortnight I have myself been asked to name principals for three colleges in the West and South . . . One who does not stand at some educational center can hardly realize how great is the pressure for high qualifications, in scholarship, character, and training, for those who are to undertake an educational leadership among women.

"But women are now intrusted with other public duties than

education . . . For insane asylums, hospitals, prisons, reformatories, almshouses, in fact for all places where sickness, misery, and sin are gathered for safety or for reformation, these women of self-control, of intelligent resource, of varied training, are a necessity . . .

"The new organizations which aim at saving the children of the criminal classes, those which furnish friends and advisers to the helpless, those which establish clubs for amusement and aid in the neighborhood of dreary homes, in short, the numberless social, moral, and religious reform movements at home and abroad, need, more than anything else, men and women with resources of mind ample enough to match their generous devotion . . . The elaborate curriculum of the modern college can hardly be described in a newspaper article. I merely desire to call attention to general influences, often overlooked, by which the woman's college is powerfully shaping its students for their new work of to-day.

"In the first place, the woman's college has from its beginning emphasized the value of strong health . . . It has insisted upon regular and simple modes of life. It has founded gymnasiums and encouraged athletic sports for girls. It has had field and lake and river at the service of its students, and has employed salaried physicians and directors for their safety and guidance . . .

"Now, it is an inestimable boon, not merely to college girls, but just as truly to women who have nothing to do with colleges, that a large and rapidly increasing body of women are taught to believe in the sacred duty of getting and keeping vigorous health . . . This company of the better taught are teaching these hardly learned lessons to their daughters, their pupils, their friends; and as a consequence we may hope that the next generation will show us girls of clearer brains, larger lungs, and calmer nerves . . .

"In the second place, the social influence of college life deserves special consideration in these days when class is arrayed against class and the important questions are, first or last, questions of social status. It is safe to say that no place can be found so truly democratic as the American college . . . The North and South, the East and West, with foreign lands as well, send earnest girls into the same college class . . . Is anything of more consequence than that our women should learn in early life what are the really valuable possessions, the abiding interests, the things that last? And college life, with its inspiring four years, gives these lessons to every open mind . . . But it gives its young women also something better than a well-stored mind; it gives them disciplined and discriminating powers, method, economy of force, and adaptability to meet the unknown demands of the future. Such powers are important for the woman of any social class. Indeed, she who has them is exalted above the influence of social classes. A truly educated woman need not fear shipwreck in the changing fortunes of modern times. She has won freedom from fear for herself and her family."

3 Education is Life.

On August 20, 1890, Mrs. Palmer delivered this Recognition Day address at Chautauqua to the Chautuaqua Literary and Scientific Circle's Class of 1890.

"There has been no happier moment in all my life before than this in which I see your white banners and have the great honor to speak the congratulations and the blessings and the good wishes of all your friends and the friends of dear old Chautauqua on this day . . . You have done so much work so bravely; you have looked forward so long to the proud day which crowns you with its splended sunshine. First of all we give you our good wishes, our blessing, our recognition as belonging now to the great army of those who have promised themselves to be scholars in the largest sense of the word . . .

"We have, some of us, thought she [Chautauqua] ought to have recognized you four years ago when you entered upon this course of training you set for yourselves . . . She knew better, so wise is she; she waited until she had tested your patience, your power, your will, your bravery . . . If Chautauqua has done any thing for our land she has done this, that she has showed us . . . 'Education ends only with life' . . . She says more to you and to those about you. She says, 'Education is life' . . . The college of Chautauqua, a greater college now than all, has been wise in bringing you up to-day to enter upon life, to come into the new birth, to come on the roll of scholars on your Recognition Day . . .

"Your earnest eyes and purpose show that you more firmly enter to-day than four years ago upon the education that is life. What is it? Let us draw a sharp contrast by saying that with Chautauqua the life is contrasted with the humdrum and more commonplace life. There can be none of us who have not passed through days when the skies were low above us, when it seemed that the earth had no stone under our feet, when duty was drudgery, when the dearest friends seemed uninteresting, when books were not opened to us, when no music sounded in our ears, when the humdrum of life and its daily round of duties made no bright outlook for us . . . And is it not so that Chautauqua has lifted us up by the thousand and given us something to think of besides what the fingers are doing and what has to be done over and over again? . . . You cannot be true Chautauquans unless life is to-day to you more beautiful, no matter what your hands are doing, and though not one of you could earn your bread because of what you have learned in your homes and in your books, every mouthful you eat ought to be sweeter because of the work you have done together. That is, then, what I mean by a life that is education . . .

"Now, you have not gone through this little list of four years' reading without having felt yourselves in a beautiful archway, members of the whole world. The Greeks have spoken to you out of their beautiful old life that has gone. The Romans have given you their ideas and you are better for them. You know the witty, bright, scintillating, fresh thinkers; you know something of the solemn, philosophical German mind; you have come to see what the stars have to say to you in the heavens at night; what the rocks have to say to you in the sun by day. You cannot, I am sure, not one of you on the farm, go out in the evening and look after your cattle, and if you are a live man, with God's truth in your heart, you cannot go in without a sweet touch in the heart of the Source of all . . .

"No man or woman is educated unless he or she out of all the learning puts himself or herself more in touch, more keenly alive, more sensitive to the life and the need of the time just round him. America has so many problems just now to solve. There are ethical questions that the newspapers from day to day are teeming with — theology, education, politics, every thing is stirring in the new land; and the questions will be settled before the little boys and girls here have grown to manhood and womanhood; and they will be settled by the men and the women who believe in this education, through this daily life, whether these men and women stand in high places or in humble places; they will be settled by these fathers and mothers who discuss them rationally about the dinner tables in the hearing of their children. God made us brave enough to settle these things in His way and not ours, before the new century comes in . . . We have promised ourselves to add every day to knowledge; but aye, beyond that, we have promised ourselves to be our best always, and what is better, to give our best and only our best always to the world that waits for it . . .

"I have just come home from many lands where Chautauqua has not conquered [*sic*] or its ideals. I come from where I have been asked by German professors, whose names you have already been hearing upon this platform, if it is really possible that in America a boy would be sent to college who expected to be a farmer. The idea to them was very shocking, for, as they viewed it, education was for the preachers and teachers, professional and learned men. I think, even in dear old England, there are too many people who suppose that Oxford and Cambridge are for gentlemen's sons. In Athens that good man who is ruling there in place of the king, sent for me last spring to ask me if I would not tell him how to get the boys and the girls educated there as this Indian name was doing over here.

"The old idea that education was for the gentlemen's sons, for a certain class or for learned professions, you have struck a death-blow in the face, and you have said that because you are men and women and because the little children around your table are human beings and are going to last forever, therefore you would know and be and do the greatest thing in the world that lay in your power. Now, for this, I can give you my blessing out of the colleges and tell you that at last you have conquered the colleges and universities. They now only ask you to be good to them and to send your boys and girls to them and let them do for your sons and daughters, Chautauqua men and women, something of what you have done for them . . ."

4 A Review of the Higher Education of Women.

Alice Freeman Palmer had a busy month of August in 1891. In addition to writing this article (in Boxford), she gave four talks at Chautauqua in Fryeburg, Maine, and the Recognition Address at Chautauqua in Epping, New Hampshire.

She begins this article: "American College education in the quarter century since the Civil War has undergone more numerous and more fundamental changes than befell it in a hundred years before. These changes have not occurred unnoticed. A multitude of journals and associations are busy every year discussing the results of the experiments in teaching which go on with increasing daring and fruitfulness in nearly all our colleges and schools. There still exists a wide divergence of opinion among the directors of men's colleges in regard to a variety of important questions . . . The advanced education of young women is exposed to all the uncertainties which beset the education of men, but it has perplexities of its own in addition . . . No educational convention meets without a session devoted to the difficulties in 'the higher education of women'; so important has the subject become, and so hard is it to satisfy in any one system the varieties of its needs . . . But already three tolerably clear, consistent, and accredited types of education appear . . . The nature of each with its special strengths and weaknesses will be set forth in no spirit of partisanship, but in the belief that a cool understanding of what is doing at present among fifty thousand college girls may make us wiser and more patient in our future growth . . .

"These, then — co-education, the woman's college, and the annex — are the three great types of college in which the long agitation in behalf of women's education has thus far issued . . . To this business I now turn, and I may naturally have most in mind the University of Michigan, my own *Alma Mater*, Wellesley College, with whose government I have been connected for a dozen years, and the Harvard Annex, whose neighbor I now am.

"Co-education involves, as its name implies, the education of a company of young men and women as a single body. To the two sexes alike are presented the same conditions of admission, of opportunities during the course, of requirements for the degrees, of guardianship, of discipline, of organization . . . [I]n most of the higher co-educational institutions the principle has from the first been assumed that students of both sexes become sufficiently matured by eighteen years of home, school, and social life — especially under the ample opportunities for learning the uses of freedom which our social habits afford — safely to undertake a college course, and advantageously to order their daily lives . . . [see 41n2 for a long excerpt from this point in the article] In my time in college the little group of girls, suddenly introduced into the army of young men, felt that the fate of our sex hung upon proving that 'lady Greek' involved the accents, and that women's minds were particularly absorptive of the calculus and metaphysics. And still in those sections, where, with growing experience, the anxieties about co-education have been allayed, a healthy and hearty relationship and honest rivalry between young men and women exists. It is a stimulating atmosphere, and develops in good stock a strength and independent balance which tell in after life . . .

"The weaknesses of this system are merely the converse of its strengths. It does not usually provide for what is distinctively feminine. Refining home influences and social oversight are largely lacking; and if they are wanting in the home from which the student comes, it must not be expected that she will show, on graduation, the graces of manner, the niceties of speech and dress, and the shy delicacy, which has been encouraged in her more tenderly nurtured sister.

"The woman's college is organized under a different and far more complex conception. The chief business of the man's college . . . is to give instruction of the best available quality in as many subjects as possible; to furnish every needed appliance for the acquirement of knowledge and the encouragement of special investigation. The woman's college aims to do all this, but it aims, also, to make for its students a home within its own walls, and to develop other powers in them than the merely intellectual . . . [T]he arrangements of the woman's college, as conceived by founders, trustees, and faculty, have usually aimed with conscious directness at building up character, inspiring to the service of others, cultivating manners, developing taste, and strengthening health, as well as providing the means of sound learning . . .

"By setting its students apart in homogeneous companies, [the woman's college] seeks to cultivate common ideals . . . Harvard and Johns Hopkins can ask their pupils to attend the lectures of a great scholar, however brusque his bearing or unbrushed his hair. They will not question their geniuses too sharply, and will trust their students to look out for their own proprieties of dress, manners, and speech. But neither Wellesley nor any other woman's college could find a place in its faculty for a woman Sophocles [see **GHP**-16] or Sylvester. Learning alone is not enough for women . . .

"The influence of hundreds of mentally eager girls upon the characters of one another when they live for four years in the closest daily companionship is most interesting to see. I have watched the ennobling process go on for many years among Wellesley students, and I am confident that no more healthy, generous, democratic, beauty-loving, serviceable society of people exists than the girls' college community affords. That choicest product of modern civilization, the American girl, is here in all her diverse colors . . . Side by side in the boats, on the tennis grounds, at the table, arm in arm on the long walks, debating in the societies, vigorous together in the gymnasium and the library, girls of every grade gather the rich experiences which will tincture their future toil, and make the world perpetually seem an interesting and friendly place. They here learn to 'see great things large, and little things small' . . .

"It is said that [woman college] students never escape from themselves and their domestic standard, that they do not readily acquire a scientific spirit, and become individual in taste and conduct. Is it desirable that they should? That I shall not undertake to decide. I have merely tried to explain the kinds of human work which the different types of higher training schools are best fitted to effect for women. Whether the one or the other kind of work needs most to be done is a question of social ethics which the future must answer . . ."

See 76n4, for a long excerpt from this article about "the 'annex,' a recent and interesting experiment in the education of girls, whose future it is yet difficult to predict."

Alice Freeman Palmer concludes: "The result of all these diversities is the most instructive body of experiment that the world has seen for determining the best ways of bringing woman to her powers. While the public mind is so uncertain, so liable to panic, and so doubtful, whether, after all, it is not better for a girl to be a goose, the many methods of education assist one another mightily in their united warfare against ignorance, selfish privileges, and antiquated ideals. It is well that for a good while to come woman's higher education should be all things to all mothers if by any means it may save girls. Those who are hardy enough may continue to mingle their girls with men; while a parent who would be shocked that her daughter should do anything so ambiguous as to enter a man's college may be persuaded to send her to a girl's. Those who find it easier to honor an old university than the eager life of a young college, may be tempted into an annex. The important thing is that the adherents of these differing types should not fall into jealousy, and belittle the value of those who are performing a work which they themselves cannot do so well. To understand one another kindly is the business of the hour — to understand and to wait."

5 The Higher Education of Women.

Alice Freeman Palmer delivered this address in the Ampitheatre to the Chautauqua Political Equality Clubs on Saturday, July 22, 1893. Regarding Chautauqua: see 82n5. The local newspaper printed the whole address and reported that the "mighty host of Political Equality forces invade Chautauqua, but it is a peaceful invasion and Chautauqua welcomes them." Not until twenty-seven years later, on August 26, 1920, was the 19th amendment to the Constitution of the United States, providing for woman suffrage, ratified.

On the same day, Professor Palmer delivered the last of his lectures on "The Ethical Doctrine of Pleasure" (**GHP**-30).

A reporter who interviewed Mrs. Palmer after the talk, wrote: "Her life work is the education of girls. She is not a woman suffrage lecturer nor a temperance advocate, nor the exponent of any special reform, although she is in hearty sympathy with all these great movements . . . She speaks in high terms of the outlook for women in the co-educational regime of the Chicago University [where she was Dean of Women]. About twenty-five per cent. of its students are women" (*Chautauqua Assembly Herald*, 1893; July 24:1).

Mrs. Palmer begins: "Ladies of the Equality Clubs of Chautauqua County: You have done me a great honor and a great kindness to invite me to meet with you today, to have the pleasure of talking of my own subject to you, a company of earnest women and men. It is an age of specialization, and you, who commit yourselves to one reform, reach kind hands to us, who have been so busy with our other little and great reforms, when you invite us to join your association and work with you.

"But while we have been busy in educating the girls we cannot help feeling that we are closely united with you. Whether we like it, or whether we do not like it, no serious man or woman can possibly study the conditions of society to-day, can read aright the drift of opinion and purpose of the last half-century in this country, and not see perfectly well that the time is drawing on apace when the women are to take into their hands the greatest political responsibilities.

"In society, in the school, in the church, in the state, at the ballot box as in the nursery, these American women of ours, we are perfectly sure, have in the immediate future such work to do, such burdens to bear, as their grandmothers never dreamed of. Since this is so, and since it is true that there is a great and growing number of serious men . . . who are . . . becoming converted to this idea that women for their own sakes and for the sake of the public ought to vote, it seems to me that you will not feel that you have misspent the afternoon, if you will let me talk about *my special hobby* [compiler's italics] and tell you how important I feel it to be, that the girls should be, as fast and as far as possible, made ready to take these great and new responsibilities and carry them wisely and efficiently.

". . . My sweet neighbor, Lucy Stone [1818–1893, "sent out call for the first national woman's-rights convention, in 1850"], off by the Atlantic, has been a blessed influence among the college girls in Boston. She is our saint in college halls, as well as in your suffrage associations, and she tells the young girls to-day, who find it so simple and natural to go into the great colleges and universities, what a great struggle it was to win this privilege for them . . .

"While you have been organizing clubs, while your women leaders have been asking that the responsibilities of suffrage shall be put in your hands, all over the country our hands are being loaded with responsibilities. Is it not true that in Massachusetts women settle all questions touching education? They are doing the teaching, they are going on school-boards, and they may vote and elect those boards if they will. Many of them will not, and many of them do not do it intelligently because they do not understand how dignified and important and essential this work is and must ever be. Therefore I ask that education be emphasized. Therefore I ask whether you will not try at once to see that better salaries are paid our teachers, better opportunities for education put in their hands, and that public spirit demands a fine training for these women who stand five days in the week to mould the life of the little boy or girl, (applause,) particularly the boy and girl not in your home, but from that poor, forlorn home where there is no beauty, where there is no book and no love of fine things.

"It is not simply for our own sake, or the sake of the home, or the sake of the school, that I ask that our women may have the best possible education, it is for the sake of these reforms in our society . . . If there is an enthusiasm among them it is to do something to solve these terrible problems that are confronting us, while the rich and the poor stand confronting each other, while East and West and North and South stand on sectional questions, and our great churches stand apart and struggle over dogma instead of fighting sin . . .

"It is going to take a great deal of brains for us women to be good and true during the coming twenty-five years. It is going to take not only sympathy, but brains, a great deal more thinking to do our duty, to decide what forces should be put into missions, and what into public schools, and what we should give to the Indians, and what to the wretched people over in that awful street, without doing them more mischief than we do them good . . .

Mrs. Palmer ends her address: "Don't be afraid to trust your splendid American girls. Don't be afraid that conceit of scholarship, that any low aims will enter in if you give them the best. You may be sure that they will not lose their sense of beauty and their love of gracious, refined living, or that they will be the less loving, lovely girls. They will have the calmer nerves, the full, deep lungs, the warm heart, the clear brain, the tried will, and they will be ready humbly and calmly to take the many heavy burdens the new century will surely throw on them when you and I who talk of these things have left our places to be filled by them. I cannot think, therefore, that I magnify too much my office as a teacher of girls when I take your time to urge you to give your girls the best education that they be bright-minded, gaining independence, sound judgment, high training, that they may the more quickly bring in your and further great reforms. [Applause.]"

6 Some Lasting Results of the World's Fair.

As described in 87n3, Alice Freeman Palmer had an important role at the 1893 World's Columbian Exposition in Chicago. As one of the Board of Managers for Massachusetts, she was responsible for the organization of exhibits to "worthily represent the educational features of the State."

This article appeared in December, soon after the Exposition closed on October 30th.

She begins: "Few persons have stood in the Court of Honor at Chicago and felt the surpassing splendors gathered there, without a certain dismay over its swiftly approaching disappearance. Never in the world before has beauty been so lavish and so transient. Probably in all departments of the Fair a hundred million dollars have been spent. Now the nation's holiday is done, the little half-year is over, and the palaces with their widely-gathered treasures vanish like a dream."

(When the Exposition closed, wrecking companies bought many of the buildings. The Massachusetts State Building, for example, like the other large structures, could not be moved. Although it seemed to be built of granite, it was really made of staff — "a building material having a plaster of Paris base and used in exterior wall coverings of temporary buildings." The cost of construction had been $46,550.41; it was sold to a wrecking company for $300.) (*Massachusetts Board of Managers.*)

Mrs. Palmer goes on: "Is all indeed gone? Will nothing remain? Wise observers perceive some permanent results of the merry-making. What these will be in the busy life of men, others may decide: I point out chiefly a few of the beneficial influences of the great Fair on the life of women . . .

"The Government appointed an independent Board of Lady Managers who, through many difficulties, gathered from every quarter of the globe interesting exhibits of feminine industry and skill. These they gracefully disposed in one of the most dignified buildings of the Fair, itself a woman's design. Here they attractively illustrated every aspect of the life of women, domestic, philanthropic, commercial, literary, artistic, and traced their historic advance . . . Their halls were crowded, their dinners praised, their reception invitations coveted. Throughout they showed organizing ability on a huge scale; they developed noteworthy leaders; what is more, they followed them, and they have quarreled no more, and have pulled wires less, than men in similar situations; their courage, their energy, their tact in the erection of a monument to woman were astonishing; the efforts of their Central Board were efficiently seconded by similar companies in every State . . .

"But the very triumph does away with its further necessity. Having amply proved what they can do when banded together, women may now the more easily cease to treat themselves as a peculiar people. Henceforth they are human beings. Women's buildings, women's exhibits, may safely become things of the past. At any future Fair no special treatment of women is likely to be called for. After what has been achieved, the self-consciousness of women will be lessened, and their sensitiveness about their own position, capacity, and rights will be naturally outgrown. The anthropologist may perhaps still assemble the work of a single sex, the work of people of a single color, or of those having blue eyes. But ordinary people will find less and less interest in these artificial classifications, and will more and more incline to measure men's and women's products by the same scale. Even at Chicago large numbers of women preferred to range their exhibits in the common halls rather than under feminine banners, and their demonstration of the needlessness of any special treatment of their sex must be reckoned as one of the most considerable of the permanent gains for women from the Fair . . .

Mrs. Palmer ends the article: "Such are the permanent results of the Fair most likely to affect women. They fall into three classes: the proofs women have given of their independent power; their ability to organize and to work toward a distant, difficult and complex end, the enlargement of their outlook, manifesting itself in a new sense of membership in a nation, a more willing obedience to law, and a higher appreciation of beauty; and, lastly, the direct assistance given to women in their more characteristic employments of housekeeping, teaching, and ministering to the afflicted. That these are all, or even the most important, results which each woman will judge she has obtained, is not pretended. Everybody saw at the Fair something which brought to individual him or her a gain incomparable.

"And, after all, the greatest thing was the total, glittering, murmurous, restful, magical, evanescent Fair itself, seated by the blue waters, wearing the five crowns, served by novel boatmen, and with the lap so full of treasure that as piece by piece it was held up, it shone, was wondered at, and was lost again in the pile. This amazing spectacle will flash for years upon the inward eye of our people, and be a joy of their solitude."

7 Introduction to *Wellesley Lyrics.*

Cordelia C. Nevers was a member of the Wellesley College class of 1896.

Alice Freeman Palmer's Introduction: "Every college has its two sides. On the one hand, it is a place of lectures, libraries, laboratories, professors, studying students; a place for the acquisition of knowledge, and for increasing the extent of what is already known. Science dominates it, irrespective of temperaments, wishes, and emotions. On the other hand, it is a place where live the chosen and ardent young; where life is maturing, friendships forming, aspirations taking shape, the ideals of the home for the first time comparing themselves with those of the larger world. Here dwell hope, admiration, intimacy with noble books and persons, while gladness in these, and a daily new sense of personal power, spread everywhere an air of romance and of expanded existence. On the former of these two sides, the studious, examinations report, and the college records. Such little books as this collection of verses tell the story of the other, — the human and romantic.

"For in these poems we catch sight not only of a multitude of incidents in the daily life of a company of brilliant girls, but we are permitted to know the girls themselves, to share their dreams, their friendships, their merriment, their religious aspiration, their ordered thought, natural English, and charming rhythms. He would be a hard person to please who did not enjoy society so cultured, so witty, so truly womanly, too. Let whoever fears that college life will render girls unfeminine, read and be reassured. And let him, too, read who already knows that an earnest, intellectual life furnishes the proper nutriment to vigorous health, happy dispositions, warm affections, winning graces, and devout hearts. This is the soil and these the products of the College Beautiful."

Bertha Palmer, class of 1891, niece of George Herbert Palmer, has a poem, named Friendship, in the collection.

8 *Why Go To College.*

The title page describes this publication as "An Address by Alice Freeman Palmer formerly president of Wellesley College," but no entry in the Chronicles tells where or when she delivered the address. A sentence from this address (on page 23) was inscribed on the tablet near the bust of Mrs. Palmer in the Hall of Fame for Great Americans: "The smallest village, the plainest home, give ample space for the resources of the trained college woman" (see 286n1). For Professor Palmer's comment on this piece, see **AFPann**-17.

Mrs. Palmer begins: "To a largely increasing number of young girls college doors are opening every year. Every year adds to the number of men who feel as a friend of mine, a successful lawyer in a great city, felt when in talking of the future of his four little children he said, 'For the boys it is not so serious, but I lie down at night afraid to die and leave my daughters only a bank account.' Year by year, too, the experiences of life are teaching mothers that happiness does not necessarily come to their daughters when accounts are large and banks are sound, but that on the contrary they take grave risks when they trust everything to accumulated wealth and the chance of a happy marriage. Our American girls themselves are becoming aware that they need the stimulus, the discipline, the knowledge, the interests of the college in addition to the school, if they are to prepare themselves for the most serviceable lives.

"But there are still parents who say, 'There is no need that my daughter should teach; then why should she go to college?' I will not reply that college training is a life insurance for a girl, a pledge that she possesses the disciplined ability to earn a living for herself and others in case of need; for I prefer to insist on the importance of giving every girl, no matter what her present circumstances, a special training in some one thing by which she can render society service, not amateur but of an expert sort, and service too for which it will be willing to pay a price . . . "

Paragraph openings follow: "While it is not true that all girls should go to college any more than that all boys should go, it is nevertheless true that they should go in greater numbers than at present. They fail to go because they, their parents, their teachers, do not see clearly the personal benefits distinct from the commercial value of a college training . . . It is undoubtedly true that many girls are totally unfitted by home and school life for a valuable college course. These joys and successes, these high interests and friendships, are not for the self-conscious and nervous invalid, nor for her who in the exuberance of youth recklessly ignores the laws of a healthy life . . .

"Pre-eminently the college is a place of education. That is the ground of its being . . . The first of [the collateral advantages of going to college] is happiness . . . Yet a girl should go to college not merely to obtain four happy years, but to make a second gain, which is often overlooked, and is little understood even when perceived; I mean a gain in health . . . It is significant that already statistical investigation in this country and in England shows that the standard of health is higher among the women who hold college degrees than among any other equal number of the same age and class. . . .

"Until a girl goes away from home to school or college, her friends are chiefly chosen for her by circumstances . . . To-day above all things we need the influence of men and women of friendliness, of generous nature, of hospitality to new ideas, in short, of social imagination. But instead, we find each political party bitterly calling the other dishonest, each class suspicious of the intentions of the other, and in social life the pettiest standards of conduct. Is it not well for us that the colleges all over the country still offer to their fortunate students a society of the most democratic sort,—one in which a father's money, a mother's social position, can assure no distinction and make no close friends? . . . To some people the shaping ideals of what character should be, often held unconsciously, come from the books they read; but to the majority they are given by the persons whom they most admire before they are twenty years old. The greatest thing any friend or teacher, either in school or college, can do for a student, is to furnish him with a personal ideal . . .

"Emerson in writing of beauty declares that 'the secret of ugliness consists not in irregular outline, but in being uninteresting. We love any forms, however ugly, from which great qualities shine. If command, eloquence, art, or invention exists in the most deformed person, all the accidents that usually displease, please, and raise esteem and wonder higher. Beauty without grace is the head without the body. Beauty without expression tires' . . .

"Yet even if that which is the profession of woman *par excellence* be hers, how can she be perennially so interesting a companion to her husband and children as if she had keen personal tastes, long her own, and growing with her growth? . . . Even with the help of a permanent business or profession . . . the most interesting men I know are those who have an avocation as well as a vocation. I mean a taste or work quite apart from the business of life. This revives, inspires, and cultivates them perpetually. It matters little what it is, if only it is real and personal, is large enough to last, and possesses the power of growth . . . There are two reasons why women need to cultivate these large and abiding interests even more persistently than men. In the first place, they have more leisure

. . . [T]here is a second reason why a girl should acquire for herself strong and worthy interests. The regular occupations of women in their homes are generally disconnected and of little educational value, at least as those homes are at present conducted . . .

"What, then, are the interests which powerfully appeal to mind and heart, and so are fitted to become the strengthening companions of a woman's life? I shall mention only three, all of them such as are elaborately fostered by college life. The first is the love of great literature . . . But there is a second invigorating interest to which college training introduces its student. I mean the study of nature, intimacy with the strange and beautiful world in which we live . . . But it is a short step from the love of the complex and engaging world in which we live to the love of our comrades in it. Accordingly the third precious interest to be cultivated by the college student is an interest in people . . . But if that life includes a love of books, of nature, of people, it will naturally turn to enlarged conceptions of religion — my sixth and last gift of college life . . ."

Mrs. Palmer ends: "Such are some of the larger influences to be had from college life. It is true all the good gifts I have named may be secured without the aid of the college. We all know young men and women who have had no college training, who are as cultivated, rational, resourceful, and happy as any people we know, who excel in every one of these particulars the college graduates about them. I believe they often bitterly regret the lack of a college education. And we see young men and women going through college deaf and blind to their great chances there, and afterwards curiously careless and wasteful of the best things in life. While all that is true, it is true too that to the open-minded and ambitious boy or girl of moderate health, ability, self-control, and studiousness, a college course offers the most attractive, easy, and probable way of securing happiness and health, good friends and high ideals, permanent interests of a noble kind, and large capacity for usefulness in the world. *It has been well said that the ability to see great things large and little things small is the final test of education* [compiler's italics]. The foes of life, especially of women's lives, are caprice, wearisome incapacity, and petty judgments. From these oppressive foes we long to escape to the rule of right reason, where all things are possible, and life becomes a glory instead of a grind. No college, with the best teachers and collections in the world, can by its own power impart all this to any woman. But if one has set her face in that direction, where else can she find so many hands reached out to help, so many encouraging voices in the air, so many favoring influences filling the days and nights?"

9 What Women Can Do For The Public Schools.

An editorial entitled Woman's "Open Door" in Education, in the same issue of the *Independent* (page 355–356) introduces Mrs. Palmer's article:

> "There are no limitations of sex in American activity or enterprise. No one who knows the women of our country will suspect them of having little to do or of being self-indulgent as to the tasks and responsibilities they assume.
>
> "Yet defining leisure as that happy condition in life which leaves one with a good large fraction of time and energy free from imperative preoccupations, there is nothing more remarkable in our civilization than its tendencies to the endowment of women with the opportunities, the power, and the boundless influence of the leisure class in society. It brings to them possibilities which are beyond computation and which owe their existence directly to the fact that by the unwritten laws and the realities of social life American women are in possession of the freedom to think and act and organize, which is the essence of what we mean by leisure. In their hands it is a power greater than capital, more potent than Legislatures, and more effective than the ballot, and owes its significance to the fact that it stands outside, above and free of them all.
>
> "Not only are these great opportunities coming more largely and more securely to women, but they are training themselves as never before in the history of the world to the administration of the trusts and the responsibilities which go with them. This explains the phenomenal growth of colleges for women and annexes for women in the established universities. It is not that the distinctions of sex are fading out, not that women are becoming men, not that a readjustment between the sexes is called for,

> but simply that women are rising to the opportunities which their freedom from the engrossing occupations and responsibilities of men give them, and fitting themselves to use them with a skill and fidelity which promise great things for the future.
>
> "This movement is part of that readjustment to new conditions which is taking place all along the line or lines of social life and which is destined, without revolution, and with no greater overturnings and no more friction than we have already had, to settle the vexed problems of capital and labor, of municipal government, of social development and individual right and freedom.
>
> "The teacher's profession is far from being an avocation of leisure; but the efficiency, discipline and general conduct of the schools will depend very largely on the number of citizens who have leisure at their command, and with what degree of public spirit and intelligence they use that leisure. This is where the new social function of women, growing out of the intelligent and public-spirited use of their leisure, comes in. The subject is brilliantly discussed in our columns to-day by Mrs. Alice Freeman Palmer. What she says so well as applied to education might be extended over the wide and important fields of art, religion, morals, manners, and all the other social interests which depend so much for their development on the citizens' leisure to attend to such things."

When she wrote this article in 1898, Mrs. Palmer had been an active member of the Massachusetts State Board of Education since 1889 (see 74n2).

Writing in Boxford, she begins: "In discussions of public education there are three considerations of grave consequence which must not be overlooked.

"The first is the imperative need of improvements in our schools in order to adapt them to the rapidly changing conditions of life. Never before have the schools been more sharply criticised both by their friends and foes.

"People are asking whether we are getting our full return for the one hundred and ninety millions we are spending annually; the experts are keenly at work on new methods and questions of reorganization; but if the public schools are to accomplish for the next generation the fundamental work we may fairly demand of them, the decisions of these and other weighty matters must not be left solely to the teachers and officers of administration. Doing their best, they must largely fail without the steady sympathy and intelligent co-operation of the homes.

"Therefore the second point must be continually emphasized—that with us in this country none of the much-needed improvements can be made in education except through the power of an aroused and enlightened public opinion . . . We must elevate public sentiment before we can give the schools the new opportunities, already the happy inheritance of the more active-minded communities. Politics in the city and stupidity in the country are formidable foes of education . . .

"Women compose at least half, and in many parts of the country much more than half, of the community. In many sections they have had, on the average, a more generous education than the men. They are, moreover, the only leisure class in this country, and must, therefore, undertake much of the unremunerated work of society, in education, in charity, in reform. They are in close and constant contact with the growing children, and know, or may know, the conditions of school life, more intimately than any one else can know them. They are now well organized in clubs and societies, so that their convictions, if carefully formed, can speedily be made effective upon public sentiment, and influential in the management of the schools . . .

"The first thing that women can do is to study the schools. No woman should fail to have an intelligent acquaintance with the schools of her neighborhood, whether she has children in them or not. All women should feel that they fail in patriotism if they fail here. They are not good citizens unless they definitely assist some work of education . . . Mothers will be astonished to learn how tremendous is the influence of a teacher, hitherto unknown, upon the whole life of their child . . . The Public Education Associations now being formed are doing much, but nothing better than in bringing teachers and parents into frequent and friendly intercourse and discussion of all the interests of the children . . .

"When the intelligent women of any community take an active interest in the schools, and are in close relation with the teachers, they will certainly wish to do something for them. They will find certain definite needs . . . Of these needs none is more urgent than the improvement of the sanitary conditions of the school buildings.

"Women must carry over their ideas of good housekeeping into the public homes of their children . . . [W]omen can occupy themselves with no more efficient and far-reaching charity than the bettering of the health conditions of the school children, omitting nothing that can improve the drainage, the air, the light; control the heat; provide suitable desks and absolute cleanliness, especially of cellars and lavatories, and protect against contagious disease . . .

"But women can give more than health; they can give beauty, a matter as important to the growing child as fresh air . . . If our people are to make living a fine art, if the next generation is to rise above coarse, rude ways to the love of beautiful things and the power to create them, then the little children must have beauty about them in the schools when they are very young . . .

"Women can provide training in domestic science and household arts. [See 80n4] This should include not only the practical and theoretical work of the cooking school and the sewing class, but some knowledge of plumbing, heating, drainage, cleaning, household buying and accounts . . . Such experiments, wisely carried out at private cost and under private direction, soon show that money spent on kindergartens, domestic science, manual training and vacation schools for city children, will save far more than their cost to the community in truant and reform schools, in prisons, almshouses and hospitals. Such considerations as I have been urging make daily war upon the grim quartet that prey upon society—ignorance, poverty, sickness and sin . . . "

10 The History of the Case.

This long poem by Alice Freeman Palmer is included here because it is buried in a book, *The Story of the Bee*, by her sister-in-law (Frederic Palmer's wife), Mary Towle Palmer (a copy is in the Special Collections at the Wellesley College Library).

The occasion was the engagement of her friend, Lilian Horsford, daughter of Eben Horsford, to William G. Farlow, Professor of Cryptogamic Botany at Harvard. Mary Towle Palmer, Alice Freeman Palmer, and Lilian Horsford were all members of the Cambridge Bee (see 260n1). The opening quotation is the first of the four stanzas in Alfred Tennyson's poem, Lilian. The map on page 512 will help the reader to follow Dan Cupid's movements on Quincy Street!

In **aboutAFPann**-16, Professor Laughlin at the University of Chicago describes a side of Mrs. Palmer that is revealed in this poem: "Her love of fun was only a part of her general cheerfulness. Never was a nature more joyous, more buoyant, more optimistic than hers. No one ever gave as much happiness to as many people as she."

The History Of The Case
November 3, 1899
On Lilian Horsford's Engagement to the
Professor of Cryptogamic Botany

Long years ago, a famous poet sang
This eager song of love to Lilian:
  "Airy, fairy Lilian,
  Flitting, fairy Lilian,
  When I ask her if she love me,
  Claps her tiny hands above me,
  Laughing all she can;
  She'll not tell me if she love me,
  Cruel little Lilian."
She would not tell him that she loved him. No.
Poet and prince and painter knelt, and though
Doctor and lawyer, merchant, priest, they came,
She stood, the unconquered girl, whom none could tame,
A new Diana on the mountains lone,
And every year more fair and stately grown.
From round the land men come to Cambridge town.
Learning and maidens gave the place renown.
But none so fair as queenly Lilian,
And none so haughty since the world began.
On staid Professors she would sweetly smile,
And dance with simple students for a while.
But huntress Dian with her silver bow

Was not more cruel to the men laid low.
Yet heartless was she not. 'Twas plain to view
From her calm heights, she looked men through and through,
And none she found in all the seeking band
So wise and strong and good to win her hand.
So then she journeyed oft across the sea,
To North and South and East and West went she,
Bicycling tried, and many things to please,
But none so loved as her own faithful Bees.
To Providence on business oft she went,
On management of large affairs intent.
To poor men's homes her presence lent a grace,
For nieces and for nephews made a place;
The Wellesley girls she treated royally;
Her name is better than their best degree.
But Radcliffe led by her so straight a path
That Barrett Wendell rose in mighty wrath
And called on all the gods to save the place,
From falling victim to such power and grace.
Harvard Professors were his fondest care,
His piercing eye forsaw the hidden snare,
Saw Harvard men's tender virility
Go tottering down before such maids as she.
For, one sweet night Dan Cupid ran away
And came to Quincy Street for pleasant play.
He needed rest from anxious care, because
So many Boston girls defied his laws.
So quite dispirited he roamed along
Past the Colonial Club's old bachelor throng,
Until he came to number twenty-four,
And slipped in softly through the open door.
The little god on mischief deep was bent.
Who was this famous man? What had he meant
By the strange mysteries through all this room?
He peeped through microscopes, found the brush-broom
And swept some precious mushrooms in the fire,
Heard C. J. overhead. Began to tire.
Turned to the table then and down he sat.
Letters and cards and finally a hat
Gave him the clue, and in the Harvard book

It did not take him very long to look.
"Oho!" said Dan, "a Botanist is this,
And learnéd too, I'll wager many a kiss.
What 'cryptogamic' is, I cannot guess.
If I could catch him once, he should confess.
It must be something secret about flowers
That botanists play with in leisure hours.
Perhaps what flowers are good for. Clearly he
A practical wise housekeeper must be."
With that he fell into a lingering gloom,
And studied all the pleasant mannish room;
Books, busts, collections, everything could see
Except one touch of femininity.
He pondered long, and every moment saw
Some fresh surprise, till wonder mixed with awe
Fell on his spirit, and he sadly said,
"Ye gods! Such learning in one human head!
My hands would tremble should I lift my bow.
This is no place for me. I'd better go!"
But Venus on the doorstep met her son,
And saw his melancholy air, and won
The story from him. "Silly boy!" she cried,
"Slip back, and in the doorway quickly hide!
How young you are! You surely can't suppose
He likes his fungi better than a rose!
Or did you think such flowers were made to tease
Poor botanists? Why, child, they're made for bees.
Where flowers are loved, the bees are sure to come.
Where flowers grow, they make their dearest home.
Forget the 'cryptogamic.' Trust to me.
It takes a botanist to catch a bee!
I know the sweetest bee in all the hive.
The loveliest lady ever yet alive!"
Young Cupid jumped for joy. Caught up his bow,
Polished his arrow, rushed inside; and so
His lady mother left him with a smile,
Crossed over to the Shalers for a while
To watch how things were going there, until
She heard a tapping on the window-sill.
"Sweet mother, you are right. He had a heart.

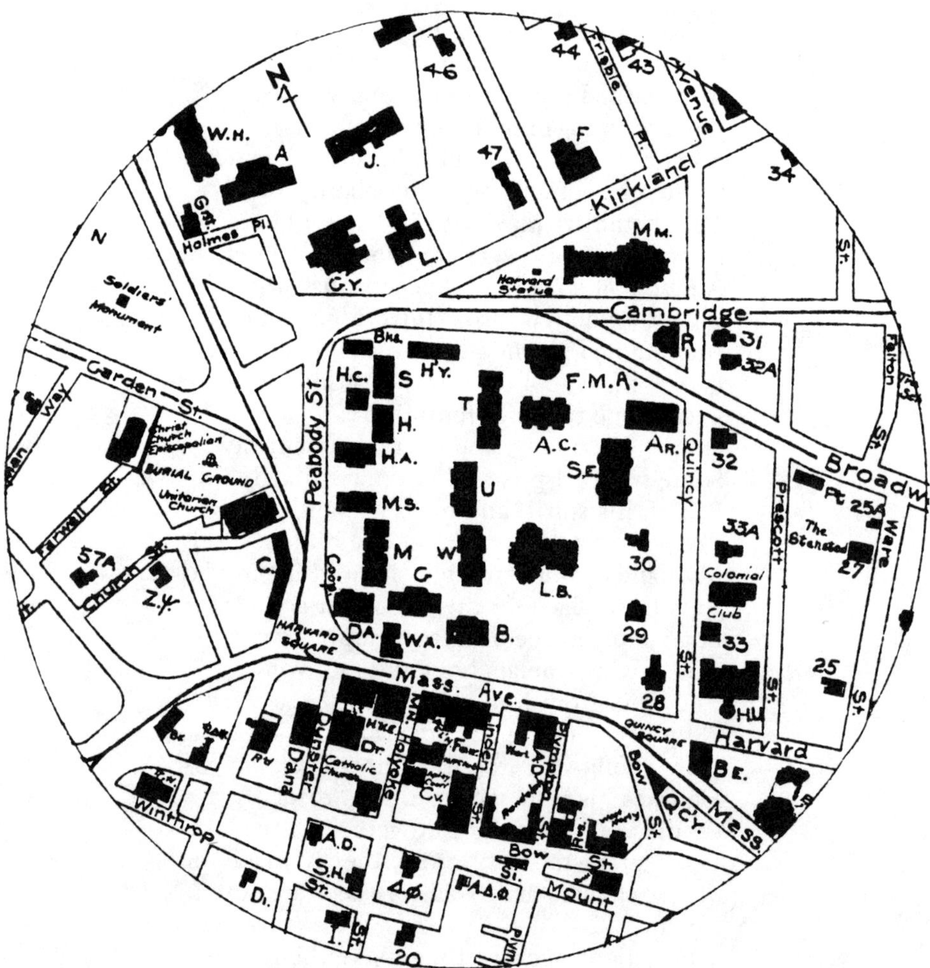

An enlarged section from a map of Cambridge in the vicinity of Harvard College, 1900–1901. The circle, centered at University Hall (U), has a radius of one-quarter mile. The key to the numbers (below) and the letters (on the facing page) are transcribed from the border of the map.

The seventeen numbers within the circle identify the homes of these individuals (see Biographical Summaries): 20 F. Bôcher; 25 H. Münsterberg; 25A F. Russell; 28 G.H. Palmer; 29 C. W. Eliot; 30 N. S. Shaler; 31 C. C. Langdell; 32 A. Agassiz; 32A J. H. Wright; 33 F. C. de Sumichrast; 33A W. G. Farlow; 34 S. M. Mcvane; 43 J. H. Arnold; 44 J. B. Ames; 46 W. C. Lane; 47 F. G. Peabody; 57A M. H. Bailey.

The letters identify buildings, often with the date of origin:

A Austin Hall, Law School, 1883; A.C. Appleton Chapel, 1858; A.D. A.D. Club House; A.D.Δ.Φ. Alpha Delta Phi Club House; Ar. Architecture Building, 1901; B. Boylston Hall, 1857; Be. Beck Hall, 1876; Bks Phillips Brooks House, 1898; Br Brewer's Block; C. College House, 1832; DA. Dane Hall, 1832; Δ.Φ. Delta Phi Club House; Di. Digamma Club; Dr. Dunster House, 1897; F. Foxcroft House, 1888; Fair. Fairfax Hall; F.M.A. Fogg Museum of Art, 1895; G. Gray's Hall, 1863; Gnt. Gannet House; Gy. Gymnasium, 1879; H. Hollis Hall, 1763; Ha Harvard Hall, 1765; H.C. Holden Chapel, 1744; H'ke Holyoke House, 1870; H.P. Club Hasty Pudding Club House, 1888; H'y Holworthy Hall, 1812; H.U. Harvard Union, 1901; I. Institute of 1770; J. Jefferson Physical Laboratory, 1884; L. Lawrence Hall, 1848; Lb. Library Gore Hall, 1841; Lit. Little's Block, 1854; M. Mathhews Hall, 1872; Mm. Memorial Hall, 1874; Mn. Manter Block, 1882; Ms. Massachusetts Hall, 1720; P'C'L'n Porcellian Club House, 1891; ΦΔΦ Phi Delta Phi Club House; θH Pi Eta Society; Pt. Prescott Hall, 1896; Q'cy Quincy Hall, 1892; R. Rogers Building, 1860; R'd Read's Block, 1886; Sh. Shepherd Block; Si. Signet Club House; T Thayer Hall, 1870; U University Hall, 1815; W Weld Hall, 1872; Wa. Wadsworth House, 1776; Warl. Warland Block; W.H. Walter Hastings Hall, 1890; Z. Zeta Psi Club House.

Forever more it carries Cupid's dart."
A moment more you might have seen the lad
Running up Brattle Street like one gone mad.
It proved a match,—the gods' peculiar care,
And not at all a mere mushroom affair.
So this is why you hear the hum of bees
These autumn days on all our Cambridge trees;
Why airs are mild, and all our gardens bring
Sweet buds to blossom, dreaming it is Spring.
For Lilian is caught, is caught at last,
And all her honey-bee's free life is past.
Now she to Quincy Street must quickly come.
"Heaven bless the lady!" every Bee must hum.
Alice Freeman Palmer

11 Women's Education in the Nineteenth Century.

This report of her scholarly study reminds the reader that Alice Elvira Freeman first came to Wellesley College as professor of history (in 1879). Except for its publication in a New York newspaper, the report is available only in an out-of-print volume (**GHP**-65, **AFP**-17); accordingly it is presented here in its entirety.

"One of the most distinctive and far-reaching movements of the nineteenth century is that which has brought about the present large opportunities for the higher education of women. Confining itself to no country, this vast movement has advanced rapidly in some, slowly and timidly in others. In America three broad periods mark its progress: first, the period of quiescence, which ends about 1830; second, the period of agitation, ending with the civil war; third, though far as yet from completion, may be called the period of accomplishment.

"For the first two hundred years in the history of our country little importance was attached to the education of women, though before the nineteenth century began, twenty-four colleges had been founded for the education of men. In the early years of this century private schools for girls were expensive and short-lived. The common schools were the only grades of public instruction open to young women. In the cities of Massachusetts, where more was done for the education of boys than elsewhere, girls were allowed to go to school only a small part of the year, and in some places could even then use the school-room only in the early hours of the day, or on those afternoons when the boys had a half-holiday. Anything like a careful training of girls was not yet thought of.

"This comparative neglect of women is less to be wondered at when we remember that the colleges which existed at the beginning of this century had been founded to fit men for the learned professions, chiefly for the ministry. Neither here nor elsewhere was it customary to give advanced education to boys destined for business. The country, too, was impoverished by the long struggle for independence. The Government was bankrupt, unable to pay its veteran soldiers. Irritation and unrest were everywhere prevalent until the ending of the second war with England, in 1815. Immediately succeeding this began the great migration to the West and Southwest which carried thousands of the most ambitious young men and women from the East to push our frontiers farther and farther into the wilderness. Even in the older parts of the country the population was widely scattered. The people lived for the most part in villages and isolated farms. City life was uncommon. As late as 1840 only nine per cent of the population was living in cities of 8000 or more inhabitants. Under such conditions nothing more than the bare necessities of education could be regarded.

"But this very isolation bred a kind of equality. In district schools it became natural for boys and girls to study together and to receive the same instruction from teachers who were often young and enthusiastic. These were as a rule college students, granted long winter vacations from their own studies that they might earn money by teaching village schools. Thus most young women shared with their brothers the best elementary training the country afforded, while college education was reserved for the few young men who were preparing for the ministry or for some other learned profession.

"From the beginning it had been the general custom of this country to educate boys and girls together up to the college age. To-day in less than six per cent of all our cities is there any separate provision of schools for boys and girls. This habitual early start together has made it natural for our men and women subsequently to read the same books, to have the same tastes and interests, and jointly to approve a large social freedom. On the whole, women have usually had more leisure than men for the cultivating of scholarly tastes.

"The first endowment of the higher education of women in

this country was made by the Moravians in the seminary for girls which they founded at Bethlehem, Pennsylvania, in 1749. They founded another girls' seminary at Lititz in 1794. Though both of these honorable foundations continue in effective operation to-day, their influence has been for the most part confined to the religious communion of their founders. In 1804 an academy with wider connections was founded at Bradford, Massachusetts, at first open to boys and girls, since 1836 limited to girls. From that time academies and seminaries for girls increased rapidly. One of the most notable was Troy Seminary, founded by Emma Hart Willard and chartered in 1819. Miss Willard drew up broad and original plans for the higher education of girls, laid them before President Monroe, appealed to the New York Legislature for aid, and dreamed of establishing something like collegiate training. More than three hundred students entered her famous seminary, and for seventeen years she carried it on with growing reputation. Her address to the President in 1819 is still a strong statement of the importance to the republic of an enlightened and disciplined womanhood.

"Even more influential was the life and work of Mary Lyon, who in 1837 founded Mount Holyoke Seminary, and labored for the education of women until her death, in 1849. Of strong religious nature, great courage and resource, she went up and down New England securing funds and pupils. Her rare gift of inspiring both men and women induced wide acceptance of her ideals of character and intelligence. Seminaries patterned after Mount Holyoke sprang up all over the land, and still remain as centres of powerful influence, particularly in the Middle West and on the Pacific Coast.

"With this development, through the endowment of many excellent seminaries, of the primary education of girls into something like secondary or high-school opportunities, the period of quiescence comes to an end. There follows a period of agitation when the full privilege of college training side by side with men was demanded for women. This agitation was closely connected on the one hand with the anti-slavery movement and the general passion for moral reform at that time current; and, on the other, with the interest in teaching and that study of its methods which Horace Mann fostered. From 1830 to 1865 it was becoming evident that women were destined to have a large share in the instruction of children. For this work they sought to fit themselves, and the reformers aided them. Oberlin College, which began as a collegiate institute in 1833, was in 1850 chartered as a college. From the beginning it admitted women, and in 1841 three women took its diploma. Antioch College, under Horace Mann's leadership, opened in 1853, admitting women on equal terms with men. In 1855 Elmira College was founded, the first institution chartered as a separate college for women.

"Even before the Civil War the commercial interests of the country had become so much extended that trade was rising into a dignity comparable to that of the learned professions. Men were more and more deserting teaching for the business life, and their places, at first chiefly in the lower grades, were being filled by women. During the five years of the war this supersession of men by women teachers advanced rapidly. It has since acquired such impetus that at present more than two thirds of the training of the young of both sexes below the college grade has fallen out of the hands of men. In the mean time, too, though in smaller numbers, women have invaded the other professions and have even entered into trade. These demonstrations of a previously unsuspected capacity have been both the cause and the effect of enlarged opportunities for mental equipment. The last thirty or forty years have seen the opening of that new era in women's education which I have ventured to call the period of accomplishment.

"From the middle of the century the movement to open the state universities to women, to found colleges for men and women on equal terms, and to establish independent colleges for women spread rapidly. From their first organization the state universities of Utah (1850), Iowa (1856), Washington (1862), Kansas (1866), Minnesota (1868), Nebraska (1871) admitted women. Indiana, founded in 1820, opened its doors to women in 1868, and was followed in 1870 by Michigan, at that time the largest and far the most influential of all the state universities. From that time the movement became general. The example of Michigan was followed until at the present time [1900] all the colleges and universities of the West, excepting those under Catholic management, are open to women. The only state university in the East, that of Maine, admitted women in 1872. Virginia, Georgia, and Louisiana alone among all the state universities of the country remain closed to women.

"This sudden opening to women of practically all universities supported by public funds is not more extraordinary than the immense endowments which during the same period have been put into independent colleges for women, or into colleges which admit men and women on equal terms. Of these privately endowed colleges, Cornell, originally founded for men, led the way in 1872 in opening its doors to women. The West and South followed rapidly, the East more slowly. Of the 480 colleges which at the end of the century are reported by the Bureau of Education, 336 admit women; or, excluding the Catholic colleges, 80 per cent of all are open to women. Of the sixty leading colleges in the United States there are only ten in which women are not admitted to some department. These ten are all on the Atlantic seaboard and are all old foundations.

"This substantial accomplishment during the last forty years of the right of women to a college education has not, however, resulted in fixing a single type of college in which that education shall be obtained. On the contrary, three clearly contrasted types now exist side by side. These are the independent college, the coeducational college, and the affiliated college.

"To the independent college for women men are not admitted, though the grade, the organization, and the general aim are supposed to be the same as in the colleges exclusively for men. The first college of this type, Elmira (1855), has been already mentioned. The four largest women's colleges — Vassar, opened in 1861; Smith, in 1875; Wellesley, in 1875, and Bryn Mawr, in 1885 — take rank among the sixty leading colleges of the country in wealth, equipment, teachers and students, and variety of studies offered. Wells College, chartered as a college in 1870, Woman's College of Baltimore, opened in 1888, and Mt. Holyoke, reorganized as a college in 1893, have also large endowments and attendance. All the women's colleges are empowered to confer the same degrees as are given in the men's colleges.

"The development of coeducation, the prevailing type of education in the United States for both men and women, has already been sufficiently described. [for example, in **AFP**-4] In coeducational colleges men and women have the same instructors, recite in the same classes, and enjoy the same freedom in choice of studies. To the faculties of these colleges women are occasionally appointed, and, like their male colleagues, teach mixed classes of men and women. Many coeducational colleges are without halls of residence. Where these exist, special buildings are assigned to the women students.

"The affiliated colleges, while exclusively for women, are closely connected with strong colleges for men, whose equipment and opportunities they are expected in some degree to share. At present there are five such: Radcliffe College, the originator of this type, connected with Harvard University, and opened in 1879; Sophie Newcomb Memorial College, at Tulane University, opened in 1886; the College for Women of Western Reserve University, 1888; Barnard College, at Columbia University, 1889; the Woman's College of Brown University, 1892. In all these colleges the standards for entrance and graduation are the same as those exacted from men in the universities with which they are affiliated. To a considerable extent the instructors also are the same.

"During the last quarter-century many professional schools have been opened to women — schools of theology, law, medicine, dentistry, pharmacy, technology, agriculture. The number of women entering these professions is rapidly increasing. Since 1890 the increase of women students in medicine is 64 per cent, in dentistry 205 per cent, in pharmacy 190 per cent, in technology and agriculture 194 per cent.

"While this great advance has been accomplished in America, women in England and on the Continent, especially during the last thirty years, have been demanding better education. Though much more slowly and in fewer numbers than in this country, they have everywhere succeeded in securing decided advantages. No country now refuses them a share in liberal study, in the instruction of young children, and in the profession of medicine. As might be expected, English-speaking women, far more than any others, have won and used the opportunities of university training. Since 1860 women have been studying at Cambridge, England, and since 1879 at Oxford. At these ancient seats of learning they have now every privilege except the formal degree. To all other English and Scotch universities, and to the universities of the British colonies, women are admitted, and from them they receive degrees.

"In the most northern countries of Europe — in Iceland, Finland, Norway, Sweden, Denmark — the high schools and universities are freely open to women. In eastern Europe able women have made efforts to secure advanced study, and these efforts have been most persistent in Russia and since the Crimean war. When denied in their own land, Russian women have flocked to the Swiss and French universities, and have even gone in considerable numbers to Finland and to Italy. Now Russia is slowly responding to its women's entreaties. During the last ten years the universities of Rumania, Bulgaria, Hungary, and Greece have been open to women; while in Constantinople the American College for Girls offers the women of the East the systematic training of the New England type of college. In western, central, and southern Europe all university doors are open. In these countries, degrees and honors may everywhere be had by women, except in Germany and Austria. Even here, by special permission of the the Minister of Education, or the professor in charge, women may hear lectures. Each year, too, more women are granted degrees by special vote and as exceptional cases.

"In brief, it may be said that practically all European universities are now open to women. No American woman of scholarship, properly qualified for the work she undertakes, need fear refusal if she seeks the instruction of the greatest European scholars in her chosen field. Each year American women are taking with distinction the highest university degrees of the Continent. To aid them, many fellowships and graduate scholarships, ranging in value from $300 to $1000, are offered for foreign study by our colleges for women and by private associations of women who seek to promote scholarship. Large numbers of ambitious young women who are preparing themselves for teaching or for the higher fields of scientific research annually compete for this aid. Three years ago an association was formed for maintaining an American woman's table in the Zoölogical Station at Naples [79n2]. By paying $500 a year they are thus able to grant to selected students the most favorable conditions for biological investigation. This association has also just offered a prize of $1000, to be granted two years hence, for the best piece of original scientific work done in the meantime by a woman. The American Schools of Classical Studies in Athens and Rome admit women on the same terms as men, and award their fellowships to men and women indifferently. One of these fellowships, amounting to $1000 a year, has just been won by a woman.

"The experience, then, of the last thirty years shows a condition of women's education undreamed of at the beginning of the century. It shows that though still hampered here and there by timorous restrictions, women are in substantial possession of much the same opportunities as are available to men. It shows that they have both the capacity and the desire for college training, that they can make profitable and approved use of it when obtained, and that they are eager for that broader and more original study after college work is over which is at once the most novel and the most glorious feature of university education to-day. Indeed, women have taken more than their due proportion of the prizes, honors, and fellowships which have been accessible to them on the same terms as to men. Their resort to institutions of higher learning has increased far more than that of men. In 1872 the total number of college students in each million of population was 590. Last year it had risen to 1270, much more than doubling in twenty-seven years. During this time the number of men had risen from 540 to 947, or had not quite doubled. The women rose from 50 in 1872 to 323 in 1899, having increased their former proportional number more than six times, and this advance has also been maintained in graduate and professional schools.

"The immensity of the change which the last century has wrought in women's education may best be seen by setting side by side the conditions at its beginning and at its close. In 1800 no colleges for women existed, and only two endowed schools for girls — these belonging to a small German sect. They had no high schools, and the best grammar schools in cities were open to them only under restrictions. The commoner grammar and district schools, and an occasional private school dedicated to 'accomplishments,' were their only avenues to learnng. There was little hostility to their education, since it was generally assumed by men and by themselves that intellectual matters did not concern them. No profession was open to them, not even that of teaching, and only seven possible trades and occupations.

"In 1900 a third of all the college students in the United States are women. Sixty per cent of the pupils in the secondary schools, both public and private, are girls —*i.e.* more girls are preparing for college than boys. Women having in general more leisure than men, there is reason to expect that there will soon be more women than men in our colleges and graduate schools. The time, too, has passed when girls went to college to prepare themselves solely for teaching or for other bread-winning occupations. In considerable numbers they now seek intellectual resources and the enrichment of their private lives. Thus far between 50 and 60 per cent of women college graduates have at some time taught. In the country at large more than 70 per cent of the teaching is done by women, in the North Atlantic portion over 80 per cent. Even in the secondary schools, public and private, more women than men are teaching, though in all other countries the advanced instruction of boys is exclusively in the hands of men. Never before has a nation intrusted all the school training of the vast majority of its future population, men as well as women, to women alone."

12 A poem from Alice Freeman Palmer to Anna Hooker Morse (1 year and 9 months old).

About fourteen years ago, in a Boston used book store, tipped into a copy of the *Life of Alice Freeman Palmer* (**GHP**-57), I found this poem in Mrs. Palmer's handwriting (AJL Collection); I present it here for the first time.

When the wind blows cold, my Anna,
and the dust flies down the street,
Can your baby heart remember
Boxford breezes fresh and sweet?
When nurse takes you, nicely bundled,
walking down the Avenue,
Can you think how tall the pine trees
in the blessed forests grew?
You have not forgotten, sweetheart,
how the faithful Hobson horse
Used to bring me, through the woodlands,
laughing little Anna Morse,
How the birds sang all the summer,
how the flowers and grasses grew,
How the waters smiled to heaven,
bluer when the skies were blue.
Blue as little Anna's eyes, and rosy
in the sunset glow, —
All the dear delights of summer, in
the winter days you know.

So there comes from me who loves you
something to remind you, dear,
Of the spring time and and [*sic*] the gardens,
and the songs of all the year.

And perhaps when you are older, you
can hear the pages say
God bless my little Anna, and
make her glad today!

Christmas,
1900

Anna Hooker Morse, born on April 5, 1899, later a member of the Wellesley College class of 1921, was the daughter of Annie Hooker Capron (Wellesley, class of 1882) and Lewis Kennedy Morse. The Palmer and Morse families were close friends (see 127n2).

13 A letter from Alice Freeman Palmer to Anna Hooker Morse (2 years and $9^{1/2}$ months old).

This handwritten letter was found in the same volume as the poem in **AFPann**-12, and, like the poem, is presented here for the first time. Arthur Webster Morse, Anna's brother, who is mentioned in the letter, was born on March 9, 1900. "Little Stella" in the letter was Estelle Freeman, born in December 1900, the daughter of Fred Warren Freeman, Alice Freeman Palmer's brother.

January 18th 1902
11 Quincy Street [Saturday]
Cambridge.

My darling little Anna,

How very much I like your nice long letter that came to me this morning! I read every word and then I showed it to Mr. Palmer and he liked it too, almost as well as I did! Your beautiful big lines made me think of the days when I used to study calculus, and I feel sure you are planning the orbits of comets you mean sometime to tell the world all about. Or is it butterflies' flights on long summer afternoons that you want to tell me about, little girl? But whether stars or butterflies, it's all a new heaven and a new earth to you, isn't it, dear? And you make all things new to those who love you so!

And I have a new picture this morning from my dear big girl, Lucy Sprague, who went with you and Arthur and me in the woods and by the big pond last summer, when I took your pictures there, don't you remember? You must all come out and see how lonely and sad she looks. She painted me a little picture of a pretty girl that I am sure you would like, so I send it to you with my love. You will soon grow up to be a College girl as tall as that!

Rex [see 216n1] lies here in the sunshine on the rug by me, and I said to him just now, "Do you want to see Anna and Arthur?" and he jumped up on the window and looked up at the cars that go into Boston and waved his tail, and said "bow-wow" as loud as he could, which means that you children must come soon, and make him a visit. Then I will tell you more about my little Stella, who goes every day to see my mother because she is sick, and sits on the bed, and shows her pictures in a big book, and says "all right" so often and so cheerfully that it makes her almost well. Just think what little girls can do by smiling on people! Tell your mamma not to forget to come to see me Tuesday [as she notes in her diary, chapter 4, Mrs. Palmer received visitors "at home" on Tuesday afternoons], and give Arthur a kiss right in the middle of his forehead for your loving,

Alice Freeman Palmer

14 The Need of Well Educated Teachers and Adequate Salaries in the Elementary Grades of our Public Schools. II. The Practical Side of Adequate Salaries.

This address and a preceding one by Professor Hugo Münsterberg were delivered before the Boston Branch of the Association of Collegiate Alumnae, on May 11, 1901. (For a description of the Association of Collegiate Alumnae, see 75n3.) The addresses "were taken down in short-hand and are printed from the stenographic report with the consent of the authors."

Professor Münsterberg spoke first, on The Need of Well Trained Teachers in the Elementary Schools. He told the group of college trained women that "it is simply your duty to go into the primary schools as much as you can. I know well that there are two somewhat important arguments always against this. The first is, that the pupils of the primary schools do not need such elaborate teaching for their simple work and do not need teachers who have learned as much as you have learned. And the second is, that it is a kind of waste of energy for students who have passed a college course to have to go into the class-rooms of the primary schools, instead of devoting their brilliant attainments to the higher classes—to the better teaching. I think this is an illusion . . . The food for your mental life is not to come from what you are teaching . . . You must give up teaching any subject, unless you don't need to look it up in the books the day before . . . Your private interests have to go far beyond that work, until the greatest possible contrast is reached . . . Inspire yourself with the deepest wisdom from books and your private study, and you will thus, even from the teaching in the primary class-room, get the inspiration of contrast. You will feel as you do your work in every class-room the effect of that kind of teaching which has nothing to do with your own problems, and which thus becomes a blessing to you and a blessing to the pupils and certainly a blessing to the whole country, which needs you far more than you yourself imagine."

After Professor Münsterberg, Mrs. Palmer spoke on The Practical Side of Adequate Salaries. Except for an introductory paragraph, her address is presented here in its entirety:

"Now, what was it which faced us practically as we listened to the appeal of Professor Münsterberg? When I graduated from college, twenty-five years ago, the supply of college women was much behind the demand. There were only a few of us coming out each June, and it was much simpler and easier than now to be called to a good position with a good salary, because we were so few.

"At present in Massachusetts, which I am going to use as an illustration, I find as I go about as a member of the Board of Education [see 74n2], that even in small high schools the superintendents everywhere are making it a practical rule that college men and women shall be employed when new positions are open in high schools. This is so in Oregon, it is so in California, it is so everywhere; and ordinarily when these new positions are open, it is to the college women. But is this so promising as it sounds? Of the half million children in the public schools and academies of Massachusetts only 33,000 are in high schools; and of about 14,000 teachers, in round numbers 1,400 are high-school teachers. Only 1,400 possible chances in the entire State to teach in high schools next year! And are all these 1,400 positions those to which the ambitious and eager college graduate can look as affording large opportunities of usefulness? Remember, I am speaking of the practical side of things as they are, and not what would be best for you or the children. One thousand four hundred positions in round numbers, 262 high schools in little Massachusetts with her 380 towns and cities. Two hundred and sixty-two high schools! This is a very large proportion, but of these only 65 have more than 150 pupils in them; and you know that a high school of 150 pupils cannot give opportunity for much specialization or much opportunity for higher work in your immediate profession. And only 72 in the whole State employ more than 5 teachers, including the special teachers of drawing, music, and the like. There are among these high schools 32 which have only one teacher for all the work done in the whole school, while 59 have only 2 teachers and 37 have only 3 teachers; and this includes all these special teachers. That is the situation at present in a State which offers as good opportunities, in proportion to its population, for advanced teaching as any of our States. You know this who come from other parts of the country.

"At this time of the year the presidents and deans of the colleges are having long interviews with those of you who want to be teachers; and I know well what you are saying to them, for when my bell rings (and I am always glad to have it ring) and a college senior comes in and asks me, 'Don't you know of a position? You are on the State Board of Education, so I thought, perhaps, you could tell me.' I know what she is going to add, in ninety-nine—no, let me be cautious, and say in ninety-eight cases out of a hundred. But still I ask her always, because it is always a pleasure to hear her answer, 'What do you want to teach, and where?' She 'wants to teach within thirty miles of Boston!' She thinks she might have to go a little farther away, but not much. [For an example, see Mrs. Palmer's diary for March 27, 1900, page 192.] She would like to teach in a college or a private school, perhaps in a high school, and that is the end. Even that is the third choice, with private schools as second and colleges as first. 'What do you want to teach?' I ask, and this answer, too, is perfectly predictable always. She 'likes something immensely' and she wants to teach it.

"Then I have to face the practical situation. Twenty-five years ago we could say what we 'liked' and where we 'wanted' to go. The supply at present is much in excess of the demand.

The colleges are very few where we are wanted. Colleges always demand a successful past in teaching, and the high schools are too few for the teachers, though, as I have said, the number of public high schools is growing where practically all the teachers are to be college men and women. Already in this State there are 1,416 high-school teachers, of whom 914 are college graduates, men and women, 23 are graduates of scientific and 207 of normal schools; and when the new appointments are made they will practically all be college graduates.

"But the salaries of many of those positions are inferior to the salaries of the best grammar-school positions in the larger cities. Of course, when our President asks me to discuss this subject we enter upon so large and complicated a problem that single individuals cannot solve it. It must be solved first by public sentiment, which must stand behind all school reform and regulate all school government. Whenever we touch any reform which involves the political situation and the management of our city governments, we have entered upon a very long reform which needs much patience.

"We women are the only class that is a leisure class in our American community; it is a pretty serious thing. You wonder where the leisure is; but all there is we can control if we will. There is no company of women that has ever had so much leisure, so much money to spend and so much independence in spending it, as we have. The men of our homes intend to give all the women they love time and money, to spend as they will. We have only two companies of men in this country who are not at work: one a few club men who sit at the windows of Fifth avenue club houses, and who count for nothing; and the other, the great army of the unemployed.

"We women have leisure; can we not see that it depends largely on us during the next ten years in our city and country life to say what shall be the public sentiment about teaching, what the kind of teachers shall be and what the management of the charities and the philanthropies which our overworked fathers and brothers are putting into our hands. It is a question that involves politics. I hope every college woman has it laid upon her heart to feel *noblesse oblige* ; she is bound to belong to a public school association, and wherever she is, in the city or in some district school, to have an interest and a share in getting the public schools under non-partisan conditions. The moment that is done, and an honorable and high-minded and efficient class of men and women put in charge of the schools, then an economical adminstration of the money that is spent on the schools can be brought about, and enough will be saved in almost every case to pay better salaries and to have fewer children in each schoolroom.

"These are the two chief reasons why you do not wish to teach the lower grades. You must have too many children in the rooms, and the rooms are badly ventilated and dirty, and the salaries are small. You object to teaching fifty children in a building that is not perfectly clean. But we never can build schools that are good on a basis which supplies no learned teachers, and which stands in opposition to training for teaching as a profession. That, too, is a long reform. I do not know how to answer the question as to how we can get adequate salaries, unless you go into the schools as they are. If we could once show by experience that it paid to have cultivated, thoroughly trained and even professionally trained, enthusiastic women as teachers, it would be done. Twenty-five years ago, people did not think it would pay to have cooking and sewing in the schools. Mrs. Hemenway showed that it would pay. It needed Mrs. Shaw to show that kindergartens would pay. We know now that vacation schools will pay: it is bad economy to turn our little children loose on the street during the summer, and the school committees of the cities are seeing that it will pay better to teach these little girls and boys on the street than to tax ourselves for reform schools afterward. Now, ladies, we women have got to show that it will pay to have thirty-five rather than sixty children in a room; that it will pay to have young college Ph.D's teach the little children as they do in Germany, from which we have still so much to learn; that it lifts the ideals, and that never can be done till we frankly go and show that it will pay.

"A lady came to me lately and said, 'You have persuaded Mabel that she wants to teach in the grammar school.' (Mabel was her daughter, a senior.) 'She did not see why Mabel should waste her time teaching little dirty children in the grammar school. She would like to teach in private school, but she could teach and work in a college settlement if she chose.' Carlyle said in his brutal way, 'You can't cure cancers by sprinkling rose water on them.' I have taught in both college settlements and public schools, and if a college girl really wants to put her life in where it will count, where it will last, where it will make such an impression that young lives will never get away from it, let her take a chance to teach where she has the children five days in the week. Let her put her life right in solidly there. We college women, like our brothers, cannot afford to pick and choose. It is a question of where you can put your lives so that they will count the most. I know of no place where they will count as they will in the big rooms of our grammar schools and primary schools in the cities. There must be a change in the words we use; we have got to find now *our interest in our work*, not *our work in our interests*. We must take our work seriously, and acknowledge and face the fact that at least nine-tenths of all work that is worth doing is drudgery. All life is drudgery, if you choose to make it so. I find that ministers do not get much time to write books, if they are good ministers, especially those in the cities; and I know some lawyers who cannot get much time to keep up their special tastes in Greek. They do the work as drudgery, and they make it divine by putting their whole lives into it. So we must get our interest in our work, not our work in our special interest. Then if we are only good enough and wise enough and are willing to take enough professional training, we can do a great public service to our country, especially if only we can be intelligent, sympathetic, energetic enough to train ourselves to do the hardest work of all and the most permanent—the teaching of little children. And when we have done it, the salaries will adjust themselves to the teachers and not the teachers to the salaries."

15 Why I Am An Optimist.

This piece is dated only eight months before Alice Freeman Palmer died at the age of forty-seven.

"I am a 'confirmed optimist' by birth, by training, by temperament, by faith and by experience.

My childhod among the Susquehanna hills and valleys early taught me the love of nature, the daily glory of sunrise and sunset, the yearly miracle of spring.

The beauty and the wonder and the power,
The shapes of things, their color, lights and shades,
Changes, surprises — and God made it all.

My training as the child of a country doctor in a home where the daily interests of every member of the family centered in caring for the sick, the poor, the aged—where everybody brought his needs and his anxieties—this was the true training for an optimist. For no one can be permanently hopeful who merely looks at life, criticizing those who work. To see clearly the tragedies and to spend self in trying to save makes an optimist.

All my life has been spent in contact wth the children and young men and women in our schools and colleges. The longer I have watched them the more hopeful I am for the future of the world soon to be in their keeping. In spite of the amusement theory of life so many temporarily follow, 'they mean intensely and mean good,' they are idealists, they are training for service, they respond eagerly to great leadership.

My experience with plain, uneducated people in many lands, as with the young, confirms my belief in the kindness and upward-toiling goodness of men and women, in their responsiveness to the best, in their readiness to follow noble leaders. The influence of these moral leaders is eternal; the world is different and better for each of them, and their number increases steadily. No one can despair of a nation that gives such reasons as ours has done for passionately loving Phillips Brooks and President McKinley.

We celebrate the birthdays not of the men who build railroads or make millions, but of those who write us great poems, or free the slaves, or teach us to 'look up and not down, out and not in, forward and not backward, and lend a hand,' [see **AFPann-**1] until

> In the darkest, meanest things,
> There alway, alway something sings."

Alice Freeman Palmer died on December 6, 1902. (See 217n3)

16 Some Religious Verse of Alice Freeman Palmer.

The title of this publication is too restrictive. Actually, along with nine of his wife's poems, Professor Palmer presents more biographical material than in **aboutAFPann**-7. He tells the story of her life at much greater length in **aboutAFPann**-9 and **GHP**-57, and he presents many more of her poems in **AFP**-18.

Professor Palmer introduces "a busy women of affairs . . . [who] devoted her brief years to occupations far from poetic, occupations calling chiefly for practical sagacity." He specifies some of these activities and then, with regard to her poems, says that "[i]t is hard to see how a woman doing . . . the work of several men, and at the same time living with singular fullness the usual life of her sex, could find leisure to gain the technical training required by the most exacting of the arts. And probably it would have been impossible if it had not been for what I call Mrs. Palmer's habit of instantaneous excellence." He went on to describe his wife's fondness for verse as a child, her extensive "acquaintance with the long line of English poets," and "how her hospitable and precise taste would discriminate the good from the middling in authors with whom she was only then becoming acquainted.

"That she was in the habit of writing verse herself, [Professor Palmer says], I did not know until the year before her death. On her last wedding anniversary in America [December 23, 1901] she brought me a volume of twenty poems celebrating our happy life in the country." After Alice Freeman Palmer died, her husband found many more poems that she had written, including, he says, "certain hymns and religious verses, which seem to me to possess a peculiar combination of simplicity, depth, and veracity. These qualities may give them general interest . . . I may add that several of those here given were written during an illness which followed a serious accident [see page 139], and all of them during the last five years of her life."

The paper concludes with nine poems.

17 *The Teacher: Essays and Addresses on Education.*

In his preface, Professor Palmer writes that he and Mrs. Palmer had "often talked of preparing together a book on education. Now, alone, I gather up these fragments."

After his own papers [see **GHPann-**65], the volume has four by Alice Freeman Palmer in the following order: Three Types of Women's Colleges, **AFP**-4; Women's Education in the Nineteenth Century, **AFP**-11; Women's Education at the World's Fair, **AFP**-6; and Why Go to College, **AFP**-8. "All these papers [Palmer writes as he introduces this section, page 311] are printed precisely as she left them, without the change of a word. I have not even ventured on correction in the printed report of one of her addresses, that on going to college. Its looser structure well illustrates her mode of moving an audience and bringing its mothers to the course of conduct she approved."

18 *A Marriage Cycle.*

(See correspondence between George Herbert Palmer and Houghton Mifflin Company about this publication, pages 471–77).

In his preface, George Herbert Palmer explains how he happened to be publishing a volume of poems by his wife, Alice Freeman Palmer, thirteen years after she died: "That is a long time to deliberate . . . Throughout it I have been questioning what to do with her verses. Describing them in my *Life* of her [**GHP**-57], I said they were too intimate for publication. But time and circumstance change judgments. To destroy the sacred papers, as she commanded, my hands will never move. If left till my death [he lived for eighteen more years], they will be pretty sure to find their way into fragmentary and disordered print. To me it belongs to fix their final form. If she is ever again to speak in public, I must be present with attending care."

He goes on to tell that his wife first showed him some of her poems on their last wedding anniversary (December 23, 1901), that she had planned to record in poetry "the steps through which two glad souls become one," and that she had not been able to complete this *Marriage Cycle.* In Paris, a few days before her death, she said to him, "In that cabinet you will find a roll of papers. Burn them. They are unfinished poems of mine, merely sketches. For our coming wedding day [seventeen days after she died] I hoped to complete my *Marriage Cycle,* but now—"

Professor Palmer printed several of her poems in **AFP**-16 and **GHP**-57. "The reception of these selected groups [he says] convinced me it would be wrong to accept Mrs. Palmer's decision and destroy writings at once so interpretative of marriage and so characteristic of herself." Accordingly, for this publication, he edited forty-eight of her poems, gave them titles, and arranged them in three groups — The Approach, Together, and The Parting.

"In verse, as in all else, [he writes,] Mrs. Palmer created her own methods, having almost a genius for imparting to others her ardent and generous feelings. Something of that genius appears in these poems. If not great, they possess, I believe, a dignity, naturalness, and appealing power unlike anything else. Her friends will prize them because here they will once more find Mrs. Palmer engaged in her magical art of transmuting our usual and necessary experiences into occasions of wonder, romance, and gladness."

See related comments in **AFPann**-20.

Paul and Meta Sachs wrote to Professor Palmer, on November 24, 1915, from Shady Hill, Cambridge: "Please do not consider it an intrusion, if as strangers [Paul Sachs, Harvard College class of 1900, had just come to Harvard as assistant director of the Fogg Art Museum], we are bold enough to yield to an impulse, at the close of a very wonderful evening, to take pen in hand to thank you for giving to the world the beautiful poems of Alice Freeman Palmer. 'A Marriage Cycle' must in many hearts, as in ours, strike a deeply responsive note. We have just read the poems aloud this precious anniversary evening and we are so profoundly grateful, that we feel impelled, quite frankly, to tell you so. Surely you will understand! In gratitude and great respect,"—

And Sara Norton, the daughter of Charles Eliot Norton, also wrote to Professor Palmer, on November 28, 1915, from 83 Mount Vernon Street: "Your most kind & beautiful gift has touched me deeply. I can never forget the evenings at Shady Hill, when you read to my Father [who died in 1908], as it advanced, your life of Mrs. Palmer — & then the first sight of these poems which I had when you lent them to my father.

"It is a moving & inspiring little book; & I am glad you now let the world have it, with your words to explain, & the lovely portrait [of Mrs. Palmer] at the beginning. Who that will read it could misread it? Such a record, so direct, so veracious in its simplicity; so expessive in every suggestion of a high noble nature, must always be deeply interesting, and delightful.

"One wishes she might have made the work even more complete, but it is complete enough under your skilful editing to give one a sense of her power in handling verse. In some of the poems one feels she achieved just what she wished to say — as in 'The Present Heaven,' & the lines leap into one's mind with a sense of truth & reality.

"But there is more than accomplishment of a rare kind in the book — when human relations have been so happy, it is to enrich life for others to let the story be told — so many readers will be grateful to you anew; & cherish the thought of her life & yours.

"Thank you again—"

(Both letters are in the Wellesley College Archives, folder 2 BI, George Herbert Palmer.)

Eight verses by Alice Freeman Palmer are presented in this compilation. Five of the eight are in *A Marriage Cycle*: The Poets (206n3), The Present Heaven (206n3), A Spring Journey (255n1), Myself (255n1), and Meeting (**AFP**-19). The other three: Four Mottoes (**AFP**-1), The History of the Case (**AFP**-10), and To Anna Hooker Morse (**AFP**-12).

19 Meeting.

Martha Hale Shackford was Professor of English Literature at Wellesley College. A graduate in the class of 1896, with a Ph.D. from Yale University, she had been a member of the department of English literature since 1901.

From the preface: ". . . When Mr. Durant chose the shore of Lake Waban for the site of his college for young women, he predetermined in many ways the interests of those who were to spend four years in this region of great natural beauty. Lake and woods, green orchard and open meadow have quickened in many of our poets that love of nature which is evident in the following pages . . . The poems are arranged in two groups,— the first consisting of those writen by officers of the college who are not Wellesley graduates; the second, of those poems written by graduates or former students [Professor Palmer's niece, Bertha Palmer Lane, has a poem in this second section]."

This poem, entitled Meeting, by Alice Freeman Palmer is included in the first group, number 14; it also appears in *A Marriage Cycle* (**AFP**-18).

One day we gave each other, one more day.
In the hot city streets we found a way
To meet, and listen to the roar and din,
And know we two sat safely folded in.

The poets brought us their grave, chastening word,
Brought murmurs of the river, breeze and bird;

Till a strange gladness rested in the heart,
Of all our coming years to be a part.

And he had changed. Through days of absence still
More masterful and tender; steady will
Ruled all his face, and love looked through his eyes,
And noble speech grew freer and more wise.

Oh, more than conqueror he seemed that day!
He stood beside me, turned, and went away.
Then I knelt down, and for his sake I prayed
To meet our future glad and unafraid.

20 *An Academic Courtship: Letters of Alice Freeman and George Herbert Palmer, 1886–1887.*

Ella Freeman Talmage, Alice Freeman Palmer's sister, who arranged this publication, writes in her Foreword: "In the introduction to his life of my sister, Alice Freeman Palmer, her husband, George Herbert Palmer, said in reference to her poems that they were 'too intimate' to be published during his lifetime. A few years later, however, he published a small volume of these poems entitled *A Marriage Cycle* (**AFP**-18). He tells us in the preface to this volume that 'time and circumstance change judgments' and that he had come to feel with a number of other literary critics of note to whom he had submitted the verses that there was 'too much beauty . . . , too just and important an understanding of wedded love, too profound an exhibit of a woman already a kind of national figure, to permit the book to be treated as a private possession.'

"Seven years after the death of this beloved philosopher, and impelled by reasons similar to those responsible for his change of judgment in regard to the poems, I have come to believe that the letters now in my possession written by him to my sister while she was president of Wellesley College, those written by her in return, and especially the letters written by them after marriage, contain too much of general interest and rare spiritual beauty to remain longer a 'private possession.'

"Their correspondence, beginning in May 1886 and ending with Alice Freeman Palmer's death in December 1902, covers an important period in the history of the higher education of women, one which included the making of Wellesley College and the birth of the University of Chicago. In addition, the letters are so filled with great and worth-while convictions, so delicately and often so humorously expressed, as to be both a stimulus and a delight to the reader. So numerous are they, however, that no attempt has been made here to cover the entire period of sixteen years. This book contains a selection from the letters written by the Palmers during the years 1886–1887, before their marriage—sufficient, it is hoped, to trace the history of their courtship and to give some impression of the character and personality of both these rare people."

At the end of her introduction to this volume, Caroline Hazard, former President of Wellesley College, writes: "If any surviving friends question the propriety of publishing these intimate letters, let them read Professor Palmer's own Apologia, written to me in 1915 when he published his wife's beautiful *Marriage Cycle.* 'I am sure you will understand how distasteful it is to me to turn Alice loose on the street, and yet how impossible to feel justified in shutting up such beauty to myself. These poems are more herself than anything that has survived. They surely must bless all who are capable of either passion or delicacy.' What he wrote of her verse is profoundly true of them both in these love letters."

Chapter 13

Publications about Alice Freeman Palmer, annotated

identified as **aboutAFPann**-number

So much has been written about Alice Freeman Palmer that this list is undoubtedly incomplete.

1 Norumbega Hall.

Norumbega Hall at Wellesley College, opened in April 1886, with rooms for President Freeman, was named in honor of Eben Norton Horsford who "had just published an essay claiming the discovery of the site of the somewhat mythical city of Norumbega." On the occasion, Alice E. Freeman read a sonnet written and dedicated to her by John Greenleaf Whittier (*The Complete Poetical Works of John Greenleaf Whittier*, Cambridge Edition, Boston, Houghton Mifflin and Co., 1894: 239–240):

> Not on Penobscot's wooded bank the spires
> Of the sought City rose, nor yet beside
> The winding Charles, nor where the daily tide
> Of Naumkeag's haven rises and retires,
> The vision tarried; but somewhere we knew
> The beautiful gates must open to our quest,
> Somewhere that marvellous City of the West
> Would lift its towers and palace domes in view,
> And, lo! at last its mystery is made known—
> Its only dwellers maidens fair and young,
> Its Princess such as England's Laureate sung;
> And safe from capture save by love alone,

It lends its beauty to the lake's green shore,
And Norumbega is a myth no more.

In **GHP**-57 (page 172), George Herbert Palmer writes: "Miss Freeman's youth and beauty ruling so skilfully the fairyland of Wellesley had often brought her the title of 'The Princess,' and Tennyson's poem of that name had become associated with her work."

Later, in his study of English poetry (**GHP**-88), Professor Palmer devotes a chapter to Alfred Tennyson; he and Robert Browning were "[t]wo gigantic figures [who] dominate English poetry of the nineteenth century."

"The Princess," Palmer points out, was published in 1847, only three years before "the Laureateship was conferred on [Tennyson]." This poem marks the beginning of Tennyson's "social studies in narrative form . . . In his treatment of the great problems which agitated the nineteenth century Tennyson was almost a prophet. Before the idea of evolution had appeared as a scientific doctrine it was put forth by Tennyson hypothetically in 'In Memoriam.' The intellectual advancement of women too (the evolution of half the human race) was announced by him before the question had even been seriously agitated. The fantastic dream of 'The Princess' has become for us an every-day reality."

An editor of "The Princess" says: "At the time of the publication of *The Princess* the surface-thought of England was intent solely on Irish famines, corn-laws and free-trade. It was only after many years that it became conscious of anything being wrong in the position of women. . . . No doubt such ideas were at the time 'in the air' in England, but the dominant, practical Philistinism scoffed at them as 'ideas' banished to America, that refuge for exploded European absurdities. I believe the *Vindication of the Rights of Women*, by Mary Wollstonecraft (1792), first turned the attention of the people of England to the 'wrongs of women' . . . The plan of *The Princess* may have suggested itself when the project of a Women's College was in [Tennyson's] mind (1839) . . . " (Alfred Lord Tennyson, *The Princess and Maud,* London, Macmillan and Co., The Eversley Edition, volume 4: 245–246).

Some lines from the Prologue to *The Princess; A Medley* (page 2–3, 6) clearly relate this poem to the crusade for the higher education of women, to Wellesley College, and to Alice Freeman Palmer:

> 'O miracle of women,' said the book,
> 'O noble heart who, being strait-besieged
> By this wild king to force her to his wish,
> Nor bent, nor broke, nor shunn'd a soldier's death,
> But now when all was lost or seem'd as lost—
> Her stature more than mortal in the burst
> Of sunrise, her arm lifted, eyes on fire—
> Brake with a blast of trumpets from the gate,
> And, falling on them like a thunderbolt,
> She trampled some beneath her horses' heels,
> And some were push'd with lances from the rock,
> and part were drown'd within the whirling brook:
> O miracle of noble womanhood!'
>
> . . .
>
> 'Where' asked Walter . . . lives there such a woman now?'
>
> Quick answer'd Lilia 'There are thousands now
> Such women, but convention beats them down:
> It is but bringing up; no more than that:
> You men have done it: how I hate you all!
> Ah, were I something great! I wish I were
> Some mighty poetess, I would shame you then,
> That love to keep us children! O I wish
> That I were some great princess, I would build
> Far off from men a college like a man's,
> And I would teach them all that men are taught;
> We are twice as quick!' . . .

Alice Freeman Palmer died in Paris on December 6, 1902, about two and one-half months before her forty-eighth birthday (see 217n3).

2 Alice Freeman Palmer, Editorial, *Outlook*, 1902; 72 (December 13): 871–872.

This tribute appeared exactly one week after Mrs. Palmer died: "The announcement is made of the death of Alice Freeman Palmer abroad, but with no details of her illness. Mrs.

Palmer had been as prominently identified with the movement for the higher education of women as any other woman of her generation. A graduate of the University of Michigan, she early imbibed an enthusiasm for the widest and freest activity for women and the largest and most stimulating opportunities. Called to the presidency of Wellesley College at a time when that institution was in a formative stage, she brought to her work entire faith in its prime importance, its dignity, and its practical usefulness. She brought also many womanly graces; a skill in dealing with affairs and with people which was the highest form of tact, sound judgment, and capacity not only for attracting others but making them allies in the work to which she had given her heart.

"She was not only the head of Wellesley College, she was its hostess; and in that early experimental period no woman could have filled with more judgment and success the difficult position of a hostess. She converted almost every one to whom she explained the college; and one of her greatest services to the college was the charm of interpretation which she placed at its command. She rendered another great service in broadening the conception of religion and of education in the institution.

"Her marriage to Professor George H. Palmer, of Harvard University, took her into another sphere without curtailing her larger activities for education or diminishing her influence. The death of Mrs. Palmer will bring with it a sense of personal loss to her very wide group of friends and former students in this country."

3 Alice Freeman Palmer, Editorial, *Outlook*, 1902; 72 (December 27): 975–976.

Two weeks after the previous piece, a longer editorial was published in the same periodical: "We are glad to learn that the friends of Mrs. Alice Freeman Palmer are planning to provide a memorial of her in connection with Wellesley College. There is something pathetic in the quick forgetfulness of the human race; in the fact, so often illustrated in death, that 'the place which once knew him shall know him no more' . . . [These] friends . . . are rightly resolved that her name shall not remain unknown to the future generations of students, who but for this memorial would share in the fruits of her influence often without knowing whence it came . . .

"Equally equipped to teach Greek, Latin, Mathematics, and History, and teaching all in succession, her career might indicate one who put scholarship above womanhood. Neither ambition as a controlling motive, nor scholastic attainments as the preeminent characteristic, make an attractive woman. Alice Freeman Palmer was fascinating to all who met her and beloved by all who knew her because her standard of greatness was Christ's standard — 'He that would be greatest among you, let him be servant of all,' and she regarded learning as she did every other acquisition, valuable chiefly as an equipment for service. The present President of Wellesley College [Caroline Hazard] well says: 'Her instinct was to help, and she spared neither time nor strength in her efforts.'

"A character so finely proportioned and so closely and harmoniously knit together puts analysis at defiance; yet it is only by analysis that the friends who loved her can describe her to others. Her will was as steel, bending but never breaking; so clear of the alloy of pride that she aroused no hostility; so guided by good judgment and tempered by conscience that she habitually discriminated between the ultimate end and the immediate means, and knew how gracefully to yield her judgment on the second if she could attain the first . . .

"[S]he never fell into the folly of those who put a career above the home; and was never more pleased than when she could tell the story of what some Wellesley College graduate was doing as wife and mother, through some humble home, to give to others the broadening and inspiration which Wellesley College bestowed upon her students. So, too, she counted it a promotion to leave the presidency of Wellesley College . . . [for] a new sphere in the home over which she so gracefully presided . . . Alice Freeman Palmer was seen at her best, not by those who knew her only as the strong executive, the wise administrator, the scholarly teacher, the brilliant platform speaker, the engaging conversationalist, but by those who were admitted to her home to share in its restfulness and its inspiration."

4 *Alice Freeman Palmer in Memoriam MDCCCLV–MDCCCCII*, Association of Collegiate Alumnae, MDCCCCIII, Boston, D. B. Updike, The Merrymount Press. 42 pages, 7x10$^{1/2}$ inches.

As soon as possible after Alice Freeman Palmer died, and

before her husband returned from Paris, their close friend, Lewis Kennedy Morse, "arranged a memorial meeting which was presided over by President Eliot. Mr. Morse secured all the speakers. He presided over the meeting and introduced President Eliot who formally took charge. Mr. Morse assembled all the addresses. He asked the Collegiate Alumnae if they would publish the same. This they gladly agreed to do and Miss Florence Cushing assumed the responsibility working with Mr. Morse" (from sheet tipped into a copy of the memorial with Lewis Kennedy Morse's bookplate, in AJL Collection).

The handsome volume is a record of that meeting, "held at Boston, December 29, 1902, to plan for memorials of the life and work of Alice Freeman Palmer." Mrs. Palmer, a founding member of the Association of Collegiate Alumnae in 1882, had been twice the president of the association, and when she died she "held its most responsible office as General Secretary." [see 75n3]

As frontispiece, the volume has a 1901 photograph of Mrs. Palmer in academic gown. Then an unsigned memorial sketch of her life has this ending: "No one can describe her personality. Exceptionally sensitive to beauties of form and color, intimately at home with living creatures, she was yet more intimately and simply at home in the heart of a child. With a child she was boundlessly in love. [see **AFP**-12 and 13] For the children of larger growth, her work was among men as well as among women, and in it all she was always and everywhere capable of a great sincerity. Hers was convincing sympathy and earnest foresight, which made her judgment so true that to her many owe not merely their success but the right choosing of a life-work. Hers was the capacity to give to others at innumerable moments, courage and gladness. Hers was a self-effacement that raised fellow-workers and friends to the level of achievement and then to them gave the credit of victory."

Next, Marion Talbot spoke about Alice Freeman Palmer "as a member of the Association of Collegiate Alumnae." [see 75n3, 79n2, 80n3, and 240n1] Talbot had been Mrs. Palmer's assistant and then successor (in 1895) as Dean of Women at the University of Chicago.

Then, the record of the meeting opens with a call to order by Mr. Kennedy who asked President Eliot of Harvard University to preside. Eliot began by reading "some lines by Richard Watson Gilder [American poet], sent by him for this meeting":

When fell, to-day, the word that she had gone,
Not this my thought: Here a bright journey ends,
Here rests a soul unresting; here, at last,
Here ends that earnest strength, that generous life—
For all her life was giving. Rather this
I said (after the first swift, sorrowing pang):
Hence, on a new quest, starts an eager spirit—
No dread, no doubt, unhesitating forth
With asking eyes; pure as the bodiless souls
Whom poets vision near the central throne
Angelically ministrant to man;
So fares she forth with smiling, Godward face;
Nor should we grieve, but give eternal thanks—
Save that we mortal are, and needs must mourn.
December 6, 1902

President Eliot then addressed the purpose of the meeting: ". . . We want to devise some means of holding up this life to the admiration of succeeding generations. It was devoted to education, the education of the young. We want some educating memorial of her which will say to coming generations, 'Go, and do thou likewise.' We wish to make her life continue to teach the noble lesson which she gave while she walked among us."

After some remarks of his own about Mrs. Palmer's life, Eliot introduced others, each of whom presented special memories of Alice Freeman Palmer:

Mr. Samuel B. Capen, president of the American Board of Commissioners for Foreign Missions, and president of the International Institute for Girls in Spain
Bishop William Lawrence, president of the Board of Trustees of Wellesley College
President Caroline Hazard of Wellesley College
President Elmer Hewitt Capen, president of Tufts College and a member of the State Board of Education
President Mary Emma Woolley of Mount Holyoke College
Dean Alice Hanson Luce of Oberlin College and a student at Wellesley College when Mrs. Palmer was teacher and then president
Mrs. Helen H. Backus, a former president of the Association of Collegiate Alumnae

President William Herbert Perry Faunce of Brown University
President William Jewett Tucker of Dartmouth College

A committee, appointed at the meeting, decided later on nine memorials which would require $425,000: An endowment for the Presidency of Wellesley College, $150,000; the enlargement of the Alice Freeman Palmer scholarship at Wellesley College (now $5,000), $20,000; a fellowship fund to be administered by the Association of Collegiate Alumnae, $30,000; twelve scholarships of $6,000 each in as many institutions, partly separate Colleges for Women, partly co-educational institutions, $72,000; Professorship at Wellesley College of Social Science and Home Economics, $50,000; A fund at Radcliffe College for supporting instruction in education, $50,000; Four scholarships at Wellesley College to be held by graduates of any Massachusetts Normal School, selected one every year by the State Board of Education, $25,000; A contribution to the new building of the International Institute for Girls in Spain, $15,000; and Portraits or busts, with tablets, at Michigan University, Chicago University, Wellesley College, Bradford Academy, The Massachusetts Board of Education, and the Massachusetts Normal Schools at Bridgewater, Lowell, and Hyannis, $13,000.

And the committee added a comment: "Mrs. Palmer's sympathy was quick, her service generous, her interests and influence wide; and her memorials should have like qualities; her career was truly memorable; and the methods of perpetuating her beneficent influence should be adequate and lasting." (Memorials to Alice Freeman Palmer, *College News*, Wellesley, volume 2, number 14, February 4. 1903: 1).

Mr. Morse ended the meeting by reading a message, which he considered fitting for the occasion, that Mrs. Palmer had delivered at the memorial service for her close friend, Mrs. Mary B. Claflin, the wife of ex-Governor Claflin, who died in June 1896:

> This is my message:
> All life is one. All service is one, be it here or there. Death is only a little door from one room to another. So she begs us in all her rich and radiant life and memory not to make much of trouble, not to be weighed down here by sorrow, not to think much or to be afraid of death for ourselves

> or for those who are dear to us; but to make life here and now, so rich and kind and sweet and noble, that this will be heaven. **W**e need no other until **H**e comes and calls us into a larger life with a fresher opportunity.

This message brings to mind a poem by Alice Freeman Palmer, entitled The Present Heaven. [see 206n3]

5 *A Service in Memory of Alice Freeman Palmer held by her Friends and Associates in Appleton Chapel, Harvard University, January Thirty-First MDCCCCIII,* Boston, Houghton Mifflin & Co., [April] MDCCCCIII. 95 pages. $5x8^{3/8}$ inches. 75 cents, *net* ; postage 7 cents.

After Alice Freeman Palmer died in Paris, on December 6, 1902, her husband did not arrive home until December 31. When Professor Palmer returned, he writes, "I was asked to allow a service to be held in Cambridge in memory of Mrs. Palmer. I gladly did so, and a large company of her friends assembled in the chapel of Harvard College on January 31, 1903. Every part of the service was in charge of those who had known and loved her. Few strangers were in the audience. The ushers were teachers and students who had been much in her home. A chorus of Harvard men and another of Wellesley girls furnished the music, singing her hymn, 'The Tempest,' [see 206n1] and others which were especially dear to her. Professor Peabody read the Scripture and offered prayer; and four college presidents — Presidents Angell, Hazard, Tucker, and Eliot — made addresses. At the beginning of the programme . . . was placed Mr. Gilder's exquisite lament [see **aboutAFPann**-4]; and at the end, some lines adapted from Richard Crashaw, a poet of whom she had long been fond. . . . Each of the four speakers, looking back on [her] life tells what he [or she] has seen in it" (**GHP**-57, page 328–329).

This charming volume, designed by Bruce Rogers (*The Work of Bruce Rogers,* Catalogue of Exhibition, New York, Oxford University Press, 1936, page 17, #98), was published on April 12, 1903. In his preface, dated February 21, 1903 — which was his late wife's forty-eighth birthday — Professor Palmer writes: "This volume contains both programme and report of a memorial service at Cambridge in honor of Mrs. Palmer. The report is made complete in order that her friends who were present may preserve, and those who were absent may experience, the feelings of beauty, thankfulness, and courage inspired by thoughts of her on that unique occasion. Here everything is presented except the music." He goes on to identify the five photographs in the volume, selected to trace "the development of her character and features during the past forty years. . . . Any adequate representation of that face is impossible. No instrument was swift and subtle enough to catch its perpetual change or to mark the strange combination in it of humor with seriousness, duty with enjoyment, nimbleness of the physical senses with high spirituality, sainthood with vivacious interest in every moving thing."

Caroline Hazard, president of Wellesley College since 1899, ended her remarks (see also 141n3) with a poem that she had written:

> We loved her for the loving thoughts which
> sped
> Straight from her heart until they found
> their goal
> In some perplexed or troubled human soul
> And broke anew the ever living bread.
> We loved the mind courageous which no dread
> Of failure ever daunted, whose control
> Of gentleness all opposition stole;
> We loved herself and all the joy she shed.
> Oh Leader of the Leaders! Like a light
> Thy life was set, to counsel, to befriend;
> Thy quick and eager insight seized the right
> And shared the prize with bounteous hand,
> and free.
> Fed from the fountains of infinity
> Thy life was service, having love to spend.

Miss Hazard's address was also published in Caroline Hazard, *From College Gates*, Boston, Houghton Mifflin Company, 1925:187–193.

Dr. Richard C. Cabot describes Professor Palmer at the service: "How little he has allowed the thought of sadness to be connected with her is always clear but never more strikingly than on the occasion of the service in memory of her held in the college chapel . . . That day he seemed determined that his wife's radiant and joyful spirit should permeate everything within his control and especially his own words and actions.

In his bearing as he greeted his friends and hers after the service, he did not allow a trace of regret or sorrow to appear. His gladness in the praise of her voiced by the speakers at that service, his welcome to all who spoke to him, conveyed to me the most convincing and contagious awareness of a life called 'dead' that I have ever known. So she would have had him bear himself. He knew it and with his consummate self-control acted out that knowledge in the full" (**aboutGHPann**-3).

6 Alice Freeman Palmer, *Wellesley Magazine*, 1903; 11 (No. 4. February 1): 145–150, 176–180.

This issue of the magazine, dated less than two months after Mrs. Palmer died, has several pieces about her, including resolutions from the New York and the Philadelphia Wellesley Clubs.

One entire article (pages 146–149), entitled, simply, Alice Freeman Palmer, is presented below. Helen Barrett Montgomery, a member of the class of 1884 and a distinguished alumna, wrote this piece. On Alumnae Day in June 1904, she spoke at dinner on "The College Woman and the Public Schools." From 1908 to 1916 she was a trustee of the college, and at the Semi-Centennial in 1925, she was one of three alumnae who received Wellesley's rare honorary degrees, LL.D. Her citation: "Helen Barrett Montgomery — Who adds to a wise and brilliant Christian leadership the achievement of a scholar in the Centennial Translation of the New Testament from the Greek text." The other alumnae recipients were Annie Jump Cannon, also class of 1884, ". . . the foremost woman astronomer in the United States . . .," and Katherine Lee Bates, class of 1880, ". . . scholar, poet, and author of the greatest of our national hymns . . ." (See also 290n1. Wellesley College Archives: 6C/1884 class of 1884; Alumnae, badges, reunions (1885–1909); 7B/1884, Barrett, Helen. Jean Glasscock, gen. ed., *Wellesley College, 1875–1975, A Century of Women*: page 356).

"It seemed as if it could not be true, that brief dispatch in the morning paper. Wellesley women everywhere read it with a throb of incredulous and startled pain. It had never occurred to one of us that we could go on living in a world in which she was not.

"No one who was not at Wellesley in the splendid decade of the Eighties can understand quite how it seemed to us who were. It was not only that we were young, the College was young, too, and so was our President. An atmosphere of youth and aspiration and high adventure enfolded us all together. We were flushed with the feeling of power and privilege. It was such a new thing to go to college; some of us were the first girls to do it in our town and the awe and delight of it lay fresh on our spirits. Wellesley is doubtless a greater college now; wiser, more learned, a better organized institution, more mature and saner but, — there was something about those first years that can never come again, the thrill and vision of her first youth. And of it all Miss Freeman was the centre.

"When we heard that Miss Freeman, the new Professor of History [appointed in 1879, only one year before this class matriculated], had been made acting president, very few of the girls in the lower classes knew her. Our only impression of her had been that she was a slender little lady, with a delicate throat [probably referring to her chronic cough; see 52n3], who wore a red scarf wrapped closely about her shoulders. When she began, as acting president [in November 1881, three months before her twenty-seventh birthday], to hold office-hours and to lead chapel [at which attendance was required], all at once the girls discovered her, rose to her with an enthusiasm that comes to few women.

"There was a beautiful simplicity about college chapel, just the reading of a few words of scripture, a hymn or two, a prayer, with sometimes, not often, a brief talk on some topic of college interest. But chapel was one of the great forces in the college. There is many a woman, who, to-day looks back at those few moments spent in the morning chapel as among the chief formative influences of her life. It is hard to analyze the secret of the wonderful power which Miss Freeman undoubtedly had over the majority of the students. It was not alone that there was earnest and simplicity in the services as she conducted them, for these qualities had never been absent. A subtle sort of vitality seemed to permeate it all under her leadership. There was such range and unexpectedness in the Bible selections and often a fresh application of truth in the very bringing together of portions that we had never thought of as vitally connected! We used to wonder if her Bible and ours were just the same. Her prayers, too, we never forgot, for though informal they found out and expressed our best aspirations.

"Miss Freeman's social influence was marked. She enjoyed

the part of hostess and was never seen to better advantage than when entertaining some distinguished guest of the college. She used every opportunity to bring the girls into contact with people who had done a great work or had spoken a noble message. Informal teas and receptions were given, to which now this class, now that, was invited. Shall we ever forget the visits of Phillips Brooks and of Whittier, of Oliver Wendell Holmes, Matthew Arnold, James Bryce, Harriet Beecher Stowe and a score of others, whose coming made red-letter days in the college calendar?

"Entertainment at the college in those days was of the simplest. The president's table was in the bay-windowed end of the long dining-room [in College Hall], but somehow she created an atmosphere altogether homelike and charming. The fortunate girls assigned to this table, it is true, found life a little strenuous at times. All table service was performed by the students and when there were eight or ten guests, and food and dishes had to be carried the length of the dining-room and through the long corridors from 'domestic hall,' dinner was not entirely a season of repose. Yet how the girls exulted, how proud they were to have the service at the president's table above reproach, how eagerly they listened to the talk, grave, gay and brilliant, that made the dinner hour so delightful! It was worth while even to miss the material dinner if one could see Miss Freeman in process of converting a guest who was not quite sure that he approved of a woman's college. The missionary work in aid of the higher education of women that was accomplished by Miss Freeman can never be fully stated. She disarmed criticism in so many points that those who came to scoff remained to praise.

"In the evening gatherings, the informal receptions in the first floor centre, and in her own room, Miss Freeman was always cordial and friendly. She entered by a genius of sympathy, into our lives. She knew our problems, understood our aspirations better than we did ourselves and in our gratitude we determined to achieve great things for the college and for her.

"It would far exceed the limits of this brief sketch to speak of the many lines of Miss Freeman's work at Wellesley. She gave us a fresh and powerful ideal of womanhood. We exulted in her brilliancy of intellect, her marvelous memory, the remarkable career that had placed her, hardly more than a girl herself, at the head of the college. She made real to us the possibility of a rounded and symmetrical womanhood. To add to one's attainment in scholarship, culture; to culture, social tact; to conjoin high enthusiasm with a sense of proportion; it was this that we believed should belong to the ideal of every college woman. As with all creeds we have mangled it a good deal in the living, but the ideal abides, which, with the help of many brave and noble women of the faculty, Alice Freeman Palmer gave to her girls."

7 *Twenty-Five Portraits of Alice Freeman Palmer, 1855–1902, Ph. D. (Michigan), L. H. D. (Columbia), LL. D. (Union), Sometime President of Wellesley College, Dean of Women in the University of Chicago, Member of the State Board of Education in Massachusetts*, by George Herbert Palmer. Twenty copies printed, Cambridge, 1904. $10^{1/2}$x$12^{3/4}$ inches.

The pictures in this volume include those that are printed elsewhere. Here, each print is mounted on a separate page.

In his introduction, dated February 21, 1904, when Alice Freeman Palmer would have been forty-nine years old, Professor Palmer continues to write about her life, as he began to do in **aboutAFPann**-5 and 9.

"I have prepared this volume as a gift to certain colleges which were special objects of Mrs. Palmer's devotion and regard. For some years at these centres of her influence there may be a desire to recall what manner of woman she was. I hope so. It would be sad to think that one who in life was so specific and individual must now in remembrance shrink to the meagre outlines of a public character, an educator, or a saint. In reality, she was a very woman; and it was through her gracious and abounding womanhood that she sent forth her largest influence.

"The times were critical when she appeared. Social transformations were in progress. Girls were just emerging from sheltered homes, desirous of education and of whatever else might help to enlarge their lives. Many feared that such desires might dispose them to drop the quietness, refinement, and spiritual power which were theirs in the home, and to admit into their natures the ruder forces of our turbulent world. Most social changes involve danger. Mrs. Palmer did much to lessen this danger and to quiet these fears. Persuasively and in her own person she showed how a deepened intelligence and wider knowledge of affairs may heighten the characteristic and ancestral traits of woman and greatly add to her charm. To the many colleges which she served she brought financial aid, improved administration, firmer scholarship, and the help that comes through a popular name. But her best gift to them all and to the community was her own rich, exquisite, and elusive personality which helped to fix the standard for college girls of what they would desire to be.

"In commemorating such a woman it is not enough to put on record what she did and said. Somewhere material should be at hand from which those who would hereafter reconstruct her may learn how she looked and bore herself. Traits like hers can better be seen then read. I accordingly gather here a set of evolutionary portraits. They are not chosen as her most pleasing pictures, but rather to show her many-sidedness and her constant advance. Substantially, they are arranged in chronologic sequence, though I am unable to verify all their dates. Whoever examines them will notice that Mrs. Palmer sometimes appears younger in the later ones than in the earlier; so solemnly and in such hardship did she begin, so successful was she in winning through experience wide freedom, swift usefulness, and glad accord with her world."

8 Personal Recollections of Alice Freeman Palmer, by Caroline Hazard. *Association of Collegiate Alumnae Magazine*, Series III, No. 9, February 1904, pages 62–70.

Also published in Caroline Hazard, *From College Gates*, Boston, Houghton Mifflin Company, 1925:194–223.

President Hazard of Wellesley College delivered this address to the Association of Collegiate Alumnae in Milwaukee, Wisconsin, on November 7, 1903. She spoke at greater length than in the two earlier memorials, and she commented on both of them (**aboutAFPann**-4 and 5).

In particular, she said, "[t]hese meetings to perpetuate her name and commemorate her work resulted in the movement to found memorials in the various institutions with which she was most closely connected. As the first object suggested, the endowment of the presidency of Wellesley was presented, and I am happy to announce that at the present time the sum of $28,307.35 has been received . . . The total amount which was mentioned by the committee having the matter in charge was $150,000. The second object . . . was the endowment of the

Alice Freeman Palmer Scholarship at Wellesley College, enlarging it to a fellowship, to be endowed in the sum of $25,000. This has already been accomplished [and] this fellowship [is] to be awarded next spring . . . A fellowship fund, to be administered by the Association of Collegiate Alumnae is the third upon the list . . . [And there are] other objects also: scholarships at the normal schools with which Mrs. Palmer was connected; the contribution to the new building for the Industrial Institute for Girls in Spain, a cause for which she worked with untiring zeal; [and] a fund for professorships at Wellesley and at Radcliffe which should recognize her interest in both institutions."

In conclusion, President Hazard said: "It is a life which can bear the light of common day; a life of such simple goodness, nourished by unseen springs, that all who came near her felt its power; a life of such sympathy that it was unstintedly poured out. Her high courage faced and conquered adverse conditions. She opened new doors for women and was among the very first to pass through them. She reconciled the new and the old conceptions of women; for in her own life she combined in a very remarkable degree the traditional feminine virtues and the wider activities of women for the ideals of life, for freedom, for truth, for the highest development of the individual."

9 Alice Freeman Palmer, by George Herbert Palmer. Reprinted from the *Oberlin Alumni Magazine*, 1906; No. 10, Commencement Number: 330–351). 45 pages.

This address by Palmer to the graduating class of Oberlin College was delivered on June 20, 1906, during the period when he was writing *The Life of Alice Freeman Palmer* (**GHP-**57). The talk was recorded stenographically and published with his permission but without his revision. Although the magazine titled the address "Alice Freeman Palmer," Professor Palmer entered it in the Chronicles (page 232) as "A Fortunate Life (Alice)."

"Instead of delivering you an oration today [Palmer begins], I propose to tell you a story; for I am very anxious that you should carry away what I say. Anxious, I say, because, though I have seen thirty-five successive classes pass away from my own college doors, I never fail to be thrilled on seeing this group of departing students . . . We who have watched them going forth again and again say to ourselves, And are they to be successful? Is life for them to be fortunate? . . . It is to [the] necessary factors of a fortunate life to which I wish to turn your attention today."

Then, in the body of the address, he described in some detail "the fortunate life of Alice Freeman Palmer—the most fortunate life that it has been my lot to carefully study. I give it to you not merely in a biographic way; I give it to you as a typical life. . . . There was nothing in it that could not be in the lives of every one of us . . ."

After a long description of the life of Alice Freeman Palmer, he summarizes: "Now, that I call a fortunate life. Here are the four great periods, each lived to the full. The family life is lived through and through. This little girl is lost in the life of the family. She comes to college, eager, greedy, never having any chance to do anything for herself, and here finds the wealth of a great university. She goes forth into service. She has most complicated acts of service to perform, calling out all her powers. She goes forward, exulting in these powers for the rest of her life, unable to distinguish from the service she is doing for others the service she is doing for herself. For she has kept the innocence of the eye, the innocence of the feelings. Romance had run through her life, and in the small things she could find joy."

Finally, Professor Palmer has an unusual ending: "One of [Mrs. Palmer's] last acts before her death was to speak in commemoration of one of her friends. I surreptitiously got a stenographer to be present on that occasion, for the friend was in many ways like herself, and I was confident that in interpreting this friend she would record her own character. Let me read her words on this occasion:

"'This woman was not afraid of herself. She knew how to live herself out, and to give her heart its way. She had the power of expression and would trust her enthusiasm. So there was nothing dull in her, no commonplace thread in her composition. By this, do I mean that she had natural genius? Not at all, only a rich nature, richly cultivated. Her child heart had an avidity to be pleased. I have driven with her on a June morning when I knew that she was weighed down with perplexity and care. Yet no bird flew from bush to shrub that her quick eyes did not see, and she smile it an answer. The flowers by the wayside she knew and rejoiced in. Few women have I known so equipped for all circumstances and conditions. She was never so harassed that the sunset would not rest her, that the stretch of the sea off the Beverly shore would not bring a thrill of joy. To nature as to human beings, she brought a strong heart and a keen mind. I never knew her to consider a duty, a duty, nor to think how little of thought or love or time or care she could put into everything she had to do. She was never satisfied to do little things in a little way but she did all things largely.'"

Professor Palmer adds: "That is the thought I want to leave with you today. To do all things, even the little things, largely."

10 *The Life of Alice Freeman Palmer*, by George Herbert Palmer. (**GHP**-57)

(See correspondence between George Herbert Palmer and Houghton Mifflin Company, page 465)

To open his introduction, Professor Palmer presents three reasons for writing this book [underlining by the annotator]. "[T]he insatiability of love . . . [A]ffection first of all. Mrs. Palmer was my wife, deeply beloved and honored. Whatever perpetuates that honor brings me peace. To leave the dead wholly dead is rude. Vivid creature that she was, she must not lie forgotten. Something of her may surely be saved if only I have skill. Perhaps my grateful pen may bring to others a portion of the bounty I myself received. [T]he general desire for portraiture . . . A second and more obvious summons comes from the fact that in herself and apart from me Mrs. Palmer was a notable person. Somebody therefore may be tempted to write her life if I do not; for her friends were numbered by the ten thousand . . . Few women of her time, I have come to think, were more widely loved. And now these people are recalling her influence and asking for an explanation . . . [T]he rights of history . . . One more aim remains, weighty, yet lying on the surface. In some of the social movements of her time Mrs. Palmer had a considerable share . . . It is well to follow such movements in the lives of their leaders and to understand the situation in which those leaders found themselves . . . As Mrs. Palmer was sometimes forced into such leadership, she may be said to have a certain historical importance . . .

"In reference to one feature of my book a little warning may be well [he states at the end of the introduction]. This is a prejudiced story. I am far from a dispassionate, or even a detached observer of her whom I would make known. She and I had become pretty completely one. Often my only way of telling about her is to tell about myself. The book, therefore, while ostensibly a biography, claims many privileges of an autobiography, and might properly enough be called the autobiography of a friend. In it I must be allowed abundant egotism, reminiscence, admiration, personal disclosure. But perhaps such a compound method will not be thought inappropriate in a portrait of one whose constant habit it was to mingle her abounding life with that of others."

A contemporary reviewer gives some idea as to how well Professor Palmer succeeded in his task. ". . . In biography the subject is often of less importance than the biographer. A dull man can make the most brilliant career seem dull; a great biographer, on the contrary, like a great portrait painter, can immortalize . . . We feel in reading Mrs. Palmer's life that it owes at every point an incalculable debt to Mr. Palmer's telling. The remarkable character, the striking career were there to be described, but only he could have produced such a description of them. We can recall no other husband who has paid such a tribute to his wife. The husband-biographer is usually to be shunned. But Mr. Palmer has almost unique qualifications for achieving the impossible. His various scholarship has not sterilized his imagination, experience has not jaded his affections; he looks at his wife with a lover's sensitiveness, but also with the large interest of a man of culture. On the side of his affections she fascinates him; but she perpetually delights his intellect, which watches her not only as wife, but as comrade, as woman of many contacts with the world, as large and uplifting influence. So we see her as she lives in both his heart and his head. He has no reserves . . . It was indispensable that we should behold Mrs. Palmer through the medium of *his* spirit in order to see her most significantly. Power can be measured by achievement, but charm is so elusive that it must be conveyed in biography through subtle suggestion. This is what Mr. Palmer has done. He makes an eager, joyous, human temperament to live again. This, we repeat, is the biographer's triumph" (Professor Palmer's Life of Mrs. Palmer, *HGM,* 1907–1908; 16 (June 1908): 654–656).

And, in complete agreement, a later reviewer writes that "among shining tributes offered by hubands to wives this book perhaps ranks second only to Shah Jehan's Taj Mahal" (A. D. Dickinson, *The World's Best Books*, H. W. Wilson Co., 1953: page 265).

In 1930 (**GHP**-104), along with his 'Homer' and 'George Herbert,' Palmer names this biography as one of his "books of affection and gratitude [which] may live for half a century." And at the same time, he writes "[m]ore than fifty thousand copies of Mrs. Palmer's 'Life' have been sold" (see table, page 480).

11 *The Life of Alice Freeman Palmer*, edition for the blind. (**GHP**-58)

The Wellesley College Archives has a set of the two volumes, given by Professor Palmer in 1913. They are printed in the raised type of the New York Point system. The compositor finished the work of making the embossed stereotype plates on April 9, 1910.

Tipped into volume 1 is a letter that Ellen Scott Davison wrote to Professor Palmer from Lexington, Kentucky, on January 1, 1911:

"I saw yesterday my dear old friend Mr. Huntoon, head of the Institute for the blind here, and of the National Printing House for the blind.

"He asked me to express to you his own personal gratification that it has been possible to put into the hands of blind people the 'Life' of Mrs. Palmer. He asked me also to tell you what the circumstances were which put it in his power so to print the book he has wanted for his blind pupils ever since he first read it.

"The money appropriated by the government for this printing house may be used only to print text-books. For all other books money must come from other sources. One of these sources is the Library of the State of New York which nowadays appropriates a thousand dollars a year for this purpose. Last year the Library authorities specified that the 'Life' of Mrs. Palmer should be printed; and they themselves have twenty-five copies. I wish Mr. Huntoon might meet you. He is a Harvard man, class of 1856, and one of the most beautiful people I know. He is not well now, I grieve to say; but I hope he may grow stronger again."

Also tipped in is a letter fom Mr. Huntoon on January 14, 1911, to T. Y. Crowell, the first publisher of Palmer's *Self-Cul-*

tivation in English (**GHP**-34), requesting permission to print that book for the blind. The New York Library, he adds, has already ordered 15 copies. (The annotator has been unable to get further information about these printings, either from the American Printing House for the Blind, the New York State Library, or the Perkins School for the Blind.)

12 *The Life of Alice Freeman Palmer*, Hall of Fame edition. (**GHP**-59)

Alice Freeman Palmer was elected to the Hall of Fame on November 10, 1920, a tablet was dedicated there on May 21, 1921, and a bust of her was installed on May 13, 1924 (see 286n1).

Katherine Lee Bates, Professor of English at Wellesley College and author of "America the Beautiful," wrote an introduction to this edition: " . . . [W]hat she was, garnered in this volume by him who knew her best, has accomplished more than even her living achievement. Her voice reached many hundreds; this book speaks to many thousands. Seldom in the history of human love has sore bereavement wrought for its saint a memory so potent.

"That Professor Palmer has donated the royalties of this Hall of Fame edition to Wellesley's Semi-Centennial Endowment Fund is characteristic. *Ever since the day when he won away her president he has been making to the College continual restitution* (annotator's italics). He has given to the Wellesley library books beyond all our resources of gratitude, — rarities wisely selected, even unique copies and manuscripts, gradually accumulating in our treasure room a marvelous collection, to be ever more precious as the centuries pass, of first editions of the English poets. But in all his books, he has given to Wellesley for all time what life gave for but a few swift years — Alice Freeman Palmer."

13 *The Life of Alice Freeman Palmer*, translated into Japanese. (**GHP**-60)

The translator, twenty-seven years old, was a graduate of Tokyo Imperial University with a great interest in girls' education. He wrote to Professor Palmer: "Japanese women are now awakening from their long asleep of ignorance, and I believed that your book should be just worth introducing to them. Her strong and beautiful life must be the best model for girls of the Far East, too" (letter from K. Sugimoto to George

Herbert Palmer, December 7, 1923, tipped into the volume in the Wellesley College Archives).

14 *The Life of Alice Freeman Palmer*, New Edition with Appendix.

(**GHP**-61)

In Appendix I, entitled The Story of the Slum Girl, to "celebrate the coming of my book to its fiftieth thousand," Professor Palmer reports an "almost incredible tale . . . a strange and romantic sequel" to a story in the book. This story describes how Alice Freeman Palmer "used to leave her peaceful, calm retreat in the country and go to Boston to talk to children of the slums at a vacation school." In particular, the story relates her conversation about "how to be happy" with one of the girls, who knew Mrs. Palmer only as "My Beautiful Lady." Years later, after George Herbert Palmer "addressed a Harvard Club in a Western city," a member of the club, who had studied philosophy with Palmer at Harvard College, took the professor to meet his wife, who was that very girl, and their baby named "Alice." The man had given his wife a copy of The Life of Alice Freeman Palmer; "[s]he opened it, saw Mrs. Palmer's face, read of her own childhood, and learned for the first time who had been her guardian angel"!

Appendix II, entitled The Hall of Fame, presents in some detail the story of Alice Freeman Palmer's election to this group of famous Americans (see 286n1).

15 *The Life of Alice Freeman Palmer*.

(**GHP**-62)

George Herbert Palmer died in 1933. This printing was copyrighted in 1936 by his nephew, Frederic Palmer, Jr. The publication differs from **GHP**-61 in the use of heavier paper, the inclusion of five photographs instead of eleven, and the absence of "New Edition with Appendix" on the title page although the two appendixes are included.

A copy (with the dust jacket which identifies "A new edition with additional material") from a usedbook shop in Boston has this inscription by an unidentified person, dated December 25, 1941: "This story of Alice Freeman Palmer is, to my mind, easily the outstanding biography of American Women — (whom I have ever known). And, one of the things that makes it facinating [*sic*] is that the secret of this most alluring personality is so simple — and, also, so easy of imitation! From the earliest years, Mrs. Palmer cultivated thinking and caring about the happiness of others more than about herself, until their welfare became the subconscious habit and directing force of her extraordinary life" (AJL Collection).

16 James Laurence Laughlin, Alice Freeman Palmer, *University Record* (Chicago), 1908;13 (No.1, July 1908):11–16.

This was the second of two addresses delivered at the University of Chicago during the Dedication of the Alice Freeman Palmer Chimes on June 9, 1908 (see 238n2). The first (pages 9–11), by George Edgar Vincent, Dean of the Faculties of Arts, Literature, and Science, was a presentation about Bells and Bell Ringing. The bells for Chicago "were ordered from the Whitechapel Foundry of East London, an establishment which traces an unbroken history back to the year 1570. From this foundry came the great bell of Westminster, 'Great Peter' of York, and 'Great Tom' of Lincoln . . . the Palmer Chimes are the fourteenth set of bells which this firm has sent to this side of the Atlantic . . . Throughout England today there are guilds of bell ringers who without payment take the keenest delight in ringing the parish and cathedral bells. They form a freemasonry with honorable traditions. They take pride in their profession, which combines music, mechanics, and athletics . . . Already there is promise that a small group of Englishmen in this city will renew their allegiance to the ancient and honorable art of change ringing [i.e., the order in which a set of bells is struck] . . . Those who knew Mrs. Palmer can easily imagine how much pleasure it would give her if the bells set up in her honor might be rung as the years go on by a band of eager, loyal students."

Professor Laughlin, head of the Department of Political Economy at the University of Chicago, had been at Harvard from 1869 to 1888, and had joined the Chicago faculty in 1892 (see 93n1), the same time when Mrs. Palmer became Dean of Women there. In 1894–1895, his daughter, Agatha, fourteen years old, lived with the Palmers while she went to school in Boston.

He begins: "At the end of many years of waiting the Memorial Committee of Chicago has succeeded in carrying out the plan to erect at this University an enduring monument to the memory of Alice Freeman Palmer. This has been the outcome of the devotion of her friends in this city both in and out of the University. Here she was the first Dean of Women; but more than that she was pre-eminently a great moral force, whose influence has not ceased with the close of her life. Here it was she gave lavishly of her inspiration and sympathy; and here shall she be recalled to generations yet unborn, by the sound of these bells which today we offer in her honor to the University of Chicago. This result has been accomplished independently of any committees elsewhere, and without any suggestion from her nearest relatives. The memorial is a spontaneous offering from a large number of her friends in and around Chicago. Only, after the plan was achieved, we have applied to Professor Palmer for the inscriptions which he has selected for us . . . [see 238n2]

"It was this young girl, who had to struggle hard for an education, that founded in this city an organization known as the Students' Fund Society for the University of Chicago. Out of her experience she had learned how to lighten the burdens of future students. So it is that a new benefaction once opened goes on with its quickening stream of help far into the indefinite future. In this Students' Fund Society, it sometimes occurs to me that she has unconsciously raised up to herself a greater monument than we can give to her in this peal of bells. Since she struck the rock with her rod, and this society sprang forth, more than five hundred persons have already been helped on to an education, who would have fallen by the way without this help . . .

"Mrs. Palmer had this genius for leadership — divine, elusive, but compelling, as genius always is. She always seemed one of us, sympathetic, persuasive, simple; yet in her hands we were but as the potter's clay. And the glory of it was, she always used this amazing power to stimulate the good that was in all of us, and to bend us to higher uses . . . It is one of the things which makes 'her career unmatched by any other American woman' — and it is a very rare thing — that she never had an enemy. Nay, more than that, never did she stir the suspicion of envy. Her power of leadership, in truth, was always controlled by an equal power of unselfish service to others . . .

"[I]t was she who laid the foundations for the education of women at college, and who began the series of experiments which have broadened into the present phases of women's training. Therefore, although she was the president of Wellesley College she was in truth the builder of woman's education, not only in America, but in Spain and throughout the world. Her heart was large; but the boundaries of the world were not too large for her sympathetic and enthusiastic activities. She established a college spirit which aimed to give to woman not merely learning, but 'helpfulness, modesty, intelligence, and grace' . . .

"Together with her quick resourcefulness, she brought to bear on every question a subtle, powerful, and virile intelligence. While she was a most effective and persuasive debater, she was at the same time under the control of a practical good sense, a sagacity, and a sense of humor which never failed . . . Her love of fun was only a part of her general cheerfulness . . . [See **AFPann**-10]

"Mrs. Palmer put her emphasis on the acquisition by others of the things of the spirit, as the only permanent, the only real things of life: on kindliness, sympathy, courage, truth, and honor. Whatever we may think of the present social régime, she has proved to us that hardship and work are compatible with the highest spiritual advancement — possibly the inevitable conditions of it . . . If I were to state the most important lesson of her career in a word, I should say that she had outflanked the position of the materialistic reformers, and showed us their ineffectiveness, by practically demonstrating that the progress of the world goes on best, or goes on only, by a growth in things of the spirit. Not that she was an extremist: she recognized the subsidiary uses of wealth; but she would have scorned the thought that the attainment of happiness, or the means of making others happy, lay chiefly through a struggle for material rewards. She centered her hopes in that education which gave self-mastery, poise, courage in standing by a principle, and the best idealism. After all, she had a working theory of constructive beneficence, based on her wide experience with the world and with human nature . . . President Eliot [of Harvard] said of her: 'Mrs. Palmer's career was devoted to positive constructive labors in promoting the well-being of the people, and cultivating their best mental and spiritual faculties . . . We cannot but believe that in the long run the surest way to cure evils is to supplant evil by good.'

"President [Harry Pratt] Judson, we commemorate today a great woman. Memorials are being established to her in several places. At Wellesley a monument in marble by the sculptor, Daniel Chester French, is being prepared, representing a young, unformed girl lighting her lamp at the college altar, and brooded over by a splended protecting figure typifying Mrs. Palmer. [See 244n5 and frontispiece] In Chicago it has been decided by her friends that the remembrance of her should be placed in this institution on which she left the impress of her character. In behalf of the Chicago Memorial Committee I have the honor to present to the University of Chicago this peal of ten bells, as a memorial to Alice Freeman Palmer . . . By placing these bells in the tower above us . . . we hope that, whenever their music is heard, they will interpret the lofty standards of Mrs. Palmer's life, and set a measure for the conduct of us, and of all who come after us, which she would approve."

17 Lyman Abbott, Alice Freeman Palmer — A Sketch, *Outlook*, 1916; 112 (January 12): 88–90.

This short sketch is expanded in **aboutAFPann**-19.

18 Mary R. Parkman, *Heroines of Service*, New York, Century Co., 1917. 322 pages.

This book for young readers has eleven biographical sketches of prominent women in a wide variety of fields. A Foreword introduces the selection: "From time immemorial women have been content to be as those who serve. *Non ministrari sed ministrare* — not to be ministered unto but to minister [Mark 10:45] — is not alone the motto of those who stand under the Wellesley banner, but of true women everywhere.

"For centuries a woman's own home had not only first claim, but full claim, on her fostering care . . . Changed days have come, however, with changed ways. The development of science and invention, which has led to industrial progress and specialization, has radically changed the woman's world of the home . . . Many women, whose energies would have been, under former conditions, inevitably monopolized by home-keeping duties, are to-day giving their strength and special gifts to social service . . . The service of the true woman is always 'womanly.' She gives something of the fostering care of the mother, whether it be as nurse, like Clara Barton; as teacher, like Mary Lyon and Alice Freeman Palmer; or as social helper, like Jane Addams. So it is that the service of these 'heroines' is that which only women could have given to the world . . ."

The chapter on Alice Freeman Palmer, titled "The Princess" of Wellesley, opens with this paragraph: "This is the story of a princess of our own time and our own America — a princess who, while little more than a girl herself, was chosen to rule a kingdom of girls. It is a little like the story of Tennyson's 'Princess,' with her woman's kingdom, and very much like the happy, old-fashioned fairy-tale." (See **aboutAFPann**-1)

The chapter ends: "There are many memorials speaking in different places of her work. In the chapel at Wellesley, where it seems to gather at every hour a golden glory of light, is the lovely transparent marble by Daniel Chester French, eternally bearing witness to the meaning of her influence with her girls [244n5 and frontispiece]. In the tower at Chicago the chimes 'make music, joyfully to recall' her labors there [238n2]. But more lasting than marble or bronze is the living memorial in the hearts and minds 'made better by her presence.' For it is, indeed, people that count, and in the richer lives of many the enkindling spirit of Alice Freeman Palmer still lives."

19 Alice Freeman Palmer, Teacher, in Lyman Abbott, *Silhouettes of My Contemporaries*, New York, Doubleday, Page & Co., 1921, page 59–80.

In his preface, Lyman Abbott describes this volume as "a gallery of shadow pictures . . . of fellow-men whom I have known and whose careers I have studied, as looking back, they now appear to me. Leaders of their generations have usually some one characteristic which distinguishes them from their contemporaries. This distinctive characteristic I have sought to portray. To that extent these portraits are partial and imperfect, as all portraits, whether painted by the brush or the pen, are and must be. They are all portraits of men who I believe have contributed something toward the progress which is making out of this world a better world — one of justice, liberty, and peace . . .

"Depressed and discouraged as we are apt to be by the flood of filth and falsehood, of corruption and crime, which the daily paper offers us for our daily food, it is well sometimes to stop, take a quieter and less partial view, and realize the right we have as Americans for pride in our past and for hope in our future."

The chapters portray eighteen men and, as the fifth presentation, one woman, Alice Freeman Palmer.

"From the first [Abbott writes] she fascinated me. Whether a sculptor would consider her features beautiful I do not know . . . But through her always-expressive face shone a beautiful spirit. Native refinement, scholarly culture, intuitive imagination, unhesitating courage, womanly grace and spontaneity of life combined to make that beauty. Profoundly interested in the movement to widen the intellectual horizon of woman and open to her the long-locked doors of opportunity to public service, she was then and always feminine."

This lengthy chapter includes a "paragraphical abstract" of **AFP**-8. And Abbott describes his own experience during Alice Freeman's presidency, when he "spent a week or ten days in [Wellesley] college preaching on the two Sundays, lecturing nearly every day during the intervening week, and giving daily 'office hours' to girls coming with questions, sometimes in twos or threes, sometimes in larger groups, oftenest alone . . .

"Walking through the college corridors with [Alice Freeman] almost daily, her personal familiarity with her three hundred pupils filled me with ever-increasing amazement. She not only seemed to know them all by name: she knew their families and their interests . . . 'How ever do you do it?' I asked her. 'I never could.' 'Oh, yes!' she replied; 'you could if you had to. It is simply that you never had to. Whatever we have to do, we can always do' . . . This quiet confidence in the ability to do what needs to be done seems to me one of the secrets of her power . . .

"No doubt this power to carry in her busy mind these details of the lives of others was in part a native gift; but it was one which she had assiduously cultivated, and she told me once what she did to cultivate it. She kept a memorandum book in her bedroom in which were the names of all the freshman class. Under each name she wrote whatever information she from time to time acquired. These notes of her pupils' characters and experiences she studied as they studied their notes of the lectures of their instructors . . . This was no compulsory or professional study. She delighted in it. She wished to know every pupil that she might better befriend every pupil. It was true for her then, as it was true for her always: 'It is people that count.'"

Abbott ends the chapter: "It was customary in the 'eighties for Wellesley College girls to elect honorary members to their classes. That honor was conferred upon me [see 64n1]. Thus enrolled among the pupils of Alice Freeman Palmer I venture to represent them as well as myself by writing beneath this simple pen-picture of our honoured teacher:

Thy gentleness hath made me great."

20 Edith S. Tufts, I Remember —II, Miss Freeman through Undergraduate Eyes, *Wellesely Alumnae Magazine*, 1924; 9 (No. 2. December): 55–57.

President of Wellesley's class of 1884, Edith Tufts extends her own comments about Alice Freeman in 1903 (64n1) and adds to the recollections by Helen B. Montgomery, a member of the same class (**aboutAFPann**-6).

"There . . . comes to me the picture of [Alice Freeman] as lecturer on English history in the old chapel, when I first experienced that power over words which enabled her to place before a class episodes and whole periods with a vividness that made the characters step out from the printed page and move as flesh and blood before us. Other teachers of my undergraduate years impressed me as greater scholars and roused in me more keenly a desire for scholarly attainment, but no one had so strongly this magic power of presentation . . .

"[Then there] were the times when we had the President to ourselves, and she related to us with most delicious humor some episode of the day's work or some experience of a trip taken in behalf of the college, to secure the interest of some prominent person. Who could forget her tale of her dismay when, as she came up New York harbor on the deck of a Fall River boat, a sudden gust of wind snatched off the new hat bought especially to impress some great personage, and she could only gaze at its ostrich plumes gaily nodding as it floated down the tide . . .

"Once, I remember, some one placed on the table to welcome her home, a toy cart full of pansies. She was delighted with the conceit, which made the pansy faces look like a gay load of passengers. When we left the table she dragged the cart down the long dining room with childish fun, while we trailed along behind in laughing delight at her abandonment, for the time, of presidential dignity.

"A more serious remembrance, and one deeply cherished from those undergraduate days, comes with the thought of daily chapel. The same gift which made Miss Freeman a vivid interpreter of history gave her great power as a chapel leader.

Her selections of Scripture were peculiarly appropriate to our daily needs. Her prayers expressed, as we could not ourselves, our desires and our aspirations. Compulsory attendance became voluntary when she led . . .

"We lived so closely together in those days when the President's suite was on a main corridor of the big building, that there were constant contacts in our daily walk and conversation, contacts which added to the joy of living. Remembering Miss Freeman as she went in and out among us, perhaps I can best sum up these stray remembrances in the words which signify the highest praise of the present generation, — she was 'so human.'"

21 Caroline Hazard, Alice Freeman Palmer: Address in the Brick Church, New York, May 20, 1921, before the Hall of Fame Unveiling; in Caroline Hazard, *From College Gates*, page 209–223. (See 286n1.)

After a review of Alice Freeman Palmer's life, her many activities, and her contributions, Miss Hazard ends the address: "To-morrow the tablet which inscribes her name in our American Hall of Fame is to be unveiled. To-morrow we Wellesley women will rejoice, for Wellesley was very dear to her. She gave much and she owed much to Wellesley. Who that ever heard her can forget her chapel services there—the full rich voice in the Scripture reading, and the outpouring of the soul in prayer? We entered into the very presence of God in those hallowed moments. She had a peculiar 'gift in prayer'; it seemed a native language, welling up spontaneous, full of devout nobility. In those moments the secret of her power was proclaimed, for through her earthly dress the 'bright shoots of everlastingness' were clearly visible."

22 Alice Fleming, *Alice Freeman Palmer: Pioneer College President*, Englewood Cliffs, New Jersey, Prentice-Hall, 1970. 143 pages.

This biography, for young readers, is one of a series about American women and men who have been elected to the Hall of Fame of New York University (see 286n1).

Biographical Summaries

Index to Notes in the Chronicles

Biographical Summaries

These summaries include most of the individuals named in the compilation. Some names in the Index to Notes in the Chronicles are not included here.

A.B. & B.A. = Bachelor of Arts
A.M. & M.A. = Master of Arts
B.Litt. = Bachelor of Literature (Oxford)
Litt.D. = Doctor of Letters (honorary)
LL.B. = Bachelor of Laws
LL.D. = Doctor of Laws (honorary)
Ph.D. (-) = Doctor of Philosophy (special field)
ΦBK = Phi Beta Kappa
Ph.B. = Bachelor of Philosophy
B.S. & S.B. = Bachelor of Science
S.T.B. = Bachelor of Divinity
S.T.D. = Doctor of Sacred Theology (honorary)
("-") = as name may appear in the compilation

Abbot, Edwin Hale (1834–1927)
Harvard: A.B., ΦBK, 1855; A.M., 1858; LL.B., 1861; tutor, Latin and Greek, 1857–1861
Wellesley, trustee, 1892–1921
Abbot, Edwin Hale, Jr. ("Ned") (1881–1966)
Harvard: A.B., ΦBK, 1903; LL.B., 1907; A.M., 1908
Abbot, Philip Stanley (1867–1896)
Son of Edwin Hale Abbot
Harvard: A.B., ΦBK, 1890; LL.B. and A.M., 1893

Abbott, Lyman (1835–1922)
Congregational clergyman
Harvard: S.T.D., 1890; preacher, 1889–1893, 1900–1909
Agassiz, Alexander (1835–1910)
Harvard: A.B., ΦBK, 1855; S.B., 1857, 1862; Museum of Comparative Zoology-curator, 1875–1898, director, 1892–1898; University Museum, director, 1902–1910; overseer, 1873–1878, 1885; fellow, 1878–1884; LL.D., 1885
Agassiz, Elizabeth Cary (Mrs. Louis Agassiz) (1822–1907)
Radcliffe: a founder, 1879; first president, 1894–1902
Aguinaldo, Emilio (1869–1964)
Commander of Filipino forces in rebellion against Spain (1896–98); led insurrection against American authority (1899–1901)
Allen, Alexander Viets Griswold (1841–1908)
Episcopal clergyman
Andover Theological Seminary, graduate, 1865
Harvard: Divinity School, lecturer, 1889–1890; S.T.D., 1886; ΦBK (honorary), 1895
Episcopal Theological School, professor, ecclesiastical history, 1867–1908
Amen, Harlan Page (1853–1913)
Harvard: A.B., 1879; overseer, 1913
Phillips Exeter Academy, principal, 1895–1913
New England Association of Colleges and Preparatory Schools, president, 1906–1908
Ames, James Barr (1846–1910)
Harvard: A.B., A.M., ΦBK, 1868; LL.B., 1872; tutor, 1871–1872; instructor, history, 1872–1873; assistant professor, law, 1973–1877; professor, law, 1877–1879; Bussey Professor of Law, 1879–1903; Dane Professor of Law, 1903–1910; dean, Law School, 1895–1910
Angell, James Burrill (1829–1916)
Brown: A.B., 1849; A.M., 1853; professor, modern languages and literature, 1853–1860
University of Vermont, president, 1866–1871
University of Michigan, president, 1871–1909
Wellesley, board of visitors, 1887
Harvard, LL.D., 1905
Angell, James Rowland (1869–1949)
Son of James Burrill Angell
University of Michigan: A.B., 1890; A.M., 1891
Harvard: A.M., 1892; LL.D., 1921
Yale, president, 1921–1937

Arnold, John Himes (1839-?)
Harvard: Law School, librarian, 1872–1913; A.M. (honorary), 1902
Arnold, Matthew (1822–1888)
English poet and critic
Avery, Helen Palmer ("Linette") (Mrs. William H. Avery) (1910-living in Maryland in 1994)
Daughter of Frederic Palmer, Jr. and Helen Wallace Palmer
Sister of Frederic Palmer, 3rd.
Granddaughter of Frederic Palmer
Grandniece of George Herbert Palmer
Wellesley, B.A., 1932

Bachelder, Augustus Edwin ("Aug" "A.E.B.") (1824–1904)
Married Lucy Ann Palmer (1853)
Married Elizabeth Wilkinson (1887)
Bachelder, Elizabeth Wilkinson ("Lily," "Aunt Lily") (Mrs. Augustus Edwin Bachelder) (1848–1909)
Sister of Katherine Wilkinson French
Aunt of Katherine French and Barbara French
Bachelder, Lucy Palmer ("Luc") (Mrs. Augustus Edwin Bachelder) (1831–1880)
Sister of George Herbert Palmer
Bailey, Marshall Henry (?)
College of Physicians and Surgeons (Baltimore), M.D., 1893
Harvard, medical adviser, 1899–1928
Baker, George Pierce (1866–1935)
Harvard: A.B., ΦBK, 1887; instructor, English, 1888–1889; instructor, forensics, 1889–1892; instructor, English, 1892–1895; assistant professor, English, 1895–1905; professor, English, 1905–1924
Yale, professor, history and technique of drama, 1925–1933
Bakewell, Charles Montague (1867–1957)
University of California: A.B., 1889; professor, philosophy, 1903–1905
Harvard: A.M., 1892; Ph.D. (philosophy), 1894; instructor, philosophy, 1896–1897; lecturer, philosophy, 1912–1913
Yale, professor, philosophy, 1905–1933
Baldwin, James Mark (1861–1934)
Princeton: A.B., 1884; professor, psychology, 1893–1903
Studied in Germany, 1884–1885
University of Toronto, professor, psychology, 1889–1893
Johns Hopkins, professor, psychology, 1903–1909
National University of Mexico, professor, psychology, 1909–1913
Barrows, John Henry (1847–1902)
Congregational clergyman

Olivet, B.A., 1867
Andover Theological Seminary, graduate, 1875
Oberlin, president, 1899–1902

Bates, Katharine Lee (1859–1929)
Wellesley: B.A., 1880; M.A., 1891; professor, English Literature, 1891–1925; LL.D., 1925

Bellamy, Edward (1850–1898)
"American author . . . His Utopian romance *Looking Backward* (1888) presented a method of economic organization, socialistic in nature, guaranteeing material equality corresponding to political equality of citizens. Its enormous success inspired an unsuccessful sequel *Equality* (1897)."

Berkeley, George (1685–1753)
Irish philosopher

Bigelow, Helen (see Helen Bigelow Merriman)

Bingham, Millicent Todd (Mrs. Walter Van Dyke Bingham) (?)

Bingham, Walter Van Dyke (1880–1952)
Beloit, A.B., 1901
Harvard, A.M., 1907
University of Chicago, Ph.D. (psychology), 1908
Dartmouth, assistant professor, psychology, 1910–1915
Carnegie Institute of Technology, dean and professor, psychology, 1915–1924
Married Millicent Todd (1920)

Blaisdell, James Arnold (1867–1957)
Beloit: A.B., 1889; A.M., 1892
Hartford Theological Seminary, graduate, 1892
Pomona, president, 1910–1928

Bôcher, Ferdinand (?–1902)
Harvard: instructor, modern languages, 1861–1865; university lecturer, 1864–1866; professor, modern languages, 1870–1902; A.M. (honorary), 1872
Massachusetts Institute of Technology, professor, modern languages, 1869–1871

Bowditch, Henry Ingersoll (1808–1892).
Harvard: A.B., A.M., ΦBK, 1828; M.D., 1832; Jackson Professor of Clinical Medicine, 1859–1867
Practice, special interest in consumption
American Medical Association, president, 1876

Bowen, Francis (1811–1890)
Harvard: A.B., A.M., ΦBK, 1833; tutor, 1835–1839; instructor, natural, intellectual, and moral philosophy, 1836–1839; Alford Profes-

sor of Natural Religion, Moral Philosophy, and Civil Polity, 1853–1889; LL.D., 1879

Bradford, Carrie Locke (Mrs. Emery Lucius Bradford) (?–1940)

Bradford, Emery Lucius (1859–1941)
Congregational clergyman
Andover Theological Seminary, graduate, 1892

Bradford, Ruth (1893–1982)
Daughter of Emery Lucius Bradford and Carrie Locke Bradford
Wellesley, B.A., 1915

Brandeis, Louis Dembitz (1856–1941)
Harvard: LL.B., 1877; A.M. (honorary), 1891; instructor, evidence, 1882–1883
United States Supreme Court, associate justice, 1916–1939

Bremer, John Lewis (1874–1959)
Harvard: A.B., 1896; M.D., 1901; instructor, histology and embryology, 1902–1906; demonstrator, histology, 1906–1912; assistant professor, histology, 1912–1915; associate professor, histology, 1915–1931; Hersey Professor of Anatomy, 1931–1942

Briggs, LeBaron Russell (1855–1934)
Harvard: A.B., ΦBK, 1875; A.M., 1882; tutor, Greek, 1878–1881; instructor, English, 1883–1885; assistant professor, English, 1885–1890; professor, English, 1890–1904; dean, Harvard College, 1891–1902; dean, Faculty of Arts and Sciences, 1902–1925; Boylston Professor of Rhetoric and Oratory, 1904- 1925; LL.D., 1900
Radcliffe, president, 1903–1923

Brooks, John Graham (1846–1938)
Harvard: S.T.B., 1875; lecturer, socialism, 1885–1886; instructor, political economy, 1889–1891
Roxbury Latin School, trustee, 1878–1882

Brooks, Phillips (1835–1893)
Harvard, A.B., ΦBK, 1855
Wellesley, trustee, 1891–1893

Brown, Rollo Walter (?)
Harvard: A.M., 1905; visiting lecturer, English, 1923; lecturer, English, 1923–1924
Wabash, professor, rhetoric and composition, 1906–1920
Carleton, professor, rhetoric and composition, 1920–1923

Bryce, James (1838–1922)
British jurist, historian, diplomat
Author of *The American Commonwealth* (1888), classic work on American government

Buckham, John Wright (1864–1945)
Congregational clergyman

University of Vermont, B.A., 1885
Andover Theological Seminary, graduate, 1888
Pacific School of Religion, professor, Christian Theology, 1903–1937
Bumstead, Horace (1841–1919)
Yale: A.B., ΦBK, 1863
Andover Theological Seminary, graduate, 1870
Atlanta University, president, 1888–1907

Cabot, Richard Clarke (1868–1939)
Harvard: A.B., ΦBK, 1889; M.D., 1892; professor, clinical medicine, 1918–1933; professor, social ethics, 1920–1934
Caird, Edward (1835–1908)
Glasgow, professor, moral philosophy, 1866–1893
Oxford, Balliol College, master, 1893–1906
Calkins, Mary Whiton (1863–1930)
Smith, A.B., 1885
Wellesley: tutor, Greek, 1887–1891; founded psychological laboratory, 1891; instructor, psychology, 1891–1898; professor, philosophy and psychology, 1898–1929
Cannon, Annie Jump (1863–1941)
Wellesley: B.A., 1884; LL.D., 1925
Harvard Observatory: assistant, 1896–1911; curator, astronomical photographs, 1911–1938
Capen, Samuel Billings, (1842–1914)
Merchant
English High School (Boston), graduate, 1858
Congregational Sunday School and Publication Society, president, 1882–1899
American Board of Commissioners for Foreign Missions, president, 1899–1914
Boston School Committee: member, 1888–1892; president, 1892–1893
International Institute for Girls in Spain, president
Wellesley, board of trustees, president, 1905–1914
Capron, Annie Hooker (see Annie Capron Morse)
Carter, Franklin (1837–1919)
Williams: A.B., 1862; professor, Latin and Greek, 1865–1872; president, 1881–1901
Yale, professor, German, 1873–1880
Massachusetts Board of Education, member, 1896–1900
Caswell, Mary (?–1926)
Wellesley: special student, 1879–1880; instructor, botany, 1881–1888; presidential secretary, 1890–1919

Cavell, Edith Louise (1865–1915)
English nurse in Belgium during European war. Executed by Germans for helping soldiers escape to Holland

Chesnutt, Charles Waddell (1858–1932)
African-American author, educator, and lawyer

Chute, Arthur Lambert (1869–1934)
Harvard, M.D., 1895

Claflin, Adams Davenport (1862–1933)
Son of William Claflin and Mary Claflin
Harvard, A.B., 1886

Claflin, Mary (Mrs. William Claflin) (1825–1896)
Wellesley, trustee, 1873–1896

Claflin, William (1819–1905)
Governor of Massachusetts, 1869–1871
Harvard, LL.D., 1869
Wellesley, trustee, 1873–1905

Clarke, Lucia Fidelia (?–1911)
Wellesley: instructor, Latin, 1875–1891; instructor, biblical history, 1891–1897; superintendent, Simpson Cottage, 1882–1900

Clement, Edward Henry (1843–1920)
Tufts, A.B., 1864
The Boston Evening Transcript, editor, 1881–1902

Clough, Anne Jemima (1820–1892)
Active in the movement to promote the higher education of women
Newnham College, Cambridge, England, first principal

Coes, Mary (1861–1913)
Radcliffe: B.A., 1887; M.A. (history and English), 1897; assistant secretary, 1890–1894; secretary, 1894–1910; dean, 1910–1913

Cole, Samuel Valentine (1851–1925)
Bowdoin: A.B., 1874; A.M., 1877; LL.D., 1912
Andover Theological Seminary, graduate, 1887
Wheaton, president, 1897–1925

Comstock, Clara Elizabeth (see Clara Comstock Everett)

Conant, Ernest Lee (1857–1948)
Harvard: A.B., ΦBK, 1884; LL.B. & A.M., 1889; instructor, forensics, 1887–1889, history, 1893–1894, and law, 1894–1895

Crothers, Samuel McChord (1857–1927)
Unitarian clergyman
Wittenberg College (Ohio), graduate, 1873
College of New Jersey (now Princeton), graduate, 1874
First Parish Church, Cambridge, minister, 1894–1927
Harvard: preacher, 1893–1896; ΦBK (honorary), 1894; S.T.D., 1899

Cummings, Edward (1861–1926)
Protestant clergyman
Harvard: A.B., ΦBK, 1883; A.M., 1885; Divinity School, student, 2 years; instructor, English, 1885–1888; instructor, political economy, 1891–1892; instructor, sociology, 1892–1893; assistant professor, sociology, 1893–1900

Davis, Olive (1862–1921)
Wellesley: B.A., 1886; superintendent of dormitories, 1900–1917; lecturer, domestic science, 1900–1915
Davison, Ellen Scott (1864–1921)
Wellesley, B.A., 1887
Western Reserve, M.A., 1894
Columbia, Ph.D., 1907
de Sumichrast, Frederick Caesar (?)
Harvard: instructor, French, 1887–1889; assistant professor, French, 1889–1899; associate professor, French, 1899–1911
Durant, Henry Fowle (1822–1881)
Harvard, A.B., 1841 (received degree, 1842)
Wellesley: founder; trustee, 1870–1881
Durant, Pauline Fowle (Mrs. Henry Fowle Durant) (1832–1917)
Wellesley, trustee, 1870–1917
Dutton, Samuel Train (1849–1919)
Yale: A.B., 1873; A.M. (honorary), 1900
Brookline (Massachusetts), superintendent of schools, 1891–1900
Harvard: lecturer, school supervision, 1896–1897; lecturer, organization and management of schools, 1897–1898
Teachers College (Columbia), professor, school adminstration, 1900–1914
Dye, Electa P. (?)
Daughter of John P. Dye and Sarah Higley Dye
Maternal niece of Elizabeth Higley Freeman
First cousin of Alice Freeman Palmer
Dye, John P. (1820–1876)
Married Sarah Higley (1845)
Father of Electa P. Dye
Dye, Sarah Higley ("Aunt Sarah") (Mrs. John P. Dye) (1825-?)
Mother of Electa P. Dye
One of Elizabeth Higley Freeman's four sisters
Maternal aunt of Alice Freeman Palmer

Dyer, Louis (1851–1908)
  Harvard: A.B., ΦBK, 1874; tutor, 1878–1881; assistant professor, Greek and Latin, 1881–1887
  Oxford: B.A., 1878; M.A., 1893

Eastman, Sarah Porter (1839–1930)
  Mount Holyoke, Doctor of Literature, 1861
  Wellesley, instructor, history and English literature, 1875–1881
  Dana Hall School, founder, associate principal, 1881–1899
Eliot, Charles William (1834–1926)
  Harvard: A.B., ΦBK, 1853; A.M., 1856; assistant professor, chemistry and mathematics, 1858–1863; president, 1869–1909; LL.D., 1909
  Massachusetts Institute of Technology, assistant professor, chemistry, 1865–1869
  Married Grace Mellen Hopkinson (1877)
Eliot, Grace Hopkinson (Mrs. Charles William Eliot) (1846–1924)
Emery, Augustus B. ("Gus," "A.B.E.") (?)
  Grandson of Joshua Emery and Harriet Peabody Emery
Emery, Florence (?)
  Granddaughter of Joshua Emery and Harriet Peabody Emery
Emery, Harriet (see Harriet Emery Herrick)
Emery, Harriet Peabody ("Aunt Hattie") (Mrs. Joshua Emery) (1812–1896)
  Daughter of Jacob Peabody and Lucy Manning Peabody
  Sister of Lucy Peabody Palmer
  Maternal aunt of George Herbert Palmer
Emery, Joshua (1807–1882)
  Congregational clergyman
  Amherst, A.B., 1831
  Andover Theological Seminary, graduate, 1834
  Married Harriet Peabody (1836)
Eucken, Rudolf Christoph (1846–1926)
  German philosopher
  Nobel Peace Prize, 1908
  Harvard, exchange professor, philosophy, 1912–1913
Everett, Charles Carroll (1829–1900)
  Unitarian clergyman
  Bowdoin: A.B., 1850
  Harvard Divinity School: graduate, 1859; Bussey Professor of Theology, 1869–1900; dean, 1878–1900
  Harvard: S.T.D., 1874; preacher, 1891–1893

Everett, Clara Comstock (Mrs. Walter Goodnow Everett) (1866–1955)
Pembroke (Women's College at Brown): Ph.B., ΦΒΚ, 1895; A.M., 1897
Stepmother of Helen Everett Meiklejohn
Everett, Helen (see Helen Everett Meiklejohn)
Everett, Walter Goodnow (1860–1937)
Brown : A.B., ΦΒΚ, 1885; A.M., 1888; Ph.D., 1895; instructor, Greek and Latin, 1894–1896; associate professor, philosophy, 1894–1896; associate professor and then professor, philosophy and natural theology, 1896–1930; acting president, 1912–1913; LL.D., 1935
American Philosophical Association, president, 1922
Father of Helen Everett Meiklejohn
Married Clara Elizabeth Comstock (1918)

Farlow, Lilian Horsford (Mrs. William G. Farlow) (1848–1927)
Member, committee of seven women who organized the program that became the Harvard Annex, 1879
Wellesley, trustee, 1886–1922
Farlow, William Gilson (1844–1919)
Harvard: A.B., A.M., 1866; M.D., 1870; assistant professor, botany, 1874–1879; professor, cryptogamic botany, 1879–1919; LL.D., 1896
Massachusetts General Hospital, surgical intern, 1869–1870
Finck, Henry Theophilus (1854–1926)
Harvard, A.B., ΦΒΚ, 1876
Finley, John Huston (1863–1940)
Knox: A.B., 1887; president, 1892–1899
Princeton, professor, politics, 1900–1903
City College of New York, president, 1903–1913
State of New York, Commissioner of Education, 1913–1921
Fiske, John (1842–1901)
Harvard: A.B., A.M., ΦΒΚ, 1863; LL.B., 1865; assistant librarian, 1872–1879; overseer, 1879–1891, 1899–1901; instructor, history, 1869–1870; university lecturer, 1869–1871; lecturer, campaigns of the Civil War west of the Alleghanies, 1895–1896; lecturer, Colonial Virginia and the other Southern Colonies, 1896–1897; LL.D., 1894
Washington University (Missouri), professor, American history, 1885–1901
Fitzgerald, Desmond (1846-?)
Phillips Academy, Andover, graduate
Topographical Commission of Massachusetts, chairman

Brookline Park Commission, chairman
Hydraulic engineer, practice for many years, principally in construction and maintenance of Boston's water supply system

Fletcher, Agnes Herrick (Mrs. Jefferson Butler Fletcher) (?)
Wellesley, 1891–1892

Fletcher, Jefferson Butler (1865–1946)
Married Agnes Peabody Herrick
Harvard: A.B., 1887; A.M., 1889; ΦBK, 1901; instructor, English, 1890–1902; assistant professor, comparative literature, 1902–1904
Columbia, professor, comparative literature, 1904–1939

Folsom, Norton (1842–1903)
Harvard, M.D., 1864
Massachusetts General Hospital, superintendent, 1872–1876
Practiced in Boston and Cambridge

Foster, William Trufaut (1879–1950)
Harvard: A.B., 1901; A.M., 1904
Columbia, Ph.D., 1911
Bowdoin, professor, English and argumentation
Reed, president, 1910–1919

Fowle, Pauline (see Pauline Fowle Durant)

Freeman, Alice Elvira (see Alice Freeman Palmer)

Freeman, Elizabeth Higley (Mrs. James Warren Freeman) (1837–1910)
Daughter of Elvira Frost
Mother of Alice Freeman Palmer

Freeman, Ella Louise (see Ella Freeman Talmage)

Freeman, Estelle (see Estelle Freeman Novy)

Freeman, Fred Warren (1856–1942)
Windsor Academy (New York), graduate
University of Michigan, M.D., 1882
Brother of Alice Freeman Palmer
Father of Estelle Freeman Novy

Freeman, James Warren (1828–1909)
Albany Medical School, M.D., 1864
Married Elizabeth Josephine Higley (1854)
Father of Alice Freeman Palmer, Fred Warren Freeman, Roxy Estelle Freeman, and Ella Freeman Talmage

Freeman, James Warren (1937-living in New York State in 1994)
Grandnephew of Alice Freeman Palmer
Grandson of Fred Warren Freeman
Great-grandson of James Warren Freeman

Freeman, Roxy Estelle ("Stella") (1860–1879)
Sister of Alice Freeman Palmer

French, Barbara (1882-?)
  Daughter of Peter French and Katherine Wilkinson French
  Twin sister of Katherine French
  Niece of Elizabeth Wilkinson Bachelder
French, Daniel Chester (1850–1931)
  American sculptor
French, Katherine (see Katherine French Rockwell)
French, Katherine Wilkinson (Mrs. Peter French) (?)
  Mother of Barbara French and Katherine French
  Sister of Elizabeth Wilkinson Bachelder
French, Peter (?–1912)
  Married Katherine Wilkinson
  Father of Barbara French and Katherine French
Frost, Elvira (?)
  Mother of Elizabeth Josephine Higley
  Maternal grandmother of Alice Freeman Palmer
Frothingham, Paul Revere (1854–1926)
  Unitarian clergyman
  Harvard: A.B., 1886; S.T.B. and A.M., 1889; preacher, 1899–1902, 1909–1910, 1914–1926; ΦBK, 1909; overseer, 1904–1910, 1918–1924
Frye, Alexis Everett (1859–1936)
  Harvard: LL.B, 1890; A.M., 1897

Gilder, Richard Watson (1844–1909)
  Poet and editor
  Harvard: A.M. (honorary), 1890; ΦBK (honorary), 1890
Gilman, Arthur (1837–1909)
  Society for the Collegiate Instruction of Women, first secretary, 1882–1894
  Radcliffe, regent, 1894–1895
  Harvard: A.M. (honorary), ΦBK (honorary), 1904
Gilman, Daniel Coit (1831–1908)
  Yale, A.B., 1852; A.M., 1855; professor, physical geography, 1856–1872
  University of California, president, 1872–1875
  Johns Hopkins, first president, 1875–1901
  Harvard, LL.D., 1876
Goodwin, William Watson (1831–1912)
  Harvard: A.B., ΦBK, 1851; tutor, Greek, 1856–1860; Eliot Professor of Greek, 1860–1901
  University of Göttingen, Ph.D., 1855

American School of Classical Studies, Athens, first director, 1882–1883

Gordon, George Angier (1853–1929)

Congregational clergyman

Harvard: A.B., ΦΒΚ, 1881; preacher, 1886–1890, 1906–1909; S.T.D., 1895; overseer, 1897–1916, 1925–1929

Grant, Elihu (1873–1942)

Boston University: A.B., 1898; M.A., 1900; Ph.D., 1906

Smith, associate professor to professor, Biblical Literature, 1907–1917

Haverford: professor, Biblical Literature, 1917–1938; director, Graduate School, 1923–1927

Grant, Robert (1852–1940)

Lawyer, essayist, and novelist

Harvard: A.B., ΦΒΚ, 1873; Ph.D. (philology), 1876; LL.B., 1879; overseer, 1895–1921; Litt.D., 1922

Probate Court, Boston, associate justice

Gray, George Zabriskie (1838–1889)

Episcopal Theological School, dean, 1876–1889

Wellesley: board of visitors, 1877–1878; trustee, 1885

Grenfell, Wilfred Thomason (1895–1940)

English physician and missionary.

Developed programs of health care in Labrador and Newfoundland

Grinnell, Angeline Palmer ("Aunt Angeline") (Mrs. Thomas Bailey Grinnell) (1805–1899)

Sister of Julius Auboyneau Palmer, Sr.

Aunt of George Herbert Palmer

Gross, Charles (1857–1909)

Williams: A.B., 1878; A.M., 1881

Harvard: instructor, history, 1888–1892; assistant professor, history, 1892–1901; professor, history, 1901–1908; Gurney Professor of History and Political Science, 1908–1909; A.M. (honorary), 1901

Gulick, Alice Gordon (Mrs. William Hooker Gulick) (1847–1903)

Congregational missionary

Mount Holyoke Female Seminary, graduate, 1867

Gurney, Ephrain Whitman (1829–1886)

Harvard: A.B., ΦΒΚ, 1852; tutor, 1857–1863; assistant professor, Latin, 1863–1867; assistant professor, intellectual philosophy, 1867–1868; assistant professor, history, 1868–1869; university professor, history, 1869–1886; dean, college faculty, 1870–1876; fellow, 1884–1886; McLean Professor of Ancient and Modern History, 1886

Hahnemann, Mrs. Samuel (?)
Samuel Hahnemann (1755–1843) expounded the homœopathic system of medicine
Hale, Edward Everett (1822–1909)
Unitarian clergyman
Harvard: A.B., A.M., ΦBK, 1839; S.T.D., 1879; overseer, 1866–1887
Roxbury Latin School, trustee, 1872–1894
Hale, Swinburne (1884–1937)
Son of William Gardner Hale
Harvard: A.B., 1905; LL.B., 1908
Hale, William Gardner (1849–1928)
Harvard: A.B., ΦBK, 1870; tutor, 1874–1880
Cornell, professor, Latin language and literature, 1880–1892
University of Chicago, professor, Latin language and literature, 1892–1919
American School of Classical Studies, Rome, first director, 1895–1896
Hall, Granville Stanley (1846–1924)
Williams, A.B., 1867; A.M., 1870
Harvard: A.M., Ph.D. (philosophy), 1878; instructor, English, 1876–1877; lecturer, 1880–1883
Johns Hopkins, professor, psychology and pedagogy, 1881–1888
Clark, president and professor, psychology, 1888–1924
Hanus, Paul Henry (1855–1941)
University of Michigan, S.B., 1878
University of Colorado, professor, mathematics, 1881–1886
Harvard: assistant professor, history and art of teaching, 1891–1901; professor, history and art of teaching, 1901–1921
Harper, William Rainey (1856–1906)
Muskingum College, A.B., 1870
Yale: Ph.D. (philology), 1875; professor, Semitic languages, 1886–1891; Woolsey Professor of Biblical Literature, 1889–1891
Theological Seminary, Morgan Park: instructor, Hebrew, 1879–1880; S.T.B., 1880; professor, Hebrew, 1880–1886; lecturer, Hebrew, 1887–1888
Chautauqua: College of Liberal Arts, principal, 1886–1891
University of Chicago, first president, 1891–1906
Harris, George (1844–1922)
Congregational clergyman
Amherst, A.B., 1866; president, 1899–1912
Andover Theological Seminary, graduate

Hart, Albert Bushnell (1854–1943)
Harvard: A.B., ΦBK, 1880; instructor, American history, 1883–1887; assistant professor, history, 1887–1897; professor, history, 1897–1910; Eaton Professor of Science and Government, 1919–1926
University of Freiburg, Ph.D., 1883

Haynes, Anna Morse (Mrs. Winthrop Perrin Haynes) (1899–1992)
Daughter of Lewis Kennedy Morse and Annie Capron Morse
Wellesley, B.A., 1921

Haynes, Winthrop Perrin (1887–1979)
Married Anna Hooker Morse (1925)
Harvard: A.B., 1910; A.M., 1912; Ph.D. (geology), 1914; instructor, geology, 1913–1914; visiting professor, petroleum geology, 1948–1958
Wellesley, instructor, geology and geography, 1914–1916
University of Kansas: assistant professor, geology, 1916–1918; associate professor, geology, 1919–1920

Hazard, Caroline (1856–1945)
Wellesley: president, 1899–1910; LL.D., 1925

Hazard, Roland (1829–1898)
Brother of Caroline Hazard
Brown, A.B., 1849 – classmate and close friend of James B. Angell who wrote: A "moving spirit in the development and management of great business enterprises . . . and a prime force in a multitude of activities for the public good . . . His character, so sincere and truth-loving, so full of charity, found its most beautiful fruitage in his religious faith . . . It bore the marks of the transparent Quaker spirit which came to him from his ancestors."

Head, Franklin Harvey (1835–1914)
Manufacturer, banker, lawyer, author
Hamilton: A.B., 1856; A.M., 1859; LL.D., 1896
Chicago Exposition, 1893, director
Newberry Library, trustee
Chicago Historical Society, president, 1898–1899

Herrick, Agnes Peabody (see Agnes Herrick Fletcher)

Herrick, Alice Palmer (1896-?)
Daughter of Robert Herrick and Harriet Emery Herrick

Herrick, Harriet Emery (Mrs. Robert Herrick) (?)

Herrick, Harriet Peabody (1900–1901)
Daughter of Robert Herrick and Harriet Emery Herrick

Herrick, Robert (1863–1938)
Harvard, A.B., ΦBK, 1890

Massachusetts Institute of Technology, faculty, English, 1890–1893
University of Chicago: faculty, English, 1893–1923; professor, English, 1905–1923
Married Harriet Emery (1894)

Herrick, Samuel Edward (1841–1904)
Congregational clergyman
Amherst, A.B., 1859
Mt. Vernon Church, Boston, pastor, 1871–1904

Hibben, John Grier (1861–1933)
Princeton: A.B., 1882; A.M., 1885; Ph.D., 1893; professor, logic, 1907–1912; president, 1912–1932
Harvard, LL.D., 1917

Higginson, Thomas Wentworth Storrow (1823–1911)
American clergyman (Unitarian), army officer (in Civil War, colonel of first Negro regiment in Union army), and writer
Harvard: A.B., ΦΒΚ, 1841; Divinity School, graduate, 1847; A.M., 1869; LL.D., 1898

Higley, Elizabeth Josephine (see Elizabeth Higley Freeman)

Higley, Sarah (see Sarah Higley Dye)

Hocking, William Ernest (1873–1966)
Harvard: A.B., 1901; A.M., 1902; Ph.D. (philosophy), 1904; instructor, philosophy, 1905–1906; professor, philosophy, 1914–1919; Alford Professor of Natural Religion, Moral Philosophy, and Civil Polity, 1919–1943
Yale, professor, philosophy, 1913–1914

Hodges, George (1856–1919)
Hamilton: A.B., 1877; A.M., 1882
Episcopal Theological School, dean and professor, homiletics and pastoral theology, 1894–1919
Harvard, preacher, 1896–1899
Wellesley, trustee, 1896–1898

Hooker, Richard (1554?–1600)
"English theologian . . . Chief work *The Laws of Ecclesiastical Polity* (4 books, 1594; 5th book, 1597; 3 more added after his death.)"

Hopkins, Mark (1802–1887)
Williams: B.A., 1824; professor, moral philosophy and rhetoric, 1830–1887; president, 1836–1872
Berkshire Medical School, M.D., 1829
American Board of Commissioners for Foreign Missions, 1857–1887
Harvard: S.T.D., 1841; LL.D., 1886

Hopkinson, Charles Sydney (1869–1962)
Portrait painter

Hopkinson, Grace Mellen (see Grace Hopkinson Eliot)
Horsford, Eben Norton (1818–1893)
Harvard: A.M. (honorary), ΦBK (honorary), 1847; Rumford professor and lecturer, application of science to the useful arts, 1847–1863; dean, Lawrence Scientific School, 1861–1862
Wellesley, board of visitors, president, 1885–1893
Father of Lilian Horsford Farlow
Horsford, Lilian (see Lilian Horsford Farlow)
Howard, Ada Lydia (1829–1907)
Mount Holyoke Seminary, A.B., 1849
Wellesley, president, 1875–1882
Howe, Julia Ward (1819–1910)
Prominent Bostonian, leader in woman-suffrage movement, participant in movement to promote international peace, author, lecturer, composed and published *The Battle Hymn of the Republic*
Howells, William Dean (1837–1920)
American man of letters
Harvard: A.M. (honorary), 1867; university lecturer, 1869–1871
Huntoon, Benjamin Bussey (1836–1919)
Harvard, A.B., A.M., 1856
Kentucky Institute for Education of the Blind, superintendent, 1871–1913
American Printing House for the Blind, superintendent, 1871–1913
Hurlbut, Byron Satterlee (1865–1929)
Harvard: A.B., 1887; A.M., 1888; instructor, English, 1891–1901; recording secretary, 1895–1902; assistant professor, English, 1901–1906; dean, Harvard College, 1902–1916; ΦBK, 1902; professor, English, 1906–1929
Hyde, William DeWitt (1858–1917)
Congregational clergyman
Harvard: A.B., ΦBK, 1879; S.T.D., 1886; preacher, 1897–1899; overseer, 1915–1917
Andover Theological Seminary, graduate, 1882
Bowdoin, president and professor, mental and moral philosophy, 1885–1917

Irvine, Julia Josephine Thomas (1848–1930)
Cornell: B.A., 1875; M.A., 1876
Wellesley: professor, Greek language and literature, 1890–1899; acting president, 1894–1895; president, 1895–1899

James, William (1842–1910)
Harvard: M.D., 1869; ΦBK (honorary), 1873; instructor, physiology,

1872–1873; instructor, anatomy and physiology, 1873–1876; assistant professor, physiology, 1876–1880; assistant professor, philosophy, 1880–1885; professor, philosophy, 1885–1889; professor, psychology, 1889–1897; professor, philosophy, 1897–1907; LL.D., 1903

Jayne, Anselm Helm (1856–1915)
Harvard, A.B., 1877

Jordan, David Starr (1851–1931)
Cornell, M.S., 1872
Indiana Medical College, M.D., 1875
Lombard University, professor, natural history, 1872–1873
Butler University, professor, biology, 1875–1879
Indiana University: professor, zoology, 1879–1885; president, 1885–1891
Stanford University, president, 1891–1913

Kimball, David (1870–1948)
Harvard: A.B., 1893; A.M., 1897

Kimball, Mary Annie (see Mrs. Jacob Peabody Palmer)

Knight, Frederick Irving (1841–1909)
Yale, A.B., 1862
Harvard: M.D., 1867; clinical professor, laryngology; specialty, diseases of throat and chest

Lane, Bertha Palmer (Mrs. William Coolidge Lane) (1869–1954)
Daughter of Jacob Peabody Palmer and Mary Kimball Palmer
Mother of Margaret Lane and Rosamond Lane
Sister of Arthur Kimball Palmer, Franklin Sawyer Palmer, and Robert Manning Palmer
Niece of George Herbert Palmer
Wellesley: B.A., 1891; M.A., 1893; trustee, 1904–1908

Lane, Caroline Coolidge (Mrs. William Homer Lane) (1835–1921)
Mother of William Coolidge Lane

Lane, Margaret (1905-living in Boxford, Massachusetts, in 1994)
Daughter of William Coolidge Lane and Bertha Palmer Lane
Sister of Rosamond Lane Lord
Granddaughter of Jacob Peabody Palmer
Grandniece of George Herbert Palmer
Wellesley, B.A., 1926

Lane, Rosamond (see Rosamond Lane Lord)

Lane, William Coolidge (1859–1931)
Married Bertha Palmer (1903)

Father of Margaret Lane and Rosamond Lane Lord
Harvard: A.B., ΦBK, 1881; A.M. (honorary), 1928; assistant librarian, 1887–1893; librarian, 1898–1928; lecturer, history of printing, 1910–1913
Boston Athenaeum, librarian, 1893–1898

Langdell, Christopher Columbus (1826–1906)
Harvard: A.B., ΦBK, 1851; LL.B., 1853; professor, law, 1870–1900; Law School, dean, 1870–1895

Laughlin, James Laurence (1850–1933)
Harvard: A.B., ΦBK, 1873; Ph.D. (history), 1876; instructor, political economy, 1878–1883; assistant professor, political economy, 1883–1888
Cornell, professor, political economy, 1890–1892
University of Chicago, professor, political economy, 1892–1916

Lawrence, Sallie ("Sarah") (see Sallie Lawrence Slattery)

Lawrence, William (1850–1941)
Episcopal clergyman
Episcopal Theological School, dean, 1888–1893
Bishop, diocese of Massachusetts, 1893–1926
Harvard: A.B., ΦBK, 1871; preacher, 1888–1891, 1910–1913; overseer, 1894–1906, 1907–1913; fellow, 1913–1931; S.T.D., 1893; LL.D., 1931
Wellesley, trustee, 1893–1916

Lee, Christabel (Mrs. Christabel Lee Safford) (1865–1952)
Wellesley: B.A., 1888; president, class of 1888

Lee, James Hattrick (1843–1903)
Amherst, A.B., ΦBK, 1864
Andover Theological Seminary, graduate, 1867
Episcopal Theological School, 1868–1869
Father of William Frazar Lee

Lee, William Frazar (1872–1900)
Harvard, A.B., 1894

Lewis, Clarence Irving (1883–1964)
Harvard: A.B., 1906; Ph.D. (philosophy), 1910; visiting lecturer, philosophy, 1920–1921; assistant professor, philosophy, 1921–1924; associate professor, philosophy, 1924–1930; Edgar Pierce Professor of Philosophy, 1930–1953; ΦBK (honorary)
University of California: instructor, philosophy, 1911–1914; assistant professor and then associate professor, philosophy, 1914–1920

Lindsay, Nicholas Vachel (1879–1931)
Harvard, ΦBK (honorary), poet, 1922

Livingston, Mrs. Luther S. (?)
Harvard: assistant to George Parker Winship, 1915–1926; succeeded him as librarian, Harry Elkins Widener Collection
Longfellow, Alexander Wadsworth (1854–1934)
Harvard, A.B., 1876
Architect
Cousin of William Pitt Preble Longfellow
Longfellow, William Pitt Preble (1836–1913)
Architect
Nephew of Henry Wadsworth Longfellow
Harvard: A.B., ΦBK, 1855; S.B., 1859
Lord, Frances Ellen (1835–1920)
Wellesley: professor, Latin, 1876–1897; acting president, 1881
Lord, Milton Edward (1898–1985)
Married Rosamond Lane (1928)
Harvard, A.B., 1919
American Academy, Rome, librarian, 1926–1932
Boston Public Library, director, 1932–1965
Lord, Rosamond Lane (Mrs. Milton Edward Lord) (1907–1992)
Daughter of William Coolidge Lane and Bertha Palmer Lane
Mother of Peter Lord, Joan Lord, Mary Lord, Anne Lord, and Sarah Lord
Sister of Margaret Lane
Wellesley, B.A., 1927
Loring, Charles Greeley (1828–1902)
Harvard, A.B., A.M., 1848
Union Army in the Civil War, First-Lieutenant to Major-General, 1861–1865
Museum of Fine Arts (Boston), executive head, 1876–1902
Lowell, Abbott Lawrence (1856–1943)
Harvard: A.B., ΦBK, 1877; LL.B., 1880; lecturer, existing political systems, 1897–1899; professor, science of government, 1900–1903; Eaton Professor of the Science of Government, 1903–1909; president, 1909–1933
Lowell, Amy (1874–1925)
Poet and critic
Lowell, James Russell (1819–1891)
Harvard: A.B., A.M., ΦBK, 1838; LL.B., 1840; LL.D., 1884; Smith Professorship of the French and Spanish Languages and Literature, and Professor of Belles Lettres, 1855–1886; lecturer, 1863–1864; overseer, 1887–1891

Luce, Alice Hanson (1861–1940)
Wellesley: B.A., 1883; instructor, English, 1897–1898; instructor, English literature, 1898–1900
University of Heidelberg, Ph.D. (philosophy and philology), 1896
Smith, instructor, English, 1896–1897
Oberlin, Dean of Woman and professor, English, 1900–1904

McKenzie, Alexander (1830–1914)
Congregational clergyman
Harvard: A.B., A.M., ΦBK, 1859; Divinity School, lecturer, 1881–1882; preacher, 1886–1889; board of overseers, secretary, 1875–1901; S.T.D., 1901
Andover Theological Seminary, graduate, 1861
Wellesley: trustee, 1883–1914; president of trustees, 1893–1902; president emeritus of trustees, 1902–1914

McKinley, William (1843–1901)
Elected president of the United States in 1896 and 1900; assassinated in September 1901

McKinney, May (see May McKinney Palmer)

Macvane, Silas Marcus (1842–1914)
Harvard: A.B., ΦBK, 1873; instructor, political economy, 1875–1878; instructor, history, 1878–1883; assistant professor, history, 1883–1886; professor, history, 1886–1887; McLean Professor of Ancient and Modern History, 1887–1911
Roxbury Latin School, faculty, 1873–1875

Makepeace, Eunice (see Eunice Makepeace Towle)

Manning, Lucy (see Lucy Manning Peabody)

Manning, Lydia (see Lydia Manning Peabody)

Marcou, Philippe Belknap (1855–1927)
Harvard: A.B., ΦBK, 1876; A.M., 1879; tutor, 1890–1893; instructor, Romance languages, 1893–1899; assistant professor, Romance languages, 1899–1907
University of Berlin, Ph.D., 1888

Marsh, Arthur Richmond (1861–1937)
Harvard: A.B., ΦBK, 1883; lecturer, ancient art, 1884–1885; assistant professor, comparative literature, 1891–1898; professor, comparative literature, 1898–1899
University of Kansas, professor, English and Belle Lettres, 1886–1889

Meiklejohn, Alexander (1872–1964)
Brown: A.B., 1893; dean, 1901–1912

Cornell, Ph.D., 1897
Amherst, president and professor, logic and metaphysics, 1912–1924
Married Helen Everett (1926)
Meiklejohn, Helen Everett (Mrs. Alexander Meiklejohn) (1892–1982)
Bryn Mawr, A.B., 1915
Radcliffe, M.A., 1918
London School of Economics, special student, 1922–1923
Washington University (St. Louis), Ph.D. (Economics), 1924
Daughter of Walter Goodnow Everett
Merriman, Helen Bigelow (Mrs. Daniel Merriman) (?)
In March 1900, her son, Roger Bigelow Merriman, was an instructor in history at Harvard
Miller, Adolph Caspar (1865–1953)
Married Mary Sprague (1895)
University of California: A.B., 1887; professor, economics and commerce, 1902–1913
Harvard: A.M., 1888; instructor, political economy, 1889–1890
University of Chicago, associate professor, economics, 1892–1902
Miller, Dickinson Sergeant (1868–1963)
Harvard: A.B., A.M., 1892; instructor, philosophy, 1899–1904
Halle-Wittenberg, Ph.D., 1893
Columbia, professor, philosophy, 1907–1919
General Theological Seminary, professor, Christian Apologetics, 1911–1924
Smith, professor, philosophy, 1924–1926
Miller, Mary Sprague (Mrs. Adolph Caspar Miller) (1872–1957)
Sister of Lucy Sprague Mitchell
Mitchell, Lucy Sprague (Mrs. Wesley Clair Mitchell) (1878–1967)
Daughter of Otho S. A. Sprague and Lucia Atwood Sprague
Sister of Mary Sprague Miller, Albert Sprague, Nancy Sprague
Radcliffe, A.B., 1900
Mitchell, Sprague (1915-?)
Son of Wesley Clair Mitchell and Lucy Sprague Mitchell
Mitchell, Wesley Clair (1874–1948)
Married Lucy Sprague (1912)
University of California, professor, economics, 1909–1912
Columbia University, professor, economics, 1914–1919, 1922–1944
Montgomery, Helen Barrett (1861–1934)
Wellesley: B.A., 1884; LL.D., 1925; trustee, 1908–1916

Moore, Clifford Herschel (1866–1931)
  Harvard: A.B., ΦΒΚ, 1889; assistant professor, Greek and Latin, 1898–1905; professor, Latin, 1905–1925; exchange professor with Western Colleges, 1913; Ingersoll Lecturer, 1917–1918; Graduate School of Arts and Sciences, acting dean, 1918–1919; Faculty of Arts and Sciences, dean, 1925–1931; Pope Professor of Latin, 1925–1931
  University of Munich, Ph.D., 1897

Morrison, Nathan Jackson (1828–1907)
  Congregational minister
  Dartmouth, A.B., 1853
  Oberlin, studied theology, 1854–1857
  Olivet, president, 1865–1872
  Drury (Springfield, Missouri), president, 1873–1888
  Marietta, professor, philosophy, 1888–1895
  Fairmount, president, 1895-?
  In 1895 was sent by the Congregational Education Society (Boston) to develop Fairmount Academy into Fairmount College

Morse, Anna Hooker (see Anna Morse Haynes)

Morse, Annie Capron (Mrs. Lewis Kennedy Morse) (1860–1909)
  Mother of Anna Hooker Morse and Arthur Webster Morse
  Wellesley, B.A., 1882

Morse, Arthur Webster (1900–1975)
  Son of Lewis Kennedy Morse and Annie Capron Morse
  Roxbury Latin School, 1911–1915, with class of 1917
  Harvard, A.B., 1923

Morse, Ednah Rich (Mrs. Lewis Kennedy Morse) (?)
  State College, Santa Barbara, California, president

Morse, Lewis Kennedy (1869–1930)
  Married Annie Hooker Capron (1897)
    Father of Anna Hooker Morse and Arthur Webster Morse
  Married Ednah A. Rich (1916)
  Roxbury Latin School, graduate, 1888
  Harvard: A.B., 1891; LL.B., 1895
  Wellesley, trustee, treasurer, 1912–1928

Münsterberg, Hugo (1863–1916)
  Harvard: professor, experimental psychology, 1892–1897; professor, psychology, 1897–1916; A.M. (honorary), 1901; director, psychological laboratory, 1905–1916

Myers, Charles Samuel (1873–1946)
  Cambridge (England), psychology laboratory, director

Neilson, William Allan (1869–1946)
Harvard: A.M., 1896; Ph.D. (philology), 1898; instructor, English, 1900–1904; professor, English, 1906–1917; ΦBK (honorary), 1913
Smith, president, 1917–1939
Newton, Alfred Edward (1863–1940)
Bibliophile and author
Nixdorff, Charles Edward ("Edward") (1879–1965)
Harvard: A.B, 1900; LL.B., 1904
Norton, Charles Eliot (1827–1908)
Harvard: A.B., A.M., ΦBK, 1846; instructor, French, 1851; lecturer, 1863–1864; lecturer, history of the fine arts as connected with literature, 1874–1875; professor, history of art, 1875–1898; LL.D., 1887
Novy, Estelle Freeman (1900–1990) (Mrs. Frank Novy)
Daughter of Fred Warren Freeman
Niece of Alice Freeman Palmer
Mother of Elizabeth Novy Proulx and Barbara Novy Webster
Wellesley, B.A., 1923

Packard, Horace (1855–1936)
Boston University: M.D., 1880; professor of surgery
Surgical practice in Boston, 1885–1925
Massachusetts Homœopathic Hospital, consulting surgeon
American College of Surgeons, fellow
Paine, John Knowles (1839–1906)
Studied music in Germany, 1857–1861
Harvard: lecturer, 1862–1864; assistant professor, music, 1873–1875; professor, music, 1875–1905; A.M. (honorary), 1869
Paine, Robert Treat, Jr. (1835–1910)
Philanthropist
Harvard, A.B., A.M., ΦBK, 1855
Associated Charities of Boston, president, 1878–1907
Palmer, Alice Freeman (Mrs. George Herbert Palmer) (1855–1902)
Daughter of James Warren Freeman and Elizabeth Higley Freeman
Siblings (from oldest to youngest): Fred Warren, Ella Louise, Roxie Estelle
Wellesley: see 61n1
Palmer, Angeline (see Angeline Palmer Grinnell)
Palmer, Arthur Kimball (1860–1879)
Son of Jacob Peabody Palmer and Mary Kimball Palmer
Brother of Franklin Sawyer Palmer, Bertha Palmer, and Robert Manning Palmer
Nephew of George Herbert Palmer

Palmer, Bertha (see Bertha Palmer Lane)
Palmer, C. D.(?)
See 127n1
Palmer, Charles Ray (1834–1914)
Son of Ray Palmer
First cousin of George Herbert Palmer
Andover Theological Seminary, graduate, 1859
Yale: A.B., 1855; fellow of the corporation, 1880–1910; Doctor of Divinity (honorary), 1889
American Board of Commissioners for Foreign Missions, 1871–1901
Tabernacle Church, Salem, Massachusetts, minister, 1862–1872
First Congregational Church, Bridgeport, Connecticut, minister, 1872–1895
Palmer, Effie Wood (Mrs. Julius Auboyneau Palmer, Jr.) (?–1893)
Palmer, Ellen Wellman ("Nell") (Mrs. George Herbert Palmer) (1835–1879)
Daughter of William Augustus Wellman and Susan Prescott Wellman
Sister of Henry Cleveland Wellman
Half sister of Francis Lewis Wellman
Palmer, Emily Jane ("Em") (1845–1907)
Sister of George Herbert Palmer
Palmer, Franklin Sawyer (1865–1935)
Son of Jacob Peabody Palmer and Mary Kimball Palmer
Brother of Bertha Palmer Lane, Arthur Kimball Palmer, and Robert Manning Palmer
Grandnephew of George Herbert Palmer
Married May McKinney (1899)
Father of Paul Sawyer McKinney Palmer
Harvard: A.B., 1886; M.D., 1890
Palmer, Frederic ("Fred") (1848–1932)
Episcopal clergyman
Brother of George Herbert Palmer
Married Mary Towle (1877)
Harvard: A.B., A.M., ΦBK, 1869; Divinity School, lecturer, 1913–1916
Andover Theological Seminary, graduate, 1872
Palmer, Frederic, Jr. ("Eric") (1878–1967)
Son of Frederic Palmer and Mary Towle Palmer
Nephew of George Herbert Palmer
Married Helen Wallace (1907)
Father of Frederic Palmer, 3rd. and Helen Wallace Palmer
Harvard: A.B., 1900; A.M., 1904; Ph.D. (physics), 1913; lecturer, physics, 1918–1919

Haverford College; ΦBK (honorary), instructor, physics and astronomy, 1904–1909; associate professor, physics, 1909–1916; dean, 1908–1929; professor, physics, 1916–1945

Palmer, Frederic, 3rd. ("little Eric") (1908–1992)
Son of Frederic Palmer, Jr. and Helen Wallace Palmer
Brother of Helen Palmer Avery
Grandnephew of George Herbert Palmer

Palmer, George Herbert (1842–1933)
Son of Julius Auboyneau Palmer, Sr. and Lucy Peabody Palmer
Siblings (from oldest to youngest): Harriet Amanda, Lucy Ann, Jacob Peabody, Julius Augustus (died in infancy), Julia Augusta, Julius Auboyneau, Emily Jane, Frederic
Nephew of Ray Palmer, Angeline Palmer Grinnell, Harriet Peabody Emery, and William Augustus Peabody
Married Ellen Margaret Wellman (1871)
Married Alice Elvira Freeman (1887)
Harvard: see 74n1
Wellesley: board of visitors, 1889–1893; lecturer, philosophy, 1902–1903; trustee, 1912–1933

Palmer, Harriet Amanda ("Hattie") (1828–1872)
Sister of George Herbert Palmer

Palmer, Helen Wallace (Mrs. Frederic Palmer, Jr.) (1877–1949)
Mother of Frederic Palmer, 3rd. and Helen Palmer Avery

Palmer, Helen Wallace (see Helen Palmer Avery)

Palmer, Jacob Peabody (1833–1901)
Brother of George Herbert Palmer
Married Mary Annie Kimball (1859)
Father of Arthur Kimball Palmer, Bertha Palmer, Franklin Sawyer Palmer, and Robert Manning Palmer

Palmer, Julia Augusta (1838–1881)
Sister of George Herbert Palmer

Palmer, Julius Auboyneau, Sr. (1803–1872)
Son of Thomas Palmer and Susanna Palmer Palmer
Married Lucy Manning Peabody (1827)
Father of George Herbert Palmer and his siblings
Brother of Ray Palmer

Palmer, Julius Auboyneau, Jr. ("Jule") (1840–1899)
Married Effie Wood (1864)
Brother of George Herbert Palmer

Palmer, Julius Augustus (1836–1837)
Brother of George Herbert Palmer

Palmer, Lucy Ann (see Lucy Palmer Bachelder)

Palmer, Lucy Peabody (Mrs. Julius Auboyneau Palmer, Sr.) (1805–1877)
Mother of George Herbert Palmer and his siblings
Niece of Lydia Manning Peabody
Half sister of William Augustus Peabody
Palmer, Mary Kimball (Mrs. Jacob Peabody Palmer) (1834–1882)
Mother of Arthur Kimball Palmer, Bertha Palmer, Franklin Sawyer Palmer, and Robert Manning Palmer
Sister-in-law of George Herbert Palmer
Palmer, Mary Towle (Mrs. Frederic Palmer) (1846–1936)
Mother of Frederic Palmer, Jr.
Sister-in-law of George Herbert Palmer
Palmer, May McKinney (Mrs. Franklin Sawyer Palmer)
Mother of Paul Sawyer McKinney Palmer
Palmer, Paul Sawyer McKinney (1900-?)
Son of Franklin Sawyer Palmer and May McKinney Palmer
Great-grandnephew of George Herbert Palmer
Harvard, A.B., 1922
Palmer, Ray (1808–1887)
Son of Thomas Palmer and Susanna Palmer Palmer
Father of Charles Ray Palmer
Brother of Julius Auboyneau Palmer, Sr.
Uncle of George Herbert Palmer
Yale, A.B., 1830
Andover Theological Seminary, board of visitors, 1865–1878
Congregational clergyman, writer of hymns and poetry
Palmer, Robert Manning (1867-?)
Son of Jacob Peabody Palmer and Mary Kimball Palmer
Brother of Bertha Palmer, Franklin Sawyer Palmer, and Arthur Kimball Palmer
Nephew of George Herbert Palmer
Palmer, Susanna Palmer (Mrs. Thomas Palmer) (1779–1815)
Mother of Julius Auboyneau Palmer, Sr. and Ray Palmer
Paternal grandmother of George Herbert Palmer
Palmer, Thomas (1773–1857)
Married Susanna Palmer (1800)
Father of Julius Auboyneau Palmer, Sr. and Ray Palmer
Paternal grandfather of George Herbert Palmer
Parker, Willard (1800–1884)
Harvard, A.B., A.M., ΦΒΚ, 1826; M.D., 1830
Columbia, College of Physicians and Surgeons, New York, professor, clinical surgery, 1870–1880

Peabody, Andrew Preston (1811–1893)
Harvard: A.B., A.M., ΦBK, 1826; Divinity School, graduate, 1832; S.T.D., 1852; preacher and Plummer Professor of Christian Morals, 1860–1881; overseer, 1883–1893
Peabody, Charles Henry (1810–1892)
Brother of Lucy Peabody Palmer and Harriet Peabody Emery
Maternal uncle of George Herbert Palmer
Peabody, Endicott (1857–1944)
Episcopal clergyman
Harvard: preacher, 1899–1902; S.T.D., 1904
Peabody, Francis Greenwood (1847–1936)
Harvard: A.B., A.M., ΦBK, 1869; S.T.B., 1872; overseer, 1877–1882; Divinity School, lecturer, 1880–1881; Parkman Professor of Theology, 1881–1886, 1893–1894; Plummer Professor of Christian Morals, 1886–1913; Divinity School, dean, 1901–1906; preacher, 1905–1906
Peabody, Jacob (1778–1856)
Married Lucy Manning (1804)
Father of Lucy Manning Peabody
Maternal grandfather of George Herbert Palmer
Married Lydia Manning (1814)
Father of William Augustus Peabody
Peabody, Josephine Preston (1874–1922)
Poet and playwright
Wellesley, instructor, English literature, 1901–1903
Married (1906) Lionel Simeon Marks (1871–1955) Harvard: assistant professor, mechanical engineering, 1900–1909; professor, mechanical engineering, 1909–1935; Gordon McKay Professor of Mechanical Engineering, 1935–1940
Peabody, Lucy Manning (Mrs. Jacob Peabody) (1780–1813)
Mother of Lucy Manning Peabody
Maternal grandmother of George Herbert Palmer
Peabody, Lucy Manning (see Lucy Peabody Palmer)
Peabody, Lydia Manning (Mrs. Jacob Peabody) (1786–1845)
Sister of Lucy Manning Peabody
Mother of William Augustus Peabody
Maternal aunt of Lucy Peabody Palmer
Great-aunt of George Herbert Palmer
Peabody, William Augustus (1816–1850)
Son of Jacob Peabody and Lydia Manning Peabody
Half brother of Lucy Peabody Palmer
Maternal uncle of George Herbert Palmer

Amherst: A.B., 1835; professor, Latin and modern languages, 1849–1850

Andover Theological Seminary, graduate, 1842

Pearmain, Alice Upton (1863–1946)

Wellesley: B.A., 1883; M.A., 1890; president, Alumnae Association, 1912–1914; trustee, 1918–1928

Peirce, James Mills (1834–1906)

Harvard: A.B., A.M., ΦBK, 1853; graduate, Division of Science, 1859; tutor, 1854–1858, 1860–1861; university professor, mathematics, 1869–1885; Perkins Professor of Astronomy and Mathematics, 1885–1906; Graduate School of Arts and Sciences, dean, 1890–1895; Faculty of Arts and Sciences, dean, 1895–1898

Pendleton, Ellen Fitz (1864–1936)

Wellesley: B.A., 1886; A.M., 1891; faculty, mathematics, 1886–1911; president, 1911–1936

Perry, Bliss (1860–1954)

Williams: A.B., 1881; A.M., 1883

Harvard: lecturer, English literature, 1904–1905; professor, English literature, 1907–1925; Francis Lee Higginson Professor of English Literature, 1925-?; Litt.D., 1925.

Perry, Ralph Barton (1876–1957)

Princeton, A.B., 1896

Harvard: A.M., 1897; Ph.D., 1899; instructor, philosophy, 1902–1905; assistant professor, philosophy, 1905–1913; professor, philosophy, 1913–1946

Williams, instructor, philosophy, 1899–1900

Peterson, Ellis (1830–1904)

Harvard: A.B., A.M., ΦBK, 1853; assistant professor, philosophy, 1870–1872

Pickering, Edward Charles (1846–1919)

Harvard: S.B., 1865; director, astronomical observatory, 1877–1919; Phillips Professor of Astronomy, 1876–1887; professor, geodesy, 1876–1887; Paine Professor of Practical Astronomy, 1887–1919

Massachusetts Institute of Technology, professor, physics, 1868–1877

Pratt, Joseph Hersey (1872–1956)

Johns Hopkins, M.D., 1898

Harvard, A.M., 1901

Tufts College Medical School, professor of clinical medicine, 1929–1947

Proulx, Elizabeth Novy (1932-living in Michigan in 1994)

Daughter of Estelle Freeman Novy

Grandniece of Alice Freeman Palmer
Granddaughter of Fred Warren Freeman
Great-granddaughter of James Warren Freeman

Rand, Benjamin (1856–1934)
Harvard: A.B., ΦBK, 1879; A.M., 1880; Ph.D. (philosophy), 1885; instructor, philosophy, 1897–1902; librarian, philosophical library, 1906-?
Rand, Edward Kennard (1871–1945)
Harvard: A.B., 1894; professor, Latin, 1909–1942
University of Munich, Ph.D., 1900
Reid, Elizabeth (Mrs. Whitelaw Reid) (1858–1931)
American Red Cross, acting head, nursing division, Spanish War (1898); chairman in London, World War I
Rich, Ednah A. (see Ednah Rich Morse)
Rieber, Charles Henry (1866-?)
University of California, A.B., 1888; professor, philosophy, 1910–1921
Harvard: A.M., 1899; Ph.D. (philosophy), 1900
Rieber, Winifred Smith (Mrs. Charles Henry Rieber) (1872-?)
Portrait painter
Robinson, Fred Norris (1871–1966)
Harvard: A.B., ΦBK, 1891; A.M., 1892; Ph.D. (philology), 1894; instructor, English, 1894–1902; assistant professor, English, 1902–1906; professor, English, 1906-?
Rockefeller, John Davison (1839–1937)
Oil magnate and philanthropist
Rockwell, Katherine French (Mrs. Alfred E. P. Rockwell) (1882–1980)
Daughter of Peter French and Katherine Wilkinson French
Twin sister of Barbara French
Niece of Elizabeth Wilkinson Bachelder
Vassar, A.B., 1905
Boston University, M.D., 1910
Married, 1915
Rogers, Bruce (1870–1957)
Artist and book designer
Roosevelt, Theodore (1858–1919)
Harvard: A.B., ΦBK, 1880; LL.D., 1902; overseer, 1895–1901, 1910–1916
United States: vice-president, 1901; president, 1901–1909
Ropes, James Hardy (1866–1933)
Harvard: A.B., ΦBK, 1889; instructor, new testament criticism and

interpretation, 1895–1898; assistant professor, new testament criticism and interpretation, 1898–1903; Dexter Lecturer, 1903–1933; Bussey Professor of New Testament Criticism and Interpretation, 1903–1910; Department of University Extension, dean, 1910–1916; Hollis Professor of Divinity, 1910–1933

Andover Theological Seminary, graduate, 1893

Ross, Denman Waldo (1853–1935)

Harvard: A.B., ΦBK, 1875; A.M., 1880; Ph.D. (early German land tenure), 1880; lecturer, theory of design, 1899–1935; Fogg Art Museum, honorary fellow, 1922–1935

Royce, Josiah (1855–1916)

Harvard: instructor, philosophy, 1882–1884; instructor, philosophy and forensics, 1884–1885; assistant professor, philosophy, 1885-1892; ΦBK (honorary), 1893; professor, history of philosophy, 1912–1914; Alford Professor of Natural Religion, Moral Philosophy, and Civil Polity, 1914–1916

Russell, Frank (1867–1903)

Harvard: A.B., 1896; A.M., 1897; Ph.D. (American Archaeology and Ethnology), 1898; instructor, anthropology, 1897–1903

Sabine, Wallace Clement (1868–1919)

Ohio State University, A.B., 1886

Harvard: A.M., 1888; instructor, physics, 1890–1895; assistant professor, physics, 1895–1905; professor, physics, 1905–1914; Lawrence Scientific School, dean, 1906–1908; ΦBK (honorary), 1907; Graduate School of Applied Science, dean, 1908–1914; Hollis Professor of Mathematics and Natural Philosophy, 1914–1919

Sachs, Paul Joseph (1878–1965)

Harvard: A.B., 1900; assistant director, Fogg Art Museum, 1915–1923; assistant professor, fine arts, 1917–1922; associate professor, fine arts, 1922–1927; associate director, Fogg Art Museum, 1923–1948; professor, fine arts, 1927–1948

Wellesley, lecturer, art, 1916–1917

Sampson, Elizabeth Burling (Mrs. William Thomas Sampson) (?)

In March 1900, her husband was commandant of the Boston Navy Yard. A rear admiral, he had commanded the North Atlantic squadron in the war with Spain

Sanderson, Robert Louis (?)

Harvard: instructor, French, 1885–1889; assistant professor, French, 1889–1895

Santayana, George (1863–1952)

Harvard: A.B., ΦBK, 1886; Ph.D. and A.M. (philosophy), 1889; instructor, philosophy, 1889–1898; assistant professor, philosophy, 1898–1907; professor, philosophy, 1907–1912

Savery, William Briggs (1875–1945)
Brown, A.B., 1896
Harvard, Ph.D. (philosophy), 1899
Fairmount (Kansas), professor, philosophy, 1900–1902
University of Washington (Seattle), professor, philosophy, 1902–1945

Schaeys, Helene A. (1845–1922)
Wellesley: instructor, French, 1895–1900; associate professor, French, 1900–1904; professor, French, 1904–1905

Schliemann, Heinrich (1822–1890)
German archaeologist, "studied Homeric sites, conducted excavations in Asia Minor and opened up what he believed to be ruins of ancient Troy"

Schurman, Jacob Gould (1854–1942)
University of London: B.A., 1877; M.A., 1878
Acadia (Nova Scotia), professor, English literature, political economy, psychology, 1880–1882
Dalhousie (Nova Scotia), professor, metaphysics and English literature, 1882–1886
Cornell: professor, philosophy, and dean, Sage School of Philosophy, 1886–1892; president, 1892–1920
Harvard, LL.D., 1909

Scudder, Horace Elisha (1838–1902)
Atlantic Monthly , editor, 1890–1897
Houghton Mifflin Company, editorial department until 1902
Wellesley, trustee, 1887–1902

Scudder, Vida Dutton (1861–1954)
Smith, B.A., 1884; M.A., 1889
Wellesley: instructor, English literature, 1887–1892; associate professor, 1892–1910; professor, 1910–1928

Seelye, Julius Hawley (1824–1895)
Amherst: professor, philosophy, 1858–1876; president, 1876–1890

Shafer, Helen Alvira (1839–1894)
Wellesley, president, 1888–1894

Shaler, Nathaniel Southgate (1841–1906)
Harvard: S.B., 1862; ΦBK (honorary), 1870; S.D. (natural history), 1875; professor, paleontology, 1869–1888; professor, geology, 1888–1906; LL.D., 1903; dean, Lawrence Scientific School, 1891–1906

Shepherd, Samuel (1850–1904)
Congregational clergyman

Harvard, A.B., ΦBK, 1878
Chicago Theological Seminary, graduate, 1882
Sidgwick, Henry (1838–1900)
Cambridge University, England, professor, philosophy, 1883–1900
Sidgwick, Eleanor Mildred (Mrs. Henry Sidgwick) (1845–1936)
Supporter of the movement for the higher education of women
Slattery, Charles Lewis (1867–1930)
Episcopal clergyman
Married Sallie Lawrence (1923)
Harvard: A.B., ΦBK, 1891; preacher, 1920–1927; overseer, 1924–1926
Wellesley, trustee, 1923–1930
Bishop, diocese of Massachusetts, 1927–1930
Slattery, Sallie Lawrence (Mrs. Charles Lewis Slattery) (?)
Daughter of William Lawrence
Wellesley, trustee, 1916–1923, 1930–1935
Smith, Judson (1837–1906)
Congregational clergyman
Oberlin, professor, 1866–1884
American Board of Commissioners for Foreign Missions, secretary, 1868–1906
Mount Holyoke, president of trustees, 1900
Spaulding, Henry George (1847–1920)
Harvard: A.B., ΦBK, 1860; Divinity School, graduate, 1866
Sperry, William Learoyd (1882–1954)
Yale, M.A., 1908
Harvard: preacher, 1921–1928; professor, homiletics, 1922–1929; Divinity School, dean, 1925–1953; board of preachers, chairman, 1928–1953; Plummer Professor of Christian Morals, 1929–1953
Sprague, Albert (1874–1924)
Brother of Lucy Sprague Mitchell
Harvard, A.B., 1898
Sprague, Henry Harrison (1841–1920)
Harvard: A.B., ΦBK, 1864; A.M., 1867; overseer, 1890–1896
Sprague, Lucia Atwood (Mrs. Otho S. A. Sprague) (1849–1901)
Mother of Mary Sprague Miller, Albert Sprague, Nancy Sprague, Lucy Sprague Mitchell
Sprague, Lucy (see Lucy Sprague Mitchell)
Sprague, Otho S. A. (1838–1909)
Father of Mary Sprague Miller, Albert Sprague, Nancy Sprague, and Lucy Sprague Mitchell
Stearns, William Augustus (1805–1876)
Harvard: A.B., 1827; LL.D., 1853
Amherst, president, 1854–1876

Stokes, Anson Phelps, Jr. (1874–1958)
Episcopal clergyman
Yale: A.B., 1896, A.M., 1900; secretary, 1899–1921
Episcopal Theological School, B.D., 1900
Wellesley, trustee, 1899–1906
Stone, Galen L., (1862–1926)
Wellesley, trustee, 1915–1925
Stone, Lucy (Mrs. Henry Brown Blackwell) (1818–1893)
American woman suffragist; aided in forming American Woman Suffrage Association, 1869
Stoops, John Dashiell (1873–1973)
Dickinson (Pennsylvania), A.B., 1894
Harvard, A.M., 1897
Boston University, Ph.D., 1899
Mt. Union (Ohio), professor, philosophy and psychology, 1899–1900
Grinnell (Iowa), professor, philosophy, 1904–1943
Stowe, Harriet Beecher (1811–1896)
Abolitionist, author of *Uncle Tom's Cabin,* or *Life Among the Lowly*
Stringham, Irving (1847–1909)
Harvard, A.B., ΦBK, 1877
Johns Hopkins, Ph.D., 1880
University of California: professor, mathematics, 1882–1909; dean, 1886–1909
Suzzallo, Henry (1875–1933)
Stanford, A.B., 1899
Columbia: M.A., 1902; Ph.D., 1905; Teachers College, professor, philosophy of education
University of Washington, president, 1915–1926
Carnegie Foundation for the Advancement of Teaching, 1930–1933

Talbot, Marion (1858–1948)
Boston University: B.A., 1880; M.A., 1882
Massachusetts Institute of Technology, B.S., 1888
Wellesley, instructor, domestic science, 1890–1892
University of Chicago: Dean of Women, associated with Alice Freeman Palmer, 1892–1895, succeeded Mrs. Palmer as dean, 1895–1925; assistant professor, sanitary science, 1893–1895; associate professor, sanitary science, 1895–1904; professor, household administration, 1904–1925
Talmage, Charles Horace (?–1925)
Married Ella Louise Freeman (1878)
Harvard, A.M., 1900

Talmage, Ella Freeman (Mrs. Charles Horace Talmage) (1858–1942)
Sister of Alice Freeman Palmer
Tarbell, Frank Bigelow (1853–1920)
Yale: A.B., 1873; Ph.D., 1879
Harvard: instructor, Greek, 1889–1890; instructor, Greek and Latin, 1890–1892
University of Chicago: associate professor, Greek, 1892–1894; professor, classical archaeology, 1894–1918
Thorp, Joseph Gilbert (?)
Harvard: A.B., ΦBK, 1879; LL.B., 1882
Thwing, Charles Franklin (1853–1937)
Congregational clergyman
Harvard, A.B., ΦBK, 1876
Andover Theological Seminary, graduate, 1879
Western Reserve, president, 1890–1921
Todd, David Peck (1855–1939)
Smith, professor, astronomy and higher mathematics, 1882–1887
Amherst: teacher, astronomy, 1881; professor, astronomy, 1892–1917
Married Mabel Loomis (1879)
Father of Millicent Todd
Todd, Mabel Loomis (Mrs. David Peck Todd) (1856–1932)
Author
First editor of the poems and letters of Emily Dickinson
Mother of Millicent Todd
Todd, Henry Alfred (1854–1925)
Philologist
Todd, Millicent (see Millicent Todd Bingham)
Towle, Eunice Makepeace (Mrs. Nathaniel Carter Towle) (1806–1894)
Mother of Mary Towle Palmer
Portrait painter
Descendent of William Makepeace Thackeray
Towle, Mary (see Mary Towle Palmer)
Towle, Nathaniel Carter (1805–1898)
Father of Mary Towle Palmer
Tucker, William Jewett (1839–1926)
Congregational clergyman
Dartmouth: A.B., 1861; president, 1893–1909
Andover Theological Seminary: graduate, 1866; professor of sacred rhetoric and lecturer on pastoral theology, 1879–1893
Tufts, Edith Souther (1862–1935)
Wellesley: B.A., 1885; president, class of 1884; M.A., 1895; instructor, Greek, 1893–1894, 1902–1909; registrar, 1909–1919; dean of residence, 1919–1930)

Very, Jones (1813–1880)
Transcendentalist poet and essayist
Harvard, A.B., ΦBK, 1836
Vincent, George Edgar (1864–1941)
University of Chicago: Ph.D., 1896; faculty, 1895–1911; Faculty of Arts, Literature and Science, 1907–1911
University of Minnesota, president, 1911–1917
Rockfeller Foundation, president, 1917–1929
Vinton, Frederic Porter (1846–1911)
American portrait painter

Wadlin, Horace Greeley (1851–1925)
Massachusetts Bureau of Statistics of Labor, chief, 1888–1903
Wallace, Helen (see Helen Wallace Palmer)
Walton, George Lincoln (1854–1941)
Harvard: A.B., 1875; M.D., 1880; clinical instructor, diseases of the nervous system, 1885–1886
Practiced neurology in Boston, 1883–1916
Ward, Elizabeth Stuart Phelps (Mrs. Hubert Dickinson Ward) (1844–1911)
American author
Warren, Gretchen Osgood (Mrs. Fiske Warren)
Husband, Harvard, A.B., 1884, paper manufacturer
Warren, William Fairfield (1833–1929)
Methodist Episcopal clergyman
Wesleyan, A.B., 1853
Andover Theological Seminary, graduate, 1856
Boston University, president, 1873–1903
Waugh, Karl Tinsley (1879–1971)
Ohio Wesleyan: A.B., 1900, A.M., 1901
Harvard, Ph.D. (philosophy), 1906
Beloit, professor, mental science and philosophy, 1909–1918
Wayland, Francis (1796–1865)
Father of Francis Wayland (1826–1904)
Andover Theological Seminary, graduate
Brown, president, 1827–1855
Wayland, Francis (1826–1904)
Son of Francis Wayland (1796–1865)
Brown, A.B., 1846
Yale, Law School, dean, 1873–1903
American Socal Science Association, president
Prominent in charitable work and prison reform

Wellman, Ellen Margaret (see Ellen Wellman Palmer)
Wellman, Francis Lewis ("Frank") (1854–1942)
Son of William Augustus Wellman and Matilda Ogden Wellman
Half brother of Ellen Wellman Palmer and Henry Cleveland Wellman
Father of Roderic Wellman
Harvard, A.B., 1876
Wellman, Henry Cleveland (1844–1866)
Brother of Ellen Wellman Palmer
Harvard, A.B., 1865
Wellman, Hiller Crowell (1871–1956)
Son of Joseph Hiller Wellman and Ellen Maria Crowell
Harvard, A.B., ΦBK, 1894
Brookline Public Library, librarian, 1898–1902
Wellman, Joseph Hiller ("Jo") (?)
Father of Hiller Crowell Wellman
Wellman, Roderic (1882–1948)
Son of Francis Lewis Wellman
Nephew of George Herbert Palmer
Harvard: A.B., 1903; LL.B., 1906
Wellman, Susan Prescott (?)
Mother of Ellen Wellman Palmer
Wellman, William Augustus (?–1878)
Married Susan Prescott
Father of Ellen Wellman Palmer and Henry Cleveland Wellman
Married Matilda Ogden
Father of Francis Lewis Wellman
Wendell, Barrett (1855–1921)
Harvard: A.B., ΦBK, 1877; instructor, English, 1880–1881, 1882–1888; assistant professor, English, 1888–1898; professor, English, 1898–1921
Wheeler, Benjamin Ide (1854–1927)
Brown: A.B., 1875; A.M., 1878
University of Heidelberg, Ph.D., 1885
University of California, president, 1899–1919
Harvard, LL.D., 1900
Whiting, Sarah Frances (1846–1927)
Wellesley: professor, physics and physical astronomy, 1876–1904; professor, physics, and director, observatory, 1904–1916
Whitman, Frank Perkins (1853–1919)
Brown, A.B., 1874
Western Reserve, professor, physics, 1886–1918

Whitney, Anne (1821–1915)
  Sculptress
  Wellesley, art department, taught modeling, February–May, 1885
Whittier, John Greenleaf (1807–1902)
  Harvard: overseer, 1858–1864; A.M. (honorary), 1860; LL.D., 1886; ΦBK (honorary), 1888
Wilkinson, Elizabeth (see Elizabeth Wilkinson Bachelder)
Wilkinson, Katherine (see Katherine Wilkinson French)
Willcox, Mary Alice (1856–1953)
  Wellesley, professor, zoology, 1883–1910
Willcox, Walter Francis (1861–1964)
  Harvard, lecturer, United States Census of 1900, 1899–1900
  Cornell, professor, political economy and statistics, 1891–1931
Willcox, William Henry (1821–1904)
  Congregational clergyman
  New York University, A.B., 1843
  Union Theological Seminary, graduate, 1846
  Wellesley: trustee, 1878–1904; executive committee, chairman, 1884–1904
Williams, Henry Willard (1821–1895)
  Harvard: M.D., 1849; A.M. (honorary), 1868; ΦBK (honorary), 1871; professor, ophthalmology, 1897–1891
Williams, Theodore Chickering (1855–1915)
  Unitarian clergyman
  Roxbury Latin School: graduate, 1872; headmaster, 1907–1909
  Harvard: A.B., ΦBK, 1876; S.T.B., 1882; preacher, 1888–1890
  Married Velma Curtis Wright (1882)
Williams, Velma Wright (Mrs. Theodore Chickering Williams) (?)
Winship, George Parker (1871–1952)
  Harvard: A.B., 1893; A.M., 1894; librarian, Harry Elkins Widener Collection, 1915–1926; ΦBK (honorary); lecturer, history of printing, 1915–1926; assistant librarian, 1927–1932
Winter, Irvah Lester (1857–1934)
  Harvard: A.B., 1886; instructor, elocution, 1899–1903; assistant professor, elocution, 1903–1908; assistant professor, public speaking, 1908–1913; associate professor, public speaking, 1913–1925
Wolcott, Roger (1847–1900)
  Harvard: A.B., ΦBK, 1870; tutor, 1870–1871; LL.B., 1874; overseer, 1885–1895
  Governor of Massachusetts, 1896–1899
Wood, Effie (see Effie Wood Palmer)

Wood, Leonard (1860–1927)
Harvard: M.D., 1884; LL.D., 1899
United States Army, Major General
Military governor of Cuba, 1899–1902

Woodberry, George Edward (1855–1930)
Harvard: A.B., ΦBK, 1877; Litt.D., 1911; Woodberry Poetry Room
University of Nebraska: professor, English and history, 1877–1878; professor, Anglo-Saxon and rhetoric, 1880–1881; professor, English language and literature, 1881–1882
Columbia: professor, literature, 1891–1899; professor, comparative literature, 1899–1904

Woods, James Haughton (1864–1935)
Harvard: A.B., 1887; instructor, anthropology, 1900–1902; instructor, philosophy, 1901–1902, 1904–1908; instructor, philosophical systems of India, 1903–1904; assistant professor, philosophy, 1908–1913; professor, philosophy, 1913–1934

Woolley, Mary Emma (1863–1947)
Brown: B.A., 1894; M.A., 1895
Wellesley: instructor, biblical history, 1895–1896; associate professor, biblical history, 1896–1899; professor, biblical history, 1899–1900
Mount Holyoke, president, 1900–1937

Wright, John Henry (1852–1908)
Dartmouth: A.B., 1873; A.M., 1876; associate professor, Greek, 1878–1886
Johns Hopkins, professor, classical philology, 1886–1887
Harvard: professor, Greek, 1887–1908; Graduate School of Arts and Sciences, dean, 1895–1908

Wyeth, Newell Convers (1882–1945)
Illustrator and mural painter

Wyman, Bruce (1876–1926)
Harvard: A.B., ΦBK, 1896; LL.B., 1900; Law School, lecturer, 1900–1903; assistant professor, law, 1903–1908; professor, law, 1908–1914

Sources

Chapters 3, 4, and 5; many of the institutions and organizations listed in the Preface; and the following publications:

Joyce Antler, *Lucy Sprague Mitchell: The Making of a Modern Woman,* New Haven, Yale University Press, 1987.

Catalogue of Phi Beta Kappa, Alpha of Massachusetts, Harvard University, Cambridge, W. H. Wheeler, 1891. The front cover of this catalogue is the source for the style of the Greek letters for Phi Beta Kappa —ΦBK— that are used in this compilation.

Catalogue of the Harvard Chapter of Phi Beta Kappa — Alpha of Massachusetts, Cambridge, Riverside Press, 1933.

Dictionary of America Biography, New York, C. Scribner's Sons, 1934

Dr. Freeman 85, passes on, Beloved physician served Saginaw half century, *Saginaw News,* January 21, 1942.

General Catalogue of the Theological Seminary, Andover, Massachusetts, 1808–1908, Boston, Thomas Todd, printer, 1909.

Jean Glasscock, ed., *Wellesley College 1875–1975: A Century of Women,* Wellesley, Wellesley College, 1975.

Alice Payne Hackett, *Wellesley: Part of the American Story,* New York, E. P. Dutton & Co., 1949.

Harvard College, *Class Reports*

Harvard University, *Quinquennial Catalogue of the Officers and Graduates, 1636–1930,* Cambridge, Harvard University Press, 1930.

Historical Register of Harvard University, 1636–1936, Cambridge, Harvard University, 1937.

Notable American Women, 1607–1950, A Biographical Dictionary, 4 vols, Cambridge, Belknap Press of Harvard University Press, 1971.

Owen H. Gates, *General Catalogue of the Andover Theological Seminary, 1927, with Biographical Data for 1908–1927,* Boston, Fort Hill Press.

The Palmer Family, in *Little Compton Families,* from records compiled by Benjamin Franklin Wilbour, Little Compton (Rhode Island) Historical Society, 1967, pages 444–466.

Palmer Families in America, vol III, compiled and arranged by Horace W. Palmer, edited by Richard N. Palmer and Eunice W. Palmer, New Hampshire, Somersworth, 1973, pages 62, 63, 105, 106.

Peabody Genealogy compiled by Selim Hobart Peabody, LL.D., edited by Charles Henry Pope, Boston, Charles H. Pope publisher, 1909.

Roxbury Latin School (founded in 1645, West Roxbury, Massachusetts), *Quinquennial Catalogue and Alumni Directory,* 1645–1976. The compiler, a graduate of this school in 1933, identifies here two trustees (Edward Everett Hale and John Graham Brooks), a faculty member (Silas Marcus Macvane), the only alumnus-headmaster (Theodore Chickering Williams), and two other alumni (Arthur Webster Morse and Lewis Kennedy Morse).

H. P. Smith, *History of Broome County,* D. Mason & Co., Syracuse, 1885, page 564 (BCHSoc.).

Shirley W. Smith, *James Burrill Angell: an American Influence,* Ann Arbor, University of Michigan Press, 1954.

Charles F. Thwing, *Guides, Philosophers and Friends,* New York, Macmillan and Co., 1927.

Webster's Biographical Dictionary, Springfield, G.&C. Merriam Co., 1969

Wellesley College Bulletin, 1942 Record Number, Volume 32, Number 1, September, 1942.

Who Was Who in America, volume 1, 1897–1942, Chicago, A. N. Marquis, 1942.

Who's Who in America, series of volumes starting in 1899–1900, Chicago, A. N. Marquis.

Helen M. Winslow, *Literary Boston of To-day,* Boston, L. C. Page & Co., 1902.

Frank Yoder, *The University of Chicago Faculty: A Centennial View,* Chicago, The University of Chicago Library, 1991.

Index to Notes in the Chronicles

(Chapters 3 and 5 with a few other references)

Key: page number n note number